Innovations in Organizational IT Specification and Standards Development

Kai Jakobs
RWTH Aachen University, Germany

Information Science
REFERENCE

Managing Director:	Lindsay Johnston
Editorial Director:	Joel Gamon
Book Production Manager:	Jennifer Romanchak
Publishing Systems Analyst:	Adrienne Freeland
Assistant Acquisitions Editor:	Kayla Wolfe
Typesetter:	Henry Ulrich
Cover Design:	Nick Newcomer

Published in the United States of America by
Information Science Reference (an imprint of IGI Global)
701 E. Chocolate Avenue
Hershey PA 17033
Tel: 717-533-8845
Fax: 717-533-8661
E-mail: cust@igi-global.com
Web site: http://www.igi-global.com

Library of Congress Cataloging-in-Publication Data

Innovations in organizational IT specification and standards development / Kai Jakobs, editor.
    p. cm.
  Summary: "This book provides advancing research on all current aspects of IT standards and standardization"--Provided by publisher.
  Includes bibliographical references and index.
  ISBN 978-1-4666-2160-2 (hardcover) -- ISBN 978-1-4666-2161-9 (ebook) -- ISBN 978-1-4666-2162-6 (print & perpetual access) 1. Information technology--Standards. 2. Standardization. I. Jakobs, Kai, 1957-
  T58.5.I56474 2013
  004.02'18--dc23
                          2012019565

British Cataloguing in Publication Data
A Cataloguing in Publication record for this book is available from the British Library.

The views expressed in this book are those of the authors, but not necessarily of the publisher.

Table of Contents

Section 6
Standards for Learning Technology

Detailed Table of Contents

Section 1
IPR Issues

Chapter 1

Anne Layne-Farrar, Compass LexEcon, USA

Cooperative standard setting may be burdened by "over patenting". Because standards may convey market power to firms whose patents are implicated, "strategic" patenting may enable opportunistic behaviors. Thus, particular concerns have been raised over patenting that takes place after the first versions of a standard are published, as these patents may be aimed at the acquisition of market power. This is a reasonable concern, but another possibility also may be likely: "ex post" patenting may be driven by genuine innovation. Which is more prevalent? To begin answering this question, the author empirically assesses the patenting that occurs within a standard setting organization. The author rejects the first stage hypothesis that all ex post patenting must be opportunistic and conclude instead that such patenting is likely a mixed bag of (incremental) innovative contributions along with some strategic ones. As a result, standard setting policy prescriptions should proceed with caution so that the good is not eliminated with the bad.

Chapter 2

Anne Layne-Farrar, Compass LexEcon, USA
A. Jorge Padilla, LECG, UK

Some policymakers, courts, and academics have expressed concerns that when a firm's patents are incorporated into a standard, the patents gain importance and can bestow on the patent holder market power that can be abused when the standard is commercialized. This paper extends the existing literature on the effect that standards can have on patents. This analysis has two aims: first, to better understand how an SSO might confer importance on included patents and second, to move closer to an empirical understanding of the impact of a standard on included patents. The authors create a dataset of patents named to voluntary standard setting organizations, as well as the patent pools that sometimes develop around such standards. The authors rely on proxies to capture a patent's importance or value.

Chapter 3

Roger G. Brooks, Cravath, Swaine & Moore, USA

Damien Geradin, Tilburg University, The Netherlands

Although often debated as though it were public law, a FRAND undertaking is a private contract between a patent-holder and an SSO. Applying ordinary principles of contract interpretation to the case of ETSI IPR policy reveals that "interpretations" of FRAND advocated by some authors—including cumulative royalty limits, royalties set by counting patents, or a prohibition on capture by the patent-holder of any gains created by standardization—cannot be correct (ETSI, n.d.). Rather, a FRAND obligation leaves wide latitude to private parties negotiating a license. However, this does not mean that a FRAND commitment has no substance to be enforced by courts. In this paper, the authors review how, consistent with both contract principles and established judicial method, courts can enforce a contractual obligation to offer licenses on FRAND terms, without becoming IPR price regulators. Similarly, ordinary principles of contract interpretation reveal that the "non-discriminatory" portion of FRAND cannot be interpreted to be coextensive with common "most favored nations" provisions, but instead contemplates substantial latitude for private parties to negotiate terms suited to their particular situations.

Section 2
Competing Standards

Chapter 4

Tineke M. Egyedi, Delft University of Technology, The Netherlands

Aad Koppenhol, Sun Microsystems, The Netherlands

A strong belief exists that competition between de facto standards stimulates innovation and benefits consumers because it drives down the costs of products. The tenability of this belief, and its preconditions and limits, has been widely scrutinized. However, little has been written about competition between negotiated, de jure (i.e., committee) standards. Are competing de jure standards a good thing? Blind (2008) equals de jure to de facto standards and concludes that competition between de jure standards increases social welfare. In this paper we argue that it is important to distinguish between de jure and de facto standards; therefore, that Blind's basic assumption is incorrect. We illustrate our argument with the same example as Blind, that is, the standards war between the document formats of ODF and OOXML. In our view, the implications of condoning—and even encouraging—competition between de jure standards will have far-reaching consequences for public IT-procurement. It will hinder innovation and counteract supplier-independent information exchange between government and citizens.

Chapter 5

Håkon Ursin Steen, University of Oslo, Norway

This paper addresses the concept of internal standards fragmentation in networked technologies - occurring when two or more products remain non-interoperable for an intended service, even though being perfectly compliant to the same core interface compatibility standard. Two main sources of internal fragmentation are identified ("configurational" and "competitive"). A case study is done on the historically observed internal fragmentation within the DVB-H and T-DMB mobile digital multimedia broadcasting standards. It is argued that internal standards fragmentation has important consequences hitherto unaddressed in the literature, including potentially undermining the effects of interoperability and economies of scale expected to follow from the adoption of a single standard. Implications for research, policy and practice are discussed, and advice for further research is provided.

Section 3
Standards Education

Chapter 6

This paper explores how standardization education can be implemented at the national level. Previous studies form the main source for the paper. This research shows that implementation of standardization in the national education system requires policy at the national level, a long term investment in support, and cooperation between industry, standardization bodies, academia, other institutions involved in education, and government. The approach should combine bottom-up and top-down. The paper is new in combining previous findings to an underpinned recommendation on how to implement standardization education.

Chapter 7

The role of standards is increasing, and as a result the role of education about standards should also increase. At the same time, there are a set of requirements—accreditation criteria—toward engineering programs. The close relationships between the accreditation criteria and standards education is not fully recognized, even by accreditation bodies and educators. The goal of this paper is to uncover these relationships. Furthermore, the paper establishes connections between other components of engineering education such as ethics, engineering design, labs, and integrated courses, on one hand and standards education on another. The conclusion from these relationships is that standards education is more important than previously realized. The paper also discusses how standards education can be incorporated in engineering and technical curricula.

Section 4
Consumers in Standardization

Chapter 8

The expansion of international standardization has reinforced enduring questions on the legitimacy of standards. In that respect, the participation of all stakeholders, including the weakest ones (unions, NGO, consumers' associations) is crucial. Given the recognized role of consumers' associations to express legitimate objectives, the question of their representation becomes central. In order to get a deeper understanding of their participation, this article explores the evolution of their representation within the Swiss national mirror committees of international standardization between 1987 and 2007. It probes the extent to which their participation is determined by the distinctiveness of issues supposedly related to consumers' concerns and by their own use of standards. The empirical findings of our study indicate an underrepresentation of consumers' associations and confirm the topical specificity of their implication in standardization processes. Finally, we found evidence that the use of standards in an association's activities supports and encourages its participation in standardization committees.

> *Jean-Christophe Graz, Université de Lausanne, Switzerland*
> *Christophe Hauert, Université de Lausanne, Switzerland*

This paper presents a pilot project to reinforce participatory practices in standardization. The INTER-NORM project creates an interactive knowledge center based on the sharing of academic skills and experiences accumulated by the civil society, especially consumer associations, environmental associations and trade unions to strengthen the participatory process of standardization. The first objective of the project is action-oriented: INTERNORM provides a common knowledge pool supporting the participation of civil society actors to international standard-setting activities by bringing them together with academic experts in working groups and providing logistic and financial support to their participation in meetings of national and international technical committees. The second objective is analytical: the standardization action provides a research field for a better understanding of the participatory dynamics underpinning international standardization. This paper presents three incentives that explain civil society (non-)involvement in standardization that overcome conventional resource-based hypotheses: an operational incentive related to the use of standards in the selective goods provided by associations to their membership; a thematic incentive provided by the setting of priorities by strategic committees created in some standardization organization; and a rhetorical incentive related to the discursive resource that civil society concerns offers to the different stakeholders.

Section 5
Shaping Factors

> *Anique Hommels, Maastricht University, The Netherlands*
> *Tineke M. Egyedi, Delft University of Technology, The Netherlands*

This paper analyzes the role of 'irreversibility' in the decision-making process for a standard for the national Dutch emergency communication network. In the late 1980s, ETSI, the European Telecommunication Standards Institute, started the development of the so-called Tetra standard. Tetra is a standard for digital radio communication and is mostly applied in emergency communication (for police, ambulance, and fire brigade). In the early 1990s, several European governments decided to replace their analogue radio equipment for emergency communication by advanced digital communication systems. The Dutch involvement in Tetra started around 1992, but it took until November 2001 before the official governmental decision to launch the national C2000 network was taken. This paper argues that at that moment the 'point of no return' of the C2000 project had already passed (in the mid 1990s). We explain this using the concept of 'constructed irreversibility'. We analyze a number of core decisions and choices of the Dutch government in the C2000 project that resulted in irreversibility. We conclude by discussing the disadvantages and the advantages of irreversibility in this innovation project.

Chapter 11

The Significance of Government's Role in Technology Standardization: Two Cases in the Wireless
Communications Industry 183

DongBack Seo, University of Groningen, The Netherlands

For first generation (1G) wireless communications technology standards, the Japanese government's early decision provided an opportunity for its national manufacturers to be first movers in the global market, while the late development of wireless communications in Korea made the Korean market dependent on foreign manufacturers by adopting the U.S. standard (AMPS). Moving toward the 2G wireless technology market, both countries decided to develop standards instead of adopting a technology from outside their regions. Japan developed its own standard, PDC, while Korea developed CDMA systems with Qualcomm, the U.S. technology provider. Although these governments' decisions on technologies looked only slightly different, the socio-economic consequences were greatly distinctive. The Korean success brought not only the rapid development of its domestic market but also opportunities for its manufacturers to become global leaders, while the PDC standard only provided the fast growth of the Japanese domestic market without any opportunities for the Japanese manufacturers to grow further internationally in the 1990s. By the end of 1990s, two nations again had to decide a 3G technology standard with vast challenges and pressures.

Chapter 12

An Exploratory Analysis of the Relationship between Organizational and Institutional Factors
Shaping the Assimilation of Vertical Standards 193

Rubén A. Mendoza, Saint Joseph's University, USA
T. Ravichandran, Rensselaer Polytechnic Institute, USA

Vertical standards describe products and services, define data formats and structures, and formalize and encode business processes for specific industries. Vertical standards enable end-to-end computing, provide greater visibility of the organization's supply chain, and enable transactional efficiencies by automating routine tasks, reducing errors, and formally defining all parameters used to describe a product, service, or transaction. Research on standards diffusion has explored either firm-level and institutional variables, without integration of the two areas. This study develops scales for 11 constructs based on concepts culled from diffusion of innovations theory, organizational learning theories of technology adoption, institutional theory and network effects theory. The scales are validated with data collected from the membership of OASIS, a leading international standards-developing organization for electronic commerce technologies. Using data cluster analysis, relationship patterns between the 11 constructs are investigated. Results show that low fit between vertical standards and existing organizational business processes and data formats, low levels of anticipated benefits, and inadequate momentum with critical business partners contribute to slower vertical standards assimilation. However, organizational involvement with influential standards-development organizations, and the right set of technologies, skills, and structures to readily benefit from vertical standards spur their assimilation.

Section 6
Standards for Learning Technology

The paper presents a model for the analysis, comparison and validation of standards, specifications and in particular reference models in the field of Technology Enhanced Learning (TEL). The Reference Model Analysis Grid (RMAG) establishes categories of reference models and standards. Based on those categories, a set of criteria for the analysis and validation of standards was elaborated as a part of the ICOPER project that aims at interoperable open content for competency-based TEL. The analysis of standards in this context is targeted at developing a set of validated approaches that lead to a new reference model. Four standards were investigated, taking into account a broad range of aspects like practical and semantic interoperability and integration issues. In the case study, the authors analyzed both, the standards and specifications and the usefulness of the RMAG. The results of this case study can be used for further analyses of TEL standards as well as for reference models targeted at interoperability.

This paper considers key challenges that learning technology standards must take into account: the inherent connectedness of the information and complexity as a cause of emergent behavior. Some of the limitations of historical approaches to information systems and standards development are briefly considered with generic strategies to tackle complexity and system adaptivity. A consideration of the facets of interoperability—organizational, syntactic and semantic—leads to an outline of a strategy for dealing with environmental complexity in the learning technology standards domain.

This paper explores the issues and opportunities for specifications that develop outside of the traditional governance processes of industry consortia or formal standards organisations through a discussion and comparison of three specifications developed in the education sector: XCRI (eXchanging Course-Related Information), SWORD (Simple Web service Offering Repository Deposit), and LEAP2.0 (Learner Portfolios 2.0). In each case study, there are challenges, opportunities, and accomplishments, and the experiences of each project are compared to identify commonalities and differences. Based on these case studies, the paper applies the framework developed by Wilson and Velayutham (2009) to position the specifications against similar specifications from established consortia and formal standards. Finally, the topic of incubating specifications is discussed, with implications for funding agencies with an interest in supporting interoperability.

Chapter 16

Simon Grant, JISC CETIS, UK

Rowin Young, JISC CETIS, UK

This paper reviews terminology, motivation, history and current work in areas relating to skill or competence. Many useful services, clarifying pathways within and from education to employment, self-assessment, and selection would be facilitated by better standardization of the format in which related definitions are represented, and also by a standard approach to representing the structured sets often called frameworks. To be effective, information models underlying interoperability specifications must be based on common conceptual models; the authors propose one such model as a work in progress. The authors see the way forward as reaching greater consensus about the components of competence, including intended learning outcomes, agreement on a model for frameworks allowing reuse of and comparison between components in and between frameworks, and investigation of how requirements and claims for skill and competence can be coordinated in the light of common practice in recruitment.

Chapter 17

Ingo Dahn, University Koblenz-Landau, Germany

Sascha Zimmermann, University Koblenz-Landau, Germany

This article examines the potential of application profiles and domain profiles as means to adapt technical specifications of data structures to particular needs. The authors argue that application profiling is better suited to increase the use of formal specifications than the creation of new specifications. The authors also describe a method to generate specific conformance test systems for machine-readable application profiles. The authors describe the respective tool set of the SchemaProf Application Profiling Tool and the Generic Test System and report on the experience of their usage in developing and introducing the IMS Common Cartridge domain profile.

Chapter 18

Jad Najjar, WU Vienna, Austria

Michael Dernt, University of Vienna, Austria

Tomaž Klobučar, WU Vienna, Austria

Bernd Simon, WU Vienna, Austria

Michael Totschnig, WU Vienna, Austria

Simon Grant, JISC CETIS, UK

Jan Pawlowski, University of Jyväskylä, Finland

Employers seek people that match particular qualifications and graduates seek jobs that match their qualifications. This market is currently managed primarily using paper certificates and heterogeneous university management systems that capture achieved learning outcomes as well as corporate information systems that capture required qualifications. In light of trends toward increased student mobility, employability and lifelong learning, this situation is less than satisfactory. Therefore, in this paper, the authors propose a schema that facilitates interoperable storage and management of Personal Achieved Learning Outcomes (PALO) based on a common data model. This paper presents use case scenarios and implementations addressing these challenges and demonstrating the added value of using such a common model.

Preface

Research into standards and standardisation in the field of Information and Communication Technology (ICT) continues to fascinate me, and the collection of papers in this volume may give you an impression why. For one, it is an extremely heterogeneous and multi-disciplinary field. There are papers written by lawyers, political scientists, and social scientists; by mathematicians, computer scientists, information systems people, and engineers. The list could go on for quite a while, but this gives an idea of the broadness of perspectives in this book alone. The breadth is extremely helpful, if not downright necessary, if you want to get an at least reasonably complete picture of what is going on in ICT standards and standardisation research. It also helps you to broaden your own perspective, to take on board tools, methodologies, and approaches from disciplines other than your own. I guess I am a rather good example for that – in an earlier life I was trained to become an electrical engineer, these days I'm entitled to call myself a computer scientist (although I rarely ever do that) and am with a Computer Science department. Yet, the work I'm trying to do could also easily be associated with a department of Social Sciences or of Information Systems. Working in this field definitely helps to avoid tunnel vision.

Of course, there's no such thing as a free lunch, and the benefits you get from working in such a multi-disciplinary field also come at a price. For one – as those of you who have chosen to at least more or less abandon mono-disciplinarity will have noticed – it is becoming increasingly difficult, for example, to publish your findings or to get funding for your research ideas in the first place. Today, the vast majority of journals have a strong mono-disciplinary focus and an equally focussed Editorial Board. And they will (have to) evaluate your findings accordingly. Sadly, few of us are e.g. excellent enough engineers and competent enough sociologists to publish in journals from both disciplines. Perhaps even worse, judging by my own experiences as well as by stories I've heard from others funding for project proposals in standardisation research is very hard to get. I remember a fairly large German proposal in which basically all senior figures with a background and an interest in ICT standardisation research were involved. It was rejected and until today I wonder where on Earth the funding organisation had found competent evaluators.

Be that as it may, and despite all the downsides, ICT standardisation research remains a fascinating field. And unlike the more technical disciplines (where I come from) where the shelf-life of most findings is measured in months rather than years, insights and findings in our field remain valid for quite a while (I quite regularly consult books from the 1980s and 1990s). Likewise, the papers in this book have probably been written in 2009/2010, but remain highly relevant until this day (and will probably stay so for another couple of years).

Yet, this is not to say that the field is static – quite the contrary. Here in Europe, for instance, the European Commission has recently published a Communication' on a strategic vision for European standards. If accepted by Parliament and Council it will quite massively change the current situation in a number of respects. Among others, the Communication addresses the aspects of the need for an improved awareness of and education about standards and calls for an increased participation of consumers and other members of what I quite like to call the third estate' in standardisation[1] (these aspects are also addressed in Sections 3 and 4 of this book, respectively). What exactly it takes to implement the proposed changes and to meet the requirements laid out in the document is a most interesting topic and will attract researchers' attention for a while. The same holds for the likely implications to be expected. Specifically, the foreseen use of consortium standards poses the question of how to maintain the contradiction-free European standards system (the issue of competing standards is discussed in Section 2).

The new proposed regulation not least aims to strengthen the role of Europe in the ICT standardisation arena. One of the crucial recent developments there is the increasing importance of the emerging markets of, for example, China, India, and Brazil. Especially China has well understood the importance of standards and the associated Intellectual Property Rights (IPR) and has for a while been strengthening its position in various standards bodies. What the traditional incumbents can do not to loose out and how to mutually beneficially co-operate with the new players are other highly relevant and timely questions (IPR issues are addressed in Section 1).

The policy developments in Europe outlined above are to no small extent based on findings of the research community. This is another benefit of the work we are doing – there is a very realistic chance that its outcome will find its way into policy making, even if it may occasionally take some time.

Yet, in addition to the grand' topics like IPR and standards battles there a number of perhaps less obvious aspects that frequently escape public and research's attention. These include, for example, the various external and internal factors that shape the standardisation process in a more, say, informal' way. My hobby horse – the influence of the individual – would fall into this category. While this specific aspect is only touched upon in this book, two papers of section 5 look at other such shaping factors).

But now over to the papers.

All papers included in this compilation have gone through a thorough review process. My normal policy is to have at least three reviews per paper; quite frequently I've got four. I try to assign not just specialists as reviewers to a particular paper, but try to also have a *multi-disciplinary review process.* That is, I normally try to have at least also one "layperson" review a paper (i.e. someone with a general background in standardisation but from a different background). I have found that this adds another valuable dimension to the review – the average computer scientist, for example, may neither be able nor inclined to check the equations in an economist's paper, nor may s/he be in a position to check the suitability of the approach chosen. But s/he may well be able to look at, for example, underlying assumptions from another discipline's point of view and thus highlight potential issues, problems, but also, of course, specific strengths.

I have grouped the papers into six topical fields.

1. IPR issues
2. Competing standards
3. Standards education
4. Consumers in standardisation
5. Shaping factors
6. Standards for Learning Technology

Out of these, five are quite natural choices. Only the Shapers' heading may be a bit far-fetched; I hope not overly much so.

SECTION 1: IPR ISSUES

The discussion about how to best incorporate IPR into standards and about the ramifications of the different approaches has been high on the agenda for a number of years now. The three papers of this part also address these issues but have one common characteristic – they challenge widely held views and perceptions.

The first paper, *Innovative or Indefensible? An Empirical Assessment of Patenting within Standard Setting*, by Anne Layne-Farrar (Compass LexEcon, USA), starts off with the observation that co-operative standard setting frequently suffers from over patenting. It discusses problems and issues many claim to be associated with a specific form of what may be called strategic patenting – ex-post patenting. This occurs once the first versions of a standard have been published. Concerns have been raised over this form of patenting as it allegedly only serves to acquire or increase market power, without actually contributing anything to the value of the associated standard. In contrast, the author argues that also such ex-post patenting may be driven by genuine innovation. To try and answer the question which form can be observed more frequently, she analyses the case of UMTS (Universal Mobile Telecommunications System). She shows that around 91% of US patents and around 82% of EPO patents were filed before 2002, i.e. prior to the commercialisation period of UMTS. The analysis suggests that a vast majority (up to 70% - 80%) of the remaining patents – that have been applied for ex-post – represent at least incremental innovations and, therefore, contribute value to the standard. Accordingly, the claim that ex-post patenting is entirely driven by strategic motives has to be rejected.

The second paper was written by Anne Layne-Farrar (Compass LexEcon, USA) and A. Jorge Padilla (LECG, UK), and is entitled *Assessing the Link between Standards and Patents*. It has a closer look at the question whether or not its inclusion in a standard has an effect a patent's importance? This is done against the background of policy makers, courts, and academics having expressed concerns about the increasing importance a patent acquires once it has been incorporated into a standard, and about the resulting significantly increased market power of the patent holder that can be abused if and when the standard is commercialised. The authors' findings suggest that a patent does not necessarily increase in value because of its inclusion in a standard. If it does, frequently the value gain is very small. Especially the values of those patents that cover a highly valuable innovation do not gain much through standards, as they are valuable in any case. Moreover, the authors find that patents included in a patent pool tend to be less important than otherwise comparable patents. The authors rely on proxies to capture a patent's importance or value.

The third paper of this section is *Interpreting and Enforcing the Voluntary FRAND Commitment*, by Roger G. Brooks (Cravath, Swaine & Moore, USA) and Damien Geradin (Tilburg University, The Netherlands). It discusses one of the currently most contentious issues in ICT standardisation research, i.e. the legally precise meaning of a commitment by the holder of patents essential' for a standard to license such patents on fair, reasonable, and non-discriminatory (FRAND) terms and conditions. The authors argue that any FRAND agreement is a private contract between a patent-holder and a standards body, and that a FRAND commitment on the one hand and the limitations that competition law may impose on IPRs on the other are two separate things each of which needs to be considered in its own right. Accordingly, any attempts to e.g. cap royalties or to apply certain algorithms to calculate maximum acceptable royalties are without basis. Nonetheless, the authors review how courts can enforce a contractual obligation to offer licenses on FRAND terms – consistent with both contract principles and established judicial method – without becoming IPR price regulators.

SECTION 2: COMPETING STANDARDS

Standards wars or battles have attracted researchers' attention for quite a while now. Probably the most popular case is the competition between VHS and BetaMax standards for Video Cassette Recording systems, which is still frequently cited today (not least by both papers in this section).

In the paper *The Standards War between ODF and OOXML: Does Competition between Overlapping ISO Standards Lead to Innovation?*, Tineke M. Egyedi (Delft University of Technology, The Netherlands) and Aad Koppenhol (Sun Microsystems, The Netherlands) argue against the belief that competition between de-jure standards (i.e. those negotiated inside a committee) stimulates innovation and benefits consumers because it drives down the costs of products as competition between de-facto standards (i.e. proprietary ones owned by a company) does. Using the example of the two ISO standards on document formats – ODF and OOXML – they maintain that competition between two de-jure standards eliminates the advantages of de-jure standardisation. They claim such competition to result in a non-transparent market, raise transaction costs, and hamper interoperability. They observe that the objective of ODF, the first of the two competing standards, was to ease interoperability between different office suites, increase supplier independence, and improve accessibility and digital sustainability of documents. The approval of OOXML, the second standard (originally developed by Microsoft), is said to not add extra value. Rather, they say, it will hinder innovation and impede supplier-independent information exchange between government and citizens.

The second paper of this section is entitled *The Battle Within: An Analysis of Internal Fragmentation in Networked Technologies Based on a Comparison of the DVB-H and T-DMB Mobile Digital Multimedia Broadcasting Standards*, and was written by Håkon Ursin Steen (University of Oslo, Norway). The author argues that having a standard is not a guarantee for interoperability. Rather, it is just a step in this direction. One major reason for this is the possibility of what he calls internal standards fragmentation. This may happen in two ways – configurational fragmentation will occur if a standard is not 100% non-ambiguous; for instance, it may offer some flexibility through e.g. functional options. This way, two implementations may be fully standard-compliant, but not interoperable. Competitive fragmentation may occur if a vendor or service provider enhances' a standard, thus locking-in customers. A case study of the DVB-H and T-DMB mobile digital multimedia broadcasting standards is used to highlight both variations of internal fragmentation. The author argues that this form of fragmentation has the potential to undermine the effects of interoperability and economies of scale expected to follow from the adoption of a single standard. He discusses the implications of this observation for research, policy, and practice are discussed, and offers advice for further research.

SECTION 3: STANDARDS EDUCATION

Education about standardisation has become a fairly hot topic. Especially standards bodies, including among others ISO, the ESOs (CEN/CENELEC and ETSI), and IEEE have developed in interest in the field and have launched numerous initiatives, from a repository of teaching material to model curricula to en eZine on standards education.

The papers in this section look a various aspects relating to standards education, from its implementation at a national level to accreditation issues to a practical application to strengthen consumer participation in standardisation.

The first paper, authored by Henk J. de Vries (Erasmus University, The Netherlands) in entitled *Implementing Standardization Education at the National Level*. Looking at the developments in standards education in Korea (the world leader in the field) and the Netherlands, the author shows that any initiatives to implement standards education in a national education system requires policy support at the national level, a long term investment in the support of the initiative, and co-operation between all major stakeholders – industry, standardisation bodies, academia, other educational institutions, and the government. In industry, the lack of awareness of the strategic importance of standards needs to be improved. Along similar lines, the desirable professionalisation of standardisation call for better educated technical officers in the standards bodies. The analogous argument applies to many civil servants, e.g. those who work on innovation or technology policy. Accordingly, especially universities need to incorporate standards education in the technical, business oriented and legal curricula. The barriers to be overcome here include making the topic of standardisation more appealing to students, to stimulate teachers' willingness to include the topic in their courses, and to raise the awareness of the importance of standardisation education for industry and government representatives. The author outlines ways how these barriers might be overcome.

Focussing on the engineering sector in the US, the paper by Todor Cooklev (Indiana University – Purdue University Fort Wayne, USA) on *The Role of Standards in Engineering Education* looks at the relation between accreditation criteria and education about standards and standardisation. The author argues that the relation between accreditation requirements and engineering, computing, and technology education on the one hand, and standards education on the other is not fully recognised, not even by accreditation bodies and educators. In the US, accreditation requirements on engineering programmes cover both hard skills and soft skills. The author claims that teaching standards is one particularly efficient way to achieve the integration of soft skills and design thinking in the engineering curriculum. He also states that through standards education both the hard skills and the soft skills can be taught at the same time. Specifically, he claims that the education about standards leads to several important benefits, including the motivation to learn in other engineering science courses, an enhanced performance in capstone design courses, a likewise enhanced student interest in engineering, the encouragement and support of collaborative work, and an enhanced design thinking.

SECTION 4: CONSUMERS IN STANDARDISATION

Consumers are probably the weakest part of the third-estate in standardisation. From my point of view their participation is not necessary in some cases (discussing the finer technical points of, for example, a new version of the Internet Protocol will be beyond both the technical expertise and the interest of most consumers) but crucially important in others, like in the standardisation of e.g. user interfaces, smart cards, or many aspects of the Internet of Things.

The paper *Where Are You? Consumers' Associations in Standardization: A Case Study on Switzerland*, by Christophe Hauert (University of Lausanne, Switzerland), is looking for consumers in standards setting. One of their roles would be to increase the legitimacy of a standard; to this end, participation of all stakeholders, including the weakest ones (unions, NGO, consumers' associations) is crucial. Yet, for consumers the question of their representation is important – individuals will hardly go to the lengths of becoming active members of standards committees. In this article the author explores the evolution of consumer representation in Swiss national mirror committees between 1987 and 2007. It probes the extent to which their participation is determined by issues supposedly related to consumers' concerns and by their own use of standards. The empirical findings clearly demonstrate the weakness of consumer representation, resulting from both a lack of material resources and – perhaps especially – their lack of technical expertise. On the other hand, the actual deployment of standards by associations (e.g. for testing and certification) offers a fairly strong incentive for participation.

The paper about *The INTERNORM Project: Bridging Two Worlds of Expert- and Lay-Knowledge in Standardization*, by Jean-Christophe Graz and Christophe Hauert, (University of Lausanne, Switzerland) presents a pilot project that aims to strengthen participatory practices in standardisation by better enabling civil society to take part in this process. To this end, the project creates an interactive knowledge centre that enables sharing of academic skills and experiences accumulated especially by consumer associations, environmental associations, and trade unions to strengthen their respective constituencies' participation in standardisation. At the same time, it provides a useful research tool to develop a better understanding of the role of these stakeholders in the setting of the technical specifications that govern globalisation. The authors identify three incentives which explain the dynamics of association's (non-) involvement in standards setting. These include an operational incentive that is related to the use of standards in the product and services provided by associations to their members. A thematic incentive, which is provided by the setting of priorities by strategic committees created in some standardisation organisations, and a rhetorical incentive, related to the discursive resource that civil society concerns offers to stakeholders. These three incentives are illustrated using the case of the consumers association as a precursory civil society association. The paper also shows that lack of technical expertise is not necessarily such an overriding issue,

SECTION 5: SHAPING FACTORS

Standards are shaped by a variety of actors and influences. Very subjective aspects like, for instance, preferences and abilities of individual members of a standards committee may play a role, as may highly objective aspects like new technical developments and corporate strategic interests. The first two papers of this section look at the shaping power of government in standards setting, albeit from very different perspectives. In contrast, the third paper analyses the factors that shape the adoption of a standard.

In their paper *Beyond the Point of No Return: Constructing Irreversibility in Decision Making on the Tetra Standard in Dutch Emergency Communication*, Anique Hommels, (Maastricht University, The Netherlands) and Tineke M. Egyedi (Delft University of Technology, The Netherlands) analyse the role of irreversibility' in the decision-making process for a standard for the national Dutch emergency communication network. In the 19902, a decision had to be made between Tetra (standardised by ETS) and Tetrapol (a proprietary system favoured by France) had to be made. The authors show that the official political decision to implement the Tetra-based network was more of a rubber-stamping of the outcome of an innovation process that had grown irreversibly long before. They argue that irreversibility did not occur because of any characteristics of the technology or because of investments of individual actors. Rather, this was a constructed' irreversibility, shaped by the actions and interactions of several key governmental actors. For one, reports, correspondence, and actions of Dutch government officials revealed a strong commitment to Tetra and to the idea of a common European standard from the early 1990s onwards. Moreover, strong personal commitment of the Dutch officials further contributed to the attractiveness of Tetra. The authors provide arguments pro and con irreversibility in their case. Sticking to a choice even if the subsequent implementation may be problematic. Moreover, an early irreversibility of large scale projects may undermine the democratic nature of the underlying political decision process. On the other hand, path dependence may also create new possibilities. In this case, the persistence of some key players led to the eventual nationwide implementation.

In the above paper government referred to the role of individual civil servants. In the paper *The Significance of Government's Role in Technology Standardization: Two Cases in the Wireless Communications Industry*, by DongBack Seo (University of Groningen, The Netherlands) it actually refers to the *entity government*. The author observes that governments, like companies, can bet on the wrong standard. This paper illustrates the importance of the government's role in standards setting through two cases: the choices of South Korea and Japan, respectively, for a national technology standard for wireless communications. In the late 1980s, both governments decided to upgrade their respective telephone networks to a 2G standard. However, the largely home-grown Japanese specification PDC was only implemented domestically but never became an international success. Eventually, this lead to the decline of the Japanese wireless communication industry. In contrast, CDMA, the proprietary technology selected by the Korean government subsequently fared very well internationally and gave Korean manufacturers a head start in the wireless handset market. The paper offers two explanations for this outcome – for one, it was known that CDMA was technologically more advanced than PDC. More importantly, CDMA offered a natural migration path to third generation (3G) mobile communication technology.

Rubén A. Mendoza (Saint Joseph's University, USA) and T. Ravichandran (Rensselaer Polytechnic Institute, USA) are the authors of the paper *An Exploratory Analysis of the Relationship between Organizational and Institutional Factors Shaping the Assimilation of Vertical Standards*. The papers focus on the adoption of vertical standards. Such standards define industry-specific vocabularies for product and service descriptions, operating and interface system parameters, and semantic data definitions for specific industries. Their adoption has generally been treated as a single event indicated by a public announcement of the acquisition or first deployment of these technologies. However, the authors note that wide-scale industry acquisition of new technologies is sometimes followed by sparse deployment within the acquiring firms, resulting in a gap between reported adoption and internal deployment of the technologies. The authors explore the assimilation of vertical standards as a progression from first awareness through complete deployment in production environments in order to reduce the effect of assimilation gaps. They develop scales for 11 constructs based on concepts from different theories such as diffusion of innovations theory, organisational learning theories of technology adoption, institutional theory and network effects theory. An investigation of relationship patterns between the 11 constructs using data cluster analysis shows that a low fit between vertical standards and existing organisational business processes and data formats, low levels of anticipated benefits, and inadequate momentum with critical business partners contribute to slower vertical standards assimilation. However, organisational involvement with influential standards-development organisations, and the right set of technologies, skills, and structures to readily benefit from vertical standards spur their assimilation.

SECTION 6: STANDARDS FOR LEARNING TECHNOLOGY[2]

Standards in the Technology-Enhanced Learning (TEL) domain, also denoted as Learning Technology Standards, have over the past decade been the subject of increased attention. As the education and training sector gains importance and technologies are ubiquitous within educational processes, it is natural that these standards are located within the conversation However, the adoption and deployment of standards in education is not meeting the expectations of the learning technology standards community, this is in marked contrast to other vertical industries.

What is the current status of development in Learning Technology standardization? What are the main developments and how are these developments adopted, or not, by the TEL-community and what is the future potential of this field? The papers in this section represent an attempt to answer these questions.

The paper *Analysis and Validation of Learning Technology Models, Standards and Specifications: The Reference Model Analysis Grid (RMAG)* by Jan M. Pawlowski and Denis Kozlov (University of Jyväskylä, Finland) addresses how standards, specifications and, more general, reference models can be evaluated and assessed. As there is currently no widely accepted assessment framework, this paper provides an insight into potential categories and criteria for assessment. It should be noted that there will be no one-fits-all framework. The outlined framework provides a basis, to be adapted for the purpose of evaluations and assessments in different contexts.

Is the learning technology domain unique in going through standardisation, or does it differ? This is a crucial question posed by Adam R. Cooper (University of Bolton, UK) in his paper on the *Key Challenges in the Design of Learning Technology Standards: Observations and Proposals*. His observations are compared to a business enterprise; he argues that the workings of the education system as a whole are rather more complicated than other domains. Consequently, you require more than the engineering heritage to deal with the complex challenges presented. Further he argues of the need to account for the inherent complexity of the domain. Therefore, LT standards should be developed to accommodate diversity and change and to be part-of the systemic processes from which learning technology emerges. Both the organisational aspects of standardisation and the technical aspect of how standards are written need to be addressed.

One approach to this challenge is pragmatic *Community-Driven Specifications: XCRI, SWORD, and LEAP2A*, described in the paper by Scott Wilson (University of Bolton, UK). He analyses three UK projects developing specifications independent of the traditional governance processes of either industry consortia or formal standards organisations. From a technical perspective, these specifications there are inspired by open web standards and semantic technologies, rather than repository vertical standardisation. From an organisational point of view, even though they are anchored in specific user communities and nursed by project funding from the educational sector, they are fed into formal standardisation as part of a broader sustainability strategy.

Two of the specifications Wilson explored are related to a new field of interest for ITLET standardisation, areas related to skill and competence. This is the starting point for Simon Grant and Rowin Young (JISC CETIS, UK), entitled *Concepts and Standardization in Areas Relating to Competence*. They offer a common conceptual model to guide the discussion towards the kind of useful specifications and standards that can enable the many real services that may well be demanded in this area. The aim is through collaborative modelling involving educators, trainers, employers, learners, assessors / evaluators, professional bodies, awarders of licenses or certificates, customers / clients, careers advisors, and any other stakeholders to come up with agreed concepts. The advocated approach consistent with the increased diversity in this field is to recognise quite small units of ability, and to be able to build these up in different ways to express the needs of different roles and positions. Grand and Young point to semantic web technology, in particular W3C's Simple Knowledge Organisation System, SKOS, as an enabler for this kind of standardisation work.

While Grant & Young start where concepts need to be negotiated to gain a clear meaning, the point of departure for Ingo Dahn' and Sascha Zimmermann' (University Koblenz-Landau, Germany) paper on *Application Profiles and Tailor-Made Conformance Test Systems* is where we already have precisely defined and testable concepts, i.e., in mature specifications and standards. They discuss the potential of application profiles and domain profiles as means to adapt technical specifications of data structures to particular needs. Dahn & Zimmerman argue that application profiling may be better suited to increase the take-up of formal specifications than the creation of new specifications. They support their claim by referring to successful examples of conformance test systems for machine-readable application profiles.

Profiling, if not conformance testing, plays an important role in the paper of Jad Najjar (WU Vienna, Austria) et al., proposing a *Data Model for Describing and Exchanging Personal Achieved Learning Outcomes (PALO)*. This specification is a step towards a common model supporting the exchange of date about knowledge, skills and competencies, to enhance interoperability of personal learning outcome information between, for example, learning management systems, e-portfolios, social applications and recruitment systems. The model builds on the result of a European project that builds on the premises of the European Qualification Framework (EQF), extending and profiling existing standards and specifications as IEEE LOM, IEEE RCD, et cetera.

Kai Jakobs
RWTH Aachen University, Germany

ENDNOTES

[1]   In pre-revolutionary France everyone who was neither clergy nor aristocracy (i.e., about 98% of the people) belonged to the Third Estate. They didn't have any say at all in state affairs. In standardisation, the 'Third Estate' comprises primarily SMEs, users, and consumers.

[2]   The following is an adaptation of the editorial preface to the special issue 'Learning Technology Standards' entitled 'On the Status of Learning Technology Specifications and Standards', by Tore Hoel (Oslo University College, Norway), Paul A. Hollins (University of Bolton, UK), and Jan M. Pawlowski (University of Jyväskylä, Finland).

Section 1
IPR Issues

Chapter 1
Innovative or Indefensible? An Empirical Assessment of Patenting within Standard Setting

Anne Layne-Farrar
Compass LexEcon, USA

ABSTRACT

Cooperative standard setting may be burdened by "over patenting". Because standards may convey market power to firms whose patents are implicated, "strategic" patenting may enable opportunistic behaviors. Thus, particular concerns have been raised over patenting that takes place after the first versions of a standard are published, as these patents may be aimed at the acquisition of market power. This is a reasonable concern, but another possibility also may be likely: "ex post" patenting may be driven by genuine innovation. Which is more prevalent? To begin answering this question, the author empirically assesses the patenting that occurs within a standard setting organization. The author rejects the first stage hypothesis that all ex post patenting must be opportunistic and conclude instead that such patenting is likely a mixed bag of (incremental) innovative contributions along with some strategic ones. As a result, standard setting policy prescriptions should proceed with caution so that the good is not eliminated with the bad.

INTRODUCTION

Much has been written — especially in recent years — regarding the perceived problem of "over patenting" within cooperative standard setting. Because standards can convey market setting. Because standards can convey market power to those firms whose patented technologies are included in the standard, the concern is that "strategic" patenting, driven not by innovation but by rent seeking, will enable firms to license their intellectual property (IP) opportunistically. Hence, theories of IP "anti-commons", "patent

DOI: 10.4018/978-1-4666-2160-2.ch001

thickets", and "royalty stacking" have been proposed in the academic literature, along with policy ideas aimed at reducing such problems (Shapiro, 2001; Mueller, 2001; Lemley & Shapiro, 2006). Much of the attention has focused on the sheer rise in patent numbers. With more and more patents being declared as potentially "essential" for the implementation of any given standard, what are the possible detrimental effects on the standardization process? How could the commercialization of the standard be affected? And what are the implications for overall innovation within standard setting contexts?

While several scholars have recognized a link between standards and innovation when considering the benefits of standardization, this story is traditionally one of research and development in anticipation of a new standard (e.g., Farrell & Saloner, 1985). That is, the chance to increase the end market size through cooperative standardization can provide enhanced incentives to innovate, meaning higher expenditures on R&D, which of course can be accompanied by patenting.

Increased patenting that takes place *during* standardization, however, and especially patenting that takes place *after* the first versions of a standard are published, tends to be viewed differently. Such "ex post" patenting is often seen as opportunistic and aimed at the unwarranted acquisition of market power. The logic behind this concern is that once a standard is defined, the key pioneering innovations have already taken place and thus any additional patenting is likely aimed at shifting rents and staking a larger (unjustified) claim of the standard's IP licensing revenues.

Several scholars have raised concerns over such opportunistic patenting. For example, in their empirical analysis of the 3G mobile telecom standard UMTS (Universal Mobile Telecommunications System), Bekkers and West (2009) caution that

A key form of standards-related strategic patenting is when a firm deduces the direction that a standardization effort is proceeding [in] and then

attempts to create patents to read on that standard. One way such strategic patenting might be evidenced would be if the patents were filed well after the corresponding standardization effort had begun.

Likewise, Hunt, Simojoki, and Takalo (2007) posit that "... firms may anticipate the outcome of the standard-setting process and apply for patents that would be infringed by users conforming to the standard." And Dewatripont and Legros (2007) use strategic patenting as motivation for their theoretical assessment of patent "padding" within a standard.

It seems safe to surmise that firms do engage in opportunistic patenting, particularly when the commercial stakes are high, as they often are. But another possibility exists in tandem: that at least some ex post patenting is driven by genuine innovation. This follows from the incremental nature of the standardization process. Once the path of a new standard is chosen, much work may still remain to define the precise implementation details. For example, at the time the technology for the UMTS mobile telecoms standard was selected, the document specifying a crucial component was only 30 pages long, but by the time the standard was ready for commercial implementation the page count had increased to over 13,000.[1] This suggests considerable additional work was necessary to move from the theoretical concept of the chosen technology to the reality of putting that technology to work in the field. This interpretation is corroborated in an industry analyst report, which although focused on mobile telecom notes that the difficulties in moving from concept to implementation are felt in all industries involving complex products and cooperative standards: "Implementation IPR ... actually makes up the vast majority of all IPR filed in any technical standard. ... In many ways it is just as important ... just as a window is of no use unless it can be effectively placed in the space that has been designed for it."[2]

Participating firms have strong incentives to solve specific technical problems related to the optimal implementation of a standard so as to move to commercialization as quickly as possible, to increase consumer acceptance and to maximize overall profits. Thus the period of time just after a standard's initial publication, when the general technology path has been chosen, could be a highly innovative one.

A second possibility for ex post innovation lies in market structure. Consider an early generation standard dominated by a relatively small set of firms. If that standard achieves commercial success, other firms (outside the standard organization) with closely related operations or skill sets could have incentives to innovate in the space in order to join the standard and share in the profits. The existing standard demonstrates commercial success and a perception of supra-competitive pricing for incumbents suggests profits to be made for new entrants. This is how markets are supposed to work: high profits lure entry and competition. Outside firms cannot join an existing standard, however, without a valuable contribution to offer; incumbents will not relinquish their positions easily and must see something in exchange. Offering new innovations for consideration in the next generation of a standard can provide outside firms with an entrée into the evolution of an existing standard.

The above reasoning raises the possibility that ex post patenting within cooperative standard setting reflects innovative efforts *and* opportunistic motives. While we cannot disregard potential problems associated with opportunistic patenting and patent proliferation, understanding that cooperative standards can also spur legitimate innovation throughout the standardization process provides a mitigating effect to concerns over strategic patenting. This paper represents a first attempt at measuring whether and to what extent mid-standard patenting might reflect incremental innovations or purely opportunistic motives.

The paper offers an empirical assessment of the patenting that occurs within an SSO. Under the most cynical view of rent-seeking behavior, all (or the vast majority of) patenting that occurs after the initial version of a standard has been published is opportunistic. While no one has taken the extreme position that *all* ex post patenting is opportunistic, this simple hypothesis offers a good starting point for analysis. Thus the null hypothesis tested here is that *none* of the ex post patenting is innovative. If the data cannot reject this hypothesis, then clearly most ex post patenting is indeed strategic. If the available data can reject this hypothesis, then we can move on to the more nuanced question of how much ex post patenting is strategic.

Taking the 3G mobile telecom standard as a test case,[3] consider indicators of innovation. Measuring "innovation" is extremely difficult, and none of the measures used here are perfect. The goal is to look at innovation from several different objective angles to obtain a reasonable indication of innovation in the aggregate. The first measure is R&D expenditures, which should correlate closely with patent application filings if such filings represent innovation. The second measure relies on innovation proxies developed in the IP literature (Trajtenberg, 1990). In particular, the number of claims per patent and the number of forward citations a patent receives are evaluated. These measures provide reasonable proxies for the value of patents and can thus be used for the purpose of weeding out innovative patents from standard "padding". The third measure considers the technical specifications that SSO members (typically engineers) submit for consideration to technical working groups. Firms may not be inclined to incur the costs necessary to make the technical case for a patent if it holds little technical merit. Note that technical submissions are not required before making patent declarations to a standard.

The next section presents the quantitative analysis. It begins with a definition of the dataset, which includes patents declared as potentially "essential" for the implementation of the 3G mobile standard developed under the European Telecommunications Standards Institute (ETSI).[4] Patent declarations are categorized according to the phase of standardization at the time the patent application is filed: early development, after the technology path has been chosen, or during commercialization. These categorizations define the extent of ex post patenting. The section then turns to an assessment of innovation. As an initial test, patent declarations are tracked against the proxy measures of patent value. Next, the correlation between patent declarations and technical specification filings is considered. The last tests are more rigorous: regressions are run on patent filings, R&D expenditures, technical submissions, an indicator variable for whether the patent application was filed ex post or not, and other controls. Finally, some preliminary analysis on the extent of opportunistic versus innovative ex post patenting is presented. Finally, we conclude the paper.

Given the complexity of standard setting and patenting, empirical investigation is especially important. I find that ex post patent filings fall into a grey area and cannot be dismissed as entirely rent seeking; many ex post patents do appear valuable on the basis of reasonable measures.[5] Seen in the context of how standards are developed, this finding is not surprising: moving from the forest of the general technology path to the trees of specific implementation is bound to raise a host of unresolved technological problems. If ETSI's UMTS standard is representative of complex standardization in general, the broader lesson is that caution should be exercised when considering policies aimed at "late" patents, from either competition/regulatory agencies or from standard setting bodies. The next research steps should be aimed at better determining the extent of strategic as compared to innovative patenting.

SEPARATING INNOVATIVE FROM STRATEGIC PATENTING

Determining whether patents filed after a standard's general path has been selected have any innovative merit or whether they are merely tools for rent extraction is a difficult empirical matter. Both theories are plausible, so the question must be answered by examining the available data. Because no one measure is perfect, the analysis here considers several measures of innovation.

The Data

The dataset used contains patents declared as potentially essential for the 3G mobile telecom standard UMTS (aka WCDMA).[6] Measures meant to capture the value of the patented technology are added to identify defensible patenting of innovations from patenting intended only to extract additional licensing revenues. These measures are evaluated over time, in relation to key milestones in standardization. Figure 1 identifies key standardization dates for UMTS.

The first UMTS working groups were created in December 1998. These groups evaluated several overarching technologies that could have formed the 3G standard.[7] One of these technology paths was voted as the standard in December 1999, when UMTS Release 1999 took place. This is the "selection" date for the path of the standard. At this point, the other broad technologies that had been competing were taken off the table. From December 1999 to late 2001, working groups filled in the many details required to flesh out the standard within the chosen path. It was not until enough of these details were settled that the firms hoping to implement the standard — handset makers, network equipment makers, network operators, etc. — began their commercialization efforts in earnest and were able to introduce the first commercial network based on UMTS in late 2001.

Figure 1. UMTS timeline

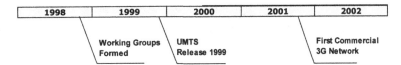

The UMTS standard is a reasonable candidate for investigating strategic patenting. First, ETSI is a very large SSO with member firms across the globe.[8] Second, the UMTS standard involves *many* patents — probably around 1500 – 2000, although an exact count is difficult to attain.[9] Third, ETSI appears to do a relatively good job of publicly listing on its website all patents declared as potentially essential. Fourth, ETSI members do a relatively good job of declaring specific IP, as opposed to making blanket declarations pertaining to "any relevant patents" a firm might hold that might be deemed to read on the standard. Other large SSOs, such as the Institute for Electronics and Electrical Engineers (IEEE), tend to have far more blanket declarations than specific ones, rendering empirical analysis infeasible.

The final dataset contains 1247 US patents and 341 EPO patents,[10] declared by 31 different entities. Some of the entities included are subsidiaries of others; these were merged. One non-profit government research institute was deleted, since the hypothesis involves rent-seeking behavior on the part of patent holders. The final sample therefore has 27 for-profit firms holding UMTS patents, 25 of which have at least one US patent.[11] For each firm in the sample, company data on yearly R&D expenditures and total company patent filings were added.

R&D Statistics

Figure 2 shows how the R&D expenditures of the 6 ETSI member firms with the highest annual R&D expenditures change over time.[12] Unfortunately, all of the firms report *aggregate*

R&D expenditures; they do not break spending out into technology fields or product lines. As a result, the R&D figures for firms with widely diversified operations, such as Panasonic and Intel among others, will include R&D on many projects wholly unrelated to UMTS. The chart includes an industry benchmark[13] as a comparison point. Observe that the industry benchmark peaks right before the dot-com bubble burst and then begins to recover again starting in 2002.

No general pattern is discernible in R&D spending over time. For 7 of the 25 firms for which we have sufficient data, average R&D spending is not statistically different for the period before versus after commercialization. Of the remaining 18 firms, 9 have a statistically higher average R&D spend for the period prior to commercialization, while 9 have a lower average.

Measures to Identify Innovation

The key to the analysis is distinguishing between innovative and strategic patenting. Relying on the literature, I calculate a number of proxies for patent value or innovative content. Among these are the subsequent citations that the ETSI-declared patents have received thus far.[14] As established by Trajtenberg and others (Trajtenberg, 1990; Harhoff et al., 1999), an accepted method for objectively quantifying a patent's value involves calculating the number of times that patent is cited by later patents (forward cites).[15]

When filing a patent in the US, inventors and assignees typically provide the patent examiner with a list of "prior art" (backward citations). Prior art

Figure 2. Inflation adjusted R&D expenditures (top third)

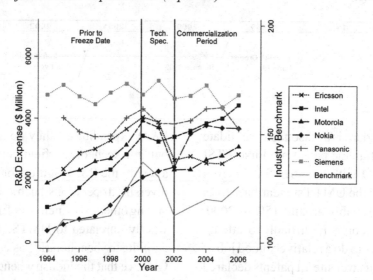

—comprised of earlier patents, academic articles, trade press, or textbooks — is the foundation of innovations that influenced the invention seeking a patent. Patent examiners also search through patent office records to determine whether other patents bear on the patent application. Patent prior art is carefully considered as it defines the breadth of the current patents' claims and can affect validity examinations and litigation outcomes (Jaffe & Trajtenberg, 1999; Hall et al., 2005). A patent that is subsequently cited by several later patents is therefore taken as influential or valuable. Thus, future citations for a patent provide an objective and readily available indication of a patent's value.

Additional patent value measures are based on citations as well.[16] For example, the "generality" measure assesses the extent to which the patented invention is employed across a wide array of technologies or is instead useful in a narrow band of applications (Trajtenberg et al., 1997). More general patents tend to be more valuable and can generate higher licensing revenues since the technology is applicable for a larger number of fields. Trajtenberg et al. observe that this measure

"presumably capture[s] important determinants of the *social* returns to innovation".

"Originality" is an analogous measure that looks to backward citations, measuring the breadth of technology fields the patent draws from in its prior art (Harhoff, et al., 1999; Jaffe & Lerner, 2001). When a patent's prior art falls into a relatively large number of classes, it signals that the patent drew from a broad range of technologies, rather than a narrow field. Thus, it is considered to be more original, and less likely to be an incremental improvement.

Yet another value measure, this one unrelated to citations, considers the total number of claims made within a patent. Claims define a patent's scope — the more claims, the broader the patent rights are on average (Lanjouw et al., 1999).

As the final measure of innovation, consider the count of distinct technical contributions made by the 27 firms to working groups within the SSO. Technical contributions are useful in identifying innovative efforts as they are typically documents describing specific technical suggestions for modifying and improving a standard made by a firm's representative to an SSO working group. These contributions do not convey IP rights so firms with purely opportunistic motives may be less likely to make the investment necessary to create contributions of this sort because they are not necessary for patent declarations. I therefore consider technical contributions a measure of incremental innovative activity within a standard that is reasonably insulated from strategic concerns.[17] I collected technical contributions made to those groups that worked on at least one specification that applied to key components of the UMTS standard.[18]

The UMTS working groups held their first meetings in mid-December 1998 so the data includes yearly contribution counts from 1999 onward for the 27 firms in the dataset. If patent filings and technical contributions are positively correlated, more technical contributions can be interpreted to indicate more innovative patents.

The following charts show the number of technical contributions over time for all the firms that made at least 100 contributions in at least one year from 1999-2006. As the scales on Figure 3, Figure 4 and Figure 5 demonstrate, contributions

per firm range from zero to the many thousands in any given year.

The charts reveal that most firms either continued to make roughly the same number of contributions to the working groups over time or increased their contributions after the path of the standard was selected.[19] Similarly, during the commercialization phase most firms tended to maintain contributions made. Although there is variation from year to year, no firm's contributions significantly decreased over time.[20] For 15 of the 21 firms with 100-plus contributions,[21] the average number of technical contributions made to working groups before commercialization was no different than after commercialization. Thus work on the UMTS standard did not appear to end with the adoption of a particular technology path.

The Extent of Ex Post Patenting

Before assessing the innovative merits (or lack thereof) of ex post patenting, consider first how prevalent ex post patenting is in practice. Figure 6 shows the distribution of US and EPO UMTS patents by application year. Of the 1247 US pat-

Figure 3. Total contributions to 3GPP working groups (top third)

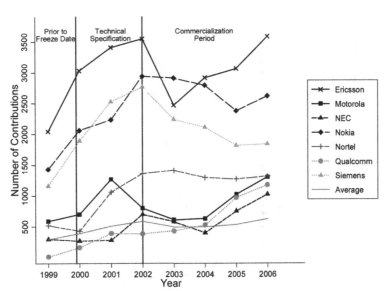

Figure 4. Total contributions to 3GPP working groups (middle third)

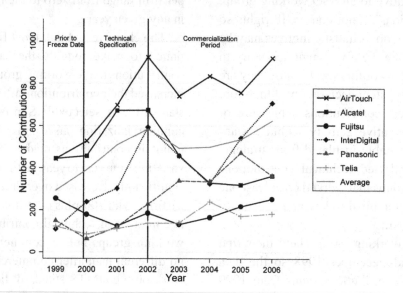

ents/applications, 56% (697) were applied for before the standard path was selected. Similarly, 42% (142) of the 341 EPO patents have an application year of 1999 or before. Both the US and EPO distributions peak around the time when the standard was selected. Nonetheless, the chart shows that patenting activity continued well after the UMTS standard was chosen. While patenting continued into the commercialization period the majority were applied for much earlier. In particular, 35% (441) of US UMTS patents were applied for during the technical specification period while 40% (136) of EPO patents have application years 2000-2002. Around 91% of US patents and around 82% of EPO patents were filed prior to the commercialization period.

Figure 5. Total contributions to 3GPP working groups (bottom third)

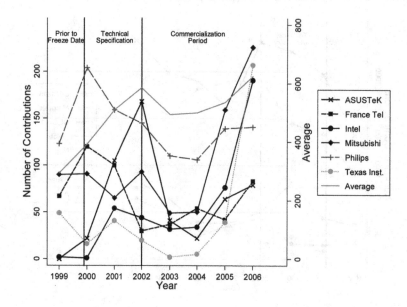

Figure 6. US and EPO UMTS patents by application year

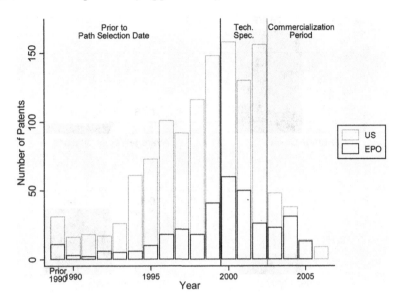

Are Ex Post Patents Innovative or Indefensible?

Under the null hypothesis of pure rent-seeking patenting, the patents filed after the standard path was chosen should be of less-than-average value. In terms of our proxy measures, this means that ex post patents should have fewer than expected claims and earn less than average citations over time.[22] If a sizeable portion of the patents filed after the selection date either meet expectations or are of above-average value, then this evidence would indicate that at least some of the ex post patents reflect genuine innovation. Define expectations in terms of average patents granted at the same time (to control for the number of possible forward citations) and in the same technology class (to control for differences across fields), but not included in the UMTS standard.

Comparing Average Patent Measures

First, patents declared ex post to UMTS are compared against a group of patents that have the same grant year and US technology class,[23] but which were not declared to the standard. Figure 7 presents the results.

All of the differences are slight and none is statistically significant. Thus while the UMTS patents are not valued at a premium compared to otherwise similar patents not declared to the standard, neither are they any less valuable.

Comparing Patent Filing with Technical Submissions

Next, consider the relationship between technical submissions to a working group and patent filings. Technical submissions are assessments, proposals, or discussions of particular technical issues that arise within a working group in relation to the development of a standard. The submissions are typically written by engineers for engineers. They may cover a firm's proprietary technology, making the firm's case for that technology's inclusion in the standard, or they might compare the workings of two or more options currently under consideration by the working group, or they may simply raise technical concerns in an effort to open discussion.

Because technical submissions must pass muster among other technical specialists, can be time consuming to prepare, and carry no property rights per se, it seems likely that purely opportunistic

Figure 7. Comparing UMTS with same cohort, non-UMTS patents

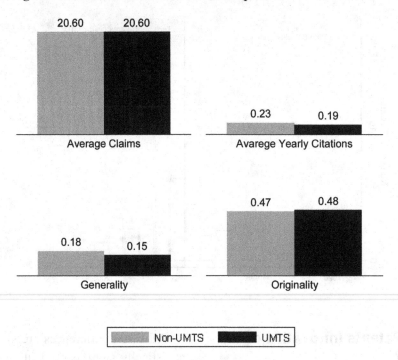

patenting would not be associated with technical submissions. Moreover, it is likely to be difficult to make a technical case for patents that have little or no technical merit and are declared to a standard solely for rent-seeking purposes. On this premise, I calculate the correlation between the timing of a technical submission and the timing of patent filings. Firms may, however, be reluctant to reveal any proprietary information in a submission that has not already been (or soon will be) covered by property rights, which suggests lagging patent filing dates.

I consider three correlations. First is a contemporaneous comparison of technical submissions and patent filings within a given year, which yields a statistically significant correlation of 0.37. For patents filed the year prior to a technical submission, the correlation is higher at 0.49, also statistically significant. Finally, patents filed two years prior to a technical submission yield an even higher positive correlation of 0.55, which is

again statistically significant.24 These correlations support the overall picture that has emerged from the analysis thus far: a reasonable portion of the ex post patents appear to have innovative content.

Regression Analysis-UMTS Patents by Declaration Year

The number of UMTS patents filed in a given year by a given firm is the dependent variable. Because this variable is a count measure and must be non-negative, I follow standard practice in the literature and employ a Negative Binomial regression model.[25] The independent variables are annual inflation adjusted R&D expenditure, total number of US patents the given firm applied for in the given year, year dummies, a post-standardization dummy when the year is greater than 1999, and an interaction variable between R&D expenditure and the post-standardization dummy.[26]

The hypothesis being tested is one flavor of the ex-post opportunistic patenting theory: firms patenting after 2000 have increased their patent propensity in relation to the early period, reflecting "patent mining". In other words, I test whether these firms are filing for more patents per dollar of R&D expenditure than they did before the standard was set, as an indication of rent seeking within an established standard.

For this test, the estimated coefficient on the interaction between R&D expenditures and patent filings is the key parameter. The R&D variable captures the well established positive relationship between investments and patenting. The dummy variable for post-2000 captures any increase in patent filing that takes place after the selection date. The interaction between the two variables then captures any incremental patenting per R&D dollar that might occur in the post-2000 period. If the interaction coefficient is positive and significant, we can conclude that firms increased their patent filing for a given dollar of R&D investment. If, on the other hand, the interaction coefficient estimate is negative or not statistically different from zero, we can conclude that firms' R&D patent propensities have not increased with patent mining after the standard selection date. Table 1 presents the regression results.

As expected, the more R&D investments made, the higher the number of patent filings. The total number of US patent applications, in the second row, captures a firm's propensity to patent in general, and it is also positive and significant. The post standardization dummy is also positive and significant, indicating that patent filings declared to the UMTS standard as potentially essential rose after 1999. The key variable, the interaction term, is slightly positive but not statistically significant from zero at the 5% level.[28] This test corroborates the earlier measures: firms are not significantly increasing their rate of patenting after standardization in an effort to patent mine.

Regression Analysis- Technical Contributions

As a final test, consider model specifications that account for the relationship between technical specifications and patenting. If there is a positive relationship between the number of UMTS patents applied for in year t-k and the number of technical contributions made in year t, then patents likely form the basis of technical specifications. Since, as explained above, strategic patents are less likely to be presented in technical specifications this evidence can be seen as supporting the hypothesis that ex post patenting can be innovative.

Table 1. Negative binomial regression estimates, dependent variable is annual UMTS patent filings[27]

Independent Variables:	Coefficient	P-Value
Inflation Adjusted R&D ($M)	0.000213*	0.04
Total # of Applied US Patents	0.000577**	0.00
Post Standardization Dummy	1.36527*	0.05
Interaction R&D/Standardization Dummy	0.000024	0.76
Year 1994	0.806308	0.26
Year 1995	0.641318	0.37
Year 1996	0.94449	0.18
Year 1997	1.012887	0.15
Year 1998	1.232287	0.08
Year 1999	1.63293*	0.02
Year 2001	-0.76513**	0.01
Year 2002	-0.94814**	0.00
Year 2003	-1.14029**	0.00
Year 2004	-1.3435**	0.00
Year 2005	-1.73652**	0.00
Year 2006	-2.89275**	0.00
Constant	-1.03909	0.13

Notes: ** Denotes significance at the 1% level or better; * denotes significance at the 5% level.

First consider the simple correlation between the number of technical contributions made in a given year and the number of UMTS patents applied for in a given year, lagged, along with the total number of US Patents applied for in a given year.

As Table 2 demonstrates, there is a strong relationship between the number of UMTS patents declared to ETSI and technical contributions made. The correlation peaks at a 2 year lag, suggesting that technical submissions are often based on R&D underlying patent applications from two years prior. There is no such correlation for total US patents applied for.

For the regression (presented in Table 3), the hypothesis is whether the number of technical contributions diverges from the number of UMTS patents declared, indicating less connection between the two and hence less valuable patents. The variable of interest is the number of UMTS patents applied for in a given year, lagged 2 years. A positive coefficient indicates that increased patenting leads to increased contributions to technical committees — suggesting that ex post patenting contains some innovative content given the assumption that technical submissions are likely to reflect genuine contributions and are not purely strategic. If, the relationship had been negative, then firms' patenting would not be matched by contributions to the working groups, consistent with the purely strategic patenting hypothesis.

Table 2. Pairwise correlations between the number of technical contributions and the given variable with certain lags

Number of Years Lagged	UMTS Patent Count	Total Number of US Patents
No Lag	0.40	0.06
1 Year	0.51	0.10
2 Years	0.58	0.11
3 Years	0.58	0.12
4 Years	0.56	0.14

The positive coefficient on the R&D variable is consistent with the patenting variable: increased R&D is associated with increased technical submissions, suggesting innovative content for those submissions.

These results corroborate those from above, reinforcing that ex post patenting is not necessarily opportunistic. The coefficient on the number of UMTS patents by application year is positive and highly significant. This indicates that patenting firms are making concrete contributions to the technical groups, further suggesting that ex post patents have some innovative content.

Quantifying Innovative Contributions

While the analysis thus far suggests a significant fraction of ex post patents are innovative rather than opportunistic, the question still remains as to the extent of innovative ex post patenting. Quantifying that degree is, of course, a difficult empirical task.[30] As an initial step, I present two proxy calculations that attempt to separate ex post patents into innovative and strategic.

The first calculation is an extension of the analysis above, comparing the number of forward cites received by the ex post UMTS patents to those received by patents in the same time/technology cohort but not declared to UMTS. If the UMTS patent received at least as many forward cites as the median of the cohort, then I consider that patent innovative; if the number falls below the cohort median than the patent is classified as strategic. Figure 8 shows the difference between the UMTS patents and the median of the cohort.

As the figure shows, the majority of ex post patents (over 80%) have at just as many forward cites as their corresponding cohort median (the zero column). The difference is positive for 71 out of 297 patents, indicating the UMTS patents have more forward cites than the general cohort, while it is negative for half that figure, 33 patents. This analysis therefore suggests that, considering only those patents with a positive or negative

Table 3. Negative binomial regression estimates, dependent variable is annual technical contributions[29]

Independent Variables:	Coefficient	P-Value
UMTS Patents Lagged 2 Years	0.0092**	0.0035
R&D Lagged 2 Years	0.00035**	0.00006
Year 2000	0.4163	0.2206
Year 2001	0.3337	0.2033
Year 2002	0.4098*	0.2020
Year 2003	0.3526	0.2038
Year 2004	0.4362*	0.2014
Year 2005	0.7277**	0.1945
Year 2006	0.9842**	0.1927
Year 2007	-0.7408**	0.2584
Constant	-0.2520	0.2070

Notes: ** Denotes significance at the 1% level or better; * denotes significance at the 5% level.

difference as compared to the general cohort, roughly one third of the ex post patents are opportunistic (33 of 104).[31]

The second classification considers the combination of forward citations and the number of technical specifications.[32] If the number of technical contributions (weighted by firm revenues) is higher than the median for the given year and the patent also was classified as innovative under the first scheme above, then I consider this as additional evidence that the patent is innovative. Table 4 gives the counts of patents falling into each of the four possible combinations.

This analysis indicates that the majority of patents fall in the high/high category, suggesting that 80% are innovative, with 11% most likely to be strategic (the "Low" citations row). Taking both calculations in tandem suggests that between 10% and 30% of the ex post UMTS patents are primarily opportunistic. Again, these calculations are rough at best, but they provide a start at quantifying the extent of opportunistic ex post patenting.

CONCLUSION

This paper has focused on the issue of opportunistic patenting within standard setting. Some have voiced concern that SSO members filing patents after a standard's technology path has been chosen have strategic rent seeking as a primary motivation. A close look at how standards evolve over time raises another possibility, though —incremental innovation. The analysis presented here attempts some first steps toward detangling these two possibilities with an empirical assessment of patenting that occurs after a standard has been published.

In particular, I examined the relationship between ex post patent filing and R&D expenditures along with measures meant to proxy patent value and thus indicate innovation. As a first step, the null hypothesis is that ex post patents are purely strategic and have no value; that hypothesis can be rejected. Instead, the results here suggest that a sizable portion of the ex post patents — perhaps as much as 70% - 80% — are at least incrementally innovative and therefore contribute value to the standard. We cannot determine precisely how many ex post patents are valuable, or which ones are truly innovative, but we can reasonably conclude that innovation does indeed continue as the standard develops and moves through commercialization.

In addition to the realities of standard development, which tends to occur slowly over time, I find this result conforms well to an understanding of how many firms license their patents. In particular, firms frequently license their patents

Figure 8. Distribution of differences in forward cites between ex-post patents and the appropriate cohort median

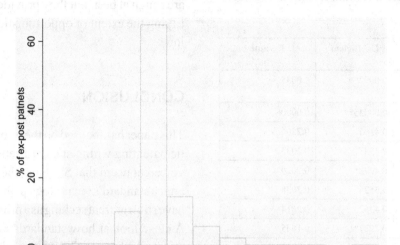

on a portfolio basis, as opposed to individually, especially within standard setting contexts. If a relatively small portion of a firm's patents were applied for after standardization then one cannot argue that the firm's patent *portfolio* as it relates to the standard is opportunistic. To the extent that firms license their patents on a portfolio basis, they have less incentive to apply for valueless patents — either ex ante or ex post. Since these firms negotiate their royalty rates based on the strength of their entire portfolio, "padding" the portfolio with trivial ex post patents offers little incremental revenue but does cost the firm in patent filing expenses. As Figure 6 showed, the major-

ity of firms with patents declared as potentially essential to UMTS filed at least some portion of their patents pre-standardization.

Unless there is reason to believe UMTS is a special case, which is unfortunately difficult to determine empirically given the lack of data available at other SSOs, then the findings presented here suggest that ex post patent filing should not automatically be considered strategic rent seeking. Certainly I do not mean to imply that all ex post patenting is valuable and driven entirely by innovation. That would be taking the other extreme view. Rather, the truth appears to lies somewhere in the middle. Some late patenting activity is likely to be opportunistic, meant to extort additional licensing fees from the standard, especially among firms that license on an individual patent basis. But at least some significant portion of late patenting, enough to lead to a rejection of purely strategic patenting in the statistical analysis above, is valuable and makes an innovative contribution to the standard. The tentative analysis above indicates that between 70% and 80% may fall into this latter category. Future research should further consider the more nuanced question of the extent of opportunistic ex post patenting.

Table 4. Number of patents grouped by technical contributions & forward citations

	Technical Contributions	
Patent Forward Cites	High	Low
High	239 (80%)	25 (8%)
Low	31 (10%)	2 (1%)

Notes: The high category includes all those patents/firms that had forward cites/technical contribution at least as large as the appropriate median value.

ACKNOWLEDGMENT

The author wishes to thank Rudi Bekkers, Daniel Garcia-Swartz, Bob Hunt, A. Jorge Padilla, Pekka Sääskilahti, and an anonymous reviewer, along with participants at the 9th Annual Bank of Finland/CEPR Conference on Innovation and Intellectual Property in Financial Services for helpful comments and Sokol Vako for research assistance. Financial support from Qualcomm is also gratefully acknowledged. All errors remain my own.

REFERENCES

Bekkers, R., & West, J. (2009). Standards, patents and mobile phones: Lessons from ETSI's handling of UMTS. *International Journal of IT Standards and Standardization Research, 7*(1). doi:10.4018/jitsr.2009010102

Blind, K., Cremers, K., & Mueller, E. (2008). The influence of strategic patenting on companies' patent portfolios. *Research Policy, 38,* 428–436. doi:10.1016/j.respol.2008.12.003

Blind, K., & Thumm, N. (2004). Interrelation between patenting and standardisation strategies: Empirical evidence and policy implications. *Research Policy, 33*(10), 1583–1598. doi:10.1016/j.respol.2004.08.007

Dewatripont, M., & Legros, P. (2008). *'Essential' patents, FRAND royalties and technological standards.* Retrieved from http://ncomprod.nokia.com/NOKIA_COM_1/Press/Legal_News_(IPR_news)/IPR_News/pdf/Dewatripont_Legros-frand-march16-2008.pdf

Farrell, J., & Saloner, G. (1988). Coordination through committees and markets. *The Rand Journal of Economics, 19*(2), 235–252. doi:10.2307/2555702

Goldstein, L., & Kersey, B. (2004). *Technology patent licensing: An international reference on 21st century patent licensing, patent pools and patent platforms.* Boston, MA: Aspatore Inc.

Hall, B., Jaffe, A., & Tratjenberg, M. (2001). *The NBER patent citation data file: Lessons, insights and methodological tools.* Retrieved from http://www.nber.org/patents/

Hall, B., Trajtenberg, M., & Jaffe, A. (2005). Market value and patent citations. *The Rand Journal of Economics, 36*(1), 16–38.

Harhoff, D., Narin, F., Scherer, F. M., & Vopel, K. (1999). Citation frequency and the value of patented inventions. *The Review of Economics and Statistics, 81*(3), 511–515. doi:10.1162/003465399558265

Hausman, J., Hall, B. H., & Griliches, Z. (1984). Econometric models for count data with an application to the patents-R&D relationship. *Econometrica, 52,* 909–938. doi:10.2307/1911191

Hunt, R., Simojoki, S., & Takalo, T. (2007). *Intellectual property rights and standard setting in financial services: The case of the single European payments area.* Retrieved from http://www.philadelphiafed.org/files/wps/2007/wp07-20.pdf

Jaffe, A., & Lerner, J. (2001). Reinventing public R&D: Patent policy and the commercialization of national laboratory technologies. *The Rand Journal of Economics, 32*(1), 167–198. doi:10.2307/2696403

Jaffe, A., & Trajtenberg, M. (1999). International knowledge flows: Evidence from patent citations. *Economics of Innovation and New Technology, 8,* 105–136. doi:10.1080/10438599900000006

Lanjouw, J., & Schankerman, M. (1999). *The quality of ideas: Measuring innovation with multiple indicators.* Retrieved from http://www.nber.org/

Lemley, M., & Shapiro, C. (2006). Patent holdup and royalty stacking. *Texas Law Review, 85*, 2007.

Lerner, J., Tirole, J., & Strojwas, M. (2003). *Cooperative marketing agreements between competitors: Evidence from patent pools*. Retrieved from http://www.nber.org/

Mueller, J. (2001). No 'dilettante affair': Rethinking the experimental use exception to patent infringement for biomedical research tools. *Washington Law Review* (Seattle, Wash.), 76.

Rysman, M., & Simcoe, T. (2008). Patents and the performance of voluntary standard setting organizations. *Management Science, 54*(11), 1920–1934. doi:10.1287/mnsc.1080.0919

Shapiro, C. (2001). Setting compatability standards: Co-operation or collusion? In Dreyfuss, R., Zimmerman, D., & First, H. (Eds.), *Expanding the boundaries of intellectual property*. New York, NY: Oxford University Press.

Trajtenberg, M. (1990). A penny for your quotes: Patent citations and the value of innovations. *The Rand Journal of Economics, 21*(1), 172–187. doi:10.2307/2555502

Trajtenberg, M., Henderson, R., & Jaffe, A. (1997). University versus corporate patents: A window on the basicness of invention. *Economics of Innovation and New Technology, 5*, 19–50. doi:10.1080/10438599700000006

ENDNOTES

[1] Technical Specification TS25.xxx.

[2] Nomura International plc, "Equipment Matters, IPR: The Master Craftsman" at 14.

[3] As explained in greater detail, we select this standard because of the relative richness of the data available.

[4] Declaring a patent as potentially essential does not mean that it will be deemed essential when the standard is implemented commercially. Thus declared patents tend to be overinclusive in terms of genuine essentiality, as determined at implementation.

[5] This conclusion is consistent with other empirical findings in the literature. For instance, Blind and Thumm (2004) present survey evidence that indicates "Gaining a better bargaining position in standard setting" is among the reasons for obtaining patents, but one that falls well below other reasons. Blind and Thumm conclude that it is of "low importance".

[6] Patent data collected in January, 2008; includes only US and European patents. ETSI is an organizational partner and founding member of 3rd Generation Partnership Project (3GPP)

[7] Five radio interfaces for mobile telecom were considered: cdma-2000, W-CDMA, TD-CDMA, TDMA-EDGE and DECT (Goldstein & Kearsey, 2004).

[8] Nearly 700 member firms from about 60 countries; See http://www.etsi.org/WebSite/AboutETSI/structure/members.aspx.

[9] The ETSI dataset includes both exact duplicates and jurisdictional "duplicates" filed with multiple patent offices. Both types are removed, keeping as the first choice US patents. Patents with the same title and company name but declared to different jurisdictions are considered equivalent. US patents are favored since the USPTO maintains an extensive, publicly available database. If there was no US patent, the second priority is EPO patents. Should a patent have been declared only to an EU member nation, we found the corresponding EPO patent whenever possible. Note that this might introduce bias as a patent could have been applied for earlier in a jurisdiction other than the US. We tested a sample of patents and found in over 95% that the application year was the same/earlier for the US version of the patent when compared to its EPO counterpart. We

do not have access to other patent offices databases.

10   Note that this number includes all patents for which we were able to find an application year. Our USPTO database contains all the patents granted up to the end of 2005, while our EPO database runs till September 2006. For consistency, we limited our patent specific analysis to patents declared before 2005 regardless of jurisdiction. Also note that only 968 of the 1252 US patents and/ or application were granted prior to 2005. Thus the patent specific analyses are based on this subsample.

11   Two firms, Telia AB and Axalto, have only EPO patents.

12   We plot the 21 firms that rank highest when looking at the maximum R&D expenditures over the 1994-2006 time period. Note that for some of the firms we were unable to get R&D numbers for some of the earlier years.

13   Sources are company 10-K or 20-F or annual reports as filed with either the SEC or other nations respective authorities. We calculate the benchmark by looking at the change in average inflation adjusted R&D expenditures from a given year to our benchmark year, 1994, for all the firms in our sample. In particular, since we don't have data for all the firms over the entire time period, we calculated the relative change by assuming that a given firm had R&D expenditures similar to the year prior. (For ex. France Telecom had R&D expenditures of $737 million in 1998; we assumed the same for 1997. We however made no assumptions for years before 1997.) We did this to ensure that we used the same firms in our year to year calculation which were then benchmarked against 1994.

14   Citation analysis is based on US patents only.

15   Consistent with the view that forward citations proxy for patent value is the conclu-

sion in Blind et al. (2008): "We find that the more intensively companies use patents to achieve a protection objective, the higher is the average number of citations their patent portfolio receives. Conversely, in cases here strategic motives, such as blocking and exchange, dominate, portfolios receive less citations."

16   Note that we only use US patents here. It is our experience that citation based calculations on EPO patents have little meaning since prior cites for EPO patents are determined primarily by the patent examiner.

17   On the other hand, as one reviewer pointed out, contributing technical submissions could be aimed at supporting low-value IP in an effort to increase the odds that it is accepted in a standard. To separate this possibility from the one described in the text above, one would need to assess the merit of the technical contributions themselves. Researchers with the technical expertise to make such an assessment may want to tackle this question in a future study.

18   UTRAN contributions are considered, which include all working groups under the following technical specification groups (TSG): CN, CT(active), RAN(active), SA(active), and T.

19   At the end of 2004 ETSI approved release 6 of the UMTS standard which may explain the uptick i contributions in 2005 and 2006.

20   We ran regressions of the number of contributions on the year and got positive slope for 20 out of the 28 firms, with one value being significantly different from zero. In the other 8 cases we got a negative slope which was not significantly different from zero.

21   5 of the remaining firms have a higher post commercialization average, while only France Telecom contributed less on average after commercialization.

22 Averages are calculated for all patents in the same grant year and USPTO technology class (i.e., overall) and all patents declared to the SSO (i.e., within standard). Comparing ex post filed patents to ex ante filed patents is difficult given the time difference: patents filed earlier have a longer time to garner cites and differences in early years may simply indicate different time paths.

23 We also compared the UMTS patents with the group of patents that were in the same class and had the same application year. The results were qualitatively identical.

24 Note that the sample size falls as the lags on patent filing increase.

25 I also tested a Poisson model, but it did not fit the data as well. For a classical paper on this topic see Hausman, Jerry, Bronwyn H. Hall, and Zvi Griliches (1984).

26 I considered lagging R&D on the theory that it tends to take time to move from research findings to submitted patent filings. That is, the research for any given patent typically occurs well before the application date of that patent. I find, however, that the correlation between the total number of applied patents and R&D expenditures is roughly the same regardless of whether R&D is lagged by one year (correlation of 0.70), two years (0.70), or is contemporaneous (0.69). Given that corporate R&D programs tend to be fairly consistent over time, this finding makes sense.

27 The results in this table are for the fixed effect model (assuming random effects yields similar results). We also ran a variety of robustness checks, including models excluding the year dummies and other models using permutations of the other explanatory variable. In all models our variable of interest, the interaction between R&D and standardization, was not significant.

28 With lagged R&D the estimated coefficient on the interaction term was also not statistically different from zero.

29 The results in this table are for the fixed effect model (assuming random effects yields similar results). We also ran a variety of robustness checks. The sign and level of significance of the variable of interest is stable across all the models we ran. In particular we ran the model lagging the independent variables from 0-3 periods and qualitatively results do not change; we do see changes in the magnitude of the variables but such changes are remarkably relatively small. We also ran simple fixed and random effect models lagging the independent variables from 0 to 3 year, and in all but one of the models our variable of interest was positive and significant.

30 There is no objective method that I am aware of which gives a definitive answer as to whether a given patent is innovative or not.

31 If one were to take a more extreme view and include the zero difference patents as opportunistic, then about three quarters of the patents would be opportunistic. 193 patents exhibit zero difference in contrast to the corresponding cohort median, while 33 are below it and 71 are above it.

32 For each firm we divide the number of technical contributions by the revenues that the firm earned in the given year as a control firm size and resources.

This work was previously published in the International Journal of IT Standards and Standardization Research (IJITSR), Volume 9, Issue 2, edited by Kai Jakobs, pp. 1-18, copyright 2011 by IGI Publishing (an imprint of IGI Global)

Chapter 2
Assessing the Link between Standards and Patents

Anne Layne-Farrar
Compass LexEcon, USA

A. Jorge Padilla
LECG, UK

ABSTRACT

Some policymakers, courts, and academics have expressed concerns that when a firm's patents are incorporated into a standard, the patents gain importance and can bestow on the patent holder market power that can be abused when the standard is commercialized. This paper extends the existing literature on the effect that standards can have on patents. This analysis has two aims: first, to better understand how an SSO might confer importance on included patents and second, to move closer to an empirical understanding of the impact of a standard on included patents. The authors create a dataset of patents named to voluntary standard setting organizations, as well as the patent pools that sometimes develop around such standards. The authors rely on proxies to capture a patent's importance or value.

1. INTRODUCTION

It is widely recognized that voluntary standard setting efforts are pro-competitive and welfare enhancing.[1] Even so, the full competitive implications for firms choosing to participate in a standard setting organization (SSO) are not entirely clear and have been the subject of considerable debate. In particular, some policymakers, courts, and academics have expressed concerns that when a firm's patents are incorporated into a standard, the inclusion can enable patent holders to abuse their position when the standard is commercialized.[2] The argument can be summarized as follows. Prior to the definition of a standard, many firms may compete over technologies, but once the standard is defined and the technologies are chosen, that competition ceases. Since the components of a

DOI: 10.4018/978-1-4666-2160-2.ch002

standard are complementary, they are all "essential" for implementing the standard. Thus, under this view, even firms with patents that read on relatively minor components of a standard will be able to "hold up" licensees for excessive royalties by threatening not to license on any other terms.[3]

In the theoretical academic literature, quite a bit of attention has been focused on the consequences of standard-granted market power, namely patent hold up, but very little has been devoted to the workings of *how* standards might enable patent holders to practice such hold up. For instance, what is the particular mechanism responsible for conveying ex post market power? Is it simply the hold up of switching costs that essential patents can provide patent holders for extorting licensees after a standard is defined, as noted above?[4] Do the broadened consumer markets that can be enabled by standards have any effect? Does publicity, where patents essential for a standard are disclosed and more widely advertised than would otherwise be the case, play any role? Moreover, how broad might an ex post effect might be? That is, does the effect hold for every single patent declared essential for a standard? Is naming a patent to a standard as potentially essential enough, or must the patent actually *be* essential? Since SSOs tend not to conduct essentiality determinations, actual essentiality would introduce considerable uncertainty into the process.

This paper has two goals: first, to help shrink the gap in the current literature regarding how an SSO can confer importance on included patents and second, to build on the handful of empirical papers in the literature that assess the link between standard setting and patent importance or value. We examine voluntary standard setting organizations, as well as the patent pools that sometimes develop around such standards, with the aim of providing some detailed measurements of the effect standardization might have on included patents.

Citations present a reasonable proxy of patent importance or value. Holders of patents representing follow on research are often compelled to cite the key patents that came before them and patent examiners include key patents in the prior art of the patents they review.[5] In addition to recognizing key predecessors, cites can be an important defensive measure: the citations included in a patent application circumscribe that patent's claims but they can also provide safe harbor for claims of infringement from other patent holders – a factor that is especially important for U.S. patents where private litigation is more common.[6] Because citations offer readily available objective measures, forward citations have been used extensively in empirical studies as proxies for patent value or importance.[7] Nevertheless, while the literature has established a clear link between citations and patent value, it appears that citations explain only a small portion of patent value. In particular, Gambardella, Harhoff, and Verspagen (2008) observe that:

Citations explain value as much as the other three indicators combined, and the right tail of citations is correlated with the right tail of our value measure. Yet, the four indicators only explain 2.7% of the variance of patent value. Thus, while the use of these indicators as proxies for value, particularly citations, may be justified, predictions based on these indicators carry significant noise. After using country, technology, and patent class fixed effects, we only explain 11.3% of the variation in patent value. The 'measure of our ignorance' about the determinants of patent value is then still sizable, which calls for additional research to fill the gap.[8]

The question we consider is a different, although related one. Instead of trying to explain the private value of patents to their holders, we examine the importance that a standard may confer on a patent, which in turn might affect the bargaining power of the patent holders whose patents are named to the standard. At the most fundamental level, separating the legitimate importance created by the standardization process from any illegitimate patent importance that might enable a patent holder to hold up implementers of the standard is difficult to do both conceptually and empirically. In examining measurable effects on patent importance, we find that some SSOs appear to enhance some included patents' importance or value, but most do not. Moreover, the effects change over time, across standards, and across patents. Thus, we conclude that for any given patent a broad range of SSO effects is possible, some even negative but most equal to zero.

The paper proceeds as follows. In section 2 we describe how standard setting works in practice as a means of moving beyond the general switching cost hold up theory to identify when and how an SSO could grant or enhance a patent's importance. As part of that analysis, we consider the alternatives to cooperative standard setting, which form the benchmarks against which SSO-conveyed importance should be compared. In section 3 we review the existing empirical evidence on patents included in standards—the few empirical studies that exist offer some provocative findings. Section 4 then turns to our empirical analysis of SSO inclusion and patent importance. Section 5 concludes the paper.

2. STANDARD SETTING, LICENSING, AND PATENT IMPORTANCE

We begin our study by considering standard setting operations and how they might confer the power to practice patent holdup. This section describes the workings of standard setting organizations, their intellectual property policies, and the competitive environment in which they operate. With an understanding of the typical workings of standard setting, we identify the routes through which patents might gain in importance during or after the process.

A. SSO Operations

The first point to understand is that SSOs are voluntary organizations. In a typical scenario, firms interested in developing or defining a technical solution that will enable multiple products or components to work together choose to collaborate in standard setting efforts. For example, the 3G mobile telecom standard WCDMA defines how mobile phone chipsets work within mobile phone handsets, how those handsets communicate with base station towers, how the calls are then routed through cellular and/or landline networks, and how the call is finally received on the other end. Thus, semiconductor designers and fabricators, handset manufacturers, mobile network operators, and firms focused on R&D related to mobile communications are among the many members of the European Telecommunications Standards Institute (ETSI) working on the 3G standard.

Next, consider how technologies are usually chosen for a standard.[9] Most SSOs form working groups at the start of the standardization process. These groups are comprised of representatives from member firms (most often engineers or other technical specialists) and they focus on evaluating the technical options for narrow aspects of a perceived industry problem. Existing technology is reviewed, with individual members often proposing specific alternatives based on their firm's proprietary intellectual property. If extant solutions are seen as inadequate, the group may decide that some technical answer needs to be developed de novo. Once all of the options have been set forth and debated, the members typically vote on the proposed options according to SSO rules to select the technology (or most likely, the group of complementary technologies) that will be included in the standard.[10] Many SSOs require a supermajority to approve a technological solution. Since the vast majority of standards are comprised of multiple interoperating technologies, the proposals and debates take place for each component in light of the components already settled. The goal of this frequently cumbersome process is generally to select the best technologies available, although practical concerns like anticipated costs and ease of implementation are typically factored in.

Finally, consider the commitments that an SSO requests of its members. Companies that hold IP rights that might be relevant for a proposed standard (i.e., potentially "essential" IP) are typically asked to disclose those rights before the standard is finalized. For example, the IEEE IPR policy states that

The Submitter of the Letter of Assurance may, after Reasonable and Good Faith Inquiry, indicate it is not aware of any Patent Claims that the Submitter may own, control, or have the ability to license that might be or become Essential Patent Claims. If the patent holder or patent applicant provides an assurance, it should do so as soon as reasonably feasible in the standards development process once the PAR is approved by the IEEE-SA Standards Board. This assurance shall be provided prior to the Standards Board's approval of the standard. This assurance shall be provided prior to a reaffirmation/stabilization if the IEEE receives notice of a potential Essential Patent Claim after the standard's approval or a prior reaffirmation/stabilization. An asserted potential Essential Patent Claim for which an assurance cannot be obtained (e.g., a Letter of Assurance is not provided or the Letter of Assurance indicates that assurance is not being provided) shall be referred to the Patent Committee.[11]

Once a company has disclosed that it holds IP it feels may be essential for an upcoming standard, the SSO then typically asks the company to commit to licensing the related patents on reasonable and non-discriminatory terms (referred to as RAND,

or FRAND with "fair" added). IEEE's policy is again instructive:

When A Letter of Assurance shall be either:

a) A general disclaimer to the effect that the Submitter without conditions will not enforce any present or future Essential Patent Claims against any person or entity making, using, selling, offering to sell, importing, distributing, or implementing a compliant implementation of the standard; or

b) A statement that a license for a compliant implementation of the standard will be made available to an unrestricted number of applicants on a worldwide basis without compensation or under reasonable rates, with reasonable terms and conditions that are demonstrably free of any unfair discrimination. At its sole option, the Submitter may provide with its assurance any of the following: (1) a not-to-exceed license fee or rate commitment, (2) a sample license agreement, or (3) one or more material licensing terms.[12]

By pushing essential IP holders to commit to license on RAND terms before the standard is adopted, the members of the SSO are trying to deter essential IP holders from exercising any otherwise legally permissible power to deny a license after adoption.[13] No SSO, to our knowledge, provides a definition of RAND or FRAND.[14] Instead, particular licensing terms are usually left to confidential bilateral negotiations between the members,[15] although the courts and competition agencies often step in when disputes arise.[16]

If an essential IP holder refuses to commit to RAND licensing, SSOs generally impose a consequence. For example, without a FRAND commitment ETSI moves to consider alternative technologies:

Where a MEMBER notifies ETSI that it is not prepared to license an IPR in respect of a STANDARD or TECHNICAL SPECIFICATION, the General

Assembly shall review the requirement for that STANDARD or TECHNICAL SPECIFICATION and satisfy itself that a viable alternative technology is available for the STANDARD or TECHNICAL SPECIFICATION which is not blocked by that IPR; and satisfies ETSI's requirements.[17]

B. Competition and Alternatives

If the voluntary standardization process breaks down, perhaps because key IP holders refuse to commit to license on RAND terms and conditions, or if a standardization effort never gets underway, the alternative use of the relevant IPRs depends, at least to some degree, on the specifics of the industry and its players. For instance, the Wi-Fi standard, which defines wireless networking, began with "a fragmented market populated by small players" who took seven years to coordinate their efforts in the form of a working standard.[18] Thus, when a clear industry leader is lacking, firms may have a difficult time cooperating, making the most likely alternative to a voluntary standard no standard at all.

When a clear market leader does exist, however, the likely alternative may be a de facto standard championed by the firm with sufficient market clout or a clearly superior product.[19] For example, the QWERTY keyboard design is a de facto standard that emerged during the typewriter era but has remained with computers and PDAs because as of yet no one has offered an alternative that is enough of an improvement to offset the switching costs for users to learn a new design.[20]

A single firm promulgating a de facto standard, however, is only possible if industry coordination is not a critical element of the end product. For example, keyboard design does not require cooperation from different kinds of firms, but communications standards do. When no one firm holds all of the components necessary for an end product, a solo-firm de facto standard is not a realistic option.

De facto tactics can nonetheless still be important. The 802.11 wireless standard promulgated at IEEE provides an illustration. When progress within the IEEE committee working on the 802.11 standard stalled and consensus seemed unlikely, "a group of influential semiconductor companies" formed their own committee, outside of IEEE, and began promoting their own proprietary solution.[21] This outside group, a sort of hybrid de facto/cooperative alliance, forced IEEE's hand and a consensus standard that combined the breakout group's proposal with elements of the proposal that had bogged down in IEEE committee finally emerged through the SSO. This example shows the gradations of de facto standard possible and suggests that patented technologies with little ex ante competition will have an importance and value of their own, regardless of the ultimate form that standardization takes.

Finally, note that in markets with several strong players it is also possible to get multiple standards. For example, in the U.S. mobile phone market, customers can opt for the CDMA standard offered through network carriers Sprint and Verizon or the GSM/EDGE standard through AT&T Wireless and T-Mobile.[22] The networks for these two standards are distinct and the standards are technically incompatible, although customers can connect with anyone who has a phone regardless of the network. Enough mobile operators had sufficient market presence in the U.S. that they could establish comprehensive mobile networks on their own, without coordinating with other network providers. The providers therefore chose to differentiate on mobile standards, rather than coordinate on a single one.[23] While the single standard adopted in Europe has the benefit of ensuring compatibility for consumers as they travel across the member states, there is a downside as well in the lost competition across standards that can encourage innovation and maintain high R&D investments levels.[24] Of course, as explained above, even U.S. mobile network providers needed to coordinate with semiconductor firms and handset manufacturers, among many others, to define each of the two competing mobile standards, but this example further illustrates that an entire industry need not agree—one powerful coalition can be enough.

C. Standardization Benefits, Patent Value, and Importance

Standards, when successful, can offer a number of benefits.[25] First and foremost, stakeholders in an emerging technology—such as network operators, equipment manufacturers, software developers, and users—benefit because standards facilitate interoperability and technology adoption. A recognized standard provides assurances to end users that compliant products will work together as described, which increases buyer confidence and can therefore increase total purchases. As a result, it is generally agreed that standardization grows a market, increases technology dissemination, and can translate into higher revenues for the firms involved.

These benefits are not limited to formal cooperative standards. A de facto standard emerging from competition *for* a market can inspire consumer confidence and increase sales as well. And de facto standards have some advantages over cooperative standards, namely in terms of speed. Formal standard setting by an SSO is recognized as relatively slow compared to a de facto standard—not surprising given the consensus building and voting required.[26]

On the other hand, formal cooperative standards can offer some benefits over de facto standards. Some authors maintain that formal cooperative standards may be more precisely defined and of higher quality than de facto standards as a result of pooling technologies from multiple sources.[27] Cooperation can also enable multiple firms to supply the end product in the case of a compatibility standard, which provides consumers with both interoperability and choice among implementers.[28] Moreover, international

SSOs can help smooth standardization across multiple geographic areas, especially in the face of language and jurisdictional barriers.[29]

Certainly if formal standard setting organizations did not offer at least some private benefits, companies would not incur the substantial transaction costs involved in participating.[30] ETSI, for example, has an annual fee that can be over €150,000 for certain large corporations.[31] Depending on the number of working groups in which a given company participates, it may have to send dozens of employees all over the globe for regular meetings and to contribute to the standard setting process. As a result, the cost of active participation can be significant, which suggests that the private benefits must be significant as well or firms would not join.

In some instances the benefits of formal standard setting may extend beyond increased consumer confidence and larger potential markets to market power derived from the standard. That is, the adoption of a firm's patents in a formal standard may confer market power on the patent holder. The market power thus acquired could then be translated into ex post opportunistic behaviors, such as unreasonable licensing terms (patent hold up). For example, Shapiro and Varian (1999)[32] argue that once patents are included in a standard; firms wishing to implement the standard are "locked in" to licensing those patents. The authors thus propose that licensing terms should not be allowed to take advantage of the lock-in: "[r]easonable [as the "R" in RAND] should mean the royalties that the patent holder could obtain in open, upfront competition with other technologies, not the royalties that the patent holder can extract once other participants are effectively locked in to use technology covered by the patent."[33]

The U.S. courts, in the few cases directly addressing the issue, have to date taken a different view of standards and market power. For example, in *Brent Townshend v. Rockwell International Corp.*, the U.S. District Court of the Northern District of California argued that "The adoption of an industry standard incorporating such proprietary technology does not confer any power to exclude that exceeds the exclusionary power to which a patent holder is otherwise legally entitled."[34] The Court went on to observe that the complainant had not presented any allegations that the adoption of the standard at issue would in any way impede the development of alternative or competitive technologies, akin to barriers to entry in traditional market analysis. In other words, the *Townshend* Court maintained that U.S. patent law grants limited "monopoly" power to patent holders and the standard setting context did nothing to alter that fact.

While a number of U.S. district courts have followed the *Townshend* precedent,[35] more recently the Third Circuit broke with the *Townshend* reasoning in its opinion for *Broadcom v. Qualcomm.*[36] It accepted that the standard setting context changed the equation. In fact, that court recognized the potential for patent hold up stemming from standard lock in.

In Europe there is a far slimmer relevant court record. While the 2010 Nokia GMBH v. IPCom GMBH & Co. KG involved patents that were named as essential to the GSM telecom standard, the UK decision from High Court of Justice Chancery Division Patents Court did not touch on the issue of whether the patents' inclusion in the standard augmented IPCom's hold up power. The German federal court case involving the same parties has been put on hold.

At the European Commission (EC) level, while the EC has investigated both Qualcomm and Rambus in connection with patent licensing within a standard setting organization, neither of those investigations led to a decision. The Qualcomm matter was dropped after several years, with the Commission observing in its closing statement "The Qualcomm case has raised important issues about the pricing of technology after its adoption as part of an industry standard. In practice, such assessments may be very complex, and any antitrust enforcer has to be careful about overturning

commercial agreements."[37] About the same time as the Qualcomm announcement, the EC reached a settlement with Rambus: the EC made no finding of liability and imposed no fine and in exchange Rambus committed to lower certain of its royalty rates.[38] Of course, the U.S. and European courts' and Commissions' views of patent rights need not square with an economic interpretation of SSOs, patent importance, and patent holder market power—either theoretical or empirical. The economic logic behind the holdup concern relies not on any legal power granted by a jurisdiction's patent law, but rather on the increased and presumably inelastic demand for patents that are deemed essential for a standard. In order to implement the standard essential patents must be licensed, by definition. Moreover, member commitments to an SSO, such as a RAND promise, could reasonably be viewed as constraining a patent holder's normal rights as bestowed by patent law.[39]

That being said, an important but implicit link in the SSO hold up chain of logic is that any enhanced patent importance that emerges as a result of the standardization process necessarily confers increased market power for the patent holder, power that can then be abused in licensing negotiations. The only legitimate price a patent holder can charge, according to this theory, is the one determined by competition in the development stage prior to any standard being set. Under this theory, anything else *must* be supra-competitive and an exploitation of market power.

The problem with this kind of reasoning is that it is at odds with our earlier discussion of the standardization process and the costs and benefits involved. Being adopted by a standard may enhance the value or importance of a patent, which we would expect given the investments in time, effort and money that firms make in the cooperative standard setting process. Viewed in this light, enhanced patent value or importance can be seen as one of the returns to a risky investment in standard setting. It does not necessarily follow, however, that the standard has granted the patent holder any market power enabling supra-competitive pricing. This is a subtle but crucial point. To see it more clearly, consider two simple examples of patents included in a standard.

Consider first a technology that is indispensable for some product. The patent on that technology will be essential regardless of whether it is included in a cooperative standard. If the technology has a capable champion, a de facto standard (either solo or oligopolistic) might have built up around it instead, in which case it would have legitimately earned importance and/or value in the marketplace through the patent holder's business acumen, leaving no room for SSO-conferred importance. In this scenario, any value is inherent in the ownership of the patented technology itself, not in the ultimate form of the standardization effort. Being included in an SSO might nonetheless enhance this patent's market *value* or *importance* even as it reduced its holder's market *power* as compared to the de facto standard benchmark since, as noted above, the voluntary standard might broaden the commercial market beyond the de facto standard level. In this scenario, the SSO would be "crowning a winner" not creating one.

Consider next a patented technology that faces a number of competitive alternatives, not necessarily perfect substitutes but close ones. Such a technology would have a slim chance at winning a non-cooperative competition in the marketplace. If—say due to happenstance or to the persuasive nature of the firm's representatives at an SSO—this technology were chosen for inclusion in a cooperative standard, the patent protecting it will have both enhanced market value and its holder may have potentially enhanced market power. We still say "potentially" because even here market power will hinge on additional factors. For instance, if the patent covers an optional feature of a standard (or, more likely, some portion of an optional feature, given that most components of standard are covered by numerous patents), it might be "essential" in a strict sense of the word (for commercial reasons) but still be easily

avoidable. Another mitigating factor lies in the cost of switching to an alternative technology after a standard is defined. If the patent covers an element of the standard that can be swapped at little cost, then if the patent holder attempted to exercise any market power after the standard vote the members would simply refuse to pay and credibly counter with a threat to redefine the standard around one of the patent's earlier competitors. Many standards bodies even have such work-around statements codified in their policy statements.[40] Yet another limiting factor is whether the standard itself faces competition from another standard—as CDMA and EDGE/WCDMA do in the U.S. If so, all patent holders in the standard will face pricing constraints.

As these two simple examples illustrate, from a theoretical standpoint the extent to which patents included in standards gain in importance or to which their holders gain in market power is a matter of degree. SSO standards can and do compete with de facto standards, or even on occasion with other SSO standards. And too, standards can fail in the marketplace, meaning all of the essential patents defining the standard have little commercial value, at least in the context of the standard. All of these factors provide additional checks on the possibility that an SSO confers importance or value on included patents. Thus, the question of SSOs and patent value or importance is just that, a question, and one that must be analyzed empirically.

3. EXISTING EVIDENCE ON SSO EFFECTS

Two prior studies have considered the impact that SSOs can have on patents included in standards.[41] The first, by Lerner, Tirole, and Strojwas (2003), focuses on whether higher quality patents are more likely to be included in a patent pool, the vast majority of which evolve from formal cooperative standards. This is clearly relevant to the debate over SSOs and their affect on patents because it tests the extent to which standards and their associated patent pools are crowning winners as opposed to creating them. The more we find that pools and SSOs select the best patents, the less room there is for SSO created importance.

The Lerner et al. hypothesis raises an important empirical issue: selection bias. If standards and patent pools are indeed crowning winners then we need a method to separate the effect of being included in a standard or a pool from the effect of being a higher value patent to begin with. A similar problem faces labor economists who want to separate out the effects of innate ability (nature) from skills acquired during schooling (nurture) on subsequent workforce earnings. In this field, a solution emerged in the literature during the late 1970s that relied on twin siblings to control for nature's contributions to income.[42] In particular, these economists created a dataset comprised of matched people—twins with identical genetic make-up but who differed on some other observable measures, such as years of education or college attended. Whatever differences appeared in their earned income as adults could then be attributed to the observable differences as opposed to some unobservable intelligence factor.

A similar approach has been developed in the intellectual property literature. Of course, by definition no patent has an identical twin. The various patent offices around the globe are supposed to grant patents only to inventions that are novel, non-trivial, and non-obvious. The task, then, is to match patents on observable traits to create close "fraternal" twins since identical twins are not possible.[43]

Lerner et al. follow this method and examine the patents included in a patent pool associated with a standard as compared to "similar" patents outside of the pool. They define similarity in two different ways. First, they identify patents awarded to the same firm and at the same time as the pool patent. This matching procedure controls for firm

fixed effects (akin to matching on parents) and allows for an equal amount of time for the patents to garner cites (recall that the longer a patent is public, the more time it has to collect citations). For the second match, Lerner et al. identify patents that were awarded to the same kind of assignee (university, firm, etc.) within the same patent technology class and at the same time as the pool patent. This approach controls for the technology field (akin to matching on college major), time (again to control for citation potential), and assignee type, which might affect the disclosure and marketing of the technology.

In comparing the pool patents to their matches, Lerner et al. conclude that pools accept more important patents and that inclusion in the pool triggers more patent utilization (i.e., more citations, more importance). Using difference-in-differences tests,[44] the authors find for all matching approaches that patents included in the pools receive more citations and that those citations come from a broader range of technical functions than the match patents not included in any patent pool. In the jargon of the IP literature, the pool patents are both more important and more general than their matches.[45] This was true both before the pool formed and after the pool formed. Lerner et al. explain the reason for considering both time periods' as follows:

The number of citations received before the pool was formed served as a measure of the importance of a patent that can reasonably be assumed to be unaffected by its inclusion in a pool. The number of citations received after the pool was formed reflects factors such as the intrinsic significance of the patent, the increased attention received due to its inclusion in the pool, and potentially the decreased concerns about blocking patent issues that arise in follow-on innovations.[46]

Lerner et al. also find that pool patents are somewhat broader in scope as measured by the number of claims made. They do not, however, find that pool patents are more "original", a measure that examines the number of technology classes the patent refers to in its prior art cites.[47] Regression analysis confirms their findings.

Interestingly, Lerner et al. find that the pool effect on patent importance is concentrated over a relatively narrow time span. They note that "the difference is confined to the years immediately before the pools' formation and the years subsequent to the pool's establishment."[48] This too emphasizes that both effects—nature and nurture—are evident.

The second paper that considers the SSO-patent-importance question is Rysman and Simcoe (2008).[49] In particular, they analyze two possible effects, a selection effect and a marginal effect. Under the former, "SSOs identify or attract technologies that are more significant (or about to become so), and therefore more frequently cited." Under the latter, SSOs "by fostering consensus and creating an open standard," "cause firms to begin using and citing a patented technology when they otherwise would not have, thus altering its citation profile."[50]

To measure these two effects, Rysman and Simcoe analyze patents declared as essential for a standard promulgated by one of four of the largest SSOs. Their primary method is to compare patent citations before and after inclusion in a standard, although they also consider patents declared to a standard with a group of comparable patents not declared to a standard.[51]

Rysman and Simcoe find that SSO patents are cited twice as frequently as the average patent, and continue to receive citations for a longer period of time than expected. And they find that disclosure to a standard increases citations by 19 to 47 percent. They conclude "that SSOs can indeed have a significant impact on the value of a technology", although they recognize that that impact is likely to differ across standard setting organizations.[52]

4. EXTENDING THE EMPIRICAL LITERATURE

Both Lerner et al. and Rysman and Simcoe focus on the selection/causation (or nature/nurture) question in its totality. The papers clearly establish that SSOs tend to attract more important and valuable patents. This implies that some sizable portion of the patents included in a standard is more likely to fall into our first scenario of crowning winners. Both papers also conclude that SSOs can have a significant impact on subsequent patent importance, meaning that SSOs can create or augment winners as well.

We start our empirical analysis from their findings, taking as given that SSOs tend to include higher value, more important patents. We then take a more detailed look at the second effect, the impact that being included in a standard can have on a patent's value and importance. In particular, we follow Lerner et al. and compare SSO patents to non-SSO patents,[53] but we define the match as closely as possible on observable value and importance measures prior to the SSO patent's declaration. Thus we attempt to find matches that are identical to SSO patents on as many observable importance measures as possible, so that (contrary to Lerner et al.) our "before disclosure" comparison of paired patents should show no significant difference between an SSO patent and its match. Then any "after disclosure" differences in patent importance can be more readily attributed to a disclosure effect.[54]

A. Comparative Statistics

We start by creating a database of patents disclosed as essential to some standard within an SSO.[55] We first identify all SSOs that provide public lists of the patents and patent applications declared as essential for their standards; we have eleven such SSOs.[56] We also include patents assigned to the eight currently operational patent pools that have emerged from standard setting efforts at these

SSOs[57] and whose participation in an SSO we can infer from pool membership. We then review all of the patents and patent applications disclosed to these SSOs, discarding any declarations that do not specify a date of disclosure to the SSO.[58] This leaves us with 11,683 declarations issued by 75 different jurisdictions. We filtered this list by removing declarations that were not marked as published in the April 2010 edition of the EPO's worldwide patent database (PATSTAT); we also removed patents from jurisdictions for which the PATSTAT database did not provide prior art citations or patent class data. This process yields 5588 valid patents from 11 jurisdictions, for which we collect prior art citations, IPC (International Patent Class), international patent family identifiers, patent file and grant years, and forward citations received.

For these SSO patents we construct a matched dataset. In particular, for each SSO patent we identify a patent from a different patent family with the same:

- IPC, to control for technology; as part of our robustness checks we also matched on IPC subclasses;[59]
- Filing year, to control for the development state of that technology; as part of our robustness checks we also matched on grant year; and

- Number of forward citations up to the date of disclosure to the SSO, as an observable measure of ex ante patent importance.

While the number of prior art cites do not have to be the same, we match as closely as possible on this variable, minimizing the absolute difference between the patent named to an SSO and its match. In the event of multiple matches after this step, we randomly selected a single match for each SSO patent from the set of possibilities. By construction, then, the SSO patent and its match have received identical patent citation counts at the time the SSO patent is publicly linked to an SSO.

Table 1 summarizes our data. Overall, we have information on 10452 patents, 5226 of which were declared to a standard and 5226 of which were not.[60] In order to separately test the effect that patent pools might have on a patent's subsequent citations, we further break the data down into patents that were included in a patent pool and those that were not. Of the 5226 SSO patents, 1192 are also included in a patent pool. All of the citation statistics in Table 1 are for the time of data collection, after the SSO patent had been disclosed to a standard. Looking at the last column, reporting average citations per patent, it is clear that in general patents included in a standard receive more citations than their matches

Table 1. SSO patent match summary

Patent Category	# of Patents	Total # of Citations[+]	Maximum Cites/patent	Average Cites/patent
SSO	4244	71066	736	16.7
SSO Match	4255	52699	467	12.39
Pool	1192	16322	324	13.69
Pool Match	1192	5898	125	4.95
Non-Pool	4034	66375	736	16.45
Non-Pool Match	3971	50533	467	12.53

Notes: [+] Total number of citations for all patents in that category, as of data collection.

not included in a standard, consistent with the empirical literature.

The patents in our dataset were by and large declared to an SSO within the last eighteen years, although some were reported in the late '70s and '80s. Figure 1 reports disclosure dates, by SSO. ETSI emerges as the SSO with the largest set of publicly declared patents.

Table 2 presents summary statistics that further describe the data. As the table illustrates, patents declared to an SSO tend to have higher citations on average, after declaration. The same is true regardless of whether the patents are also subsequently named to a patent pool or not.

Table 3 presents a preliminary test of the overall hypothesis that SSOs increase a patent's citations, and thus enhance its importance and potentially its holder's bargaining power. In particular, following the literature in the use of a

difference-in-differences approach, we compare the SSO patents with their matches and test the difference in forward citation counts for the period *after* the SSO patent is publicly declared as potentially essential for a standard. Recall that by construction the difference *before* SSO disclosure is zero for all but the pool versus non-pool comparison, which pits one group of SSO patents against another instead of comparing SSO patents to their non-SSO matches.

Note that in the final row of Table 3 we compare patents that eventually end up in a patent pool to patents included in the SSO but not in an associated pool rather than to their non-SSO matches. Here we find that pool patents come into a standard with fewer citations than other SSO patents.[61] That difference remains even after the pool patents have joined the pool, although it is lowered somewhat. Thus, patents included in a

Figure 1. Distribution of disclosure dates, 1992 - 2005

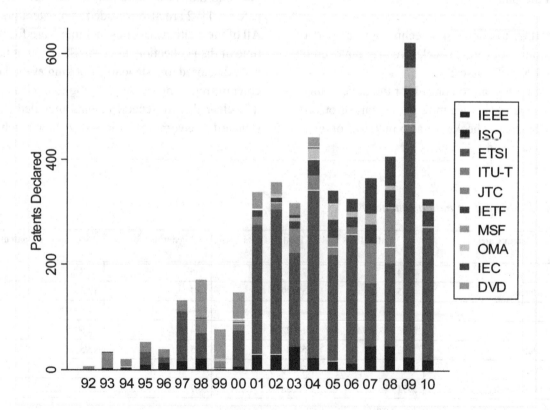

Table 2. Summary statistics

	Application year, mode	Grant year, mode	Average prior art citations	Average Pre-SSO forward citations	Average Post-SSO forward citations
SSO+	1999	2002	15.28	4.67	12.03
Match	1999	2000	14.6	4.67	7.71
Pool	2000	2004	20.59	0.48	13.22
Match	2000	2008	20.52	0.48	4.47
Non-Pool	1999	2002	14.52	4.87	11.58
Match	1999	2002	13.8	4.87	7.65

Notes: +SSO patents, both in a pool and not in a pool.

pool appear to be generally weaker than other patents in a standard before inclusion but those, differences are reduced after inclusion.

In regard to the match assessment, all three comparisons find statically higher citation average counts for SSO patents as compared to matches after disclosure to a standard. These statistics suggest that being declared essential for a standard provides a modest but statistically significant increase for the average included patent's importance, even after controlling for a number of observable ex ante quality measures. This finding is consistent with the results reported in both Lerner et al. and Rysman and Simcoe. As we will show, however, a far more complex picture emerges when the patents are evaluated on a more granular level.

Table 3. Difference-in-differences forward citation comparisons

Patent Category	Difference Pre-SSO Declaration	Difference Post-SSO Declaration
SSO vs. Match	0	4.32**
Pool vs. Match	0	8.74**
Non-Pool vs. Match	0	3.93**
Pool vs. Non-Pool+	-4.40**	-1.64*

Notes: + Not compared to their matches but to each other.
*Denotes statistically significant at the 5% level and **denotes statistically significant at the 1% level or better.

1. Heterogeneity across SSOs

The comparison in Table 3 masks a great deal of variation across SSOs. We consider heterogeneity among standard setting organizations in Table 4.

The results in Table 4 illustrate the broad range of effects hidden by the overall SSO statistics presented earlier. Certain standard organizations appear to significantly enhance average patent citations, but others do not.[62] In particular, the International Electrotechnical Commission (IEC) effects are not statistically different from zero (neither is the MultiService Forum, or MSF, but it is based on an extremely small sample). The JTC, and ETSI effects are all positive and statistically significant, but still modest—around 2 additional cites over the life of the patent (to date).

The biggest effects are found for the Digital Video Drive Forum (DVD), International Organization for Standardization (ISO), Open Mobile Alliance (OMA), Internet Engineering Task Force (IETF), IEEE, and the International Telecommunications Union (ITU). These six SSOs are the key drivers of the overall results reported earlier. The relatively large average effects for these SSOs are not surprising since several provide international guidance, with buyers in many countries looking to ITU and ISO standards before purchasing equipment.[63] Moreover, these latter two institutions act

Table 4. Difference-in-differences forward citation comparisons, by SSO

SSO	# of Patent Pairs	Avg. Cites / Patent – SSO	Avg. Cites / Patent – Match	Difference
MSF	5	24.8	22	2.8
ISO	50	28.94	14.74	14.20**
OMA	164	25.21	15.34	9.87**
IEC	241	12.59	11.64	0.95
IETF	273	21.86	12.41	9.45**
JTC	217	18.61	16.29	2.32*
DVD	271	20.43	10.52	9.91**
IEEE	342	32.92	19.58	13.35**
ITU	310	26.2	15.4	10.82**
ETSI	2673	13.27	11.47	1.80**

Notes: *Denotes statistically significant at the 5% level and ** denotes statically significant at the 1% level.

as a bridge between the public and private sectors, and some of their standards are mandated by national government agencies. In fact, Rysman and Simcoe (2008) speculate that different standards forums possess different comparative advantages, with some better able to coordinate market players than others. Our findings are consistent with their hypothesis.

2. Heterogeneity across Application Year

Another source of variation can come from time effects. The age of a patent is an important determinant of the number of cites that a patent receives since the longer a patent is public the more time it has to collect citations. Note that our patent matching process controls for this effect.

Table 5 illustrates that even for pairs of patents applied for in the same year (and thus with roughly the same amount of time to receive forward cites) a wide range of SSO effects on citations is nonetheless evident. Out of 20 year-groups, 15 are statistically significant at the 1% level, while 2 more are significant only at the 5% level. The difference in citations between SSO patents and their matches is insignificant in the remaining 3

application year groups. A patent's time cohort therefore emerges as potentially important in determining differences in citations between SSO patents and their matches. This result might be capturing a time-specific technology aspect or specific standards that are especially important. We explore this latter hypothesis next.

3. Heterogeneity across Standards

It is possible that the individual standard itself exerts a great deal of influence on included patents, with the SSO behind that standard being less important. As we noted earlier, not all patents declared to a standard under development are actually deemed essential for a ratified standard. Moreover, some early declarations are likely to turn out irrelevant either because the standard for which they were declared was abandoned (which evidently happens with some regularity) or because the standard subsequently took a different technical direction that did not involve the earlier declared patent. Even among officially approved standards, some will become commercially successful while others will not.[64] All of this suggests that the standard itself is likely to matter a great deal in terms of any ex post effect.

Table 5. Difference-in-differences forward citation comparisons, by year

Application Year	# of Patent Pairs	Avg. Cites / Patent – SSO	Avg. Cites / Patent – Match	Difference
<1990	527	21.11	16.47	4.64**
1991	103	33.30	24.37	7.92
1992	121	35.79	16.55	19.23**
1993	177	35.47	23.59	11.87**
1994	228	33.79	21.51	12.29**
1995	268	30.22	24.08	6.14*
1996	370	26.36	16.73	9.62**
1997	410	23.04	16.20	6.83**
1998	411	16.22	13.20	3.01*
1999	447	13.21	10.61	2.60**
2000	507	11.22	3.90	7.32**
2001	402	5.39	3.58	1.80**
2002	327	3.56	2.48	1.07**
2003	236	2.05	0.85	1.19**
2004	192	1.40	0.71	0.69**
2005	128	0.85	0.69	0.16**
2006	106	0.44	0.23	0.22**
2007	133	0.92	0.12	0.80**
2008	111	0.1	0.03	0.08
2009	22	0.04	0	0.04

Notes: *Denotes statistically significant at the 5% level or better and ** denotes statically significant at the 1% level or better. We skip any year for which there is not sufficient data to compare SSO patents to their matches. Note that the last column sometimes does not match the actual difference between columns 3 and 4 due to rounding.

Unfortunately, we are not able to associate every SSO patent with the standard for which it was declared essential. Very few declarations provide that level of specificity. Nor do most SSOs report the relevant standards for the patents they publicize as potentially essential. We are, however, able to examine this issue for a subset of our data. For this analysis we identified 16 standards and a total of 3512 patent pairs. Table 6 summarizes our results.

Looking over the results presented in Table 6 we find that roughly a third of the differences are not statistically significant (5 out of 16). Among those that are statistically significant, most are positive and 5 are in the double digits (MG-PEG1394, MPEG2, Bluetooth, DTS, and GPRS). Surprisingly, two of the significant differences

show a *negative* effect of inclusion in a standard (LTE and DVB, both of which are at ETSI).[65]

The results in Table 6 emphasize the importance of the specific standard involved, demonstrating that a particular SSO does not have a consistent effect on included patents. Consider the measured effects for ETSI, which range from about -3 citations (statistically significant) for two standards, to not statistically different from zero for five standards, to positive but modest (3 to 5 citations) for two other standards, to positive and sizeable (9 to 26 citations) for four other standards. Thus a single standard setting organization can exhibit remarkable diversity in its average impact on included patents' importance depending on the standard under development.

Table 6. Difference-in-differences forward citation comparisons, by standard

Standard	# of Patent Pairs	Avg. Cites / Patent – SSO	Avg. Cites / Patent – Match	Difference
MPEG1394 (JTC)	75	30.88	12.45	18.42**
MPEG4 (JTC)	174	9.35	4.21	5.15**
MPEG2 (JTC)	119	25.39	6.14	19.24**
DVD (DVD Forum)	271	20.43	10.52	9.91**
Bluetooth (IEEE)	262	16.58	4.33	12.26**
AVC (ITU)	218	5.03	1.83	3.20**
DTS (ETSI)	9	32.56	6.00	26.56*
DECT (ETSI)	11	11.91	13.09	-1.18
BRAN (ETSI)	16	14.13	7.75	6.40
TETRA (ETSI)	42	14.83	14.81	0.02
DVB (ETSI)	66	10.20	13.21	-3.02*
GMR (ETSI)	33	14.33	16.73	-2.30
GPRS (ETSI)	106	24.42	13.68	10.74**
GSM (ETSI)	563	11.56	10.56	1.00
3G (ETSI)	1147	16.59	12.78	3.81**
LTE (ETSI)	400	3.47	6.14	-2.67**

Notes: *Denotes statistically significant at the 5% level or better and ** denotes statically significant at the 1% level or better. Note that the last column sometimes does not match the actual difference between columns 3 and 4 due to rounding. Note that some patents are declared to multiple standards.

4. Heterogeneity across Patents

A final variable to consider in evaluating ex post SSO effects is heterogeneity across individual patents. All of the difference comparisons presented above are averages, either across an SSO, across an application year cohort, or across a standard within an SSO. As the analysis below illustrates, within each standard some patent citations receive a boost from inclusion in the standard (as compared to their match) while others do not, or

receive only a modest boost. In fact, oftentimes the patents named as potentially essential for a standard receive *fewer* citations than their matches. Figure 2 presents the distribution of citation differences between an SSO patent and its match for the period after disclosure to an SSO.

As the figure illustrates, an SSO's affect on a particular patent's importance covers a huge range. Both tails of the distribution are quite long. Thus, a very small number of patents appear to receive a substantial boost to citations from being declared to a standard, but the vast majority does not. The mode occurs at zero, meaning that most of the time matched patents receive the same number of citations as the corresponding SSO patent.. The next two highest frequencies occur at 1 and -1. The median effect is also zero, meaning that half of all SSO patents receive the same or fewer citations than their match after their inclusion in a standard.

Even when we look at some of the SSO's with the highest average difference in cites between SSO patents and their match, considering the distribution of the data presents a very different picture than the averages reported earlier. Take for example patents declared to ISO. Although the average difference in post-declaration cites is 14.20, the median is roughly one fifth of that at 3. The differences are even more pronounced if we look at an SSO with a larger number of patents, such as ITU. Recall that the average difference in post-declaration citations between ITU patents and their matches is 10.82 citations. Further examination of this subset of patents reveals that out of 310 patents declared to ITU, 91 (29%) have a non-positive difference. The median difference for ITU patents is 6.5 additional cites; the mode is zero. As before, the range of effects is extensive.

Parsing the data even further by focusing on just those standards within an SSO that exhibit some of the highest average differences in cites we nonetheless find negative differences when we examine individual patent pairs. In particular if we consider the JTC's MPEG2 standard, in

Figure 2. Frequency distribution of citation difference (SSO-Match) [Notes: For display reasons the range of this graph is truncated. It illustrates the differences for 4116 observations out of 5226 (78.8%). 786 observations (15%) fall above the value of 15, while 324 observations (6.2%) lie below -15. The lower bound for the dataset is -415 and the upper bound is 689.]

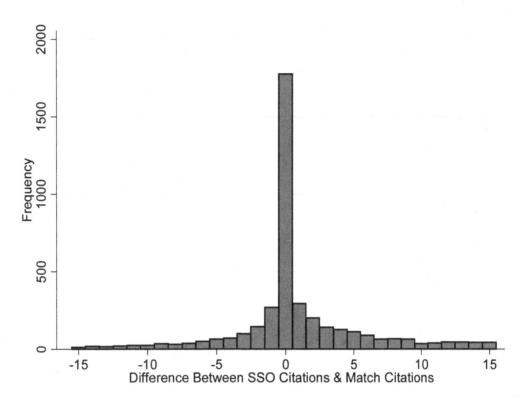

72 pairs (60.5%) the matched non-SSO patents have just as many or more citations as their SSO counterpart. Although the average difference for this particular standard is 19.24 cites, as reported above, the median is about half as much as 11 additional cites.

5. Heterogeneity across Patent Jurisdictions

As a final check, we consider whether the office issuing the patent has any affect on the analysis. Table 7 presents difference-in-difference comparisons according to the jurisdiction of the SSO patent. Of the eleven jurisdictions covered, only three exhibit a statistically significant SSO effect on citations: USPTO, Australia, and WIPO. Of these three, the SSO effect on Australian patents

is negative, while for WIPO patents the effect is modest, at 1.4. It appears that USPTO patents are largely responsible for any significant positive effects.

Taking all of the analysis into account, we can conclude that a positive SSO effect is not inevitable, even for patents declared to the international standards bodies with some compulsion authority. Instead, it appears that a subset of patents within a select group of SSOs drive the averages reported above.

B. Regression Analysis

The analysis above considers each potential determining factor one at a time: first SSO effects, then year cohorts, then standard effects, then individual patent effects, and finally jurisdiction effects. However, the various factors might interact with one another. For example, cohort effects might appear important only because they capture specific standard effects. To address this issue, we estimate a regression.

We consider the entire data set of 5226 SSO patents and their 5226 matches. In particular we consider each patent and each match as a separate data point of our dataset; hence our dataset consists of 10452 patents. Since our dependent variable is the number of post declaration citations, we calculated the value of that variable for each non-SSO patent based on the year in which its corresponding SSO patent match was declared.[66]

Table 8 shows the results of our regression analysis on the entire dataset. In order to properly correct for non-constant variance in our dependant variable, we use the logarithmic transformation of the number of post declaration cites.[67]

The model displays the effects of three key explanatory variables: years since declaration, prior art count, and pre-declaration forward cites.

Table 7. Difference-in-differences forward citation comparisons, by jurisdiction

Patent Jurisdiction (SSO Patent)	# of Patent Pairs	Avg. Cites / Patent – SSO	Avg. Cites / Patent – Match	Difference
USPTO	3511	22.68	15.30	7.39**
EPO	599	3.14	2.94	0.21
Australia	353	0.74	0.39	-0.32**
WIPO	321	2.18	0.82	1.35**
Germany	183	1.52	1.88	-0.36
Japan	134	0.11	0.17	-0.06
France	86	1.72	2.02	-0.30
Netherlands	21	0.10	0.81	-0.71
Singapore	12	0.00	0.08	-0.08
Turkey	5	0.00	0.00	0.00

Notes: *Denotes statistically significant at the 5% level or better and ** denotes statically significant at the 1% level or better. We skip Spain which only has 1 patent pair. Note that the last column sometimes does not match the actual difference between columns 3 and 4 due to rounding.

Four categories of patents are considered in the model: those declared to just one SSO, those declared to multiple SSOs, those included in pools, and lastly, matched patents. The three explanatory variables are interacted with dummies for patent categories to examine potential differential effects between categories. The intercept terms for each of the patent categories have no physical interpretation since none of the covariates are ever zero; they are included in the model, however, since there is an a priori difference in prior art counts between matched patents and SSO patents. Dummy variables are also included for each of the issuing jurisdictions to control for unobserved country specific heterogeneity between patents.

As expected, years since declaration has a positive and significant effect on the accumulation of cites post declaration. For matched patents, this effect is estimated as an 8.95% increase in forward cites per year. For patents declared to just one SSO, we observe a 17.4% increase in forward cites per year; for patents declared to multiple SSOs and pools, the effect is estimated to be more rapid at 18.24% and 18.17% per year respectively. These findings suggest that SSO effects (and pool effects) are cumulative.

Prior art does not have a significant effect on the accumulation of forward cites for matches or pool patents. However, for SSO patents the effect of prior art cites appears to be weakly positive – we see a significant effect of 0.31% for single SSO patents and 0.93% for multiple SSO patents. Perhaps this finding reflects the fact that patents declared to a standard build upon one another, and in the aggregate may make the standard more successful.

Finally, we observe that the number of pre-declaration cites has a positive and significant effect for matches: one additional cite prior to declaration increases the number of post declaration cites by 4.68%. The effect is equivalent for both patents declared to multiple SSOs as well as those included in pools. However, the model estimates slightly weaker effects of 3.20% for

Table 8. Regression analysis[68]

Coefficient	Citations Post Declaration
Single SSO Patent	-0.104***
	(0.0339)
Multiple SSO Patent	-0.105
	(0.103)
Pool Patent	-0.207**
	(0.0811)
Years Since Decl'n	0.0895***
	(0.00354)
Single SSO & Years Since Decl'n	0.0841***
	(0.00540)
Multiple SSO & Years Since Decl'n	0.0929***
	(0.0149)
Pool & Years Since Decl'n	0.0922***
	(0.00918)
Prior Art	-0.000984
	(0.000691)
Single SSO & Prior Art	0.00311***
	(0.000945)
Multiple SSO & Prior Art	0.00929**
	(0.00368)
Pool & Prior Art	-0.000354
	(0.00143)
Citations Pre Decl'n	0.0468***
	(0.00229)
Single SSO & Citations Pre Decl'n	-0.0148***
	(0.00286)
Mult SSO & Citations Pre Decl'n	-0.00439
	(0.00368)
Pool & Citations Pre Decl'n	-0.0115
	(0.0143)
Jurisdiction Dummies	Negative Significant
Constant	0.813***
	(0.0309)
Observations	10,452
R-squared	0.519

Robust standard errors in parentheses
*** p<0.01, ** p<0.05, * p<0.1
The omitted jurisdiction dummy in the model is for the USPTO

patents declared to just one SSO. This finding is intuitively consistent with our initial discuss of SSOs crowning winners: patents that come into a standard as important will continue to gain in importance over time, distinct from any SSO effect.

In contrast to the USPTO, the dummies for other patent issuing jurisdictions are all negative and significant. This is consistent with the statistics presented in Table 7, which shows that U.S. patents appear to be driving a bulk of the apparent differences between SSO patents and their matches.

The implications of the model are best summarized by comparing the predicted number of post declaration cites for each group of patents identified. At the average value of the covariates, the model predicts 4.5 forward cites for matched patents, 6.2 forward cites for patents declared to just one SSO, 8.6 forward cites for patents declared to multiple SSOs, and 6.1 forward cites for pool patents. At the 90th percentile of the covariates, the model predicts 11.8 forward cites for matched patents, 28.1 forward cites for patents declared to one SSO, 55.8 cites for patents declared to multiple SSOs and 13.3 forward cites for patents declared to pools.

What these predictions illustrate quite clearly is that matched patents and SSO patents tend to exhibit substantial differences only when patents are declared to multiple SSOs. Furthermore, patents declared to pools and patents declared to only one SSO appear to receive only marginally more forward cites than their matches.

1. Heterogeneity across Patents

The largest positive coefficient in the overall regression presented in Table 9 is the number of years since the patent was declared to the SSO. It may be the case, then, that the results are driven largely by the few patents that were declared to an SSO long ago. In the table that follows we test this conjecture by limiting our regression to those patents that were declared to an SSO less than 15, 10 and 5 years from 2010 respectively.

For matched patents, the time effect, which is estimated as a 9.9% to a 10.4% increase in forward cites per year, is more or less equal across the three models. For patents declared to both single and multiple SSOs, we observe an increasing effect as the time window is shortened from 15 years to 10 years; however, the effect is either weakened in the 5 year window (for single SSO patents), or not statistically significant (for multiple SSO patents). A similar result is evident for patents included in pools: the strongest effects are seen for patents declared less than 10 years ago, weaker effects are seen for patents declared less than 15 years ago, and no significant effects are seen for patents declared less than 5 years ago. It appears, therefore, that a cohort of SSO patents declared between 5 and 10 years ago appear to drive the largest differences in citation counts, followed closely by those patents declared between 10 and 15 years ago. Thus, we conclude that higher citation counts for SSO patents are not being driven by a linear function of time, but rather by a more complex effect which appears to have emerged between 5 and 15 years ago.

2. Heterogeneity across SSOs

The comparative statistics reported earlier suggested that certain SSOs, particularly the larger international ones with governmental ties, were more likely to have an impact than other SSOs. We consider that question again using regression analysis. In particular, we restrict our sample to just those patents declared to an SSO (i.e., we drop the matches) and examine the average number of cites those patents receive after joining an SSO. Table 10 presents the results.

In Table 10 we find significance for 7 of the 9 SSO dummies included in the model. Comparing SSOs presented in the model with the omitted dummy for ETSI, we see that two SSOs, ISO and JTC, have coefficients that are not significantly different from zero. In contrast, the coefficients for ITU and DVD are negative and significant indicating that patents declared to ITU and the DVD forum generally garner fewer cites than those declared to ETSI. For the five remaining SSOs, the effects for IEEE, IETF, MSF, OMA, and IEC are all positive and significant, indicating that patents at these SSOs are stronger in terms of post declaration citation counts than those declared to ETSI. The coefficient for pool patents is negative, indicating that these patents accumulative fewer cites than the ones declared to ETSI. In this model, the coefficient for years since declaration is positive and significant; it indicates that in general patents declared to the included SSOs gather 18.9% more forward cites for each year since their declaration. The coefficient for pre-declaration forward cites is also positive and significant; it indicates that each additional cite gathered pre-declaration raises the number of post declaration cites by 3.01%. As in Table 8, prior art appears to have no significant effect on post declaration cites. All three of these estimates are generally consistent with the pooled model presented in Table 8.

3. Robustness Analysis

In this section we check the robustness of our analysis (Table 11) by changing some of the criteria used in the matching process. Specifically we generate three separate sets of matches in increasing order of selectivity: the first where we match based on filing year and IPC subclass; the second based on filing year, grant year, and IPC class; and the third based on filing year, issuing country, and IPC class.

The most selective matching criteria equalize the pre-declaration forward cites, filing years, and IPC subclasses of the SSO and matched patents. Using these matching criteria, we reduce the size of our dataset from 10452 patents to 8840 patents. The next most selective criteria equalize pre-declaration forward cites, filing years, grant years

Table 9. Regression analysis-keeping only patents declared within given time period

Coefficient	(1) Less than 15 Years	(2) Less than 10 Years	(3) Less than 5 Years
Single SSO Patent	-0.116***	-0.263***	-0.319***
	(0.0335)	(0.0340)	(0.0397)
Multiple SSO Patent	-0.232*	-0.344**	-0.382**
	(0.128)	(0.134)	(0.193)
Pool Patent	-0.164**	-0.284***	-0.273***
	(0.0819)	(0.0906)	(0.0788)
Years Since Decl'n	0.0994***	0.104***	0.100***
	(0.00368)	(0.00524)	(0.0150)
Single SSO & Years Since Decl'n	0.0884***	0.131***	0.199***
	(0.00559)	(0.00726)	(0.0195)
Multiple SSO & Years Since Decl'n	0.129***	0.163***	0.237***
	(0.0272)	(0.0336)	(0.0754)
Pool & Years Since Decl'n	0.0846***	0.148***	0.0674**
	(0.00957)	(0.0159)	(0.0302)
Prior Art	-0.000961	-0.00117	-0.000796
	(0.000688)	(0.000731)	(0.000798)
Single SSO & Prior Art	0.00315***	0.00445***	0.00204**
	(0.000934)	(0.000940)	(0.000959)
Multiple SSO & Prior Art	0.00945**	0.0104***	0.00408
	(0.00380)	(0.00378)	(0.00422)
Pool & Prior Art	-0.000433	-0.00231	-0.000464
	(0.00143)	(0.00153)	(0.00141)
Citations Pre Decl'n	0.0469***	0.0488***	0.0586***
	(0.00231)	(0.00251)	(0.00481)
Single SSO & Citations Pre Decl'n	-0.0154***	-0.0180***	-0.0281***
	(0.00286)	(0.00300)	(0.00527)
Mult SSO & Citations Pre Decl'n	-0.00453	-0.00504	-0.0121**
	(0.00372)	(0.00395)	(0.00603)
Pool & Citations Pre Decl'n	-0.0121	-0.0799*	0.462***
	(0.0144)	(0.0435)	(0.167)
Jurrisdiction Dummies	Negative		
	Significant		

continued on following page

Table 9. Continued

Coefficient	(1) Less than 15 Years	(2) Less than 10 Years	(3) Less than 5 Years
Constant	0.760***	0.677***	0.531***
	(0.0310)	(0.0337)	(0.0437)
Observations	10,176	8,544	4,292
R-squared	0.515	0.512	0.450

Robust standard errors in parentheses
*** p<0.01, ** p<0.05, * p<0.1
The omitted jurisdiction dummy in the model is for the USPTO

and IPC classes. Using these criteria reduces the size of our dataset to 10098 patents. Finally, we match on pre-declaration forward cites, filing years, IPC class, and filing jurisdiction. This method reduces the size of our data set to 10402 patents.

Running the main specification on these datasets does not substantially alter the coefficient for time effects, which continues to have the largest absolute impact on forward cites. The baseline estimates for time effects are robust to changes in matching criteria, as are the estimates of the interactive terms associated with patents declared to just one SSO, multiple SSOs, and pool patents. In general, we see that patents declared to multiple SSOs and pool patents exhibit the biggest difference compared to matches, whereas patents declared to just one SSO are a little closer to matches in terms of post declaration forward cites.

In contrast, the estimates for prior art cites exhibit some sensitivity across matching criteria. In columns (1) and (3) we observe a significant negative effect associated with increased prior art counts; however, in column (2) the effect is not statistically significant. For SSO patents, the estimates of the interactive terms are consistent with the results in the main model: we see a small but net positive contribution associated with increased prior art. While we do not see any significant effect for prior art for pool patents in columns (1) and (3), we do, however, see a negative effect in column (2). Overall, these results are ambiguous in relation to the effects of prior art on post declaration forward cites.

The effect associated with the number of forward cites accumulated pre declaration appears to be largely consistent with the main model: for matched patents, we observe a positive and significant effect. In the main model, we observed a significant and negative effect for patents declared to a single SSO and no differences for patents declared to multiple SSOs and pool patents. In the robustness checks presented above, the negative effect for single SSO patents appears in column (3) but does not appear in column (1) or (2). For multiple SSO patents and pool patents, the estimates for the pre declaration citation effect are not different from zero, a result which is consistent with the main model.

5. CONCLUSION

We began this research with questions: does inclusion in a standard affect a patent's importance? Does a patent's inclusion in a standard affect the patent holder's market power or bargaining position, and if so how? Most antitrust inquiries

Table 10. Regression with SSO effects

Coefficient	Log Transformed Citations Post Declaration
Pool Patents	-0.125***
	(0.0401)
Years Since Decl'n	0.189***
	(0.00430)
Prior Art	-0.000589
	(0.000631)
Citations Pre Decl'n	0.0301***
	(0.00161)
IEEE	0.223***
	(0.0576)
ISO	0.192
	(0.153)
ITU	-0.225***
	(0.0611)
JTC	-0.0537
	(0.0720)
IETF	0.316***
	(0.0588)
MSF	0.745**
	(0.340)
OMA	0.357***
	(0.0808)
IEC	0.223***
	(0.0654)
DVD	-0.315***
	(0.0777)
Jurisdiction Dummies	Negative
	Significant
Constant	0.743***
	(0.0352)
Observations	5,226
R-squared	0.614

Robust standard errors in parentheses

*** $p<0.01$, ** $p<0.05$, * $p<0.1$

The omitted jurisdiction dummy in the model is for the USPTO, the omitted SSO dummy is for ETSI

before competition agencies and the courts look at indicators and effects of market power, but do not attempt to measure it directly. While this approach works well for studying an individual firm accused of anticompetitive foul play, it is not a practical route for a broader analysis of thousands of firms participating in cooperative standard setting. The many difficulties likely explain the dearth of empirical analyses testing the effect on a patent holder of naming patents as potentially essential to a standard. While a number of theoretical papers start from the presumption of SSO-conferred importance on included patents and market power for the patent holders and then consider the potential anticompetitive effects, such as ex post patent hold up, only two studies, to our knowledge, consider measures of the effect an SSO might actually have on patents included in an SSO, and hence on patent holders whose patents are declared as potentially essential to a standard. Those two studies ask whether inclusion in a standard augments patents' importance or value, as measured by forward citations. In this paper, we extend that research by analyzing a larger and more detailed database of patents named to standards (and a subset named to patent pools associated with standards).

We find a spectrum of possibilities. Inclusion in a standard need not have any affect at all on patent value as the modal effect we found was zero. Moreover, if inclusion in a standard does have a positive effect, that effect is oftentimes small. This will be especially true for those patents that are chosen for a standard precisely because they cover a highly valuable innovation. In other words, as common sense suggests and as the existing empirical literature corroborates, SSOs tend to "crown winners" because the more influential technologies will naturally suggest themselves for inclusion in standards. The instances of a standard "creating" a winner appear relatively more isolated according to our data.

We conclude that the question of an SSO effect on included patents is a matter of degree. In light

Table 11. Robustness regressions

Coefficient	(1) Filing Year & Subclass Match	(2) Filing Year, Class & Grant Year Match	(3) Filing Year, Class & Jurisdiction Match
Single SSO Patent	0.0666*	-0.0259	-0.0807**
	(0.0348)	(0.0336)	(0.0332)
Multiple SSO Patent	-0.0279	-0.0563	-0.0721
	(0.116)	(0.105)	(0.104)
Pool Patent	-0.129	-0.176**	-0.188**
	(0.0839)	(0.0803)	(0.0791)
Years Since Decl'n	0.122***	0.115***	0.0987***
	(0.00358)	(0.00358)	(0.00362)
Single SSO & Years Since Decl'n	0.0410***	0.0560***	0.0751***
	(0.00565)	(0.00547)	(0.00540)
Multiple SSO & Years Since Decl'n	0.0752***	0.0645***	0.0848***
	(0.0189)	(0.0150)	(0.0154)
Pool & Years Since Decl'n	0.0652***	0.0699***	0.0855***
	(0.00948)	(0.00911)	(0.00912)
Prior Art	-0.00277***	0.000819	-0.00178***
	(0.000954)	(0.000733)	(0.000684)
Single SSO & Prior Art	0.00271**	0.000399	0.00421***
	(0.00112)	(0.000973)	(0.000936)
Multiple SSO & Prior Art	0.00982**	0.00678*	0.0104***
	(0.00417)	(0.00395)	(0.00378)
Pool & Prior Art	-8.88e-05	-0.00289**	0.000776
	(0.00163)	(0.00144)	(0.00141)
Citations Pre Decl'n	0.0444***	0.0343***	0.0455***
	(0.00336)	(0.00231)	(0.00204)
Single SSO & Citations Pre Decl'n	-0.00616	-0.00358	-0.0129***
	(0.00504)	(0.00310)	(0.00267)
Mult SSO & Citations Pre Decl'n	0.00439	0.00680	-0.00436
	(0.0102)	(0.00519)	(0.00369)
Pool & Citations Pre Decl'n	-0.0714	-0.00836	-0.00794
	(0.0653)	(0.0135)	(0.0119)
Jurisdiction Dummy	Negative		
	Significant		
Constant	0.737***	0.799***	0.766***
	(0.0324)	(0.0300)	(0.0304)
Observations	8,840	10,098	10,402

continued on following page

Table 11. Continued

	(1)	(2)	(3)
Coefficient	**Filing Year & Subclass Match**	**Filing Year, Class & Grant Year Match**	**Filing Year, Class & Jurisdiction Match**
R-squared	0.537	0.533	0.530
Adj.R-squared	0.536	0.532	0.529

Robust standard errors in parentheses
*** p<0.01, ** p<0.05, * p<0.1
The omitted jurisdiction dummy in the models is for the USPTO

of the wide ranging effects on patent importance, and considering idiosyncrasies across industries, technologies, standards, patent offices, and SSOs, we argue that the question of SSO effects should be considered separately for each individual SSO, standard, and patent.

As for patent pools, our analysis confirms findings elsewhere in the literature: the patents included in pools tend to be less important than otherwise comparable patents named to a standard, although they do have more citations than patents not named to a standard. The comparative statistics indicate that patents joining a pool associated with a standard tend to be of relatively lesser quality than their counterparts named to a standard but not to the pool. While they have higher citation counts upon entering a standard, they garner fewer additional cites after joining the pool as compared to non-pool patents over the same period. In our overall regression we find that the pool dummy variable is negative and statistically significant.

The analysis we present in this paper furthers our understanding of cooperative standard setting organizations, the patent pools sometimes associated with them, and the effects of a patent's inclusion in either. It was already well understood that patents exhibit considerable variation in value and importance. We find that this same broad ranging pattern holds for patents named to a standard as well. As Mark Lemley explains, "Patents differ in their likely validity, their importance to the standard, and the ease with which they can

be designed around. Further, standards differ in their importance and the price that can be charged for products or components that incorporate the standard."[69] With such inherent variation in patents and standards, the wide variation in SSO effects on patents that we find in our empirical analysis appears only natural.

A second, and equally important, reason to closely examine how and when SSOs might enhance included patents value or importance rests with firm investment decisions. Unraveling legitimate value created by the standardization process from illegitimate market power that leads to hold up can be extremely difficult—both conceptually and empirically. Participating in cooperative standard setting efforts is time consuming, costly, and risky for firms since there is no guarantee that a useful, commercially successful standard will emerge at the end. In this light, increased patent importance can be seen as one of the returns to a risky investment in standard setting and not simply an exercise in market power abuse.

REFERENCES

Alcácer, J., & Gittelman, M. (2006). Patent citations as a measure of knowledge flows: The influence of examiner citations. *The Review of Economics and Statistics, 88*(4), 774–779. doi:10.1162/rest.88.4.774

Allison, J., & Lemley, M. (2002). The growing complexity of the United States patent system. *Boston University Law Review, 82*, 77.

Allison, J., & Tiller, E. (2003). The business method patent myth. *Berkeley Technology Law Journal, 18*(987), 1082.

Baumol, W., & Swanson, D. (2005). Reasonable and nondiscriminatory (RAND) royalties, standards selection, and control of market power. *Antitrust Law Journal, 73*(1).

Behrman, J., & Taubman, P. (1976). Intergenerational transmission of income and wealth. *The American Economic Review, 66*(2), 436–440.

Belleflamme, P. (2002). Coordination on formal vs. de facto standards: A dynamic approach. *European Journal of Political Economy, 18*(1). doi:10.1016/S0176-2680(01)00073-8

Burkart, M. (1995). Initial shareholdings and overbidding in take-over contests. *The Journal of Finance, 50*(5), 1491–1515. doi:10.1111/j.1540-6261.1995.tb05186.x

Cabral, L., & Salant, D. (2008). *Evolving technologies and standards regulation*. Retrieved from http://ssrn.com/abstract=1120862

Chiao, B., Lerner, J., & Tirole, J. (2005). *The rules of standard setting organizations: An empirical analysis*. Retrieved from http://ssrn.com/abstract=664643

Chowdry, B., & Jegadeesh, N. (1994). Pre-tender offers share acquisition strategy in takeovers. *Journal of Financial and Quantitative Analysis, 29*, 117–129. doi:10.2307/2331194

DeLacey, B., Herman, K., Kiron, K., & Lerner, J. (2006). *Strategic behavior in standard-setting organizations*. Retrieved from http://ssrn.com/abstract=903214

European Telecommunications Standards Institute. (2006). *ETSI directives: Version 20*. Retrieved from http://portal.etsi.org/directives/

Farrell, J., Hayes, J., Shapiro, C., & Sullivan, T. (2007). Standard setting, patents, and hold-up. *Antitrust Law Journal, 603*(3).

Farrell, J., & Saloner, G. (1988). Coordination through committees and markets. *The Rand Journal of Economics, 19*(2), 235–252. doi:10.2307/2555702

Furman, J., & Stern, S. (2006). *Climbing atop the shoulders of giants: The impact of institutions on cumulative research*. Cambridge, MA: National Bureau of Economic Research. doi:10.1257/aer.101.5.1933

Greenstein, S., & Rysman, M. (2007). Coordination costs and standard setting: Lessons from 56K modems. In Greenstein, S., & Stango, V. (Eds.), *Standards and public policy*. Cambridge, UK: Cambridge University Press. doi:10.1017/CBO9780511493249.005

Harhoff, D., Narin, F., Scherer, F. M., & Vopel, K. (1999). Citation frequency and the value of patented inventions. *The Review of Economics and Statistics, 81*(3), 511–515. doi:10.1162/003465399558265

Heckman, J., Ichimura, H., Smith, J. A., & Todd, P. E. (1998). Characterizing selection bias using experimental data. *Econometrica, 66*, 1017–1098. doi:10.2307/2999630

Heckman, J., Ichimura, H., & Todd, P. E. (1997). Matching as an econometric evaluation estimator: Evidence from evaluating a job training programme. *The Review of Economic Studies, 64*, 605–654. doi:10.2307/2971733

Jaffe, A., & Lerner, J. (2001). Reinventing public R&D: Patent policy and the commercialization of national laboratory technologies. *The Rand Journal of Economics, 32*(1). doi:10.2307/2696403

Jennings, R., & Mazzeo, M. (1993). Competing bids, target management resistance and the structure of takeover bids. *Review of Financial Studies, 6*, 883–909. doi:10.1093/rfs/6.4.883

Johnson, D., & Popp, D. (2003). Forced out of the closet: The impact of the American inventors protection act on the timing of patent disclosure. *The Rand Journal of Economics, 34*(1), 96–112. doi:10.2307/3087445

Lanjouw, J., & Schankerman, M. (2001). Characteristics of patent litigation: A window on competition. *The Rand Journal of Economics, 32*, 129. doi:10.2307/2696401

Layne-Farrar, A., & Lerner, J. (2010). To join or not to join: Examining patent pool participation and rent sharing rules. *International Journal of Industrial Organization, 29*(2), 294–303. doi:10.1016/j.ijindorg.2010.08.006

Layne-Farrar, A., Padilla, A. J., & Schmalensee, R. (2007). Pricing patents for licensing in standard setting organizations: Making sense of FRAND commitments. *Antitrust Law Journal, 74*(3).

Lee, K. (1996). Cooperative standard-setting: The road to compatibility or deadlock? The NAFTA's transformation of the telecommunications industry. *Federal Commission Law Journal, 487.*

Leibowitz, S., & Margolis, S. E. (2002). *Winners, losers, and Microsoft.* Oakland, CA: The Independent Institute.

Lemley, M. (2002). Intellectual property rights and standard-setting organizations. *California Law Review, 90*, 1889. doi:10.2307/3481437

Lemley, M. (2006). *Ten things to do about patent holdup of standards (and one not to).* Retrieved from http://ssrn.com/abstract=923470

Lemley, M., & Shapiro, C. (2006). *Patent holdup and royalty stacking.* Retrieved from http://ssrn.com/abstract=923468

Lerner, J., Tirole, J., & Strojwas, M. (2003). *Cooperative marketing agreements between competitors: evidence from patent pools.* Retrieved from http://www.nber.org/papers/w9680.pdf

Miller, J. (2006). Standard setting, patents, and access lock-in: RAND licensing and the theory of the firm. *Indiana Law Review, 40.*

Moore, K. (2005). Worthless patents. *Berkeley Technology Law Journal, 20*, 1521.

Patterson, M. (2003). Antitrust and the costs of standard-setting: A commentary on Teece and Sherry. *Minnesota Law Review, 87*, 1995.

Roe, M. (1996). Chaos and evolution in law and economics. *Harvard Law Review, 109*, 641. doi:10.2307/1342067

Rysman, M., & Simcoe, T. (2005). Patents and the performance of voluntary standard setting organizations. *Management Science, 54*(11), 1920–1934. doi:10.1287/mnsc.1080.0919

Shapiro, C. (2001). Setting compatability standards: Co-operation or collusion? In Dreyfuss, R., Zimmerman, D., & First, H. (Eds.), *Expanding the boundaries of intellectual property.* New York, NY: Oxford University Press.

Shapiro, C., & Varian, H. (1999). *Information rules: A strategic guide to the network economy.* Boston, MA: Harvard Business School Press.

Stulz, R., Walking, R., & Song, M. (1990). The distribution of target ownership and division of gains in successful takeovers. *The Journal of Finance, 45*, 817–833. doi:10.1111/j.1540-6261.1990.tb05107.x

Taubman, P. (1976). Earnings, education, genetics, and environment. *The Journal of Human Resources, 11*(4), 447–461. doi:10.2307/145426

Taubman, P. (1976). The determinants of earnings: Genetic, family, and other environments: A study of white male twins. *The American Economic Review, 66*(5), 858–870.

Thomson, P., & Fox-Kean, M. (2005). Patent citations and the geography of knowledge spillovers: A reassessment. *The American Economic Review, 95*(1), 450–459. doi:10.1257/0002828053828509

Trajtenberg, M. (1990). A penny for your quotes: Patent citations and the value of innovations. *The Rand Journal of Economics, 21*(1). doi:10.2307/2555502

Trajtenberg, M., Henderson, R., & Jaffe, A. (1996). University versus corporate patents: A window on the basicness of invention. *Economic Innovation New Technology, 5.*

U.S. Department of Justice and FTC. (2000). *Antitrust guidelines for collaborations among competitors.* Retrieved from http://www.ftc.gov/os/2000/ 04/ftcdojguidelines.pdf

Walking, R. (1985). Predicting tender offer success: A logistic analysis. *Journal of Financial and Quantitative Analysis, 20*, 461–478. doi:10.2307/2330762

ENDNOTES

[1] As recognized by the European Commission in its Guidelines on the applicability of Article 101 of the Treaty on the Functioning of the European Union to horizontal co-operation agreements, Section 7 on Standardisation Agreements, at para. 258: "Standardisation agreements generally have a positive economic effect, for example by promoting economic interpenetration on the internal market and encouraging the development of new markets and improved supply conditions." *See also*, U.S. Dep't of Justice & FTC, Antitrust Guidelines for Collaborations Among Competitors (2000), available at http://www.ftc.gov/os/2000/04/ftcdojguidelines.pdf. The U.S. courts have tended to agree: In Allied Tube v. Indian Head, Inc., 486 U.S. 492 (1988), the U.S. Supreme Court stated that "…private standards can have significant procompetitive advantages…" *See also*, Mark A. Lemley, "Intellectual Property Rights and Standard-Setting Organizations," California Law Review, Vol. 90, p. 1889, 2002.

[2] For an academic endorsement of this view, *see* e.g., Mark Lemley, "Ten Things to Do About Patent Holdup of Standards (and One Not to)", 2006; *see also* Mark A. Lemley and Carl Shapiro, "Patent Holdup and Royalty Stacking," 2006; J. Farrell, J. Hayes, C. Shapiro and T. Sullivan, "Standard Setting, Patents, and Hold-Up," 74 Antitrust L.J. 603, (Issue 3, 2007).

[3] For a discussion of hold up, see Anne Layne-Farrar and Klaus Schmidt, ""Licensing Complementary Patents: 'Patent Trolls', Market Structure, and 'Excessive' Royalties", forthcoming in Berkeley Technology Law Journal, 2010.

4   Which assumes, implicitly, that licenses are not and cannot be negotiated ex ante, before any switching costs come into play.

5   Ideally, our empirical assessment of citations would distinguish between those inserted by the patent filer and those inserted by the patent examiner. According to one empirical study, as much as 63% of prior art citations in the average U.S. patent is inserted by examiners; approximately 40% of citing patents have all citations imposed by examiners; and only 8% of patents have no examiner-added citations at all. (See Juan Alca´cer and Michelle Gittelman, "Patent Citations as a Measure of Knowledge Flows: The Influence of Examiner Citations", *The Review of Economics and Statistics*, November 2006, 88(4): 774–779.) The percentage of citations added by examiners is even higher for EPO patents. While USPTO data began distinguishing between filer and examiner prior art citations in 2001, the EPO's PAT-STAT dataset which we rely on here does not accommodate this distinction. Because, however, we are concerned with patent importance, rather than knowledge flows from inventors, which party inserted a prior art citation to an earlier patent is less important for our purposes.

6   *See* Kimberly A. Moore, "Worthless Patents," *Berkeley Technology Law Journal*, 20, 1521, 2005.

7   See, e.g., Manuel Trajtenberg, "A Penny for Your Quotes: Patent Citations and the Value of Innovations," Rand Journal of Economics 21(1), 1990; Dietmar Harhoff, Francis Narin, F.M. Scherer, and Katrin Vopel, "Citation Frequency and the Value of Patented Inventions," *The Review of Economics and Statistics*, August 1999, 81(3), 511-515; Adam Jaffe and Josh Lerner, "Reinventing Public R&D: Patent Policy and the Commercialization of National Laboratory Technologies," *Rand Journal of Econom-*ics 32(1), 2001; Daniel Johnson and David Popp, "Forced Out of the Closet: The Impact of the American Inventors Protection Act on the Timing of Patent Disclosure", *Rand Journal of Economics* 34(1), Spring 2003, pp. 96-112.

8   Alfonso Gambardella, Dietmar Harhoff, Bart Verspagen, "The value of European patents", *European Management Review* (2008) 5, 69–84.

9   *See* Lemley, *supra* note 1; Brian DeLacey, Kerry Herman, David Kiron, and Josh Lerner, "Strategic Behavior in Standard-Setting Organizations" 2006, available at http://ssrn.com/abstract=903214; Shane Greenstein and Marc Rysman, "Coordination Costs and Standard Setting: Lessons from 56K Modems," in *Standards and Public Policy*, Cambridge: Cambridge University Press, 2007.

10 Voting rules can range from one-member-one-vote to sales-apportioned votes. *See* Lemley, *supra* note 1, for a discussion SSO voting approaches.

11 IEEE-SA., *IEEE-SA Standards Board By-laws*, January 2008, Section 6.2

12 *Id.*

13 *See* Anne Layne-Farrar, A. Jorge Padilla and Richard Schmalensee, "Pricing Patents for Licensing in Standard Setting Organizations: Making Sense of FRAND Commitments," *Antitrust Law Journal*, 74 (2007).

14 Note that the two terms RAND and FRAND are used interchangeably in this paper.

15 VITA is an exception. This SSO requires all members disclosing potentially essential IP to also disclose the most restrictive licensing terms they intend to seek from those implementing the standard. VITA STANDARDS ORGANIZATION, *VSO Policies and Procedures*, January 2008, Revision 2.4, Sect. 10.3.2. IEEE has a voluntary licensing term disclosure policy, as the above quote makes clear; *see* IEEE-SA., *supra* note 12.

[16] See, for instance, the EC's investigation of Rambus, CASE C-3/38.636—Rambus, which followed the U.S. FTC's Rambus investigation, Rambus, Inc., No. 9302, at 4-5, (F.T.C. Aug. 2, 2006), http://www.ftc.gov/os/adjpro/d9302/060802commissionopinion.pdf. The FTC likewise investigated Negotiated Data Solutions, LLC, regarding patent licensing within an SSO: FTC File No. 051 0094, available at http://www2.ftc.gov/os/caselist/0510094/index.shtm.

[17] European Telecommunications Standards Institute. 2006. *ETSI Directives*, Version 20, July 2006, Annex 6 "ETSI Intellectual Property Rights Policy," ¶ 8.1.1.

[18] DeLacey et al., *supra* note 9.

[19] *See*, e.g., the discussion in Paul Belleflamme, 'Coordination on formal vs. de facto standards: a dynamic approach,' *European Journal of Political Economy*, 18(1), 2002, pp. 156-157.

[20] *See*, e.g., Mark Roe "Chaos and evolution in Law and Economics," 109 *Harvard Law Review* 641, January, 1996. *See also*, Stan J. Leibowitz and Stephen E. Margolis, *Winners, Losers, and Microsoft*, 1999, Oakland, CA: The Independent Institute. Bottom of Form

[21] DeLacey et al., *supra* note 9.

[22] *See* Reinhardt Krause, "Corporate America A Key Nokia Target; Needs To Make Inroads; Cell phone leader's been slowed by failure to gain in U.S. enterprise market," Investor's Business Daily, & Technology; Q & A; National Edition; pp. A04, March 17, 2005. In Europe, the EC preferred a single standard to harmonize offerings across EU nations. See Iversen, E. (1999). Standardisation and intellectual property rights: conflicts between innovation and diffusion in new telecommunications systems. In K. Jakobs (Ed.), Information technology standards and standardization: a global perspective (pp. 80–101). Hershey, PA [etc.]: Idea Group Pub.

[23] In Europe this was deemed undesirable. Thus, in 1988 the European Commission created ETSI to harmonize European telecommunication standards and then pressured the then-responsible body, the Conférence Européenne des Administrations des Postes et des Télécommunications (CEPT), to transfer mobile phone standards efforts to ETSI. See Rudi Bekkers and Joel West, "The Limits to IPR Standardization Policies as Evidenced by Strategic Patenting in UMTS", Telecommunications Policy 33 (2009) 80–97.

[24] See Luis Cabral and David Salant, *Evolving Technologies and Standards Regulation* (Working Paper, 2008), *available at* http://ssrn.com/abstract=1120862.

[25] Note that standards are not always successful. The VL-bus standard, for instance, never took off, despite the efforts of its developers. *See* Carl Shapiro, "Setting Compatibility Standards: Co-operation or Collusion?" In R. Dreyfuss, D. Zimmerman & H. First (Eds.) *Expanding the Boundaries of Intellectual Property*, New York, NY: Oxford University Press, 2001.

[26] Joseph Farrell & Garth Saloner, 'Coordination through Committees and Markets,' *RAND Journal of Economics*, 19(2), 1988, p. 235-252. *See also*, Shapiro, *supra* note 18.

[27] Belleflamme, *supra* note 19.

[28] Shapiro, *supra* note 25.

[29] Greenstein and Rysman argue that the International Telecommunications Union (ITU) plays such a function. Greenstein and Rysman, *supra* note 9, p. 19.

[30] Mark R. Patterson, "Antitrust and the Costs of Standard-Setting: A Commentary on Teece and Sherry," *87 Minnesota Law Review* 1995 (2003); DeLacey et al., *supra* note 9; Greenstein and Rysman, *supra* note 9, p. 19; Knut Blind and Nikolaus Thumm, "Interrelationship between patenting and standardization strategies: empirical evi-

dence and policy implications", *Research Policy* 33 (2004), 1584-1598.

[31] *See* ETSI Fee structure available at http://www.etsi.org/WebSite/Membership/fees.aspx

[32] *See also* Joseph Miller, "Standard Setting, Patents, and Access Lock-In: RAND Licensing and the Theory of the Firm," 40 *Indiana Law Review*, 2006.

[33] Carl Shapiro & Hal Varian, *Information Rules: A Strategic Guide to the Network Economy*, 1999, Boston, MA: Harvard Business School Press, at p. 241.

[34] Townshend v. Rockwell Int'l Corp., 2000 U.S. Dist. LEXIS 5070 (D. Cal. 2000).

[35] See e.g., Broadcom Corp. v. Qualcomm, Inc., No. 05-3350, (D. N.J. Aug. 31, 2006);

[36] Broadcom Corp. v. Qualcomm, Inc., No. 06-4292, (3rd Cir. filed Sept. 4, 2007).

[37] Commission Press Release, "Antitrust: Commission closes formal proceedings against Qualcomm", 24 November 2009, available online at http://europa.eu/rapid/pressReleasesAction.do?reference=MEMO/09/516.

[38] Rambus Press Release, "Rambus Reaches Tentative Settlement with European Commission", 11 June 2009, available online at http://www.rambus.com/us/news/press_releases/2009/090611.html.

[39] This is a controversial point, however. *See*, e.g. Damien Geradin & Miguel Rato, "Can Standard-Setting Lead to Exploitative Abuse? A Dissonant View on Patent Hold-Up, Royalty Stacking and the Meaning of FRAND" (April 2006), available at http://ssrn.com/abstract=946792.

[40] See, e.g., the ITU IP Policy, which stipulates that if "The patent holder is not willing to comply with the provisions of either paragraph 2.1 or paragraph 2.2 [i.e., is not willing to license the patent on RAND terms]; in such case, the Recommendation/Deliverable shall not include provisions depending on the patent." See http://www.itu.int/en/ITU-T/ipr/Pages/policy.aspx.

[41] Jeffrey L. Furman and Scott Stern, "Climbing Atop the Shoulders of Giants: The Impact of Institutions on Cumulative Research", NBER Working Paper No. 12523, March 5, 2006, considers a similar question in relation to biological resource centers.

[42] *See for example*, Paul Taubman, "The Determinants of Earnings: Genetic, Family, and Other Environments; A Study of White Male Twins," *The American Economic Review* 66(5): 858-870, 1976; Jere R. Behrman, and Paul Taubman, "Intergenerational Transmission of Income and Wealth," *The American Economic Review* 66(2): 436-440, 1976; Paul Taubman "Earnings, Education, Genetics, and Environment," *Journal of Human Resources* 11(4): 447-461, 1976.

[43] Another route is to consider the patents over time, measuring the impact of inclusion in a standard through a before-and-after comparison. This is problematic, however, because the standard itself may change over time, increasing or decreasing in importance and commercial success. And standards often have multiple iterations, with the early rounds frequently representing the pioneering changes while later rounds may be only incremental improvements, and yet later rounds may again be pioneering. It would be extremely difficult to separate the effects of the evolution of technology from the impact of the cooperative standard setting process in a before-and-after analysis.

[44] *See* James J. Heckman, H. Ichimura and P.E. Todd, "Matching as an Econometric Evaluation Estimator: Evidence from Evaluating a Job Training Programme," *Review of Economic Studies* 64, 605-654, 1997. *See also*, James J. Heckman, H. Ichimura J.A. Smith and P.E. Todd, "Characterizing Selection Bias Using Experimental Data," *Econometrica* 66, 1017-1098, 1998.

45 That is, patent "importance" and "generality" were both statistically higher for the pool patents as compared to their matches, regardless of the matching technique. The generality measure is a standard one in the IP literature. It examines the technology classes of the citing patent. The more classes represented among citing patents, the more technology fields the cited patent is applicable for, hence the higher its generality measure. *See* Manuel Trajtenberg, Rebecca Henderson and Adam Jaffe, "University Versus Corporate Patents: A Window on the Basicness of Invention," *Economic Innovation New Technology*, 5: 19-50, 1997.

46 Josh Lerner, Jean Tirole, and Marcin Strojwas, "Cooperative Marketing Agreements Between Competitors: Evidence from Patent Pools," NBER Working Papers 9680, 2003, p. 25-26. The published version of this paper (see "The Design of Patent Pools: The Determinants of Licensing Rules" (with Marcin Strojwas and Jean Tirole), Rand Journal of Economics, 38 (2007), 610-625) contains less complete empirical analysis as compared to the working paper version.

47 The more technology classes included among prior art cites, the more "original" a patent is. This measure is based on the premise that relatively minor incremental innovations will cite prior art in a narrow field, while pioneering or ground breaking innovations will draw from many diverse technologies.

48 Lerner et al., *supra* note 46, at p. 26.

49 Rysman, M. and Tim Simcoe (2008), "Patents and the Performance of Voluntary Standard Setting Organizations," 54 *Management Science*.1920.

50 Id. p. 1921.

51 The authors study patents declared for ETSI, the Internet Engineering Task Force (IETF), the Institute of Electrical and Electronics Engineers (IEEE), and the International Telecommunication Union (ITU). Note that they are only able to identify those patents reported to an SSO. There is no way to ascertain whether the declared patents were subsequently included in a final, approved standard.

52 Id, p.1921.

53 We find the within patent over time approach taken by Rysman and Simcoe (2008) problematic for our purposes. In particular, an SSO's effect is likely to vary across standards, as some will be more influential than others, and even within a single standard over time, as later generations of a given standard have more or less of a commercial impact.

54 Of course, unobservable value may still be a factor. To the extent that the observable proxies are accurate indicators of true patent importance and value, the cleaner this test will be.

55 As with Rysman and Simcoe, *supra* note 41, for many of the patents we can only identify those patents firms have reported as potentially reading on a standard. For these patents, we do not know which ended up as actually essential for a standard. We conduct additional analysis on the subset of patents that we are able to match to particular standards.

56 In particular, our dataset includes patents declared to IETF, IEEE, ETSI, ITU, OMA, JTC, MSF, ISO, IEC, W3C, and DVD. Though JTC–Joint Technical Committee–is not officially an SSO, it is a joint effort of IEC and ISO that has published technological standards including MPEG2, MPEG4, and JPEG. The DVD forum does not list patents in the standard (the forum only publishes the names of standard members), but by following the procedure used by Layne-Farrar and Lerner (2009) we are able to construct a set of patents eligible for this SSO. Only US patents were collected for the DVD forum because of a lack of assignee names in the PATSTAT data. *See* Anne Layne-Farrar and

Josh Lerner in, "To Join or Not to Join: Examining Patent Pool Participation and Rent Sharing Rules," *International Journal of Industrial Organziation*, forthcoming., available at http://ssrn.com/abstract=945189.

[57] These include the following: MPEG2, MPEG4, MPEG1394, AVC, DVB-T, Bluetooth, DVD1, and DVD2. As was the case with the DVD standard, patents included in the Bluetooth pool were not listed in public sources. We relied on the same process mentioned in note 38 to determine a set of US patents included in the Bluetooth pool.

[58] For pool patents that were not "officially" declared to the SSO, we use pool formation year as the SSO declaration year. If the formation date is before the application data, we took the declaration year as one year after the grant year.

[59] A majority of U.S. patents in our sample did not have IPC class identifiers; for these patents we use U.S. patent classes and subclasses instead.

[60] As we matched by patent characteristic, the number of SSO patents in our dataset dropped from 5588 to 5226. We were unable to match 362 patents based on the 3 criteria above. No patents for the W3C SSO remained after the filtering and matching process; therefore, we are left with ten SSO's and eight pools.

[61] This result is consistent with the findings reported in Layne-Farrar and Lerner *supra* note 46

[62] All patents are limited to those with declaration dates, but there is no reason to expect clarity in declaration date to be correlated with patent quality in any way.

[63] Rysman and Simcoe, *supra* note 41, p. 19.

[64] See Shapiro, *supra* note 25.

[65] Consistent with this finding, Knut and Blind observe that "...the value of the patent portfolio of a company can either be increased or decreased by this engagement [participation in a standard] in the same way as in R&D co-operations." Knut and Blind, 2004, *supra* note 30.

[66] Implicitly we assume that the matched patent has the same value for the variable years since declaration as its SSO counterpart. This variable is defined as the number of years elapsed between the declaration year and 2010.

[67] We use a log(var+1) transformation so as not to lose those data points that have zero post declaration cites.

[68] We considered adding indicator variables based on the IPC class of the patents. Including such variables in the regressions does not change our conclusions. We also ran a negative binomial regression model (dependent variable not transformed), and once again the results were comparable to the model presented in Table 8.

[69] Mark Lemley, "Intellectual Property Rights and Standard-Setting Organizations" *California Law Review* 90, 1965 (2002).

This work was previously published in the International Journal of IT Standards and Standardization Research (IJITSR), Volume 9 Issue 2, edited by Kai Jakobs, pp. 19-49, copyright 2011 by IGI Publishing (an imprint of IGI Global)

Chapter 3
Interpreting and Enforcing the Voluntary FRAND Commitment

Roger G. Brooks
Cravath, Swaine & Moore, USA

Damien Geradin
Tilburg University, The Netherlands

ABSTRACT

Although often debated as though it were public law, a FRAND undertaking is a private contract between a patent-holder and an SSO. Applying ordinary principles of contract interpretation to the case of ETSI IPR policy reveals that "interpretations" of FRAND advocated by some authors—including cumulative royalty limits, royalties set by counting patents, or a prohibition on capture by the patent-holder of any gains created by standardization—cannot be correct (ETSI, n.d.). Rather, a FRAND obligation leaves wide latitude to private parties negotiating a license. However, this does not mean that a FRAND commitment has no substance to be enforced by courts. In this paper, the authors review how, consistent with both contract principles and established judicial method, courts can enforce a contractual obligation to offer licenses on FRAND terms, without becoming IPR price regulators. Similarly, ordinary principles of contract interpretation reveal that the "non-discriminatory" portion of FRAND cannot be interpreted to be coextensive with common "most favored nations" provisions, but instead contemplates substantial latitude for private parties to negotiate terms suited to their particular situations.

INTRODUCTION

A. Overview

Technical standards are far from a new phenomenon. Since the late eighteenth and early twentieth centuries, national and international bodies—in many cases purely private and voluntary bodies—have been promulgating standards in a wide array of commercially important technical fields. Over the years, thousands of such standards have been developed, approved, and used in industry. Until recently, all this was very largely the domain of engineers; until the last decade, despite their commercial and international importance, technical standards attracted very little litigation or legal commentary.

DOI: 10.4018/978-1-4666-2160-2.ch003

But times have changed. Now, lawyers are studying intensively each stage of the standardization process: membership rules of standards-setting organizations ("SSOs"), policies concerning disclosure of potentially relevant patents, licensing of "essential" patents, and enforcement in the case of alleged violations of SSO policies—all are now transformed into legal topics.

In this new world of standards, one of the currently most contentious issues concerns the meaning of a commitment by the holder of patents "essential" to the practice of a standard to license such patents on "fair, reasonable, and nondiscriminatory" (FRAND) terms and conditions. The body of legal literature addressing this question is by now substantial, and growing. While not necessarily reaching similar conclusions, a number of authors have addressed this issue as a question of economic theory: what limitations (if any) on the freedom of the parties negotiating a licence to essential patents will best ensure efficient outcomes?

As a response to this question, authors have variously argued that, in order to satisfy a "fair and reasonable" commitment, a patent holder:

- Must charge no more than the incremental value of his invention over the next best technical alternative (Lemley & Shapiro, 2007; Dolmans, 2008; Temple Lang, 2007);

- Must not negotiate for a royalty-free cross-licence as part of the consideration for a license (Dolmans, 2008);

- Must set his royalty rate based on a mathematical proportion of all patents essential to the practice of a standard (Chappatte, 2009; Temple Lang, 2007);

- Must set his royalty rate in such a way as to prevent cumulative royalties on the standardised product from exceeding a low percentage of the total sale price of that product (Lemley & Shapiro, 2007);

- Must not raise requested royalty rates after the standard has been adopted, or after the relevant market has grown to maturity (Chappatte, 2009; Shapiro & Varian, 1999; Swanson & Baumol, 2005);

- Is not entitled to seek injunctive relief against a standard implementer should they fail to agree on licence terms (Farrell et al., 2007; Temple Lang, 2007).

The types of economic arguments relied on by these authors to justify these restrictive regimes may well be useful in debating public policy and the proper application of antitrust rules – although one of the present authors and others have elsewhere critiqued the merits of many of these calls for what is essentially government intervention in the private licencing process.[1] But in this paper we step back to ask a different question: What do these arguments and proposed regimes have to do with the contract which is the source of the FRAND obligation?

This paper is divided in four section. Section 1 reviews the basic fact that a FRAND commitment is the result of a voluntary contract between essential patent holders and a standards-setting organization, with the important corollary that the meaning of that commitment must be determined through the legal methods of contractual interpretation. Using a FRAND undertaking to ETSI as an example, it identifies the main categories of information potentially relevant to contract construction, including for instance the contract language itself, and the "negotiation history" of the ETSI IPR Policy (ETSI, n.d.). Section 2 shows that none of these categories of information support any of the restrictive limitations listed at the opening of this introduction. On the contrary, "fair and reasonable" are on their face flexible terms the specific content of which is substantially left to the negotiation between the parties. Our research also shows that all attempts made subsequent to the ETSI IPR Policy's adoption to alter the balance of interests between essential patent holders and implementers by changing the meaning of FRAND have been rejected by the ETSI membership. Section 3 addresses issues regarding the judicial enforcement of a FRAND undertaking. First, we demonstrate that, when it is alleged that a patentee has failed to offer "fair and reasonable" terms, the role of a court is not to determine what "fair and reasonable" terms would be, but whether the terms offered, taking into account all of the specific circumstances between the parties and prevailing market conditions, fall outside the range of reasonableness contemplated by the FRAND commitment. Second, we conclude that a licencee should not be able to collaterally attack the enforceability of a licence based on a prior FRAND commitment. Third, we note that what is "fair and reasonable" after full adjudication of infringement and validity may be higher than what would have been "fair and reasonable" in the context of pre-litigation negotiations. Section 4 offers a few observations as to the "intent of the parties" with respect to the "non-discriminatory" component of FRAND based on the deliberative record surrounding the adoption of the ETSI IPR policy, concluding that while the "ND" of FRAND does impose requirements that in some contexts will go beyond the requirements of national competition law, it cannot be read as requiring the equivalent of universal "most favored licensee" rights for all licensees.

B. Methodology

We focus our analysis on the ETSI IPR policy for two reasons. First, the ETSI policy in particular is a subject of great economic importance and current controversy with the European Union. The WCDMA standard adopted by ETSI was, for instance, at the core of a couple of a competition law investigations initiated by the European Commission, which ended with no finding of infringement at the end of 2009.[2] (European Commission, 2009a, 2009b). Second, ETSI has maintained an unusually comprehensive and accessible archival

history of its deliberations concerning IPR policy. ETSI was by no means the first SSO to request FRAND (or RAND) commitments from members, but it engaged in and has preserved records of meaningful discussion of its IPR policy at the time of its original adoption, and of proposed changes in subsequent years, leaving a valuable resource for those wishing to learn how industry participants actually understand FRAND – at least in the context of one major SSO.

For context and broader perspective, we have also looked to the IPR policy of the American National Standards Institute (ANSI, 1959), an organization founded in 1918 and a founding member of the International Standards Organization (ISO). ANSI is not itself an SSO, but rather is an organization that encourages standardization and accredits SSOs. ANSI has promulgated a patent policy since at least 1959, and requires as a condition of accreditation that an SSO comply with ANSI's patent policy (ANSI, 2010, Sections 3.0, 3.1, 3.3). More than 200 SSOs (responsible for more than 9000 standards) are now accredited by ANSI and thus operate under its patent policy (ANSI, n.d.). As will be seen, the ANSI IPR policy language is closely consistent with that of the ETSI policy. However, so far as we have been able to determine, ANSI has not maintained archives capturing the deliberations surrounding the original adoption of its RAND-based IPR policy.

1. THE CONTRACTUAL BASIS OF FRAND OBLIGATIONS

A. FRAND as a Voluntary Contract

The core right and definition of a patent is the power to exclude others from practicing the invention. Obviously, an agreement to licence on FRAND terms is a critical restriction of that right. What is equally obvious is that a FRAND obligation is *solely* the result of a *voluntary* contract entered into by the patent owner on an identifiable date

(Miller, 2007; Lemley, 2002).[3] And it is voluntary in at least two ways. First, a patent-holder may decline membership in an SSO, and thus have no obligations under its rules.

Second, based on our non-exhaustive review, it appears that at least most major SSOs make a FRAND commitment voluntary even for members. That is, members are requested – not required – to commit to licence patents on FRAND terms, and may elect to do so, or not, on a patent-by-patent basis. While there are SSOs that require a blanket FRAND commitment as a condition of membership, such requirements have in some instances created "nonparticipation" problems, ETSI and ANSI are representative in their explicitly voluntary policies, under which an obligation to licence a patent on FRAND terms arises not by automatic operation of the entity's policy, but (at the earliest) only if and when the patent owner agrees, in writing, to licence on FRAND terms.[4]

If a member patentee wishes to retain its right to exclude, and so declines to make a FRAND commitment with respect to a particular patent, then the SSO generally will simply adopt a standard that does not use that patented technology,[5] leaving the SSO no worse off than if the excluded innovation had never been developed, and potentially advantaging consumers by setting up competition between standardised and proprietary solutions.

We note that the draft "Guidelines on the applicability of Article 101 of the Treaty on the Functioning of the European Union to horizontal co-operation agreements" (European Commission, 2010) (the "Horizontal Cooperation Guidelines") recently issued by DG Comp would radically change this landscape, imposing a *de facto* requirement (on pain of competition law liability) that *all* SSOs require mandatory blanket FRAND commitments from members (SEC (10) 528/2 draft para. 282). With respect to SSO members, this policy would for the first time impose an *involuntary* termination of the basic patent "right to exclude", with the only "voluntary" option left being the choice to abstain from participation in the SSO. As a by-product, the ability of an SSO

member to elect to compete against a standard by means of a proprietary solution would be eliminated as a practical matter.

B. Interpreting FRAND as a Contract

If a FRAND undertaking is a contract, then there are legally proper methods for determining what that contract means, and they do not include lengthy flights of economic theory. On the contrary, both the Civil Law and Common Law traditions of contract interpretation and enforcement fundamentally look to discern and give effect to *the intent of the parties* (Corbin, 1952, p. 538).[6]

In that context, we note that the "parties" to a FRAND undertaking are the patent owner and the SSO, while the "parties" that developed and agreed upon the underlying IPR Policy were the diverse set of industry participants that make up the membership of the SSO – not academic economists or competition authorities. As a result, there is no reason at all to suppose that the "founding fathers" of ETSI (for example) settled on IPR policies that are functionally interchangeable with EU competition law, as some authors more or less suggest (Dolmans, 2008) ("Article 82 obligations are substantially similar to the contractual obligations under FRAND commitments."). Nor is there any reason to suppose that the agreement they reached did or was intended to implement idealized economic theory.

We propose, then, to take the FRAND obligation seriously as a contract. Using a FRAND undertaking to ETSI as an example, we will ask when the contract was formed, and what the parties actually agreed to.

Acknowledging the relevance of the "intent of the parties" to the meaning of a FRAND commitment raises the possibly troubling spectre that FRAND could mean different things in different SSOs. As a theoretical matter, this is true. As a practical matter, there are good reasons to believe that the memberships of major SSOs do *not* mean different things by "FRAND". First, the major players in major SSOs are generally multi-national corporations that participate in multiple SSOs; one would expect their employees to carry a generally consistent expectation of what "FRAND" means from one context to the next. Second, as will be seen in our review below, individual SSOs have not infrequently explicitly referred to the IPR policies of longer-established SSOs as precedent to explain or justify their own IPR policies. And third, as an empirical matter to the limited extent commentary bearing on the intent of ANSI's RAND licensing policy can be identified, it reveals no evidence of any significant divergence in intent with respect to FRAND commitments. Thus, while one must always bear in mind the possibility of divergent "intents" among different SSOs, it is considerably more likely that the record provided by the well-documented history of the ETSI IPR policy is giving us a window into how active participants in standardised high-technology industries generally understand FRAND.

C. Locating the Intent of the Parties

It is easy to refer to "the intent of the parties", but in the case of a voluntary FRAND commitment, locating that intent is by no means a simple matter. A particular FRAND obligation comes into existence as the last step in a lengthy history. Taking ETSI as our working example, the relevant terms of the ETSI IPR Policy were fixed by vote of the ETSI membership in 1994. However, the adoption of the ETSI IPR Policy did not create any FRAND commitment; it merely set out the terms under which ETSI may (if it follows its rules) consider member-owned IPR for inclusion in standards. No contract is formed, no FRAND commitment is created, until a patent holder voluntarily submits a written agreement to licence identified patents (whether identified individually or categorically) on FRAND terms. Certainly it is this written agreement or "undertaking" that is the contract (in the words of ANSI, it is the written undertaking that "creates a commitment by the patent holder and third-party beneficiary rights in implementers of the standard" (ANSI, 2006), but

since such undertakings commonly repeat or refer to the "fair, reasonable, and nondiscriminatory" terminology of the pre-existing IPR Policy, and are written against the background of that policy, such an undertaking cannot be construed as a free-standing document, but must be construed (as it was written) with reference to the IPR Policy.

In sum, we identify four main categories of information potentially relevant to contract construction: (i) the contract language itself; (ii) information as to the pre-existing "understanding of the industry" as to what a FRAND undertaking to an SSO meant, at the time the FRAND concept was incorporated into the SSO IPR Policy; (iii) information concerning the actual deliberation and debate by the ETSI members at the time the policy was adopted; and (iv) subsequent comment and action relating to the meaning of FRAND by the relevant SSO.

The specific language of a particular declaration made by a patent holder would of course also be relevant. However, since this class of evidence of intent would by its nature pertain only to individual declarations, we will not give it any further consideration in this discussion of general principles.

It is indeed possible that economic theory might make additional contributions by enabling us to better *understand* the course of the contract negotiations, or the contemporaneous industry practices, but nothing in either the Civil Law or Common Law tradition could permit economic theory to *substitute* for or overrule evidence of the actual intent of the parties. Further, if one did wish to use economic theory to predict or better understand the IPR Policy compromises actually reached by the members of ETSI or any other SSO, one would need to look to game theory models that take into account the institutional interests and bargaining power of the member organizations, and we have not seen that complicated game attempted.

2. THE CONTRACTUAL MEANING OF "FAIR AND REASONABLE"

In this section, we look to the main categories of information potentially relevant to contract construction identified above to determine the meaning of "fair and reasonable" in connection with the ETSI IPR policy in particular. On occasion, we also cite to ANSI materials as well for broader industry context.

A. The Plain Language

The starting point of any contract interpretation must be the language of the contract itself. The terms "fair and reasonable" are on their face terms implying wide latitude; they are permissive words to which there is even conceptually no one right answer.[7] For example, in connection with the sale of a relatively illiquid property such as a house or a tract of real estate, negotiations between the seller and one or more potential buyers could result in a considerable range of prices (perhaps differing depending on the urgencies of the parties), any one of which the outside observer would have to concede to be at least "fair" or "reasonable". The same is surely true of prices and terms for patent rights.

But we can say more. When a patent holder commits to licence on "fair, reasonable, and nondiscriminatory" terms in response to and pursuant to Section 6.1 of the ETSI IPR Policy, it is appropriate that, when considering the "plain meaning", we look to what was before the declarant: the "plain meaning" of FRAND as it appears in context within the IPR Policy.

The ETSI IPR Policy states as its "Policy Objectives" the following:

3.1 It is ETSI's objective to create STANDARDS and TECHNICAL SPECIFICATIONS that are based on solutions which best meet the technical objectives of the European telecommunications sector, as defined by the General Assembly. In order to further this objective the ETSI IPR POLICY seeks to reduce the risk to ETSI, MEMBERS, and others applying ETSI STANDARDS and TECHNICAL SPECIFICATIONS, that investment in the preparation, adoption and application of STANDARDS could be wasted as a result of an ESSENTIAL IPR for a STANDARD or TECHNICAL SPECIFICATION being unavailable. In achieving this objective, the ETSI IPR POLICY seeks a balance between the needs of standardization for public use in the field of telecommunications and the rights of the owners of IPRs.

3.2 IPR holders whether members of ETSI and their AFFILIATES or third parties, should be adequately and fairly rewarded for the use of their IPRs in the implementation of STANDARDS and TECHNICAL SPECIFICATIONS.

3.3 ETSI shall take reasonable measures to ensure, as far as possible, that its activities which relate to the preparation, adoption and application of STANDARDS and TECHNICAL SPECIFICATIONS, enable STANDARDS and TECHNICAL SPECIFICATIONS to be available to potential users in accordance with the general principles of standardization. (emphasis added)

The above language makes clear that the rationale behind the FRAND commitment – and the "fair and reasonable" terms that are part of it – is twofold: (i) to ensure dissemination of the essential IPR contained in a standard, thereby allowing it to remain *available* for adoption by members of the industry, whilst at the same time (ii) making certain that holders of those IPR are able to reap *adequate and fair rewards* from their innovations.

The fact that IPR holders should be "adequately" rewarded is listed as the first criterion, and is by no means a synonym of "fair". One may ask, "adequate for what purpose?" In the context of the wireless industry in which continual innovation is the lifeblood of the entire industry, the answer is utilitarian and reasonably clear: "adequate to motivate the investment and risk necessary to create the next generation of innovation".

This is as one would expect: the goal to motivate future investment lies at the heart of the patent system, and is essential to the success of the standards enterprise. A Communication of the European Commission issued in 1992 (European Commission, 1992) – just at the time ETSI began developing its IPR policy – emphasized the prospective, motivational imperative specifically in the standards context:

[T]he incentive to develop new products and processes on which to base future standardization will be lost if the standard-making process is carried out without due regard for intellectual property rights (European Commission, 1992)

Recent (2006) commentary from ANSI highlights the same policy goal of motivating new R&D investment:

In return for "sharing" its patented technology (including making it available to competitors), the patent holder may receive reasonable compensation from implementers of the standard in a non-discriminatory manner. The patent laws were designed in part to stimulate innovation and investment in the development of new technologies, which can be shared at reasonable rates with all those wishing to implement a standardized solution to an interoperability or functionality challenge (ANSI, 2006) (emphasis added).

Given a goal of compensation that will "adequately" motivate next-generation innovation, the ETSI IPR Policy's reliance on the undeniably loose terms "fair and reasonable" will be seen as inevitable rather than a "defect". The reason is that the circumstances surrounding the negotiation of particular licencing agreements differ widely;[8] the scale of R&D investment which must be induced in order to bring in the next generation of innovation in a timely fashion may escalate from one generation to the next; the investment-discouraging risk that R&D investment will result in failure may vary from one setting to the next. Given this radical

and irreducible variability in the real world, only flexible terms such as "fair and reasonable" – the precise content of which is left to negotiation between the parties on a case-by-case basis – can ensure the widest availability of the technology embodied in the standard in the widest possible variety of circumstances, without unduly diminishing the innovation incentives that patent law was designed to create.[9] Thus, as pointed out by the European Commission in its Communication on "Intellectual property rights and standardization" that was issued while the ETSI IPR Policy was being negotiated, beyond the broad goal that essential technology be *available*, "it is not feasible or appropriate to be more specific as to what constitutes "fairness" or "reasonableness" since these are subjective factors determined by the circumstances surrounding the negotiation" Communication of the Commission "Intellectual Property Rights and Standardization" (European Commission, 1992).

By contrast, the above extracts of the ETSI IPR Policy do not contain any language hinting at *any* of the very specific and restrictive limitations listed at the opening of this paper, which other authors attempt to read into "fair and reasonable".[10]

Also in at least potential contrast to the pragmatic and prospective policy purposes embodied in the goal of "adequate" compensation to IPR owners found in Section 6.1 of the ETSI IPR Policy is the Horizontal Cooperation Guidelines proposal to measure what is "fair and reasonable" by reference to "the economic value of the patents" (Horizontal Cooperation Guidelines para 284). While "economic value" could be defined so many ways that it may in practice be as open as "fair and reasonable", on its face it introduces terminology foreign to the IPR policy of ETSI (and that of ANSI), and suggests a retrospective focus (on the "value" of past innovation) rather than the prospective and motivational focus that is native to the theory of patents. Certainly the "plain language" of the ETSI IPR Policy does not point in that new direction.

B. "Fair and Reasonable" in the Standards Context Prior to the ETSI IPR Policy

While focusing on the ETSI IPR Policy in our discussion above, we have also cited to ANSI-related sources where available as providing a separate "datapoint". However, the IPR policies of major SSOs are in truth not "independent". No SSO IPR policy adopted in recent decades has arisen *ex nihilo*; quite the contrary, they are adopted by sophisticated industry participants against a global background of decades of successful precedent. In the case of ETSI, the framers of its IPR policy very explicitly picked up the "FRAND" concept from the pre-existent "RAND" policy of the International Standards Organisation (ISO). For example, a document submitted by the ETSI Technical Assembly Chairman in 1991 proposed that "The licens[or] is required to grant licences on fair and reasonable non discriminatory terms as for the ISO policy" (12 TA TD 7 4 (attached to ETSI/GA11(91) TD 20).[11] Similarly, the ETSI Director submitted the ETSI Annual Report to the 12th ETSI General Assembly in 1992, which stated that ETSI was "developing a policy, based on that of the International Standards Organisation (ISO) and the International Electrotechnical Commission (IEC)" (ETSI/GA12(92)TD 15 6). IPR policies very similarly worded to that of the ISO were at that time already in place at other internationally important SSOs as well. It is reasonable, then, to suppose that the understanding of technology industry companies as to what "fair and reasonable" meant in this context was informed by the usage in those other SSOs.

One could review that context at length, but we will limit ourselves here to only a few illustrations. For instance, an ISO document circulated by the ISO/IEC Secretariat in 1999 stated that, even by that date, "ISO has no guidelines as to what constitutes 'reasonable' since each patent holder sets its own fee which is based upon commercial considerations at the time" ("Issues

Relating to Patents – SC17's Patent Policy" (Sept. 21, 1999) ISO/IEC JTC1/SC17 N 1585). Similarly, the patent policy of the International Telegraph and Telephone Consultative Committee (CCITT) (now known as ITU-T) in place in 1994 aimed to ensure that patentees "would be willing to negotiate licences with other parties on a non-discriminatory basis on reasonable terms and conditions", but emphasized that the "detailed arrangements arising from patents (licencing, royalties, etc.) are being left to the parties concerned, as these arrangements might differ from case to case" (ETSI/GA15(93)18).[12] Finally, in a 1992 letter to ETSI, ANSI noted that "under the ISO/IEC and ANSI policies licensors remain free to negotiate such license terms as they may deem appropriate so long as such licenses are fair and non-discriminatory" (ETSI/GA12(92)TD3 4). Obviously, by the time ETSI set out to adopt its own IPR policy, the ISO, ITU, and ANSI between them had (or their members had), promulgated numerous economically important standards which had been widely and successfully implemented, within the framework of this generally consistent and unrestrictive conception of "F/RAND".

Here again, what our research has *not* found is any indication, by the time ETSI adopted its current FRAND policy in 1994, that "fair and reasonable" in the context of the ISO – or other SSOs – had ever been held by the ISO or by any court to imply *any* of the detailed restrictions recently hypothesized by various authors.

C. "Negotiation History" of the ETSI IPR Policy

As we have noted, the relatively recent history of the adoption of ETSI's IPR policy is well documented, and key points in the negotiation and adoption of that policy may also shed light on what ETSI members (including major multinational technology companies[13]) understand that they are agreeing to when they make a FRAND undertaking.

ETSI as an organization was established in 1988, by the European Conference of Postal and Telecommunications Administrations ("CEPT"). As discussed in the previous section, when it set out to adopt an IPR policy in the early 1990s, ETSI looked to the ISO IPR policy in general, and in particular with respect to FRAND licensing. However, in other respects ETSI's draft policy initially aimed at what the ETSI Technical Assembly Chairman believed would be an "advance" over the ISO IPR policy (12 TA TD 7 3). This proposed package of heightened restrictions on IPR owners included what became referred to as an "automatic licencing" or "licencing by default" provision, a requirement of advance declaration of maximum royalty rates, a rule precluding required cross-licences, and a mandatory arbitration requirement (ETSI/GA12(92)3).

Commencing at the 12th ETSI General Assembly meeting in April 1992, fierce controversy broke out over these proposed heightened restrictions. We find in this debate an interesting intersection of ETSI and ANSI, as ANSI submitted to ETSI a letter containing strong warnings about the impact of the proposed restrictions on licensing freedom on incentives for innovation:

If holders of IPRs are deprived of the ability freely to determine the terms and conditions upon which they will (or will not) make their IPRs available to others, the incentive for investing in innovative research and development will be significantly compromised. Furthermore, the incentive for leaders in the development of technological advancements to participate in the ETSI standardization process will be dramatically undermined (ETSI/GA12(92)TD3 4).

Nevertheless, at the March 1993 15th ETSI General Assembly, an IPR Policy and Undertaking including some of the novel provisions noted above was approved over heated opposition including threats by some participants to withdraw from ETSI.[14]

However, following the approval, even louder opposition broke out. Several important IPR owners objected strongly to the "automatic licencing" provision, and the Computer and Business Equipment Manufacturers" Association ("CBEMA") filed a complaint with the European Commission asserting that novel aspects of the policy (including the requirement of advance disclosure of royalty rates) were anticompetitive. Important participants threatened to withdraw from ETSI if the policy was implemented (Iversen, 1999);[15] so serious was the dissention among the membership that the ETSI Technical Assembly Chairman warned that "other entities with simpler rules may have ambitions to take over ETSI work and ETSI could be out of business in five or ten years" (ETSI/GA20(94)22 Rev.1 4).[16] On 22 July 1994, the ETSI General Assembly voted to "abandon the IPR Undertaking as adopted by the General Assembly meeting during its meeting on 18 March 1993" (ETSI/GA20(94)20; ETSI/GA20(94)22 Rev. 1). The 1993 draft IPR Policy and Undertaking was never actually implemented by ETSI, and following the July 1994 vote ETSI was again without an IPR policy.

Finally, at the 21st ETSI General Assembly in November 1994, the ETSI membership approved an IPR policy from which the heightened restrictions described above had been removed, placing ETSI's IPR policy squarely in the main stream of the policies of other major international SSOs (ETSI/GA21(94)3; ETSI/GA21(94)39 Rev.2 17-18). The 1994 policy remains in effect today, with minor changes.

What this history documents is that not merely was FRAND a concept borrowed in its inception from prior use by the ISO, but that the ETSI membership did not pour *new* meaning into FRAND, as all attempts to do so were rejected. Thus, any one who wishes to argue some restrictive or idiosyncratic meaning for an *ETSI* FRAND undertaking, whether based on economic argument or idiosyncrasies of EU or French law, should face a substantial burden of proof as a matter of contract interpretation.

D. Post-1994 ETSI Comment on the FRAND Undertaking

Post-adoption ETSI commentary and actions establish that the ETSI membership has consistently rejected subsequent efforts to alter the balance of interests between IPR owners and licencees by changing the meaning of FRAND.

In 2003, a number of ETSI members promoted an effort to make FRAND less flexible and discretionary by defining or giving examples of practices that would violate FRAND. The ETSI General Assembly authorized the creation of an Ad Hoc Group (AHG) to consider and report on such proposals (ETSI/GA42(03)20). During this process, multiple participants in the ETSI AHG noted their understanding that the meaning of FRAND was a matter of global consensus, not an ETSI question. A representative of Microsoft observed that "FRAND is a standard principle throughout all SDOs", while a representative of Motorola asserted that the "FRAND term is identical in ITU policy, Japan SDO, US SDO . . . and this ['FRAND'] is the standard way to express it" (ETSI/GA/IPR02(03)05 3).

But even if FRAND had historically been a global concept, other AHG participants argued that ETSI should nevertheless endorse new specific restrictions under the FRAND umbrella for its own purposes. Proposals included prohibitions on licences that require a royalty-free cross licence, prohibitions on requiring "grantbacks" of rights to improvements, and prohibitions on licencing for certain regions of the globe at rates different from those charged for other regions. But none of these restrictions ever were agreed to, whether by the AHG or by the ETSI General Assembly. Instead, the AHG reported to the ETSI General Assembly that "The ETSI IPR Policy does not define FRAND", and that "The ad hoc group was unable to define FRAND conditions" (ETSI/GA42(03)20 8). Further, it reported that "holders of big IPR portfolios" "saw no sense in . . . attempts" "to indirectly define FRAND conditions by giving several examples of bad practices" (Ibid at p.9). The AHG provided with its report an "Annex A" that contained a list of supposed "bad practices" that had been proposed by those members who advocated additional restrictions, while noting that these had *not* been agreed to by the AHG. The ETSI GA, while accepting the report itself, went farther and deleted this Annex A entirely (ETSI/GA42(03)20 Rev.1; ETSI/GA42(03)34 4-5).

In 2006 another effort to tighten the permissive nature of "fair and reasonable" was made within ETSI, with Nokia and two other manufacturers advocating that ETSI should "make changes to the [ETSI] IPR regime and practices" by "introduc[ing] the principles of AGGREGATED REASONABLE TERMS and PROPORTIONALITY into the FRAND definition" (ETSI/GA/IPRR01(06)08 2-3).[17] The proposal was once again intensely controversial within ETSI, and was not adopted by the General Assembly (ETSI GA/IPRR06(06)24 Rev.1 14).

Thus, any party contemplating making a FRAND commitment that looks to the ETSI record to understand what such a commitment would mean will find the ETSI membership *declining* to approve restrictions or interpretations identical or analogous to many of those advocated today by the proponents of the restrictive FRAND regimes.

Most recently, ETSI's "Guide on IPRs", published in 2007, once again specifically disclaims any notion that ETSI does or intends to impose any more specific (and therefore more restrictive) definition of FRAND terms and conditions, stating instead that "such commercial terms are a matter for discussion between the IPR holder and the potential licensee, outside of ETSI" (§ 2.2), and "Specific licensing terms and negotiations are commercial issues between the companies and shall not be addressed within ETSI" (§ 4.1).

3. ENFORCING FRAND CONTRACTUAL COMMITMENTS

A. Who Decides, and How? The Role of Courts

Business people—those who actually develop and use standards—inhabit a world ruled not by theoretic constructs, but by interests, negotiation, and endless and thoroughly pragmatic compromise. But lawyers, academics, and regulators breathe different air, and have a strong desire for certainty and consistency: What exactly constitute FRAND license terms? What formula or rule may we use to determine whether offered terms are or are not FRAND? Are particular terms for a particular portfolio FRAND, or are they not?

This desire for clear rules is understandable, but it cannot be reconciled with the concept of FRAND as adopted and understood by the industry participants who use it. The terms "fair and reasonable" are on their face terms of wide latitude and discretion, and as we have seen, that latitude has been emphasized rather than restricted by commentary from multiple SSOs, and the membership of ETSI has more than once rejected efforts to add more specific and therefore more constricting limitations into the meaning of FRAND.

Given the endless and wide variety of market and technological circumstances in which FRAND commitments are made, it may well be that any less flexible obligation would prove a procrustean bed, potentially discouraging SSO participation, or damaging incentives for beneficial R&D investment. But whether or not this is true as a policy matter, the fact remains that the meaning of FRAND (if construed as a voluntary contract) is such that there *can be* no mathematical rules for determining what is or is not FRAND, because there is not and was not intended to be a precise answer to that question.

If FRAND is intended to provide wide latitude to be resolved by individual parties in individual negotiations (as SSOs have repeatedly stated), two questions naturally arise: (1) Does a FRAND commitment really mean anything at all? and, (2) Who decides what it means? The answer to the first question is "yes", and the two questions are importantly related. It is only by careful attention to the question of process, the question of "who decides, and how?", that one can preserve both the intended reality and the intended flexibility of a FRAND commitment.

A legal dispute concerning compliance with a FRAND commitment is most likely to arise on one of two ways. If an essential patent holder and a standard implementer[18] are unable to agree on licencing terms, the standard implementer, once accused of infringement, may simply wait and assert defensively that the IP owner has failed to satisfy its obligation to offer fair and reasonable terms, or possibly (depending on the procedures available in a given jurisdiction) could seek a determination through a breach of contract action that FRAND terms have not been offered, and an order requiring compliance with that obligation (Geradin & Rato, 2007, p. 119).

As we have seen, however, a court confronting such a claim radically misunderstands the FRAND commitment that the IP owner has made, and misunderstands the court's own role, if it seeks to answer the question "What is the reasonable royalty for this IPR?" In agreeing to licence on FRAND terms, the IP owner has not agreed to constrain its licencing terms more tightly than the "range of reasonableness". Thus, if an offer has been made and refused, then the only contractual question to be adjudicated is whether the terms offered, taking into account all of the specific circumstances between the parties and prevailing market conditions, fall outside the *range* of reasonableness contemplated by the FRAND commitment.

This type of analysis is not foreign to courts. Under US patent law, for example, after a jury has awarded "reasonable royalty" damages, the appeals court does *not* seek to second guess that decision and substitute its own view of what is "most reasonable". Rather, the appeals court engages in a deferential review, asking only whether the jury's award falls outside the range of what could be considered reasonable (*Micro Chem., Inc. v Lextron, Inc.*; *Rite-Hite Corp v Kelley Co., Inc.*; *Monsanto Co. v Ralph)*[19] Similarly, European courts[20] use a "going rate" or benchmarking method to identify a range of reasonable royalty rates that can serve as the basis for the calculation of damages after a finding of patent infringement, and the trial court enjoys significant judicial discretion in its appraisal. Where a decision awarding damages is appealed, the task of the appeals court is not to determine *ex novo* what the "reasonable rate" and resulting damage award is, but only to examine whether the lower court exceeded its considerable discretion in awarding reasonable damages (Cour de Cassation (Ch. Comm.) (France), *Sté Ets Delaplace et Sté Sicma c. Sté Van Der Lely*; Sampson, 2007). [21]

In the case of FRAND licencing, the initial discretion as to what is "reasonable" is entrusted to the negotiating parties or, in the absence of agreement, to the IP owner. If the would-be licencee "appeals" to a court, that court's task is comparable to that of the appeals court in the US and European patent systems. And, as the party advancing the proposition that specific offered terms fall outside the range of reasonableness and thus do not satisfy the FRAND commitment, one would expect that the burden of proof would rest with the potential implementer. This allocation of burden is perhaps all the more reasonable given that, even with this "procedural safeguard" against aggressive manufacturers, the FRAND commitment represents a very significant concession by the IPR owner as compared to the pre-existing statutory right to exclude inherent in its patent.

In order to determine whether offered terms and conditions pass this "range of reasonableness test", while there can be no mathematical rules, there is no reason that courts should not make use of analytical tools already existing in the law. For instance, while the question of what is "reasonable" continues to be a flexible inquiry, the much-cited *Georgia-Pacific* case identifies a (non-exhaustive) list of 15 specific factors that US courts routinely consider,[22] and the factors from the *Georgia-Pacific* list have been invoked as useful in other jurisdictions. Interestingly, in one discussion paper created by the ETSI General Assembly Ad Hoc Group in 1993, the reporters (themselves representatives of RIM, not a US corporation) wrote that "If one were to read the important *"Georgia-Pacific"* case cited in United States law as a method to determine a "reasonable royalty", it can readily be seen to be a test that closely parallels the concept of "fair, reasonable, and non-discriminatory" license obligations" (ETSI GA/IPR02(03)05 1).

Of course other important jurisdictions use different language, but we believe that they fundamentally agree that, when a court must determine a royalty rate, it may and should consider the wide range of information that would be relevant to a business decision-maker confronting the same question (*General Tire & Rubber Co. v Firestone Tyre & Rubber Co.*; *Cofrinex v Helary*; German Patent Act, Sec. 139 Para. 2).[23] Similarly, we believe that non-US jurisdictions can also find within their own structures examples of the type of deferential review that is appropriate where a court is tasked not to decide what the "right" answer is, but to decide whether terms offered fall entirely outside the *range* of possibility contemplated by the word "reasonable" (*Flint v Lovell*).[24]

Not all of the *Georgia-Pacific* factors will necessarily be relevant to the question of whether proffered licence terms are within the range of reasonableness, and peculiarities of a particular industry or standardised industries in general may properly enter into the equation. Nevertheless, a court may well find that the *Georgia-Pacific* list provides a useful framework or starting point for the inquiry.[25] Notably, royalties received under prior and existing licences for the very patents being litigated often represent the most influential factor in determining "reasonableness" under the *Georgia-Pacific* framework, and should arguably have the same role in the context of FRAND litigation.

B. FRAND Commitments and Challenges to Executed Licences

If a would-be licencee refuses offered terms and objects that those terms do not satisfy the patent owner's agreement to offer FRAND terms and conditions, then the court must undertake the analysis discussed above. However, *after* the parties have negotiated and executed a licence agreement, a complaint by the licencee that the terms of that licence are not FRAND presents very different issues.

While the doctrinal description will differ in different jurisdictions, the point is not complicated: It cannot be proper for a party, aware of rights it is entitled to claim under an existing contract (here, the FRAND commitment), to negotiate and sign a licence, enjoy the benefit of that licence for as long as it pleases, and then collaterally attack the licence as unenforceable (and perhaps claim past damages) on the theory that the licence terms violated the preceding contractual commitment. Within the Common Law tradition, this is a result of the doctrine of integration (*Restatement (Second) of Contracts* (1981) § 213),[26] or alternatively of the rule that, even in the absence of complete integration, a collateral contract may not be used to contradict the terms of a subsequent agreement (Lord, 2009, § 33:26).[27]

An extremely important economic truth underlies this principle. It is widely understood that uncertainty itself imposes an economic cost; accordingly, businesses often use the "stabilizing force of contracts" to reduce or eliminate unpredictability (*NRG Power Marketing v Main Public Utilities*). For this reason, companies commonly negotiate long-term licence agreements at fixed royalty rates, giving the two parties predictability as to revenues and costs, respectively. As the US Supreme Court has explained, "Markets are not perfect, and one of the reasons that parties enter into . . . contracts is precisely to hedge against the volatility that market imperfections produce" (*Morgan Stanley Capital Group, Inc. v Public Utility District 1 of Snohomush County*, p. 2746).

Private parties are of course free to negotiate short-term licence agreements, or agreements under which the royalty rate is subject to frequent re-negotiation, or periodic modification based on some external criteria. But they don't do this, precisely because predictability is extremely important to many aspects of the conduct of a business, including, e.g., decisions about investments in research and development. As a result, uncertainty relating to "contract sanctity can have a chilling effect on investments and a seller's willingness to enter into long-term contracts and this, in turn, can harm customers in the long run" (*Morgan Stanley Capital Group, Inc. v Public Utility District 1 of Snohomush County*, p. 2749 (quoting *Market Based Rates*, para. 6, 72 Fed. Reg. 33906-33907). Yet, a rule that would permit a licencee to collaterally attack a licence agreement—potentially years after the fact—on the theory that its terms violate a prior FRAND commitment, would make it *impossible* for licencing parties to negotiate for long-term predictability.

C. What is "Fair and Reasonable" Will be Higher After Adjudication of Infringement and Validity

US courts and commentators routinely recognize that a "reasonable royalty" will be higher after a patent has been held valid and infringed in court than it was before that adjudication.[28] Providing empirical and theoretical support for this judicial view, Lemley and Shapiro have demonstrated that nearly half of patents litigated to a final determination in the US are held invalid, while a significant number of those held valid are held to be not infringed (Lemley & Shapiro, 2005, 2007). They report in a later paper that average "reasonable royalty" damage awards set rates more than *double* estimated average negotiated patent royalties, and conclude that this difference is at least in part attributable to the uncertainty surrounding the strength and value of untested patents (Lemley & Shapiro, 2007).

Shapiro points out that, in light of these facts, what is "fair and reasonable" in the context of an offer to licence patents that have not been tested in litigation should be something lower than would be awarded after adjudication of infringement and validity, because of the uncertain strength of the patents (Farrell, 2007). But the reverse is equally true: After a patent has been tested and the uncertainty eliminated, then what is "fair and reasonable" no longer needs to include any "uncertainty discount", and should be substantially *higher* than would have been the case pre-litigation.

This "that was then, this is now" aspect of FRAND is not only theoretically correct, it stands as a critically important deterrent to excessive litigation. Lemley and Shapiro have also noted that, in the ordinary licencing context, the risk of injunction and complete exclusion from the market motivates prospective infringers to obtain a licence instead of litigating (Lemley & Shapiro, 2005). However, if an infringer of essential patents is entitled to the *same* terms after unsuccessful litigation as he was entitled to before, then this incentive disappears; the infringer will have strong incentives to litigate even a weak case in the hopes of "getting lucky" with an invalidity or non-infringement ruling, and will face no downside risk beyond attorneys" fees. The former Chief Judge of the Federal Circuit has noted exactly this incentive problem in the context of *Georgia-Pacific* royalty determinations, explaining that an infringer who, after unsuccessful litigation, "could count on paying only the normal, routine royalty non-infringers might have paid . . . would be in a "heads-I-win, tails-you-lose" position" (*Panduit Corp v Stahlin Bros. Fibre Works,* 1978, p. 1158). Thus, a static definition of "fair and reasonable" unaffected by litigation would expose FRAND declarants to a much greater risk of non-meritorious litigation than faces parties unconstrained by FRAND. It is unlikely that any standards-setting organization intended, by requiring FRAND declarations, to create this perverse incentive to attack rather than to pay for the intellectual property of its members.

D. "Durable FRAND": Can FRAND Commitments Survive the Sale of Patents?

Some commentators have raised the spectre that to acknowledge the contractual nature of a FRAND commitment could enable such a commitment once made to be evaded by selling the patent to a third party. However, despite decades of SSO operation in reliance on contractual FRAND commitments, the only three instances we are aware of in which a purchaser of patents has claimed not to be bound by a prior FRAND (or similar) commitment are (a) the position taken but more recently abandoned by IPCom in connection with patents purchased from Bosch,[29] (b) N-Data's attempt to ignore a prior owner's agreement to license certain essential patents for $1000 (*N-Data Complaint,* 2008, para 28),[30] and (c) an effort by Funai Electronic Co. to charge "non-FRAND" royalties for patents purchased from Thomson Licensing (*Vizio Inc. v Funai Elec,* 2010).

None of these efforts appear to have succeeded, and more than one theory provides protection against "FRAND evasion" while respecting the contractual nature of a FRAND commitment. First, an argument can be made that, given the on-line publication of FRAND declarations by major SSOs and the sophistication of participants in such industries, a purchaser of a patent which has been made subject to a FRAND declaration takes with either actual or constructive notice of that declaration and can be presumed to have negotiated a price taking that "encumbrance" into account, and should therefore be equitably estopped from asserting the patent in a manner inconsistent with that undertaking. This was essentially the result reached by the FTC in the *N-Data* case (Federal Trade Commission, 2008). Second, the court in *Vizio v. Funai* held that an allegation that Thomson sold patents to Funai as part of an *intentional* "scheme to circumvent Thomson's FRAND commitment" stated a claim for unlawful conspiracy under Section 1 of the Sherman Act (*Vizio Inc. v*

Funai Elec., 2010). Of course, the details of such approaches must be worked out within the legal doctrines of particular jurisdictions.

The draft Horizontal Cooperation Guidelines provide that, in order to fall outside the scope of the prohibition contained in Article 101(1) of the Treaty on the Functioning of the European Union (which prohibits anti-competitive agreements), all SSOs should require that members (who under the Guidelines proposed structure would be subject to mandatory FRAND obligations) "take all necessary measures to ensure that any [entity] to which the IPR owner transfers its IPR . . . is bound by that commitment" (Horizontal Guidelines, para. 286). Given the experience and theory reviewed above, this requirement would possibly be harmless, but certainly addresses a "problem" which thus far has been solvable with existing legal tools.

4. Non-Discrimination: The Other Half of FRAND

We have focused in this paper on the "fair and reasonable" component of FRAND, because the meaning of "fair and reasonable" has attracted far more controversy than the meaning of "non-discriminatory". But important questions remain in this area as well. Most significantly, one may ask whether the "ND" in FRAND really adds any obligation as a practical matter, or whether it is instead a platitude that imposes no obligations over and above what the competition law of most jurisdictions – such as the Robinson Patman Act in the United States or Article 102(c) of the Treaty on the Functioning of the European Union – would require in any case. Or, conversely, one may ask whether the "ND" imposes the same sort of obligations that are created by the type of "Most Favoured Licensee" (MFL) clause that parties commonly include in licenses by agreement.

Perhaps because it has not been at the centre of much controversy, we have found far less documentary history in the ETSI archives relating to the meaning "non-discriminatory" than exists with

regard to the meaning of "fair and reasonable", but there is enough to offer a few observations about the "intent of the parties" with respect to "non-discriminatory" in the ETSI context.

A. The ETSI IPR Policy Was In Significant Part Designed to be "Non-Discriminatory" as to Nationality and Membership-Based Discrimination

It is clear that from the start, one class of "discrimination" about which ETSI and stakeholders were concerned was classic protectionist discrimination, which might erect "barriers to trade" (ETSI/GA11(91)8),[31] and even violate the then called "GATT obligations" of the European Community member states (ETSI/GA12(92)TD 16 3; ETSI/GA12(92)TD 3 2; ETSI/IPR/GA(92)TD 5 3).[32] Emphasis was also put on the need to ensure that license terms did not discriminate in favour of ETSI members and against non-members (ETSI/GA12(92)TD 19 5; ETSI/IPR/GA(92)TD5 3; ETSI/GA14(92)TD 20 3).[33] These goals were stated repeatedly during the development of the initial ETSI IPR policy, and attracted no significant disagreement then or in later disputes about IPR policy within ETSI, so far as we find in the records. It is also the case that we do not find any sign in these records – nor are we aware from any other source – of any later incident in which an ETSI member was alleged to have discriminated in its licensing terms based on the nationality of the licensee, or based on its status as a non-member of ETSI. Whether credit belongs to the "non-discriminatory" clause of the FRAND commitment or to market forces is an open question—although one suspects the latter, since where rules and market forces are at odds, one would expect to find telltale signs of ongoing controversy and "cheating". Be that as it may, in the case of ETSI standards, these leading goals of the "non-discrimination" requirement appear to have been achieved.

B. "Non-Discriminatory" Is Not the Equivalent of a "Most Favoured Licensee" Guarantee

Interestingly, the first IPR Policy adopted by ETSI – the 1993 policy adopted but then withdrawn amidst controversy, as reviewed previously (in section II(C), above) – went beyond the "non-discriminatory" requirement inherited from the ISO precedent by including, as part of an "Undertaking" that each member was to sign, what was in essence a rather straight-forward "MFL" requirement, requiring that licenses (at least licenses to other parties to the Undertaking)

include a clause requiring the licensor to promptly notify a licensee of any license granted by the it to a third party for the same IPRs under comparable circumstances giving rise to terms and conditions that are clearly more favourable, in their entirety, than those granted to the licensee and allowing the licensee to require replacement of the terms and conditions of its license, in their entirety, either with those of the third party license, or with such other terms and conditions as the parties may agree" ("ETSI Intellectual property Rights Undertaking, ETSI/GA15(93)TD 25 para 3.1) (emphasis added).

However, the IPR policy that was finally adopted and made effective in 1994 did not include the undertaking, nor anything similar to the MFL requirement quoted above, and we find no suggestion in the records of discussions of IPR policy within ETSI, at any time after the rescission of the 1993 policy, that any member argued that the "notice" and "substitution of terms" rights that had been contained in the Undertaking remained implicit in the "non-discriminatory" requirement. Given this history, we conclude that any attempt to equate the "non-discriminatory" component of an ETSI FRAND commitment with thoroughgoing "Most Favoured Licensee" obligations would be mistaken as a matter of intent-based contract interpretation.

C. "Non-Discriminatory" Does Not Require Identical Terms

In fact, when the ETSI membership turned to developing the replacement policy that was ultimately adopted in 1994, the conversation turned in quite a different direction. Where the Undertaking had specified that similarly situated licensees had a right to *identical* terms, the final text of the "Common Objective" document annexed to the final report of the Special Committee on IPR stated, under the heading "Concerns about most favoured licensee provision," that while "License terms and conditions should be non-discriminatory," "this does not necessarily imply identical terms". Instead, under the heading "Commercial freedom", the document asserted, "Licensing terms and conditions should allow normal business practices for ETSI members. ETSI should not interfere in licensing negotiations" (ETSI/GA 20(94)2 (SC Final Report), ANNEX XII). Indeed, in subsequent discussion in which the members of the Special Committee were divided into four groups to report views on various issues, three out of the four groups reported agreement that non-discriminatory "does not necessarily imply identical terms", and the fourth group did not comment on that topic (ETSI/GA 20(94)2 (SC Final Report), ANNEX XVIII, at 4-5).

The sum of these observations is not dramatic. One the one hand, the "non-discriminatory" component of FRAND is more than merely an affirmation of national competition law, because such law may indeed permit outright discrimination in certain circumstances – for example, in favour of exclusive or preferred distributors.[34] On the other hand, in the case of ETSI at least,[35] "ND" clearly means less than a Most Favoured Licensee clause, with an MFL clause having been explicitly repealed, and comment at the time of adoption of the present policy signalling an intention to leave members wide flexibility in agreeing to particular terms with particular licensees depending on the commercial circumstances.

CONCLUSION

The effort to conflate a contractual FRAND commitment with either idealized economic theory or the competition law of any jurisdiction is ill-conceived. In short, a FRAND commitment and the limitations that competition law may impose on intellectual property rights are simply two separate things, and intellectual clarity requires that each be considered in its own right, and according to the analytical methods appropriate to it.

Our research shows that, if a FRAND commitment is taken seriously as a contract – as it should be – then efforts to look to FRAND as a source of cumulative royalty caps, particular formulas for calculating or apportioning royalties, or limitations on remedies against unlicensed infringers are not only without basis, but are contradicted by the ordinary methods of contract interpretation.

REFERENCES

ANSI. (1959). *ANSI patent policy*. Retrieved from http://publicaa.ansi.org/sites/apdl/Reference%20 Documents%20Regarding%20ANSI%20Patent%20Policy/02-Apr1959%2011.6PatentsASA. pdf

ANSI. (2006, June). *Activities Related to IPR and Standards*. Paper presented to the Global Standards Collaboration-11, IPR Working Group Meeting, Chicago.

ANSI. (2010). *ANSI essential requirements*. Retrieved from http://publicaa.ansi.org/sites/apdl/Documents/Standards%20Activities/American%20National%20Standards/Procedures,%20 Guides,%20and%20Forms/2010%20ANSI%20 Essential%20Requirements%20and%20Related/2010%20ANSI%20Essential%20Requirements.pdf

ANSI. (n.d.). *Domestic programs (American National Standards Overview)*. Retrieved from http://www.ansi.org/standards_activities/domestic_programs/overview.aspx?menuid=3

Case C-336/07 Kabel Deutschland [2008] ECR I-10889 para 46.

Chappatte, P. (2009). FRAND commitments—The case for antitrust intervention. *European Competition Journal, 5*, 319–340. doi:10.5235/ecj.v5n2.319

Cofrinex v Helary, Paris Court of Appeal 12 July 1977; Sec. 139 Para. 2 German Patent Act.

Corbin, A. L. (1952). *Corbin on contracts*. St. Paul, MN: West Publishing Company.

Cour de Cassation. (1991). Sté Ets Delaplace et Sté Sicma c. Sté Van Der Lely. *Annales de la Propriété Industrielle, 4*.

DeNicolo, V. (2008). Revisiting injunctive relief: interpreting *ebay* in high-tech industries with non-practicing patent holders. *Journal of Competition Law & Economics, 4*, 571. doi:10.1093/joclec/nhn028

Dolmans, M. (2008). Standards, IP, and competition: How to avoid false FRANDs. *Fordham IP Law Institute, Standard Setting — The Interplay With IP and Competition Laws,* 12-13.

E & L Consulting, Ltd. v. Doman Indus. Ltd., 472 F.3d 23 29 [2d Cir. 2006].

Endress & Hauser, Inc. v Hawk Measurement Sys. Pty. Ltd. 892 F. Supp 1123, 1130 [S.D. Ind. 1995].

ETSI. (n.d.). *ETSI IPR policy*. Retrieved March 7, 2010, from http://www.etsi.org/WebSite/document/Legal/ETSI_IPR-Policy.pdf

European Commission. (1992). *Communication of the Commission: Intellectual property rights and standardization*. Brussels, Belgium: Author.

European Commission. (2007). *Memo/07/389*. Retrieved from http://europa.eu/rapid/pressReleasesAction.do?reference=MEMO/07/389

European Commission. (2009a). *MEMO/09/516*. Brussels, Belgium: Author.

European Commission. (2009b). *MEMO/09/549*. Retrieved from http://europa.eu/rapid/pressReleasesAction.do?reference=MEMO/09/549&format=HTML&aged=0&language=EN

European Commission. (2010). *Guidelines on the applicability of Article 101 of the Treaty on the Functioning of the European Union to horizontal co-operation agreements (DRAFT)*. Retrieved from http://ec.europa.eu/competition/consultations/2010_horizontals/guidelines_en.pdf

Farrell, J. (2007). Standard setting, patents, and hold-up. *Antitrust Law Journal, 74*, 603–638.

Federal Trade Commission. (2008). *Negotiated Data Solutions LLC, Order and Decision, No. C-4234*. Retrieved on March 7, 2010, from http://www.ftc.gov/os/caselist/0510094/080923ndsdo.pdf

Flint v Lovell (1935) 1 K.B. 354 (CA) (Greer, L.J.)

Fr. Civil Code Art. 1121

General Tire & Rubber Co. v Firestone Tyre & Rubber Co. (1975) F.S.R. 273

Georgia-Pacific Corp v US Plywood Corp. 318 F Supp 1116 1120-21 (SDNY 1970)

Geradin, D. (2006). Standardization and technological innovation: Some reflections on ex-ante licensing, FRAND, and the proper means to reward innovators. *World Competition, 29*, 511.

Geradin, D. (2009). Pricing abuses by essential patent holders in a standard-setting context: A view from Europe. *Antitrust Law Journal, 76*, 329.

Geradin, D. (2008). Competing away market power? An economic assessment of ex ante auctions in standard setting. *European Competition Journal, 4*, 443. doi:10.5235/ecj.v4n2.443

Geradin, D. (2008). The complements problem within standard setting: Assessing the evidence on royalty stacking. *Boston University Journal of Science & Technology Law, 14*, 144.

Geradin, D., & Rato, M. (2007). Can standard-setting lead to exploitative abuse? A dissonant view on patent hold-up, royalty-stacking and the meaning of FRAND. *European Competition Law Journal, 3*, 101.

Geradin, D., & Rato, M. (2009). *FRAND commitment and EC competition law: A reply to Philippe Chappatte*. European Competition Journal. doi:10.5235/ecj.v6n1.129

Grundmann, S., & Mazeaud, D. (Eds.). (2006). *General clauses and standards in European contract law – Comparative law, EC law and contract law codification*. Frederick, MD: Aspen Publishers.

Iversen, E. J. (1999). *Standardization and intellectual property rights: ETSI's controversial search for new IPR-procedures*.

Lemley, M. (2002). Intellectual property rights and standard-setting organizations. *California Law Review, 90*, 1889–1909. doi:10.2307/3481437

Lemley, M.A., & Shapiro, C. (2005). Probabilistic patents. *The Journal of Economic Perspectives*. doi:10.1257/0895330054048650

Lemley, M. A., & Shapiro, C. (2007). Patent holdup and royalty stacking. *Texas Law Review, 85*, 1991–1996.

Lord, R. A. (2009). *Williston on Contracts*. St. Paul, MN: West Publishing Company.

Market Based Rates, para. 6, 72 Fed. Reg. 33906-33907.

Maxwell v J. Baker, Inc. 86 F 3d 1098, 1109-10 [Fed. Cir. 1996]

Micro Chem., Inc. v Lextron, Inc. 317 F 3d 1387, 1394 [Fed Cir 2003].

Miller, J. (2007). Standard setting, patents, and access lock-in: RAND licensing and the theory of the firm. *Indiana Law Review, 40,* 351.

Monsanto Co. v Ralph 382 F 3d 1374, 1383 [Fed Cir 2004].

Morgan Stanley Capital Group, Inc. v Public Utility District 1 of Snohomush County 128 S Ct 2733, 2746 [2008].

Nigel Christopher Blayney (t/a Aardvark Jewellery) v (1) Clogeau St Davids Gold Mines [2003] F.S.R. 19.

NRG Power Marketing v Main Public Utilities S Ct 693, 696 [2010].

O'Brien, V. E. (2000). Economics & key patent damages cases. *University of Baltimore Intellectual Property, 9.*

Panduit Corp v Stahlin Bros. Fibre Works 575 F 2d 1152, 1158 [6th Cir 1978].

Rahnasto, I. (2003). *Intellectual property rights, external effects and anti-trust law.* Oxford, UK: Oxford University Press.

Restatement (Second) of Contracts (1981) § 213.

Rite-Hite Corp v Kelley Co., Inc. 56 F 3d 1538, 1554-55 [Fed Cir 1995].

Sampson, T. (2007). The "adjusted future free income ratio": A new methodology for determining IPR royalty rates? *European Intellectual Property Review, 1*(371), 377.

Shapiro, C., & Varian, H. (1999). *Information rules: A strategic guide to the network economy.* Cambridge, MA: Harvard University Press.

SS Tech., Inc. v PC–Tel, Inc., No. C-99-20292, 2001 WL 1891713, 3–6 [N.D. Cal. November 28, 2001].

Stickle v Heublein, Inc. 716 F 2d 1550, 1563 [Fed Cir 1983].

Swanson, D. G., & Baumol, W. J. (2005). Reasonable and Nondiscriminatory (RAND) royalties, standards selection, and control of market power. *Antitrust Law Journal, 73*(1), 10.

Temple Lang, J. (2007, April 13-14). Licensing, antitrust and innovation under European competition law. In *Proceedings of the Fordham IP Property Conference* (pp. 2-6).

Troxel Mfg. Co. v Schwinn Bicycle Co. 465 F 2d 1253, 1257 [6th Cir 1972].

Vizio Inc. v Funai Elec. Co. No. CV-09-0174, 2010 U.S. Dist. LEXIS 30850 [C.D. Cal. February 3, 2010].

Volvo Trucks N. Am., Inc. v. Reeder-Simco GMC, Inc., 546 U.S. 164 176 [2006].

ENDNOTES

[1] Damien Geradin has published a series of articles in combination with other authors, including Anne Layne-Farrar, Jorge Padilla and Miguel Rato, which criticise the various arguments raised in the papers cited in the preceding footnotes on the grounds that these papers were not supported by legal and economic analysis, but instead merely reflected the policy preferences of their authors. See, eg, D Geradin & M Rato, "FRAND Commitment and EC Competition Law: A Reply to Philippe Chappatte" (2009) European Competition Journal (forthcoming 2010); D Geradin, "Pricing Abuses by Essential Patent Holders in a Standard-Setting Context: A View from Europe" (2009) 76 Antitrust Law Journal 329; D Geradin et al., "Competing

Away Market Power? An Economic Assessment of Ex Ante Auctions in Standard Setting" (2008) 4 European Competition Journal 443; D Geradin et al., "The Complements Problem Within Standard Setting: Assessing the Evidence on Royalty Stacking" (2008) 14 Boston University Journal of Science & Technology Law 144; V DeNicolo et al., "Revisiting Injunctive Relief: Interpreting *eBay* in High-Tech Industries with Non-Practicing Patent Holders" (2008) 4 Journal of Competition Law and Economics 571; D Geradin & M Rato, "Can Standard-Setting Lead to Exploitative Abuse? A Dissonant View on Patent Hold-up, Royalty-Stacking and the Meaning of FRAND" (2007) 3 European Competition Law Journal 101.

2   In the *Qualcomm* case, six firms active in the mobile phone equipment sector filed complaints with the European Commission in the latter part of 2005 alleging that Qualcomm's licensing terms and conditions for its patents essential to the WCDMA standard did not comply with Qualcomm's FRAND commitment and, therefore, breached EU competition rules. "Commission initiates formal proceedings against Qualcomm", Memo/07/389, (1 October 2007), available at http://europa.eu/rapid/pressReleasesAction.do?reference=MEMO/07/389. After a long and thorough investigation, the Commission eventually decided to close its formal proceedings against Qualcomm. "Commission closes formal proceedings against Qualcomm", MEMO/09/516, (24 November 2009).

3   J Miller, "Standard Setting, Patents, and Access Lock-In: RAND Licensing and the Theory of the Firm" (2007) 40 Indiana Law Review 351 ("The RAND promise, embedded in SSO bylaws to which participants agree, is primarily a matter of contract law."); M Lemley, "Intellectual Property Rights and Standard-Setting Organizations" (2002) 90

California Law Review 1889, 1909 ("SSO IP rules have legal significance only to the extent they are enforceable. Because the IP policies are at base agreements by members of the SSO to abide by certain rules regarding IP ownership, their enforceability is initially a question of contract law.").

4   Section 6.1 of ETSI's IPR policy provides that when essential IPR is disclosed, ETSI will request—but not oblige—the owner of the IPR to undertake in writing that it is prepared to grant irrevocable licences on FRAND terms and conditions, and as such to waive its right to refuse to offer a licence to those seeking one. Under the ANSI Patent Policy, "disclosure may be made by a patent holder or third party with actual, personal knowledge of relevant patents. Once such a disclosure is made, ANSI requires a written statement in order to determine whether the patent holder will provide licenses (a) on reasonable and non-discriminatory ("RAND") terms and conditions or (b) on a compensation-free basis (that may include other RAND terms and conditions). If the patent holder submits a patent statement to the effect of either (a) or (b) above, then this creates a commitment by the patent holder and third-party beneficiary rights in implementers of the standard." ANSI, *ANSI Activities Related to IPR and Standards*, submitted to the Global Standards Collaboration, IPR Working Group Meeting, Chicago, June 2006 (GSC11/IPRWG(06)10) at p.4.

5   Section 8 of the ETSI IPR Policy contains a mechanism for dealing with the "non-availability of licences" including a member's refusal to licence on FRAND terms. Where an IPR owner informs ETSI of such a refusal prior to the publication of a standard, the General Assembly first tries to find a "viable alternative technology". If none exists, and the IPR owner refuses to reconsider its position, there is a procedure for ETSI to decide

whether ETSI "should pursue development of the concerned parts of the STANDARD or a TECHNICAL SPECIFICATION based on the non-available technology and should look for alternative solutions." (§ 8.1.3) Similarly, ANSI has said that under the ANSI Patent Policy, if "[licensing] assurances are not forthcoming or if potential users can show that the policy is not being followed, the standard may be withdrawn either by the consensus committee or through the appeals process." GSC11/IPRWG(06)10 at p.5.

6   The intent of the parties also plays a fundamental role in the interpretation of contracts in Civil Law systems. See, for instance, Article 1156 of the French Civil Code whereby the judge must search for the intent of the parties when the contract was concluded or modified. Under this provision, the "subjective intent" of the parties ("what they really meant") is more important than the literal language of the contract itself.

7   See for instance Case C-336/07 *Kabel Deutschland* [2008] ECR I-10889 para 46 (discussing the notion of "reasonable" "must carry" obligations that may be imposed by EU Member States upon cable operators on the basis of the Universal Service Directive).

8   Not all standard implementers seeking to obtain a license from a given essential patent holder will be similarly situated. Generally, a range of variables will traditionally be negotiated between licensors and licensees, all of which may be of appreciable value, such as cross-licencing, volume of licensed products, exhaustion of patent rights, technology transfer, technical support, upfront fees, jurisdiction, scope of license (eg, products, territory, have made rights, etc.), possible product purchases, the formation of broader business relationships and cooperation, etc. Granting a license cannot be confused with selling a product at a standard price (which would be the royalty). Because licensors

and licensees seek to exchange a potentially diverse assortment of "value" (the royalties being just one possible elements of consideration), any interpretation of a FRAND commitment as "dictating or specifying a particular licencing result" would prove a Procrustean bed.

9   In this respect, FRAND is very much akin to a general clause, albeit a contractual one. "General clauses or standards ('Generalklauseln', 'clauses générales') are legal rules which are not precisely formulated, terms and concepts which in fact do not even have a clear core. They are often applied in varying degrees in various legal systems to a rather wide range of contract cases when certain issues arise such as abuse of rights, unfairness, good faith, fairness of duty or loyalty or honesty, duty of care, and other such contract terms not lending themselves readily to clear or permanent definition." S Grundmann & D Mazeaud (eds), *General Clauses and Standards In European Contract Law – Comparative Law, EC Law and Contract Law Codification*" (2006).

10   For instance, nothing can be read in such extracts as suggesting that FRAND imposes any specific and concrete obligations on the owner of standard essential patents with regard to the actual level of royalties or any other terms and conditions provided for in licencing agreements. Nokia's Vice President for Intellectual Property Rights, Dr. Ilkka Rahnasto, makes a similar observation. He explains that "the [FRAND] rule leaves the determination of exact terms for the parties to decide. This case-by-case determination allows parties to a particular licencing transaction to find their own interpretation of 'fair and reasonable'." I. Rahnasto, *Intellectual Property Rights, External Effects and Anti-trust Law* (OUP, 2003) 4.105. He further adds: "In connection with standardization, the term "fair and reasonable"

is usually understood as a reference to the economic reality. Generally, a licence is fair and reasonable if the terms would be acceptable in arm's-length-negotiations." *Ibid* 6.34. "Fair and reasonable" licencing terms would therefore consist of those terms determined through fair, bilateral negotiations between individual IPR owner and standard implementer in accordance with the market conditions prevailing at the time of such negotiations.

11 We use the ETSI nomenclature to identify ETSI documents. Thus, this ETSI Technical Assembly ("TA") document was attached to "Temporary Document" number 20, submitted at the 11th ETSI General Assembly meeting in 1991.

12 Enclosure to letter dated 29 October 1992 from CCITT to Eurobit.

13 For example, an ETSI Special Committee on IPR appointed in 1994 to propose provisions for an IPR policy included representatives of AT&T, Bosch, IBM, Motorola, Nokia, Philips, and Siemens, in addition to a number of less multi-national corporations. See ETSI/GA 20(94)2, ANNEX IV, at 89.

14 For example, IBM called the proposal "a source of deep divisions within the ETSI membership" and stated that for "many members it is the company's strategic assets and policies which are at stake". ETSI/GA15(93)26. IBM said "IBM has to evaluate now its future involvement in ETSI". ETSI/GA15(93)6. Other companies said words to the same effect. ETSI/GA15(93)23.

15 "ETSI received between 12-14 letters from parties . . . who threatened to pull out of ETSI if it implemented the 1993 Policy." E J Iversen, "Standardization and Intellectual Property Rights: ETSI's controversial search for new IPR-procedures" (September 1999) (Paper presented at the first IEEE conference on standardisation and innovation in information technology, Aachen, Germany).

16 The threats of participants such as IBM to withdraw from ETSI, and the Chairman's comment quoted above, raise the interesting point that an SSO—even an SSO such as ETSI which has been granted a supposed monopoly position by law or regulation—does not have an unconstrained ability to set restrictive IPR policies. Development of successful next-generation standards in high technology fields can only be accomplished through the intensive efforts of the industry leaders, and unpalatable SSO IPR policies may cause key players to channel those efforts through other SSOs. See also Communication of the Commission "Modernising ICT Standardisation in the EU - The Way Forward" (3 July 2009) Com (09) 324 final para 1 (noting the emergence of global fora and consortia as "world-leading [Information and Communication Technology] standards development bodies," and stating that "the EU risks becoming irrelevant in ICT standard setting").

17 For a discussion of this proposal and the negative impact it would have had, see D Geradin, "Standardization and Technological Innovation: Some Reflections on Ex-ante Licensing, FRAND, and the Proper Means to Reward Innovators" (2006) 29 World Competition 511.

18 The intended beneficiaries of a FRAND declaration appear to be any parties who wish to perform actions identified in Paragraph 6 of the ETSI IPR Policy with respect to a standard-compliant product. This includes those who wish to "manufacture, including the right to make or have made customized components and sub-systems to the licensee's own design for use in manufacture". The ability of intended third party beneficiaries of a contract to enforce their rights under that contract is well recognized within the Common Law Tradition, while Civil Law jurisdictions provide comparable enforce-

ment rights under (in the case of France, for example) the doctrine of "stipulation pour autrui". Fr. Civil Code Art. 1121.

19   *Micro Chem., Inc. v Lextron, Inc.* 317 F 3d 1387, 1394 [Fed Cir 2003] (discussing the differences between the experts" opinions regarding royalty rates and affirming jury's determination as reasonable); *Rite-Hite Corp v Kelley Co., Inc.* 56 F 3d 1538, 1554-55 [Fed. Cir. 1995] (noting range of possible royalties and affirming lower court's determination of royalty rate as reasonable); *Monsanto Co. v Ralph* 382 F 3d 1374, 1383 [Fed. Cir. 2004] (giving deference to jury's determination of royalty rate based on expert testimony regarding *Georgia-Pacific* factors).

20   It must, however, be noted that in Europe, by contrast with the United States, injunctive relief is considered the primary remedy for patent infringement, over and above monetary compensation. Moreover, any damages awarded must only be compensatory in nature and may not have a punitive character. For these reasons, many cases are settled out of court after a finding of patent infringement and the existing case law on the calculation of damages is therefore very sparse.

21   Cour de Cassation (Ch. Comm.) (France), *Sté Ets Delaplace et Sté Sicma c. Sté Van Der Lely*, 19 February 1991, [1991] Annales de la Propriété Industrielle, 4 (noting that the lower court had correctly exercised its judicial discretion in determining the royalty rate serving as the basis for damages after a finding of patent infringement). See also the example given of a "notional" royalty rate set by the UK Court of Appeal in a copyright case: *Nigel Christopher Blayney (t/a Aardvark Jewellery) v (1) Clogeau St Davids Gold Mines* [2003] F.S.R. 19.

22   The non-exhaustive list of 15 factors identified by the *Georgia Pacific* court is provided in the Appendix.

23   *General Tire & Rubber Co. v Firestone Tyre & Rubber Co.* [1975] F.S.R. 273 (H.L) ("[E]vidence may consist of the practice, as regards royalty, in the relevant trade or in analogous trades; perhaps of expert opinion expressed in publications or in the witness box; possibly of the profitability of the invention; and any other factor on which the judge can decide the measure of loss."); Sec. 139 Para. 2 German Patent Act (royalty rate of a hypothetical license agreement must be determined in the light of all relevant circumstances).

24   *Flint v Lovell* [1935] 1 K.B. 354 (CA) (Greer, L.J.) (explaining that an award of damages is reversible only if "the amount awarded [is] an entirely erroneous estimate of the damage to which the plaintiff is entitled").

25   At least one US court has adopted the *Georgia-Pacific* factors to assess the reasonableness of a licencing offer challenged on FRAND grounds. *ESS Tech., Inc. v PC–Tel, Inc.*, No. C-99-20292, 2001 WL 1891713, 3–6 [N.D. Cal. Nov. 28, 2001].

26   "(1) A binding integrated agreement discharges prior agreements to the extent that it is inconsistent with them. (2) A binding completely integrated agreement discharges prior agreements to the extent that they are within its scope. (3) An integrated agreement that is not binding or that is voidable and avoided does not discharge a prior agreement. But an integrated agreement, even though not binding, may be effective to render inoperative a term which would have been part of the agreement if it had not been integrated" (*Restatement (Second) of Contracts* (1981) § 213).

27   RA Lord 11 *Williston on Contracts* (4th ed 2009) § 33:26 ("[E]vidence of a collateral agreement is not barred by the parol evidence rule if such evidence does not contradict the written contract.").

28 See for example *Maxwell v J. Baker, Inc.* 86 F 3d 1098, 1109-10 [Fed. Cir. 1996] ("[T] hat an infringer had to be ordered by a court to pay damages, rather than agreeing to a reasonable royalty, is also relevant" to "an amount sufficient to adequately compensate the patentee for the infringement"); *Stickle v Heublein, Inc.* 716 F 2d 1550, 1563 [Fed. Cir. 1983]; *Endress & Hauser, Inc. v Hawk Measurement Sys. Pty. Ltd.* 892 F. Supp 1123, 1130 [S.D. Ind. 1995] ("Although courts employ the "willing licensor/willing licensee" model as the basis for determining a reasonable royalty, they do so with the understanding that a "reasonable" royalty after infringement is likely to be higher than that arrived at between truly willing patent owners and licensees."); V. E. O'Brien, "Economics & Key Patent Damages Cases" (2000) 9 University of Baltimore Intellectual Property 1, 19 & 20 n.70 (observing that "the hypothetical negotiation already has a built-in bias toward a royalty rate that is higher than those observed in practice" and that the Federal Circuit often sustains awards "based on a royalty several times that observed in the real world").

29 For a discussion of the dispute see "Antitrust: Commission welcomes IPCom's public FRAND declaration", MEMO/09/549, Brussels (Dec. 10, 2009) (European Commission welcoming "the public declaration by German IP licensing company IPCom, following discussions with the Commission, that it is ready to take over Bosch's previous commitment to grant irrevocable licenses on fair, reasonable and non-discriminatory (FRAND) terms to patents held by IPCom which are essential for various standards set by the European Telecommunications Standard Institute (ETSI) and Universal Mobile Telecommunications System (UMTS)"), http://europa.eu/rapid/pressReleasesAction. do?reference=MEMO/09/549&format=HT

ML&aged=0&language=EN> accessed on Mar. 7, 2010.

30 N-Data refers to NEGOTIATED DATA SOLUTIONS LLC.

31 ETSI/GA11(91)8 was an agreement between ETSI and the Standards Institution of Israel approved at the 11th ETSI General Assembly in 1991.

32 ETSI/GA12(92)TD 163 (expresses concerns that ETSI standards "must in principle be made available on a national treatment basis in order to meet the Community's international obligations"); ETSI/GA12(92)TD 3 2 (ANSI submission expressing concern that "ETSI members have the apparent ability to decline to license IPRs to certain manufacturers . . . based on the manufacturer's country of residence or the origin of the manufactured goods"); ETSI/IPR/ GA(92)TD 5 3 (Statement of Commission Representative emphasizing that, under the Technical Barriers to Trade Agreement, "the parties to that Agreement are entitled to treatment equal to that given to Community nationals and to equal treatment as between one another.").

33 See ETSI/GA12(92)TD 19 5 (Submission of the Chairman of the ETSI Technical Assembly, asserting that, under the then-proposed policy, "In particular members and non members within the Community are treated the same."); ETSI/IPR/GA(92) TD5 3 (Statement of the Commission of the European Communities ("CEC") noting that "there is the question of the position of non-ETSI members", and asserting that "standards, including IPR's, must be available to all potential users within the Community on equivalent or comparable terms . . . ."); ETSI/GA14(92)TD 20 3 (Letter of the CEC to ETSI stating, "The Commission considers that non-members of ETSI should not receive less favourable terms merely because they are not members.").

34 See, e.g., *Volvo Trucks N. Am., Inc. v. Reeder-Simco GMC, Inc.*, 546 U.S. 164 176 [2006] (approving preferred dealership discounts); *E & L Consulting, Ltd. v. Doman Indus. Ltd.*, 472 F.3d 23 29 [2d Cir. 2006] [a lower Federal court case] ("It is not a violation of the antitrust laws, without a showing of actual adverse effect on competition market-wide, for a manufacturer to ... appoint an exclusive distributor." (internal quotation marks and citation omitted)).

35 However, in this respect the ETSI reading of "non-discriminatory" appears to be consistent with that of ANSI, which has said explicitly that "RAND does not mean that each licensee will receive exactly the same set of terms and conditions because other considerations (such as reciprocal cross-licensing) may be a factor." GSC11/IPRWG(06)10, at p.7. [xxxvi] *Georgia-Pacific Corp v US Plywood Corp.* 318 F Supp 1116 1120-21 [SDNY 1970].

APPENDIX

The *Georgia-Pacific* court listed the following as "the factors mutatis mutandis seemingly more pertinent to the issue" of what royalty is reasonable:

1. The royalties received by the patentee for the licensing of the patent in suit, proving or tending to prove an established royalty.
2. The rates paid by the licensee for the use of other patents comparable to the patent in suit.
3. The nature and scope of the license, as exclusive or non-exclusive; or as restricted or non-restricted in terms of territory or with respect to whom the manufactured product may be sold.
4. The licensor's established policy and marketing program to maintain his patent monopoly by not licensing others to use the invention or by granting licenses under special conditions designed to preserve that monopoly.
5. The commercial relationship between the licensor and licensee, such as, whether they are competitors in the same territory in the same line of business; or whether they are inventor and promoter.
6. The effect of selling the patented specialty in promoting sales of other products of the licensee; that existing value of the invention to the licensor as a generator of sales of his non-patented items; and the extent of such derivative or convoyed sales.
7. The duration of the patent and the term of the license.
8. The established profitability of the product made under the patent; its commercial success; and its current popularity.
9. The utility and advantages of the patent property over the old modes or devices, if any, that had been used for working out similar results.
10. The nature of the patented invention; the character of the commercial embodiment of it as owned and produced by the licensor; and the benefits to those who have used the invention.
11. The extent to which the infringer has made use of the invention; and any evidence probative of the value of that use.
12. The portion of the profit or of the selling price that may be customary in the particular business or in comparable businesses to allow for the use of the invention or analogous inventions.
13. The portion of the realizable profit that should be credited to the invention as distinguished from non-patented elements, the manufacturing process, business risks, or significant features or improvements added by the infringer.
14. The opinion testimony of qualified experts.
15. The amount that a licensor (such as the patentee) and a licensee (such as the infringer) would have agreed upon (at the time the infringement began) if both had been reasonably and voluntarily trying to reach an agreement; that is, the amount which a prudent licensee- who desired, as a business proposition, to obtain a license to manufacture and sell a particular article embodying the patented invention- would have been willing to pay as a royalty and yet be able to make a reasonable profit and which amount would have been acceptable by a prudent patentee who was willing to grant a license.

Section 2
Competing Standards

Chapter 4

The Standards War between ODF and OOXML:
Does Competition between Overlapping ISO Standards Lead to Innovation?

Tineke M. Egyedi
Delft University of Technology, The Netherlands

Aad Koppenhol
Sun Microsystems, The Netherlands

ABSTRACT

A strong belief exists that competition between de facto standards stimulates innovation and benefits consumers because it drives down the costs of products. The tenability of this belief, and its preconditions and limits, has been widely scrutinized. However, little has been written about competition between negotiated, de jure (i.e., committee) standards. Are competing de jure standards a good thing? Blind (2008) equals de jure to de facto standards and concludes that competition between de jure standards increases social welfare. In this paper we argue that it is important to distinguish between de jure and de facto standards; therefore, that Blind's basic assumption is incorrect. We illustrate our argument with the same example as Blind, that is, the standards war between the document formats of ODF and OOXML. In our view, the implications of condoning—and even encouraging—competition between de jure standards will have far-reaching consequences for public IT-procurement. It will hinder innovation and counteract supplier-independent information exchange between government and citizens.

INTRODUCTION

In the neo-classic economic line of reasoning competition is held to benefit consumers because it lowers the price of products, increases product supply and stimulates innovation. That is, it im-

proves the price/performance ratio of products. Furthermore, through the workings of the free market the most innovative and competitively priced products will automatically drive out lesser products. The market has a self-regulatory capac-

DOI: 10.4018/978-1-4666-2160-2.ch004

ity: by means of competition it will purge itself and stimulate innovation.

The neo-classic line of reasoning is temptingly clear. Its implications are relatively easy to handle by policy makers faced with non-transparent and complex processes. Moreover, in many situations this line of argument may hold. But in some important other situations it does not. As the current economic crisis shows, in the financial sector competition also leads to fraudulent financial innovations. The self-regulatory capacity of the financial market has failed for it does not address the quality of products and services, and currently cannot cope with long term societal values and interests.

At present much more is known about the conditions under which competition between products and de facto standards has a positive effect on innovation. For example, a market with many small competing parties is not necessarily innovative; an oligopoly generally appears to be more so (Scherer, 1992). Many case studies exists about extremely competitive situations and in particular about wars between de facto standards (Stango, 2004). But little is known about whether these insights also apply to de jure standards. Recently Knut Blind (2008), a German economist, addressed the topic in a EURAS paper called 'A welfare analysis of standards competition: The example of the ECMA OpenXML Standard and the ISO ODF Standard'. There, he concludes that market competition is a good thing and no less so for de jure standards: competition between de jure standards leads to technology innovation.

Looking at a classic example in standardization, the variety of national standards for electrical plugs and the impediments which this causes, Blind's conclusion is hard to grasp. The implications of his conclusion are too far-reaching and the example he uses, that of two overlapping ISO-standards for document formats, is of too much consequence to gloss over our difference of view. The two ISO-standards are ODF, the Open Document Format, which was formalised in 2006,

and a second competing standard, Microsoft's OOXML, which was approved in November 2008. Because document formats play a key role in, for example, the way governments exchange information with their citizens, the consequences of having two overlapping ISO standards will be felt by citizens globally. Moreover, the development of two overlapping ISO standards draws into question the fundamental purpose of de jure standardisation.

In this article we will argue that competition between overlapping de jure standards leads to unnecessary confusion. It adds to social and economical costs without offering anything in return—least of all innovation.

An Ill-Founded Assumption

Blind's key question is how competing standards should be theoretically evaluated in particular in respect to their effect on innovation.[1] He identifies eight parameters[2] that are relevant to determine whether one should immediately choose between standards or prolong the period of competition before making a choice.

Our objections to Blind's view do not so much concern the arguments he uses, but rather the underlying assumptions and implicit shift in research question. Blind claims that it makes no difference whether we are dealing with de facto standards like Blu-Ray or formal de jure and consortium standards like ETSI's GSM standard and W3C's XML standard. In developing his argument he extensively uses the Anglo-Saxon body of economic literature on standardisation, which centres on de facto standards (Blind, 2004). In doing so, he confines his discussion to situations and problems which are typical for de facto standards and obscures answering the initial research question.

For example, a recurrent problem addressed by economic literature is the risk that consumers prematurely get locked into a certain technology whereas its quality is not yet evident. According to Blind such uncertainty calls for a prolongation of standards competition until the technologies have taken shape and it has become clear which is technically superior.[3] We have two objections to this view. Firstly, in most standards wars technical superiority—which is hardly objectifiable in any case—is not at stake. Different technologies merely represent a different solution. Which technology 'wins' is primarily attributable to the availability of products, the forming of alliances and successful marketing. Prolonging the period of competition may even adversely influence the market. We may bear in mind here the war between Blue-Ray and HD-DVD in the market for High Density DVDs. This market stagnated for a long time because consumers feared to be left stuck with a 'losing' system and therefore postponed their purchases.

Our second objection, and the most important one for this article, is that what may possibly apply to de facto standards does not necessarily apply to de jure standards. The nature of both types of standards is too fundamentally different.

Difference between 'De Facto' and 'De Jure'

The best-known international organisation for standardisation, the ISO, uses the following definition of 'de jure' standard: "a document established by consensus and approved by a recognized body, that provides, for common and repeated use, rules, guidelines or characteristics for activities or their results, aimed at the achievement of the optimum degree of order in a given context" (ISO/IEC, 2004, p. 8). What is important in this definition is that standards are, whenever possible, accepted by consensus—and consequently without fundamental objections—and that democratic procedures are followed in developing them. The latter element characterizes a 'recognised organisation'.

The 'optimum degree of order in a given context' offers ample room for interpretation. In principle, this order could include competitive standards. But given that the ISO generally rejects the development of overlapping standards, this does not seem plausible.[4]

De jure standards are meant for voluntary use, even though the term 'de jure'—Latin for 'legal, according to the law'—seems to suggest that such standards are used in the context of law and regulation and as such are compulsory.[5] In general the term de jure standard is used for standards developed within committees of official standards organisations like the ISO.

In the ICT area increasingly standards are also being developed by committees of standards consortia. Three such consortia are particularly important for the standards war discussed here: the W3C (World Wide Web Consortium) that is in charge of the XML-standard to which the two standards for document format conform, and the standards consortia OASIS and Ecma International, which have initially standardised the two competing document formats.

A third important source of committee standards are umbrella organisations and public authorities. These fall outside the scope of this article. For the sake of convenience all committee standards are in the following referred to as 'de jure standards'.

In daily life, the term standard usually refers to a de facto standard. De facto standards are products and services with such a large market share that 'de facto' (literally: in fact, in actual practice) they function as a standard. Their market share induces other companies to develop interoperable products and services. Clear examples of this are the Office products of Microsoft and Adobe's PDF.

For some de facto standards there is a demand to formalise them as a 'de jure' standard. In order to do so, the specifications of the de facto standard must be made public. From then on other companies will have the possibility to implement the specifications into their own products. This was, for instance, the case for Adobe's PDF which by now has been formalised as an ISO standard (ISO 32000).

Summarising, whereas the term de facto standard refers to a significant market share, a de jure standard is based on a collective agreement. As such they are innately different, as are their value and effect on the market.

Effect on the Market

De jure standards are points of reference. Referring to standards saves us the time and effort we would otherwise need to explain exactly what we mean. As such they reduce what economists term the *informational transaction costs* because 'both parties to a deal mutually recognize what is being dealt in' (Kindleberger, 1983, p. 395).

The characteristics of the standard-conform product are known, and therefore buyers are less likely to be disappointed (Reddy, 1990). Furthermore, the costs of finding the desired product are reduced because less time and money is needed to evaluate different products (Jones & Hudson, 1996). In other words, standards provide information which makes the market more transparent.

In the case of compatibility standards—among which document format standards—these standards allow products to interoperate and components to be replaced (compatibility, interoperability[6], exchangeability). Especially in anonymous markets, where parties do not know each other, complementary products can be used together once the interfaces have been standardised. For instance, the ISO standard for paper formats (ISO 216) is an important design specification in the paper processing industry (e.g. printers, photocopiers and fax machines). Standards structure markets and thus can lay the foundation for new clusters of economic activity.

The important contribution of standardisation is that it reduces the type of variety which has little extra to offer to consumers. Here we may think of the many national electricity plugs and of the metrical and imperial systems of measurement. Reducing unprofitable variety not only results in a more transparent and smoothly running market— the functions of compatibility and information respectively. It also brings with it the advantages of large scale industrial production (economies of scale). The functions and their effects of de jure standards are summed up in Table 1. They are typical of de jure standards and are, consequently, not automatically applicable to de facto standards.

In the example which Blind discusses and which we adopt as well, he initially addresses the competition between a formal standard and a consortium standard (ISO's ODF standard vs. Ecma's OOXML standard 1st edition, respectively). Later, he generalizes his initial findings to competition between formal standards (the situation in November 2008: ISO's ODF standard and ISO's OOXML standard).

Because ISO is a pre-eminent de jure standards organisation, its standards should in principle meet the above-mentioned requirements and have the said effects. However, both the way in which the OOXML standard came into being, its contents and its approval as a second standard seem to undo all market advantages of de jure standardisation.

Table 1. The main functions of de jure compatibility standards (Egyedi & Blind, 2008, p. 4).

Function of standards	Effect on the market
Information	Reduces transaction costs Corrects adverse selection[7] Facilitates trade
Compatibility	Creates network externalities[8] Avoids lock-ins
Variety reduction	Allows economies of scale Builds critical mass

How the Two Standards Came into Being

The key problem in the standards war between document formats is Microsoft's monopoly position in the software market. Estimations vary, but 90 to 95% of all digital documents may be presumed to be stored in 'old' Microsoft document formats. There is a danger to this.

Monopolies are in a position to capture (or internalise) the value of network externalities – although this value is by definition not an attribute of an individual user's product or service, a monopoly or dominant player is in a position to raise the price of an individual user's access beyond its inherent value, based on the external value of the network effect (Ghosh, 2005)

In other words, it is hardly possible for individual as well as business consumers to change providers without high costs (high barrier to exit). They are, as it were, stuck with their provider (lock-in). In principle, standardisation puts a stop to this dependence. However, as we will see, some standards are more provider-independent than others.

The two standards for document formats, ODF and OOXML, aim to store digital documents made with word processors, spreadsheet programmes, or presentation programmes in XML[9] (see Table 2).

The big advantage of XML-adherence is that the standards thereby comply with widely supported international coding conventions for information structure and character set. Another advantage is that the documents are separated from the applications that created them, which then makes it possible to process documents with competing applications. This makes it easer to exchange documents between similar office applications. In addition, an important side-effect is that by encoding documents in compliance with a public standard it will also be possible to retrieve their contents in the future, regardless of any further updates to the software application. In short, the future accessibility of the contents of XML documents is better secured. Applying XML in software products thus enhances supplier-independence of citizen consumers and business consumers, and improves the digital sustainability of electronic documents.

There is a catch, however. For, whereas the scope of the ODF standards committee explicitly

Table 2. Comparing ODF and OOXML

	ODF	OOXML
Originally submitted by	Sun Microsystems[10]	Microsoft
Standards consortium	OASIS	Ecma International
XML-based	Yes	Yes
Aim of supplier independence	Yes	No
ISO/IEC standard	ISO/IEC 26300	ISO/IEC 29500
Year	2006	2008
ISO/IEC standard corresponds to	OpenDocument v1.0 Specification (OASIS, May 2005)	ECMA-376 2nd edition (Ecma, Dec. 2008)
Accelerated ISO/IEC JTC1 procedure	Publicly Available Specification (PAS): PAS submitter	Fast Track
• Access to accelerated procedure	Bureaucratic and recurring process	One-time application for A-liaison
• Ballot period	6 months	5 months
Year	2006	2008

supports supplier independence[11], OOXML aims '[to be] fully compatible with the existing corpus of Microsoft Office documents' (ECMA-376 Part 1, Introduction, p. X).

The large amount of already existing Microsoft Office documents (legacy) was the main justification to enter the competing OOXML standards trajectory. Allegedly, ODF did not sufficiently take this legacy into account.

Although Microsoft did not take part in the development of ODF in OASIS, the standards committee noted that 'transformability into potential Microsoft office XML formats could be sensible'. However, the committee agreed to refrain from making this a formal requirement in the standardisation process.[12] In fact, to do so would have been difficult because at the time Microsoft's doc-specifications had not yet been made public. This in itself is not very surprising because, in order to protect their market share, specifications of a de facto standard are seldom released.

The 'legacy argument' seems reasonable at first sight. However, the following qualifications can be made. First, the fast track JTC1 procedure that was used to formalise ECMA-376 is generally used to formalise specifications that are already widely accepted. Such specifications are usually mature and therefore undergo few changes. For the ECMA-376 standard, however, the situation was entirely different. This standard had many flaws. In other words, if the faulty ECMA-376 had been adopted without alterations, as it would normally be in a fast track procedure, the future of Microsoft's legacy documents would have been all but secure.

Secondly, the legacy argument could equally have been a reason for Microsoft to take part in the ODF process, and thus make ODF suitable for its document formats. Would it have been possible at the time to formulate the later OOXML specifications as an extension to the ODF standard? That question will unfortunately remain unanswered as Microsoft did not take part. At the time it did not seem to be in Microsoft's interest to release its specifications.

Currently Microsoft has indicated its willingness to actively support the ODF standard.[13] This step might have been motivated by the fact that the legacy argument largely seems to have become a thing of the past anyway. For example, in principle OpenOffice.org can both read and write Microsoft's .doc documents. Furthermore, document converters are now able to translate between different document formats. Examples are those of Centric, one of the most important software suppliers to the Dutch authorities, and the open source converter of Xout. Moreover, OpenOffice.org itself includes converting functions for all current document formats (see Figure 1).

At first sight the ways in which both standards have come into being are quite similar. Both standards have passed from being a (product) specification to become a consortium standard and via an accelerated procedure an ISO/IEC standard.[14] In the case of ODF, however, the standards process took place much more in the open and lasted much longer (3 years)[15]; the quality of the consortium process and the document was checked beforehand by JTC1 (PAS procedure[16]); and the standards process proceeded without much ado.

In the case of OOXML, on the other hand, the initial specification increased in size during the Ecma process from roughly 1900 to 6000 pages over the period of December 2005 to December 2006; the due to a historic privilege the Ecma standard could enter the Fast Track procedure without impediment[17]; but the standards process caused much concern. Both the proposed standard content (ECMA-376 edition 1) and the JTC1 process were heavily attacked with over a thousand comments, accusations of attempts at bribery and changes to the JTC1 procedures during the process[18] (Koppenhol & Egyedi, 2008). Eventually, the OOXML standard was approved as ISO/IEC 29500 in November 2008 and adopted unaltered a month later by Ecma as ECMA-376 edition 2 (7342 pages).

Figure 1. For the purpose of illustration the figure shows two recent office packages: OpenOffice.org 3.0 and Microsoft Office 2007. Note that the OOXML mentioned in the figure is the specification which served as input for the Ecma standardisation process and is as such not the outcome of this process (i.e. ECMA-376 edition 1) or the recently approved ISO OOXML standard (ISO/IEC 29500).

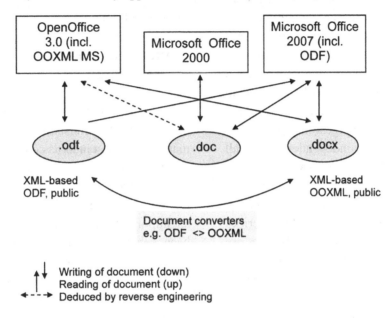

Although much more could be said about the JTC1 process, this falls outside the scope of the current article. Important for our research question in this article is the observation that two XML-oriented document formats have been standardised by the same standards body. Furthermore, it is highly unorthodox for JTC1, which champions implementation-independent standardisation, to have approved a standard which refers explicitly to a product supplier.

Stakes in the War

In a way the war between ODF and OOXML is similar to those between de facto standards for these, too, compete to set the standard for technology development and markets (Besen & Farrell, 1991). Where ODF and OOXML differ,

however, is that they wage their war not merely in the market but have turned de jure standardisation into a battlefield as well.

What stake do the players have in de jure standardisation? The formalisation of product specifications in JTC1 generally serves to increase their visibility and acceptance worldwide. A de jure standard implies stability which increases its support. In addition it facilitates access to the considerable market of public IT procurement[19] (Egyedi, 2001). ISO and IEC have a good reputation. They are international organisations with democratic procedures, in the sense that they and their national counterparts, the national standards bodies, aim to involve all parties concerned in the standards negotiations and encourage decisions to be taken in consensus. These are two important process characteristics of 'open standards'. They imply a fair process. ISO and IEC's good reputation earns JTC1, their joint technical committee, and therefore JTC1 standards much credit.

In the case of public IT procurement a standard for document formats is especially relevant because government authorities will want to avoid implicitly forcing citizens, companies and other organisations to purchase software from a certain provider, for instance, in order to be able to read government websites. The only way to meet the need for document exchangeability, interoperable systems and supplier-independence is for all software providers to conform to a standardised document format. In the action plan 'The Netherlands in Open Connection' the Dutch government, for example, chooses JTC1's ODF and prescribes that from 2008 onward all public authorities are to support ODF-conform exchanges (EZ, 2007, 2008). Adding a second standard does not improve market transparency.

Competition between de facto standards in the consumer electronics market is already problematic:

There's no denying that consumer electronics format wars are a nuisance. The rules of engagement are particularly cruel for the buying public, asking them to make an expensive bet on a technology that could be obsolete in a few years time. They emerge with remarkable frequency: 78 rpm discs versus 45 rpm in the 1940s, 8-track versus cassette in the 70s, Betamax versus VHS in the 80s, digital audio tape versus the compact disc in the 90s. Not to mention, of course, the ongoing QuickTime versus Windows Media versus RealMedia struggle (Warner, 2008)

But in the case of ODF and OOXML public values are also at stake such as equal access for citizens to public information and free choice of software suppliers. Document formats determine how public authorities and citizens exchange information and the extent to which archived information remains accessible (digital sustain-

ability). Having two largely overlapping JTC1 standards not only hinders information exchange and digital sustainability, it also flatly contradicts JTC1's own views[20] and to those of the World Trade Organisation.[21]

Standard as a Platform for Innovation

The essence of de jure standardisation is that the fight for the consumer is not fought in the market but in a standards committee. The agreed specification generally represents a compromise between the different parties concerned. No one will be entirely satisfied with the result, but an important aim of standardisation will have been achieved: the conditions are created for a market with interoperable and exchangeable standard-conform products. Standards create a level playing field for all parties. They lower the threshold for newcomers because interoperability and exchangeability issues have been taken care of by the standard. Competition can then focus on how best to implement the standard and other product features. As such de jure standards are a platform for innovation. All this leads to the consumer advantages mentioned earlier: a better price/performance ratio and a larger variety of products. The desired economic effect of a de jure standard is 'supporting full competition in the marketplace for suppliers of a technology and related products and services' (Ghosh, 2005).

By focusing competition on products rather than standards consumers also benefit from a lower barrier to entry and a lower barrier to exit. The purchase of standard-conform products reduces the risk of a bad bargain and cuts down the costs of switching providers precisely because the products are more easily replaceable and exchangeable. In other words, competition should not take place between de jure standards but between standard-conform implementations.[22]

CONCLUSION

Blind makes a plea for competition between ODF and OOXML because also in this case competition is to lead to innovation. He thereby assumes that de facto standards and de jure standards may be regarded as equal and accordingly fails to make a distinction between products and agreements. This ill-founded assumption leads to an equally ill-founded conclusion.

'De jure' and 'de facto' standards fundamentally differ. De jure standards for document formats aim to foster interoperability, create network externalities, prevent lock-in, cut transaction costs, create a transparent market and reduce variety. The impact of de facto standards on the market tends to be the exact opposite. Indeed, in the Office environment supplier-dependence and a non-transparent market are the main problem.

Competition between two de jure standards undoes all the advantages of de jure standardisation. It results in a non-transparent market, raises transaction costs and hampers interoperability. This also holds for the two ISO standards for document formats. The objective of ODF, the first ISO standard, was to ease interoperability between different office suites, increase supplier *in*dependence and improve accessibility and digital sustainability of documents. The approval of OOXML, the second standard, does not add extra value. On the contrary, it reduces it.

As noted, there are good reasons to question the sincerity of Microsoft's legacy argument, which was the main argument to justify the ISO OOXML standard. Furthermore, the argument appears to have been largely overtaken by recent developments. Nonetheless some governments will feel obliged to refer to both standards in their IT-procurement, and software vendors will have to anticipate on this situation by implementing both standards.

If one disregards the increased costs and system vulnerability due to increased complexity, adapters, converters, plug-ins, multi-protocol stacks, and 'multiple implementations' of competing standards in one products may seem an easy solution. However, such solutions also lead to performance degradation (Shapiro & Varian, 1999). Werner Langer (2008) has quantified the performance costs of document format conversion.

Moreover, converters may offer a fairly good solution for the legacy problem of *.doc* formats, that is, for making accessible the old static documents. But for a number of reasons they do not provide a systematic solution for the interoperability and conversion problems of the 'live' documents that are exchanged. The most important reason is that converters are built to translate between implementations of certain versions of different standards. However, in practice these standards are subject to changes. Consequently, conversion solutions are not a once and for all cure. They need maintenance and updates. Another important reason not to make light of having two overlapping standards is more complicated. As most computer users will have experienced at one time or another, conforming to a standard does not always guarantee interoperability of products. This is because - intentionally or unintentionally - standards are often implemented differently (Egyedi, 2008). Therefore, not only conformance tests are needed to indicate whether a product complies to the standard but also interoperability tests. Where this causes problems with one and the same standard, the problem aggravates exponentially with two standards. Converters cannot offer solace for this problem.

In short, having two overlapping de jure standards merely creates extra costs for citizens, companies, government authorities and others without offering anything in return. It leads to frustration and waste, and certainly not to innovation, as Blind argues.

ACKNOWLEDGMENT

We sincerely thank Arjan Loeffen (Valid/Vision), Alfred Kleinknecht (Delft University of Technology), the editors of the Dutch version of this article (Egyedi & Koppenhol, 2009), Hans Sleurink and Jan Stedehouder, and the anonymous EURAS reviewers for their valuable suggestions.

REFERENCES

W3C. (2006). *Extensible Markup Language (XML) 1.0* (4th ed.). Author.

Besen, S. M., & Farrell, J. (1991). The role of the ITU in standardization. Pre-eminence, impotence or rubber stamp? *Telecommunications Policy*, *15*(4), 311–321. doi:10.1016/0308-5961(91)90053-E

Blind, K. (2004). *The Economics of Standards: Theory, Evidence, Policy*. Cheltenham, UK: Edward Elgar.

Blind, K. (2008). A Welfare Analysis of standards Competition: The example of the ECMA OpenXML Standard and the ISO ODF Standard. In K. Jakobs & E. Soederstroem (Eds.), *Proceedings of the 13th EURAS Workshop on Standardisation* (pp. 1-17). Aachen, Germany: Wissenschafts Verlag Mainz.

Egyedi, T. M. (2001). Why JavaTM was -not-standardized twice. *Computer Standards & Interfaces*, *23*(4), 253–265. doi:10.1016/S0920-5489(01)00078-2

Egyedi, T. M. (2008). An implementation perspective on sources of incompatibility and standards' dynamics. In Egyedi, T. M., & Blind, K. (Eds.), *The dynamics of standards* (pp. 181–189). Cheltenham, UK: Edward Elgar.

Egyedi, T. M., & Blind, K. (2008). Introduction. In Egyedi, T. M., & Blind, K. (Eds.), *The dynamics of standards* (pp. 1–12). Cheltenham, UK: Edward Elgar.

Egyedi, T. M., & Koppenhol, A. (2009). Concurrerende standaarden een goede zaak? In Sleurink, H., & Stedehouder, J. (Eds.), *Open Source Jaarboek 2008-2009* (pp. 119–130). Gorredijk, The Netherlands: Media Update Vakpublicaties.

EZ. (2007). *Nederland Open in Verbinding: Een actieplan voor het gebruik van Open Standaarden en Open Source Software bij de (semi-)publieke sector*. 's-Gravenhage: Ministerie van Economische Zaken.

EZ. (2008). *Actielijn 6 ODF-invoering Toelichting op actieplan Nederland Open in Verbinding*. 's-Gravenhage. The Netherlands: Ministerie van Economische Zaken.

Farrell, J., & Saloner, G. (1985). Standardization, Compatibility and Innovation. *The Rand Journal of Economics*, *16*, 70–83. doi:10.2307/2555589

Ghosh, R. (2005). *Free/Libre/OpenSource Software: Policy Support: An Economic Basis for Open Standards*. Maastricht, The Netherlands: MERIT, University of Maastricht, FLOSSPOLS Project. Retrieved from http://flosspols.org/deliverables.php

ISO/IEC. (1991). *Guide 2*. Geneva, Switzerland: Author.

ISO/IEC. (2004). *ISO/IEC Directives, Part 1, Procedures for the technical work* (5th ed.). Geneva, Switzerland: Author.

ISO/IEC. (2008). *ISO/IEC Directives, Part 1, Procedures for the technical work* (6th ed.). Geneva, Switzerland: Author.

Jones, P., & Hudson, J. (1996). Standardization and the Cost of Assessing Quality. *European Journal of Political Economy*, *12*, 355–361. doi:10.1016/0176-2680(95)00021-6

JTC1. (2007). *ISO/IEC JTC 1 Directives, Version 3.0* (5th ed.). Geneva, Switzerland: ISO/IEC JTC1.

Kindleberger, C. P. (1983). Standards as Public, Collective and Private Goods. *Kyklos*, *36*, 377–396. doi:10.1111/j.1467-6435.1983.tb02705.x

Koppenhol, A., & Egyedi, T. M. (2008, April 9). Een standaardenoorlog met alleen verliezers. *Automatisering Gids*.

Langer, W. (2008, February 28). Open Standards, Open Source, Open Documents: Experiences in Format Conversion. In *Proceedings of odfworkshop.nl*. Retrieved from http://www.odfworkshop.nl/files/20080228-ODFworkshop-WernerLanger.pdf

Reddy, N. M. (1990). Product of Self-Regulation. A Paradox of Technology Policy. *Technological Forecasting and Social Change, 38*, 43–63. doi:10.1016/0040-1625(90)90017-P

Scherer, F. M. (1992). Schumpeter and Plausible Capitalism. *Journal of Economic Literature, 30*(3), 1416–1433.

Shapiro, C., & Varian, H. R. (1999). *Information rules - A Strategic Guide to the Network Economy*. Boston: Harvard Business School Press.

Stango, V. (2004). The Economics of Standards Wars. *Review of Network Economics, 3*(1), 1–19. doi:10.2202/1446-9022.1040

Warner, B. (2008, January 9). HD-DVD v Bluray: Is the battle over? *Times Online*. Retrieved from http://technology.timesonline.co.uk/tol/news/tech_and_web/the_web/article3159432.ece

WTO. (1994). *Agreement on Technical Barriers to Trade of the WTO Agreement: Annex 3: Code of Good Practice for the Preparation, Adoption and Application of Standards*. Geneva, Switzerland: Author. Retrieved from http://www.wto.org/english/docs_e/legal_e/17-tbt.pdf

ENDNOTES

[1] 'How should multiple parallel existing standards, which exist in the same technological area, be fundamentally evaluated in terms of theoretical – static welfare, and most importantly with respect to their dynamic effect on innovation and competition?' (Blind, 2008, p.1)

[2] The parameters are: 'preference for network effects, local network effects, heterogeneity of the preferences, cost of the development and maintenance of standards, uncertainty regarding the technical quality, length of the life cycle, development potential, uncertainty regarding future user preferences.' (Blind, 2008, p.7)

[3] Blind (2008) frequently mentions the possibility of making the wrong decision ('wrong decision' p.6, 9, 'maintaining the standardisation competition' p.7, 'delay the market from committing' p.5), and draws comparisons with classic *de facto* standards (e.g., p. 1, 5, 9).

[4] See par. 1.3.1, 1.16.1, B.4.2.1, C.4.6.2 in ISO/IEC Directives (ISO/IEC, 2008).

[5] This makes the term 'de jure' a confusing one and is the reason why we usually prefer to speak about committee standards.

[6] 'Interoperability' and 'compatibility' refer to: "the suitability of products, processes or services for use together under specific conditions to fulfil relevant requirements without causing unacceptable interactions.' (ISO/IEC, 1991)

[7] Adverse selection takes place if a supplier of inferior products gains market share through price competition because the supplier of high quality products has no means to signal the superior quality of its products to consumers. Quality standards support the latter in signalling activities, foster the co-existence of low and high quality market segments, and therefore minimise the likelihood that consumer selection is based on wrong assumptions.

[8] The term *network externalities* refers to the situation that every new user in the network increases the value of being connected to the network (Farrell & Saloner, 1985).

[9] '[XML] describes (…) XML documents. (...). Markup encodes a description of the document's storage layout and logical structure.' (chapter 1, W3C, 2006) Nowadays XML is used for very different purposes such as electronic invoicing and publication processes. Often a distinct XML-based standard is developed because each application area has different requirements. This is also applies for office applications. In the case of ODF and OOXML, software for making and reading texts, spreadsheets and presentations is at stake.

[10] http://lists.oasis-open.org/archives/office/200212/msg00003.html

[11] http://www.oasis-open.org/committees/office/charter.php

[12] http://lists.oasis-open.org/archives/office/200212/msg00003.html

[13] December 16th 2008. http://www.microsoft.com/presspass/features/2008/dec08/12-16DougMahughQA.mspx

[14] JTC1 is as it were an organisation within an organisation has its own, partially different procedures: the JTC1 directives. JTC1 procedures result in ISO/IEC standards.

[15] http://lists.oasis-open.org/archives/tc-announce/200211/msg00001.html

[16] 'PAS Submitter gives a PAS originator the right to submit specifications into the transposition process for a period of two years with the possibility of further extensions of five year periods' (14.4.1) (JTC1, 2007)

[17] Ecma has a so-called A-liaison with JTC1, a status obtained in 1987 which allows Ecma standards immediate access to the Fast Track procedure. See also http://isotc.iso.org/livelink/livelink/fetch/2000/2489/186491/186605/Jtc1_Directives.pdf?nodeid=3959538&%2520vernum=0

[18] For example, comments were grouped together for 'block-voting' to more easily deal with the large amount of comments.

[19] Estimations vary from 16 up to 30% of the IT market in Europe.

[20] JTC1 seeks to avoid 'duplication of or conflict with the work of other ISO and IEC TCs' (JTC1, 2007, p. 13).

[21] 'Where international standards exist or their completion is imminent, the standardizing body shall use them, or the relevant parts of them, as a basis for the standards it develops, except where such international standards or relevant parts would be ineffective or inappropriate' (WTO, 1994, p. 135, F).

[22] Apart from this key point, the implementability of the Ecma-OOXML edition 1 standard is strongly questioned. This *de jure* standard therefore seems to have been published for political-economic reasons only and, as such, does not meet Ghosh's criteria of an open standard: 'If only one company -- or only that company's close partners -- can fully implement a standard, then the standard isn't really open, no matter how "reasonable" its licensing terms might be or how many people collaborated in its creation' (Ghosh, 2005).

This work was previously published in the International Journal of IT Standards and Standardization Research (IJITSR), Volume 8, Issue 1, edited by Kai Jakobs, pp. 49-62, copyright 2010 by IGI Publishing (an imprint of IGI Global)

Chapter 5

The Battle Within:
An Analysis of Internal Fragmentation in Networked Technologies Based on a Comparison of the DVB-H and T-DMB Mobile Digital Multimedia Broadcasting Standards

Håkon Ursin Steen
University of Oslo, Norway

ABSTRACT

This paper addresses the concept of internal standards fragmentation in networked technologies - occurring when two or more products remain non-interoperable for an intended service, even though being perfectly compliant to the same core interface compatibility standard. Two main sources of internal fragmentation are identified ("configurational" and "competitive"). A case study is done on the historically observed internal fragmentation within the DVB-H and T-DMB mobile digital multimedia broadcasting standards. It is argued that internal standards fragmentation has important consequences hitherto unaddressed in the literature, including potentially undermining the effects of interoperability and economies of scale expected to follow from the adoption of a single standard. Implications for research, policy and practice are discussed, and advice for further research is provided.

INTRODUCTION

The deployment of the GSM mobile phone standard has permanently raised the awareness of industry, policymakers and the public in general of the advantages of having a single interface compatibility standard for a technological service: economies of scale, interoperability and global roaming. In some respects, however, the success of GSM is a dubious yardstick as it can strengthen the conjecture that the selection and adoption of "one interface compatibility standard" *always* leads to

DOI: 10.4018/978-1-4666-2160-2.ch005

actual interoperability of products and benefits from economies of scale. This is, however, far from the case, as demonstrated in this paper. What from a distance looks like a single standard in a deployment scenario, might on closer inspection be an archipelago of isolated, non-interoperable network services.

Adding to the economic literature investigating the relationship between standardisation and policy (David & Greenstein, 1990; Stango, 2004), this paper defines "internal standards fragmentation" as when two or more products are *non-interoperable for an intended service,* even though being *perfectly compliant* to the same core interface compatibility standard. It also identifies two sources for internal standards fragmentation. The first, *fragmentation by configuration*, is when *endogenous* or *exogenous configurational flexibility* of a compatibility standard leads to non-interoperable products. The second, *fragmentation by competition*, describes the situation when interoperability between products complying with the same standard is hampered by intentionally "locking" certain devices to others.

This framework is applied for understanding the internal standards fragmentation observed in the design and adoption of the DVB-H *(Digital Video Broadcasting – Handheld)* and T-DMB *(Terrestrial – Digital Multimedia Broadcasting)* mobile digital multimedia broadcasting (MDMB) standards. The findings hopefully motivates questioning the validity of uncritically applying arguments such as "interoperability" and "economies of scale" as benefits of what is commonly (and, as the paper indicates, often imprecisely) referred to as uniform standardisation of networked technologies.

The rest of this paper is organised as follows. First I review relevant literature on standards and standards wars. Next I introduce theoretical concepts for explaining two types of internal fragmentation within networked standards. A case study of the DVB-H and T-DMB standards families are presented, including their potential for, and realisation of, internal fragmentation. I discuss consequences for research, policy and practice, before the article closes with a conclusion.

LITERATURE REVIEW

The basic matter for the economic literature on standards competition (often referred to as "standards wars") is to investigate whether or not the market settles on efficient standards – and further: whether or not public policy intervention is justified from a social welfare point-of-view (David & Greenstein, 1990; Stango, 2004). Important contributions are descriptions of how standards choice is dependent on prior historical events (Arthur, 1989) and how historical events can lead to the market locking in on (supposedly) inferior standards (David, 1985). Other important contributions are describing the effects of "the existing installed base" of users having adopted a standard (Farrell & Saloner, 1986), and how direct and indirect network effects (existing adopters' added utility of having a new user adopting a standard) influence competition outcomes (Katz & Shapiro, 1994). Particularly for "interface compatibility standards" (whose received definition is not unproblematic and is therefore discussed in the next section) is that it is generally recognised that *uniform* uptake (meaning a resolved standards war) of a single standard leads to *economies of scale* and *interoperability of products*, whereas *fragmented* uptake (meaning an unresolved standards war) of non-compatible standards negatively impacts these issues (Grindley, 1995).

A concern with the economic literature is that it is rather theoretically embedded: standards are analytically for many purposes treated as a "black boxes", and the literature in general engages restrainedly with what is actually going on *inside* standards and standardisation. This includes both the standards' technological characteristics, and also how they dynamically evolve through their interaction with the market and other institutions. Whilst distance from concrete instances of empirical matter may be pertinent to some types of analysis (like devising game-theoretic approaches to understand standardisation outcomes e.g., Besen & Farrell, 1994), it is highly inadequate for others – to the extent that it may result in a skewed and occasionally erroneous empirical foundation for the production of theory. An object lesson is that two of the hallmark examples a considerable portion of the theoretical literature on *standards lock-in* is based on, *keyboard layouts* and *video-cassette formats*, are founded in such arms-length engagement with the empirical matter. The treatment of the cases in the literature is therefore worth briefly reviewing as motivation for the strategy of in-depth examination of empirical standards and standardisation necessary for appreciating the concept of "internal fragmentation".

In both cases, it was in the literature assumed that the market had, because of lock-in effects, erroneously adopted two inferior standards: respectively the "QWERTY" keyboard layout and the "VHS" video cassette format. This conjecture was made on the assumption that the "Dvorak" keyboard layout (Arthur, 1989; David, 1985; Farrell & Saloner, 1985) and the "Beta" video format (Arthur, 1990) were technologically superior to respectively QWERTY and VHS. However, a second consideration of the evidence indicates that these assumptions of any clearly discernable superiority probably are false. In more rigorous reviews, the Dvorak keyboard is found to hold little – if any – efficiency advantage over QWERTY (Liebowitz & Margolis, 1990). Similarly with video cassette formats: a series of technological tests with different outcomes could *not* conclude if either of the standards were better than the other with regards to the main point in question – picture quality (Klopfenstein, 1989; Liebowitz & Margolis, 1995).

Whilst these revisionist findings by Klopfenstein, Liebowitz and Margolis of course also

can be questioned, the imminent lesson is in any case that research into standards is dependent on rigorous attention to the actual implementation and dynamics of technologies in real life. If not, researchers run the danger of developing invalid theory based on incomplete premises. Taken into consideration that "lock-in" into standards is one of the more important concepts of the economic standards discourse (and has given rise to one of the more uncontested presumptions about the properties of standards and standardisation); when Stango after reviewing the case studies in the literature argues that "there exists little hard empirical evidence of lock-in" to the extent that "conducting empirical tests of lock-in stands as one of the most important areas for future research in standards" (Stango, 2004, p. 8), this should be a reminder that received concepts not necessarily are as unproblematically valid as one could like them to be.

This lack of adequate supporting evidence for the "lock-in" concept emphasises the importance of immersing in the empirical specifics of the technologies described by standards. However, empirical research into standards is a complex discipline. It requires a combination of technological, economical and political knowledge. Adding significant complexity is that the constellations of standards, markets and institutions studied are in continuous change. This means that even the "standard itself" cannot be expected to be a fixed variable and leverage point in the analysis – the standard *in use* (which is what is interesting as it is what actually gives rise to economic effects) is usually always evolving and changing by means of formal or informal alterations by market players. This may again potentially affect its economic performance, and accordingly the rationale for any potential policy development related to the standard.

Paul David argues in 1995 that because of the dynamic characteristics of the market and network technology evolution, there are no quick fixes for standards policy. Simplified approaches to either *laissez-faire*, strict control or negotiated "middle positions" are not viable for David. This is because he simply questions much of the canon of economic standards research on the grounds that the "classic welfare analytical exercises that economists have conducted" are the wrong approach to dynamic problems altogether (David, 1995, p. 33). Rather, he argues that technologies and market particularities are highly contingent, precluding arrival at "policy recommendations that have a simple, non-contingent and time invariant form" (David, 1995, p. 34). He argues that *dynamic* problems must have *dynamic*, empirically informed solutions, allowing for "oscillations" in policy development. He terms such a strategy a "best policy flux" (David, 1995, p. 35).

In such a "flux", policy evolution is best informed by studies embracing the complexity observed – where both the specifics of the (changing) standards and technologies, as well as dynamic institutional contexts, are studied concurrently. Within the field of standards a number of such studies already exist, including studies of alternating (AC) versus direct (DC) electric current in the electrification of society (Hughes, 1983), AM versus FM radio (Besen, 1992), colour TV standardisation (Crane, 1979; Fridenson, 1991), OSI versus TCP/IP networking protocols (Hanseth, 2001), first-generation cellular communication standards (Lyytinen & Fomin, 2002) and MDMB standards (Steen, 2009). However, as these studies focus on fragmentation and competition *between* standards, they have largely precluded adequate attention to another important phenomena of standards and standardisation: fragmentation and competition *within* standards[1].

THEORETICAL CONCEPTS

A much-quoted definition of a "standard" is David and Greenstein's, describing it as "a set of technical specifications adhered to by a producer, either tacitly or as a result of a formal agreement"

(1990, p. 4). They further subtype into three types of standards: *reference*, *minimum quality* and *interface compatibility* standards.

This paper discusses challenges with *interface compatibility* standards. These are described by David and Greenstein (1990, p. 4) as "assur[ing] the user that an intermediate product or component can be successfully incorporated in a larger system comprised of closely specified inputs and outputs". This definition is, however, inadequate for the purposes of this paper. What is regarded as "successful" incorporation of a component *per se* (that is, conforming to a set of defined inputs and outputs at some layer of an architectural stack), does not mean that the product as a whole provides the overall *interoperability* typically expected from the end user of the product. As a consequence the relationship between *interface compatibility* and *interoperability of products* must be more closely specified.

"Interface Compatibility" versus Interoperability of Products

Products may be perfectly *interface compatible* according to what is specified in a standard, yet they may at the same time be perfectly *non-interoperable* for certain (or even all) practical uses. From this follows that interoperability is not an attribute guaranteed by the standard itself, but rather an attribute of the observed *implementation* and *use* of the standard. In this sense, an interface compatibility standard does *not* guarantee interoperable products – but interoperable products will for practical purposes *always* need (explicitly or implicitly) to comply with an interface compatibility standard to be interoperable.

There can be different degrees of interoperability for products implementing the same standard(s), ranging from "none" to "full". The according relationship between compatibility and interoperability is schematically illustrated by Figure 1. It seeks to illustrate that product Q (for instance a broadcasting receiver) may have varying

Figure 1. The relationship between interface compatibility and interoperability

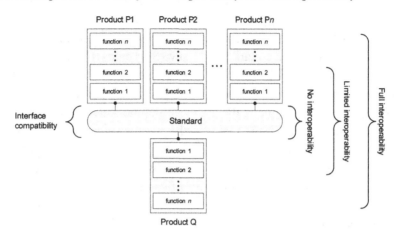

degrees of interoperability (including complete non-interoperability) with varying implementations of product P (for instance broadcasting networks), even if product Q and all instances of product P formally perfectly adhere to the exact same interface compatibility standard.

External versus Internal Fragmentation

When treating fragmentation, the economic literature is implicitly concerned with *external* fragmentation of standards. This is the situation when multiple non-compatible standards co-exist, inhibiting interoperability between products and economies of scale (Grindley, 1995, p. 28). We define *economies of scale* in the received sense with Silberston as the average reduction in production costs achieved "at larger scales of output" (Silberston, 1972, p. 370). We also follow Silberston's general thesis that the level of standardisation (understood as lack of variation) of products is positively correlated with the technical possibilities for getting benefits from economies of scale (Silbertson, 1972, p. 373).

Fragmentation can be either temporary or permanent. *Temporary* fragmentation is a normal feature of a "standards war". *Permanent* fragmentation, however, manifests if the standards war

does not resolve, and multiple, non-compatible standards coexist for a longer period of time. Fragmentation *within* standards may take place when interoperability between products is hampered or non-existent, despite products formally complying with the "same" standard. Economically, this may have many of the same consequences as external fragmentation. In addition to impeding possibilities for economies of scale, this reduces (or eliminates altogether) the potential for *network effects* commonly associated with interface compatibility standards. In the following, two sources of internal fragmentation are introduced: technical configurational flexibility and competitive incentives[2].

Configurational Flexibility

Internal fragmentation due to configurational flexibility of a standard has largely been a disregarded feature of historical examples of alleged uniform standardisation in the economic literature. This occurs when two different products, perfectly implementing the same standard, are configured in a (either internally, or in relation to other components of the product) so that the products become non-interoperable.

The configurational flexibility of a standard can have *endogenous* or *exogenous* sources.

Intentionally in the design phase introducing configurational flexibility that later may allow non-interoperable implementation (for example with the intention of catering to diverse market demands), increasing the risk of the standard fragmenting, is an example of an *endogenous* source of fragmentation. One historical example is the possibility to use either NTSC or PAL/SECAM signal processing methods on VHS video cassette recorder tapes (Shiraishi & Hirota, 1978). Another example is the European standard for satellite-based digital TV broadcasting, DVB-S (ETSI, 1997), where the configuration of key parameters (e.g. the supported radio carrier symbol rate) was at implementers' discretion, resulting in non-interoperable, DVB-S-compliant products (Nolan, 1997).

The second source for configurational fragmentation is *exogenous* to the standard. The standard itself may become a component in a product that induces non-interoperability with other products implementing the same standard, because of different configurations of associated components[3]. A historical example is also here DVB-S, which in addition to the endogenous fragmentation mentioned in the paragraph above, experienced exogenous fragmentation because of the incompatibility of the different systems for conditional access implemented in different devices for digital pay-TV systems (Levy, 1997).

Competitive Incentives

Competitive fragmentation is an explicit consequence of competitive strategy. Competitive fragmentation, however, happens when implementations are interface compatible (and potentially fully interoperable, with no variations in components between implementations) but interoperability of products is *intentionally* reduced by means of e.g. "locking" a product to a particular vendor or network operator. A well-known example of competitive fragmentation is the propensity of GSM operators to make the mobile phone handsets non-interoperable with competitors' networks, most often for a time-limited period (usually by pre-programming the phones to only accept their own SIM cards) (Valletti & Cave, 1998). Another example is regional coding on DVDs, which limits playback of discs to devices sold in specific geographic areas (Stone, 2007). Whilst affecting the user through a smaller or larger degree of non-interoperability, competitive fragmentation usually will not affect economies of scale significantly (on the production side) as production lines would be equal, and e.g. locking phones to a given operator would be a trivial additional task in the general software market preparation procedures of the device that anyway would have to be performed.

Mitigation and Resolution of Internal Fragmentation

Several effects may mitigate, even resolve, internal fragmentation. First, if fragmentation is the consequence of deliberate attempts by competing actor groups to promote their own specific version of a standard (rather than configuration as bound to e.g. territorial factors), an "internal standards war" may arise. The dynamics of such internal standards competition may be positive, in that resolution would mean the end of internal fragmentation. However, in the presence of a non-resolving internal standards war, policy intervention can also be a way to encourage actors to coalesce around one standard (however, the success of this is contingent).

In the presence of entrenched internal fragmentation not amendable by internal standards competition and/or policy intervention, markets may still mitigate negative impacts on network effects through introducing interoperability with multiple configurations of the standard at the user side. Such instances of "end-system-induced interoperability"[4] can e.g. manifest in multimode approaches to coverage of multiple radio parts of the radio spectrum (like seen with GSM cellular handsets covering multiple frequency bands). However, supporting multiple variations of a standard is a trade-off between the perceived added value to the consumer and the additionally incurred costs – for less critical and more price-sensitive technologies (like mobile TV) this may be an intolerable expense.

INTERNAL FRAGMENTATION IN T-DMB AND DVB-H

Both configurational and competitive fragmentation are observed in MDMB standards. After briefly reviewing the status of mobile TV technology worldwide, the current section presents the generic architectural stack of a MDMB carrier standard, and discusses the general potential for configurational fragmentation within such a stack. Then specific sources of *configurational* fragmentation in respectively the T-DMB and DVB-H standards will be presented, before a review of currently deployed services illustrates instances of internal fragmentation brought forward by *competitive* strategy.

External Fragmentation in Mobile Digital Multimedia Broadcasting

There are generally two ways of transmitting live multimedia content (required for mobile TV) to devices in the mobile environment: various modes of point-to-point or point-to-multipoint (Bakhuizen & Horn, 2005; Elsen, Hartung, Horn, Kampmann, & Peters, 2001) streaming within existing mobile phone networks, or direct broadcasting by means of radio carrier standards solely designed for the purpose. The latter, which this paper concerns, usually implies significant extra start-up costs because of the need to establish a dedicated network. Once beyond that, MDMB on dedicated radio carriers have distinct economic advantages. First, it is a way for society to have more diversified infrastructural competition in the

mobile environment – operators both outside and within the traditional telecommunications industry may start their own service, and thus potentially create a healthy, competitive climate for delivering rich media to mobile devices. Second, once deployed, dedicated mobile television networks are a cost-efficient way to broadcast the same content simultaneously to principally an unlimited number of users within reception range.

Since 2005, a relatively high number of standards have emerged enabling MDMB on dedicated radio carriers. The two standards studied in this paper, DVB-H and T-DMB, represent parts of the current *external* fragmentation of MDMB standards worldwide. DVB-H is predominantly deployed in Europe, but deployments are also reported elsewhere, including select countries in Africa, Asia and the Middle East (DVB-H.org, 2010). T-DMB is commercially only deployed in Norway, South Korea and China, although trials are ongoing in several countries (Poland, Netherlands and Italy). In the U.S., *Qualcomm*'s MediaFLO (TIA, 2006) and the *Advanced Television Systems Committee*'s ATSC-Mobile (ATSC, 2009) are the most notable standards. Japan uses the native mobile support of their digital terrestrial television (DTT) standard *Integrated Service Digital Broadcasting – Terrestrial* (ISDB-T) to permit broadcasting of content adapted to reception in mobile terminals (Asami & Sasaki, 2006). In China the domestically developed *China Mobile Multimedia Broadcasting* (CMMB) standard is deployed in over 200 cities nationally (CMMB, 2009).

Two Sources of Internal Fragmentation

Adding to the external fragmentation of MDMB standards is a considerable level of *internal* fragmentation. In this subsection we will briefly present how the concepts of *configurational* and *competitive* fragmentation specifically apply to MDMB standards.

Configurational Flexibility

Figure 2 shows a depiction of an architectural stack of a MDMB standard. This is a generic depiction – some standards do not implement all layers. However, as we will see there is often configurational flexibility allowed by standard specifications in up to four layers of the model: the radio frequency band (layer a), the coding/decoding (codec) layer (layer g), and the service provision layers, which are grouped to include both the *Digital Rights Management* (DRM) system (layer h), as well as the *Electronic Service Guide* (ESG) (layer i).

First, the configurational flexibility of the radio frequency band is motivated by variations in frequency availability from country to country. Typically, MDMB standards are designed to permit deployment in either VHF, UHF or L-Band. Either of these parts of the radio spectrum, however, need distinct radio frequency modulation and demodulation equipment. There is thus an economic incentive to implement only the equipment needed for the frequency band a given broadcast service is already running (or planned) on. For instance, in a country supporting only L-Band broadcasts, there will be a reduced incentive to implement circuitry for enabling e.g. VHF and UHF reception in receiving units because of the added cost it poses.

Second, choice of audiovisual codec technology may, or may not, be specified by the standard. If not one codec technology is required by the standard, different options are usually specified. However, most often the standard requires only one of these options to be chosen.

Third, the service provision layers (not specified by all standards), typically add support for DRM systems (enables service operators to protect content and enable payment-based services), and ESG (enabling the display of e.g. a program guide). Some standards define in detail one or multiple DRM and ESG systems (like FLO, CMMB and DVB-H), whilst others leave this optional (like T-DMB). A variation in either one of the above mentioned layers can thus render devices – whilst still conforming perfectly to the given standards specification – completely *non-interoperable*.

Incentives for Competitive Fragmentation

Although the consumer would benefit from accessing as large a selection of content as possible, a service operator may consider in its interest (depending on business model used) to lock consumers into its own service only. Locking consumers into a given service for competitive reasons (and conversely locking competing service providers "out") can implicitly be done by using any of the

Figure 2. Generic mobile TV standard carrier stack (sequence illustrational)

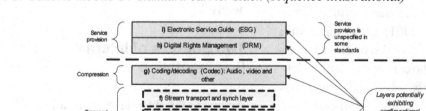

layers of configurational fragmentation above. However, if services are equally configured and actually interoperable, non-interoperability with other services can still be controlled by means of the DRM system, and/or other specific adaptations to the handset.

DVB-H

Whilst the *DVB Project* (the industry consortium responsible for the DVB family of standards) since 1998 had been experimenting with mobile reception of the DTT standard DVB-T, this was found inadequate for needs of the mobile environment with regards to reception quality and battery life. As a consequence, in 2002 a DVB working group was incepted with the specific mandate of making a standard suitable for the mobile environment. Work concluded in late 2004 with the finished DVB-H standard (ETSI, 2004; Faria, Henriksson, Stare, & Talmola, 2006).

Sources of Internal Fragmentation

DVB-H emerged as the product of a focused standardisation effort. A great deal of flexibility was intentionally embedded in the standard from the start. DVB-H was explicitly designed to be used for UHF radio frequencies (but could technically also be applied in VHF and L-Band) (ETSI, 2009). The core carrier-level standard (ETSI EN 302 304) in isolation, however, specifies only layer *b)* to *e)* in of the stack in Figure 2 (ETSI, 2004), and makes no recommendations for spectrum deployment. Thus, whilst the carrier in isolation is coherent and with no endogenous possibilities for configurational fragmentation, any real-life DVB-H implementation would need specific decisions on what radio spectrum to deploy in and how to implement the higher layers – also deciding on the stream transport and codec layers being a minimum for providing a mobile TV service. Although formally being exogenous to the DVB-H radio carrier, it is thus not meaningful with regards to achieving interoperability to see DVB-H in isolation from the DVB Project's recommendations for the higher layers, specified by the "DVB-IPDC" standard (ETSI, 2007b; Faria et al., 2006).

Following DVB-IPDC, DVB-H gets a high degree of configurational flexibility. For video codec, it has two options: *MPEG-4 H.264/AVC* and *Microsoft VC-1* – and the standard specifically says that only one of the codecs has to be implemented by the receiving device (ETSI, 2007a). As for audio codecs, this flexibility is even greater. A valid implementation can use either one (or a combination) of the following codecs: *MPEG-4 (HE) AAC (v2)*, *3GPP AMR-WB+*, or *Dolby Digital AC-3/Enhanced AC-3* (ETSI, 2007a).

The DVB-IPDC specification (ETSI, 2007b) also describes a specific set and configurations of ESG (ETSI, 2010) and DRM (ETSI, 2007c) systems to be used. However, the *Open Mobile Alliance* (OMA - a standardisation consortium where the majority of actors are mobile operators from the telecommunications industry) has concurrently specified "OMA BCAST". Although having its roots in DVB-IPDC, this competing standard for the service provision layers offers alternative and predominantly non-compatible[5] DRM and ESG implementations: OMA DRM 2.0 (OMA, 2009a) and OMA BCAST ESG 1.0 (OMA, 2009b).

With multiple options at various layers, and no requirement to implement more than one option at any layer, there are many possibilities for creating non-interoperable devices that still perfectly comply with DVB-H as interface compatibility standard. With, as a minimum – but to illustrate a point – three frequency domains, two video and four audio codecs, DVB-H is *sui generis* possible to fragment into no less than 24 distinct and non-interoperable implementations – and adding the possibilities for using OMA BCAST as the service provision layer, this number is doubled.

Deployment and Internal Fragmentation

Most commercial deployments seen in Europe have in practice – despite the plethora of options in the standard at the radio and codec layers – used a pretty uniform setup with UHF radio spectrum deployment combined with H.264 video and (HE) AAC v2 audio coding (DVB-H.org, 2010). What is seen of internal fragmentation in DVB-H has taken place in the *service provision* layers. In 2006 to 2009 there was internal fragmentation between DVB-IPDC and OMA BCAST. The three services launched in Italy by respectively *3 Italia*, *TIM* and *Vodafone* all used the DVB-IPDC standard for service provision. However, most deployed services elsewhere – e.g. Finland, Switzerland, Austria and The Netherlands, used OMA BCAST. This meant that, in general, DVB-H devices bought in Italy could not be used for mobile TV reception when travelling to other countries using DVB-H.

However, one could assume that when all Italian services ran DVB-IPDC, it would be at least possible for consumers within Italy to enjoy offerings from competing operators running DVB-H. But competitive fragmentation stopped this. Apart from some shared content, consumers were locked into the channels that the service provider offered (La3tv, 2007).

An interesting observation is that the competitive fragmentation of DVB-H in Europe was reduced when *3 Italia* decided in 2008 to broadcast a set of channels free-to-air. Additionally, the configurational fragmentation was reduced when the same operator in 2009 upgraded its head-end equipment to be able to transmit a OMA BCAST-compatible service provision layer concurrently with its original DVB-IPDC services (Cable & Satellite International, 2009). Surprisingly, it seems that the OMA BCAST standard (and not the original DVB-IPDC standard) for ESG and DRM largely has won the service provision battle within DVB-H, as newer handsets, like e.g. the *Nokia*

N96 have been released supporting OMA BCAST only (Nokia, 2010), and traditional vendors of DVB-IPDC-only handsets are now supporting both standards (Samsung, 2008).

T-DMB

Rather than being the output of one working group, the T-DMB standard is the result of uncoordinated, distributed technological evolution. It uses the *Digital Audio Broadcasting* (DAB) system as the transmission layer. Whilst commercial deployments of T-DMB weren't seen before 2005, early experiments with multimedia broadcasting over DAB took place already in the early 1990ies at *Bosch* in Germany (Hallier, Lauterbach, & Unbehaun, 1994). Bosch evolved and refined their version of the system, and, taking advantage of concurrent advances within the *Motion Pictures Expert Group* (MPEG), presented in 1996 a solution based on DAB and streaming of multimedia content using the MPEG-2 suite of standards (Müller-Römer, 1997). The system was further elaborated by the concurrently emerging MPEG-4 codec standards, and in 2001 Bosch published the general architectural design for DMB (Grube, Siepen, Mittendorf, Boltz, & Srinivasan, 2001).

Sources of Internal Fragmentation

Bosch never commercialised their 2001 version. In 2002, however, a group of representatives from the South Korean *Electronics and Telecommunications Research Institute* (ETRI) met with Bosch in Germany and had the technology demonstrated (Tunze, 2005). Based on the general architecture of the Bosch design (DAB radio carrier, MPEG-2 transport stream and MPEG-4 codecs, specifically with H.264/AVC for video compression) they implemented a fully operational technology – later deployed commercially in 2005 as "T-DMB". ETRI did only minor alterations to the original

Bosch design. In fact, the only major difference is that they chose the *Bit-Sliced Arithmetic Coding* (BSAC) audio codec instead of the Bosch choice of *Advanced Audio Coding – Low Complexity* (AAC-LC). BSAC had some technological advantages over AAC-LC – but, another motivation was that Samsung held a significant amount of intellectual property rights (IPR) in BSAC (Telecoms Korea, 2006).

In early 2005, ETRI submitted its domestic version of T-DMB with BSAC to ETSI (which by then already had been ratified as a domestic South Korean standard by the national standards organisation *Telecommunications Technology Association*). Importantly, in the meantime, the *High Efficiency* AAC v2 audio codec had matured within the MPEG. HE-AAC v2 is technologically superior to both BSAC and AAC-LC, and several actors involved in the ETSI standardisation process strongly recommended it to be a part of the ETSI-ratified version of T-DMB. The resulting ETSI-approved T-DMB standard thus had two different "profiles"; one using BSAC ("Profile 1") and the other using the full HE-AAC v2 ("Profile 2") (ETSI, 2005a, 2005b), endogenously being a source for configurational fragmentation.

As T-DMB does not specify any technologies in the service provision layer and does not include IP encapsulation of content, it has lower design complexity than e.g. DVB-H. However, unlike DVB-H, T-DMB is readily deployed in all three relevant radio frequency bands: VHF, UHF and L-Band –VHF and L-Band being the ones typically used in practice. This is also an endogenous source for fragmentation in T-DMB, as VHF, UHF and L-Band are all specified as options in DAB (ETSI, 2006), cited by T-DMB (ETSI, 2005a). From configurational flexibility, it is thus theoretically possible to fragment T-DMB into six non-interoperable standards (two different audio codec profiles, and three different spectrum bands.)

Deployment and Internal Fragmentation

Despite T-DMB's limited configurational flexibility compared to DVB-H, in actual deployments it has seen considerable fragmentation. The first commercial installation of T-DMB in South Korea used Profile 1 (BSAC) in VHF. The 2006 deployment in Germany by *Mobiles Fernsehen Deutschland*, however, used L-Band and Profile 2 (HE-AAC). The T-DMB service deployed in Beijing in 2006 used VHF and HE-AAC: the same configuration also used in the later 2009 deployment in Norway. Both the Chinese and Norwegian services were thus non-interoperable with typical handsets offered in South Korea. The impact on interoperability for the consumer varied. Most handsets sold in South Korea implemented only VHF and BSAC support. However, at the German L-Band launch, two devices were introduced: *Samsung SGH-P900* and *LG V9000*. The SGH-P900 supported only L-Band. The LG V9000, however, was a true multi-mode handset, supporting both L-Band and VHF, as well as HE-AAC v2 and BSAC (LG Mobile, 2005). This handset can thus be seen as an exception to the general observation that manufacturers prefer to support the lowest possible number of configurations needed for a market (as multi-mode support generally adds to unit price).

A COMPARISON

Table 1 holds a comparison of the theoretical, and actually observed internal fragmentation in the T-DMB and DVB-H standards. It should, however, be mentioned that the theoretical potential for fragmentation is a non-absolute number, and merely illustrational to indicate the potential for compliant, yet non-interoperable configurations of the standard. If potential fragmentation due to

Table 1. Potential and actually observed internal fragmentation due to configuration

	Potential for non-interoperable configurations of standard as full service	Observed internal fragmentation with non-interoperability
DVB-H	48	2 (OMA BCAST deployments vs. DVB-IPDC deployments)
T-DMB	6	3 (South Korean, German and Norwegian/Chinese deployments)

different ESG and DRM systems deployed within T-DMB was included, this would easily raise the number of potential non-interoperable configurations of T-DMB accordingly.

This table does not account for non-interoperability caused by competitive fragmentation, which was an important feature of the services deployed in Italy in 2006 – where handsets basically were locked in to the content of the respective operators. Because TIM and Vodafone are no longer promoting their Italian DVB-H service, they are not active market players in this respect – and, as mentioned above, this eliminates the impact of competitive fragmentation on new consumers. Another important aspect is that the business models of most mobile TV services operating today are not focusing primarily on subscription and payment-based services, but rather on providing content free-to-air and drawing revenues on advertising. Examples of such business models are the deployments in China (both with the CMMB and T-DMB standards), Japan (ISDB-T), Norway and South Korea (T-DMB).

The empirical picture interestingly shows that, whilst being a predominant problem in the early deployments in 2005-2006 and onwards, non-interoperability stemming from configurational and competitive sources seems to cease gradually for both T-DMB and DVB-H. This is due to a mix of explicit moves towards harmonisation, but just

as much trouble with revenue generation – leading to services going out of business. For DVB-H, 3 Italia's move towards concurrently supporting both the OMA BCAST and DVB-IPDC service provision layers directly facilitated harmonisation (especially as that the two other Italian DVB-IPDC operators stopped promoting DVB-H.) Internal fragmentation for T-DMB was reduced when the L-Band-based service of *Mobiles Fernsehen Deutschland* disbanded in 2008, however, the issues of non-interoperability between T-DMB Profile 1 and Profile 2 prevails for devices supporting only one of the profiles (typically the case for devices sold in South Korea).

DISCUSSION

The Tension between Flexibility and Interoperability

Internal fragmentation arises in the interplay between the actors that develop (often committees, but also companies in isolation) and implement (usually companies) standards. Committees (like those of the DVB Project) may intentionally embed endogenous configurational flexibility in the development of a standard, and market actors may exacerbate this fragmentation exogenously by using the standard in configurations not initially endorsed by the developers.

As mentioned with the example of DVB-S in the mid-1990s, it is interesting to note that endogenously inducing a possibility for configurational fragmentation has been an accepted strategy within the DVB Project to accommodate varying market requirements. This attitude prevailed into the new millennium when the commercial requirements for the (then emerging) DVB-H standard were elicited by a special task force within DVB. These requirements specifically stated, with the intention of facilitating rapid roll-out of services, that implementations would not have to support all configurations of the resulting standard (DVB Project, 2002).

After the deployment experiences with DVB-H, however, the official DVB Project development policy was changed. In early 2010, the "Rules and Procedures of the DVB Project" were expanded to specifically address endogenously induced internal fragmentation, stating "[i]n general, the preparation of a specification should provide a single technical solution for each function. A 'toolbox approach', allowing multiple technical solutions, is discouraged" (DVB Project, 2010, article 8.7). However, "[a] 'toolbox approach' may be considered if it allows flexibility without compromising interoperability or if responds to different requirements in different territories [...]" (DVB Project, 2010). This still ambivalent position captures the difficult balance between the need for interoperability, on one side, and the need for flexibility, on the other.

Notwithstanding such institutional arrangements by a standards consortium aimed at controlling endogenous configurability, there is in practice no effective way to protect against *exogenous* fragmentation caused by a standard being applied in varying implementations in the market. This is seen in the example of DVB-H where mobile operators with OMA BCAST added a *competing* standard for service provision, rather than the recommended DVB-IPDC. This illustrates that what ultimately conditions the potential for non-interoperability of a standard, is not in the control of a developing consortium (like the DVB Project) or the approving ratification agency (like ETSI). Rather, it can be decided exogenously in an *ex post* evolutionary fashion by a competing standards organisation (like OMA), and other market players.

A similarly unruly evolution was what caused configurational fragmentation within T-DMB. BSAC was chosen in deployments in the South Korean market, as BSAC in the early 2000s was an advanced and suitable codec technology – and a way to promote national IPR. However, when transferring T-DMB to Europe, it was natural to include HE-AAC v2 into this standard as well to reflect the latest advances for ensuing deployments. Interestingly, this shows how the variations in *exogenous* configuration of Bosch's DMB standard later would manifest as an *endogenous* source of fragmentation in the ETSI-ratified version of T-DMB.

The Impacts of Internal Fragmentation

The Effects of Non-Interoperability

The co-existence of interface compatibility and device non-interoperability has asymmetric impacts on various groups of market actors. On one side, at least in the short run, the equipment producers (of chipsets, handset and infrastructure) and IPR holders related to the architectural layers of the standard still unfragmented, will get a fair share, even if internal fragmentation is present at other layers. But the consumers are the ones that will suffer.

The first disadvantage is that user choice is limited to a set of service offerings provided by a single (or minimal set of) service provider(s). This can be further accentuated in the case of subscription-based mobile TV solutions which commonly are marketed with a handset bundling plan (often for as long as a year). If user choice is limited to a selection of channels offered by one provider, this conversely excludes that user from the selection of channels from another provider – some of, or all of, may be exclusive. This short-term consideration by service providers runs the risk of, in the longer run, making the mobile TV market less interesting and dynamic both for users and content providers, as *de facto* non-interoperability will cause users to know that they cannot access all possible content by means of the interface compatibility standard. Conversely, content providers cannot access all possible users.

The second disadvantage is that the user cannot expect the receiving terminal to work with services provided in other regions. Does it matter? On one hand it can be argued that as televised content often is localised (i.e. national language, special interest programming etc.), the lack of "roaming" features is less of an issue with reception of mobile television than it is with e.g. cellular phone service (where connection to the network gives approximately the same utility – save for costs – no matter where the connection is initiated.) On the other hand, international travellers can be expected to draw benefit from international news, sports and entertainment channels. So, in this respect, non-interoperability can still be a considerable disadvantage.

The Question of Economies of Scale

In the context of this paper, implications on economies of scale of internal standards fragmentation must be based on theorising. Effects would primarily depend on configurational (and not competitive) fragmentation. Here, there are two primary effects that affect economies of scale on the terminal side. Because different reception circuitry has to be utilised for the VHF, UHF and L-Band (and any multi-band solutions increase cost), configurational fragmentation at the radio frequency layer will likely be an impediment to economies of scale. However, circuitry dealing with demodulation and various forms of error coding can typically be shared in all configurations of a mobile TV standard, as can e.g. IP capsulation (when applicable, as with DVB-H) and the stream transport and synch layers (if the latter are embedded in hardware.) Codecs are, however, generally realised in dedicated units anyway (application-specific integrated circuits or modular software components) to be available to all applications needing codec functionality on a device, and would – at least from this architectural design consideration – not be subject to savings gained from integrating logic in a single chip. However, when licensing codec technologies,

the attractiveness of licensing terms in general increases with the volume of licenses requested (see e.g., MPEGLA, 2010), so savings benefiting economies of scale would theoretically follow from lack of fragmentation also here.

Whilst the strongest possibilities for economies of scale typically can be achieved when a limited number of competing producers manufacture large amounts of a single chipset dedicated to a single configuration (preferably combined with mature and stable implementations of codecs, ESG and DRM systems), multi-mode handsets will in general be more expensive. Depending on the layers in question, multi-mode approaches can require more chips (or more complex versions of the chipsets already present), and even additional antennas. Second, especially if multiple codecs, DRM and/or ESG is to be supported, all else being equal the increased total licensing costs for applicable IPR will typically increase the final product's price.

Implications for Research, Policy, and Practice

Research

That the claim "compatible with standard S" is not synonymous with the claim "interoperable with all other devices implementing standard S", requires researchers to work towards more precise definitions and pursue in-depth examination of standards. As the empirical example of this paper illustrates, in the presence of internal fragmentation, the mere reference to a standard easily becomes ambiguous in the presence of internal fragmentation – and it follows that interoperability issues aren't necessarily resolved by simply selecting "one" standard. With respect to a precise specification of interoperability, any reference to the standard "itself" becomes inadequate – literally only the semantic tip of an iceberg which may hold potential for significant configurational and/or competitive standards fragmentation. For the historically observed fragmentation within DVB-H, this is illustrated in Figure 3.

Rather, uniquely identifying a configuration of a standard that ensures interoperability (void of competitive fragmentation) means that explicit and unequivocal choices must be made for all layers where configurational flexibility of a standard can exist. Returning to the example of DVB-H, such a job has been done by the "Broadcast Mobile Convergence Forum" (BmcoForum), an organisation of companies with a common interest in commercialising media broadcasting technologies (BmcoForum, 2008). Adding to the complexity of the institutional ecology surrounding DVB-H, BmcoForum is an independent actor, not formally associated with the DVB Project, ETSI or OMA. BmcoForum has created a set of recommendations for the implementation of all layers of a DVB-H service, such as to maximise the probability of actual interoperability in deployed services (BmcoForum, 2010).

The BmcoForum recommendations could potentially be what DVB-H needs to stave off configurational fragmentation in the long run. However, the mere fact that the first version of these recommendations did not appear until late 2007 (BmcoForum, 2009, p. 13) – about 3 years after the DVB-H standard was initially published and in the midst of deployed internal fragmentation in DVB-H – emphasises the particular dynamism of the challenges facing researchers. To meaningfully theorise about interoperability, network effects and economies of scale, researchers need stable leverage points in terms of identified configurations. When both the potential for these configurations (in terms of options at the various layers) and the actual configurations preferred by the market are in a state of rapid flux, this requires the researcher to carefully investigate the empirical arena beyond mere nominal references to standards. And whilst competition within standards at first glance may exert many of the same characteristics of "normal" standards wars, the dynamics between competing groups in "internal standards wars" may be much more complex as interests can be conditioned by a delicate mix of competing interests at some layers of the standard (e.g. the service provision layers), and overlapping interests at other layers of the standard (e.g. a common radio layer).

Figure 3. Example of historical internal fragmentation observed in the service provision layers of DVB-H

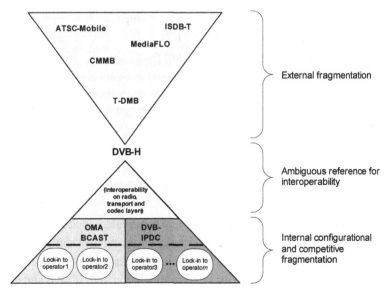

Policy

The findings of this paper seem to support David's view of standardisation as an "integral aspect of the process of technological development [...] that cannot be managed successfully without acknowledging its intrinsic uncertainties" (1995, p. 34). One such uncertainty is the potential internal fragmentation following endogenous and exogenous configurational flexibility of a single network standard. Policy for standardisation should thus not only be about harnessing and controlling *external* fragmentation – it should just as much be concerned about understanding, harnessing and controlling *internal* fragmentation. To this end, policy intervention aimed at setting a standard that is, or could be, internally fragmented, may not yield the desired results for the market and society at large. In 2006-08, the *European Union*'s Commissioner for *Information Society and Media*, Viviane Reding, ran a policy campaign voicing increasingly stronger support for DVB-H (Reding, 2007b). Noted rhetoric was such as "[mobile TV] could create economies of scale through the adoption of a general open standards policy which ensures interoperability" (Council of the European Union, 2007) and "[...] all EU Member States will have to support and encourage the use of DVB-H for the launch of mobile TV services, thus avoiding market fragmentation and allowing economies of scale" (Reding, 2007a). These representative quotes arguably implicitly created an impression that interoperability and economies of scale were to follow from the selection of a single interface compatibility standard.

The Commission's support of DVB-H apexed in 2008 when it was added to the official "List of standards and/or specifications for electronic networks, services and associated facilities and services" (European Commission, 2002b, 2008). In the context of policy vis-à-vis internal fragmentation, this addition provides an interesting example. This is because what was added was purely a reference to the DVB-H radio carrier

and transport layer (layers *b)* to *e)* in Figure 2) – that, as we know, definitively could not guarantee interoperability. No comments or configurational information was included (European Commission, 2008) – even if such additional information is not unusual with other standards present in the very same list. This omission could be understood in the light of the addition taking place in the midst of the internal fragmentation between DVB-IPDC and OMA BCAST. Despite this, the addition throws into stark relief the formal *raison d'être* of this list, which is stated as to "ensure interoperability of services and to improve freedom of choice for users" (European Commission, 2002a, p. 45).

Reviewing the received policy paradox pertaining to standardisation from the economic literature, one would, on one side, prefer intervention (be it on technological, economic and/or political grounds) before the market becomes too entrenched in one or more unwanted standards, whilst on the other side give the market time to potentially sort issues out, and if intervening, not intervening prematurely with the possible consequences of selecting inferior technology and/or causing unnecessary negative economic impacts for the parts of industry supporting the "losing" technology. This is as effective public policy intervention necessarily comes at a price. For example, the industrial ecologies with interests in a losing standard may risk that investments in IPR, infrastructures and technological expertise are partly or fully lost.

To warrant such losses for one side of the industry (which can be considerable), it is important that it is not merely the *production* side of the winning standard that benefits. Rather, it is the policymaker's obligation to consumers and society at large that the intervention actually leads to interoperability of services and freedom of choice for *users*. For policymakers to succeed and not create added confusion in this respect, not only choosing the "right" standard, but also opening the "black box" and acquiring knowledge of relevant configurational and competitive sources of internal fragmentation, are issues of rather great importance.

But how should one intervene in the possible presence of internal fragmentation – which for the remainder of the standard's lifecycle threatens to erode many of the positive effects typically associated with arriving at a single standard? As seen with DVB-H, the potential for different configurations continued to evolve long after the core standard was stabilised in late 2004, first with the matured DVB-IPDC specifications, then with OMA BCAST, and ultimately with the BmcoForum configurational profiles. If the dynamics of the DVB-H standardisation process, as a single and potentially anecdotal case, can be used to inform future policy development, it can possibly be inferred that to facilitate uniform adoption of *actually* interoperable standards through intervention in the face of internal fragmentation from configurational flexibility, policymakers must evolve their strategy from just considering the intervention/non-intervention dichotomy, to appreciate more complex trajectories of intervention based on dynamic learning throughout the process; hopefully combining the strengths of both "early" and "late" intervention in the standardisation process.

"Early" intervention could in this context be to early signal support for a single standard, and wait until internal fragmentation possibly resolves by itself (or not caring about internal fragmentation at all). "Late" intervention would conversely signal support for a single standard, but not before there exists a mature configuration of the standard that by a high degree of likelihood maximises interoperability at all layers (such late intervention may, of course, be far too late for the intervention to have any impact).

However, a combination of both early *and* late intervention selects a general standard at an early stage, waits for any variations of internal fragmentation to evolve (if not resolve), and, if necessary, intervenes again with a recommended configuration. Some element of dynamism and

possibility for policy learning is built into such a "policy oscillation" between the "poles of authoritarian regimentation and anarchic freedom" (David, 1995, p. 35), possibly with greater finesse (and accordingly, yields) than static, middle-ground compromises.

Practice

The need for multi-staged policy intervention could be diminished by removing sources for configurational flexibility as early as possible. A potential remedy is to specify a vertical minimum reference configuration crosscutting all layers that all devices claiming to implement the interface compatibility standard are required to support. Whilst this formally would remove the possibilities for internal configurational fragmentation of the standard, it could of course not guarantee against competitively induced non-interoperability. Additionally, when wanting to benefit from significant technological evolution (e.g. improved codecs and service provision layers), the need to keep backwards compatibility with a legacy reference implementation would add to the implementation complexity and cost.

In such a scenario, "fragmentation or not" becomes a question of for how long it is economically feasible to retain backwards compatibility. This is conditioned by the economic and technological specifics on a layer-by-layer basis. Taking the example of the DVB-H case, despite OMA BCAST and DVB-IPDC's formal incompatibility in the service provision layers, the service provision layers represent such a small amount of data that the cost of supporting both is negligible.

At e.g. the codec layer, however, backwards compatibility is usually much harder to realise. With a more efficient compression algorithm that is not backwards compatible, the only way to retain full interoperability with devices only supporting the "old" standard is to concurrently broadcast ("simulcast") the same services with both codecs. However, as the total amount of data is increased rather than decreased, this obviously voids any efficiency advantage associated with using the new, improved codec. Reaping benefit in such a case thus invariably means that non-interoperability would have to be permitted. Exemplified by the T-DMB case, this led to the mentioned internal fragmentation based on the non-interoperable BSAC- and HE-AAC v2-based "profiles".

A similar problem was solved differently in the case of T-DMB's audio-only cousin, DAB (at its 1995 release specified with the *MPEG-1 Layer 2* as audio codec.) In 2007 an improved version of DAB was ratified (ETSI, 2007d), with only HE-AAC v2 at the codec layer. In a laboratory setting, the efficiency increase was large, as the new codec allowed twice as many radio channels as the old in an equal slice of radio spectrum. But the already existing installed base of MPEG-1 Layer 2-based DAB devices could not decode the broadcasts based on the HE-AAC v2 configuration of DAB. It was thus decided to market the HE-AAC v2-based configuration as an entirely new standard: "DAB+". To cater to those already having bought DAB-only receivers, simulcasting of both DAB and DAB+ was necessary. This has, however, resulted in an embarrassing paradox: whilst digitalisation of radio was supposed to lead to more efficient use of radio spectrum, the current result is the diametrical opposite. A good illustration is the situation in Germany. In August 2010, 58% (83) of the DAB and 73% (8) of the DAB+ services are mere simulcasts of what is *already* is being broadcasted using FM or AM networks (WorldDMB, 2010).

For practitioners, the DAB/DAB+ example shows that strictly defining a vertical configuration for all layers in a stack is no "silver bullet" against non-interoperability. Whilst in the short run potentially stopping *internal* fragmentation, in the presence of attractive enough efficiency improvements in a given architectural layer of a technology, interoperability may not hold as fragmentation is manifested *externally* instead.

CONCLUSION

Rather than being a guarantor for interoperability, formal ratification in standardisation organisations may only be a discrete step in a prolonged, unpredictable trajectory of technological shaping, potentially including internal fragmentation. This does, however, not mean that the risk of internal fragmentation cannot be mitigated. Developers of standards ought to strive towards removing sources for configurational flexibility during development. To the extent multiple configurations are possible, a fully specified reference implementation clearly signalling minimum requirements for an interoperable service should ideally be provided at ratification time.

Internal fragmentation requires policymakers to be attentive to the nuances of actual technological evolution, also after ratification. Potential issues of fragmentation should be adequately investigated so that any intervention is unambiguous and meaningful. Finally, the concept of "internal fragmentation" potentially adds an important new dimension of (internal) conflict to traditional analysis of standards. An interesting venue of further research would therefore be to direct studies at exploring more in detail the dynamics of loyalty and rivalry between constellations of various interest groups "within" standards, particularly considering how these dynamics may, or may not, facilitate internal fragmentation.

ACKNOWLEDGMENT

My gratitudes to *Lindsay Cornell* (BBC Research and Development; WorldDMB Technical Committee Leader), *Carter Eltzroth* (DVB Project; Legal Director), *Stephan Gauch* (at the Chair of Innovation Economics, Berlin University of Technology), *Dr. Juhani Huttunen* (Nokia; former Vice-Chairman of DVB-CBMS, specifying DVB-IPDC), *Dr. James Stewart* (at the Institute for the Study of Science, Technology and Innovation, The University of Edinburgh), *Pekka Talmola* (Nokia; member of the original DVB-H Specification Group) and three anonymous reviewers for extremely useful comments on earlier versions of this paper. I am also very grateful to those that have provided important information along the way on key issues in T-DMB standardisation and deployments worldwide: *Gunnar Garfors* (Norwegian Broadcasting Corporation; President of the International DMB Advancement Group), *Jørn Jensen* (Norwegian Broadcasting Corporation; President of WorldDMB), *Markus Prosch* (Fraunhofer IIS; participant in the ETSI ratification process of T-DMB), *Thomas Wächter* (Media Broadcast GmbH) and *Hanns Wolter* (Club DAB Italia; WorldDMB Regulatory and Spectrum Committee Leader). Additionally, special thanks to *Dr. Jukka Henriksson* (Nokia; leader of the original DVB-H Specification Group) for the affluence of information provided and facilitation of contact with other key players in the DVB-H standardisation process.

REFERENCES

Arthur, W. B. (1989). Competing technologies, increasing returns, and lock-in by historical events. *The Economic Journal*, *99*(394), 116–131. doi:10.2307/2234208

Arthur, W. B. (1990). Positive feedbacks in the economy. *Scientific American*, *262*(2), 92–99. doi:10.1038/scientificamerican0290-92

Asami, H., & Sasaki, M. (2006). Outline of ISDB systems. *Proceedings of the IEEE*, *94*(1), 248–250. doi:10.1109/JPROC.2005.859690

ATSC. (2009). *Mobile DTV standard, part 1 – ATSC mobile digital television system*. Retrieved from http://www.atsc.org/cms/standards/a153/a_153-Part-1-2009.pdf

Bakhuizen, M., & Horn, U. (2005). Mobile broadcast/multicast in mobile networks. *Ericsson Review, 1*.

Besen, S. M. (1992). AM versus FM: The battle of the bands. *Industrial and Corporate Change*, *1*(2), 375–396. doi:10.1093/icc/1.2.375

Besen, S. M., & Farrell, J. (1994). Choosing how to compete: Strategies and tactics in standardization. *The Journal of Economic Perspectives*, *8*(2), 117–131. doi:10.1257/jep.8.2.117

BmcoForum. (2008). *The bmcoforum articles of association*. Retrieved from http://www.bmcoforum.org/fileadmin/user_upload/Forms/bmcoforum_Articles_2008_06_17_English.pdf

BmcoForum. (2009). *Recommendation for implementation profile: OMA BCAST system adaptation: IPDC over DVB-H*. Retrieved from http://www.bmcoforum.org/fileadmin/user_upload/Downloads/Implementation_profiles/bmcoforum_profile_-_DVB_Adaptation_V1.2_20090107-A_-_OMA_BCAST_V1.0.pdf

BmcoForum. (2010). *Profile documents, version 2.0*. Retrieved from http://www.bmcoforum.org/index.php?id=191

Cable & Satellite International. (2009). *3 Italia launches OMA BCAST service*. Retrieved from http://www.csimagazine.com/news-19-02-2009-oma.php

China Mobile Multimedia Broadcasting (CMMB). (2009). *List of promulgated industry standards*. Retrieved from http://www.cmmb.org.cn/knowledge/105/

Council of the European Union. (2007). *Draft council conclusions on "strengthening the internal market for mobile television (Mobile TV)" (15201/07)*. Retrieved from http://register.consilium.europa.eu/pdf/en/07/st14/st14398.en07.pdf

Crane, R. J. (1979). *The politics of international standards: France and the color TV war*. New York, NY: Ablex Publishing.

David, P. A. (1985). Clio and the economics of QWERTY. *The American Economic Review*, *75*(2), 332–337.

David, P. A. (1995). Standardization policies for network technologies: The flux between freedom and order revisited. In Hawkins, R., Mansell, R., & Skea, J. (Eds.), *Standards, innovation and competitiveness - The politics and economics of standards in natural and technical environments*. Aldershot, UK: Edward Elgar.

David, P. A., & Greenstein, S. (1990). The economics of compatibility standards: An introduction to recent research. *Economics of Innovation and New Technology*, *1*(1), 3–41. doi:10.1080/10438599000000002

DVB-H.org. (2010). *DVB-H global mobile TV: Services, trials & pilots*. Retrieved from http://www.dvb-h.org/services.htm

Egyedi, T. M. (2007). Experts on causes of incompatibility between standard-compliant products. In G. Doumeingts, J. Müller, G. Morel, & B. Vallespir, (Eds.), *Enterprise interoperability* (pp. 553–563). Berlin, Germany: Springer-Verlag. doi:10.1007/978-1-84628-714-5_51

Egyedi, T. M. (2007). Standard-compliant, but incompatible?! *Computer Standards & Interfaces*, *29*(6), 605–613. doi:10.1016/j.csi.2007.04.001

Egyedi, T. M., & Hudson, J. (2005). A standard's integrity: Can it be safeguarded? *IEEE Communications Magazine*, *43*(2), 151–155. doi:10.1109/MCOM.2005.1391516

Elsen, I., Hartung, F., Horn, U., Kampmann, M., & Peters, L. (2001). Streaming technology in 3G mobile communication systems. *IEEE Computer*, *34*(9), 46–52. doi:10.1109/2.947089

European Commission. (2002a, March 7). Directive 2002/21/EC of the European Parliament and of the council on a common regulatory framework for electronic communications networks and services (Framework Directive). *Official Journal of the European Communities, L108*, 33–50.

European Commission. (2002b). List of standards and/or specifications for electronic networks, services and associated facilities and services. *Official Journal of the European Communities, C331*, 36–49

European Commission. (2008, March 17). 2008/286/EC: Commission decision amending decision 2007/176/EC as regards the list of standards and/or specifications for electronic communications networks, services and associated facilities and services. *Official Journal of the European Union. L&C, L93*, 4.

European Telecommunications Standards Institute (ETSI). (1997). *EN 300 421 V1.1.2: Digital video broadcasting (DVB): Framing structure, channel coding and modulation for 11/12 GHz satellite services*. Sophia-Antipolis, France: European Telecommunications Standards Institute.

European Telecommunications Standards Institute (ETSI). (2004). *ETSI EN 302 304: Digital video broadcasting (DVB): Transmission system for handheld terminals (DVB-H)*. Sophia-Antipolis, France: European Telecommunications Standards Institute.

European Telecommunications Standards Institute (ETSI). (2005a). *ETSI TS 102 427: Digital audio broadcasting (DAB); Data broadcasting - MPEG-2 TS streaming.* Sophia-Antipolis, France: European Telecommunications Standards Institute.

European Telecommunications Standards Institute (ETSI). (2005b). *ETSI TS 102 428: Digital audio broadcasting (DAB); DMB video service; user application specification.* Sophia-Antipolis, France: European Telecommunications Standards Institute.

European Telecommunications Standards Institute (ETSI). (2006). *ETSI EN 300 401 V1.4.1: Radio broadcasting systems: Digital audio broadcasting (DAB) to mobile, portable and fixed receivers.* Sophia-Antipolis, France: European Telecommunications Standards Institute.

European Telecommunications Standards Institute (ETSI). (2007a). *ETSI TS 102 005 V1.3.1: Digital video broadcasting (DVB); Specification for the use of video and audio coding in DVB services delivered directly over IP protocols.* Sophia-Antipolis, France: European Telecommunications Standards Institute.

European Telecommunications Standards Institute (ETSI). (2007b). *ETSI TS 102 468 V1.1.1: Digital video broadcasting (DVB); IP datacast over DVB-H: Set of specifications for phase 1.* Sophia-Antipolis, France: European Telecommunications Standards Institute.

European Telecommunications Standards Institute (ETSI). (2007c). *ETSI TS 102 474 V1.1.1: Digital video broadcasting (DVB); IP datacast over DVB-H: Service purchase and protection.* Sophia-Antipolis, France: European Telecommunications Standards Institute.

European Telecommunications Standards Institute (ETSI). (2007d). *ETSI TS 102 563 V1.1.1: Digital audio broadcasting (DAB); transport of advanced audio coding (AAC) audio.* Sophia-Antipolis, France: European Telecommunications Standards Institute.

European Telecommunications Standards Institute (ETSI). (2009). *ETSI TR 102 377 V1.3.1: Digital video broadcasting (DVB); DVB-H implementation guidelines.* Sophia-Antipolis, France: European Telecommunications Standards Institute.

European Telecommunications Standards Institute (ETSI). (2010). *ETSI TS 102 471 V1.4.1: Digital video broadcasting (DVB); IP datacast over DVB-H: Electronic service guide (ESG).* Sophia-Antipolis, France: European Telecommunications Standards Institute.

Faria, G., Henriksson, J. A., Stare, E., & Talmola, P. (2006). DVB-H: Digital broadcast services to handheld devices. *Proceedings of the IEEE, 94*(1), 194–209. doi:10.1109/JPROC.2005.861011

Farrell, J., & Saloner, G. (1985). Standardization, compatibility, and innovation. *The Rand Journal of Economics, 16*(1), 70–83. doi:10.2307/2555589

Farrell, J., & Saloner, G. (1986). Installed base and compatibility: Innovation, product preannouncements, and predation. *The American Economic Review, 76*(5), 940–955.

Fleck, J. (1995). Configurations and standardization. In Esser, J., Fleischmann, G., & Heimer, T. (Eds.), *Soziale und ökonomische Konflikte in Standardisierungsprozessen.* Frankfurt, Germany: Campus Verlag.

Fridenson, P. (1991). Selling the innovation: French and German color TV devices. *Business and Economic History. Second Series, 20,* 62–68.

Funk, J. L. (2002). *Global competition between and within standards: The case of mobile phones.* New York, NY: Palgrave MacMillan.

Grindley, P. (1995). Framework for standards strategy: Establishing standards and maximizing profits. In Grindley, P. (Ed.), *Standards strategy and policy: Cases and stories* (pp. 20–54). Oxford, UK: Oxford University Press. doi:10.1093/acpro f:oso/9780198288077.003.0002

Grube, M., Siepen, P., Mittendorf, C., Boltz, M., & Srinivasan, M. (2001). Applications of MPEG-4: Digital multimedia broadcasting. *IEEE Transactions on Consumer Electronics, 47*(3), 474–484. doi:10.1109/30.964136

Hallier, J., Lauterbach, T., & Unbehaun, M. (1994). Multimedia broadcasting to mobile, portable and fixed receivers using the Eureka 147 digital audio broadcasting system. In *Proceedings of the 5th IEEE International Symposium on Personal, Indoor and Mobile Radio Communications: Wireless Networks - Catching the Mobile Future.*

Hanseth, O. (2001). Gateways—Just as important as standards: How the Internet won the "religious war" over standards in Scandinavia. *Knowledge, Technology & Policy, 14*(3), 71–89. doi:10.1007/s12130-001-1017-2

Hughes, T. P. (1983). *Networks of power: Electrification in western society, 1880-1930.* Baltimore, MD: Johns Hopkins University Press.

Katz, M. L., & Shapiro, C. (1994). Systems competition and network effects. *The Journal of Economic Perspectives, 8*(2), 93–115. doi:10.1257/jep.8.2.93

Klopfenstein, B. C. (1989). The diffusion of the VCR in the United States. In M. R. Levy, (Ed.), *The VCR age: Home video and mass communication.* London, UK: Sage.

La3tv. (2007). *Samsung P910: Accendi il TVfonino.* Retrieved from http://www.la3tv.it/la3Live/HM/Offerta/TVfonini/Samsung_SGH-P910

Levy, D. A. L. (1997). The regulation of digital conditional access systems: A case study in European policy making. *Telecommunications Policy, 21*(7), 661–676. doi:10.1016/S0308-5961(97)00035-9

Liebowitz, S. J., & Margolis, S. E. (1990). The fable of the keys. *The Journal of Law & Economics, 33*, 1. doi:10.1086/467198

Liebowitz, S. J., & Margolis, S. E. (1995). Path dependence, lock-in, and history. *Journal of Law Economics and Organization, 11*(1), 205–226.

Lyytinen, K., & Fomin, V. V. (2002). Achieving high momentum in the evolution of wireless infrastructures: The battle over the 1G solutions. *Telecommunications Policy, 26*(3), 149–170. doi:10.1016/S0308-5961(02)00006-X

Mobile, L. G. (2005). *Mobile meets TV: LG Mobile V9000* [Product Brochure]. San Diego, CA: LG Mobile.

MPEGLA. (2010). *Summary of AVC/H.264 license terms.* Retrieved from http://www.mpegla.com/main/programs/avc/Documents/AVC_Terms-Summary.pdf

Müller-Römer, F. (1997). *DAB progress report.* Retrieved from http://www.ebu.ch/en/technical/trev/trev_274-m_romer.pdf

Nokia. (2010). *Nokia N96 tech specs.* Retrieved from http://europe.nokia.com/find-products/devices/nokia-n96/technicalspecifications-nseries#tv-lt

Nolan, D. (1997). Bottlenecks in pay television: Impact on market development in Europe. *Telecommunications Policy, 21*(7), 597–610. doi:10.1016/S0308-5961(97)00037-2

Open Mobile Alliance (OMA). (2009a). *Releases - Mobile broadcast services V1.0*. Retrieved from http://www.openmobilealliance.org/Technical/release_program/bcast_v1_0.aspx

Open Mobile Alliance (OMA). (2009b). *Service guide for mobile broadcast services (1.0)*. Retrieved from http://www.openmobilealliance.org

Project, D. V. B. (2002). *DVB-Mobile commercial requirements CM391v5: DVB-CM ad-hoc group DVB-Mobile*. Retrieved from http://www.dvb.org/groups_modules/commercial_module/cmavc/index.xml?groupID=51

Project, D. V. B. (2010). *Rules and procedures of the DVB project (SB 1699 rev. 4)*. Retrieved from http://www.dvb.org/membership/mou/Rules-and-Procedures-of-the-DVB-Project.pdf

Reding, V. (2007a). *Commission strategy for mobile TV in Europe endorsed by member states*. Retrieved from http://www.europa.eu/rapid/pressReleasesAction.do?reference=IP/07/1815&format=HTML&aged=0&language=EN&guiLanguage=en

Reding, V. (2007b). *Mobile TV: The time to act is now*. Retrieved from http://www.europa.eu/rapid/pressReleasesAction.do?reference=SPEECH/07/154&format=HTML&aged=0&language=EN&guiLanguage=fr

Samsung. (2008). *Samsung introduces P960, the first mobile TV slider phone for Europe*. Retrieved from http://www.samsung.com/uk/news/presskitRead.do?news_seq=8460

Shiraishi, Y., & Hirota, A. (1978). Magnetic recording at video cassette recorder for home use. *IEEE Transactions on Magnetics, 14*(5), 318–320. doi:10.1109/TMAG.1978.1059827

Silberston, A. (1972). Economies of scale in theory and practice. *The Economic Journal, 82*(325), 369–391. doi:10.2307/2229943

Stango, V. (2004). The economics of standards wars. *Review of Network Economics, 3*(1), 1–19. doi:10.2202/1446-9022.1040

Steen, H. U. (2009). Technology convergence, market divergence: Fragmentation of standards in mobile digital broadcasting carriers. *Information Systems and E-Business Management, 7*(3), 319–345. doi:10.1007/s10257-008-0099-8

Stone, R. (2007). Notes from Region 2. *Journal of Contemporary European Studies, 15*(1), 5–14. doi:10.1080/14782800701273292

Telecommunications Industry Association (TIA). (2006). *TIA-1099: Forward link only air interface specification for terrestrial mobile multimedia multicast*. Arlington, VA: Telecommunications Industry Association.

Telecoms Korea. (2006). *Korea has 29% of terrestrial DMB patents*. Retrieved from http://www.telecomskorea.com/service-4855.html

Tunze, W. (2005). *The DMB story. Deutschland Online: Forum für Politik, Kultur und Wirtschaft*. Retrieved from http://old.magazine-deutschland.de/magazin/OZ-IFA_5-05_ENG_E4.php?&lang=eng&lang=eng&lang=eng

Valletti, T. M., & Cave, M. (1998). Competition in UK mobile communications. *Telecommunications Policy, 22*(2), 109–131. doi:10.1016/S0308-5961(97)00063-3

World, D. M. B. (2010). *Country information for DAB, DAB+ and DMB - Germany*. Retrieved from http://www.worlddab.org/country_information/germany

ENDNOTES

[1] Internal competition in standards is discussed by Funk (2002, pp. 246-258), however without addressing effects on internal fragmentation.

[2] Although not within the scope of this article, it should be noted at a general level that loss of compatibility can also be caused by sheer errors in the ways standards are developed (e.g. interpretational ambiguities in specifications or poor structure), which in turn may increase the possibility of non-interoperable implementations (see Egyedi, 2007).

[3] This introduced notion of "exogenous configurational flexibility" can be seen as a specific application of what Egyedi and Hudson earlier have referred to as the "embrace-and-extend" strategy (Egyedi, 2007; Egyedi & Hudson, 2005) of standards (for the purpose of adding new functionality with the intentional or unintentional result of rendering standards-compliant products non-interoperable), and also be viewed as a natural consequence of socially shaped technological configurations (Fleck, 1995, p. 60).

[4] Thanks to one of the anonymous reviewers for introducing this concept.

[5] OMA defines two independent service and content protection solution alternatives in their Service and Content Protection specification: "OMA BCAST DRM profile" (based on OMA DRM 2.0) and "OMA BCAST Smartcard profile". "OMA BCAST DRM profile" has its roots in "DVB IPDC 18Crypt", and are compatible. (Thanks to Dr. Juhani Huttunen for pointing this out.)

This work was previously published in the International Journal of IT Standards and Standardization Research (IJITSR), Volume 9, Issue 2, edited by Kai Jakobs, pp. 50-71, copyright 2011 by IGI Publishing (an imprint of IGI Global)

Section 3
Standards Education

Chapter 6
Implementing Standardization Education at the National Level

Henk J. de Vries
Erasmus University, The Netherlands

ABSTRACT

This paper explores how standardization education can be implemented at the national level. Previous studies form the main source for the paper. This research shows that implementation of standardization in the national education system requires policy at the national level, a long term investment in support, and cooperation between industry, standardization bodies, academia, other institutions involved in education, and government. The approach should combine bottom-up and top-down. The paper is new in combining previous findings to an underpinned recommendation on how to implement standardization education.

INTRODUCTION

Interest in standardization education is growing. In Indonesia, for instance, the number of universities cooperating with the Indonesian national standards body BSN to address standardization has increased from none in 2007 to 23 in 2010 (Odjar Ratna Komala, 2011). South Korea is at the forefront of implementing standardization education in academic curricula and does more than Europe as a whole (Choi, 2008, Czaya et al.,

2010). Starting from scratch in 2003 (KSA, 2003) Korea has managed to get standardization education implemented at several levels, in particular universities and elementary schools, amounting to 7,490, 10,486 and 9,503 students in 2008, 2009 and 2010, respectively. Standardization education is emerging in other Asian countries as well, both at the academic level and at lower levels including secondary and even elementary schools. Standardization education increases awareness of standards and standardization and prepares

DOI: 10.4018/978-1-4666-2160-2.ch006

people for jobs in which they have standards-related tasks. In this paper, we investigate what could be done at the national level to stimulate standardization education.

The need for education about standardization has been addressed in several studies (Verman, 1973; Korukawa 2005; de Vries, 2005; de Vries & Egyedi, 2007; Krechmer, 2007; Cooklev, 2010). Implementing standardization education is not easy and despite its recent growth, it is an exception rather than a rule that the topic of standardization is included in education. A combination of barriers has to be overcome. A first barrier relates to the image of standardization. Students may perceive standardization to be 'dull' and if it is the main topic of an elective course, they may choose another, seemingly more appealing course. A second barrier is related to teachers: they may be reluctant to address standardization, because 1) they may be afraid that the topic fails to attract students (this is related to the first barrier), 2) they are not familiar with the topic, 3) they are not aware of its importance, and/or 4) the curriculum is already overloaded. The situation would be different if teachers were required to focus on standardization, but who should convince those who determine curricula and define the final attainment level for students? Standards bodies, of course, are aware of the importance of standards and standardization because it is their core business but should they take initiatives to promote standardization education? What about industry and governments? What role should they play and how aware are they of the importance of standardization as such and standardization education in particular? Lack of awareness on their side may be a third barrier (de Vries et al., 2009).

The 2006 standardization education workshop organized by the International Cooperation for Education about Standardization (ICES) concluded that if standards bodies or other stakeholders take the initiative to promote standardization education, success of implementation depends on (1) national policy, (2) the availability of resources

at the national level, and (3) close cooperation between industry, standards bodies, academia, other organizations in the field of education, and government (de Vries & Egyedi, 2007). These elements will be addressed in the subsequent sections. The concluding section describes what steps could be taken to promote and implement standardization education.

NATIONAL POLICY

Developing and deploying a national standardization education strategy and policy is a prerequisite for a systematic national approach to standardization education (Choi et al., 2009; DeNardis & Levin, 2009). The creation of a national standardization education strategy in APEC member countries was stimulated by a decision taken at the 18th APEC Ministerial Meeting in Hanoi, Vietnam, in November 2006: 'The ministers of the Asia Pacific Economic Cooperation recognized the importance of standards education and encouraged their members to develop reference curricula and materials to address the significance of standards and conformance to trade facilitation in the region' (APEC, 2006). Following this decision, a project was set up and led by the Korean Standards Association (KSA) (Choi, 2008). It includes the development of curricula and teaching materials, and the training of teachers. Most APEC member countries now have a national standardization education strategy. This strategy can be broad (addressing many areas of education) or limited and it can be detailed (specifying exactly what will be done when by whom) or global. It seems that the broader and more detailed the strategy, the more standardization education activities are in place in a country (Choi et al., 2009; Choi & de Vries, 2011). At the European level, the European Commission 'encourages the Member states to improve the position of standardisation in education programmes and academic curricula, in order to familiarise students with the strategic benefits and challenges of standardisation, drawing on the expertise of standardisation bodies' (Council of the European Union, 2008). Referring to this resolution, the CEN/CENELEC/ETSI Joint Working group on Education about Standardization (Ketchell, 2010) is preparing a standardization education policy document which can serve as an example for national standardization education policies.

INVESTING IN ONGOING SUPPORT

However, a national strategy is not sufficient. Korean and Dutch examples show that a long-term investment in time (and thus money) is needed in the form of one or more dedicated people who actively approach and support schools in developing, implementing and maintaining education.

In the Korean case, the Korean Standards Association took the lead and managed to get education about standardization implemented in bachelor programs of engineering education all over the country. They established a Standards Education Development Committee composed of participating professors and lecturers. This committee networked with standards experts from various fields in the Republic of Korea and developed a curriculum and educational materials. The Korean government provided financial support (Lee, 2007). The personal efforts of a KSA staff member, Danbee Kim, seem to have been decisive for the success of the project.

The Dutch case did not focus on standardization education but on a similar topic: intellectual property rights (IPR) in higher professional education. This subject has now been integrated in several compulsory courses in higher professional education and elective courses have been developed. It all began when the patent office approached an institution for higher professional education a few kilometres from their office. They established contacts with teachers, one of whom was offered for an internship at the patent office. He became

the patent and IPR expert within his school and developed an elective course on patents together with patent office staff. The course is open to students from all technical disciplines. Other teachers were stimulated and started to introduce the topic into their courses. Starting with this one school, this approach was used at other schools of higher professional education in the country and 100% coverage has been achieved. The patent office stays in touch with the schools to increase awareness of the topic and its importance. It does so by arranging guest lectures, and providing teaching materials co-developed with teachers, exam questions, access to the patent database, and advice about how to include the topic in the final attainment level students should reach when leaving the school. The patent office is also in close contact with school boards, the national association of schools, and the national association of engineers. Moreover, there is a link to the education officer of the FME Association, the largest organization in the Netherlands representing employers and businesses in the technology sector. To enable these activities, the patent office has a dedicated officer for higher professional education available. From this level of education, the patent office has expanded its activities to a higher level (universities) and a lower level of technical education (intermediate technical schools) for which staff capacity is also available. As a governmental agency, the patent office is funded for these tasks by the national government (de Vries, 2003, pp. 14-15) (http://www.octrooicentrum.nl/index.php/Producten-en-diensten/onderwijsmateriaal12.html).

The Korean and Dutch examples and the literature show the following typical elements of a successful national approach:

- An inventory of needs for education (de Vries & Egyedi, 2007)
- A steering group in which the most important stakeholders are represented (industry, standards bodies, government, organizations in the field of education)

- An action plan
- One or more dedicated staff members who are available for a period of years
- Funding for salaries and other costs
- Development of curricula and materials
- A train-the-teachers programme
- Promotional activities

Activities can start with one or a few teachers from one or a few schools and from there expand to a growing number of schools. Additionally, an approach for teaching practitioners is needed (Choi & De Vries, 2011; Giossi, 2010).

BRIDGING FIVE WORLDS: INDUSTRY, STANDARDIZATION BODIES, ACADEMIA, OTHER INSTITUTIONS FOR EDUCATION, AND GOVERNMENT

A third requirement for successful implementation of standardization education is to bridge five worlds that are all involved in some way with standardization but are not always aware of each others' interests and capacities: industry, standards development organizations, academia, other institutions for education, and government. At the end of the day, industry and other stakeholders need employees' awareness of standards and standardization, and industry, government, standards development organization and other organizations need qualified people to do standards-related tasks. Academic and other education is needed to provide this qualification.

Standardization can be seen as a discipline for which education is needed (Verman, 1973; de Vries, 2002). But is it a discipline? 'Standards and standardization have yet to reach the status of an academic discipline in their own right, while on the other hand they cannot be classified under one of the accepted academic disciplines, such as engineering or social sciences' (Hesser, 1997, p. 3). De Vries (1999) elaborates the idea of stan-

dardization as a discipline using the periods in the development of a scientific discipline developed by Kuhn (1962). The current trend to pay more attention to standardization education (Kurokawa, 2005; de Vries & Egyedi; 2007) should be seen as a normal step in the development of standardization into a more mature discipline (de Vries, 2002). A discipline needs professionals with professional education, and professional and scientific journals publishing results of illustrative best practice cases and scientific research.

Industry

The need for standardization education in industry is latent rather than manifest. Take the example of industry participants in international standardization. Research has revealed more than a hundred factors that contribute to successful participation in international standardization committees (Brons, 2007). Most participants in international standardization are not aware of these factors. They spend several days or weeks a year in standardization activities and have the illusion they are doing a good job but are not aware that their efforts could be much more effective.

A professional community is needed to enhance professionalization of standards experts in industry. The national members of the International Federation of Standards Users IFAN, such as the Standards Engineering Society SES in the United States and Canada, form such communities where standards experts can share knowledge and experience. However, we can observe a paradoxical situation. Membership in both IFAN and most national standards user's organizations, except in some Asian countries, has decreased recently although the importance of standards and standardization has increased (de Vries, 1999; Kurokawa, 2005; Swann, 2010). How can this paradox be explained? Traditionally, the members of these national organizations are managers of standardization departments in large companies or standards experts in medium-sized companies (Adolphi, 1997) and thus they are not only standards users (who use standards for their products, services, processes, etc.) but also standards developers (developers of company standards for use within their company or participants in standardization committees at the national or international level, in formal standards bodies or in industry consortia). However, many companies have eliminated standardization departments or reduced the number of staff. Reasons for this reduction include:

- Lack of awareness of the strategic importance of standardization.
- Standardization has an image problem. 'In Japan, there is a tendency for standardization personnel not to be assigned important roles in organizations, even in industries where standards are emphasized' (Kurokawa, 2005, p. 41). It is the author's experience that the same applies in other countries.
- Staff cost as a percentage of total cost has increased because the cost of machines and other equipment has decreased.
- Standardization requires a medium to long-term business perspective because standards, by definition, "freeze" a specification for a certain period of time until a new standard is developed, which may take several years. Cost precedes benefits. The growing emphasis on short-time financial returns makes it easy to justify cuts of standards-related activities.
- More standards-related tasks are being outsourced, e.g. updating the standards collection to a standardization body or a company.

These reasons, in particular the first one, provide a further underpinning of the need to address standards in technical but also in business education. However, the current under-evaluation of standards and standardization hinders the initiation

of standardization education activities. What is needed is a clear and strong signal from industry that such education is needed. However, as long as industry and its associations lack awareness of the importance of standardization, this is not likely to happen. So to a certain extent there is a vicious circle. This could be broken by highlighting cases of companies that have managed to gain a competitive advantage by using standards or by being involved in standardization. For example, the German ISO member DIN presents an annual award for the best entries demonstrating the benefits of standardization (Deutsches Institut für Normung, 2010).

If companies recruit fewer standards experts whereas standards and standardization are becoming more important, there should be a market for intermediary parties such as trade associations or consultancy firms to support companies in standards activities. Perhaps future standards experts will no longer be recruited by companies but by these intermediary parties instead. However, a mixed situation is more plausible, with big companies having their own experts and SMEs relying more on external advice (de Vries et al., 2009) and both companies and intermediaries represented in national associations of standards experts.

More about industry needs for standardization education can be found in Kurokawa (2005) and De Vries and Egyedi (2007). They conclude that general education should provide awareness about standards and standardization. This awareness should enable graduates, once they have a job in industry or in another sector, to recognize if they need further education. Additionally, regular education may prepare students, in particular in technical, business and economic and law studies, for their future jobs by teaching more than just awareness. And last but not least, thorough academic education is needed to prepare people who can improve the current standardization system and to further develop standardization as a discipline.

A few examples show that industry has taken initiative to stimulate standardization education. At the international level, the initiative to create the International Cooperation for Education about Standardization ICES was taken by industry (John Hill, Sun Microsystems, USA and Toshiaki Kurokawa, CSK Corporation, Japan). The International Federation of Standards Users IFAN has established a working group to stimulate standardization education. At the European level, Orgalime (European Engineering Industries Association) has emphasized the need for standardization education in policy papers (Orgalime, 2010a; Orgalime, 2010b). In the Netherlands, the FME Association, representing companies in the technology industry, has developed activities to support education including a working group of teachers in higher professional education. The Association has also stimulated the inclusion of standardization in curricula via this group (de Vries, 2003). SES, the standards users organization in Canada and the US, offers an introduction course about standardization (http://www.ses-standards.org).

Standardization Bodies

Standards and standardization are the core business of standardization bodies, so one would expect them to be centers of standardization expertise. In South Korea, it was the trade union of employees of KSA that saw the need to professionalize KSA staff and this is the reason that they initiated a workshop which formed the start of academic standardization education activities (KSA, 2003). DIN staff are required to successfully follow standardization courses (Behrens, 2010). However, such recognition of the importance of real standardization expertise for standardization bodies is not widespread.

Part of the professionalization of international standardization could thus be to better educate technical officers of standardization bodies. The system of international standardization could be upgraded by granting ISO and IEC secretariats only to technical officers with a recognized diploma in standardization. This is self-evident in other professional areas from accountants to bus drivers but so far not required for experts who provide standardization services. A first step in this direction is the certification programme established by SES to recognize people who have demonstrated a high degree of professional competency in standardization (http://www.ses-standards.org).

Many standardization organizations provide standardization activities themselves, mostly for business people but sometimes also in regular education (Choi, 2008). The academic week organized by the international standardization organizations ISO, IEC and ITU (http://www.iso.org/sites/WSCAW2010/index.html), the ISO award for Standardization in higher Education (International Organization for Standardization, 2011), the IEC lecture series (IEC, 2005, 2007) and the ITU Kaleidoscope conferences (http://www.itu.int/ITU-T/uni/kaleidoscope) are examples of how international standards bodies reach out to the academic community. National standards bodies have similar initiatives, for instance the Korean standards bodies, Korean Agency for Technology and Standards KATS and the Korean Standards Association KSA, established the Society for Standards and Standardization SSS, an academic association also open to practitioners. SSS took off in October 2010 with an international symposium on "Promotion of Research Activities on Standardization" (International Organization for Standardization, 2011).

Academia

A limited number of university professors pay attention to standardization in their education and research activities. In most cases, it is only one of the many topics they address. The number of standardization chairs is very limited. In terms of size of standardization staff, China Jiliang University in Hangzhou, winner of the first ISO Award on Higher Education in Standardization 2007, is the number one in the world (Song, 2007 and Yang, 2010). Until recently, the second largest standardization research group was at the Helmut Schmidt University in Hamburg (Hesser & Czaya, 1999). Prof. Blind's Chair at the Technical University in Berlin can be seen as a successor though its scope is broader than just standardization. In Japan, the Tokyo University of Agriculture and Technology addresses standardization in its Management of Technology programme (Furukawa, 2007; Nonaka, 2010). Other universities with standardization programs include the Belarussian National Technical University (Serenkov, 2010), the French Ecole Internationale des Sciences du Traitement de l'Information (Beauvais-Schwartz & Bousquet, 2010) and the French University of Technology of Compiègne (Caliste & Farges, 2007).

The situation in the Netherlands is unique and might serve as a benchmark for other countries. The Dutch ISO member, NEN, created an endowed chair in standardization at the Rotterdam School of Management (RSM), Erasmus University in 1994. "Endowed" means that NEN pays the professor, currently Prof. Dr. Knut Blind, for his appointment on a one-day-a-week basis. NEN provides additional funding so that he can receive support. Besides providing standardization education at its own university, the chair does the following activities:

- Supports standardization research and education at other universities (by organizing, maintaining and supporting an informal network of academic researchers in standardization encompassing nine of the 12 Dutch universities).The Netherlands Standardization Institute NEN, the Dutch Council for Accreditation RvA, the Dutch standards users organization NKN and the Dutch Ministry of Economic Affairs also participate in this network, which allows for informal links with major stakeholders.

- Gives "status" to the topic of standardization by the simple fact the university has an endowed chair.
- Further develops standardization as a scientific discipline.
- Participates in policy debates, for instance, on how to improve national environmental policy by making use of standards. In some cases, the opinion of a professor is more convincing than that of the general director of a standards body.

Additionally, RSM students help NEN with feasibility studies for new standardization topics which has resulted in new activities for NEN. Five students educated at RSM have been recruited by NEN. RSM advice has contributed to better stakeholder involvement in NEN, the number of participants has increased by 30% which has also contributed to NEN's healthy financial results (NEN, 2010). Apparently, NEN gets a return on its investment in the chair.

Establishing an academic community is essential primarily for research but also for education. The European Academy for Standardisation EURAS (http://www.euras.org) is an established community of standardization researchers although membership is open to non-academics as well. EURAS' main activity is its annual conference. A EURAS working group is currently investigating user needs for standardization education. The organization is represented in the CEN/CENELEC/EURAS Working Group on Education about Standardization, and is preparing a White Paper on Standardization Education. The SIIT conferences (Standardization and Innovation in Information Technology) form another place for standardization researchers to meet. Four countries have an academic community at the national level: Korea, the Netherlands, Bulgaria and Greece. The Bulgarian Union of Standardization for European Integration of the Republic of Bulgaria was established in 1991 to support the transition of Bulgaria from a planned/socialist economy to a market economy. Besides academic research and education, many seminars are organised for industry, in particular for SMEs (Ganeva et al., 2010). In Greece, Eneprot was established in 1997. This official organization focuses on academic research and education but supports SMEs. Eneprot took the initiative for a series of international conferences on "Standardization, Protypes and Quality: A means of Balkan Countries Collaboration" (Zachariadou et al., 2010).

Academic journals are another prerequisite for the development of a discipline. Standardization journals include the *EURAS Yearbook of Standardisation* (special issues of *Homo Oeconomicus*), the *International Journal of IT Standards and Standardization Research*, the *International Journal of Services and Standards*, and *Computer, Standards & Interfaces*. However, these journals have not yet achieved a scientific reputation in the set of management and economics journals needed to attract a sufficient number of excellent scientific contributions pushing the scientific progress in standardization research. Special issues on standardization of *Réseaux* (2000), *Knowledge, Technology, & Policy* (2001), *Telecommunications Policy* (2002), *MIS Quarterly* (2006), *Revue d'Économie Industrielle* (2006), *Organization* (2007), *Entreprises et Histoire* (2008), *Technology Analysis and Strategic Management* (2011) and *Organization Studies* (2011) have brought or are expected to bring standardization research to the attention of a broader academic audience. The more standardization is addressed in academic research, the more scientific researchers will be inclined to include it in their teaching activities.

Other Education Institutions

Standardization education is not only relevant at the academic level. In the Netherlands, the first case of successfully implementing education about IPRS was in higher professional education and this level was and is the first target group. From there, it was extended to senior secondary vocational education and universities. Also secondary schools are relevant and Thailand and Turkey are successful examples (Choi, 2008). Compared with universities, other schools have less freedom to address their preferred subjects. Therefore, including standardization in the final attainment levels will stimulate adoption. However, this can only be achieved by involving individual teachers and schools but also associations and other organizations active in the organization of education at the national level.

Government

National governments play different roles related to standards and standardization (De Vries, 1999). These include:

1 Supporting standardization as a part of their general role in stimulating business performance and international trade.
2 Creating a legal foundation for standardization – many countries have legislation setting criteria for the national standardization institute (Schepel, 2005).
3 Carrying out standardization activities themselves (in many countries, in particular in the former Soviet Union and in developing countries, the national standardization organisation is a governmental agency).
4 Supplementing, simplifying, or improving their legal system with standardization by making references to standards in laws.
5 Using standardization for specific public sector tasks (for instance, in the areas of public health, environmental protection, traffic infrastructure, army, and police. Then governmental interests are comparable to those of companies with a dominant market position or companies as main users).
6 Using standardization to improve their performance in areas that are not specifically governmental (for instance, procurement, IT systems, occupational health and safety of government workers).

In all these roles the government would benefit from better standardization education. Government officers in charge of roles 2, 3 and 4 need very specific standardization education. For role 1, standardization education is one of the policy instruments the government might use. Moreover, government has a seventh role: it is responsible for education. The government could include standardization knowledge in its criteria for accreditation of educational programs (Spivak & Kelly, 2003; Cooklev, 2010).

Many governments are insufficiently aware of these t roles and lack a policy that addresses them. An exception is the policy of the German government which focuses on the first role but also mentions all other roles except 3 (not applicable) and except the governmental responsibility for education (Die Bundesregierung, 2009).

THE PROCESS TOWARDS MORE STANDARDIZATION EDUCATION

We started this paper with three barriers for the implementation of standardization education. The first barrier might be the most difficult to overcome: how can we make the topic of standardization more appealing to students? Attractive teaching approaches and materials may partly solve this problem – and students may well pass on their enthusiasm to fellow students. De Vries and Egyedi (2007) have examined teaching materials and new materials and approaches including games are being developed. But this does not completely solve this problem. Elective courses focused on standardization only may lack appeal to students. Including it in other courses or as a compulsory part of the curriculum could be a solution.

The second barrier relates to teachers' willingness to include the topic in their courses. The Dutch and Korean examples suggest a combination of 'top-down' and 'bottom up'. The process is top-down in the sense that a decision is taken at central level, funding is available, and staff for coordination and support is available. The process

is bottom-up in the sense that individual teachers and their management need to be convinced that standardization is an important subject and should form part of the curriculum. This is not easy because the curricula are already full and the topic has to compete with other more established ones. It would be particularly convincing if industry and government acknowledged the importance and the need for standardization and strongly urged (or recommended) it be included in educational programs. This can be achieved by setting up a standardization education steering group at the national level in which industry, government, standards body and academia plus other educational institutions are represented. This group can also facilitate another 'top-down' process: to get standardization included in the official final attainment level for graduating students. This may not apply for universities, but probably does for lower levels of education. This requires considerable lobbying which will be easier if some education is in place already. Where applicable, reference to APEC or EU policies or to national standardization strategies (APEC, 2006; Choi et al., 2009; Council of the European Union, 2008) can be made. Participation in a national steering group increases awareness of the importance of standardization education for industry and government representatives – the third barrier. Their awareness and subsequent involvement is needed to gain momentum at the national level and this, in turn, may convince schools and their teachers to include standardization in the curriculum. Moreover, it may mobilize resources needed for the investment in standardization education.

Education is organized mainly at the national level so this is the natural level for starting initiatives. In some big countries, initiative taking could also occur at a regional level. Moreover, in a growing number of cases, national boundaries are no longer relevant – this applies to multinational companies and NGOs, and Internet communities. At the global level, ideas and approaches can be exchanged using the platform of the International Cooperation on Education about Standardization

ICES (http://www.standards-education.org). International standardization have an additional role in developing teaching materials and in providing assistance or even education in countries where no standardization education is in place yet (Gerundino, 2010).

In South Korea, the initiative for standardization education was taken by an unexpected stakeholder: a trade union. This shows that any party can take the initiative – the standards body, industry, government, a university or any other stakeholder. The role of the initiator is to involve other stakeholders. The APEC inventory shows that national standards bodies play an important role in each country that has successfully implemented standardization education (Choi, 2008). Next, resources are needed to employ dedicated people for some years, to develop educational materials and to organize train-the-trainer programs etc. These resources could come from industry, from standards bodies (with some delay, it will enhance their market position but cost precedes benefits), or from government (in the European case from the European Commission).

FUTURE RESEARCH

Meanwhile, initiatives for more standardization education are taken all over the world. Future research might make an inventory of initiatives and achievements and relate impact to measures taken. In-depth case studies might provide best practice examples. In particular, the Korean case deserves further investigation. Another opportunity is to benchmark the introduction of standardization education with other topics of education, such as the similar topic of IPR. Above we mentioned the example of IPR education in the Netherlands. Another country for such research is Japan where a steady increase in IPR education can be observed (Yamada, 2011). In such studies, authors might borrow from literature on 'educology' – the field of research that studies educational processes.

REFERENCES

Adolphi, H. (1997). *Strategische konzepte zur organisation der betrieblichen standardisierung.* Berlin, Germany: Beuth Verlag: DIN Normungskunde Band 38.

APEC. (2006). *The eighteenth APEC ministerial meeting joint statement.* Singapore: APEC.

Beauvais-Schwartz, N., & Bousquet, F. (2010). *France – Fostering competitive intelligence.* Retrieved from http://www.iso.org/iso/iso-focusplus_index/iso-focusplus_online-bonus-articles/the-2009-iso-award/2009-award_france.htm

Behrens, H. (2010, March 9). *Education about standardization – Competency of standards body staff.* Paper presented at the First Meeting of the CEN/CENELEC/ETSI Joint Working Group on Education about Standardization, Brussels, Belgium.

Brons, T. F. (2007). *Effective participation in formal standardization: A multinational perspective.* Rotterdam, The Netherlands: Rotterdam School of Management.

Caliste, J., & Farges, G. (2007). A French University: Encouraging hands-on experience. *ISO Focus, 4*(11), 13–14.

Choi, D. (Ed.). (2008). *APEC SCSC education guideline 1: Case studies of how to plan and implement standards education programs.* Singapore: Asia Pacific Economic Cooperation.

Choi, D., & de Vries, H. J. (2011). Standardization as emerging content in technology education. *International Journal of Technology and Design Education, 21*(1), 111–135. doi:10.1007/s10798-009-9110-z

Choi, D., de Vries, H. J., & Kim, D. (2009). Standards education policy development: Observations based on APEC research. *International Journal of IT Standards and Standardization Research, 7*(2), 23–42. doi:10.4018/jitsr.2009070103

Cooklev, T. (2010). The role of standards in engineering education. *International Journal of IT Standards and Standardization Research*, 8(1), 1–9. doi:10.4018/jitsr.2010120701

Council of the European Union. (2008, September 25). *Council conclusions on standardisation and innovation: 2891ˢᵗ competitiveness council meeting*. Brussels, Belgium: Council of the European Union.

Czaya, A., Egyedi, T., & Hesser, W. (2010, June 8-9). The current state of standardization education in Europe. In *Proceedings of the 7ᵗʰ International Conference on Standardization Protypes and Quality: A Means of Balkan Countries Collaboration*, Zlatibor, Serbia (pp. 85-90).

de Vries, H. J. (1999). *Standardization – A business approach to the role of national standardization organizations*. Boston, MA: Kluwer Academic.

de Vries, H. J. (2002). Standardization – Mapping a field of research. In S. Bollin, (Ed.), *The standards edge* (pp. 99–121). Ann Arbor, MI: Bollin Communications.

de Vries, H. J. (2003). *Kenbaarheid normalisatie en normen – Deelproject 9b HBO-onderwijs – Tussenrapportage*. Delft, The Netherlands: NEN.

de Vries, H. J., Blind, K., Mangelsdorf, A., Verheul, H., & van der Zwan, J. (2009). *SME access to European standardization - Enabling small and medium-sized enterprises to achieve greater benefit from standards and from involvement in standardization*. Brussels, Belgium: CEN and CENELEC.

de Vries, H. J., & Egyedi, T. M. (2007). Education about standardization – Recent findings. *International Journal of IT Standards and Standardization Research*, 5(2), 1–16. doi:10.4018/jitsr.2007070101

Denardis, L., & Levin, A. (2009). *Bridging the standardization gap – ITU-T research project: Measuring and reducing the standards gap*. Geneva, Switzerland: International Telecommunication Union.

Deutsches Institut für Normung. (2010). *DIN-Preise*. Retrieved from http://www.din.de/cmd?level=tpl-rubrik&menuid=47388&cmsareaid=47388&menurubricid=47468&cmsrubid=47468&languageid=de

Die Bundesregierung. (2009). *Normungspolitisches konzept der bundesregierung*. Berlin, Germany: Die Bundesregierung.

Furukawa, Y. (2007). A Japanese university: Educating standardization strategists in business. *ISO Focus*, 4(11), 15–16.

Ganeva, L., Sandalski, B., & Kotev, R. (2010, June 8-9). Contributions of the Bulgarian Union of Standardization for the European Integration of the Republic Bulgaria. In *Proceedings of the 7ᵗʰ International Conference on Standardization Protypes and Quality: A Means of Balkan Countries Collaboration*, Zlatibor, Serbia (pp. 29-38).

Gerundino, D. (2010). Standards in economic development and trade. *ISO Focus*, 1(1), 35.

Giossi, S., & Papastamatis, A. (2010, June 8-9). The effective teaching of standards in a lifelong learning world. In *Proceedings of the 7ᵗʰ International Conference on Standardization Protypes and Quality: A Means of Balkan Countries Collaboration*, Zlatibor, Serbia (pp. 118-125).

Hesser, W. (1997). *The need for interdisciplinary research on standardization*. Paper presented at the SCANCOR/SCORE Seminar on Standardization, Lund, Sweden.

Hesser, W., & Czaya, A. (1999). Standardization as a subject of study in higher education. *ISO Bulletin, 30*(6), 6–11.

IEC. (2005). *IEC lecture series – International standardization in business, industry, society and technology*. Geneva, Switzerland: International Electrotechnical Commission.

IEC. (2007). *IEC lecture series II – The importance of standards*. Geneva, Switzerland: International Electrotechnical Commission.

International Organization for Standardization. (2011). Society for standards and standardization launched. *ISO Focus, 2*(1), 36.

International Organization for Standardization. (2011). *The ISO 2011 award for higher education in standardization*. Geneva, Switzerland: International Organization for Standardization.

Ketchell, J. (2010, July 5-9) *Education about standardization – developing future generations of standardisers*. Paper presented at the WSC Academic Week, Geneva, Switzerland.

Krechmer, K. (2007). Teaching standards to engineers. *International Journal of IT Standards and Standardization Research, 5*(2), 1–12. doi:10.4018/jitsr.2007070102

KSA. (2003). *International workshop to develop a standardization education model*. Seoul, Korea: KSA.

Kuhn, T. (1962). *The structure of scientific revolutions*. Chicago, IL: University of Chicago Press.

Kurokawa, T. (2005). Developing human resources for international standards. *The Quarterly Review*, 17.

Lee, G. (2007). Universities in the Republic of Korea: Training the next generation of professionals. *ISO Focus, 4*(11), 17–18.

NEN. (2010). *Annual report 2009 – Crisis & control*. Delft, The Netherlands: NEN.

Nonaka, R. (2010, March 19-20). New approach on the pedagogy for standards education: A case of Applied Standards Education at TUAT. In *Proceedings of the International Symposium on Standardization Education and Research*, Hangzhou, China (pp. 156-167).

Odjar Ratna Komala, D. (2011, February 28). *Mechanics of developing a university level standards education program in Indonesia*. Paper presented at the PEC SCSC PAGE – ANSI CoE Workshop, Washington, DC.

Orgalime. (2010a). *Draft Orgalime comments on EP IMCO report on the future of European standardization*. Brussels, Belgium: Orgalime.

Orgalime. (2010b). *Review of the European standardization system*. Brussels, Belgium: Orgalime.

Schepel, H. (2005). *The constitution of private governance – Product standards in the regulation of integrating markets*. Portland, OR: Hart Publishing.

Serenkov, P. (2010). *Belarus – Training tomorrow's experts today*. Retrieved from http://www.iso.org/iso/iso-focus-plus_index/iso-focusplus_online-bonus-articles/the-2009-iso-award/2009-award_belarus.htm

Song, M. (2007). Guest view. *ISO Focus, 4*(11), 4–7.

Spivak, S. M., & Kelly, W. E. (2003). Introduce strategic standardization concepts during higher education studies … and reap the benefits! *ISO Bulletin, 34*(7), 22–24.

Swann, G. M. P. (2010). *The economics of standardization – An update report for the UK Department of Business, Innovation and Skills (BIS)*. London, UK: Innovation Economics Limited.

Verman, L. C. (1973). *Standardization – A new discipline*. Hamden, CT: Shoe String Press/Archon Books.

Yamada, H. (2011, February 28). *Development of education on standardization in Japan*. Paper presented at the PEC SCSC PAGE – ANSI CoE Workshop, Washington, DC.

Yang, Y. (2010). China institute of metrology's educational model for standardization. *China Standardization, 37*(1), 15–21.

Zachariadou, K., Zachariadis, A., & Latinopou-lou, M. (2010, June 8-9). Contributions of the Bulgarian Union of Standardization for the European Integration of the Republic Bulgaria. In *Proceedings of the 7th International Conference on Standardization Prototypes and Quality: A Means of Balkan Countries Collaboration*, Zlatibor, Serbia (pp. 78-82).

This work was previously published in the International Journal of IT Standards and Standardization Research (IJITSR), Volume 9, Issue 2, edited by Kai Jakobs, pp. 72-83, copyright 2011 by IGI Publishing (an imprint of IGI Global)

Chapter 7
The Role of Standards in Engineering Education

Todor Cooklev
Indiana University, USA & Purdue University Fort Wayne, USA

ABSTRACT

The role of standards is increasing, and as a result the role of education about standards should also increase. At the same time, there are a set of requirements—accreditation criteria—toward engineering programs. The close relationships between the accreditation criteria and standards education is not fully recognized, even by accreditation bodies and educators. The goal of this paper is to uncover these relationships. Furthermore, the paper establishes connections between other components of engineering education such as ethics, engineering design, labs, and integrated courses, on one hand and standards education on another. The conclusion from these relationships is that standards education is more important than previously realized. The paper also discusses how standards education can be incorporated in engineering and technical curricula.

INTRODUCTION

There is little doubt that various technical standards are the foundation of much of every part of the high-tech industry. A large part of the world trade today involves products that comply with at least one, and typically a much higher number of standards. For example, the US Congress has

estimated that standards and government technical regulations affect at least $7 trillion of world trade (U.S. House of Representatives, 2005). A study estimates the annual contribution of standards to the British economy at 3.6 billion euros (National Standardization Strategic Framework, 2008).

At the level of a single company, standards are a significant factor for business success in the long

DOI: 10.4018/978-1-4666-2160-2.ch007

term (De Vries, 2005). Some of the benefits from participation in standards-developing organization are higher market share, reduced cost and shorter time-to-market, higher visibility in the industry, and better opportunities to license intellectual property. Some companies do not sell products, but sell intellectual property. Intellectual property required for the implementation of a successful standard is generally very valuable and highly sought after by companies and businesses (Krechmer, 2007)

To remain competitive a growing number of nations have developed national standards strategies. These national standards strategies have recognized for a long time now the need to develop comprehensive standards education programs. More recently these national standards strategies have called for expanded and strengthened efforts to assist university and college programs in their efforts to educate students on standards. For example, the British National Standardization Strategic Framework specifically calls for embedding knowledge of standards into formal education curricula. The need for education about standards is discussed in several publications (De Vries, 2005; Krechmer, 2007).

Standards education has traditionally been done on the job using information on the web sites of national standards bodies and other courses and seminars generally in area of continuing education.

While continuing education activities are and will remain important, in this paper the focus is on regular education. All engineering, computing, and technology programs in the United States undergo a periodic accreditation review by the Accreditation Board for Engineering and Technology (ABET).

In the General Criteria (ABET, 2006), Criterion 5 regarding the Curriculum requires that

"Students must be prepared for engineering practice through a curriculum culminating in a major design experience based on the knowledge and skills acquired in earlier course work and incorporating appropriate engineering standards and multiple realistic constraints." As a result of these initiatives, the American National Standards Institute (ANSI) and the IEEE established committees on standards education with one of their charges to support and assist engineering and technology programs in standards education (Kelly, Bickart, & Forselius, 2006).

The accreditation criteria toward technology programs include "competence in the use of standard design practices, tools, techniques, and computer hardware and software" and "technical expertise in industry standards".

It should be noted that the accreditation requirements towards computing programs are somewhat different. ABET requires students of information technology programs to have "understanding of best practices and standards and their applications", but there is no similar explicit requirement towards students in computer science and information systems programs.

It should be noted that the above-mentioned Criterion 5 appears somewhat ambiguous: 'appropriate engineering standards' does not mean following proper engineering practices, but it actually means 'appropriate technical standards'. Furthermore the criterion does not fully describe to what extent should standards be incorporated, and more importantly does not describe how can the accreditation requirements be satisfied. The Institute of Electrical and Electronic Engineers (IEEE) is a major international standards developer and has been playing an important role in electrical and computer engineering education. In an attempt to complement the ABET requirements, the IEEE Standards Education Committee (SEC), has been trying to determine what should electrical and computer engineering students know about standards (IEEE Standards in Education Committee, 2008).

Although ABET criteria are specifically for the United States, global expectations with respect to culminating capstone projects in engineering, computing, and technology education tend to mirror the ABET expectations on global, economic, societal, and cultural issues. In fact, it should be noted that the United States does not appear to be in a leading position with respect to standards education. As reported in (Kelly, Bickart, & Forselius, 2006), the Canadian accreditation requirements (Canadian Engineering Accreditation Board, 2007a) and (Canadian Engineering Accreditation Board, 2007b) are even stronger. The Canadian Engineering Commission Accreditation Criteria requires engineering programs to participate in "multi-stakeholder forums for the development of technical standards, codes, regulations or guidelines." Canadian engineering colleges are asked to provide information "relating to staff participation in standards developing organizations at the national or international level. There is no comparable ABET requirement towards engineering programs.

Furthermore, as reported in De Vries and Egyedi (2007) incorporating standards in regular education courses has been much more actively accomplished in countries such as Korea and China and much less in the United States, with Europe being in the middle. The comprehensive Korean and Chinese programs have started off by targeting students of engineering.

While the importance of including standards in the education has been recognized, it should be noted that little has been reported about teaching standards. Some authors such as Krechmer (2007) discuss standards education, but generally do not discuss in detail why standards education is important beyond the obvious desire to prepare better the students for industry. Little, if anything, has been published on the deeper connection between accreditation requirements and engineering, computing, and technology education on one hand, and standards education on another. This is the contribution of this paper.

CHALLENGES TO STANDARDS EDUCATION

There are several significant challenges to standards education. A major challenge is the fact that in many cases the educators themselves are not familiar with standards and their role. Many engineering educators assume that standards education belongs only to the area of continuing education. A recent IEEE survey reports (ICES, 2008) that about 450 engineering schools worldwide have full access to IEEE standards through the IEEE/IET Electronic Library, but only about 10 schools make use of this feature. Another survey (Center for Global Standards Analysis, 2004) concluded that schools of engineering in the USA are largely unaware of the importance of standards and are not even trying to educate students about technical standards. Results presented at the ICES Workshop in 2008 show that most undergraduate students in the US have never read or used a standard.

Furthermore, in many cases, engineering educators wrongly assume that standards education is concerned with standards *about* education, not education about technical standards. In other words standards education should begin with educating the educators.

This suggests that the ABET criteria with respect to "engineering standards" do appear somewhat vague and therefore difficult to enforce. A clear accreditation requirement will translate into sections in engineering textbooks.

Many technical jobs list familiarity and experience with certain technical standards as a requirement. Such job announcements motivate students to learn more about the standards in their relevant areas. However standards are difficult to understand and apply for the following reasons:

1.   Standards are written in a formal language, which is very difficult to read and understand. This formal language is the reason why some

consider standards boring. The complexity of the technology compounds this difficulty.

2. The amount of material to learn is very significant. Every year, in every technical area, hundreds, if not thousands, of pages of new standards are being published.

3. Standards change and evolve rapidly. In fact standards evolve more rapidly than the underlying technical area.

4. Standards have inter-disciplinary nature. They often require expertise in more than one technical area. In addition, knowledge of and use of standards also requires understanding of issues such as government regulations, ethics, intellectual property, etc. However, Issues such as ethical and societal constraints maybe absent from engineering curricula or at best considered secondary.

As discussed here, two sets of reasons why standards education is important emerge from the above challenges. Knowledge of standards and ability to apply them is part of the "hard skills" and therefore very important. The second set of reasons is related to the so-called "soft" or professional skills. Within the hard skills, standards education has important connections to topics such as engineering design, laboratory instruction, and integrated courses. The purpose of this paper is to discuss these connections.

STANDARDS EDUCATION AND THE ACCREDITATION REQUIREMENTS TOWARDS ENGINEERING PROGRAMS

The major requirements towards engineering education have seen several major changes. Historically engineering education was focused more on practice. World War II and the ensuring Cold War were significant stimuli for unprecedented advances in science and technology. After the so-called Grinter report (Grinter, 1956), the focus of engineering education shifted towards strengthening education in mathematics and theoretical fundamentals. Knowing theory was considered paramount, and practice was viewed as less important or at least something that can be learned quickly on the job. This approach gave a solid theoretical foundation to engineers, but has the drawback that many students upon graduation may be perceived as being unable to practice in industry. The academic response has been the inclusion of a capstone design project in the curriculum.

ABET requires standards to be used in the culminating design experience or capstone course. However, this paper proposes that there are deeper connections between standards education and the ABET's requirements. ABET's Criterion 3 on Program Outcomes for engineering (ABET, 2006) requires that students attain:

a. An ability to apply knowledge of mathematics, science, and engineering

b. An ability to design and conduct experiments, as well as to analyze and interpret data

c. An ability to design a system, component, or process to meet desired needs within realistic constraints such as economic, environmental, social, political, ethical, health and safety, manufacturability, and sustainability

d. An ability to function on multidisciplinary teams

e. An ability to identify, formulate, and solve engineering problems

f. An understanding of professional and ethical responsibility

g. An ability to communicate effectively

h. The broad education necessary to understand the impact of engineering solutions in a global, economic, environmental, and societal context

i. A recognition of the need for, and an ability to engage in life-long learning

j. A knowledge of contemporary issues

k.   An ability to use the techniques, skills, and modern engineering tools necessary for engineering practice.

All 2,500 accredited engineering programs in the United States must demonstrate that their students achieve these attributes. Note that Criterion 3 has two sets of requirements - hard skills (items (a), (b), (c), (e), and (k)) and "soft" or professional skills (items (d), (f), (g), (h), (i), and (j)) (Shuman, Besterfield-Sacre, & McGourty, 2005).

Laboratory instruction is an important component of engineering education, although not specifically addressed by the accreditation criteria. Laboratories at educational institutions can be research and educational. In educational laboratories the students learn things which are already known. In research laboratories novelties are discovered and new features are devised. Laboratory exercises involving technical standards have a place in both research and educational laboratories. Furthermore, there are two main types of labs: computer simulation-based and hardware-based. Both can be used in education about standards.

Another area of research in engineering education that has been proposed is integrated or multidisciplinary courses (Froyd & Ohland, 2005). Integrated courses are better suited to complex systems, which engineering graduates are likely to encounter. Still, very little research has been made in this area and few integrated courses have been developed. Most faculty are not experts in more than one technical area and, as a result, do not offer integrated courses. It can be noted that because of their multidisciplinary nature standards naturally establish connections among different science and engineering courses and therefore are very suitable to be used as integrated courses or as the foundation of integrated courses.

As was discussed in the Introduction, knowledge of the standards and ability to use these standards are required from engineering graduates as part of the "hard skills". However, equally importantly, through standards engineering students

can learn valuable "soft", also called "professional" skills.

These professional skills have been another area of reform in engineering education since the 1990s (Smerdon, 2000). American Society for Engineering Education (ASEE)'s report (Augustine & Vest, 1994) stated that engineering education must provide the societal context of engineering. The NSF's complementary report emphasized environmental, political, social, legal and ethical issues (National Science Foundation, 1995). These professional skills have been required by ABET for over ten years now, and in the last ten years, if anything, their importance has grown. Some authors have proposed that the mastery of professional skills combined with an ability to innovate will add sufficient value to U.S. engineering graduates in the twenty-first century (Smerdon, 2000; Shuman, Besterfield-Sacre, & McGourty, 2005). While educators recognize their importance, teaching these professional skills continues to be a challenge for engineering schools worldwide.

It is well worth noting that knowledge and application of standards is an evidence of most of the above requirements. Regarding requirements (f), (h), and (j), there are few, if any, engineering courses, where the issues of professional and ethical responsibility, the impact of engineering solutions in a global context, and knowledge of contemporary issues are so prominent and are interwoven with the technical content.

The need to integrate some form of ethics instruction in the engineering curriculum is no longer debated (Fleddermann, 2000). At present, for the most part, incorporating ethics into engineering education is done by emphasizing the importance of "public safety" and the ethical dilemmas posed by conflicts between the business interests of a private enterprise and the public interests. Note that the ABET criteria require *knowledge or awareness,* not particular *values* or *beliefs.* Standards education courses include topics such as standardization bodies, government regulations, and intellectual property policy, making them a very appropriate vehicle for integration of ethics into the curriculum.

Technical standards are documents that define the solution of complex technical problems taking into account all economic, ethical, and societal constraints. Therefore standards (including codes, regulations, etc.) reflect society's requirements and expectations with respect to products, processes, and services—and, consequently, they represent, at least in part, the "societal context" (as found in Outcome h) for the design, development, and deployment of products, processes, and services. Furthermore, since many standards are increasingly global—at least, international—in their adoption, they also help satisfy the "global context" set forth in Outcome h.

The necessity for lifelong learning (item (i)) is better communicated by standards education than by traditional engineering courses. The reason is that standards evolve more rapidly than the fundamentals of the relevant technical area, taught in other courses. For many professionals a major reason to be engaged in lifelong learning is to gain knowledge about certain standards. To reinforce the need for lifelong learning (as well as other valuable concepts), standards education courses emphasize how the standards have been developed. In this way the idea of what can be expected in the future and the enthusiasm about the future technology are directly communicated.

Teaching standards touches another important area—engineering design (Dutson, Todd, Magleby, & Sorensen, 1997; Dym & Agogino, 2005). Integrating engineering design into the curriculum is considered very desirable. Most engineering science courses include "design examples" to emphasize theoretical principals. Each design example typically emphasizes a single concept. Engineering design, however, involves considerably more than these design examples (Dym & Little, 2003). There are several definitions of engineering design. One definition focuses on how engineers think and emphasizes

how engineers create, assess, and select ideas (Dym & Agogino, 2005). It is important to understand that knowledge of engineering science is not sufficient to understand the thought process that leads to successful design, and that studying these thought processes is critical to improving design education.

Another aspect of engineering design, which has been virtually ignored by educators, is that designers now are required to include social impacts in their designs. The engineers of today must understand deeply global, cultural, and societal context. The technical courses taught in engineering schools do not achieve this.

It is precisely during the process of developing standards that engineers generate, evaluate, and select novel ideas considering their legal, business, and social impacts. Because standards incorporate complex constraints and are multi-disciplinary they can be considered as the ultimate in the engineering design process. This leads to the conclusion that in standards education students get exposed to engineering design education.

INCORPORATING STANDARDS EDUCATION IN ENGINEERING PROGRAMS

Continuing education will continue to play important role in standards education, but fundamental knowledge should be provided by regular education (De Vries, 2005). Furthermore we assume that standards education includes education about the technical content of a standard, the standardization process, and the role of the standard. The goals are to prepare engineering and technology graduates to build products that comply with one or more standards, offer services based on standard, and even develop new standards.

Given that formal engineering education should provide some knowledge about standards, how should this be done? There is a choice between developing a separate course and integrating standards in other technical courses.

Stand-alone courses on standards exist, but are rare. Such an approach does not appear realistic, given the full curriculum. Rather than to create new courses, an appropriate way to incorporate standards into the engineering curriculum is to integrate standards into existing technical courses. This approach is also advocated in (Krechmer, 2007). The integration of standards in engineering, technology, and computer science curricula may be achieved indirectly (by reference) or directly:

1. It can be done by reference—indicating that there is a standard for the described technology and a citation of the standard.
2. By the direct use of a standard in classroom instruction, homework problems, laboratories, or projects.

Engineering, technology, and computer science schools at least should use every opportunity to teach standards by reference. This will significantly prepare students to use appropriate standards during their senior design project.

As an example of the second approach, the author has developed and taught a course on wireless communication substantially based on the many wireless communication standards that have emerged to dominate the wireless communication industry. Enrollment in this course has been steady. In addition to solid technical content about wireless communication systems, this course teaches how do the standards work, how did the standards evolve, and why did they evolve in the way that they did. The course is inter-disciplinary, incorporating areas of electrical engineering, computer networking, information security, and also discusses adequately government regulations. When asked about the course 73% of the students felt that they have benefited from the course, even if they do not take a job in a related area.

CONCLUSION

It is well known that standards are an application of mathematics, science and engineering. However, from the viewpoint of ABET's requirements standards are not only an excellent application of mathematics, science and engineering, but also examples of systems that meet desired needs within realistic constraints such as economic, environmental, social, political, ethical, health and safety, manufacturability, and sustainability.

The importance of the "soft skills" and design thinking has lead to the questions of how to integrate these "soft skills" and design thinking into the engineering curriculum. Teaching standards is one particularly efficient way to achieve this.

Overall, through standards education both the "hard skills" and the "soft skills" can be taught at the same time, unlike most traditional engineering courses.

The education about standards leads to several important benefits:

1. Motivates learning in other engineering science courses
2. Enhances performance in capstone design courses
3. Enhances student interest in engineering
4. Encourages and supports collaborative work
5. Enhances design thinking

Not only standards education is an efficient way to achieve these objectives, but it is difficult to identify other courses and topics that could achieve the same outcomes at the same time.

Similar arguments can be made for computing and technology disciplines. The above benefits are also desired outcomes in these disciplines.

There are significant challenges to standards education, not the least of which is the fact that engineering educators should be educated about standards. Furthermore, the accreditation requirements need clarification as they do not clearly state what the desired outcomes are.

This paper discusses for the first time the connections between components of engineering education such as ethics, engineering design, labs, and integrated courses, on one hand and standards education on another. A direct conclusion from this is that standards education is more important than previously realized. The paper also discusses how standards education can be incorporated in engineering and technical curricula.

ACKNOWLEDGMENT

The author expresses appreciation to Dr. Theodore Bickart, President Emeritus of the Colorado School of Mines, for reviewing an earlier version of the manuscript, providing a number of helpful comments, and encouraging the author to seek publication.

REFERENCES

ABET. (2006). *Criteria for the evaluation of engineering programs*. Retrieved from http://www.abet.org

Augustine, N., & Vest, C. (1994). *Engineering Education for a changing world*. Washington, DC: ASEE.

Canadian Engineering Accreditation Board. (2007a). *Canadian accreditation criteria*. Retrieved from http://www.ccpe.ca/e/files/report_ceab.pdf

Canadian Engineering Accreditation Board. (2007b). *CEAB Questionnaire for Evaluation of Engineering Programs*. Retrieved from http://www.ccpe.ca/e/acc_supp_1.cfm

Center for Global Standards Analysis. (2004). *Report on a survey of schools of engineering in the United States concerning standards education*. Washington, DC: The Catholic University of America.

De Vries, H. J. (2005). Standardization education. *Homo Oeconomicus. 22*(1), 71-91

De Vries, H. J., & Egyedi, T. M. (2007). Education about standardization: Recent findings. *International Journal of IT Standards and Standardization Research, 5*(2), 1–12. doi:10.4018/jitsr.2007070101

Dutson, A. J., Todd, R. H., Magleby, S. P., & Sorensen, C. D. (1997). A review of literature on teaching design through project oriented capstone courses. *Journal of Engineering Education, 76*(1), 17–28.

Dym, C., Agogino, A. M., Eris, O., Frey, D. D., & Leifer, L. J. (2005). Engineering design thinking, teaching and learning. *Journal of Engineering Education, 94*(1), 103–120.

Dym, C. L., & Little, L. (2003). *Engineering Design: A Project-Based Instruction*. New York, NY: John Wiley & Sons.

Fleddermann, C. B. (2000). Engineering ethics cases for electrical and computer engineering students. *IEEE Transactions on Education, 43*(3), 284–287. doi:10.1109/13.865202

Froyd, J. E., & Ohland, M. W. (2005). Integrated engineering curricula. *Journal of Engineering Education, 94*(1), 147–164.

Grinter, L. E. (1956). Report on the evaluation of engineering education. *English Education, 46*(1), 25–63.

ICES. (2008). *Workshop presentations*. Retrieved from http://www.standards-education.org/workshops/ices2008/presentations

IEEE Educational Activities Board Standards in Education Committee. (2008). *Standards education*. Retrieved from http://www.ieee.org/web/education/standards/index.html

Kelly, W. E., Bickart, T. A., & Forselius, R. (2006). *Standards education: An industry, government, university partnership*. Paper presented at the American Society for Engineering Education Mid-Atlantic Conference.

Krechmer, K. (2007). Teaching standards to engineers. *International Journal of IT Standards and Standardization Research*, *5*(2), 1–12. doi:10.4018/jitsr.2007070102

National Science Foundation. (1995). *Restructuring engineering education: A focus on change*. Arlington, VA: Author.

National Standardization Strategic Framework. (2008). *British National Standardization Strategic Framework*. Retrieved from http://www.nssf.info/resources/documents/Guide_to_NSSF.pdf

Shuman, L., Besterfield-Sacre, M., & McGourty, J. (2005). The ABET "professional skills" – Can they be taught? Can they be assessed? *Journal of Engineering Education*, *94*(1), 41–55.

Smerdon, P. (2000). *An action agenda for engineering curriculum innovation*. Paper presented at the 11th IEEE-USA Biennial Careers Conference, San Jose, CA.

U.S. House of Representatives. (2005). *Europe, and the use of standards as trade barriers: How should the US respond?* Congressional Hearing.

This work was previously published in the International Journal of IT Standards and Standardization Research (IJITSR), Volume 8, Issue 1, edited by Kai Jakobs, pp. 1-10, copyright 2010 by IGI Publishing (an imprint of IGI Global)

Section 4
Consumers in Standardization

Chapter 8
Where Are You? Consumers' Associations in Standardization:
A Case Study on Switzerland

Christophe Hauert
University of Lausanne, Switzerland

ABSTRACT

The expansion of international standardization has reinforced enduring questions on the legitimacy of standards. In that respect, the participation of all stakeholders, including the weakest ones (unions, NGO, consumers' associations) is crucial. Given the recognized role of consumers' associations to express legitimate objectives, the question of their representation becomes central. In order to get a deeper understanding of their participation, this article explores the evolution of their representation within the Swiss national mirror committees of international standardization between 1987 and 2007. It probes the extent to which their participation is determined by the distinctiveness of issues supposedly related to consumers' concerns and by their own use of standards. The empirical findings of our study indicate an underrepresentation of consumers' associations and confirm the topical specificity of their implication in standardization processes. Finally, we found evidence that the use of standards in an association's activities supports and encourages its participation in standardization committees.

INTRODUCTION

Standardization is part of the infrastructure of globalization providing cross-border nongovernmental coordination mechanisms, which formally respect state sovereignty. Various studies in organizational science and international relations have examined how voluntary and consensual standards have become crucial tools in the organization of global markets (Graz, 2004; Tamm-Hallström, 2004; Krewer, 2005).

As the increased usage of standards affects a wide range of issues, such as environmental management, psychological tests, measures of the quality of medical services, and nanotechnologies, the quantitative and qualitative expansion

DOI: 10.4018/978-1-4666-2160-2.ch008

of international standardization has reinforced enduring questions on the legitimacy of standards. In other words, who defines standard matters for the recognition of their greater use in society at large? As Ulrich Bamberg, from the German KAN (Workplace Health and Safety and Standardization Commission) emphasizes, "Standardization is characterized by a paradox of 'large minorities.' The two biggest groups concerned (370 million consumers, including 165 million salaried employees, in the EU) are in the minority on standardization committees … if represented at all" (Bamberg, 2004, p. 13). Given the recognized role of these actors, especially consumers' associations, to express legitimate objectives in matters of health, safety or environmental protection within the standardization process, the question of their representation, as well as the mechanisms governing their involvement within these arenas, becomes central (Fabisch, 2003; Biswell, 2004; Dawar, 2006).

Studies on the world of standardization never fail to stress the under-representation of civil society actors, such as consumers' associations, environmental protection organizations, unions, and NGOs, despite their recognized contribution to the process of legitimizing standards. Some case studies in distinct specific international committees have provided evidence of their under-representation (Morikawa & Morrisson, 2004). Several scholars have highlighted that including the weakest stakeholders remains important for the perception of legitimacy in decision-making procedures that respect public interest concerns (Raines, 2003; Fabisch, 2003; Dawar, 2006). Standardization studies conventionally explain the under-representation of civil society actors in international committees of standardization by lack of financial, cognitive and temporal resources (Egan, 1998; Schmidt & Werle, 1998; Tamm-Hallström, 2004). From a more sociological perspective, consumers' concerns in standardization are understood as a rhetorical resource under the control of standard-setters (Cochoy, 2000);

yet, by identifying standardization processes as topical issues related to consumers' concerns, such a rhetorical resource may in turn reinforce consumers' effective participation (Cochoy, 2000).

While studies draw attention to the resource that consumers' participation brings to standardization organization in terms of legitimacy, they largely ignore the resource that standards can in turn bring to consumers' associations themselves, through the use of for instance comparative tests. Moreover, the study of their participation in an international committee only provides a one shot picture of their implication with no clue to its evolution in the course of time. Finally, financial, temporal and cognitive resources are determinant in explaining consumers' under-representation, but these elements remain very broad and only partially take into account the dynamics governing the involvement (or not) of these actors in standardization work.

Thus, the following questions remain largely unexplored: does the evolution of consumer's participation reflect the growing importance of standardization in society? To which extent is their participation related to the specificity of the topics standardized? To which extent does the inclusion of standards in the deliverables of consumers' associations affect their participation in committees?

This article tries to answer these questions by exploring more systematically the evolution of consumers' associations' representation within national mirror committees of international standardization processes. It probes the extent to which their participation is determined by the distinctiveness of issues supposedly related to consumer's concerns and by their own usage of standards.

Our contention is that a resource-based explanation of the under-representation of consumers' associations should bring together the resource-consuming activity of standard-setting with the resource-providing activity of consumers' associations. In other words, this article argues that the propensity to use standards in the services provided by consumers' associations is likely to affect their participation. This participation incentive is operational and topical as the specificity of consumers' issues dealt with in standardization is likely to reinforce the participation of consumers' associations.

In order to test our argument, this article provides for the first time a study of a longitudinal analysis of participation in ISO and CEN national mirror committees by exploring the case of Switzerland in 1987, 1997 and 2007. A quantitative analysis completed by semi-open interviews with participants of three representatives of consumers' associations have helped to gain a deeper understanding of consumers' participation.

Our results provide clear evidence of consumers' associations under-representation: despite a slight increase in consumer participation in mirror committees, today they are present in less than one committee out of five. Moreover, our results provide evidence of the topical specificity of consumers implication: these associations are principally represented within committees dealing with transversal themes (health, safety and the environment) as Graz highlights, whose definition is "intrinsically more controversial" (Graz, 2004, p. 257), as well as concerning consumer goods and services. Finally, according to our argument, we found evidence that the use of standards in an association's activities, supports and encourages its participation in standardization committees: activities that incorporate standards such as comparative trials or the selling of quality seals to producers provide financial as well as cognitive resources to consumers' associations, raise their awareness regarding standardization, leading to sustaining their overall participation.

The following section presents a discussion of the literature on civil society participation, especially that of consumer associations in standardization arenas. Section 3 outlines our theoretical framework in order to explain why the usage of standards in consumers' associations activities is likely to shape their inclination to take part in standard processes. Section 4 presents the methodology employed and section 5 presents our principal results. The conclusion reflects on the significance and limits of our findings. It emphasizes that consumers' associations are certainly a resource in the construction of the authority of standards, but standards also constitute a resource for these associations.

CONSUMER PARTICIPATION IN THE LITERATURE

Many studies mention the degree to which companies are overrepresented and civil society is under-represented, despite its recognized role in defending legitimate interests such as access to transparent information, and protection of health, the environment or work safety conditions. Their lack of resources largely explains their under-representation as "Participation in standards development is time-consuming, resource-intensive and requires technical expertise" (Werle & Iversen, 2006, p. 36). For instance, the target time frame required for the development of a standard at the ISO is 36 months, even if this time frame may be shorter for other standard-setting bodies (NO-REST, 2005, p. 73). Furthermore, active participation involves reading and understanding the standard discussed during committee meetings, and participation in the latter further adds to the workload. In addition, participation in committees incurs a number of expenses, especially at the logistical level (travel and accommodation) and fees. Finally, technical expertise is required to comprehend and formulate propositions, since it is the basis of argumentation during deliberations. Technical language thus seems to be a "compulsory figure" for standardization (Mallard, 2000a, p. 57). While industries have access to the required technical expertise by their involvement in the production process of the goods and services subject to standardization, civil society actors find themselves far removed from the manufacturing process and its underlying technical expertise. For example, consumer associations wish to have quality condoms, particularly in regard to resistance. The standardization work implies to translate the concept of resistance in a way that enables its physical measurement. In other words, a translation work must be accomplished between public health, safety or environmental concerns made in general terms and a series of tests organized and manipulated in a laboratory (Callon, Lascoumes & Barthe, 2001). Thus, "an understanding of at least the technical basics" (Jakobs, Procter & Williams, 2006) can overcome communication problems between engineers and consumers' associations. It is against this understanding for instance that Morikawa and Morrisson (2004, pp. 18-22) provide evidence of the under-representation of NGO participation on two ISO technical committees, attaining three and five percent of delegates representing civil society.

The few studies of consumers' associations' participation emphasize the impact of their contributions on the process of legitimizing standards. Their presence permits public interest concerns to be taken into account, for example, through extending the notion of product safety beyond the foreseeable usage by an "average" consumer to guarantee consideration of more specific categories, such as children, senior citizens and the disabled (Fabisch, 2003; Biswell, 2004). Therefore, their participation may raise the quality of standards, thus contributing to their legitimization. More generally, representation of the least advantaged stakeholders is important in the perception of the legitimacy of decision-making procedures (Raines, 2003) and in the construction of the authority of standardization organizations. The concept of "inclusiveness" consequently makes us attentive to various material, cognitive and symbolic resources that different actors bring to the work of standardization and that are, in turn, mobilized by standardization bodies to bolster their credibility (Boström, 2006)

While the lack of resources explains to a certain extent consumers' associations' under-representation, in general it does not help us to understand why one association rather than another becomes involved in standardization. Moreover, the study of consumer participation in a particular international committee is very instructive, but the selection criteria of these committees examined remain implicit. Thus, case studies fail to uncover the specific areas in which consumers are involved. Finally, the contribution of consumer participation to the legitimizing process of standards often leads to perceiving these associations from the angle of the resources they provide to standardization organizations. The distinct uses that these associations are likely to make of the standards have largely been ignored despite the fact that this may as well prompt them to take part in committee work. While consumers' associations provide legitimation resources to standardization organization, standards also provide resources the other way round to these associations. The next section sets out a framework of analysis which aims to explain more fully the (lack of) involvement of consumers' associations in standardization processes.

CONSUMER'S ASSOCIATIONS' USE OF STANDARDS

According to Marcus-Steiff (1977), one of the main purposes of consumers' associations is to inform consumers. These informational tasks can be performed through comparative testing or labeling activities, which are mainly standard-based activities. However, consumers' associations' informational tasks concern not every object, but rather are concentrated on products and services of «mass» consumption as well as on broader societal issue (health, safety, environment). Consequently, the topical specificity of consumers' associations' implication in standardization committees should reflect these themes.

According to Cochoy (2000) the "consumer" offers a discursive resource to standard-setters. This author also suggests that standards are a resource for the associations, for example in terms of consumers' information through comparative trials. Comparative tests are at the intersection of two types of actions available to associations to allow for the consumption of the healthiest and safest products possible: information and collective action (Marcus-Steiff, 1977). According to Mallard (2000b), conducting comparative tests is a current practice that serves to feed "the consumer press" which represents a substantive part of consumers' associations' financing. Moreover, these trials have a number of connections to standardization. Firstly, like standardization, they are based on scientific analysis. Secondly, procedures governing these comparative tests are standardized (Cochoy, 2002). Thirdly, comparative trials mobilize standards for the products tested and thus may lead to a critical examination of technical specifications. Finally, in France for instance, it is still a standard that stipulates the possible use of test results by industries in order to prevent them being used for marketing purposes (Mallard, 2000b), which we readily understand since they might harm consumers' associations' credibility.

Comparative tests also create connections between consumers' associations and standardization. Conducting tests presupposes the collaboration of a journalist responsible for writing an article and the engineer conducting the test (Mallard, 2000b). This then permits consumers' associations to familiarize themselves with the technical language and to acquire some technical expertise. These tests being the occasion for a critical examination of standards, may trigger a campaign to set more demanding criteria or an expression of appreciation for the intrinsic quality of a standard - witness an article in *FRC Magazine*, the magazine of the French-speaking Swiss Consumers Federation (Erard, 2008). In the case of a struggle to redefine the standard, they will represent a significant source of scientific

arguments in standardization committees. Tests conducted by consumers' associations bring us back to promotional activities for standards since the latter are at the core of this critical practice. Whether these tests stem from a positive or negative critique of standards, they contribute to legitimizing recourse to standardization while providing standardization organization with new clients and objects: testing centers and their procedures. At the same time as comparative tests integrate standards at a number of levels, they also permit, for example, "an understanding of usage" (Mallard, 2000b). Therefore these tests are the occasion for a new interpretation of the standard resulting from the integration of consumer concerns, such as questions about usage. The subsequent critical examination of standards opens the way to consumers' associations' involvement for the (re-) definition of a standard. As we see, the activities of definition, promotion and interpretation of standards may thus prove to be related to conducting comparative tests that constitute a useful means of providing consumer information. In this way, these tests are shaped by standardization, while they contribute to shaping standardization through the medium of consumers' associations.

Against this background, our main argument is that the usage of standards by an association supports and encourages its participation to standard-setting activities. As the use of standards in the deliverables of a consumers' association make them aware of the importance of standards and permit them to acquire empirically based arguments as well as financial resources, they take part to the process of standard-setting/-reviewing. Certainly, the usage of standards does not necessarily mean participation in committees, but it offers consumers' associations an incentive to do so. While it provides cognitive resources known to be essential to participating in committee work, it also supports comparative tests that give them additional resources in return for the time and money spent in standardization committees.

METHODOLOGY

In order to probe our argument, we collected data inventorying all participants in ISO/CEN mirror committees established within the Swiss Standardization Association (SNV) in 1987, 1997 and 2007.[1] This temporal sequence reflects the growing importance of consumers' concerns in standardization over the last 20 years. After categorizing the participants and the mirrored technical committees (see below), the resulting data base allowed us to quantify the consumers' associations representation and its evolution as well as the topical specificity of their implication. In order to obtain a deeper understanding of consumers' participation we conducted semi-open interviews with participants of three representatives of consumers' associations to identify the use of standards within these associations' activities.

As we mentioned, after incorporating the participants into our data base, we classified them by the following categories:

- **Enterprises (E):** includes businesses, etc.
- **Professional Associations (ProfA):** includes associations representative of an industry or profession.
- **Public Actors (PublA):** includes federal, cantonal and municipal administrative bodies, universities, graduate schools, and hospitals, as well as associations representing public collective memberships (for example the public transport union) and institutions and foundations whose financing is essentially public or has strong links with public bodies.
- **Civil Society Associations (CSA):** includes associations and foundations representative of individuals' "non-professional" interests: athletic, consumer, patient, Internet user and car owner associations. As unions are also included, we did not label this group "consumers' associations."

In order to establish eventual correlations between the type of participant and the object for which standards were being set, we established the following typology of standards.

- **Definitions and Methods (D):** although these aspects are included in almost all committees, some deal only with these subjects. For example, "measurement of fluid loss in closed pipelines," "system of network grids," "modular systems," etc.
- **Management System (MS),** such as quality standards in the ISO 9000 series or environmental management systems.
- **Goods and Services for Specialists (GS):** these are goods and services whose usage is essentially professional. For example "plastic feed lines," "metallic and other inorganic coatings," etc.
- **Consumer Goods and Services (CS):** products and services that could be directly purchased and used by all consumers, such as "furniture", "textiles", or "tourist services," etc.
- **Transversal Themes (TT):** this category brings together themes which cannot be directly related to a distinct industry or the above-mentioned categories. They mainly concern safety, health, and the environment, as well as emerging technologies (for example, "nanotechnologies" and "biotechnologies"). Themes concerning the environment are, for example, "air quality" or "water quality," etc. Safety issues are, amongst others, "rescue systems" or "fire detection and fire-fighting." Health-related themes include subjects such as "surgical implants," "medical computer technology," "optical ophthalmology" or even "invitro systems of medical analysis."

Certain themes unavoidably overlap some categories: for example, a committee concerning "toy safety" could be interpreted as belonging to transversal themes since it touches on safety, but is also a consumer product. Similarly, the committee dealing with "environmental management" could well be classified with management systems, as well as transversal themes. We chose to classify the cases mentioned above in the most specific category, that of consumer products in the case of toys, and management systems in the second case. These different types of standards are not to be interpreted in connection with their possible influence on consumers. Therefore, the aim is not to say that management systems have fewer repercussions on consumer life, and their participation is less important. The purpose of this typology is to see whether the type of object for which a standard is being set has an influence on the representation of the different types of actors previously defined, and whether this is consistent with our hypotheses.

RESULTS

The Most Present but Still Under-Represented Actors

Over the entire period studied, our sample contained 91 mirror committees in which more than 600 firms and some 18 civil society associations participated. This general finding provides an initial glimpse of the weak consumer participation in standardization work, but tells us nothing about an eventual evolution of their representation. Table 1 presents the evolution over 20 years of the participation of the different types of organizations defined earlier. It takes into account the number of committees where a type of actor is present, regardless of the importance of the actor's role in the committee. For example, in 1987 there are 43 standardization committees where at least one company is present. Therefore, these are present in 98% of the mirror committees counted in this year.

These data confirm consumers' associations under-representation and the overrepresentation of companies. The quantitative and qualitative expansion of standardization coincides with an increase in participation of consumers' associations, present in an ever-increasing number of committees. Despite this evolution, in 2007 they

Table 1. Presence of different types of organizations

	1987		1997		2007	
	(N =44)	%	(N=64)	%	(N=72)	%
E	43	97.7	60	93.8	65	90.3
ProfA	34	77.3	53	82.8	47	65.3
PublA	35	79.5	58	90.6	55	76.4
CSA	6	13.6	8	12.5	14	19.4
Others	8	18.2	12	18.8	16	20.8

are present in less than one committee in five, thus having the weakest rate of participation of all categories. Observation of committees where consumers are represented indicates that their role is a minority one. They never constitute the dominant force of a committee. Our sample presents 28 committees with civil society association participation. Two thirds of the cases—19 cases out of 28—show consumer representation by a single association. In the remaining cases, they are at best represented by three associations (one case in 2007 on the committee on information technologies). The participation of more than one civil society association in the same committee could be interpreted in two ways. Firstly, the sectorial nature of certain associations' concerns makes their participation complementary. For example, the participation of the Swiss Ski Association and the Swiss Federation of Free Flight in the committee dealing with "sports material" is understandable to the extent that these actors are concerned with different aspects of standardization work. Clearly, they are not interested in the same sports equipment. Here the participation of two associations seems complementary since they are concerned with different objects within the same standardization committee. Secondly, certain committees reveal participation of associations with seemingly similar concerns. This joint presence may be explained by a different vision of consumer interests. These associations are, thus, in competition. In this manner, we may interpret the participation of the Swiss Automobile Club and the Swiss Touring Club, two associations representative of car drivers, in the committee on "road vehicles." Being classified in the same actors category—in this case, civil society association - should not, therefore, be interpreted as signifying similar interests. One has only to consider consumer preferences on electrical plugs: while identical plugs in different countries would constitute a clear advantage for consumers, again one needs to know which countries must adapt; in this case, consumers have a national interest,

each one hoping that their own national system would be adopted by other countries.

Detailed analysis of consumers' associations participation also allows us to determine the stability of their presence in committees: more than two thirds of committees where they are present in a particular period still report this representation in the next period. The involvement in standardization work seems lasting. However, the stability of their presence must not minimize the importance of associations' participation which were until then absent from standardization work. In 1987 and 1997, the extension of consumer participation in new committees almost always resulted in the involvement of a new consumers' association. It was different in 2007 when an association already active in 1987 represented consumers in four new committees. One association alone accounted for more than a quarter of consumer participation in committees! Participation in new committees in 2007 is, therefore, due more to greater participation of an association that had already participated in standardization work than to the presence of new associations. Nonetheless, qualitatively, this last period marks the addition to some committees of associations dealing more directly with health, for example, an association of patients, one for quality labeling of contraceptives or an allergy, skin and asthma foundation. Are these associations present to deal with transversal themes touching on health, as our argument suggests?

The Topical Specificity of Consumers' Participation

Now, let us examine these associations' participation in the different types of standards identified. During the period studied, certain committees were created and others disappeared, thereby reflecting technological evolutions and more extensive changes in standardization. Thus, the committees created between 1997 and 2007 mainly concern services, management systems and transversal themes. The change in the nomenclature of committees in charge of developing technical specifications within the SNV is revealing in that regard: in 2006, the label "technical committee" gave way to the more "neutral" denomination of "standardization committee", thus reflecting the fact that certain objects for which standards were being set could not be designated as purely technical (SNV, 2006)— if the SNV argument is related to "certain objects", science studies have convincingly argued that there is nothing such as "pure science" (Lelong & Mallard, 2000, pp. 16-20). We could observe that the number of committees dealing with products for specialists had diminished, contrary to those in all other fields. The areas that progressed the most were standards concerning consumer products and transversal themes, especially medical fields. To a lesser extent, the spectrum of management tasks lending themselves to standardization has also broadened as only quality and environmental management were on the agenda in 1997.

Table 2 shows the percentage of each type of committee in which consumers' associations participated. For example, in 1987, sixteen committees dealt with consumer goods or services and consumers' associations participated in five of these committees, which is less than a third of committees on the subject (31.3%). This table will allow us, therefore, to verify the topical specificity of consumers' associations involvement in standardization work.

Our empirical data confirm the specificity of the topical involvement of consumers' associations. Table 2 indicates that participation of civil society associations is concentrated mostly on standards concerning consumer goods and services. Indeed, these associations are present in almost a third of committees on this subject. It appears that growing consumer involvement in standardization committees is accompanied by a diversification of topics on which they are participating. Thus, we may observe here a growing participation in transversal areas, as well as an incursion into a committee concerning management systems. However, these associations are almost totally absent from fields touching on definitions and goods and services for specialists, with only an exception or two in 1987. This participation was due to the Swiss Institute of Household Research, which was dissolved in 1992. The reasons for the dissolution of this institute provide an indication of the rare participation of a consumers' association in a field concerning primarily specialists: "Financial difficulties, as well as the accusation of favoring manufacturers over consumers, after a media campaign in 1991, led to the dissolution of the Institute in 1992" (Joris, 2008).

Table 2. Participation of CSAs in various types of standards

	1987			1997			2007		
	(N=44)	CSA	%	(N=64)	CSA	%	(N=72)	CSA	%
D	5	0	0.0	5	0	0.0	6	0	0.0
MS	1	0	0.0	2	0	0.0	6	1	16.7
GS	12	1	8.3	16	0	0.0	13	0	0.0
CG	16	5	31.3	20	6	30.0	25	8	32.0
TT	10	0	0.0	21	2	9.5	22	5	22.7

Outside of this rather anecdotal participation, we must stress the fact that many objects falling into the categories of consumer goods and services as well as transversal themes are still standardized in the absence of consumers' associations. Committees dealing with "furniture," "toy safety" or even "nanotechnologies" reveal no presence of these actors. If we wish to remedy these shortcomings, it is then crucial to further our understanding of the mechanisms governing their participation.

The Usage of Standards, a Determining Factor

According to the above-presented literature, all interviewed consumer representatives mention the financial, temporal and cognitive constraints related to standardization work. Technical abilities are required to understand standardization work, as well as to make any proposals. Even if the users' input are aimed, as for instance in the ICT sector, at bringing real-world requirements (experiences and needs) to the committee members (Jakobs, Procter, & Williams, 1998), these requests have to be formalized: one respondent indicated the difficulty of bringing single experiences (Pia Ernst, Swiss Patients Organization, pers. comm., January 27, 2008) while another pointed to the need of formal studies in order to be heard (Françoise Michel, French-speaking Swiss Consumers Federation, pers. comm., January 31, 2008). To the necessarily technical skills required to participate in committees are added the abilities necessary to protect consumers. As one respondent maintained, having a technical expert was not sufficient. He or she must "still be familiar with patients' requirements and expectations with respect to the committee's subject." (Pia Ernst, Swiss Patients Organization, pers. comm., January 27, 2008). The importance of this unique consumers' association expertise is underscored by one of the main Swiss associations:

It is true that with respect to the average consumer who could probably adjust to something that is not ideal, we also protect the most vulnerable consumers a great deal, that is children, senior citizens, and people with disabilities, a field in which standardization is not yet well-adapted. We have devoted considerable time to developing perfect standards, but they were created for the average consumer... and we cannot say that there is a product dangerous only for healthy, intelligent and wealthy people... and that is a total innovation in the work... (Françoise Michel, French-speaking Swiss Consumers Federation, pers. comm., January 31, 2008).

Therefore, as well as technical expertise, specific skills for consumer protection are necessary, which means new requirements for representatives. This impacts the possibility of mandating an external expert to sit on such committees.

Our respondents also mention a criterion of efficiency that intervenes in the choice of investing financial, cognitive and temporal resources. These associations are confronting a dilemma in the usage of these resources as they are also selling benefits which often comprise a significant portion of their budget. Consequently, when there is expertise within an association, should it be used to participate in standardization work or for the production of benefits? The use of standards in the provision of consumers' associations' benefits allows for the reconciling of these two objectives. Thus, the standards are a resource for these associations, motivating them to participate in standardization work.

Associations' participation in developing standards may be explained by the contribution and use they make of standards in their daily activities. The most active consumers' association in standardization work in 2007 is a good illustration of this aspect. Some of this association's tasks are based on the usage of standards, through comparative tests. As a representative of the association said:

To do credible tests, you have to base them on the recognized standards of manufacturers, manufacturers that you are, in fact, indirectly criticizing... Since the tests are the bases of consumer work and information, there are no tests without standardization and without "good" standardization. (Françoise Michel, French-speaking Swiss Consumers Federation, pers. comm., January 31, 2008).

Doing these tests is, therefore, part of standardization for this association. They allow for consumers to be informed and are the occasion for a critical examination of standards. The usage of standards through the intermediary of these tests then provides cognitive resources to this association that could be mobilized to make itself heard within the committees. As our respondent explains:

If you are alone amongst 12 or 15 people on a committee, and everyone tells themselves "she doesn't know anything" or if you are someone who says: "I did tests; I had that experience; I saw that the products did not respond; this is why they didn't respond. I have a study that shows that such a percentage of the population uses this type of appliance and may suffer injuries or dangers", then someone will listen. (Françoise Michel, French-speaking Swiss Consumers Federation, pers. comm., January 31, 2008).

Taking consumers' association claims into account occurs through a technical formulation of the latter. Reliance on research allows for the translation of these general concerns into a technical language. As these different studies provide many arguments during committee work, this allows for them to be heard. We see that standards are also a resource for this association to act. The use of standards is part of consumer information and brings with it cognitive resources. Thus, an association's use of standards allows for the reconciling of participation in committees and the provision of benefits.

An association's use of standards does not only occur through comparative tests. In that respect, the Association for the Condom Quality Seal reveals another use of standards. Let us rapidly trace the history of this association:

The Association for the Condom Quality Seal was founded in 1989. It grew out of the working group responsible for contraceptives within the framework of the SNV in Zurich... Despite everything, to be able to give enough "weight" to this standard, the Swiss Consumers Federation, the Consumers Protection Foundation and the Swiss Help Against AIDS created the Association for the Condom Quality Seal." ("Qui est l'association pour le label de qualité ?", n.d.).

Among the originators of this association are personalities who were part of the technical committee, but on behalf of the Federal Office of Public Health or EMPA (Swiss Federal Laboratories for Materials Testing and Research). End-consumers are not members of this association, but are represented through affiliated consumers associations. This case is very significant because it shows how associations with broader concerns are, along with public actors, behind the creation of an association that would then guarantee consumer representation. Moreover, this association is based on standardization: on one hand, its existence stems from standardization work and the links formed between diverse consumers' associations and public representatives. On the other hand, the determination of the label is a function of the conformity of contraceptives to the corresponding standard. The association is only financed through sales of the label:

The Association for the Condom Quality Seal is naturally financed by the sale of the label. Companies wishing to use the label on their contraceptives pay the association a certain amount for each batch and this finances the association... then we buy contraceptives in Switzerland, have them tested and finance the evaluation of the results. (Dr. Johannes Gauglhofer, Association for the Condom Quality Seal, pers. comm., January 21, 2008).

This evaluation is then done by a member of the association. This case brings out two significant elements. On one hand, it confirms the links and relationships existing between the activities of definition, promotion, interpretation, and implementation of standards. Involvement in one of these activities may also lead to participation in other activities of constructing the authority of standards. Secondly, it confirms the importance of the usage of standards in an association's activities to explain its involvement in standardization work. Again, this association's utilization of standards allows for the reconciling of participation in committees and the provision of benefits. This case demonstrates that participation in standardization is not only a burden, but may also be the basis of an association's financing. Consumers' associations are certainly a resource in the construction of the authority of standards, but standards definitely provide resources to these associations too.

In contrast to these two cases, one may point to an association of patients that only participated in a single meeting of a standardization committee in 2007. The association makes no use of standards and remains skeptical of standardizing issues of a less technical nature. The representative we interviewed mentioned, however, a participation in the creation of "guidelines" formulating best practices in the medical field. This guidelines-setting activity takes place in collaboration with professional associations on issues such as "communication with the patient" or "information before intervention." Participation seems more accessible, since the association can directly refer to its own experiences, thus avoiding the technical "compulsory figure": "Discussions are less technical… we can often also come back to our experiences, for example in the matter of advice…" (Pia Ernst, Swiss Patients Organization, pers. comm., January 27, 2008). The preparation of these guides to good practice, therefore, allows

for the use, as is, of experiences and the recounting of observations, in contrast with standardization work where demands usually formulated in terms of general objectives must be translated into a technical language.

These different cases show that the frequent usage of standards by consumers' association is important in explaining their participation in standardization work. Some of the tasks of the most active association in standardization work rely on the use of standards (conducting comparative tests). Similarly, the activities of the Association for the Condom Quality Seal are based almost entirely on standardization. Thus, associations using standards in their activities have become familiar with the constraints of technical language and may make reference to research and tests to make themselves heard. This research allows them to formalize past experiences and thus be able to show their worth in committee discussions. Finally, the use of standards by these associations allows them to reconcile participation in committees and the provision of services. Therefore, we understand how the role of standards in an association's provision of services acts as an incentive to participation.

CONCLUSION

With the rich empirical material collected, we were able to test our argument about consumer participation. The results clearly demonstrate the weakness of consumer representation, resulting from both a lack of material resources, and also and perhaps especially, the lack of technical expertise. Although their participation increased in absolute terms over the period, in 2007 consumers' associations were only present in a fifth of the committees, comprising the lowest level of participation. Moreover, it remains to be seen whether their participation could achieve significant influence on the contents of the standards under elaboration.

Technical expertise clearly appears to be a major constraint for consumer participation. Technical skills are determinant even before any participation, since they are necessary to evaluate the relevance of participation in a committee. Moreover, these technical aptitudes are crucial throughout standardization work, whether it is a question of understanding propositions or formulating them. In this sense, the use of standards in consumers' associations' benefits can provide them the technical expertise through the recourse of research and tests, allowing consumers' associations to comply with the technical "compulsory figure." Comparative tests or labeling activities provide arguments during deliberations as well as an informational tool for consumers. The use of standards in consumers' associations' benefits is important in explaining their participation because it allows for a more efficient articulation of the crucial resource of time, expertise and money. This article suggests that the classical resource-based explanation of their under-representation needs some refinement. Observing the use of standards in consumers' associations' activities can provide, as we have seen, a useful perspective on the reasons of their participation.

Not surprisingly, consumers' associations participate in committees on consumer products, and always more where transversal topics are concerned, thus confirming our argument on topical incentive. It is, therefore, appropriate to ask what influence a broadening of the themes touched upon could have. Standardization of transversal themes or services seems more difficult to formulate in purely technical language. Will the appearance of these new issues allow the consumers' associations to recognize their own experiences more easily within committees? The question remains open but we may suppose that the long tradition of technicality of deliberations might contribute to closing the window of opportunity that these new fields represent.

As a concluding remark, we suggest that the use of standards may also raise consumers' associations' consciousness about the social, economical and political impacts of standards which may in turn reinforce their participation. In that way, their participation could be conceived as a political action which takes place in the realm of "political consumerism". If this holds true, questions of legitimacy and accountability of these associations promise to become an important research issue.

ACKNOWLEDGMENT

The author would like to thank the Swiss National Science Foundation (SNSF) and the Faculty of Social and Political Sciences of the University of Lausanne for the research funding. The author would also like to express deep gratitude to the following people for providing support as well as valuable comments and suggestions during the preparation of this article: Dr. Oscar Zosso, Dr. Hans Peter Homberger, Urs Fischer and Rita Schindelholz from the Swiss Standardization Organization (SNV); Jean-Christophe Graz, Professor of political science at the Institute of Political and International Studies (IEPI) of the University of Lausanne and André Mach, Tenured Senior Lecturer and Researcher at the Institute of Political and International Studies (IEPI) of the University of Lausanne. Special thanks goes to the interview respondents for the time they accorded to me: Françoise Michel, French-speaking Swiss Consumers Federation, Pia Ernst, Swiss Patients Organization and Dr. Johannes Gauglhofer, Association for the Condom Quality Seal. The three anonymous reviewers are being acknowledged for their comments.

REFERENCES

Bamberg, U. (2004). Le rôle des syndicats allemands dans le processus de normalisation national et européen. *Newsletter du BTS, 24-25*, 12-16. Retrieved December 10, 2008, from http://hesa.etui-rehs.org/fr/newsletter/files/Pages12-16.pdf

Biswell, K. (2004). Consumers and standards: increasing influence. *Consumer Policy Review, 4*(6), 177–185.

Boström, M. (2006). Regulatory credibility and authority through inclusiveness: Standardization organizations in cases of eco-labelling. *Organization, 13*(3), 345–367. doi:10.1177/1350508406063483

Callon, M., Lascoumes, P., & Barthe, Y. (2001). *Agir dans un monde incertain. Essai sur la démocratie technique*. Paris: Seuil.

Cochoy, F. (2000). De l' « AFNOR » à « NF » ou la progressive marchandisation de la normalisation industrielle. *Reseaux, 102*, 63–89.

Cochoy, F. (2002). Une petite histoire de client, ou la progressive normalisation du marché et de l'organisation. *Sociologie du Travail, 44*, 357–380. doi:10.1016/S0038-0296(02)01238-4

Dawar, K. (2006). Global governance and its implications for consumers. *Consumer policy review, 16*(1), 2-4.

Egan, M. (1998). Regulatory strategies, delegation and European market integration. *Journal of European Public Policy, 5*(3), 485–506. doi:10.1080/135017698343938

Erard, L.-O. (2008). Sécurité: Fumer n'est pas jouer. *FRC Magazine, 12*, 4.

Fabisch, G. (2003, December 8-9). *Consumers and standards: Consumer representation in standards setting*. Paper presented at the Cotswolds Conference. Retrieved December 10, 2008, from http://www.stanhopecentre.org/cotswolds/Fabisch%20Paper%202003.pdf

Farquhar, B. (2006). Consumer representation in international standards. *Consumer Policy Review, 16*(1), 26–30.

Graz, J. C. (2004). Quand les normes font loi. Topologie intégrée et processus différenciés de la normalisation international. *Revue Etudes Internationales, 35*(2), 233–260.

Jakoba, K., Procter, R., & Williams, R. (1998). User participation in standards setting – The panacea? *ACM Standard View, 6*(2), 85–89. doi:10.1145/301688.301693

Joris, E. (2008). Institut suisse de recherche ménagère. In *Dictionnaire historique de la suisse*. Retrieved December 10, 2008, from http://www.hls-dhs-dss.ch/textes/f/F16503.php

Kerwer, D. (2005). Rules that many use: Standards and global regulation. *Governance: An International Journal of Policy, Administration and Institutions, 18*(4), 611–632. doi:10.1111/j.1468-0491.2005.00294.x

Lelong, B., & Mallard, A. (2000). Présentation. *Reseaux, 102*, 9–34.

Mallard, A. (2000a). L'écriture des normes. *Reseaux, 102*, 37–61.

Mallard, A. (2000b). La presse de consommation et le marché: Enquête sur le tiers consumériste. *Sociologie du Travail, 42*, 391–409. doi:10.1016/S0038-0296(00)01087-6

Marcus-Steiff, J. (1977). L'information comme mode d'action des organisations de consommateurs. *Revue Francaise de Sociologie, 18*(1), 85–107. doi:10.2307/3320870

Morikawa, M., & Morrison, J. (2004). *Who develops ISO standards? A survey of participation in ISO's international standards development processes.* Retrieved December 10, 2008, from http://www.pacinst.org/reports/iso_participation/iso_participation_study.pdf

NO-REST. (2005). *Networked organisations – Research into standards and standardisation.* Retrieved May 10, 2008, from http://www.no-rest.org/Documents/D05&6_Final.pdf

Qui est l'association pour le lable de qualité? (n.d.). Retrieved December 10, 2008, from http://www.guetesiegel.ch/

Raines, S. (2003). Perception of legitimacy and efficacy in international environmental management standards: The impact of the participation gap. *Global Environmental Politics, 3*(3), 47–73. doi:10.1162/152638003322469277

Schmidt, S. K., & Werle, R. (1998). *Coordinating technology: Studies in the international standardization of telecommunications.* Cambridge, MA: MIT Press.

SNV. (2007). *Jahresbericht 2006.* Retrieved December 10, 2008, from http://www.mysnv.ch/document_show.cfm/Jahresbericht%202006?wm=c%28614%29cl%282%29cv%2820070618151 8%29&ext=.*

Tamm-Hallström, K. (2004). *Organizing international standardization: ISO and the IASC in quest of authority.* Cheltenham, UK: Edward Elgar.

Werle, R., & Iversen, E. J. (2006). Promoting legitimacy in technical standardization. *Science. Technology & Innovation Studies, 2*, 19–39.

ENDNOTES

[1] Our data encompass all mirrored committees in « interdisciplinary stock of standards (INB) that is under the organizational responsibility of the SNV. Standardization committees that are under the organizational responsibility of sectoral professionnal associations are not included.

This work was previously published in the International Journal of IT Standards and Standardization Research (IJITSR), Volume 8, Issue 1, edited by Kai Jakobs, pp. 11-27, copyright 2010 by IGI Publishing (an imprint of IGI Global)

Chapter 9
The INTERNORM Project:
Bridging Two Worlds of Expert- and Lay-Knowledge in Standardization

Jean-Christophe Graz
Université de Lausanne, Switzerland

Christophe Hauert
Université de Lausanne, Switzerland

ABSTRACT

This paper presents a pilot project to reinforce participatory practices in standardization. The INTERNORM project creates an interactive knowledge center based on the sharing of academic skills and experiences accumulated by the civil society, especially consumer associations, environmental associations and trade unions to strengthen the participatory process of standardization. The first objective of the project is action-oriented: INTERNORM provides a common knowledge pool supporting the participation of civil society actors to international standard-setting activities by bringing them together with academic experts in working groups and providing logistic and financial support to their participation in meetings of national and international technical committees. The second objective is analytical: the standardization action provides a research field for a better understanding of the participatory dynamics underpinning international standardization. This paper presents three incentives that explain civil society (non-)involvement in standardization that overcome conventional resource-based hypotheses: an operational incentive related to the use of standards in the selective goods provided by associations to their membership; a thematic incentive provided by the setting of priorities by strategic committees created in some standardization organization; and a rhetorical incentive related to the discursive resource that civil society concerns offers to the different stakeholders.

DOI: 10.4018/978-1-4666-2160-2.ch009

INTRODUCTION

Standardization is part of the infrastructure of globalization providing cross-border nongovernmental coordination mechanisms, which formally respect state sovereignty. Various studies in economics (Blind, 2004), in law (Schepel, 2005) in organizational science (Brunsson & Jacobsson, 2000), and international relations have examined how voluntary and consensual standards have become crucial tools in the organization of global markets (Graz, 2004, 2006; Tamm-Hallström, 2004; Krewer, 2005).

As the increased usage of standards affects a wide range of issues, such as environmental management, psychological tests, measures of the quality of medical services, and nanotechnologies, the quantitative and qualitative expansion of international standardization has reinforced enduring questions on the legitimacy of standards (Werle & Iversen, 2006, p. 20; Ruwet, 2009, pp. 12-13). In other words, who defines standard matters for the recognition of their greater use in society at large. In that respect, the participation of all stakeholders, including the weakest one (unions, NGO, consumers' associations) is crucial (Raines, 2003; Boström, 2006). Given the recognized role of consumers' associations, unions and environmental associations to express legitimate objectives, the question of their representation becomes central. Surprisingly, civil society participation in international standardization received little attention from scholars dedicated to the study of standardization (Wilcock & Colina, 2007, p. 3). Despite this lack of specific attention, studies on the world of standardization never fail to stress the under-representation of civil society actors, such as consumers' associations, environmental protection organizations, unions, and NGOs.

This paper present a pilot project called IN-TERNORM which was recently successfully submitted to the University of Lausanne in order to engage at both analytical and practical level the under-representation of civil society. INTERNORM aims to create an interactive knowledge center based on the sharing of academic skills and the experiences accumulated by the civil society, especially consumer associations, environmental associations and trade unions to strengthen the participatory process of standardization.

The INTERNORM project has a twofold objective. The first is action-oriented. At this level, INTERNORM is aimed at bridging the actors of the civil society and academics in order to sustain civil society participation in international standard-setting activities by the common pooling of the specific knowledge of these actors. Moreover the project should provide financial support to civil society actors for their participation in committees - most notably for the membership fees allowing access to national standardization bodies and for traveling and accommodation costs. The second objective of the project is an analytical one. The standardization action initiated through INTERNORM will provide a useful research field for a better understanding of the political, social and economic implications of standardization for society by studying the role of consumer associations, trade unions and environmental associations in the setting of the technical specifications governing globalization. Adopting a more long-term perspective on the links between standardization and civil society associations, we identify three incentives which explain the dynamic of their involvement. An operational incentive, related to the use of standards in the product and services provided by these associations to their members. A thematic incentive, provided by the setting of priorities by strategic committees created in some standardization organization. And a rhetorical incentive, related to the discursive resource that civil society concerns offers to stakeholders. These three incentives will be illustrated using the case of the consumers association as a precursory civil society associations (Hilton, 2008, p. 215).

In the next section, we present the rationale, the modus operandi and the different partners involved in the INTERNORM project. Then we will review the literature and outline the theoretical framework from which we analyze the dynamics governing the participation of civil society actors in international standard-setting activities. After some methodological considerations, we will conclude and discuss the strength and weakness of the project. As far as we know, no similar research-action project exists and in case of success, this project could generate parallel initiatives in other countries.

INTERNORM: RATIONALE, MODUS OPERANDI, AND PARTNERS INVOLVEMENT

Rationale of the Project

The INTERNORM project proposes to establish a platform that links knowledge and action in defining technical specifications governing the globalization of markets. It aims to develop exchanges between the scientific knowledge of academic scholars and the knowledge of civil society associations in order to support their participation in the development of international standards. The provision of academic knowledge in the construction of a "pluralistic expertise" (Kaufmann et al., 2004) and putting it into action will encourage the participation of under-represented actors in strengthening their competences. INTERNORM will thus allow a detailed analysis of the role of these actors.

One of the central issues raised by the growing role of international standards is their legitimacy regarding the participants in committees in charge of their development. In other words, who defines standards? Work on the world of standards never fail to emphasize how enterprises are over-represented. In contrast, civil society actors are under-represented, despite their recognized role in defending legitimate interests such as access to transparent information, protection

of environment or health and safety issues. The reasons commonly invoked to explain this under-representation are the lack of financial resources, knowledge and time (Schmidt & Werle, 1998; Tamm-Hallström, 2004). According to a recent study (Hauert, 2008), consumer representatives were in 2007 involved in less than one committee out of five in the Swiss standardization organization (SNV); despite a slight increase since 1987, their involvement has been confined to consumer goods and some transversal themes (such as corporate social responsibility).

It appears that many objects are standardized in the absence of consumers' and workers' representatives. In the few interviews conducted within the same study, the problem of expertise was a unanimously mentioned. A major consumer organizations in Switzerland has explicitly regretted the lack of participation of representatives from the academic world within the technical committees as well as the lack of academic support at their disposal. The highly technical nature of the deliberations in committees is an obstacle to greater involvement and effective participation of civil society associations: whether to understand or make suggestions, expertise is at the basis of the arguments mobilized in the committee deliberations. While these associations have a unique expertise in terms of consumers, workers, or environmental protection, they experience great difficulties in translating general concerns into the technical language which is a "compulsory figure" of the standard-setting activities (Mallard, 2000a, p. 57). For example, consumer associations wish to have condoms of quality, particularly in regard to resistance. The standardization work implies to translate the concept of resistance in a way that enables its physical measurement. In other words, a translation work must be accomplished between public health, safety or environmental concerns made in general terms and a series of tests organized and manipulated in a laboratory (Callon et al., 2001). Finally, in addition to technical expertise and lack of financial resources and time, the lack of knowledge of the formal and informal rules governing the standardization process has also emerged as a barrier to participation.

To improve the representation of the weakest stakeholder, some national standards bodies have established, often on the basis of public funding, consumers committees. In Switzerland no such body exists and at the government level, the Federal Office of Consumer Affairs participates in only a limited number of committees. Thus, the INTERNORM project will contribute to overcome this shortcomings in providing an interactive knowledge-building platform that sustain and support the participation of civil society associations in standard-setting activities.

Modus Operandi

INTERNORM is a four years project and will end in 2013. In order to ensure the operational activities, a project manager as well as a junior researcher will constitute the platform staff. At the operational level, the focus will be first to inform stakeholders on the objectives and functioning of INTERNORM and, if necessary, to raise their awareness of the issues of standardization. The realization of workshops will allow the different partners to select five technical committees of mutual interest on a deliberative basis. Then, the INTERNORM staff will have to manage information flows between academics, civil society and standardization bodies and provide logistical support for the organization of workshops and for the participation in SNV and ISO technical committees. Within the latter, an academic and a representative of civil society will ensure the joint implementation of prior knowledge developed during the workshops. The presence of an observer during the workshop and committees deliberations with a greater attention to the dynamics of work will feed the analysis.

We limit the purpose of participation in committees under the auspices of ISO. The delimitation of the research-action field is mainly justified by the costs of participation in international committees (travel, accommodation) as well as by the existence of the ANEC (the European consumer voice in standardization) in charge of consumer protection within the various European standardization bodies. In addition, the proximity of the central secretariat of ISO (in Geneva) facilitates the establishment of the collaboration. The participation in an ISO standard-setting committee involves the participation in the national mirror committee, where national experts to the ISO committee are appointed. Following this procedure, INTERNORM will support the representation of consumers associations, environmental associations and trade unions at the international level through the participation in the Swiss mirror committees.

To sum up, in order to strengthen the participation of civil society actors in standard-setting activities, the INTERNORM platform will:

- Disseminate information on the existence of the platform within the various associations of civil society interested in participating in standardization work.
- Provide organizational support for the exchange of knowledge between civil society actors and academics on the process and purpose of standardization.
- Materially support the access of consumer associations, environmental associations and trade unions in the work of Swiss and international standard-setting bodies.
- Analyze more precisely the standards development process with regard to the participation of different stakeholders, their resources and interests.
- Disseminate and exploit the output of INTERNORM through conferences, scientific publications, and the use of the relay provided by the media of the partners.
- And, according to the results obtained, undertake the necessary steps to sustain the operation of the platform. Various funding sources will then be considered.

Partners Involvement

INTERNORM is a pilot project. In order to create an interactive knowledge center based on the sharing of academic skills and the experiences accumulated by the civil society, especially consumer associations, environmental protection and trade, the project relies on the practical involvement of these actors in the elaboration of standards. Thus we have to identify the possible partners and ensure their support.

A first category of partners is logically constituted by standardization bodies. The ISO and the SNV showed strong interest in the project and formally support it. The involvement of these partners secures the presence of observers during the committee deliberation as well as sustains the appointment of INTERNORM representatives (an academic scholar and a civil society representative) as experts to ISO committees.

On the academic side, professors and researchers from various departments of the University of Lausanne have been contacted to act as departmental correspondent of the INTERNORM platform. Their support is vital as they will bring their own academic knowledge to the project and offer it a large and highly specialized research pool. Actually, we received support of scholars belonging to the following bodies of the University of Lausanne:

- Faculty of Law and Criminal Justice
- Faculty of Business and Economics
- Faculty of Geosciences and Environment
- Faculty of Social and Political Sciences

The identification of civil society association was facilitated by the existence of a research which identified the actual civil society actors involved in standard-setting activities in Switzerland. These actors were asked for support and we have also included actors who were not previously involved in standard-setting activities. Most contacted associations were at first glance interested in the project, but some have expressed fears in relation to the workload that an effective participation would imply. Others – most notably trade union – were not aware of the importance of their participation and of the way in which standard affect their members. A few example of standardization's impact on their field of activity have then helped to raise their awareness. Today the following associations have provided a formal support to the project:

- Swiss Trade Union (the umbrella association for most trade unions in Switzerland)
- World Wildlife Fund - Switzerland
- Swiss Patients Organization

We are also in contact with the main Swiss consumers associations, but some procedural questions are delaying their official support.

Finally we have also seek and receive support from the Federal Office of Consumer Affairs, who is active in standardization issue. This office could provide a substantial support in order to sustain the platform after the end of the project.

The practical involvement of the academics and associational partners will occur within the INTERNORM workshops and within the SNV and ISO selected committees. The INTERNORM workshops will first provide a forum where the relevant standards committees will be identified. Then, it is in these workshops that standards will be discussed and propositions elaborated. The partners are also asked to diffuse the work and achievement of INTERNORM through their specific media. They should lastly take part to different valorization action which are planned – most notably a conference at the end of the project.

Analytical Framework

INTERNORM provides an excellent opportunity to analyze the dynamic of civil society actors participation in standard-setting activities. Standardization studies conventionally explain the under-representation of civil society actors in international committees of standardization by lack of financial, cognitive and temporal resources (Egan, 1998, p. 492; Schmidt & Werle, 1998, pp. 87-89; Tamm-Hallström, 2004, p. 32). As a recent email exchange (initiated by K. Jakobs, April 3, 2009) between EURAS members about "Evaluating standards people" suggests, negotiating skills and the knowledge of procedure are also essential for effective participation of all stakeholders, and education is a major element in that regard (de Vries & Simons, 2006, p. 19). The development of a standard at the ISO can be viewed as a long-term activity, taking an average of 36 months. Active participation involves the reading and understanding of the standard discussed during committee meetings, and participation in the latter further adds to the workload. In addition, participation in committees incurs a number of expenses, especially at the logistical level (travel and accommodation) and fees. Finally, technical expertise is required to comprehend and formulate propositions, since it is the basis of argumentation during deliberations. As stated above, the technical language is a "compulsory figure" of the standardization work (Mallard, 2000a, p. 57). While industries have access to the required technical expertise by their involvement in the production process of the goods and services subject to standardization, civil society actors find themselves far removed from the manufacturing process and its underlying technical expertise.

These explanations are general and could not benefit from a real fieldwork following the ongoing process within existing committees. They provide few information about the specific dynamic of the involvement of civil society associations in standard-setting activities. It remains unclear, in particular, who participates and why, where do they participate and how do they impact upon standards definitions procedures. Why, for instance, an association rather than another is taking part to such activities? Moreover, as the thematic scope of standard-setting organizations has expanded

behind purely technical matters, it is important to evaluate the extent to which the involvement of these associations reflects this evolution. In other words, where do they participate? Finally, it seems necessary to move beyond the statement of their under-representation in order to evaluate their real impact on committee deliberations when they are present. Here, the core question to be tackled is how these associations could achieve significant impact upon the standardization work once their participation has improved?

In order to get a better understanding of the specific dynamic of the involvement of civil society associations in standard-setting activities, it is fruitful to identify the main factors which contributed to link these associations to standard-setting activities. As "civil society" is a very broad category, we focus on the case of the consumers associations to illustrate how links were established and how they are likely to impact upon their participation. These links lead to the identification of three main incentives that govern the participation of consumers in standard-setting activities: an *operational incentive*, a *thematic incentive* and a *rhetorical incentive*. These incentives constitute our analytical framework and are aimed at explaining why consumers associations participate, where, and how; in other words they help us to understand the dynamic of the involvement of consumers associations.

The participation of consumers is important in order to bring "real world requirements" to the standard-setting process (Jakobs et al., 1997). Moreover their inclusion brings various material, cognitive and symbolic resources that can be mobilized by standardization bodies to bolster their credibility (Boström, 2006, p. 361). Thus, involving consumers and taking their claims into account contribute to the construction of the authority of standardization bodies through input and throughput legitimacy. While the importance of consumer representation was recognised long ago by the creation in 1978 of the ISO Committee on consumer policy (COPOLCO), it must be noted that the input of this body cannot be equated with direct participation in technical committees in which it has for instance no voting rights. According to its terms of reference, COPOLCO only "selects areas in ISO's work that are of priority to consumers... develops publications to promote consumer participation in standards work and to train consumer representatives for this task. It coordinates training activities and representation ... organizes annual workshops that bring together representatives of consumers, public authorities, manufacturers and standardization experts" (ISO, n.d.). Whatever the positive outcomes of such procedures, they differ from potential results to be expected from the direct participation of consumers' group and civil society associations in the technical work to be sustained by the INTERNORM platform.

It is worth noting that standardization has offered a valuable tool for associations and governments in charge of consumer protection. As early as 1929, comparative testing activities were launched in order to provide the consumer with accurate information he could mobilized in his buying decision (Hilton, 2008, p. 216; Ruffat, 1987, pp. 32-33). According to Mallard (2000b, p. 392), conducting comparative tests is a current practice that serves to feed "the consumer press" which represents a substantive part of consumers' associations' financing. In other words, comparative tests belongs to products that consumers associations provide to their membership as it usually includes a subscription to a magazine with valuable consumer-oriented information. The realization of these comparative tests has encouraged consumer associations to take a closer look at the work of standardization bodies. As Arthur Kallet, director of Consumers Union put it in 1956, " Few of the testing agencies' technical problems, from brand sampling to rating, are outside the orbit of cooperatives approaches to solutions under the aegis of standardization bodies"; he consequently pointed up "(...) the need for aid by other qualified agencies, primarily through the standardization process." (Kallet, 1956, p. 288). So, "It is understood that for comparative testing to be reliable it must use testing standards and even develop future standards" (Cochoy, 2005, p. S45). As we see, consumers' associations may achieve significant benefits in using standards. In that regard, the participation in standard-setting activities is not only a resource-consuming activity, but also a resource-providing activity through its inclusion in the production of selective goods. So the usage of standards by an association in the provision of selective goods (i.e. through comparative testing) supports and encourages its participation to the committee in charge of its definition. Their involvement will thus follow an *operational incentive.*

According to Marcus-Steiff (1977, p. 88), one of the main purpose of consumers' associations is to inform consumers. These informational tasks can be performed through comparative testing or labeling activities, which are mainly standard-based activities. However, consumers' associations' informational tasks concerned not every objects, but are concentrated on products and services of mass consumption as well as on broader societal issue (health, safety, environment). Consequently, the topical specificity of consumers' associations' implication in standardization committees should reflect these themes. Moreover, the institutionalization of the consumer representation through the COPOLCO provides a framework that also oriented their thematic involvement. But "These new institutional arrangements did not, however, mean that consumers took part directly in the standardizing process. Consumer were involved in the setting of priorities, but remained outside the technical work. Consumers were, therefore, more "trustees" than "executives" in the standardization process" (Cochoy, 2006, p. 153). Even if consumers were more "trustees" than "executives", the setting of priorities in this strategic committee should be reflected in their thematic involvement in the technical committees. The topical specificity of the participation of consumers association will thus follow a *thematic incentive*.

A last and more general incentive is rhetorical. Frank Cochoy suggest that "Industrialists took consumer protection as a means to prevent unfair competition, and standardizers promoted the consumer standpoint as a way to "exist" in discussions with their industrial partners" (2006, p. 145). Following his argument, consumers provide a rhetorical resource for standardizers as well as for industrialists which in turn reinforce consumers' effective participation (Cochoy, 2000, p. 84). This rhetorical incentive refers primarily to the dynamics driving their effective involvement. We also extend this notion to the distinct way that allows consumers stakes to be taken into account during the committees' deliberations. For example, a lighter manufacturer has achieved significant success in promoting higher security standards for lighters in the name of the consumers (Ben Youssef et al., 2005, pp. 381-382). As we see, all stakeholders can talk in the name of the consumer. This suggest that the propensity to include consumers associations stakes depends of the adequacy of the different interests speaking for the consumer. The participation of consumers association will thus follow a *rhetorical incentive*.

To sum up, the lack of cognitive and material support unquestionably explains to some extent the under-representation of civil society actors in standardization. Yet, the following assumptions may well supplement such a conventional resource-based explanation:

1. The frequent use of national or international standards in the products and services provided by an association (comparative testing or labeling activities) encourages its participation (operational incentive).
2. The participation of associations is likely to be focused in committees dealing with cross-cutting themes regarded as inherently more controversial and in those relating to products or services to which it has acquired specific expertise and identified as strategic priorities (thematic incentive).
3. Taking into account demands from consumer associations, environmental organization and trade unions depends on the rhetorical resource that they represent for other stakeholders (rhetorical incentive).

These three hypotheses should contribute to a more detailed and comprehensive explanation of the participation of consumer associations, environmental organizations and trade unions in the standardization process. The first hypothesis explains *who* participates and *why* by focusing on the selectivity of the operational incentive provided by standard-based comparative testing and labeling activities; the second clarifies *where* their participation takes place by examining the thematic incentive of the distinct issues to be standardized; the third untangles *how* the influence of civil society associations in standardization is likely to be reinforced by pointing to the rhetorical incentives that their participation offers to other participants.

Methodological Considerations

The analysis of the standard-setting process is prompt to direct observation, because negotiations on distinct standards involve a limited number of places, persons, and actions allowing increasingly fine-tuned observations (Arborio & Fournier, 1999). Moreover direct observation is particularly relevant in understanding how a microcosm functions and evolves over a "long term" period and standards-setting belongs to such a microcosm. Furthermore, standard-setting in committee is a research field where the recording is a recurring activity and the presence of observers a widespread practice. Direct observation will allow us to identify participants in the international committees and to follow "step by step" the actions taking place in these committees (Peretz, 1998). Furthermore we will detect the resources mobilized during the discussions and the dynamic of the standardization work within the committee. This ethnographic approach will not be limited to the work in the deliberation room, but will also be used in coffee breaks and lunches in order to broaden our understanding of coalition building process. Access to the field research will be facilitated by the institutional membership of INTERNORM to the SNV and by the contacts already woven with the SNV during a past internship of an INTERNORM staff member. Finally, these observations will be supplemented by interviews and consultation of written documents.

DISCUSSION

Standardization actions initiated through INTER-NORM should sustain and reinforce the participatory process of standardization organization and provide a useful research field for a better understanding of the role of consumer associations, trade unions and environmental associations in the setting of the technical specifications governing globalization. This represents the major strength of the project. We have to turn now to the possible weaknesses of the project which identification can lead to a significant improvement of the project.

Concerning the rationale of the project, it could be argued that what is needed from a participation of the civil society is not so a technical competence, but more a contribution in term of real-world requirements. Following this argument, the task of civil society actors is to make other stakeholders aware of the possible (mis-) use that end users will make of the object under standardization. Consequently, academic knowledge will be of minor use in strengthening their participation – consumers' association do not need an academic to sustain the fact that small mechanical parts of toys can be eaten by kids. Being aware of that different line of reasoning will enable us to assess this argument. Even if the interviews with key representatives of civil

society actors tend to invalidate this argument, the participation in standard-setting committee will allow us to assess the extent to which these actors can bring "real world" requirement on a trivial – or non technical – basis. By so doing, we have to keep in mind that the validity of this argument is perhaps related to the thematic of the committee, as suggested by Jakobs et al. (1997).

A second weakness can be related to the tension between the two aims of project, on the one hand a practical involvement of partners in standardization activities, and on the other an analysis of the dynamic governing their involvement. As the project itself provides material and cognitive support for participation, it impacts upon the possibility to assess the operational incentive. This argument is correct, but it does not invalidate the framework of analysis. First, on epistemological ground, a non positivist understanding of social sciences takes for granted that knowledge production interferes with the reality which such knowledge refers to. Second, in providing crucial resources for participation to civil society associations, the project tries to move beyond the classical resource-based explanations. Third, the incentive provided by the project does not invalidate other incentives: if, for instance, the operational incentive is important in explaining why an association rather than another takes part to standardization processes, associations using standards in the provision of selective goods should be even more interested in taking part to the INTERNORM project than associations who do not include standards in their provisions.

To conclude, the INTERNORM project represents a great opportunity to achieve significant impact on standardization in regard to civil society concerns as well as to raise consciousness about the social, economical and political impacts of standards in society at large. If this goal is attained, the viability of the INTERNORM platform should be more easily secured through external funding. Such an outcome should in turn encourage a replication of the project in other countries.

REFERENCES

Arborio, A.-M., & Fournier, P. (1999). *L'enquête et ses méthodes: l'observation directe*. Paris, France: Nathan Université.

Ben Youssef, H., Grolleau, G., & Jebsi, K. (2005). L'utilisation stratégique des instances de normalisation environnementale. *Revue Internationales de Droit Economique, 4*, 367–388. doi:10.3917/ride.194.0367

Blind, K. (2004). *The economics of standards: Theory, evidence, policy*. Cheltenham, UK: Edward Elgar Publishing.

Boström, M. (2006). Regulatory Credibility and Authority through Inclusiveness: Standardization Organizations in Cases of Eco-Labelling. *Organization, 13*(3), 345–367. doi:10.1177/1350508406063483

Brunsson, N., & Jacobsson, B. (Eds.). (2000). *A World of Standards*. New York, NY: Oxford University Press.

Callon, M., Lascoumes, P., & Barthe, Y. (2001). *Agir dans un monde incertain. Essai sur la démocratie technique*. Paris, France: Seuil.

Cochoy, F. (2000). De l'AFNOR à NF ou la progressive marchandisation de la normalisation industrielle. *Reseaux, 102*, 63–89.

Cochoy, F. (2005). A brief history of 'customers,' or the gradual standardization of markets and organizations. *Sociologie du Travail, 47*, S36–S56. doi:10.1016/j.soctra.2005.08.001

Cochoy, F. (2006). The industrial Roots of Contemporary Political Consumerism: The Case of the French Standardization Movement. In M. Micheletti, A. Follesdal, & D. Stolle, (Eds.), *Politics, products, and markets: Exploring political consumerism past and present* (pp. 145–160). London: Transaction Publishers.

De Vries, H. J., & Simons, J. (2006). Effectiveness of participation in Standardisation. *Synthesis Journal*, 15-20.

Egan, M. (1998). Regulatory strategies, delegation and European market integration. *Journal of European Public Policy, 5*(3), 485–506. doi:10.1080/135017698343938

Graz, J. C. (2004). Quand les normes font loi. Topologie intégrée et processus différenciés de la normalisation international. *Revue. Etudes Internationales, 35*(2), 233–260. doi:10.7202/009036ar

Graz, J. C. (2006). International standardisation and corporate democracy. In K. G. Giesen, & K. van der Pijl, (Eds.), *Global Norms for the 21st Century* (pp. 118–133). Cambridge, UK: Cambridge Scholars Press.

Hauert, C. (2008). *Normalisation: Quelle place pour les consommateurs? Etude de la participation des associations de consommateurs aux comités miroirs établis en Suisse en 1987, 1997 et 2007*. Lausanne, Switzerland: Mimeo.

Hilton, M. (2008). The death of a consumer society. *Transactions of the royal historical society, 18*, 211–236. doi:10.1017/S0080440108000716

ISO. (n.d.). *What COPOLCO does*. Retreived May 22, 2009, from http://www.iso.org/iso/resources/resources_consumers/what_copolco_does.htm

Jakobs, K., Procter, R., & Williams, R. (1997, July). Users in IT-standardisation: A myth revised. In *Proceedings of the 1st International Conference on Managing Enterprise Stakeholders, Mech. Eng. Publications*, Loughborough, UK (pp. 599-604).

Kallet, A. (1956). Standards for rating consumer goods. In D. Reck, (Ed.), *National standards in a modern economy* (pp. 275–291). New York: Harper & Brother.

Kaufmann, A., et al. (2004). De la gestion à la négociation des risques: Apports des procédures participatives d'évaluation des choix technologiques. *Revue européenne des sciences sociales, 130*, 109-120.

Kerwer, D. (2005). Rules that many use: Standards and Global Regulation. *Governance: An International Journal of Policy, Administration and Institutions, 18*(4), 611–632. doi:10.1111/j.1468-0491.2005.00294.x

Mallard, A. (2000a). L'écriture des normes. *Reseaux, 102*, 37–61.

Mallard, A. (2000b). La presse de consommation et le marché. Enquête sur le tiers consumériste. *Sociologie du Travail, 42*, 391–409. doi:10.1016/S0038-0296(00)01087-6

Marcus-Steiff, J. (1977). L'information comme mode d'action des organisations de consommateurs. *Revue Francaise de Sociologie, 18*(1), 85–107. doi:10.2307/3320870

Peretz, H. (1998). *Les méthodes en sociologie: l'observation*. Paris: La découverte & Syros.

Raines, S. (2003). Perception of legitimacy and efficacy in international environmental management standards: The impact of the participation gap. *Global Environmental Politics, 3*(3), 47–73. doi:10.1162/152638003322469277

Ruffat, M. (1987). *Le contre-pouvoir consommateur aux états-unis*. Paris, France: PUF.

Ruwet, C. (2009). *Des filetages à la RSE. Normalisation et démocratie. Sociologie du processus d'élaboration d'ISO 26000*. Unpublished doctoral dissertation, Université Catholique de Louvain.

Schepel, H. (2005). *The constitution of private governance - product standards in the regulation of integrating markets*. Oxford, UK: Hart.

Schmidt, S. K., & Werle, R. (1998). *Coordinating technology: Studies in the international standardization of telecommunications*. Cambridge, MA: MIT Press.

Tamm-Hallström, K. (2004). *Organizing international standardization: ISO and the IASC in Quest of Authority*. Cheltenham, UK: Edward Elgar.

Werle, R., & Iversen, E. J. (2006). Promoting legitimacy in technical standardization. *Science. Technology & Innovation Studies, 2*, 19–39.

Wilcock, A., & Colina, A. (2007). Consumer representation on consensus standards committees: A value-added practice. *International Journal of Services and Standards, 3*(1), 1–17. doi:10.1504/IJSS.2007.011825

This work was previously published in the International Journal of IT Standards and Standardization Research (IJITSR), Volume 9, Issue 1, edited by Kai Jakobs, pp. 52-61, copyright 2011 by IGI Publishing (an imprint of IGI Global)

Section 5
Shaping Factors

Chapter 10
Beyond the "Point of No Return":
Constructing Irreversibility in Decision Making on the Tetra Standard in Dutch Emergency Communication

Anique Hommels
Maastricht University, The Netherlands

Tineke M. Egyedi
Delft University of Technology, The Netherlands

ABSTRACT

This paper analyzes the role of 'irreversibility' in the decision-making process for a standard for the national Dutch emergency communication network. In the late 1980s, ETSI, the European Telecommunication Standards Institute, started the development of the so-called Tetra standard. Tetra is a standard for digital radio communication and is mostly applied in emergency communication (for police, ambulance, and fire brigade). In the early 1990s, several European governments decided to replace their analogue radio equipment for emergency communication by advanced digital communication systems. The Dutch involvement in Tetra started around 1992, but it took until November 2001 before the official governmental decision to launch the national C2000 network was taken. This paper argues that at that moment the 'point of no return' of the C2000 project had already passed (in the mid 1990s). We explain this using the concept of 'constructed irreversibility'. We analyze a number of core decisions and choices of the Dutch government in the C2000 project that resulted in irreversibility. We conclude by discussing the disadvantages and the advantages of irreversibility in this innovation project.

DOI: 10.4018/978-1-4666-2160-2.ch010

INTRODUCTION: RISKY DECISION MAKING IN LARGE INNOVATION PROJECTS

In the early 1990s, the Netherlands was among the first countries in Europe to get involved in the development and implementation of the Tetra standard in a nationwide network for emergency communication. Large technological projects such as C2000 are often characterized by a multitude of problems: they take much longer than expected, the costs are hard to predict and often overrun, and their development is characterized by many risks and uncertainties (Flyvbjerg, Bruzelius, & Rothengatter, 2003). This can be explained by the complexity of such projects: C2000 is a project in which several technological and organizational innovations had to be combined. The heterogeneity of these projects—their interwovenness with, for instance, political ideals, social changes, user practices and financial considerations—makes them highly complex to manage. Moreover, taking into account that innovation processes are never linear and that their outcome and added value can remain highly uncertain for a long time, it is not surprising that the development of such projects is often difficult and problematic.

Many examples of such risky projects can be given in the Netherlands and worldwide. Given that large areas of the Netherlands are below sea level and the ensuing threat of floods, the Delta Plan and the Oosterschelde storm surge barrier are at present considered to be the crown jewels of Dutch water engineering. But they have been realized with a ten year delay and a budget increase of 30 percent (Bijker, 1993, 1995). The Delta Plan required technological, organizational and economic innovations: Rijkswaterstaat, the Dutch departmental ministry for waterways, established a new research institute for water management that competed with existing institutes, a new on-site training site for young engineers was introduced, and new contracts had to be made with construction and water works companies. In the 1970s,

the political circumstances changed: the taken for granted authority of institutes like Rijkswaterstaat declined and there was more attention for the environment. Political pressure rose and the closing of the Oosterschelde became a topic of heated political debate in the early 1970s. Eventually the decision was taken to build a permeable storm surge barrier that could be closed in case of high tide (Bijker, 1993). Other large technological projects in cities, such as the Boston Central Artery/ Tunnel project (Hughes, 1998), the reconstruction of Utrecht's railway station area (Hommels, 2005) and the Channel Tunnel between the UK and France (Flyvbjerg, Bruzelius, & Rothengatter, 2003) show similar processes of complexity, delays and huge technological and financial risks.

Trying to understand the complexities and risks involved in large technological projects as C2000, we foreground one important mechanism: the role of irreversibility in innovation projects. The Tetra standard, initiated by the European Telecommunication Standards Institute (ETSI) since the late 1980s, was still very much under development when the Dutch had to decide on the C2000 infrastructure they wished to implement. In the early 1990s, not many manufacturers had the expertise to develop infrastructures that complied with the Tetra standard. But the Netherlands, being a small country with a small market, wanted to engage in Tetra development because building its own national network would be far too expensive. Having chosen for Tetra around 1994, it took until 2001 before an official governmental decision was taken to start the national roll-out of the C2000 network. In this paper we argue that this 2001 decision was taken long after the "point of no return" in the C2000 project had been reached. What factors had made the choice for Tetra irreversible? We attempt to answer this question with data from archival research, i.e., by analyzing reports, correspondence between those involved in standards and policy development, minutes of meetings (e.g. standards meetings in ETSI, Schengen Telecom Group), etc. that give insight into the Dutch decision making process around Tetra and C2000. We further conducted a series of in-depth interviews with key actors in this process that are listed at the close of this article. In the running text, the interviewees are indicated by [#. number on the list].

We position this paper in the middle of a long-running debate between social constructivists, economists of innovation and standardization researchers about the degree in which technology development can be shaped by human actors.

Irreversibility in Innovation and Standardization

Economists of innovation have advanced the notions of path dependence and lock-in (Arthur, 1984). Path dependence refers to the idea that past events keep influencing the developmental path or trajectory of a technology. Path dependence develops over a longer period of time. As such, "local, short-term contingencies can exercise lasting effects" (MacKenzie & Wajcman, 1999, p. 20). Technological change is always path dependent "in the sense that it builds on, and takes for granted, what has gone before. Today's choices constrain tomorrow's possibilities" (Edwards, Jackson, Bowker, & Knobel, 2007, p. 21) Technical standards, being endogenous to technology, may also foster path dependence (Egyedi, 1996).[1] They tend to become entrenched in institutional and technological arrangements, and, as it were, locked into a specific developmental path. This can make it difficult to change them later on (Vrancken, 2008). The economic standardization literature has mainly emphasized the disadvantages of path dependence in technology development: if a specific standard is chosen too early, there is a possibility of a lock-in into an inferior technology. The aim should be to prevent a too early lock-in and allow the 'best' standard to survive (Blind, 2004). However, there is only a narrow policy window. That is, there is only limited time during which effective public policy interventions can be made. "Increasing returns implies that once the market has "chosen a path" it becomes increasingly difficult to change that path, so policy is most effective early in the process. This is the time, though, at which uncertainty is greatest and the probability of making errors is highest." (Cowan, 1992, p. 287)

Crude notions of path dependence and trajectories as developing according to an internal, "natural" logic have been criticized by social constructivist Science, Technology and Society studies (STS) scholars, who emphasize the contingent and fluid character of technology development. Social constructivists describe "trajectories" or "paths" as being actively constructed or destructed instead of being given by nature (Garud & Karnøe, 2001). The sociologist of technology Trevor Pinch (2001) has correctly pointed out the "a-symmetric" analyses of path dependence by economists, who only invoke history when addressing "inferior" technologies. In contrast, Pinch proposes a more constructivist variant that focuses both on the paths taken and alternative paths not taken. Furthermore, it is often disputed what the 'best' technology is. Whereas, if a technology has an alternative that is seen as better by many, it is unlikely that the 'inferior' technology will survive since there are many strategies (e.g. subsidizing or offering it below cost) to overcome lock-in (MacKenzie & Wajcman, 1999). At the same time, social constructivists argue that it is important to keep a technology as flexible as possible before 'obduracy', i.e., resistance to change (Hommels, 2005), occurs and the freedom of choice of actors diminishes.

To analyze the material-cognitive frame or mindset of the key actors and explain the obduracy they experience, we use Wiebe Bijker's (1995) concept of 'technological frame' and Leon Festinger's (1957) theory of 'cognitive dissonance'. Bijker (1995) developed the concept of 'technological frame' in the context of the SCOT-model (Social Construction of Technology) (Pinch & Bijker, 1984, 1987). A technological frame is built up during interactions among relevant social groups. It may consist of goals, problems, problem-solving strategies, standards, current theories, design methods, testing procedures and so forth (see Table 1 for his tentative list of elements of a technological frame). In particular the role of 'exemplary artifacts' in the technological frame is important to consider for the analysis of obduracy:

An artifact in the role of exemplar (that is, after closure, when it is part of a technological frame) has become obdurate. The relevant social groups have, in building up the technological frame, invested so much in the artifact that its meaning has become quite fixed—it cannot be changed easily, and it forms part of a hardened network of practices, theories and social institutions. From this time on it may indeed happen that, naively spoken, the artifact 'determines' social development (Bijker, 1995, p. 282).

Because technological frames are of a shared nature, they have an obduracy of their own. Avoiding the deterministic connotation of older work on path dependence, and taking a social constructivist approach to technological development while acknowledging the obdurate character of technologi-

Table 1. Tentative list of elements of technological frames (Bijker, 1995, p. 125)

Goals
Key problems
Problem-solving strategies
Requirements to be met by problem solutions
Current theories
Tacit knowledge
Testing procedures
Design methods and criteria
Users' practice
Perceived substitution function
Exemplary artifacts

cal frames, we propose the notion of 'constructed irreversibility' to understand decision making about complex multi-actor innovation projects and the C2000 project in particular. 'Constructed irreversibility' refers to a—intentionally or unintentionally—created situation in which actors who are involved in a decision process feel that they have no choice but to pursue the path previously embarked upon. Earlier behavior (i.e. actions, decisions) are experienced to be irreversible.

The concept of 'technological frame' is used to analyze the constructed nature, the direction and the obduracy of the technological path taken. To better understand the experienced 'irreversibility' of technical choices in the C2000 project, we apply the theory of cognitive dissonance developed by Leon Festinger (1957) and elaborated by colleague social psychologists.

The essence of Festinger's theory is that inconsistent sets of knowledge or cognitions give rise to the disturbing state of cognitive dissonance which people will try to lessen or avoid. Two cognitions "are in a dissonant relation if, considering these two alone, the obverse of one would follow from the other ... x and y are dissonant if not-x follows from y" (Festinger, 1957, p. 13) At stake are cognitions that have contradictory implications for behavior (Berkowitz, 1980, p. 88). Later theorists qualified Festinger's theory noting that cognitive dissonance does not always arise. Conflicting cognitions are only disturbing if an individual has publicly committed[2] herself to one of these views (Brehm & Cohen, 1962) and believes she has a personal responsibility[3] for creating the inconsistency (Wicklund & Brehm, 1976). For example, someone thinks of herself as a healthy person but she also smokes. She can, for example, reduce the cognitive dissonance she feels by stopping smoking but also by seeking information, which indicates that only heavy smokers die from smoking. More in general, people reduce cognitive dissonance by altering their beliefs or actions, and their interpretation thereof to make it more acceptable. They, for example, tend to avoid information that is inconsistent with their beliefs, attitudes and decisions ('selective exposure').

Choosing between options can also give rise to cognitive dissonance. Cognitive dissonance is all the more disturbing if the decision is important, difficult to make, has aversive consequences and is irreversible. A postdecisional conflict may then emerge. Experiments show that many people try to reduce postdecisional dissonance by altering their understanding of the alternatives they faced when they took the decision (Wicklund & Brehm, 1976, pp. 83-84). They convince themselves that the alternative they selected is even more attractive and that the rejected alternative is less attractive (Berkowitz, 1980, p. 92). There is a psychological need to reduce the uncomfortable tension created by cognitive dissonance. Once the dissonance-reducing action has been taken, 'cognitive irreversibility' (Lepper et al., 1970) may occur. That is, certain psychological processes, once initiated, are not easily reversed. According to Lepper et al. (1970), when a person engages in a dissonance-arousing action, cognitive dissonance theory predicts that he will examine the cognitions relevant at the time of commitment and proceed to reduce dissonance.[4]

We apply cognitive dissonance theories in two ways, first, as an explanation of *ex ante* conformance to and reinforcement of a shared technological frame. Second, we use it to explain perceived irreversibility of ongoing developments. Focusing on the role of the Dutch government, we highlight a number of decisions and choices that have contributed to the irreversibility of the Tetra choice in the C2000 project. We start our case study with an analysis of the technological frame that was built up by the Dutch government. Then, we show how this frame became challenged by other actors (such as members of the Dutch parliament) and developments. We will analyze how governmental actors dealt with these dissonating forces and tried to reinforce their technological frame, thus constructing an irreversible path for the development and implementation of C2000.

Constructing a Technological Frame around Tetra

In the early 1990s, the Netherlands and Belgium made plans to develop a new national radio communication network for the emergency services. In the Netherlands this project started as PCS2000 (Police Communication System 2000) but was renamed C2000 in 1994. At that time, the scope of the project had already been broadened to include not only police communication but also communication among the ambulances and fire brigades. This project fell under the responsibility of the Ministry of the Interior. Almost from the start[5], the Netherlands wanted to base its system on a common European standard and became involved in the international standardization efforts at ETSI.

Why did the Dutch government involve itself in these international initiatives? The Dutch 'Tetra feasibility study' of July 1994 mentions economic reasons for standardization: the Dutch 'market' for safety and security was too small for manufacturers to develop products only for this market. Using a single standard for all safety organizations in Europe would provide advantages of price, choice of suppliers and technical alternatives. The Dutch considered supplier-independence a main asset of international standardization (Jastrzebski, 1993). According to a report of the Dutch Fire Brigade Federation (NBF, 1993), the complexity of the technology and related development costs would anyway require a European standard. Also the Dutch police thought that a specific police standard would be too costly.[6] Moreover, the EU had to protect itself from competition by the United States and Japan (NBF, 1993).

ETSI had started the development of a mobile digital radio system in 1988. In the early days, this system was called MDTRS (Mobile Digital Trunking Radio System). In 1992, it was re-named Tetra (Trans European Trunked Radio, later when the global capacities of Tetra became clear, TErrestrial Trunked RAdio).[7] A competing standard called APCO25 had already been developed in the United States. The head of the R&D department of the ICT organization of the Dutch police was informed about the developments in the United States by his British colleague. The British had been following the developments in the United States around APCO25 for some time and had become quite enthusiastic. They also knew about the new ETSI project to develop a standard for mobile radio communication for a wide market and they informed the Dutch about this. Together, they agreed that the British would follow the developments in the United States and that the Dutch would focus on ETSI. Soon, the UK also joined ETSI. This was the start of the Dutch involvement in ETSI RES-6 where the Tetra standard was developed (#1).[8]

At the same time, a Working group of the Telecom experts of the Schengen countries[9] was established. This group would define the functional requirements for the ETSI standard that was being developed. According to one of the Dutch representatives in the Schengen Telecom group, the Dutch followed the developments in the United States quite closely. However, they finally decided that they preferred a European standard, developed by European industry. As Europeans they wanted to support the European industry, not the American. Moreover, Schengen Telecom would never accept APCO25: they clearly preferred a European standard developed by ETSI (#2). [10] According to a former high-ranked civil servant at the ministry of Justice, "In technological matters, the Netherlands has always been a country very willing to cooperate in Europe. (…) So, if there would be any chance of a European technological development and a European solution, you would go for that – for reasons of scale and impact." (#3)

In addition to economic-political reasons, the Dutch also expected a European standard to bet-ter address the needs within Europe. A telecom engineer of the Dutch police argues that European products better take the specific European circumstances into account. For instance, in Europe, the geographical distance between big cities is much smaller than in the United States. Therefore, less powerful transmitters would be needed: "We need a technology that better matches the highly populated areas we have." (#2) This line of reasoning is also expressed in the minutes of a Schengen Telecom meeting on June 23, 1992 in the Netherlands, where the Germans claim that: "the advantage of [the Tetra standard] over the APCO standard is that the latter is based on the American geographical and urban reality, which is altogether different from the European situation."[11]

The two alternative technologies that were available at time, GSM and Tetrapol, were never seriously considered by the Dutch government. Tetrapol was a French industry standard, developed by Matra and not acknowledged by ETSI. The Dutch did not want to limit themselves beforehand to one supplier (Matra) and therefore Tetrapol was not an option for them (#2, #1, # 4). GSM was rejected by police experts because it did not allow group communication and required too much time for establishing radio contact for conference calls. This made GSM inappropriate for emergency services. Finally, GSM is no dedicated network, which made this network more vulnerable to overhearing conversations (#2).

Although the Schengen Telecom group was still debating the desired functional requirements of the standard and ETSI worked hard on defining the standard, the Dutch government's preference for Tetra grew stronger and stronger. This is illustrated, for instance, by the signing of a so-called Memorandum of Understanding (MoU) in support of the Tetra standard in December 1994. The MoU signaled a collective support for Tetra. Parties that signed the MoU (manufacturers, users, regulators and accredited test houses) thereby demonstrated their intention to stimulate product development based on this standard. According to the Head of R&D of the Dutch police "Dutch participation in the Tetra-25[12] MoU was highly desirable. Not signing it could have been explained by manufacturers as lack of support and would have had an adverse effect upon what they tried to achieve with C2000, namely the acceleration of the standardization process and the concrete availability of products."[13] Although signing the MoU was not binding in the legal sense, it indicated commitment to the Tetra technology. In that sense, it was an important step for the Dutch government.

Based on these developments, we conclude that already around 1994 quite a strong technological frame had been built up by the Dutch actors involved in negotiations on Tetra and C2000 (see Table 2 for a summary). The key problem was framed as the outdated analogue communication systems of the Dutch police. The main goal was thus to implement a digital communication network in the Netherlands based on an "open

Table 2. Technological frame Dutch government

Goals	Implementing a digital communication network in the Netherlands based on a European standard, increasing public safety and improving the cooperation between emergency services
Key problems	Old analogue systems are outdated and need replacement
Problem-solving strategies	Supporting and influencing ETSI development of MDTRS/Tetra standard ("there are no alternatives")
Requirements to be met by problem solutions	European solution, multi-vendor, economically viable
Political rationale	The Netherlands in a frontline position (being first), being a loyal European country, supporting the implementation of the Schengen agreements
Exemplary artifact	Tetra as 'the GSM standard' for public safety

European standard". At that moment, Tetra was considered to be the best way to achieve this goal, even though the standard was not yet finished. The standard had to be open because the Netherlands favored a so-called 'multi-vendor' situation – a situation in which they would not be dependent on one supplier or manufacturer. The standard had to be 'European' as the Netherlands considered itself a strong supporter of Europe and European integration, wanted to contribute to meeting the Schengen objectives and wished to support European industry (rather than American, for instance). Moreover, to develop a new nationwide system by itself was not considered economically viable.

Although the Dutch government has considered some alternatives to the Tetra standard (GSM, APCO25, Tetrapol), they invested much in the Tetra standard from the beginning: representatives of the Dutch government were involved in the Schengen Telecom working group and the ETSI RES-6 committee, they shared their expertise about the public safety sector and tried to convince ETSI of the functional specifications that would be needed for the Dutch network. The Dutch were pro-active in trying to build up knowledge and expertise. They also forged strategic alliances with other European countries such as the UK. Although the Dutch kept monitoring some alternatives, from 1995 onwards no alternatives other than Tetra were seriously considered. By participating in ETSI (and, to a lesser extent, in Schengen Telecom), the Dutch choice had been made - albeit unofficially. The Dutch negotiators actively lobbied for the Tetra standard almost from the start and the Dutch had signed the MoU for Tetra, thereby publicly showing their commitment. We argue that already at this stage, that is, around 1995, the choice for Tetra had almost become irreversible. The first clear signs emerged in the Dutch parliamentary debates after 1996. We will show how critical members of parliament challenged assumptions in the government's technological frame and how these dissonating voices were dealt with.

Dealing with Dissonance I: Debating Tetra in the Dutch Parliament

In the meantime, the Dutch government had decided that they wanted to play a leading role in the implementation of public safety networks in Europe. According to a civil servant, at that time responsible for international relations at the Ministry of the Interior,

Yes, we knew that we were going to take a risk with the new technology and the new standard. But, okay, you decide you want to be a leader in that area or not, and someone has to be the first to implement them. And we invested a lot in the spreading of the Tetra standard because we found it so important to have, in Europe, a radio communication network for emergency services, comparable with GSM. (#4)

However, dissonating opinions that were critical about the government's choice to support Tetra were voiced by some members of the Dutch parliament. The appropriateness of the Tetra standard for the C2000 network became a recurring theme in Dutch parliamentary debates after 1996. The C2000 project, being the responsibility of the Ministry of the Interior was designated the status of a "large technological project". This implied closer parliamentary monitoring of the project. On December 11, 1997, van Heemst and Cornielje, members of Parliament, asked the minister of the Interior what would happen if other countries would opt for another standard, and what the Minister considered as "the point of no return" for the Dutch choice for Tetra. The Minister responded that the Netherlands preferred the Tetra standard because this would be the common European standard. The fact that France opted for a different technology was no reason for him to reconsider this. However, he added that the choice for the standard would only become irreversible after the contracts for the building of the network had been signed and a test had taken place: "Only then

the next decision about Tetra will be made: does it suit our goals or do we need to reconsider?"[14]

The discussion about the choice between Tetra and Tetrapol that originated in the early 1990s was re-opened in this parliamentary debate as well. MP van Heemst asked for a comparison of the costs of Tetra and Tetrapol. He raised uncomfortable questions: "What if Germany opts for Tetrapol? What shall we do then?" According to the Minister, the comparison of Tetra and Tetrapol should be viewed in the context of "the praise-worthy shamelessness with which France always tries to promote its own industry."[15] The Netherlands should focus on the choices of their direct neighbors (Belgium, Germany, Luxembourg). "If the consequence of France's choice for Tetrapol is that it cannot, or can only with extensive technical measures, communicate with other countries, Mr. Chirac should rethink his statements about the fight against international crime", according to the Minister. "So far, all other countries have opted for Tetra and a government that does not do so bears a heavy responsibility"[16], he argued.

These parliamentary debates and repeated public commitments of Dutch government officials to Tetra show how dependent the national C2000 project had become on the Tetra standard. Signs of irreversibility were becoming clear: the timing of activities in the C2000 project depended upon and was synchronized with the development of Tetra—not only in the Netherlands, but also in other Schengen countries. The reasoning of the Minister was in line with the Dutch government's technological frame outlined above: "Acting according to the European spirit" was one of the main arguments to justify the Dutch choice for Tetra.

In the course of 1998, it became clear that Tetra was winning terrain in Europe. In October 1998, the Netherlands, Belgium, UK, Finland, Norway, Sweden and Portugal had chosen for the Tetra standard.[17] However, the deputy minister for the Interior, Gijs de Vries, still regretted the lack of consensus within Europe about the adoption of the Tetra standard. If other countries would choose for another standard, that would hinder cross border communication. Therefore, he contacted the European Commission and requested them to stimulate the Tetra option among other European countries. The European Commission responded, however, that European public tender law does not permit an a priori choice for the Tetra standard, thereby excluding alternative technologies such as Tetrapol. This would contradict Europe's open market philosophy.[18] Therefore, de Vries also lobbied for Tetra among other European countries and (at that moment) candidate member states such as Poland and Hungary. These countries eventually decided to opt for Tetra as well.

Dutch government officials were aware of the risks they took in choosing a system that did not exist yet. They reduced cognitive dissonance by investigating alternative options besides the Tetra standard for a long time (until 2002). However, "The only conclusion of those studies always was that there was no alternative. It has to be either this standard, or we had to fall-back on analogue technology that cannot offer what a modern society needs. So yes, at a certain moment, as a government, you have to make sure that it becomes a success." (#4) The Head of R&D of the Dutch police was also convinced that there were no alternatives to Tetra: "There were no better alternatives … So my philosophy was: the best thing you can do is use all your energy and put your shoulders under it, to lobby to make this standard a success. It was as simple as that. Being convinced that there were no real alternatives." (#1) A high-ranked civil servant at the Ministry of Justice and deeply involved in international police cooperation at the time was also concerned about the loss of international prestige if the Netherlands would give up on Tetra:

You have put so much prestige in it and you are so far, there have been so many networks built, discussion networks and signs to ETSI and others. And then to change all of a sudden and say, "on second thoughts, GSM is much better", yes,

they were very scared about that. … You end up empty-handed soon. (…) Once you have chosen for a certain direction and even if better alternatives become available in the meantime, you have to be very careful to start a discussion about these alternatives. You can easily loose your credibility and you can loose coalitions that you've built up. Then you will stand isolated and that is the worst thing that can happen. (#5)

Although no official political decisions had been taken yet on Tetra, it is clear that there was no way back. The key political players involved were all convinced that turning away from Tetra would have damaging consequences for the Dutch position in Europe, its credibility as a country and its international prestige. Thus, the Dutch government tried to find more allies in support of Tetra within Europe, thus further strengthening its choice for this standard. Moreover, the choice for Tetra was rationalized by arguing that other countries (France) did not act in the right European spirit or by pointing at the importance of sticking to choices that had been announced before. These arguments reinforced the government's technological frame, thus embedding the choice for Tetra more strongly in Dutch governmental reasoning.

In 1997, the Dutch government started a tender procedure for the development and implementation of the C2000 network. After long negotiations, a contract was signed with Tetraned/Motorola in April 1999. Having selected a standard, a supplier and a manufacturer of the network infrastructure for C2000 made the process even more irreversible. Although there were still possibilities to disband the contract, this was never really considered as an option. However, the official political decision to start the national implementation of C2000 still had to be made.

In the meantime, because of the many uncertainties about Tetra development and the availability of Tetra products, the Minister of the Interior decided in 1998 that, before a "go/no go" decision could be taken about the whole C2000 project, the network would have to be tested in an operational setting.[19] As we will discuss below, the outcome of this test showed that approximately half of the planned functionality of the C2000 network actually worked. Although this test result could have challenged the government's technological frame, the government decided to start implementing the C2000 project anyway. How did the involved officials manage to bring the dissonating test results in line with their technological frame?

Dealing with Dissonance II: Go/No Go Decision

The Amsterdam region was chosen as the first test region for C2000. This choice for Amsterdam is interesting as it is the most complex and difficult region in the Netherlands when it comes to public safety (#6). The idea was that if they could prove the system to work in Amsterdam, then it could work everywhere (#7). In 1996, independent of all C2000 developments, the city of Amsterdam had made plans for a local digital communication network. They had already proceeded thus far that they were negotiating with Motorola to develop their network for them. The Ministry of the Interior considered this to be a risk for the success for the national C2000 network and therefore pressured Amsterdam to stop their plans. With success: by designating Amsterdam as the 'Start Region', the city had to follow the plans of the national government. Amsterdam was thus not only a complex region in technological and organizational terms, but also in terms of winning the support of the users for the national system.

The process of building the network in the Start Region did not go smoothly. Within six months after the contract had been granted to the Tetraned/Motorola consortium, they had to admit that they couldn't meet the deadlines for the delivery of the network for the Start Region.[20] The deputy minister De Vries illustrates the classical "lock-in" position the Dutch government was facing at that moment by stating that switching to a different

system would result in delays and higher costs. Moreover the deputy minister wanted to keep the Dutch frontline position.[21] According to De Vries, the Tetra standard was winning terrain in Europe and there was no alternative with comparable technical functionality:

As long as a hundred small communication networks exist in the Netherlands, there will be communication problems between regions as well as emergency services and the emergency response will not be optimal. For the safety of citizens it is thus of utmost importance that there is one common communication system.[22]

In 2000, the C2000 network was tested in the Amsterdam region. The test showed that only half of the planned functionalities were operational.[23] Important functionalities, such as indoor and outdoor radio coverage in the city center of Amsterdam, were not up to standard. Furthermore, the important aim of '99.99% disturbance free communication' was not reached. Moreover, the test report concluded that the new radio communication systems did not sufficiently match existing working procedures in the dispatch room.[24] Nevertheless, the minister decided for a "go". The official "go" decision was taken 9 November 2001.

Various explanations have been put forward to clarify and justify this decision. According to a former director of the Project Office C2000, the trust people had vested in the Tetra standard resulted in the "go" decision for C2000 (#6). The good reputation of the supplier, Motorola, also played a role. In those days, Motorola had become involved in the development of Tetra-networks in several countries (in the UK, Germany, the North of Spain, Portugal), which increased public confidence (#6). Moreover, the working group 'fall back options', which existed until 2002, had concluded that there were no alternatives for the C2000 network in the short term.[25] Some of the interviewees stress that the lack of alternatives was the main reason for continuing with the tetra-based C2000 project. Meanwhile so many investments had been made in the network that the 'point of no return' already passed several years before (#8):

The test in the Start Region became smaller and smaller, and I have never considered the link with the go-no go decision very realistic. We were, in my view, in the formal and judicial sense, so committed to the project, that there was no way back at all. Any story could be put together as to why it had to be continued... I have always felt that the 'go decision' had been taken even before the results of the test were available.

Another reason for deciding for a "go" might lie in the contract with Tetraned. According to the contract, Tetraned would build the network for Start region. If they did well, and this decision would be taken at the go-no go moment, Tetraned would be given the contract to build the national network. If the government decided to end the contract with Tetraned before the 'go-no go' decision took place, this would be a costly affair. If they would do so at the 'go-no go' moment on the basis of insufficient quality delivered by Tetraned this could be done without costs. If the government would change its preference while Tetraned had fulfilled all contractual requirements, then the government would have to pay 35 million guilders (about 15 million euros) to Tetraned.[26]

Although Tetraned supplied the test network in the Start Region too late and offered only half of the requested functionalities, the contract was continued. Moreover, anticipating on a positive outcome, already during the test plans were made to implement the network for real in order to prevent any delays after the "go" sign had been given. The 'Roll-out' report[27] argued that even the then current time schedule would already result in operational problems since the existing analogue equipment was vulnerable, hard to replace (because the market had only a limited supply of this old equipment) and investment decisions had

been postponed because of C2000. It calculated that postponing the implementation of C2000 would cost 5 million guilders per month.

Finally, in the year 2000 two traumatic disasters had taken place in the Netherlands which affected the Dutch stance. In May 2000, a fire work storage facility in the city of Enschede, which is close to the German border, exploded. Twenty-three people died and about 950 people were injured. On New Year's Eve of 2000-2001 an accident in Volendam took place. A big fire demolished a café in which many young people were celebrating the New Year. Fourteen young people died and 180 people were injured. The Enschede and the Volendam event were also mentioned as an argument to speed-up the national roll-out of C2000; "the disasters in Enschede and Volendam have shown that the present analogue radio communication networks of the public safety services urgently need replacement."[28] Moreover, one of the policy aims closely intertwined with the introduction of C2000 was to reorganize the dispatch rooms. Instead of each emergency service having its own dispatch room, the three emergency services were to share one common dispatch room. This policy could only succeed if there would be one national radio network for all three emergency services.

The main aim characterizing in the Dutch government's technological frame, that is, to improve public safety by implementing a new digital system, would seem to have been seriously jeopardized by the outcomes of the test. At the same time, the test in the Start Region dramatically showed how irreversible the choice for Tetra and C2000 had become around 2000: The government had locked itself into a contract with Tetraned that did not provide sufficient means to 'punish' them if they did not deliver on time. During the test phase, the acquisition of space for the C2000 radio masts was already taking place. Other policies, such as the renewal of the dispatch rooms, became intertwined with the C2000 project and depended on a successful outcome. To those involved there seemed no alternatives but to go ahead with Tetra and the C2000 project. All these factors were reasons to justify the "go" decision and to reduce cognitive dissonance by aligning the test results with the technological frame. Thus, they reinforced the irreversibility of implementing C2000.

CONCLUSION: CONSTRUCTING THE IRREVERSIBILITY OF C2000

Our analysis shows an innovation process that had grown irreversible long before the official political decision to implement the Tetra-based network had been taken. We argue that irreversibility did not occur because of characteristics of the technology or because of investments of single actors. The irreversibility we are dealing with is a constructed irreversibility, shaped by the actions and interactions of several key governmental actors.

Two main factors contributed to the irreversibility of the decision making process. First, the technological frame provided focus to and direction in the decisions of the Dutch government officials. Already from the early 1990s onwards, their communications, reports, correspondence and actions revealed a strong commitment to Tetra and to the idea of a common European standard despite the numerous uncertainties surrounding the standard and its international acceptance. Although there was fierce competition from Tetrapol, drawbacks in planning and finance, delays in the standards choice of neighboring countries, and negative test results, the Netherlands persistently adhered to the built 'technological frame' and acted accordingly.

Second, the Dutch officials showed personal commitment in trying to speed up the decision process and played an active role in increasing support for the Tetra process– in ETSI, in the Schengen Telecom Group, among the European member-states and within the European Commission. According to the cognitive dissonance theory and 'postdecisional conflict' explanations, such behavioral commitment (i.e. convincing and

lobbying for Tetra) will further confirm the attractiveness of Tetra and lessen the attractiveness of the rejected alternatives as perceived by the officials. Their public commitment and vested efforts will have fed the irreversibility of the Tetra choice.

Note also that the Dutch, who highly valued the idea of a common European standard for the emergency services, initially had to face a very difficult dilemma: choosing the vendor-independent Tetra standard would exclude France (proprietary Tetrapol) and make a true pan-European standard impossible. These two conflicting cognitions within the technology frame were mutually exclusive.

Moreover, there were also other high-dissonance arousing circumstances surrounding the Tetra choice such as the expected high societal impact (safety, health) of the decision. All these factors add up to make it very difficult for key actors to reconsider their original decision. Irreversibility is created. The actors feel that they have no choice but to pursue the path previously embarked upon.

In our view, the point of no return should be situated in the mid 1990s, when the Dutch government publicly announced its support for the Tetra standard for the first time and signed the Tetra MoU. By then, the politicians and telecom experts of the Ministry of the Interior had discarded all other technological alternatives, thus making Tetra the only 'feasible' alternative to the existing analogue systems. In the following years, although an official 'go' decision had not been taken yet, several political and operational measures were taken to consolidate and embed Tetra and C2000 (e.g., preparing the implementation, buying mast spaces). The contract with Tetraned made it also very hard for the Dutch government to deviate from the chosen direction. Official political decision making lagged behind the actual innovation and implementation process. Due to this gap in 'timing', it was hard to steer and monitor the C2000 project in a democratic way. However, paradoxically, the debates in the Dutch parliament and the close parliamentary monitoring of the C2000 project also increased the irreversibility of the Tetra choice. As we mentioned before, public commitment to a specific decision—but also the demand for transparency in political decision making and the political pressure for consistency—makes it hard to change one's opinion; 'cognitive irreversibility' is likely to occur. That is, the political setting, the public nature of parliamentary debates, and the frequent discussions between the minister, deputy minister and members of parliament will have reinforced politicians to act consistently - and increased the irreversibility of the Tetra decision.

How should we evaluate 'irreversibility' in this process? Our first intuition would be to qualify it as rather negative. It will prevent deviation from earlier choices even if the network implementation turns out to be problematic (resulting in extra costs and delays). For example, the few Tetra manufacturers participating in the tender procedure made the Dutch government's negotiation position very difficult. Its justified expectation of increasing vendor-independence and market competition via an open ETSI standard had been overtaken by mergers in the market. Moreover, early irreversibility of large scale projects may undermine the democratic nature of the political decision process. In this case the point of no return had been reached long before the official political decision making took place. These are all reasons for evaluating the "path dependence" on Tetra negatively.

However, with hindsight one can also argue that it was beneficial that the key actors constructed this irreversibility of Tetra/C2000. As Paul Edwards and others (2007, p. 17-18) have argued: "path dependence also creates new possibilities, i.e. directions that could not have been taken in the absence of technology X." They speak of the possibility of "positive path dependence", that is, the idea that "progress is possible precisely because new practices build upon old ones." (p. 18). What are, in this case, the positive dimensions of irreversibility in technology development and standardization? After all, C2000 has been implemented across the country[29]. Perhaps one

could say that without the determination and persistence of some key actors within the Ministry of the Interior (deputy minister Gijs de Vries) and the Ministry of Justice, and the IT department of the Dutch Police, this system would not have been implemented at all. Taking risks is inherent to innovation processes and the fact that projects like these are risky, should not be a reason not to undertake them at all (Hommels, Peters, & Bijker, 2007). It is, however, crucial that actors are aware of the irreversibility enhancing effects which their own technological frame and actions have. In particular, the political arena may need to rethink its own paradoxical role in constructing irreversibility while desiring a meaningful influence.

INTERVIEWEES

1. Former Head of the R&D Department of the Dutch Police, Former chairman of Schengen Telecom, former member of ETSI RES-6 representing the Netherlands; Odijk: 31-5-2006; 29-1-2009.

2. Telecom expert Dutch Police, Dutch representative Schengen Telecom, system architect C2000; Odijk: 9-5-2005; Driebergen: 29-1-2009.

3. Former high-ranked civil servant Dutch Ministry of Justice; Leiden: 16-6-2008.

4. Civil servant Ministry of the Interior, responsible for international contacts police; Den Haag: 26-9-2007.

5. Former high-ranked civil servant Ministry of Justice, Dutch delegation leader in Schengen; Leiden: 16-6-2008.

6. Former director Project Office C2000; Maastricht: 4-3-2005; Den Haag: 12-4-2005.

7. Former head Department Telecom of the Amsterdam police; Driebergen: 29-1-2009.

8. Director Safety-Region Rotterdam-Rijnmond, representative of the Dutch Fire Brigade in the C2000 decision making process; Rotterdam: 21-8-2007.

ACKNOWLEDGMENT

This research has been funded by the Dutch Research Council (NWO, project number 458-06-027). We sincerely thank the interviewees for sharing their experiences with us and in some cases granting us access to their personal archives; we thank ETSI and the Dutch standards body for facilitating access to their archives; and we thank the two anonymous reviewers of the European Academy for Standardization (EURAS) for their useful comments on an earlier draft. This article is a strongly revised version of the EURAS paper.

REFERENCES

Arthur, W. B. (1984). Competing Technologies and Economic Prediction. In D. MacKenzie, & J. Wajcman, (Eds.), *The social shaping of technology* (2nd ed., pp. 106–112). Buckingham, UK: Open University Press.

Bekkers, R. (2001). *Mobile telecommunication standards: GSM, UMTS, Tetra and Ermes*. Boston, MA: Artech House.

Berkowitz, L. (1980). *A survey of social psychology*. New York, NY: Holt, Rinehart and Winston.

Bijker, W. E. (1993). *Dutch, dikes and democracy: An Argument against democratic, authoritarian and neutral technologies*. Lyngby, Denmark: Unit of Technology Assessment, Technical University of Denmark.

Bijker, W. E. (1995). *Of Toward a Theory of Sociotechnical Change*. Cambridge, MA: MIT Press.

Blind, K. (2004). *The Economics of Standards: Theory, Evidence, Policy*. Cheltenham, UK: Edward Elgar.

Brehm, J. W., & Cohen, A. R. (1962). *Explorations in cognitive dissonance*. New York: Wiley. doi:10.1037/11622-000

Cowan, R. (1992). High Technology and the Economics of Standardization. In Dierkes, M., & Hoffmann, U. (Eds.), *New Technology at the Outset. Social Forces in the Shaping of Technological Innovations* (pp. 279–300). New York: Westview.

Edwards, P. N., Jackson, S. J., Bowker, G. C., & Knobel, C. P. (2007). *Understanding Infrastructure: Dynamics, Tensions and Design* (Report of the Workshop on History & Theory of Infrastructure: Lessons for New Scientific Infrastructures). Ann Arbor, MI: School of Information, University of Michigan.

Egyedi, T. M. (1996). *Shaping Standardization: A study of standards processes and standards policies in the field of telematic services*. Delft, The Netherlands: Delft University Press.

Egyedi, T. M., & Verwater-Lukszo, Z. (2005). Which standards' characteristics increase system flexibility? Comparing ICT and batch processing infrastructures. *Technology in Society*, *27*, 347–362. doi:10.1016/j.techsoc.2005.04.007

Festinger, L. (1957). *A theory of cognitive dissonance*. Palo Alto, CA: Stanford University Press.

Flyvbjerg, B., Bruzelius, N., & Rothengatter, W. (2003). *Megaprojects and Risk. An antomy of ambition*. Cambridge, UK: Cambridge University Press.

Garud, R., & Karnøe, P. (Eds.). (2001). *Path Dependence and Creation*. Mahwah, NJ: Lawrence Erlbaum Associates.

Hommels, A. (2005). *Unbuilding Cities. Obduracy in Urban Sociotechnical Change*. Cambridge, MA: MIT Press.

Hommels, A., Peters, P., & Bijker, W. E. (2007). Techno Therapy or Nurtured Niches? Technology Studies and the Evaluation of Radical Innovations. *Research Policy*, *36*(7), 1088–1099. doi:10.1016/j.respol.2007.04.002

Hughes, T. P. (1998). *Rescuing Prometheus*. New York: Pantheon Books.

Jastrzebski, R. (1993). Europese harmonisatie van communicatiestandaarden op komst. *Alert*, *5*, 26–27.

Lepper, M. R., Zanna, M. P., & Abelson, R. P. (1970). Cognitive Irreversibility in a dissonance-reduction situation. *Journal of Personality and Social Psychology*, *16*, 191–198. doi:10.1037/h0029819

MacKenzie, D., & Wajcman, J. (1999). Introductory Essay: the Social Shaping of Technology. In MacKenzie, D., & Wajcman, J. (Eds.), *The Social Shaping of Technology* (pp. 3–27). Buckingham, UK: Open University Press.

NBF. (1993). *Programme of requirements third generation communication networks for the fire brigade*. Author.

Pinch, T. (2001). Why Do you go to a Piano Store to Buy a Synthesizer: Path Dependence and the Social Construction of Technology. In Garud, R., & Karnøe, P. (Eds.), *Path Dependence and Creation* (pp. 381–399). Mahwah, NJ: Lawrence Erlbaum Associates.

Pinch, T. J., & Bijker, W. E. (1984). The Social Construction of Facts and Artifacts: Or How the Sociology of Science and the Sociology of Technology might Benefit Each Other. *Social Studies of Science*, *14*(3), 399–441. doi:10.1177/030631284014003004

Pinch, T. J., & Bijker, W. E. (1987). The Social Construction of Facts and Artifacts: Or How the Sociology of Science and the Sociology of Technology Might Benefit Each Other. In Bijker, W. E., Hughes, T. P., & Pinch, T. (Eds.), *The Social Construction of Technological Systems. New Directions in the Sociology and History of Technology* (pp. 17–50). Cambridge, MA: MIT Press. doi:10.1177/030631284014003004

Vrancken, J., Kaart, M., & Soares, M. (2008). Internet addressing standards: A case study in standards dynamics driven by bottom-up adoption. In Egyedi, T. M., & Blind, K. (Eds.), *The dynamics of standards* (pp. 68–81). Cheltenham, UK: Edward Elgar.

Wicklund, R. A., & Brehm, J. W. (1976). *Perspectives on cognitive dissonance*. Hillsdale, NJ: Erlbaum.

ENDNOTES

[1] Note that Egyedi and Verwater-Lukszo (2005) explore the opposite contention, i.e., to what degree standards can increase infrastructure flexibility.

[2] "A person is committed when he has decided to do or not to do a certain thing, when he has chosen one (or more) alternatives and thereby rejected one (or more) alternatives, when he actively engages in a given behaviour or has engaged in a given behaviour" (Brehm & Cohen, 1962, p. 7)

[3] "Without personal responsibility the dissonant events are psychologically irrelevant for the individual." Responsibility is defined as a combination of choice and the foreseeability of the consequences thereof. (Wicklund & Brehm, 1976)

[4] According to Festinger's original cognitive dissonance theory, when a person engages in a dissonance-arousing action he will examine the cognitions relevant at the time of commitment and proceed to reduce dissonance. If at a later moment new discrepant cognitions arise, further dissonance reduction will occur. However, according to Lepper et al (1970), "[f]urther dissonance reduction will not result, according to the irreversibility argument, for the 'dissonance-reducing' problem has already been solved and additional cognitions will not break the person's

fixation on his original act of dissonance reduction." (Wicklund & Brehm, 1976, p. 57)

[5] In minutes of one of the first meetings of the PCS2000 Technical working group, mention was made of several supplier specific systems that could be considered for the national communication network. A European standard was not mentioned at all (Minutes 6 December 1990). Less than a year later (Minutes 15th meeting of the PCS2000 preparation committee, 21 November 1991) the developments in ETSI are mentioned.

[6] Note from the Dutch delegation to Schengen Telecom Working party, 21 June 1993 (Schengen Telecom archive).

[7] Note from German delegation to Schengen Telecom Working party, 27 July 1992 (Schengen Telecom archive). See the important work by Rudi Bekkers on the early development of the Tetra standard (Bekkers, 2001).

[8] Borgonjen tried to get Ginman (as a non-Schengen country) on board of the Schengen Telecom Working Group in order to act more effectively as strategic partners (Letter R. Ginman to J.B.M. Borgonjen, 24 September 1990; #1).

[9] Initially five countries (Belgium, the Netherlands, Luxemburg, Germany and France) signed the Schengen Agreement (June 14, 1985). The Schengen Agreement expressed the ambition to create a Pan-European network for public safety and justice, and to enhance the cooperation between police services in different EU countries. The Schengen Agreement was later on officially adopted as EU policy in the Treaty of Amsterdam of 1997.

[10] This was also mentioned in an interview with the head of the Knowledge and Innovation Centre of the Dutch ICT Service Centre for Police, Justice and Security (#1). An at the time confidential note by Hans Borgonjen

(September 27, 1990) stated that if the European industries do not have a kind of structured debate with the European police organizations, there is "a risk that America will become dominant in the field of police communication" (Note H. Borgonjen to Permanent Working group Schengen, 27 September 1990, p. 2).

[11] Minutes Schengen Telecom meeting, 18 June 1992, Bilthoven (ST). According to the head of the Knowledge and Innovation Centre of the Dutch ICT Service Centre for Police, Justice and Security, they were lucky that the technical experts also had technical reasons for supporting Tetra. Otherwise, the political dimension would have made the debate on APCO25 versus Tetra more difficult.

[12] In the mid-1990s Tetra was often referred to as Tetra-25. A competing variant that was debated at that time was called Tetra-6.

[13] Note from J.B.M. Borgonjen to the Temporary Steering Group C2000. 12 December 1994.

[14] Dutch parliament, report of general meeting, 11-12-1997, 25 124, no. 5. p. 5.

[15] Ibid., p. 8.

[16] Ibid.

[17] Minutes Dutch parliament 1998-1999, 25 124, no. 7.

[18] Letter Deputy Minister of Internal Affairs to the Parliament, 16 February 2001, 25 124, no. 19, p. 11. Here, the European Commission plays an interesting 'double role': on the one hand, they want to promote common standards and a wide adoption of European standards, on the other hand, they don't want to stimulate this process because of their loyalty to an open market philosophy.

[19] A second test was devised in 2003 to evaluate the capacity of the C2000 network and the Tetra standard in particular to support international communication between emergency services in the border region of

Aachen (Germany), Liège (Belgium) and Maastricht (The Netherlands).

[20] Letter J.Kuiperi, ITO to the members of OGO, 6-6-2000, and Minutes Dutch parliament 1999-2000 25 124, nr. 14.

[21] Minutes Dutch parliament TK 1999-2000 25124, nr. 14, p. 8.

[22] Minutes Dutch parliament 1999-2000 25125, nr. 14, p. 6

[23] A conformance table in the test report shows that roughly half of the listed functionalities worked during the pilot (Testreport Test within the test (2001). Den Haag: Ministery of the Interior). A former director of the C2000 project office assesses that only ten percent of the planned functionality of C2000 actually worked at the time. (#6).

[24] Testreport Test within the test (2001). Den Haag: Ministery of the Interior.

[25] Progress report C2000 to the Parliament, 9-11-2001.

[26] Minutes Dutch parliament 1999-2000, 25124 nr. 14, p.6.

[27] Nota Voluit report (preparation nation-wide roll-out C2000)Versie 1.2 J.H. Brinkman, 8-8-2000.

[28] Progress report C2000 to the parliament, 9-11-2001, p. 3.

[29] Note that recently (2009) a number of fire brigades have switched partly back to analogue communication modes because they were not satisfied about C2000.

This work was previously published in the International Journal of IT Standards and Standardization Research (IJITSR), Volume 8, Issue 1, edited by Kai Jakobs, pp. 28-48, copyright 2010 by IGI Publishing (an imprint of IGI Global)

Chapter 11
The Significance of Government's Role in Technology Standardization:
Two Cases in the Wireless Communications Industry

DongBack Seo
University of Groningen, The Netherlands

ABSTRACT

For first generation (1G) wireless communications technology standards, the Japanese government's early decision provided an opportunity for its national manufacturers to be first movers in the global market, while the late development of wireless communications in Korea made the Korean market dependent on foreign manufacturers by adopting the U.S. standard (AMPS). Moving toward the 2G wireless technology market, both countries decided to develop standards instead of adopting a technology from outside their regions. Japan developed its own standard, PDC, while Korea developed CDMA systems with Qualcomm, the U.S. technology provider. Although these governments' decisions on technologies looked only slightly different, the socio-economic consequences were greatly distinctive. The Korean success brought not only the rapid development of its domestic market but also opportunities for its manufacturers to become global leaders, while the PDC standard only provided the fast growth of the Japanese domestic market without any opportunities for the Japanese manufacturers to grow further internationally in the 1990s. By the end of 1990s, two nations again had to decide a 3G technology standard with vast challenges and pressures.

DOI: 10.4018/978-1-4666-2160-2.ch011

ORGANIZATIONAL BACKGROUND

While it has always been true that governments play a critical role in the economy when they drive decisions about standards, today's rapidly changing and technology-dependent business environment has made the role of the government in standardization even more important. Some governments play their roles actively, whereas others leave it over to industries or a number of lobbyists.

A standard declared by a government is considered as a *de jure* standard, while a standard emerges from market competitions is *de facto*. De Vries (2006) points out that this classification is confusing and provides more detail and specific definitions and a typology of IT standards by suggesting various aspects related to subject matter, standards development, and standards use. For the cases of Korea and Japan in this paper, standards refer to governmental standards that are set by a governmental agency in the classification related to organizations, according to the category of De Vries (2006).

Governments, especially those in developing countries or with planned economies, often nurture certain industries to drive the national economy. In order to do so, some choose to use their regulatory power to mandate standards in technology-dependent industries. This eliminates the need for companies to expend resources in competing to establish a standard through market forces, allowing them to focus instead on creating economies of scale, and developing complementary products. If the standard successfully creates network externalities and is cost-effective, the standard can diffuse to other nations. Then companies enjoy the benefits of being developers or early adopters, and can use their domestic market to develop subsequent technologies and test marketing strategies to export to other countries. They have the advantage of being able to innovate and move the market to the next generation technology before later adopters can catch up. End-users in the countries that adopt the technology earlier enjoy benefits as well, with lower prices and greater variety of products or services.

However, a government has power to mandate a standard only for its juridical region. There is no international organization to force any country to adopt a particular standard. Thus, to diffuse a standard to other nations (or make an international standard), a governmental standard in one nation has to go through competition in the international market (Funk & Methe, 2001). This process is often very competitive because other nations tend to push their governmental standards to be international standards as well.

For this reason, governments, like companies, can bet on the wrong standard. In this paper, the importance of the government's role will be illustrated by looking at two cases: South Korea (Note: it will be referred to Korea in the rest of paper) and Japan, in their choice of a national technology standard for wireless communications (governmental standards). Some countries like the United States have settled on standards in their wireless communication industry through open competition (*de facto* standards through company or consortium standards); many others, however, including Korea and Japan, have had a history of tight regulation of their telecommunications industries and only privatized them in the last few decades. Because of similarities in the Korean and Japanese wireless communication markets, these two cases provide a stark comparison of governments' roles and the economic and social consequences of the governments' decisions in technology standardization.

Japan

Japan, as a defeated nation in World War II, was devastated, so the first priority of the Japanese government was reconstructing the nation. With scarce resources and capabilities, the Japanese government was heavily involved in developing certain industries such as motorcycles, sewing machine, steel, and shipbuilding through directing necessary resources (Porter, 1990). Companies in these industries were able to gain competitive advantages under the government's support, protection from foreign competitors, and policies like market liberation in a timely manner. Although there were other factors such as demand conditions and disciplined workers, the role of Japanese government was significant in reviving its industries.

The Japanese government also encouraged companies to develop related and supporting industries for the industries that it directly involved in. For example, the Temporary Measures Law for Machinery and Electronics between 1971 and 1978 contributed to develop these industries rapidly (Porter, 1990). Through these kinds of government policies, many Japanese electronics companies quickly developed their competitive capabilities to become a global firm such as Sony and NEC.

The Japanese government's role has changed as its industries have evolved. It is not involved as directly and actively as it used to be, but it still influences industries with regulations and public policies. Considering the history of the Japanese government's involvement in its industries, it is not surprising that the Japanese government has participated in the wireless telecommunications technology standardization.

Korea

During the Cold War period, Korea was not seen as an attractive country to invest in by foreign investors. After Park Chung Hee gained power with a military coup in 1961, the Korean government started to create economic development policies to achieve public support and cover their illegitimate power. The Korean market could not have free competition like the United States or western European countries, because there weren't any Korean players who could compete against foreign giant companies that had been in the market for a long time. The only way to develop the Korean economy was to execute a deliberate strategy by the Korean government to grow certain industries one by one in a protectionist manner.

The Korean government started by borrowing money from other countries and developing light industries for export, like the garment industry. With the capital accumulated from the development of this sector of the Korean economy, the Korean government was able to move into heavy industries like the auto industry. The companies that had close relationships with the Korean government were able to get into these industries and grow quickly under the government's wing.

Of course, all of this has changed dramatically through international pressure to open the Korean market, along with the political change from military dictatorship to democratic government, the Asian financial crisis in 1997, and other factors. The Korean market has become an open market and companies have become independent. The Korean government can't intervene into industries and markets directly, but they still can direct them by providing regulations as other governments do.

SETTING THE STAGE

Before the fifteenth century, people exchanged messages between distant regions through various methods such as beacon fires, messengers, and flags. The main purpose of most messages was related to military and sovereign matters of rulers. The development of the wireless telecommunications industry is an extension of the evolution of postal service, telegraphy and telephony. They were all designed to communicate more quickly over long distances as the socio-economic conditions of human activities changed.

Although individuals invented telephony technologies and founded private telephony companies, governments in many countries nationalized landline telephone networks in the late 1890s and early 1900s through World Wars I and II (Noam, 1992). Even before the liberalization and privatization of wireless telecommunications operators in the 1980s and 1990s, many governments ran their national telephone industry through their *Post, Telegraphy and Telephony* (PTT) bureaus. The timing and the development of liberalization and privatization varied across nations.

Japan

The Japanese government has played a significant role in its wireless communications industry. Japan was the first country that installed a cellular telephony system in 1979, but the market grew slowly at that time. After observing the development of wireless telecommunications technologies in Europe and the United States that moved to the second generation (2G) wireless telephony based on digital technology, the Japanese government decided to upgrade its infrastructure to 2G in 1989 (Bekkers, 2001). Instead of adopting one of the existing 2G technologies – Global System for Mobile (GSM), which would be used widely in Europe and around the world, or Time Division Multiple Access (TDMA) used in the United States—the Japanese government decided to create its own technology standard (Komiya, 1993). It felt confident in doing so, drawing on the strength of its technological capabilities and established track record in becoming the world leader in other industries, for example, consumer electronics. It also invited foreign companies such as Ericsson, Motorola and AT&T to develop the standard with its national companies like NEC. Its ambition was to make this wireless communications technology an international standard by exporting the technology to other countries, especially other Asian countries, so that Japanese companies could have benefits from this proprietary technology standard.

Japan thus developed Personal Digital Cellular (PDC) with its national manufacturers as a standard. NTT DoCoMo, which was used to be the Japanese national Post, Telegraph, Telephony

(PTT), started to provide digital wireless communication services using the PDC standard in 1993. Initially, NTT DoCoMo was not enthusiastic about moving its network to 2G (Bekkers, 2001). This attitude stimulated the Japanese government to allow two more companies to be wireless service providers (Digital Tu-Ka Kyushu and Japan Telecom Digital Phone (Garrard, 1998). This government's decision has made the Japanese domestic wireless communications market more competitive with in total five wireless service providers. In addition to the three mentioned, there were IDO and DDI. This free competition could encourage wireless service providers to competitively upgrade their networks with next generation technologies.

One thing to remember is that the standardized PDC was not as radical compared to other technologies. It was technologically close to TDMA developed in the United States (Bekkers, 2001). This technological limit also affected the prosperity of PDC. This aspect will be discussed in the next section.

The first goal for the Japanese government was to provide more advanced services to its domestic market. The Japanese domestic market was enthusiastic about the new standard and fully embraced it. The number of wireless communication subscribers grew quickly, from less than 2 million at the end of 1993, to around 9 million at the end of 1995, and then to 42 million (about 33% of the total population) by mid-1999 (Bekkers, 2001).

On the other hand, the standardization of PDC was not internationally successful. Originally, PDC stood for Pacific Digital Cellular. As you can see from this original meaning, the Japanese government had obvious ambition to make PDC as an international standard, at least for Pacific-Asian region. However, this second goal was not achieved, which will be explained more in the next section: 'CASE DESCRIPTION.'

Korea

Like the Japanese government, the Korean government has played a major role in the development of the Korean wireless industry from the beginning. The first wireless communications company in Korea was founded by the Korean government in March 1984 and named Korean Wireless Telecommunication. It started wireless telecommunications service in May 1984 through adopting the AMPS technology (Advanced Mobile Phone Service) from the United States. This adoption made the Korean wireless telecommunications market dependent on the foreign companies (e.g. Motorola) for systems.

The Korean government had four choices of technologies for its future 2G wireless industry: GSM, TDMA, PDC, and Code Division Multiple Access (CDMA). GSM, TDMA and PDC were easy to implement because they had been used in other markets, but it would have made the Korean wireless market dependent on foreign wireless companies again. The CDMA technology was developed by Qualcomm in 1989 but had not been introduced in any market at the time.

Although CDMA had not been proven in a commercial market yet, it would give a great advantage to the first company or market that tried it, by giving a chance to build CDMA networks, handsets, etc. The Korean government decided to go for CDMA to boost its electronics industry and have a better chance to keep its wireless industry independent, even though they had to pay royalties to Qualcomm for use of the CDMA technology. At that time, Pactel (former Verizon) and Southwestern Bell (former SBC), who were willing to be CDMA pioneers in United States, asked the Korean government whether it would be interested in waiting and buying a complete CDMA system from U.S. companies to deploy the CDMA technology, but the Korean government rejected this idea, even though it didn't know when it could develop its own CDMA systems (Lee, 2001). This incident indicated the willing-

ness of the Korean government as a developer, not as a simple adopter, to develop, implement, and diffuse the CDMA systems.

In May 1991, the Electronics and Telecommunications Research Institute (ETRI)—founded by the Korean government in 1976 as a research institute—and Qualcomm agreed to jointly develop CDMA systems. This agreement implied that the Korean government and industry would invest enormously in financial means and other resources to develop and commercialize all the necessary CDMA systems. When the CDMA development did not go smoothly, Ericsson approached the Korean government and offered the deployment of GSM equipment for the Korean market without initial payment, but the Korean government did not approve this proposal (Lee, 2001). The Korean government had a very strong will to develop its own CDMA system to protect its wireless communications market. If the Korean government would fail, it would end up losing a lot of investment and time, and would have to build its wireless infrastructure again using one of the other technologies (GSM, TDMA, or PDC). Although the Korean government faced many challenges in developing and implementing CDMA-based systems, through diligent efforts from 1991 to 1995, it was finally able to launch commercial CDMA wireless service in 1996.

In the same year, the Korean government licensed three more companies as Personal Communication Service (PCS) providers based on the CDMA network, totaling five number of companies to compete in the Korean wireless communications market. In 1994, when the Korean government decided to privatize government-owned Korean Wireless Telecommunication, which was renamed SK Telecom in 1997, it also allowed another company, Shinsegi Telecommunication, to enter the wireless communications market, creating two private companies. These privatization and liberalization policies brought more competition to stimulate the Korean wireless communications market.

CASE DESCRIPTION

Up until this point, Korean and Japanese wireless communications industries have seemed to be in similar positions. They both took a chance on technology standards not being used outside their country, in order to develop their domestic companies' capabilities and give them the advantage of being a first mover in the global market. At the same time, they liberalized their market to grow with free competition.

However, while CDMA was subsequently adopted by other companies and markets, PDC remained isolated in Japan. There were two main factors that made CDMA more attractive to other markets than PDC. First, it was known that CDMA was technologically more advanced (Mock, 2005). CDMA could accommodate more subscribers in the same size network due to the effective frequency usage, the more efficient battery usage in handsets, and the better security (Mock, 2005). Further more, CDMA-based networks cost less to implement and maintain (Mock, 2005). Companies in other countries had been aware of the technological advantage of CDMA, even when they did not have confidence in its commercialization (Lee, 2001). Once they saw its commercial success in Korea, some of them were willing to implement it such as several U.S. companies (e.g. Verizon and Sprint).

Second, the biggest attraction of CDMA was about the natural migration path to third generation (3G) technology. When wireless telecommunications markets, at least in the developed countries, became mass markets for large customer populations, based on the 2G technologies from niche markets in the 1G period, as well as Internet emerged with great popularity, governments and companies realized that 3G technologies should provide wireless broadband to deliver large data in a speedy manner (Seo & Lee, 2007). Considering possible migration paths from existing 2G technology standards, CDMA was the most superior technology to provide the wireless broadband at the time. Seeing the advantage of ease migration path to 3G technology along with other factors including political reason, less developed countries that were still in the 2G stage have decided to open up their markets for CDMA along with their existing GSM networks. Thus, China and India started commercial CDMA service in 2002, expanding significantly the CDMA global market due to these countries' sizes and economic growths (Seo & Mak, in press).

Consequently, the choice of CDMA as a wireless communications technology standard has greatly impacted the Korean economy, even though the commercial debut of CDMA was much later than those of GSM and TDMA. Despite the small share of the CDMA standard in the global market, Korean government's decision has allowed major Korean electronic companies like Samsung and LG to become some of the world's leading wireless handset makers. These handset manufacturers have expanded their capabilities to produce GSM handsets as well, learning from their CDMA handset experience (Figure 1).

In contrast, no other countries have adopted PDC. Although the Japanese government, NTT DoCoMo, and NEC promoted PDC for the Asian market with the helps from Ericsson and Motorola in 1992, the Japanese wireless industry became technologically isolated from the global 2G wireless communication market (Bekkers, 2001). This standard was not so attractive to other nations. First, the PDC technology was not distinguishably innovative from GSM and TDMA. Second, the GSM standard, with noticeably roaming capability and the support of many European nations, already started to gain its global market share. Third, the PDC systems were more expensive and proprietary than others (Garrard, 1998). Considering these factors in the competitive international market, other countries tended to adopt the GSM technology that could bring the economy of scale for lower costs and would provide more options for systems, unless countries had a political and economical tie with a nation that

Figure 1. Korean exports of wireless handsets and systems (1998-2002)

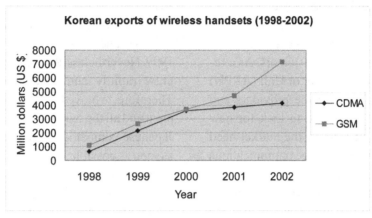

(Source, International Cooperation Agency for Korea IT, Monthly IT Export – 2003/10; Original source, Ministry of Information and Communication in Korea (MIC) 2003/09)

hosted a certain standard. For example, many countries in Central and South America used to adopt U.S. technology standards because of the historically close relationship with the U.S. government (Funk & Methe, 2001).

The failure of PDC as an international standard also influenced the Japanese telecommunications system manufacturing industry. The Japanese electronics companies had gained significant market shares for the telecommunications-related systems as first movers under the supportive policies of the Japanese government during the 1G wireless telecommunications technology period (1980s). For example, in 1989, NEC and Fujitsu were ranked 5 and 9 respectively by the telecommunications-related sales in the global market (Bekkers, 2001). However, this success was doomed by the technologically isolated standard, PDC. While the Japanese companies such as Sony and Panasonic gained leading global brand names in the consumer electronics market, Nokia, Ericsson, Samsung, and LG pushed away these Japanese companies from the center of the world wireless communications market during the 2G period (1990s). As a result of the decision to develop its own technology standard, the Japanese electronics industry did not effectively expand its

market globally, which has led to loss of economic opportunities for them and disadvantages for end-users. Because no other companies entered the Japanese market, lack of sustained competition meant higher prices and less variety of handsets and services.

CURRENT CHALLENGES

By the late 1990s, governments witnessed some standards successfully becoming international standards, while others were falling behind in the global standards competition. At the same time, the global telecommunication market evolved to be de-monopolized from the state-owned industry. In addition, the tight relationship between wireless service providers and manufacturers broke down. Considering this dynamic environment, the role of governments has become more significant than ever in standardizing the 3rd generation wireless telecommunications technologies.

As the 2G wireless telecommunications market became more mature and saturated—at least in the developed countries—the competition between companies became more intense. From the market perspective, this fierce competition naturally led to price erosion and loss of revenue. For example, wireless service providers set lower prices to attract customers from their competitors, which increased the costs for recruiting new customers and for maintaining existing customers. As a result, Average Revenue Per User or Unit (ARPU) deteriorated. Thus, both service providers and manufacturers were motivated to look for new sources of revenue. It showed the market need to develop a 3G wireless telecommunications technology. This situation has put more pressure on governments in terms of allocating necessary frequencies, opening their markets, and setting appropriate technology standards policies (Steinbock, 2003).

The questions were again what technology a government should pursue, and whom should it collaborate with for the upcoming 3G technology market. These were particularly important matters to the Korean and Japanese governments, because the CDMA and PDC markets were very small compared to the European standard, GSM, which dominated more than 70% of the global 2G market (see Figure 2).

While the European manufacturers were prospering with the success of the GSM standard, the Japanese manufacturers had to satisfy themselves with their domestic market, because Japan's 2G standard PDC was not adopted anywhere else. Even the second largest wireless service provider in Japan, KDDI abandoned its PDC infrastructure and adopted CDMA for its network in 1999. Nevertheless, the Japanese domestic market grew rapidly and became quickly saturated. Therefore, to move forward, the Japanese government and all the wireless communications related Japanese companies were keen on realizing 3G as soon as possible. The Japanese government did not want its electronics manufacturers to be again excluded from the future global 3G wireless communications market. Therefore, the Japanese government actively sponsored a study group and invited non-Japanese organizations as well as Japanese manufacturers to research and coordinate plans for 3G. The Japanese government hoped that the participation of non-Japanese organizations would help make whatever 3G technology it promoted internationally recognized. However, the Japanese government had to answer many difficult questions to move forward quickly such as:

- Whether the 3G technology should be migrated from its existing PDC market, otherwise, the switching cost would be very

Figure 2. The configuration of 2G standards in mid-1990s

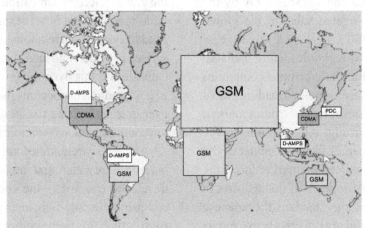

(Note: this picture is simplified and does not show all standards adopted by every country)

high for wireless service providers to implement whole new systems;

- Whether Japan should develop its own technology as it did for the 2G market, if so, then how Japan should advocate it in the global market;

- Whether Japan should adopt a technology from others, if so, then from whom, what technology, and when it should adopt the technology;

- Whether Japan should adopt a basic technology and develop it further, or wait and adopt the fully developed technology.

These questions put the Japanese government in dilemma, but it did not have time to sit and ponder the questions. The Japanese government should move very fast to provide first mover advantages to its national companies.

Through standardizing the CDMA technology, Korea has become the world's most advanced wireless market, and Korea's electronics industry grew to be highly sophisticated and successful. However, the large financial resource from this prosperity flowed to Qualcomm, because Qualcomm owned the essential Intellectual Property Rights (IPR) on the CDMA technology and the Korean manufacturers had to pay royalties to Qualcomm when they produced the CDMA systems including handsets. Although the Korean government and manufacturers participated in developing the CDMA systems further to commercialize them successfully, Qualcomm already had patents on essential technologies for CDMA. Despite the fact that the Korean government helped manufacturers to receive advantageous IPR agreements with Qualcomm, Qualcomm has been able to collect significant royalties from the Korean manufacturers.

The Korean government recognized very early that 1) the CDMA market was going to be much smaller than the GSM market and 2) many organizations on the GSM side would leverage their strategies and tactics to develop the 3G technology

that would be incompatible to the existing 2G CDMA technology to protect the GSM market from the CDMA actors encroaching on their turf.

It was a big dilemma for the Korean government, because 1) the CDMA technology it developed and implemented was technologically superior; and 2) the migration from the 2G CDMA to the future 3G CDMA would be fairly smooth with low costs; but 3) what if the rest of the world decided to adopt another incompatible technology, while the Korean government would let its industry move toward the natural migration path to the 3G CDMA. If this happened, the Korean market would be technologically isolated and its companies would stay in the niche market. Therefore, the Korean government should also consider many questions. For example:

- Whether the Korean government should propose to develop its own 3G based on the natural migration path from its existing 2G CDMA technology, while minimizing the technology dependence on Qualcomm to avoid the large royalty fees, and then try to make an international standard;

- Whether Korea should abandon its 2G standard and adapt the 3G standard that GSM actors will develop;

- If the Korean government chooses an incompatible 3G standard from the 2G CDMA, how will it persuade the Korean wireless service providers to adopt new systems based on the new standard.

- Whether it chooses its own standard or adapts a standard from others, whom Korea should cooperate with in developing the 3G standard.

These were the questions that the Korean government had to answer for building standards strategies for the 3G wireless telecommunications technology. It should decide and act soon; otherwise, the window of opportunity would be closed in a very short time period.

REFERENCES

Bekkers, R. (2001). *Mobile Telecommunications Standards: GSM, UMTS, TETRA, and ERMES.* Boston: Artech House.

De Vries, H. J. (2006). IT Standards Typology. In Jakobs, K. (Ed.), *Information Technology Standards and Standardization Research* (pp. 1–26). Hershey, PA: Idea Group Publishing. doi:10.4018/978-1-59140-938-0.ch001

Funk, J. L., & Methe, D. T. (2001). Market- and Committee-based Mechanisms in the Creation and Diffusion of Global Industry Standards: The Case of Mobile Communication. *Research Policy, 30,* 589–610. doi:10.1016/S0048-7333(00)00095 0

Garrard, G. A. (1998). *Cellular Communications: Worldwide Market Development.* Boston: Artech House.

Komiya, M. (1993). Personal Communications in Japan and its Implications for Asia. *Pan-European Mobile Communications, Spring,* 52-55.

Lee, W. C. Y. (2001). *Lee's Essentials of Wireless Communications.* New York: McGraw-Hill.

Mock, D. (2005). *The Qualcomm Equation: How a Fledgling Telecom Company Forged a New Path to Big Profits and Market Dominance.* New York: AMACOM.

Noam, E. M. (1992). *Telecommunications in Europe.* New York: Oxford University Press.

Porter, M. E. (1990). *The Competitive Advantage of Nations.* New York: The Free Press.

Seo, D., & Lee, J. (2007). Gaining Competitive Advantage through Value-Shifts: A Case of the South Korean Wireless Communications Industry. *International Journal of Information Management, 27*(1), 49–56. doi:10.1016/j.ijinfomgt.2006.12.002

Seo, D., & Mak, K. T. (in press). Using the Thread-Fabric Perspective to Analyze Industry Dynamics: An Exploratory Investigation of the Wireless Telecommunications Industry. *Communications of the ACM.*

Steinbock, D. (2003). Globalization of Wireless Value System: From Geographic to Strategic Advantages. *Telecommunications Policy, 27,* 207–235. doi:10.1016/S0308-5961(02)00106-4

This work was previously published in the International Journal of IT Standards and Standardization Research (IJITSR), Volume 8, Issue 1, edited by Kai Jakobs, pp. 63-74, copyright 2010 by IGI Publishing (an imprint of IGI Global)

Chapter 12
An Exploratory Analysis of the Relationship between Organizational and Institutional Factors Shaping the Assimilation of Vertical Standards

Rubén A. Mendoza
Saint Joseph's University, USA

T. Ravichandran
Rensselaer Polytechnic Institute, USA

ABSTRACT

Vertical standards describe products and services, define data formats and structures, and formalize and encode business processes for specific industries. Vertical standards enable end-to-end computing, provide greater visibility of the organization's supply chain, and enable transactional efficiencies by automating routine tasks, reducing errors, and formally defining all parameters used to describe a product, service, or transaction. Research on standards diffusion has explored either firm-level and institutional variables, without integration of the two areas. This study develops scales for 11 constructs based on concepts culled from diffusion of innovations theory, organizational learning theories of technology adoption, institutional theory and network effects theory. The scales are validated with data collected from the membership of OASIS, a leading international standards-developing organization for electronic commerce technologies. Using data cluster analysis, relationship patterns between the 11 constructs are investigated. Results show that low fit between vertical standards and existing organizational business processes and data formats, low levels of anticipated benefits, and inadequate momentum with critical business partners contribute to slower vertical standards assimilation. However, organizational involvement with influential standards-development organizations, and the right set of technologies, skills, and structures to readily benefit from vertical standards spur their assimilation.

DOI: 10.4018/978-1-4666-2160-2.ch012

INTRODUCTION

Accuracy and consistency in product and service descriptions are some of the biggest challenges facing organizations engaged in electronic commerce. While EDI technologies have been widely implemented, their static, document-driven approach does not provide the flexibility and transparency to meet today's dynamic data exchange needs. Vertical standards formally define industry-specific vocabularies for product and service descriptions, operating and interface system parameters, and semantic data definitions (Markus et al., 2003). Vertical standards are implemented with XML (eXtensible Markup Language), syntax rules which enable the creation of robust industry-specific vocabularies and reduce development complexity and costs for organizations. Vertical standards are made up of collections of interrelated modular standards that grow and evolve to meet dynamic business needs, a different approach from the monolithic, stable, finished-product approach of prior data exchange technologies such as EDI. Vertical standards typically consist of a set of vocabulary markup tags that accompany data in order to embed a semantic payload with the data and of data dictionaries which contain consistent definitions and formatting instructions for specific data elements. The vocabulary and data dictionaries form the bases for creating flexible modules that provide semantic consistency to individual terms associated with the data payloads exchanged by various systems. This modularity enables firms to expand and modify vertical standards to reflect changes in business processes faster, easier, and much more accurately than the document-specific transactional approach of EDI technologies. By contrast, the maintenance of fixed EDI documents to reflect business process changes requires greater development and testing effort and cost. Changes to vertical standards can be implemented by firms faster, and with much lower risks to existing compatibility and features.

An emerging body of literature has explored vertical standards adoption but has generally treated adoption as a single event indicated by a public announcement of the acquisition or first deployment of these technologies (Chen et al., 2003; Markus et al., 2006). However, it has been observed that wide-scale industry acquisition of new technologies is sometimes followed by sparse deployment within the acquiring firms, resulting in a gap between reported adoption and internal deployment of the technologies. This assimilation gap (Fichman & Kemerer, 1999) can lead to incorrect assessments of the strength of a technology's assimilation throughout an industry, depending on the event used as the measure of adoption. We explore the assimilation of vertical standards as a progression from first awareness through complete deployment in production environments in order to reduce the effect of assimilation gaps. Understanding organizational and institutional factors driving the assimilation of vertical standards requires at least partial answers to each of several potential dilemmas. First, organizational participation in the development of vertical standards is more likely to take place when the benefits of early or continued participation are clear, but such benefits are often not immediately obvious and are dependent on the firm's familiarity with the standard itself. Secondly, identifying value and extracting it from vertical standards will determine the extent to which vertical standards are assimilated, but resources needed to successfully solve the value extraction problem are not homogeneously distributed across industry members, complicating the efforts of standards-developing organizations (SDO) and industry consortia to promote a dominant vertical standard. Lastly, extracting value from deeply-entrenched business processes and data formats will be a function of firm-specific environment and skill combinations, but firms with large legacy investment to protect may decide not to invest in replacement technologies, even if they can serve to extend the useful life of legacy investment (Fichman & Kemerer, 1993).

Establishing the true extent of vertical standards assimilation across industries (Nelson et al., 2005) is particularly difficult. Most vertical standards are developed by volunteer individual and corporate members coordinated by SDOs, which make them available to industry participants who wish to use them. The easy and unmonitored availability of the standards results in an incomplete picture of industry assimilation, based primarily on anecdotal evidence. For example, little evidence exists to determine the extent of diffusion of HL7 (health care), RosettaNet (electronics and logistics), and ACORD (insurance) standards in their respective industries, though no one questions their dominance. By contrast, the real estate (MISMO.org, RETS.org, OpenMLS.org) and financial services (FIXProtocol.org, Omgeo.com, eChecks.org, FpML.org) industries have multiple competing standards, with no clear leader. More importantly, the specific factors that lead to the creation of competing vertical standards and to the establishment and assimilation of a dominant one are not well understood. Very little empirical work on vertical standards assimilation has been published, and there are no validated instruments with which to begin exploring factors that impact standard formation and establishment in an industry.

We believe our work contributes to the existing literature in several ways. While technology assimilation has been examined extensively in the information systems and technology management literatures, extending this research to the context of vertical standards has to take into account the unique characteristics of vertical standards. In this paper we attempt this by our careful choice of the factors expected to matter in understanding the assimilation of user-developed networked technologies such as vertical standards. Moreover, several new constructs not examined so far in the literature have been conceptualized, defined, and measured in this study. Finally, we profile organizations using these factors to develop an understanding of which of these factors are more

important in influencing the assimilation of vertical standards and why they are important. The development of a validated instrument with which to measure vertical standards assimilation, and the preliminary analysis of the relative importance of various constructs on assimilation are only the first steps towards a much broader body of work that will help us understand how such unique technologies as vertical standards are assimilated by organizations across several industries.

The rest of this paper is organized as follows: we first synthesize extant literature to identify both organizational and institutional factors that could be important correlates of vertical standard assimilation by firms. Second, we develop and validate a set of scales to measure these factors. We then examine patterns of association among these factors and profile organizations based on these observed patterns in an attempt to better understand broader issues that drive vertical standards assimilation. Such an examination provides a deeper understanding of the key drivers of vertical standards assimilation, and provides insights for further work aimed at developing and testing theories of vertical standards assimilation. Lastly, we summarize our findings and provide some avenues for further research on this important emerging topic.

Literature Review and Theoretical Background

Vertical standards focus on product descriptions, service information, and data structures used in specific industries (Markus et al., 2003; Steinfield et al., 2004; Wigand et al., 2005). The growing body of literature on vertical standards has centered on their technical development processes, features and benefits, and industry adoption. Vertical standards are developed using simple Internet technologies, resulting in significantly lower development and operational costs than those associated with EDI (Beck & Weitzel, 2005). The elimination of expensive value-added networks

(VANs) and specialized developers (Reimers & Li, 2005) also reduce interconnectivity costs (Wigand et al., 2005).

The same flexible features that enable benefits like system-to-system process automation (Markus et al., 2003) has been blamed for the suboptimal diffusion and eventual failure of vertical standards. Efforts to build compatibility with older technologies into emerging vertical standards for the energy markets (Wareham et al., 2005) and financial services industries (Gogan, 2005) led to inefficient, inflexible specifications that limited future growth, stunted implementation and eventually lead to failure in standardization. Themes explored in the standards development literature include the critical role of potential adopters (Nickerson & Muehlen, 2003; Zhao et al., 2005), the flow of ideas across SDOs (Nickerson & Muehlen, 2003), and development communities as standards diffusion ecologies (Nickerson & Muehlen, 2006). Individual social relationships (Markus et al., 2003) and key stakeholder participation in standards-development processes have been found to impact adoption outcomes in the telecommunications (Keil, 2002) and automotive industries (Gerst & Bunduchi, 2005).

Factors affecting diffusion explored in the emerging body of literature include technical path dependence, organizational attributes, and industry characteristics. Early technology decisions limited standards development and created path dependencies that led to standardization failure in energy markets (Wareham et al., 2005) and the financial services sector (Gogan, 2005). Ingrained business practices, such as data exchange by FAX and inappropriate technical infrastructure (Beck & Weitzel, 2005) are among the organizational factors found to shape vertical standards diffusion. Other factors constraining standards diffusion include a lack of clear competitive advantage from the use of web services (Ciganek et al., 2006), market uncertainty, and organizational learning

barriers (Mendoza & Jahng, 2003), power asymmetries and stakeholder exclusion in development activities (Gerst & Bunduchi, 2005), and the structure and density of an organization's business network, specifically influential business partners (Weitzel et al., 2006).

DoI theory examines innovation characteristics to describe how an innovation spreads in a social system. Empirical findings show complexity, compatibility, and relative advantage are the most consistently significant diffusion predictors among the characteristics typically studied (Tornatzky & Klein, 1982). Vertical standards are complex networked technologies (Damsgaard & Lyytinen, 2001) with an organizational-adoption focus, so we develop factors based on DoI theory to understand how vertical standards complexity (Knowledge Stock) and the knowledge barriers they create, compatibility with existing technology investments (Technology Fit, Legacy Technology Embeddedness), and the relative advantage vertical standards provide an organization (Benefits) affect their assimilation by firms. The complexity of vertical standards makes them learning-intensive artifacts (Lyytinen & Damsgaard, 2001), and require the firm to develop significant expertise (Webster, 1995). Also, as complex networked technologies, vertical standards create and are subject to interorganizational dependencies (Lyytinen & Damsgaard, 2001), and institutional views are necessary to understand how community dynamics affect their assimilation.

Institutional theory explores how norms and patterns of use form in communities to establish structures as legitimate and sanctioned (Emerson, 1962; Lyytinen & Damsgaard, 2001). Complex technologies are socially-constructed (Damsgaard & Lyytinen, 2001), making vertical standards subject to the development of commonly-accepted usage norms by the user community. This process of legitimation (Emerson, 1962) is not adequately understood in vertical standards.

Constructs and Scales

The majority of existing research on vertical standards focuses on either organizational or institutional views, with very little integration between the two approaches. The factors in our study were developed by integrating organizational-level theories such as diffusion of innovations (DoI) (Rogers, 1983) and organizational learning theories of technology adoption (Attewell, 1992) with community-based theories such as institutional theory (Emerson, 1962; Meyer & Rowan, 1977) and network effects (Katz & Shapiro, 1985). Research also shows the importance of bandwagon effects (Katz & Shapiro, 1985), the availability of complementary goods (Schilling, 2002), and of prior technology drag (Fichman & Kemerer, 1993) on the diffusion of technology innovations, which we also explore here. We use organizational learning theories of technology adoption to develop factors that help us understand the role of accumulated expertise in reducing knowledge barriers, which have been shown to delay technology assimilation (Attewell, 1992) due to their time-sensitive nature (Brynjolffson & Hitt, 1998; Devaraj & Kohli, 2003). We also explore factors determining how vertical standards become legitimated in an industry, the role of critical business partner adoption and standards-development participation behaviors, and of supply-side signaling. Business partner behaviors and supply-side signaling have been shown to affect technology assimilation by firms (Bouchard, 1993; Ravichandran, 2005; Wareham et al., 2005). Finally, we use network effects concepts (Katz & Shapiro, 1985) to explore the impact of bandwagon effects and complementary goods on assimilation, and of the use of vertical standards as technology bridges to reduce the drag exerted by prior technology investment on the assimilation of vertical standards. Table 1 provides a summary of the core concepts in each of the firm- and community-based theories used

in construct development and of the constructs whose development they inform.

The multiplicity of effects driving the assimilation of complex technologies like vertical standards cannot be measured directly. However, the influence of these effects on the organizational assimilation of vertical standards can be inferred from the behavior of groups of variables that can be measured directly. These groups of related measures form scales that help to identify latent variables of interest to the assimilation of vertical standards. Based on a synthesis of the technology adoption literatures, we identified eleven constructs likely to impact vertical standards assimilation in organizations. The scale items in the final eleven constructs used in this study were adapted from existing studies whenever possible and are shown in Appendix A, along with descriptions of the items removed from the final data analysis stage. We discuss these eleven constructs, and their measurement scales, in the rest of this section.

A. Assimilation

Assimilation of a technical innovation has been described as an organizational absorption process that embeds the technology into the fabric of the organization's business. Previous work on technical innovation assimilation has measured this scale using between five and seven separate stages (Ettlie, 1980; Fichman & Kemerer, 1997; Ravichandran, 2005). Our scale measures assimilation using a seven-stage scale that includes awareness, rejection, evaluation, trial, adoption, partial deployment, and full deployment.

B. Expected Benefits

We define the DoI concept of relative advantage (Rogers, 1983) as internal benefits derived by firms through the use of vertical standards. For data exchange technologies like EDI, research shows that system integration and process optimization

Table 1. Theoretical bases for constructs

Theory	Core Concepts	Constructs in This Study
Diffusion of Innovations	• Spread of an innovation throughout social systems • Most consistent diffusion predictors are complexity, compatibility, and relative advantage of innovation	• Expected Benefits • Technology Fit • Legacy Technology Embeddedness
Organizational Learning Theories of Technology Adoption	• Organizations as learning entities adapting to changing environments • Knowledge barriers – firms delay complex technology adoption until sufficient expertise is developed • Absorptive capacity – capacity to recognize, appropriate, and exploit new knowledge • Knowledge stock – related expertise helps firms overcome knowledge barriers	• Knowledge Stock • Related Knowledge – Legacy Data Exchange Technologies • Related Knowledge – Emerging Technologies
Institutional Theory	• Establishment of structures as legitimate and definitive guidelines for community behavior • Community behaviors extend beyond simple aggregation of member behaviors • Signaling by influential community members reduces uncertainty	• Standard Legitimation • Standards-Development Vendor Collaboration • Business-Partner Participation in Standards-Development Activities • Business Partner Convergence
Network Effects	• Benefits are a function of size of user network • Bandwagon or penguin effects • Critical mass in tipping markets • Prior technology drag	• Availability of Complementary Products and Services • Business Partner Convergence • Legacy Technology Embeddedness

are the greatest sources of extracted benefits for firms (Swatman et al., 1994). The potential to extract these benefits from vertical standards is equally available to all firms in an industry, but firm-specific perceptions of vertical standards value will vary according to each firm's ability to identify value from vertical standards and the firm's readiness to deploy and use them to support critical business processes. The scale used to measure the Expected Benefits (EB) construct asks directly about the level of expected business benefits vertical standards will deliver to the organization, and the importance of the business processes the vertical standards will support.

C. Legacy Technology Embeddedness

Most organizations have some data exchange technologies supporting their business processes. As organizations continue to leverage these legacy technologies they become deeply embedded in the business processes making it difficult to replace them. Such embeddedness causes a drag which could impede the adoption of potentially

new technologies. However, if new technologies can act as bridge technologies to allow firms to repurpose legacy technology assets, assimilation of the new technology is facilitated. Such compatibility, as suggested by DoI theory (Rogers, 1983), can extend the value-extraction horizon of legacy technology and thus provide a facilitating condition for the new technology.

Vertical standards allow firms to continue benefit extraction from deeply embedded technologies like EDI and other in-house applications, by providing fast, simple, and cost-effective data porting between platforms. The implications of this aspect for vertical standard assimilation will, however, vary based on the extent to which legacy technology is embedded in a firm's business processes. To assess this, we propose a construct labeled Legacy Technology Embeddedness (LTE) that measures the importance of existing legacy data exchange technologies by measuring their contributions to automational, informational, and transformational effects on the firm's internal and external business processes.

D. Technology Fit

The purpose of systems integration is to facilitate data exchange across internal and external organizational boundaries. Vertical standards facilitate *external* business integration and data portability within an industry, making external implementation homogeneous. Therefore, competition on the basis of standards implementation is not a desirable strategy since the expected result, according to the resource-based view of the firm, is competitive parity (Mata et al., 1995). It is reasonable to evaluate vertical standards benefits as a function of fit with *existing* processes and data formats. A high level of fit with existing business processes has been shown to explain organizational adoption of various technology innovations (Cooper & Zmud, 1990; Tanriverdi, 2006). We suggest that vertical standards compatibility with existing internal and external business processes and data formats is a good organizational assimilation predictor, and the scale items in the Technology Fit (TF) construct measure it directly.

E. Knowledge Stock

Organizational learning research shows organizations develop sufficient in-house expertise before they assimilate complex technologies (Attewell, 1992; Fichman & Kemerer, 1997). The assimilation of MRP systems (Cooper & Zmud, 1990), corporate travel reservation systems (Chircu et al., 2001), and most recently the Linux operating system (Dedrick & West, 2003) has been shown to be affected considerably by technological complexity (Rogers, 1983) and insufficient levels of internal expertise to address such complexity. Complex technologies present three kinds of barriers: (i) technology-, (ii) project-, (iii) and application-related (Nambisan & Wang, 1999). Technology-related barriers are created by the firm's lack of technical skills related to the technology. Project-related barriers reflect low proficiency in the management of these tech-

nologies, and application-related barriers keep the firm from capitalizing on the business benefits of a technology. Conversely, the development of factual, application, and evaluative expertise have been shown to positively affect the assimilation of complex technologies (Ravichandran, 2005). This *knowledge stock* reduces the learning burden of complex technologies and spurs the assimilation of vertical standards. Our Knowledge Stock (KS) scale includes items that directly measure the level of applicable technical and project management expertise accumulated by the firm with vertical standards.

F. Related Knowledge – Emerging Technologies

A firm's absorptive capacity is the effectiveness with which it recognizes, acquires, assimilates, and exploits valuable new knowledge, and is considered a function of prior related expertise (Cohen & Levinthal, 1990). Absorptive capacity has been shown by organizational learning theory to be a significant predictor of IT use in organizations (Boynton et al., 1994). We suggest that internal expertise with emerging data exchange technologies such as XML, and with Internet infrastructure technologies needed to support vertical standards, increase a firm's absorptive capacity, thus stimulating vertical standards assimilation. Research shows low-risk experimentation with emerging technologies (Gosain, 2003) lowers knowledge barriers (Attewell, 1992), and that firms in several industries experiment with proprietary XML-based applications and web service technologies (Ciganek et al., 2005, 2006; Mendoza & Jahng, 2003) as a means to develop expertise. Expertise developed through low-risk experiments with XML and Internet infrastructure technologies helps reduce risks associated with external dependence on third-party service providers. The capital and human resource investment made during low-risk experimentation allows companies to reduce assimilation delays that firms with lower levels of related knowledge may face. Previous research has established a link between prior investment in infrastructure technologies and higher rates of electronic commerce technology assimilation in the insurance industry (Forman & Gron, 2005). The items in the Related Knowledge – Emerging Technologies (RKET) scale measure the firm's level of investment, technical and project management expertise, and benefit-extraction ability with respect to XML and Internet infrastructure technologies. This scale differs from the scale used to measure the Knowledge Stock construct in that it measures existing expertise developed with technologies *other than* the targeted vertical standards, but which may be leveraged in the deployment and assimilation of vertical standards.

G. Related Knowledge – Legacy Data Exchange Technologies

Organizational learning research suggests organizations with significant investment in legacy data exchange technologies, such as EDI, are more likely to have easily-transferable skills to help support vertical standards than firms without similar investments (Boynton et al., 1994; Cohen & Levinthal, 1990). EDI applications help develop data modeling, file transfer, and process mapping skills that form the core of expertise needed for vertical standards assimilation. Investments made developing technical, project management, and exploitative skills with legacy data exchange technologies like EDI directly increase related knowledge redeployable with vertical standards. Scale items for the Related Knowledge – Legacy Data Exchange Technologies (RKLDET) construct measure investment levels, technical and project management expertise, and benefit-extraction ability with respect to EDI technologies and applications. This scale differs from the scale used to measure the Knowledge Stock construct in ways similar to those for the Related Knowledge – Emerging Technologies scale.

H. Standards-Development Vendor Collaboration

Lack of vendor participation and collaboration in standards development has been identified as a key barrier to standards assimilation in more than 25 industries (Intellor, 2001) and for ERP, EDI, and XML technologies (Benjamin et al., 1990; Damsgaard & Lyytinen, 2001; Sumner, 2000). During the research and development and early assimilation stages of technical standards, vendor behavior may be either collaborative or non-collaborative. Collaborative strategies seek cooperation for the common good in developing and promoting the specification that best serves the industry. Non-collaborative strategies include promoting the firm's own product as a standard over any other compromise, and outright process sabotage designed to maintain industry incompatibility (Besen, 1995). Only collaborative strategies reduce market uncertainty by signaling industry convergence on a single dominant vertical standard. While participation in standardization activities requires large financial and human resource investment from vendors (Farrell & Saloner, 1992), participation can also improve the vendor's competitive position in a standardized market (Shapiro & Varian, 1999). Favorable market positions are important enough that some suppliers hedge their bets by participating in multiple standardization efforts within the same industry (Gogan, 2005). Institutional theory views vendor collaboration in vertical standards development activities as more than simple collaboration, and as a signal to the commitment of the emergence of a single vertical standard. This collaboration reduces uncertainty (Ravichandran, 2005) and spurs vertical standards assimilation. The Standards-Development Vendor Collaboration (SDVC) construct scale gauges the level of participation, total capital and human resource investment, and collaborative behavior of software vendors in development activities, as seen by potential vertical standards users.

I. Availability of Complementary Products and Services

The availability of complementary standards-compliant products and services has been shown to be critical to the success of a technology in an industry (Dedrick & West, 2003; Schilling, 2002; Wareham et al., 2005). As industries converge on fewer vertical standards, the availability of complementary products and services increases to meet demand, signaling greater vendor commitment to a standard and reinforcing network effects (Katz & Shapiro, 1994). As the size of the complementary products and services market grows, network effects continue to attract suppliers, increasing the available pool of technical, project management, and support expertise (Hills, 2000), attracting more users to the standard and spurring its assimilation. Parallel convergence and complementarity processes eliminate the apparent chicken-and-egg problem between the emergence of winning standards and the development of complementary products and services for those winning standards. The Availability of Complementary Products and Services (ACPS) scale contains items that directly measure the number and quality of external software products and consulting services that support vertical standards chosen by the organization.

J. Standard Legitimation

Institutional theory researchers define legitimation as the process of establishing norms and patterns of acceptable use for a technical innovation by its user community (Emerson, 1962; Lyytinen & Damsgaard, 2001). Legitimation establishes the innovation, formally or through market forces, as a sanctioned or authorized solution for an industry, though not necessarily as the only option. Legitimation of any given vertical standard does not guarantee the standard will ultimately become the winning standard for the industry. This organizing vision guides user communities towards convergence on technical standards (Swanson & Ramiller, 1997) and enables vertical standards assimilation. The establishment of any given vertical standard as the preferred solution in a single industry is the result of a complex process of market signals, generated and interpreted by the members of that industry, in a self-reinforcing legitimation process. Vertical standards legitimation can be as simple as a public signal of use by influential industry members, without the need for further assessments by other industry members about the efficiency, productivity gains, or benefits provided by vertical standards. Public approval by influential business partners is a cue about the innovation's legitimacy and not following suit becomes abnormal or illegitimate behavior (Abrahamson & Rosenkopf, 1993; Meyer & Rowan, 1977). Since legitimation is a community process, the convergence of various interests is required to establish any vertical standard as legitimate (Lyytinen & Damsgaard, 2001). Standard Legitimation (SL) scale items include questions regarding the commitment of most of a respondent organization's influential customers and suppliers, and of other industry participants to the vertical standards an organization is considering for use.

K. Business Partner Convergence

Extant literature in institutional theory shows organizations considering the deployment of data exchange technologies tend to wait for signals from business partners (Bouchard, 1993), making an otherwise autonomous decision interdependent (Weitzel, 2003). The deployment of a dominant vertical standard by influential business partners is interpreted by firms as a signal about the standard's likelihood of success (Keil, 2002), increasing its legitimacy in the industry, and starting an industry-wide process of convergence. Simulations have shown that autonomous agents are influenced by the decisions of the most significant members of the agents' overall network (Weitzel et al., 2006).

We define convergence as the process through which a *single* vertical standard emerges as the dominant industry standard and is acknowledged as such by industry members through their deployment behaviors. As the process of convergence unfolds, organizations are faced with deciding which of all the competing vertical standards will become the "winner" in their industries. In a cascading process of influence, deployment decisions by major industry players and influential business partners generate imitation behaviors in peripheral industry members (Abrahamson & Fombrun, 1994; Abrahamson & Rosenkopf, 1997), spurring convergence. A lack of convergent behaviors by business partners has been identified as contributing to delays in the assimilation of web services by organizations (Ciganek et al., 2005, 2006). The items making up the Business Partner Convergence (BPC) scale specifically ask whether influential customers and suppliers have begun assimilating the "winning" vertical standard. This construct is different from the Standard Legitimation construct because it measures the extent to which influential business partners are assimilating the dominant standard in the firm's home industry, not simply the viability of an emerging standard as a sanctioned option, regardless of its current or future position as the dominant vertical standard. Previous work shows that organizations are willing to deploy as many vertical standards as their relationships with critical business partners require (Mendoza & Jahng, 2003).

L. Business Partner Participation in Standards-Development Activities

Influential business partner participation in vertical standards development activities is interpreted by community members as a strong signal of intent to deploy the vertical standard. This institutional effect has been observed in the insurance, financial services, and aerospace industries (Mendoza & Jahng, 2003). The items in the Business Partner Participation in Standards-Development Activities

(BPSA) scale measure total capital investment and level of participation in technical-development activities of influential customers, suppliers, and other industry participants for standards-making efforts in the firm's home industry.

Instrument Design and Data Collection

The survey instrument consisted of 72 items, plus demographic questions designed to help us interpret the results. Individual survey questions were adopted and modified from existing instruments whenever possible and new items were developed as needed to cover the remaining constructs. The survey was tested starting in November 2005 with members of the Organization for the Advancement of Structured Information Standards (OASIS-Open.org), widely recognized as one of the leading global, cross-industry SDOs in e-business and Internet-related technologies and standards, and sponsors of work on web services, security, and e-business standards in both the private and public sectors. OASIS was founded in 1993 and has over 5,000 individual members representing more than 600 organizations in 100 countries. Instructions included in the survey asked respondents to answer all questions in the survey in the context of XML-based vertical standards their companies have adopted or are considering for adoption. Whenever firms participated in multiple industries, respondents were asked to complete the survey with their primary industry, and with the XML-based vertical standards used in that industry, in mind. Thus, the nature of the vertical standards in question varied from company to company to provide us with the widest possible sample to draw conclusions from, but all responses were based on a single family of XML-based standards in use or in consideration by the responding firm, and sanctioned and promoted by OASIS.

The survey was conducted in two stages, beginning with a random sample of 75 OASIS members each representing individual organizations, and with official voting responsibility in OASIS affairs for their respective organizations. Potential respondents were invited to participate in the online survey, with an option to decline. Survey attempts and declined invitations were tracked automatically by the web site hosting the survey. A reminder was sent nine days later to those who had neither attempted to complete the survey nor declined to participate and a final reminder was sent three weeks after the initial invitation. Included in the survey was a request to all respondents to volunteer for a clarifying interview regarding the survey process and the instrument. Follow-up interviews revealed the survey was clear and the questions, logical flow, instrument length, and domain coverage were all appropriate. Of the responses received in the first round of testing, 22 surveys (representing 20 unique companies, with one survey missing company identification) were deemed usable and were retained, for an effective yield rate of 29.33%, above the minimum recommended level for organizational surveys (Grover, 1997).

For the second stage of the instrument test, an additional 611 individuals were selected from the OASIS membership database. Once again, with very few exceptions, all individuals were the single authorized voting representatives for their respective companies. The 75 names used in the procedural assurance portion of the instrument test were not included in the second round of data collection and, with negligible editing, the same survey was administered during the second stage. All procedures for extending an invitation to participate in the survey and for data collection were identical to those used in the first round of testing, with two reminder emails sent out twelve calendar days and three weeks after the initial invitation. Six follow up interviews with respondents did not reveal any problems with either the process or content of the survey. Of the 611 surveys sent, 124 were returned, for a yield of 20.29%, meeting the

minimum recommended level for organizational surveys (Grover, 1997). Data cleanup resulted in 89 surveys found usable for further analysis (14.56% yield). These 89 surveys represented a total of 87 unique organizations.

Since the survey instrument and all other data-gathering procedures were practically identical in both stages, it was decided it was appropriate to combine the data sets as one. The total number of usable surveys from first stage (22) were added to the 89 in the second stage, for a total of 111 surveys and a 16.18% effective yield rate. In order to comply with OASIS member communications policies, individuals participating on both the first and the second test stages and choosing to opt out of the survey or who did not respond received no further contact. Thus, analysis of nonrespondent bias is limited to a comparison of the profiles of early and late respondents. Respondents were split into three groups based on the completion date recorded by the hosting web site. The first group (early respondents) consisted of 18 surveys collected during the first data stage, while the third group (late respondents) consisted of 27 surveys collected during the last weeks of the data gathering effort. One-way ANOVA testing revealed no significant differences on demographic characteristics such as industry, revenue, IT budget, or percentage of IT work conducted in-house. Thus, pooling all surveys for further analysis will not lead to a loss in generalizability. Further data cleanup reduced the total number of surveys used in this effort to 75, for a final rate of 12.27% of the initial invite list. While the response rate is quite modest for theory-making purposes and for confirmatory analysis of an existing theory, we considered it useful enough for the purposes of developing and validating an instrument that can be tested with a high level of confidence in later work.

Five industries accounted for 68% of the reported industries in the data set, with companies reporting work with government agencies (local, state, federal, and international, software development, IT & telecommunications, financial services, and consulting services constituting the largest reported segments. A variety of other industries, ranging from manufacturing to health care, aerospace, education, and several others made up the remaining 32% of all industries reported, as seen in Figure 1. Half our sample (50.60%) was comprised of companies on the low end of the revenue scale, with reported revenue less than US$50Million, while the upper end of the scale (>US$1,000M) featured just under 30% of the total sample (29.30%). Figure 2 illustrates the results. Respondents were fairly equally divided between senior executive level positions such as CEO, CIO, CFO, etc. (29.30%), middle executive levels (Director, Senior Manager; 26.70%), and staff (38.70%). Four respondents (5.30%) did not provide information related to their job function. Figure 3 illustrates these results.

Analysis and Results

A principal components analysis (PCA) was performed on the final data set in order to guide subsequent scale validation work. The analysis done in SPSS v16 using Varimax rotation and Kaiser normalization led to a reduction in the data set from 72 to 51 items making up the eleven constructs. This reduction was iterative, testing survey items thought to be theoretically related at each stage to determine whether they would load with other items into logical constructs. An Eigenvalue greater than or equal to one was used as a guide for item retention or elimination. Survey items were eliminated through several rounds until a stable structure for the eleven constructs emerged. Means and standard deviations for the final eleven constructs are provided in Table 2. Appendix A provides sources to articles used in survey item

Figure 1. Respondent profile by industry

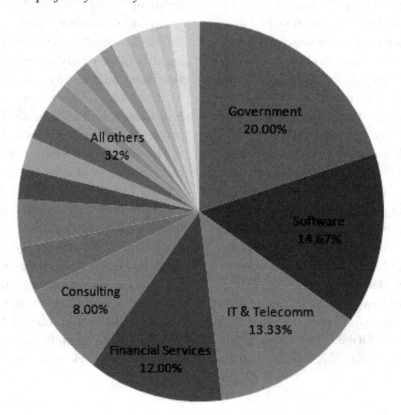

Figure 2. Respondent profile by revenue

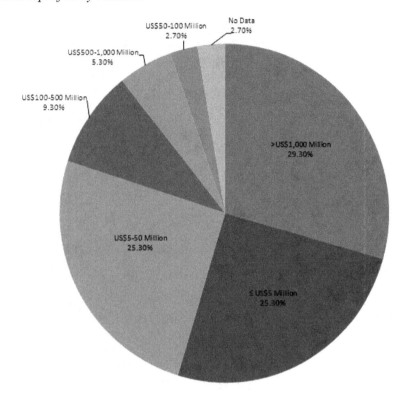

Table 2. Descriptive statistics

Construct	Mean	Std Dev
Assimilation	4.71	1.77
Expected Benefits	5.37	1.37
Legacy Technology Embeddedness	4.06	1.64
Technology Fit	5.00	1.34
Knowledge Stock	5.31	1.36
Related Knowledge – Emerging Technologies	5.10	1.58
Related Knowledge – Legacy Data Exchange Technologies	3.55	2.11
Standards-Development Vendor Collaboration	3.90	1.49
Availability of Complementary Products & Services	3.68	1.40
Standard Legitimation	5.81	1.28
Business Partner Participation in Standards-Development Activities	3.62	1.30
Business Partner Convergence	4.01	1.75

development, and a description of items not used in the final version of the instrument.

In order to validate the 51-item scale and our eleven constructs, we built and tested a structural equation model using PLS (PLS-Graph, version 3.0, build 1130) and followed the recommended practices for establishing the convergent and divergent validity of the scales in the model (Gefen & Straub, 2005). The use of PLS permits the specification of a model in which each latent construct is made up of a linear combination of its reflective indicator items, and allows an assessment of the fit of the model being tested to the existing data for all constructs. The model fit was tested with no causal paths linking the individual constructs to each other (Figure 4). In PLS, convergent validity is shown when the measurement items associated with a latent construct load on that construct with a significant t-value. Table 3 shows that t-values for all multi-item scales are significantly higher than the minimum recom-

Figure 3. Respondent profile by management level

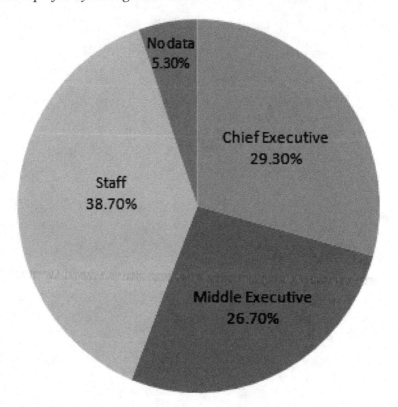

mended level, and convergent validity is established for all scales. Loadings for all items on their assigned constructs are also shown in Table 3. For discriminant validity, two conditions must be met. First, the correlation coefficient for all indicator items has to be higher within their assigned construct than across other constructs. Table 4 shows this to be the case by at least the recommended minimum of one order of magnitude (Gefen & Straub, 2005).

The second discriminant validity procedure is an analysis of the average variance extracted (AVE) for each latent construct. Specifically, the square root of the AVE for each construct must be higher than the maximum correlation coefficient between each construct and any other available construct (Gefen & Straub, 2005). Table 5 confirms this for all constructs. The values on the diagonal line correspond to the composite reliability of each scale in the instrument. As gener-

ated by PLS-Graph, composite reliability is equivalent to Cronbach's Alpha for reflective indicators (Chin et al., 1996). For all constructs measured in the instrument, Table 5 shows the composite reliability value for all instrument scales to be higher than the recommended minimum of 0.70 (Cronbach, 1951). Thus, the convergent and discriminant validity of the scales is established and the instrument is validated.

A review of the path coefficients generated by the full model revealed that the only path coefficient showing statistical significance was for the Expected Benefits construct, despite the fact that the total variance accounted for by the model was 54.70%. Given the modest size of the data set, our original goal of validating the instrument for use as part of a much broader research program into the organizational assimilation of vertical standards seems reasonable, and further theory-making will be left to continued efforts

Figure 4. PLS-G Model used for validation

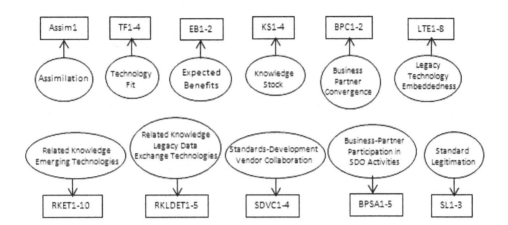

with a much more robust data set. In the interest of brevity, then, we do not report further on the results of the PLS-G model path coefficients and their significances. However, in order to extract any useful information that may guide subsequent theory-making efforts with a larger data set, we completed a cluster analysis of the data set to determine potentially useful relationships between the constructs beyond their effects on the organizational assimilation of vertical standards.

Relationships among the Constructs

We used cluster analysis to determine what relationships exist between the eleven constructs. Clusters were formed using average values for all items in each construct, and statistical-significance testing between the cluster centers for all eleven constructs was performed. The number of clusters to form was determined by examining a dendogram generated from the data. Further, we used k-means clustering with squared Euclidean distances as the cluster distance measure and Ward's method to separate the data into clusters, as suggested in previous research using cluster analysis (Bensaou & Venkatraman, 1995). Table 6 shows how the observations separated into three clusters and the significance levels of the difference in cluster centers for each pair of clusters.

Cluster 1 was dominated by organizations in the software, government service, and consulting industries, and by firms on the low end of the revenue scale (67.70% ≤ $100M) and with relatively small IT budgets (86.7% ≤ $50M, mean $8.85M). In Cluster 2, 50% of all cases were in the software and government service industries, on the low end of the revenue scale (50% ≤ $50M, mean $8.75M) and had low IT budgets (71.40% ≤ $50M, mean $7.50M). Cluster 3 was heavily populated by organizations in the government service, IT & telecommunications, and financial services industries (61.70% of all cases). Organizations in this cluster were on the high end of the revenue scale (50% ≥ $500M, mean $2867.65M), but at the low end of the IT budget scale (57.60% ≤ $50M, mean $9.08M).

A review of the means across the three clusters offers some insight into the patterns of XML-based vertical standards assimilation. Cluster 1 has the lowest average assimilation score of all three clusters, and Cluster 2 the highest. The difference in average assimilation scores between Clusters 1 and Clusters 2 & 3 is significant, but it is not significant between Clusters 2 & 3. Also, the average score for the Expected Benefits construct is significantly lower for Cluster 1 than it is for Clusters 2 & 3, but it is not significant between the latter. Cluster 1 also has the lowest Technology Fit and Knowledge Stock scores of all

207

Table 3. Item loadings and t-statistic values (convergent validity)

Constructs & Items	Loading	T-stat		Constructs & Items	Loading	T-stat
Knowledge Stock				Business Partner Participation in Standards-Development Activities		
KS1	0.852	19.877		BPSA1	0.803	18.887
KS2	0.828	10.212		BPSA2	0.809	19.297
KS3	0.901	24.154		BPSA3	0.592	4.667
KS4	0.880	25.921		BPSA4	0.785	15.425
Expected Benefits				BPSA5	0.776	9.670
EB1	0.920	50.744		Business Partner Convergence		
EB2	0.920	50.744		BPC1	0.964	73.981
Related Knowledge – Legacy Data Exchange Technologies				BPC2	0.959	76.331
RKLDET1	0.951	53.499		Availability of Complementary Products and Services		
RKLDET2	0.954	56.301		ACPS1	0.883	33.962
RKLDET3	0.919	30.850		ACPS2	0.884	30.426
RKLDET4	0.957	82.821		ACPS3	0.872	18.130
RKLDET5	0.854	15.298		ACPS4	0.866	25.091
Technology Fit				Standards-Development Vendor Collaboration		
TF1	0.866	31.136		SDVC1	0.932	60.048
TF2	0.881	34.795		SDVC2	0.961	81.266
TF3	0.859	27.420		SDVC3	0.951	62.765
TF4	0.870	34.665		SDVC4	0.804	16.517
Related Knowledge – Emerging Technologies				Standard Legitimation		
RKET1	0.789	14.197		SL1	0.973	82.622
RKET2	0.842	20.480		SL2	0.944	29.048
RKET3	0.868	21.722		SL3	0.925	17.963
RKET4	0.893	29.840		Legacy Technology Embeddedness		
RKET5	0.861	24.554		LTE1	0.839	15.789
RKET6	0.768	10.338		LTE2	0.867	19.245
RKET7	0.863	29.023		LTE3	0.845	20.613
RKET8	0.883	32.073		LTE4	0.865	23.872
RKET9	0.864	23.759		LTE5	0.890	27.122
RKET10	0.879	32.530		LTE6	0.914	38.898
				LTE7	0.835	18.629
				LTE8	0.857	16.666

three clusters. Together, these results suggest that lower levels of anticipated benefits from the use of vertical standards may result, at least partially, in lower assimilation scores. The perceived lack of benefits from vertical standards may be due to low fit between the vertical standard and the firm's existing processes and data formats, and may be exacerbated by low levels of expertise to

Table 4. Item-construct correlations (discriminant validity)

	EB	LTE	TF	KS	RKET	RKLDET	SDVC	ACPS	SL	BPSA	BPC
EB1	**0.938**	0.280	0.647	-0.028	0.134	0.149	0.217	0.224	0.109	0.337	0.310
EB2	**0.897**	0.358	0.633	-0.060	-0.041	0.200	0.201	0.122	0.114	0.280	0.273
LTE1	0.213	**0.845**	0.234	-0.290	0.169	0.440	0.175	0.373	-0.127	0.076	0.472
LTE2	0.272	**0.863**	0.280	-0.357	0.314	0.436	0.172	0.238	-0.157	0.123	0.321
LTE3	0.249	**0.831**	0.338	-0.171	0.042	0.516	0.198	0.076	0.093	0.068	0.328
LTE4	0.405	**0.848**	0.447	-0.264	0.150	0.512	0.281	0.150	0.072	0.198	0.318
LTE5	0.373	**0.901**	0.409	-0.229	0.086	0.474	0.294	0.151	0.010	0.092	0.361
LTE6	0.398	**0.916**	0.343	-0.221	0.153	0.485	0.261	0.172	-0.042	0.248	0.308
LTE7	0.256	**0.834**	0.285	-0.204	0.076	0.398	0.243	0.173	-0.036	0.089	0.295
LTE8	0.298	**0.844**	0.226	-0.325	0.202	0.521	0.129	0.192	-0.120	0.070	0.253
TF1	0.614	0.333	**0.870**	0.059	0.052	0.264	0.242	0.141	0.153	0.197	0.257
TF2	0.680	0.428	**0.892**	-0.049	0.083	0.318	0.207	0.099	0.167	0.291	0.338
TF3	0.509	0.175	**0.842**	0.063	0.070	0.142	0.133	0.137	0.139	0.175	0.174
TF4	0.633	0.333	**0.870**	0.005	0.066	0.245	0.189	0.077	0.088	0.273	0.238
KS1	0.043	-0.039	-0.080	**0.868**	0.313	-0.092	0.059	0.265	0.359	0.242	-0.095
KS2	-0.132	-0.033	-0.159	**0.882**	0.416	-0.108	0.031	0.182	0.398	0.058	-0.096
KS3	0.057	-0.150	-0.006	**0.931**	0.336	-0.101	0.147	0.129	0.394	0.135	0.005
KS4	0.047	-0.134	-0.018	**0.889**	0.368	-0.041	0.013	0.095	0.436	0.042	-0.033
RKET1	0.041	0.181	0.018	-0.016	**0.801**	0.155	0.184	0.233	0.130	0.100	-0.014
RKET2	-0.156	0.119	-0.160	0.096	**0.827**	-0.016	0.115	0.170	0.100	0.018	-0.035
RKET3	-0.130	0.187	-0.125	0.134	**0.861**	0.023	0.232	0.196	0.120	0.040	0.008
RKET4	-0.084	0.164	-0.173	0.013	**0.862**	0.042	0.146	0.169	0.155	0.088	-0.073
RKET5	-0.004	0.217	-0.066	0.106	**0.894**	0.091	0.253	0.284	0.159	0.115	0.071
RKET6	0.194	0.294	0.163	-0.023	**0.736**	0.288	0.204	0.304	0.245	0.117	0.183
RKET7	0.104	0.128	0.055	0.121	**0.780**	0.161	0.199	0.358	0.226	0.185	0.156
RKET8	0.079	0.161	0.005	0.148	**0.793**	0.189	0.322	0.375	0.162	0.208	0.221
RKET9	0.120	0.152	0.059	0.153	**0.822**	0.205	0.259	0.395	0.212	0.185	0.160
RKET10	0.148	0.202	0.062	0.160	**0.809**	0.243	0.251	0.352	0.188	0.189	0.207
RKLDET1	0.235	0.517	0.284	-0.212	0.098	**0.848**	0.200	-0.022	-0.041	0.126	0.399
RKLDET2	0.093	0.480	0.222	-0.150	0.157	**0.947**	0.140	0.153	-0.088	0.012	0.244
RKLDET3	0.107	0.490	0.199	-0.122	0.135	**0.951**	0.161	0.183	-0.063	0.030	0.280
RKLDET4	0.204	0.517	0.278	-0.189	0.036	**0.924**	0.072	0.132	-0.179	-0.005	0.186
RKLDET5	0.131	0.539	0.210	-0.123	0.111	**0.959**	0.158	0.166	-0.089	0.065	0.290
SDVC1	0.288	0.238	0.267	-0.031	0.176	0.131	**0.931**	0.263	-0.055	0.487	0.132
SDVC2	0.238	0.189	0.194	-0.058	0.212	0.096	**0.952**	0.309	-0.055	0.453	0.167
SDVC3	0.344	0.303	0.239	-0.043	0.315	0.203	**0.949**	0.346	0.004	0.510	0.223
SDVC4	0.218	0.106	0.211	-0.049	0.214	0.056	**0.775**	0.110	0.166	0.387	0.204
ACPS1	0.303	0.176	0.217	-0.063	0.173	0.143	0.111	**0.879**	-0.126	0.137	0.129
ACPS2	0.273	0.078	0.190	-0.065	0.067	0.048	0.104	**0.865**	-0.217	0.092	0.042

continued on following page

Table 4. Continued

	EB	LTE	TF	KS	RKET	RKLDET	SDVC	ACPS	SL	BPSA	BPC
ACPS3	-0.027	0.092	-0.029	-0.051	0.239	0.105	0.229	**0.861**	-0.088	0.220	0.134
ACPS4	0.095	0.030	0.040	0.006	0.246	0.007	0.250	**0.860**	-0.130	0.181	0.059
SL1	0.138	-0.055	0.128	0.350	0.159	-0.156	0.041	-0.138	**0.978**	0.212	0.203
SL2	0.041	0.011	0.048	0.335	0.193	-0.155	-0.010	-0.170	**0.952**	0.192	0.165
SL3	0.108	-0.063	0.113	0.360	0.142	-0.202	0.083	-0.132	**0.976**	0.193	0.200
BPSA1	0.402	0.220	0.348	0.081	0.219	0.142	0.368	0.278	0.343	**0.822**	0.454
BPSA2	0.362	0.262	0.255	0.181	0.239	0.149	0.376	0.309	0.381	**0.834**	0.448
BPSA3	0.388	0.222	0.285	-0.020	0.071	0.112	0.313	0.131	-0.010	**0.564**	0.291
BPSA4	0.327	0.058	0.116	0.044	0.058	-0.092	0.429	0.285	-0.110	**0.807**	0.251
BPSA5	0.339	0.182	0.249	-0.065	0.205	0.065	0.479	0.110	0.174	**0.780**	0.446
BPC1	0.409	0.514	0.310	-0.174	0.265	0.383	0.242	0.133	0.194	0.369	**0.938**
BPC2	0.384	0.465	0.268	-0.120	0.179	0.312	0.155	0.205	0.155	0.379	**0.974**

deal with the standard itself. Consistent with existing research on the links between IT investment, technology assimilation, and benefits extraction (Brynjolffson & Hitt, 1998; Devaraj & Kohli, 2003), this result may point to the existence of time lags between organizational investment in vertical standards and the development of knowledge stock and the extraction of benefits due to the fit of vertical standards technologies with existing infrastructure.

The mean for the Standard Legitimation construct is uniformly high across all clusters, with no statistically-significant differences, suggesting that involvement with OASIS lends legitimacy to efforts on behalf of the vertical standards in the respondents' respective industries. Scores for the Business Partner Participation in Standards-Development Activities and Business Partner Convergence constructs are significantly lower for Cluster 1 than for Clusters 2 & 3, indicating the vertical standard in the Cluster 1 organization's home industry does not have adequate momentum with critical business partners, slowing assimilation.

Cluster 2 has the highest average assimilation score of all three clusters. It also has the highest mean for Expected Benefits (p < 0.000), Technol-

ogy Fit (p < 0.000), and Knowledge Stock. This suggests Cluster 2 is populated by organizations with the right set of technologies and structures in place to readily benefit from vertical standards.

The Cluster 3 centers for the Related Knowledge – Emerging Technologies and Related Knowledge – Legacy Data Exchange Technologies constructs were the highest of all three clusters, suggesting that Cluster 3 organizations might perceive existing skills with data exchange technologies to be relevant expertise required to successfully assimilate vertical standards.

The combined results of our cluster analysis suggest that Knowledge Stock is a critical factor shaping the assimilation of vertical standards. The effective evaluation of the fit of vertical standards in a firm's technical and business environment, and of the expected benefits derived from vertical standards deployment, appear to vary with changing levels of organizational Knowledge Stock. In addition, association with the dominant SDO provides an organization with a frame of reference with which to evaluate the legitimacy of a vertical standard in its industry, which will increase the assimilation momentum for vertical standards with dominant firms in any given industry.

Table 5. AVE analysis (discriminant validity) and composite scale reliability (Cronbach's alpha)

	AVE	Sqrt	KS	EB	RKLDET	TF	RKET	BPSA	BPC	ACPS	SDVC	SL	LTE
KS	0.749	0.865	**0.923**										
EB	0.847	0.920	-0.012	**0.917**									
RKLDET	0.861	0.928	-0.098	0.169	**0.969**								
TF	0.755	0.869	-0.034	0.707	0.250	**0.925**							
RKET	0.726	0.852	0.331	-0.009	0.179	-0.030	**0.963**						
BPSA	0.574	0.758	0.098	0.455	0.087	0.355	0.148	**0.869**					
BPC	0.924	0.961	-0.008	0.393	0.358	0.318	0.223	0.432	**0.961**				
ACPS	0.768	0.876	0.122	0.153	0.171	0.087	0.376	0.279	0.213	**0.930**			
SDVC	0.835	0.914	0.005	0.285	0.147	0.261	0.230	0.508	0.235	0.304	**0.953**		
SL	0.898	0.948	0.368	0.024	-0.141	0.025	0.203	0.171	0.209	-0.101	0.040	**0.964**	
LTE	0.747	0.864	-0.151	0.364	0.541	0.375	0.190	0.208	0.486	0.267	0.273	-0.012	**0.959**

Limitations

As with any research effort, there are limitations to the generalizability of our findings. It is well known that technology assimilation is a heavily-contextual process, and despite the cross-industry nature of our study marked differences in findings may be present between research efforts conducted in different industries. Additionally, research has identified the time-sensitive nature of several factors shaping technology assimilation. The links between investment and benefits extraction (Brynjolffson & Hitt, 1998), and between organizational performance and actual technology utilization (Devaraj & Kohli, 2003) have been well documented. As such, the generalizability of our findings is limited by the cross-sectional nature of our study. A longitudinal effort would help clarify the validity of our findings as time-sensitive constructs such as knowledge stock

Table 6. Clustering of cross-industry assimilation drivers

Construct	Cluster 1 (n=33)	Cluster 2 (n=8)	Cluster 3 (n=34)	p 1-2	p 1-3	p 2-3
Assimilation	3.85	5.75	5.29	0.010	0.001	ns
Expected Benefits	4.576	6.929	5.824	0.000	0.000	ns
Legacy Technology Embeddedness	2.745	3.768	5.186	ns	0.000	0.015
Technology Fit	4.152	6.286	5.551	0.000	0.000	ns
Knowledge Stock	5.250	5.458	5.363	ns	ns	ns
Related Knowledge – Emerging Technologies	5.164	2.367	5.554	0.000	ns	0.000
Related Knowledge – Legacy Data Exchange Technologies	2.222	1.433	5.063	ns	0.000	0.000
Standards-Development Vendor Collaboration	3.304	3.708	4.484	ns	0.005	ns
Availability of Complementary Products and Services	3.344	3.063	4.147	ns	0.048	ns
Standard Legitimation	5.859	6.222	5.699	ns	ns	ns
Business Partner Participation in Standards-Development Activities	2.913	4.844	4.030	0.001	0.001	ns
Business Partner Convergence	2.760	4.500	4.950	0.025	0.000	ns

and benefits evolve to shape the organizational asssimilation of vertical standards.

Another limitation of our study is that the central objective of this effort was to develop and validate a survey instrument which may be redeployed as part of a larger research program. The data set collected was of modest size, limiting theory-making and reducing the potential generalizability of our findings, even as it helped validate the constructs represented in the instrument. In addition, the final constructs in the validated instrument are the result of iterative reduction based on the modest data set we collected. A larger data set may lead to a different combination of relevant items and constructs.

Finally, our data set contains significant representation from organizations in the government, IT & telecommunications, financial services, and consulting services industries. As such, any findings will reflect a bias towards the unique characteristics of the firms in these industries.

CONCLUSION

This study enables practitioners to better understand the dynamics of vertical standards assimilation by synthesizing the wide range of themes discussed in practitioner and academic literatures with respect to vertical standards acceptance and use, and by identifying a parsimonious set of factors that are likely to be important correlates of vertical standards assimilation. The assimilation of vertical standards is still in its early stages (Wareham et al., 2005), which provides opportunities to make contributions of practical significance for technical development, for creating industry best practices, and for government policy regarding these technologies.

The development and validation of an instrument to understand the role of organizational and community factors in vertical standards assimilation, as well as the resulting analysis of relationships between the constructs developed

in this research, are an important contribution to this emerging field. Our study was conducted with data collected from several industries, and while the dynamics of standardization are likely to be different in each industry, there is significant value in identifying a common set of factors that can influence standards assimilation and in testing scales for these factors using a cross-industry sample. First, the use of a cross-industry sample to validate the scales provides greater validity to the scales because the effects seen are not necessarily specific to any industry context. Second, our cluster analysis revealed patterns of association among these constructs that transcend any specific industry context. This provides some broad insights about the relative importance of the factors examined and of any association among them to guide research in individual industries. The specific manner in which these factors will interrelate to influence vertical standards assimilation in any industry could be different from the patterns observed here.

User organizations need to extract value from technical choices forced upon them by influential business partners, and to leverage those investments with existing legacy technologies. Knowledge of the factors driving the assimilation of vertical standards is useful to practitioners to avoid selecting a standard that will fail to achieve dominance in their industries. It is also useful to help them evaluate their existing knowledge stocks related to vertical standards and develop that expertise appropriately. For vendors, an awareness of vertical standards assimilation factors can help determine appropriate standards-development investment strategies and ways to influence the emergence of a dominant vertical standard. For industry consortia developing and sponsoring vertical standards, understanding the importance of standard legitimation, business partner participation, and business partner adoption convergence on the assimilation of its sponsored standards is crucial. The appropriate knowledge creation and dissemination practices can help consortia increase participation and reduce the development burden of active participants. In addition, consortia-backed vertical standards proponents can exploit the relative importance of knowledge stocks and related knowledge to highlight the relative lack of domain expertise in SDO development committees, enhancing the competitive advantage of their own standards. For their part, SDOs would benefit from an understanding of the assimilation process by identifying the most effective way to legitimate their sponsored standards in an industry. Additionally, SDOs can develop more efficient information-sharing strategies to become the official vertical standardization information source in the industries they serve and to combat the perception that their development processes take too long to be useful to fast-moving industries.

We hope these scales provide the basis for further empirical work aimed at developing and testing theories of vertical standards assimilation. It must be pointed out that development of valid scales transcends a single research study. Future research should examine the conceptual definitions of the constructs put forth here, assess the scales used to measure them, and test their psychometric properties using new data. Such cumulative research is needed to develop a body of knowledge in this emerging and important area. It is imperative that future studies follow up this initial work with industry-specific studies that examine how the factors developed in this effort interrelate to affect vertical standards assimilation.

REFERENCES

Abrahamson, E., & Fombrun, C. J. (1994). Macroculture: Determinants and Consequences. *Academy of Management Review, 19*(4), 728–755.

Abrahamson, E., & Rosenkopf, L. (1993). Institutional and Competitive Bandwagons: Using Mathematical Modeling as a Tool to Explore Innovation Diffusion. *Academy of Management Review, 18*(3), 487–517.

Abrahamson, E., & Rosenkopf, L. (1997). Social Network Effects on the Extent of Innovation Diffusion: A Computer Simulation. *Organization Science, 8*(3), 289–309. doi:10.1287/orsc.8.3.289

Al-Qirim, N. (2005). An Empirical Investigation of an e-commerce Adoption-Capability Model in Small Businesses in New Zealand. *Electronic Markets, 15*(4), 418–437. doi:10.1080/10196780500303136

Angeles, R., Corritore, C. L., Basu, S. C., & Nath, R. (2001). Success factors for domestic and international electronic data interchange (EDI) implementation for US firms. *International Journal of Information Management, 21*(5), 329–347. doi:10.1016/S0268-4012(01)00028-7

Attewell, P. (1992). Technology Diffusion and Organizational Learning: The Case of Business Computing. *Organization Science, 3*(1), 1–19. doi:10.1287/orsc.3.1.1

Beck, R., & Weitzel, T. (2005). Some Economics of Vertical Standards: Integrating SMEs in EDI Supply Chains. *Electronic Markets, 15*(4), 313–322. doi:10.1080/10196780500302781

Benjamin, R. I., de Long, D. W., & Morton, M. S. S. (1990). Electronic Data Interchange: How Much Competitive Advantage? *Long Range Planning, 23*(1), 29–40. doi:10.1016/0024-6301(90)90005-O

Bensaou, B., & Venkatraman, N. (1995). Configurations of Interorganizational Relationships: A Comparison Between U.S. and Japanese Automakers. *Management Science, 41*(9), 1471–1492. doi:10.1287/mnsc.41.9.1471

Besen, S. M. (1995). The Standards Processes in Telecommunication and Information Technology. In Hawkins, R., Mansell, R., & Skea, J. (Eds.), *Standards, Innovation, and Competitiveness: the Politics and Economics of Standards in Natural and Technical Environments*. Cheltenham, UK: Edward Elgar.

Bouchard, L. (1993). *Decision Criteria in the Adoption of EDI*. Paper presented at the Fourteenth International Conference on Information Systems, Orlando, FL.

Boynton, A. C., Zmud, R. W., & Jacobs, G. C. (1994). The Influence of IT Management Practice on IT Use in Large Corporations. *Management Information Systems Quarterly*, *18*(3), 299–318. doi:10.2307/249620

Bradford, M., & Florin, J. (2003). Examining the role of innovation diffusion factors on the implementation success of enterprise resource planning systems. *Accounting Information Systems*, *4*, 205–225. doi:10.1016/S1467-0895(03)00026-5

Brynjolfsson, E., & Hitt, L. M. (1998). Beyond the productivity paradox. *Communications of the ACM*, *41*(8), 49–55. doi:10.1145/280324.280332

Chen, A. N. K., Sen, S., & Shao, B. (2003, August 4-6). *Identifying Factors to improve effective XML adoption in Electronic Businesses*. Paper presented at the Ninth Americas Conference on Information Systems, Tampa, FL.

Chin, W. W., Marcolin, B. L., & Newsted, P. R. (1996, December 16-18). *A Partial Least Squares Latent Variable Modeling Approach for Measuring Interaction Effects: Results from a Monte Carlo Simulation Study and Voice Mail Emotion/Adoption Study*. Paper presented at the Seventeenth International Conference on Information Systems, Cleveland, OH.

Chircu, A. M., Kauffman, R. J., & Keskey, D. (2001). Maximizing the Value of Internet-Based Corporate Travel Reservation Systems. *Communications of the ACM*, *44*(11), 57–63. doi:10.1145/384150.384162

Chwelos, P., Benbasat, I., & Dexter, A. S. (1997). *The Adoption and Impact of Electronic Data Interchange: A Test of Internal and External Factors*. Paper presented at the International Conference on Information Systems (ICIS), Atlanta, GA.

Chwelos, P., Benbasat, I., & Dexter, A. S. (2001). Research report: Empirical test of an EDI adoption model. *Information Systems Research*, *12*(3), 304–321. doi:10.1287/isre.12.3.304.9708

Ciganek, A. P., Haines, M. N., & Haseman, W. D. (2005, January 3-6). *Challenges of Adopting Web Services: Experiences from the Financial Industry*. Paper presented at the Hawaii International Conference on System Sciences (HICSS 38), Waikoloa, HI.

Ciganek, A. P., Haines, M. N., & Haseman, W. D. (2006, January 4-7). *Horizontal and Vertical Factors Influencing the Adoption of Web Services*. Paper presented at the Hawaii International Conference on System Sciences (HICSS 39), Kauai, HI.

Cohen, W. M., & Levinthal, D. A. (1990). Absorptive capacity: A new perspective on learning and innovation. *Administrative Science Quarterly*, *35*(1), 128. doi:10.2307/2393553

Cooper, R., & Zmud, R. (1990). Information Technology Implementation Research: A Technological Diffusion Approach. *Management Science*, *36*(2), 123–139. doi:10.1287/mnsc.36.2.123

Cronbach, L. J. (1951). Coefficient Alpha and the Internal Structure of Tests. *Psychometrika*, *16*, 297–334. doi:10.1007/BF02310555

Damsgaard, J., & Lyytinen, K. (2001). The Role of Intermediating Institutions in the Diffusion of Electronic Data Interchange (EDI): How Industry Associations Intervened in Denmark, Finland, and Hong Kong. *The Information Society*, *17*(3), 195–210. doi:10.1080/01972240152493056

Dedrick, J., & West, J. (2003, December 12-14). *Why Firms Adopt Open Source Platforms: A Grounded Theory of Innovation and Standard Adoption*. Paper presented at the International Conference on IS Special Workshop on Standard Making sponsored by MISQ, Seattle, WA.

Devaraj, S., & Kohli, R. (2003). Performance Impacts of Information Technology: Is Actual Usage the Missing Link? *Management Science, 49*(3), 273–289. doi:10.1287/mnsc.49.3.273.12736

Emerson, R. M. (1962). Power Dependence Relations. *American Sociological Review, 27*(1), 31–41. doi:10.2307/2089716

Ettlie, J. E. (1980). Adequacy of Stage Models for Decisions on Adoption of Innovation. *Psychological Reports, 46*(8), 991–995. doi:10.2466/pr0.1980.46.3.991

Farrell, J., & Saloner, G. (1992). Converters, Compatibility, and the Control of Interfaces. *The Journal of Industrial Economics, 40*(1), 9–35. doi:10.2307/2950625

Fichman, R. G., & Kemerer, C. F. (1993). Adoption of Software Engineering Process Innovations: The Case of Object Orientation. *Sloan Management Review, 34*(2), 7–22.

Fichman, R. G., & Kemerer, C. F. (1997). The Assimilation of Software Process Innovations: An Organizational Learning Perspective. *Management Science, 43*(10), 1345–1363. doi:10.1287/mnsc.43.10.1345

Fichman, R. G., & Kemerer, C. F. (1999). The Illusory Diffusion of Innovation: An Examination of Assimilation Gaps. *Information Systems Research, 10*(3), 255–275. doi:10.1287/isre.10.3.255

Forman, C., & Gron, A. (2005, January 3-6). *Vertical Integration and Information Technology Adoption: A Study of the Insurance Industry.* Paper presented at the Hawaii International Conference on System Sciences (HICSS 38), Waikoloa, HI.

Gefen, D., & Straub, D. (2005). A Practical Guide to Factorial Validity Using PLS-Graph: Tutorial and Annotated Example. *Communications of the AIS, 16,* 91–109.

Gerst, M., & Bunduchi, R. (2005). Shaping IT Standardization in the Automotive Industry - The Role of Power in Driving Portal Standardization. *Electronic Markets, 15*(4), 335–343. doi:10.1080/10196780500302872

Gogan, J. L. (2005). Punctuation and Path Dependence: Examining a Vertical IT Standard-Setting Process. *Electronic Markets, 15*(4), 344–354. doi:10.1080/10196780500302880

Gosain, S. (2003, December 12-14). *Realizing the Vision for Web Services: Strategies for Dealing with Imperfect Standards.* Paper presented at the International Conference on IS Special Workshop on Standard Making sponsored by MISQ, Seattle, WA.

Grover, V. (1997). *A Tutorial on Survey Research: From Constructs to Theory.* Retrieved from http://dmsweb.badm.sc.edu/grover/survey/MIS-SUVY.html

Hills, B. (2000). Common message standards for electronic commerce in wholesale financial markets. *Bank of England Quarterly Bulletin, 40*(3), 274–285.

Iacovou, C. L., Benbasat, I., & Dexter, A. S. (1995). Electronic Data Interchange and Small Organizations: Adoption and Impact of Technology. *Management Information Systems Quarterly,* 465–484. doi:10.2307/249629

Intellor. (2001). *XML Adoption: Benefits and Challenges.* Retrieved from http://www.dad.be/library/pdf/intellor2.pdf

Jones, M. C., & Beatty, R. C. (1998). Towards the development of measures of perceived benefits and compatibility of EDI: a comparative assessment of competing first order factor models. *European Journal of Information Systems, 7*(3), 210–220. doi:10.1057/palgrave.ejis.3000299

Karahanna, E., Straub, D. W., & Chervany, N. L. (1999). Information Technology Adoption Across Time: A Cross-Sectional Comparison of Pre-Adoption and Post-Adoption Beliefs. *Management Information Systems Quarterly*, *23*(2), 183–213. doi:10.2307/249751

Katz, M. L., & Shapiro, C. (1985). Network Externalities, Competition, and Compatibility. *The American Economic Review*, *75*(3), 424–442.

Katz, M. L., & Shapiro, C. (1994). Systems Competition and Network Effects. *The Journal of Economic Perspectives*, *8*(2), 93–115. doi:10.1257/jep.8.2.93

Keil, T. (2002). De facto Standardization Through Alliances - Lessons From Bluetooth. *Telecommunications Policy*, *26*(3-4), 205–213. doi:10.1016/S0308-5961(02)00010-1

Lyytinen, K., & Damsgaard, J. (2001, April 7-10). *What's Wrong With the Diffusion of Innovation Theory: The Case of a Complex and Networked Technology*. Paper presented at the International Federation for Information Processing (IFIP), Banff, AB, Canada.

Markus, M. L., Steinfield, C. W., & Wigand, R. T. (2003, December 12-14). *The Evolution of Vertical IS Standards: Electronic Interchange Standards in the US Home Mortgage Industry*. Paper presented at the International Conference on IS Special Workshop on Standard Making sponsored by MISQ, Seattle, WA.

Markus, M. L., Steinfield, C. W., Wigand, R. T., & Minton, G. (2006). Industry-Wide Information Systems Standardization as Collective Action: The Case of the U.S. Residential Mortgage Industry. *Management Information Systems Quarterly*, *30*, 439–465.

Mata, F. J., Fuerst, W. L., & Barney, J. B. (1995). Information Technology and Sustained Competitive Advantage: A Resource-Based Analysis. *Management Information Systems Quarterly*, *19*(4), 487–505. doi:10.2307/249630

Mendoza, R. A., & Jahng, J. J. (2003, August). *Adoption of XML Specifications: An Exploratory Study of Industry Practices*. Paper presented at the Americas Conference on Information Systems (AMCIS), Tampa, FL.

Meyer, J., & Rowan, B. (1977). Institutionalized organizations: Formal structure as myth and ceremony. *American Journal of Sociology*, *83*, 340–363. doi:10.1086/226550

Moore, G. C., & Benbasat, I. (1991). Development of an Instrument to Measure the Perceptions of Adopting an Information Technology Innovation. *Information Systems Research*, *2*(3), 192–222. doi:10.1287/isre.2.3.192

Nambisan, S., & Wang, Y.-M. (1999). Roadblocks to Web technology adoption? *Communications of the ACM*, *42*(1), 98–101. doi:10.1145/291469.291482

Nelson, M. L., Shaw, M. J., & Qualls, W. (2005). Interorganizational System Standards Development in Vertical Industries. *Electronic Markets*, *15*(4), 378–392. doi:10.1080/10196780500303045

Nickerson, J. V., & Muehlen, M. Z. (2003, December 12-14). *Defending the Spirit of the Web: Conflict in the Internet Standards Process*. Paper presented at the International Conference on IS Special Workshop on Standard Making sponsored by MISQ, Seattle, WA.

Nickerson, J. V., & Muehlen, M. Z. (2006). The Ecology of Standards Processes: Insights from Internet Standard Making. *Management Information Systems Quarterly*, *30*, 467–488.

O'Callaghan, R., Kaufmann, P. J., & Konsynski, B. R. (1992). Adoption correlates and share effects of electronic data interchange systems in marketing channels. *Journal of Marketing, 56*, 45–56. doi:10.2307/1252041

Premkumar, G., & Ramamurthy, K. (1995). The Role of Interorganizational and Organizational Factors on the Decision Mode for Adoption of Interorganizational Systems. *Decision Sciences, 26*(3), 303–336. doi:10.1111/j.1540-5915.1995.tb01431.x

Premkumar, G., Ramamurthy, K., & Crum, M. R. (1997). Determinants of EDI adoption in the transportation industry. *European Journal of Information Systems, 6*(2), 107–121. doi:10.1057/palgrave.ejis.3000260

Ravichandran, T. (2005). Organizational Assimilation of Complex Technologies: An Empirical Study of Component-Based Software Development. *IEEE Transactions on Engineering Management, 52*(2), 249–268. doi:10.1109/TEM.2005.844925

Reimers, K., & Li, M. (2005). Antecedents of a Transaction Cost Theory of Vertical IS Standardization Processes. *Electronic Markets, 15*(4), 301–312. doi:10.1080/10196780500302740

Rogers, E. M. (1983). *Diffusion of Innovations* (3rd ed.). New York: The Free Press.

Schilling, M. A. (2002). Technology success and failure in winner-take-all markets: Testing a model of technological lock out. *Academy of Management Journal, 45*(2), 387–398. doi:10.2307/3069353

Shapiro, C., & Varian, H. R. (1999). The Art of Standard Wars. *California Management Review, 41*(2), 8–32.

Steinfield, C. W., Wigand, R. T., Markus, M. L., & Minton, G. (2004, May 13-14). *Promoting e-Business Through Vertical IS Standards: Lessons from the US Home Mortgage Industry.* Paper presented at the Workshop on Standards and Public Policy, Chicago.

Sumner, M. (2000). Risk factors in enterprise-wide/ERP projects. *Journal of Information Technology, 15*(4), 317–327. doi:10.1080/02683960010009079

Swanson, E. B., & Ramiller, N. C. (1997). The Organizing Vision in Information Systems Innovations. *Organization Science, 8*(5), 458–474. doi:10.1287/orsc.8.5.458

Swatman, P. M. C., Swatman, P. A., & Fowler, D. C. (1994). A model of EDI integration and strategic business reengineering. *The Journal of Strategic Information Systems, 3*(1), 41–60. doi:10.1016/0963-8687(94)90005-1

Tan, M., & Teo, T. S. H. (2000). Factors influencing the adoption of Internet banking. *Journal of the AIS, 1*(1).

Tanriverdi, H. (2006). Performance Effects of Information Technology Synergies in Multibusiness Firms. *Management Information Systems Quarterly, 30*(1), 57–77.

Tornatzky, L. G., & Klein, K. J. (1982). Innovation Characteristics and innovation Adoption-Implementation: A Meta Analysis of Findings. *IEEE Transactions on Engineering Management, 29*(1), 28–45.

Wareham, J., Rai, A., & Pickering, G. (2005). Standardization in Vertical Industries: An Institutional Analysis of XML-Based Standards Infusion in Electricity Markets. *Electronic Markets, 15*(4), 323–334. doi:10.1080/10196780500302849

Webster, J. (1995). *The Development of EDI*. Paper presented at the PICT/COST A4 International Research Workshop, Brussels, Belgium.

Weitzel, T. (2003, December 12-14). *A Network ROI*. Paper presented at the International Conference on IS Special Workshop on Standard Making sponsored by MISQ, Seattle, WA.

Weitzel, T., Beimborn, D., & Konig, W. (2006). A Unified Economic Model of Standard Diffusion: The Impact of Standardization Cost, Network Effects, and Network Topology. *Management Information Systems Quarterly*, *30*, 489–514.

Wigand, R. T., Steinfield, C. W., & Markus, M. L. (2005, January 3-6). *Impacts of Vertical IS Standards: The Case of the US Home Mortgage Industry*. Paper presented at the Hawaii International Conference on System Sciences (HICSS 38), Waikoloa, HI.

Zhao, K., Xia, M., & Shaw, M. J. (2005). Vertical E-Business Standards and Standards Developing Organizations: A Conceptual Framework. *Electronic Markets*, *15*(4), 289–300. doi:10.1080/10196780500302690

APPENDIX A

SURVEY INSTRUMENT

Assimilation

Please indicate the status of any vertical standards use by your company:

[a] Not interested in their use, [b] Not currently in use, but tracking their development/progress, [c] Developing expertise, with no plans for formal evaluation, [d] Actively evaluating one or more for deployment, [e] Officially adopted for internal/external data exchange but not yet in production, [f] Partially deployed in a production environment, [g] Fully deployed in a production environment (Ettlie, 1980; Fichman & Kemerer, 1993; Fichman & Kemerer, 1997; Ravichandran, 2005).

(All remaining survey items were measured using a seven-point Likert scale in which a score of one signifies strong disagreement and seven specifies strong agreement)

Expected Benefits

Vertical standards adopted, or in consideration for adoption by our company, 1) are expected to or already deliver significant business benefits to our company, 2) will be used for critical data transactions (Al-Qirim, 2005; Moore & Benbasat, 1991).

Legacy Technology Embeddedness

Prior to the adoption of a vertical standard data exchange technologies contributed significantly to the 1) integration of our company's internal business processes, 2) integration of our company's external business processes, 3) automation of our company's internal business processes, 4) automation of our company's external business processes, 5) enabled our company to develop new internal business processes, 6) enabled our company to develop new external business processes, 7) quality improvements in our company's internal business processes, 8) quality improvements in our company's external business processes (Angeles et al., 2001; Bradford & Florin, 2003; Jones & Beatty, 1998; Premkumar & Ramamurthy, 1997; Tan & Teo, 2000).

Technology Fit

Vertical standards adopted, or in consideration for adoption by our company are compatible with 1) our internal business processes, 2) our external business processes, 3) data formats used for internal purposes, 4) data formats used for external purposes (Al-Qirim, 2005; Bradford & Florin, 2003; Jones & Beatty, 1998; Moore & Benbasat, 1991; Tan & Teo, 2000).

Knowledge Stock

1) Our company has the necessary technical expertise to implement vertical standards, 2) It will not take long for our company to acquire the necessary technical expertise needed to implement vertical standards, 3) Our company has the necessary project management expertise to implement vertical standards, 4) It will not take long for our company to acquire the necessary project management expertise needed to implement vertical standards (Bradford & Florin, 2003; Karahanna et al., 1999; Moore & Benbasat, 1991; Premkumar & Ramamurthy, 1997; Ravichandran, 2005; Tan & Teo, 2000).

Related Knowledge – Emerging Technologies

Prior to the adoption of a vertical standard our company 1) had significant technical expertise with XML, 2) had significant expertise managing projects related to XML, 3) was successful in deriving benefits from XML, 4) had significant expertise managing organizational and process changes associated with the use of XML, 5) had significant technical expertise with Internet technologies, 6) had significant expertise managing projects related to Internet technologies, 7) was successful in deriving benefits from Internet technologies, 8) had significant expertise managing organizational and process changes associated with the use of Internet technologies, 9) had a significant total dollar investment in Internet technologies, 10) had a significant total dollar investment in XML technologies (Bradford & Florin, 2003; Karahanna et al., 1999; Moore & Benbasat, 1991; Premkumar & Ramamurthy, 1997; Ravichandran, 2005; Tan & Teo, 2000).

Related Knowledge – Legacy Data Exchange Technologies

Prior to the adoption of a vertical standard our company 1) had significant technical expertise with data exchange technologies like EDI, 2) had significant expertise managing projects related to data exchange technologies like EDI, 3) was successful in deriving benefits from data exchange technologies like EDI, 4) had significant expertise managing organizational and process changes associated with the use of data exchange technologies like EDI, 5) had a significant total dollar investment in EDI technologies (Bradford & Florin, 2003; Karahanna et al., 1999; Moore & Benbasat, 1991; Premkumar & Ramamurthy, 1995; Premkumar & Ramamurthy, 1997; Ravichandran, 2005; Tan & Teo, 2000).

Standards-Development Vendor Collaboration

In regards to vertical standards development activities in our industry most major industry software vendors 1) participate actively, 2) have made a significant total dollar investment, 3) have made a significant human resource investment, 4) collaborate with each other (Al-Qirim, 2005; Ravichandran, 2005; Schilling, 2002).

Availability of Complementary Products and Services

1) An adequate number of external software products exist to support the vertical standards our company has adopted or will adopt, 2) External software products that support the vertical standards our company has adopted or will adopt are of high quality, 3) An adequate number of external consulting services exist to support the vertical standards our company has adopted or will adopt, 4) External consulting services that support the vertical standards our company has adopted or will adopt are of high quality (Al-Qirim, 2005; Premkumar & Ramamurthy, 1995; Schilling, 2002).

Standard Legitimation

The vertical standard adopted or likely to be adopted by our firm is the same as that adopted by 1) most of our major customers, 2) most of our major suppliers, 3) the major players in our industry (Bouchard, 1993; Chwelos et al., 1997; Chwelos et al., 2001; Iacovou et al., 1995; O'Callaghan et al., 1992; Schilling, 2002).

Business Partner Convergence

1) Most of our company's major customers have adopted the vertical standard seen by our industry as the "winning" standard, 2) Most of our company's major suppliers have adopted the vertical standard seen by our industry as the "winning" standard (Bouchard, 1993; Chwelos et al., 1997; Chwelos et al., 2001; Iacovou et al., 1995; O'Callaghan et al., 1992; Ravichandran, 2005).

Business Partner Participation in SDO Activities

1) The total dollar investment in vertical standards of most of our major customers is significant, 2) The total dollar investment in vertical standards of most of our major suppliers is significant, 3) In regards to vertical standards development activities in our industry most of our company's major suppliers participate actively, 4) In regards to vertical standards development activities in our industry most of our company's major suppliers participate actively, 5) In regards to vertical standards development activities in our industry most of our industry's major players participate actively (Chwelos et al., 1997; Chwelos et al., 2001; Iacovou et al., 1995; O'Callaghan et al., 1992; Ravichandran, 2005).

*Items not used in final instrument include a total of 18 items exploring business partner adoption of a single vertical standard (2 items), investment in vertical standards complementary technologies (2 items), the nature of vertical standards competition and regulatory guidelines in adoption in the firm's home industry (6 items), the extent of the firm's participation in vertical standards development activities (6 items), vertical standards adoption by industry participants (1 item), and two demographic questions initially thought to be theoretically more relevant. Several iterations of principal component analysis supported the exclusion of these items, which are not listed here for brevity.

Section 6
Standards for Learning Technology

Chapter 13

Analysis and Validation of Learning Technology Models, Standards and Specifications:
The Reference Model Analysis Grid (RMAG)

Jan M. Pawlowski
University of Jyväskylä, Finland

Denis Kozlov
University of Jyväskylä, Finland

ABSTRACT

The paper presents a model for the analysis, comparison and validation of standards, specifications and in particular reference models in the field of Technology Enhanced Learning (TEL). The Reference Model Analysis Grid (RMAG) establishes categories of reference models and standards. Based on those categories, a set of criteria for the analysis and validation of standards was elaborated as a part of the ICOPER project that aims at interoperable open content for competency-based TEL. The analysis of standards in this context is targeted at developing a set of validated approaches that lead to a new reference model. Four standards were investigated, taking into account a broad range of aspects like practical and semantic interoperability and integration issues. In the case study, the authors analyzed both, the standards and specifications and the usefulness of the RMAG. The results of this case study can be used for further analyses of TEL standards as well as for reference models targeted at interoperability.

1. INTRODUCTION

A variety of models, standards and specifications is used in the field of Technology-Enhanced Learning (TEL). Many of those follow the idea of reference modeling, i.e., providing a base model or specification for solving a design or development problem. Most reference models aim at achieving interoperability between different systems and platforms. However, these models have different underlying theoretical foundations, different scopes, methodologies, and implementations. Hence, users of the reference models cannot clearly decide whether it is suitable for their purpose and

DOI: 10.4018/978-1-4666-2160-2.ch013

context. Therefore, the Reference Model Analysis Grid (RMAG) has addressed this issue.

The main research question addressed in this paper is: How can current learning technology reference models, standards and specifications be assessed and how can they be combined to provide meaningful solutions to content developers, educators and users? The main goal is to develop an analysis scheme aiming at assessing reference models as well as standards and specifications built on existing practice. Our approach is based on an extensive literature research in the field – for the construction of the reference model, we follow the Design Science Research methodology (Hevner et al., 2004), developing an artifact – the analysis grid – and evaluating those against the key objectives.

A reference model represents for example generic processes, systems, and data as well as actors of a specific domain aiming at supporting developers by adapting this model to a specific context. It is a conceptual framework that can be used as a blueprint for systems development. Reference models are also called universal models, generic models or model patterns (Fettke & Loos, 2003a; Fettke & Loos, 2003b; Fettke & Loos, 2006). Concrete examples of reference models are SAP's reference model (Keller & Teufel, 1998), Hay's data model patterns (Hay, 1998) or Scheer's reference model for production planning and control systems (Scheer, 1994).

The application of the general methodology of the reference models to the field of Technology Enhanced Learning (TEL) is relatively new. Examples are the Open Lausanne Model (Madhour & Wentland Forte, 2007), the Course Validation Reference Model COVARM (Franklin et al., 2008), or the Framework Reference Model for Assessment FREMA (Barn et al., 2006). These examples, in particular the survey of Franklin at el. (2008), show that reference models of different complexity exist: from modeling the whole domain of TEL or providing a model for a specific component like assessment. Models like IMS Common Cartridge (IMS, 2008) or SCORM (Advanced Distributed Learning, 2009) can also be seen as reference models as they provide process and data models for the TEL domain. Generally, reference models shall support and ease the implementation of systems in this domain. Therefore, we summarize a variety of models in this domain (system development models, process models, data models) under the term of reference models. The main aim is to support actors to develop TEL systems by adapting the reference model.

One of the most important issues is to analyze how various existing reference models, standards and specifications can be used or adapted for the needs of systems design and development processes. Currently, many standards and specifications are used in the TEL field. However, their distribution and adoption has not reached a critical mass yet. This is in particular the case for the design and development of systems which follow the idea of Open Educational Resources (OERs) (UNESCO, 1998) and reusability. OERs can only be successful if they reach a critical mass in terms of available content, participating users and adoption rates. In particular, interoperability achieved by the use of widely accepted standards is a critical success factor.

In particular in the TEL domain, the use of common-sense specifications and standards as well as reference models is still very low in comparison to other vertical industries (cf. Tyrväinen, Warsta, & Seppänen, 2008). This leads to a variety of proprietary systems and to inefficient development and deployment processes in this domain. There are several reasons for the lack of adoption of TEL models, standards and specifications, such as:

- **Lack of Completeness:** The reference model does not cover all the aspects of a system that a developer wants to design.
- **Complexity:** The reference model is too complex to be implemented by developers.
- **Lack of Adaptability:** The reference model is not easy to adapt, e.g., the effort for

adaptation is higher than designing a system from scratch.

- **Acceptance and Participation:** The reference model is not used by a broad community because of a lack of awareness or acceptance.
- **Lack of Documentation:** The reference model not well documented and cannot be used intuitively.
- **Lack of Coherence**: Many standards are just loosely coupled, significantly overlapping with each other or even competing.

In the TEL domain, acceptance is still the most important factor – developers are unaware or skeptical towards the use of existing models. Therefore, it seems useful to provide decision support to understand the suitability of a reference model or a standard for the stakeholders' purposes. The Reference Model Analysis Grid (RMAG) is a tool to analyze how standards and specifications used and combined to develop interoperable systems. Its main goal is to provide a solid methodology covering a broad range of aspects related to the development and deployment of TEL systems.

We use the following major definitions. A *standard* is a set of mandatory requirements employed and enforced to prescribe a uniform approach in specific are, e.g., in software development, that is, mandatory conventions and practices are in fact standards (cf., IEEE, 1990). A *specification* is a document that specifies, in a complete, precise, verifiable manner, the requirements, design, behavior, or other characteristics of a system or component, and, often, the procedures for determining whether these provisions have been satisfied (IEEE, 1990).

The paper is organized as follows. Section 2 provides the research background on analysis of reference models and TEL standards and specifications. Sections 3 and 4 present the reference model analysis grid, i.e., the methodology used to analyze TEL reference models and standards, as well as its practical implementation (case study).

Section 5 and 6 highlight the most important results of our case study. Finally, we illustrate conclusions and future directions.

2. ANALYSIS OF REFERENCE MODELS AND STANDARDS

The main objective of the paper is to present a methodology for testing and validation of TEL reference models, standards and specifications to reach interoperability for systems in the TEL domain, in particular for OERs and related tools. This section shows how reference models including standards and specifications can be analyzed and assessed. We discuss which analysis frameworks and analysis results can contribute towards a generic analysis scheme aiming at interoperability and efficient systems development in general.

2.1. Reference Models

A first class of analysis schemes assesses *reference models in general*. Reference models shall support systems developers by adapting the model for a specific organizational context. However, this aim is complex and needs a careful analysis scheme. Fettke and Loos (2003a) developed a framework for reference model evaluation. The framework is based on multi-perspective approach by taking into account various perspectives, namely:

- Plain text-based evaluation, i.e., based on the verbal characteristics, strengths and weaknesses of a reference model,
- Feature based evaluation, i.e., based on specific set of features which can be used to describe and characterize reference models,
- Metric-based evaluation, i.e., based on quantitative or qualitative characteristics of a reference model to be measured,
- Meta-model-based evaluation, i.e., based on a meta grammar model that is used to

check whether the reference model is syntactically correct,

- Master reference model-based evaluation i.e. based on a model that represents all classes of enterprise domains or industry-types,
- Paradigmatic evaluation, i.e., based on meta theoretical assumptions including ontological, epistemological, linguistic and contextual aspects,
- Contingency theory-based evaluation, i.e., based on contingency theory focusing on non-unique methods to manage an organization,
- Ontology-based evaluation i.e., based on the notion of ontological correctness of a reference model,
- Cognitive psychology-based, i.e., how a reference model supports or impedes processes of human information processing,
- Economic-based evaluation, i.e., from the business management and national economic viewpoint) empirical evaluation, i.e., survey, laboratory experiment, field experiment, case study and action research.

The study shows that there is a variety of perspectives on reference models and present useful methodological alternatives. It shows that building a reference model requires a clear set of objectives and evaluation procedures.

In a second study, Fettke and Loos (2003b) proposed a framework for classification of reference models. The classification principles for reference models include:

- Basic classification, i.e., each classification object is element of one class, all the classes are mutually disjunctive,
- Hierarchical classification, i.e., each classification object is element of one class, the classes are ordered hierarchically,

- Faceted classification, i.e., each classification object is classified according to different viewpoints, and
- Characteristic based classification, i.e., each classification object is characterized by several characteristics.

The guidelines for a classification of reference models include completeness, precision, consistency, extensibility, user friendliness, and economic effects. The identified characteristics for classification of reference models include

- General and domain independent (describe only formal attributes of a model),
- Specific and domain independent (defined in the context of a modeling language),
- General and domain dependent (characterize the application domain in general),
- Specific and domain dependent characteristics (defined in the context of a specific application domain).

A classification system in the content of a specific application area is proposed to be developed by means of procedural model. This model consists of five phases, i.e., inception, elaborating characteristics, specifying classification scheme, testing and usage and maintenance. The results of this study shows that different types of reference models exist which have to be matched to the purpose (e.g., systems development, interoperability). This can be beneficially used to elaborate a set of fine-grained criteria for analysis of standards and specifications.

A set of criteria is also given by Frank et al (2007) – the multi-perspective approach distinguished four perspectives: economical, deployment, engineering, and epistemological viewpoints. Criteria for those categories are derived for generic reference models, such as:

- **Economical:** Costs, benefits, coordination.
- **Deployment:** Understandability appropriateness.

- **Engineering:** Language features, technical model features.
- **Epistemological:** Scientific evaluation, scientific progress.

The model provides a basic scheme for reference model analysis and derives a set of criteria – however, those criteria need to be selected, adapted and extended for a specific domain.

2.2. Standards and Specifications

A second class of analysis schemes assesses *standards and specifications* and combinations and integrations of those. Vogten et al. (2006) presented a framework for the integration of e-Learning services based on two specifications, namely IMS LD (IMS, 2003) and IMS QTI (IMS, 2006). The issue of integration of those two specifications was represented as aligning LD properties and QTI variable names. Vogten et al. (2006) developed an open source architecture called CopperCore Service Integration (CCSI) that can be seen as an adapter between an existing legacy services and clients. The study is a good example how standards can be integrated to combine components.

Tomberg and Laanpere (2007) provided a critical analysis of existing industry-driven specifications (e.g., IMS QTI) and their impact on the development of online assessment tools, as well as demonstrated the new opportunities for developing next generation assessment tools with web services and business process execution language. From the viewpoint of our study the most important part of the study of Tomberg and Laanpere concerns analysis of several releases of IMS QTI (IMS, 2006). The following differences between version 1.0 and version 2.0 were identified:

- Changes in the data model, i.e., Test-Section-Item model instead of ASI (Assessment-Section-Item) model,

- Changes in visualization, i.e., support of XHTML that enables to create test to be assured in adequacy of the final visualization results,
- Introduction of question template in version 2.0,
- Changes in a feedback to the user, i.e., the feedback is divided into a modal and an adaptive,
- Revising the rules for cooperation with specification IMS Content Packaging (IMS, 2004).

This specific analysis investigates issues related to backward and forward compatibility between the versions of IMS QTI. This is one of the quality attributes to be investigated also in our study. However, the range of this analysis is very limited.

Lewis et al. (2008) carried out an in-depth analysis of limitations of e-Learning standards and specifications with respect to their ability to assure systems interoperability and proposed a number of solutions how to minimize high expectations to the interoperability of those standards. Lewis et al. identified several levels of interoperability, namely, machine level (i.e., the hardware level), syntactic (i.e., the format and structure of the data exchanged), semantic (i.e., the actual meaning of the data being exchanged) and organizational (i.e., the ability to perform actions with the data) interoperability. The current technologies, standards and tools support machine-to-machine transaction in the first two levels, and to some extent the third level. Achieving semantic and organizational levels of interoperability is often very challenging or even impossible. With respect to standards themselves, Lewis et al. identified several categories of standards, namely a) bad standards, b) conflicting standards and c) inflexible standards.

Each of those categories has several sub-categories. The solutions proposed by Lewis et al. (2008) include

- Identifying the level of interoperability required between systems,
- Understanding existing standards (in terms of usage, adaptation, domain specific extensions and specializations, vendors and products supporting the standard, standard governing body), and
- Filling the gaps of the standards, e.g., by identifying how good the standard fits the scenario requirements.

The framework of Lewis et al. (2008) is highly useful in our context as it identifies attributes to assess interoperability of TEL standards. However, it does not cover the integration of standards in a common framework.

Finally, the evaluation model of Cooper (2009) provides pragmatic criteria for standards evaluation covering the following aspects: a) business considerations / cases, b) purpose and intended use, c) context, d) provenance and governance, e) technical aspects, and f) personal requirements. Cooper's model also considers the design of a standardization project, aiming at evaluating standards throughout the development process in a common framework. The approach can be seen as very pragmatic with a broad coverage of criteria for standards. However, specific aspects for reference models are not covered. We use parts of the criteria for the RMAG approach.

As a conclusion, it can be summarized that a variety of analyses range from a broad methodological analysis of (integrated) reference models to specific analyses of single standards. However, there is currently no widely accepted analysis scheme which provides methods to assess single standards as well as their combination regarding systems development and interoperability.

3. REFERENCE MODEL ANALYSIS GRID

This section presents the methodology for analysis of TEL reference models, standards and specifications to be applied in the following sections of the paper.

The Reference Model Analysis Grid (RMAG) is a methodology to assess standards with the aim to combine them in a harmonized framework, i.e., a TEL reference model. By developing the RMAG we use and adapt the multi-perspective approaches presented by Fettke and Loos (2003a) and Frank (2007) and incorporate a broad range of assessment criteria, such as Cooper (2009).

RMAG aims at both, providing descriptive information on a reference model or standard as well as assessing those for a given purpose, e.g., designing interoperable systems. In a first step, description and classification criteria shall were derived (Table 1).

This first set of criteria aims at describing a reference model or standards, its scope, objectives and details. It covers mainly descriptive information of the reference model or standard to provide an overview and to contextualize the analysis.

A second set of criteria aims at the assessment of reference models and standards. The model is based on the generic analysis models by Frank (2007) and Fettke and Loos (2003a). Based on these generic models, we have adapted the model for the particular TEL domain. In our context, we focus mainly on the economic and deployment perspective as those two are the most relevant for decision makers as well as developers.

The following main aspects can be distinguished (Table 2):

1. **Transformation and Analysis:** How can a model be used to analyze and transform systems an organization and its processes?
2. **Maintenance:** How can the models and tools be maintained?

Table 1. Categories for the classification of TEL reference models (adapted from Fettke & Loos, 2003a, and Frank, 2007)

Category	Description
General data	Origin of the model, original authors and inventors, terms of licensing related to TEL resources and reference models, stakeholders addressed
Objectives	Main principles and objectives to design the reference model, e.g. interoperability, reusability, competency assurance.
Domain	Target domain, e.g. TEL, software development, health management
Classification	Focus area of the reference model or standard in a classification – in the TEL domain, the following classes can be distinguished based on the focus: contents, actors or stakeholders, didactics and pedagogy, management, federation, context and related standards (cf. Ehlers & Pawlowski, 2006).
Methodology	Methodology used to design the model, e.g. empirical research, constructive research. We use the reference modeling method proposed by (Fettke, Loos, 2007). The reference model development process consists 1) problem definition, development, evaluation and maintenance. In turn, the activities to apply a reference model include 1) selection, 2) adaptation, 3) utilization, and 4) integration.
Evaluation	Methodology used to evaluate the reference model from various perspectives, as well as the criteria for model application success.
Processes	Which (business) processes, e.g., a TEL lifecycle, are covered and addressed
Levels	Model of process levels that a reference model addresses, e.g., business processes, systems components, interfaces, data models.
Usage and validation	Is there proof in terms of validations and experiments in practice? How are the models used?
Documentation	Availability, accessibility and documentation of the model for different stakeholder groups.

3. **Effectiveness and Efficiency:** How does the use of the reference model impact organizations' resources?

4. **Flexibility and Integration:** How flexible is the model when adapted to the organizations context?

5. **Coordination and Knowledge Management:** How are coordination mechanisms and knowledge transfer and exchange supported?

6. **Interoperability:** How are interoperability aspects supported?

7. **Understandability and Usability:** How understandable and usable is the model in its implementation and deployment?

8. **Coherence:** Is the model coherent to other standards and specifications?

Based on those main aspects, the following table shows the refinement of the analysis grid. For each aspect, a description is given. Furthermore, we list sample criteria and metrics to assess each aspect.

The above classification criteria can be used to compare reference models in a broad range of levels: from abstract software development models to very specific standards. We use this model in particular to derive criteria for the analysis of TEL standards.

4. CASE STUDY "DEVELOPMENT OF THE ICOPER REFERENCE MODEL FOR TECHNOLOGY ENHANCED LEARNING"

In this section, we show how the Reference Model Analysis Grid (RMAG) is used to assess reference models, standards, and specifications. We show how the model can be used to assess a variety of standards using the methodology of a multiple case study (Yin, 2008). By using a case study, we show the feasibility and validity of the model in contexts.

The case study was performed in the ICOPER project (Najjar & Simon, 2009) – its main goal is to enable technology-supported, competency-based learning in Higher Education. A part of this project is to analyze the potentials of existing standards and the development of a reference model for competency-based, technology-enhanced learning. The study consists of four cases of different

Table 2. Analysis and assessment aspects and metrics (adapted from Fettke & Loos, 2003a and Frank, 2007)

Perspective	Aspect	Description	Criteria or Metrics
Economic perspective	Transformation and analysis: Suitability	Suitability of data models and prototypes for deployment	• Concepts and attributes used in data models allow for automatic transformation into implementation level specifications • Concepts and attributes of data models that are compatible with existing standards • Concepts and attributes of data models cover the whole domain
	Maintenance: Conceptual support	Maintenance of data models and prototypes from conceptual viewpoint	• Concepts and attributes of data models that support adaptation and compatibility with emerging standards and tools in a safe and convenient way • Number of person-hours spent to train stakeholders to use the models or standards
	Maintenance: Tools	Availability of tools for maintenance and management of data models and prototypes, including multiuser access	• Availability of tools that support management and further development of data models and prototypes, e.g. UML modeling tools • Number of person-hours spent to integrate data models or mock-ups into existing tools
	Maintenance: Skills	Skills required for maintenance of data models and prototypes	• Availability of experts keeping data models and prototypes up-to-date
	Efficiency and Effectiveness: Development and maintenance of further models and standards	Efficiency of data models to facilitate the development and maintenance of further models, e-learning resources, VLEs, models and standards	• Concepts and attributes of data models that support adaptation and compatibility with emerging standards and tools in a safe and convenient way
	Efficiency and Effectiveness: Business and Management	Efficiency of data models and prototypes to facilitate business processes	• Concepts and attributes of data models that support and facilitate specific scenarios
	Flexibility and Integration: Dependence from IT vendors and standardization bodies	Support of data models and prototypes by developers of services, VLEs, etc	• Relevant IT-vendors supporting prototypes • Standardization bodies and experts supporting data models • Number of end users • Degree of customization • Level of industry commitment
	Flexibility and Integration: Openness	Data models can be mapped or integrated with other standards and tools	• Amount of semantic integration required, i.e. concepts and attributes that are not supported / vaguely supported by the tools/environments • Compatibility of concepts and attributes of data models with the concepts used in other tools/environments • Concepts and attributes of data models that are compatible with existing standards • Concepts and attributes of data models that support adaptation and compatibility with emerging standards and tools in a safe and convenient way

continued on following page

Table 2. Continued

Perspective	Aspect	Description	Criteria or Metrics
	Flexibility / Integration: Expressive power	Flexibility of data models from an ontological viewpoint	• Concepts and attributes of data models that are fully understandable, partially understandable, unclear for end users • Missing attributes of data models that would enhance description and understandability of concepts by end users
	Coordination/Knowledge management	Analysis of data models and prototypes from the viewpoint of potential user organizations, organizational units, subunits and individuals	• Concepts and attributes of data models helping to overcome communication barriers and promoting knowledge exchange between end users, i.e. concepts and attributes of data models that are fully understandable, partially understandable, unclear for different types of end users
	Coordination/Knowledge management: Acceptance / Commitment	Popularity of data models and prototypes	• Number of organizations that use data models and prototypes • Number of vendors and service providers that support prototypes • Concepts and attributes of data models that are compatible with existing standards
	Coordination/Knowledge management: Technological change	Dependence of data models and prototypes on the underlying technologies	• Concepts and attributes of data models that support adaptation and compatibility with emerging technical standards in a safe and convenient way
Deployment perspective	Completeness	Data models describe the domain appropriately	• Concepts and attributes of data models cover the whole domain • Precise description of core concepts of data models with respect to corresponding real world concepts • Missing attributes of data models that enhance understandability of concepts by end users
	Technical interoperability	Data models enhance data exchange between systems	• Concepts and attributes of data models that are fully supported, partially supported, unsupported by the tools/environments • Compatibility of concepts and attributes of data models with the concepts used in the tools/environments
	Pragmatic interoperability	Data models enhance data exchange between systems and people	• Concepts and attributes of data models that are fully supported, partially supported, unsupported by the tools/environments • Concepts and attributes of data models that are fully understandable, partially understandable, unclear for end users
	Understandability	Understandability of data models for different types of users	• Concepts and attributes of data models that are fully understandable, partially understandable, unclear for different types of end users

continued on following page

Table 2. Continued

Perspective	Aspect	Description	Criteria or Metrics
	Usability	Elegance and clarity of data models and prototypes	• Concepts and attributes of data models that are fully understandable, partially understandable, unclear for different types of end users • Intuitive interface of prototypes • Intuitive, readable, sufficient/non-redundant output of search queries
	Coherence and non-redundancy	Data models are connected with each other sufficiently. The relations are non-redundant	• Non-unique attributes that are shared by several data models • Types of relations between data models, i.e. one-to-one, one-to-many, etc.

TEL standards. The goal was to analyze those standards from the viewpoint of interoperability, modifiability and other quality attributes. We have chosen these four standards as they cover a broad scope, diversity and range of methodologies in the field of TEL. The analyzed standards are the following:

- **CEN MLO-AD (CEN/ISSS, 2008):** The main goal of this specification is to provide metadata for learning opportunities, in particular advertizing information for content providers.
- **IEEE RCD (IEEE, 2007):** The specification provides a scheme to describe competencies to be re-used in different systems.
- **IMS QTI (IMS, 2003):** The specification aims at the interoperability of assessments between different learning (management) systems
- **ISO/IEC 19796-1 (ISO/IEC, 2005):** The standard aims at describing quality approaches with a common description scheme to harmonize quality approaches.

The case study was performed in three steps:

- **RMAG Adaptation:** The generic RMAG was adapted to the purpose of the context – this means that certain attributes from

the generic framework were selected and prioritized.
- **Assessment:** The above mentioned standards and specifications were assessed using the adapted RMAG
- **Feedback and Validation:** The analysis process was validated regarding the usefulness and completeness of the analysis scheme.

In the following, we will describe the results of the case studies regarding both, the analysis of the standards as well as the discussion of the usefulness of the RMAG.

4.1. Operationalizing RMAG: Deriving Assessment Criteria

The generic RMAG has to be adapted towards an operational analysis method in a specific context – the ICOPER project – including measurable and assessable criteria. To derive those, the generic analysis categories for reference models were used as a basis to define a set of criteria to classify TEL standards and specifications for the purposes of reference modeling. In the following, we show how the generic analysis grid is used to develop a concrete assessment tool, in our case a questionnaire for the analysis. Table 3 shows the criteria for classification and analysis of TEL standards and specifications. In most cases, there

Table 3. Structure of the questionnaire

Section	Reference model classification criteria	Questions or sub-sections
Basic information about the standard or specification	General data, Documentation	Full name of the standard
		Source
		Main users or target groups
		Release date
		Number of versions
Assessing the standard	Usage and validation	Maturity of the standard. Is the standard already used and validated in practice?
	Integration: Maturity	Support offered by which vendors or products?
	Domain	Main concepts: Which main concepts are used in the standard, e.g. represented in categories or attributes?
	Integration: Competing standards	Competing standards: Are there standards which cover the same scope? Are there concepts or attributes within the standard which are also covered by other standards? (e.g. LOM.educational could compete with IMS LD)
	Integration: Underlying standards	Underlying standards / technologies for this standard: Are there other standards being used (like base technologies as HTTP or XML)
	Processes, Levels	Reference model level: Data, Services, Processes
	Integration	Other relevant standards belonging to Data Level Other relevant standards belonging to Process, Service and Data level
Relations	Processes, Use cases	Use cases of your work packages, for which this standard is helpful or applicable
	Processes, Stakeholders	Stakeholders of your work package's use cases
	Usage and validation: Usefulness	Usefulness of the standard for each of those stakeholders
In-depth analysis	Interoperability: Practical interoperability and credibility	Investigate practical interoperability of the standard in terms of its credibility. It is considered to be trustworthy in the eLearning domain? Try to define the intended effect of the standard. Does the intended effect of the standard differ from its actual effect? Define also the percentage of the standard's categories or concepts that are widely used in practice. Are there any categories that are not accepted by the users?
	Interoperability: Semantic interoperability	Investigate semantic interoperability of the standard by defining whether the standard describes what it should describe. E.g.: Is competency described in a way it should have been described according to the European Qualification Framework definition? Investigate the relations between the standard and the competing or relevant standards with respect to overlaps and differences on semantic level. Pay attention to the use of metadata elements and vocabularies / ontologies / taxonomies. Are they used consistently in the standard?
	Integration: Communication	Investigate the communication of the standard by defining whether the elements of the standard are able to communicate with the elements of other relevant standards on the data level.
	Integration: Bindings and conformance	Find our whether there are any bindings provided in the standard. Provide some examples. Investigate whether the standard states conformance of its bindings to the bindings of other relevant standards. Investigate the possibility of the standard to transfer its elements to the elements of other relevant / competing standards. Are there recommendations how to do it?
	Integration: Integrity	Define mechanisms that control or protect the standard's integrity. Investigate whether it is possible to use the standard, if the technologies underlying it change significantly. Please, provide some examples.

continued on following page

Table 3. Continued

Section	Reference model classification criteria	Questions or sub-sections
Quality attributes	Integration: Seamless-ness	Seamlessness: Can the elements of the standard be used together with the elements of competing / relevant standards to satisfy specific user requirements? Are there any adapters to connect elements of those standards?
	Adaptation	Evolvability: Are there standards originating from this standard focusing on other relevant issues?
	Documentation: Guid-ance	Guidance: Does the standard provide detailed guidelines to users how to use it?
	Integration: Compat-ibility	Backward / forward compatibility: Do the standards / technologies underlying the current version of the standard differ from ones of its previous versions? If yes, are those underlying technologies compatible with the old ones?
	Extensibility, Adaptation	Modifiability: Does the standard allow adding or modifying new elements? Does the standard allow adding or modifying new properties of its elements?

are strict and obvious relations between both sets of criteria. Additionally, the model was extended adding new categories which are more specific to TEL standards rather than to reference models and which do not correspond to any of the categories of reference model classification.

We have used the previously mentioned studies to develop the questionnaire. The study of Lewis et al. (2008) was used as one of the major sources by preparing our questionnaire. In particular, such aspects as domain specific extensions and specializations, vendors and products supporting the standard, standard governing body were taken into consideration. In the future we plan to follow the recommendation of Lewis et al. (2008) and to carry out an in-depth gap analysis of the analyzed standards against the use cases.

The 'Basic information' category provides a general information about the scope, availability, accessibility, maturity in terms of the number of releases and target groups of the standard. This category helps to identify usefulness and suitability of the standards in a context.

The 'Assessing the standards' category presents high level relations between TEL standards, as well as their maturity in terms of acceptance by vendors and products and validation by prac-

titioners. One more concern of this category is to provide a clear relation between the TEL standards and reference model levels such as data, services, or processes. Those relations are described further in the 'Relations' category with respect to use cases, stakeholders and usefulness of standards for stakeholders. The character of those relations goes beyond this study and will be investigated as a separate study.

The 'In-depth analysis' category consists of the most important quality attributes of TEL standards, i.e., two different types of interoperability (semantic and practical) and integration. Semantic interoperability is crucial, since semantically coherent standards are more likely to be accepted by practitioners. Moreover, by analyzing semantic interoperability it is possible to find out whether the standard covers the whole field. Practical interoperability concerns the credibility of a standard, i.e. whether it is trustworthy and widely used in practice. Practical interoperability is related to semantic interoperability. Communication, bindings and integrity can be considered as technical interoperability. It is crucial to know whether standards can be used together in a context or not.

The 'Quality attributes' category consists of seamlessness, evolvability, learnability, forward/ backward compatibility and modifiability. All these categories are related to practical interoperability, however present different aspects. The exception is learnability whose main goal is to show whether the standard provides a guideline to users. Many criteria presented in the table below can be considered as quality attributes which describe any technical system. A majority of those quality attributes were used previously in the field of TEL by other researchers (cf., Klett, 2007).

5. RESULTS

In the following section, we describe the results of the case study for both, the analysis of standards using RMAG as well as an analysis of the usage process.

5.1. Analysis of Standards

This section presents the results of the questionnaire on analysis of TEL standards and specifications. The results are presented from general to more specific technical levels. The main concepts of the four analyzed TEL standards were identified (Table 4). The number of concepts varies considerably. For example, ISO-IEC 19796-1 has three main concepts which have been explained.

To be able to analyze and compare standards and specifications, information about competing and underlying standards is needed (Table 5). Information about underlying standards reflects also practical and semantic interoperability. ISO/IEC 19796-1 is a standard which itself aims at helping to extend generic standards. Half of the analyzed standards have competing domain standards. In the analysis, IMS QTI was deviant in a sense that formats with the questions and answers assessments functionality (e.g., DocBook, FML, QAML, SuML) can be seen as competing domain standards for IMS QTI.

Practical and semantic interoperability was analyzed through several explanatory questions. In fact the analysis of practical and semantic interoperability was not completed in a sufficient level. There was no data for practical interoperability in three cases out of four. This means that the standards were not used in practice widely.

The *measurement of communication* between the TEL standards aims at measuring technical interoperability of the standards. The most communicative standard out of four standards analyzed in the study was IMS QTI which communicates with ISO 15836 (ISO, 2003), IEEE 1484-12: 2002 (IEEE, 2002), IMS Content Packaging v1.2 (IMS, 2004) and IMS QTI (IMS, 2006) and IMS Common Cartridge Authorization Web Service v1.0 (IMS, 2008).

Integrity and seamlessness are parts of technical interoperability of the TEL standards. If

Table 4. Main concepts of the TEL standards

Standard	Main concepts
CEN MLO	Learning opportunity, Learning Opportunity Provider, Learning Opportunity Specification, Learning Opportunity Instances
IEEE RCD	Competency definitions
IMS QTI	Item, section, test
ISO/IEC 19796-1	Needs analysis: identification and description of requirements, demands and constraints of an educational project; Framework analysis: identification of the framework and the context of an educational process Conception/design: conception and design of an educational process; development/production: realization of concepts; implementation: description of the implementation of technological components; learning process: realization and use of the learning process; evaluation/optimization: description of the evaluation methods, principles and procedures

Table 5. Competing and underlying standards

Standard	Competing domain standards	Underlying technical standards
CEN MLO	IEEE 1484.12.1 Learning Object Metadata (LOM), MLO-AD	
IEEE RCD	PALO specification	Data types of some IEEE LOM elements
IMS QTI	Formats with the questions and answers assessments functionality (e.g. DocBook, FML, QAML, SuML)	XML, XML Schema, DTD
ISO/IEC 19796-1	No competing standards	Standard itself helps to extend generic standards PAS 1032-1, CEN/ISSS CWA 14644 etc. have been served as a base for international harmonization

a standard has strict control mechanisms, it is not highly reusable since the usage of different implementations and bindings becomes unfensible. The analysis of integrity is also significant to find out if the standard disintegrates in a case where its underlying standard is modified. In our study, two of the analyzed standards, CEN MLO and ISO/IEC 19796-1, were loosely integral i.e. they allowed different kind of implementations and extensions. In IEEE RCD, conformance of systems was outside the scope.

Seamlessness means the standard's capability to be used together with the elements of the competing and/or relevant standards to satisfy specific user requirements. IMS QTI can be used together wit IEEE LOM, SCORM and IMS LD. In contrast, in the case of ISO/IEC 19796-1 other relevant standards were used in the definition but not to complement it.

Backward and forward compatibility and modifiability are also parts of technical interoperability. The aim of analyzing backward and forward compatibility is to find out if the standards and technologies underlying the current version of the standard differ from ones of its previous versions and whether those underlying technologies compatible with the old ones. In case of IMS QTI, newer versions of the analyzed standards were not compatible with the older ones. The aim of analyzing *modifiability* is to find out if the standard allows adding or modifying elements and

properties. Modifiability is a crucial feature in terms of reusability and usefulness. A modifiable standard can be used for different kinds of purposes. It corresponds better to user requirements. In most cases the analyzed standards were highly modifiable. IEEE RCD was the only exception.

For the analysis of concrete standards and specifications, we have achieved a variety of analysis outcomes. We support the outcome of Vogten et al. (2006) it should be stressed that according to our results IMS QTI is able to communicate with IMS LD. We furthermore support the results of Tomberg & Laanpere (2007) showing that the versions 1.x and 2.0 of the specification IMS QTI are not compatible with each other. By comparing our study with the study of Tomberg and Laanpere it should be noted that Tomberg and Laanpere focused on analysis of the major changes of two successive releases of IMS QTI, whereas our study provides analysis of how those versions communicate with each other and with other standards.

The analysis has produced a variety of results and has been applied by different experts. We have successfully applied the analysis scheme to TEL standards and specifications tested by different users, both standardization experts as well as content providers. The analysis process has shown that those users can successfully apply the analysis grid leading to comparable, comprehensive results.

5.2. Analysis of RMAG

The standards' analysis process described above was also observed and analyzed to understand the use and usefulness of RMAG and to refine the aspects as well as criteria. The users performing the analysis grid found the RMAG useful as a basic model but too complex in its original form. Even though, it was communicated that the model is meant to be generic and comprehensive, this was one of the main weaknesses. In the following, the main findings regarding the model are summarized:

- **Completeness:** The model was seen as very comprehensive and complete and therefore a good basis for developing an adapted analysis scheme as well as a specific questionnaire. Almost all aspects needed for the analysis were derived from RMAG.
- **Adaptation Effort:** Users at first did not fully understand the adaptation process. In particular, it was not always clear that not all categories of RMAG have to be used but that appropriate categories need to be selected and prioritized. After this fact was clear, the adaptation process was simple and was done in a short time period.
- **Validity of Aspects:** This cannot be answered completely from the case study, as it depends highly on the context. Most aspects and criteria from RMAG were also mentioned by the users who performed the standard analysis.
- **Understandability:** As mentioned above, RMAG needed to be clarified and needed additional explanations. Therefore, further descriptions need to be added.
- **Ambiguity:** The model led to similar outcomes in the assessment by different users. However, it cannot be assured that all users will achieve the same outcomes (and are not meant to). It should be clear that

the model shall guide the analysis process, however, it is not intended to provide pre-defined criteria for quantitative evaluation but to facilitate a qualitative, collaborative evaluation process.

In general, it can be seen that RMAG was seen as useful for the users performing the analysis after the adaptation procedure was clear. However, only a quite small number of attributes were chosen for the analysis in the ICOPER context.

6. DISCUSSION

The Reference Model Analysis Grid provides categories to classify and assess reference models which – in a broad sense – also contain standards and specifications in the TEL domain. These aspects and assessment criteria have been used in a case study shown in the previous section. The models have been evaluated using RMAG. The evaluation led to the conclusion that RMAG is suitable for evaluating and decision support for TEL standards and specifications. We see our findings in accordance to the proposal by Frank (2007) which provides generic categories for analyzing reference models. However, there is a strong need to provide analysis schemes which are specifically designed and adapted for a certain domain, in our case the TEL domain. RMAG is a comprehensive adaptation of the generic model by Frank (2007).

However, there is also a negative side to our approach – in particular in the domain of TEL, reference models from different other domains might be used. Originally designed for other purposes, those models and specifications might be applied in this domain as well – an example is the usage of HR-XML (HR-XML, 2009) for describing competencies. When using domain-independent standards and specifications, the analysis scheme has to be adapted for the originating as well as the target domain. We recommend, for this purpose, to use the base scheme of RMAG and extend it using categories and criteria of the originating domain.

Despite of this, RMAG can be seen as a robust tool for evaluating reference models as well as specific standards and specifications for process and data models.

7. CONCLUSION

The study presented a methodology to analyze, compare, and validate TEL standards and specifications. Four well-known TEL standards were analyzed from various viewpoints including semantic and pragmatic interoperability, communication, and seamlessness. The analysis was carried out as a part of the more general methodology, namely Reference Model Analysis Grid (RMAG) which is used to build the ICOPER Reference Model. The proposed methodology for reference model classification and analysis in the TEL domain can be beneficially used in various research and development projects, especially in those that aim at achieving interoperability. For future developments, we aim at validating RMAG in different contexts as well as using the model for decision support mechanisms.

ACKNOWLEDGMENT

Parts of this work have been done in the project "iCOPER: Interoperable Content for Performance in a Competency-driven Society", funded by the European Union Ref No ECP-2007-EDU-417007. The paper only states the opinions of the authors.

REFERENCES

Advanced Distributed Learning. (2009). *Shareable Content Object Reference Model SCORM 2004* (4th ed.). Alexandria, VA: Advanced Distributed Learning.

Barn, B., Dexter, H., Oussena, S., Sparks, D., Petch, J., & Stiles, M. (2006). *COVARM – Course Validation Reference Model* (Final Report). *JISC Collections*. Retrieved March 31, 2010 from http://www.jisccollections.ac.uk/media/documents/programmes/elearningframework/covarm_final_report_v1.pdf

CEN/ISS. S (2008). *CWA 15903:2008. Metadata for Learning Opportunities (MLO) – Advertising*. Brussels, Belgium: The European Committee for Standardization.

Cooper, A. (2009). *Evaluating Standards – A Discussion of Perspectives, Issues and Evaluation Dimensions*. Bolton, UK: JISC CETIS. Retrieved April 21, 2010 from http://wiki.cetis.ac.uk/images/e/e7/ Evaluating_Standards_Public_v1p0.doc

Ehlers, U. D., & Pawlowski, J. M. (2006). Qualiy in European E-Learning – An Introduction. In Ehlers, U. D., & Pawlowski, J. M. (Eds.), *European Handbook of Quality and Standardisation in E-Learning*. Berlin: Springer. doi:10.1007/3-540-32788-6_1

Fettke, P., & Loos, P. (2003a). Multiperspective Evaluation of Reference Models – Towards a Framework. *Computer Science: Conceptual Modeling for Novel Application Domains* (LNCS, pp. 80-91). New York: Springer.

Fettke, P., & Loos, P. (2003b). Classification of Reference Models - A Methodology and Its Application. *Journal of Information Systems and e-Business Management, 1*(1), 3-53.

Fettke, P., & Loos, P. (2006). *Using Reference Models for Business Engineering - State-of-the-Art and Future Developments. Innovations in Information Technology.* Washington, DC: IEEE Computer Society Press.

Fettke, P., & Loos, P. (2007). Perspectives on Reference Modeling. In Fettke, P., & Loos, P. (Eds.), *Reference Modeling for Business Systems Analysis* (pp. 1–22). Hershey, PA: Idea Group.

Franklin, T., Beeston, M., Dexter, H., & van Harmelen, M. (2008). *Final Report of the Reference Model Projects Synthesis and Evaluation Projects.* London: JISC Collections. Retrieved March 21, 2010, from http://www.jisc.ac.uk/publications/publications/finalreportreferencemodelsynthesis, retrieved 2010-03-21

Hay, D. C. (1996). *Data Model Patterns - Conventions of Thought. New Yorks.* Dorset House.

Hevner, A. R., March, S. T., Park, J., & Ram, S. (2004). Design Science in Information Systems Research. *Management Information Systems Quarterly, 28*(1), 75–105.

HR-XML. (2009). *HR-XML 3.0 Specification.* Retrieved from http://www.hr-xml.org

IMS Global Learning Consortium. (2003). *IMS Learning Design, Version 1.0 Final Specification.* Lake Mary, FL: IMS Global Learning Consortium.

IMS Global Learning Consortium. (2004). *IMS Content Packaging Specification, Version 1.1.4 Final Specification.* Lake Mary, FL: IMS Global learning Consortium.

IMS Global Learning Consortium. (2006). *IMS Question and Test Interoperability Specification, Version 2.1 Public Draft Specification.* Lake Mary, FL: IMS Global Learning Consortium.

IMS Global Learning Consortium. (2008). *IMS Common Cartridge, Version 1.0 Final Specification.* Lake Mary, FL: IMS Global Learning Consortium.

Institute of Electrical and Electronic Engineering (IEEE). (1990). *IEEE 610.12:1990 IEEE Standard Glossary of Software Engineering Terminology.* Washington, DC: IEEE.

Institute of Electrical and Electronics Engineers. (2002). *IEEE 1484-12.1:2002 Standard for Learning Object Metadata (LOM).* Washington, DC: IEEE.

Institute of Electrical and Electronics Engineers (IEEE). (2007). *IEEE 1484.20.1 Draft Standard for Learning Technology - Data Model for Reusable Competency Definitions.* Washington, DC: IEEE.

International Organization for Standardization. (2003). [*Information and documentation - The Dublin Core metadata element set.* Geneva, Switzerland: IOS.]. *ISO, 15836,* 2003.

International Organization for Standardization/ International Electrotechnical Commission (ISO/IEC). (2005). *ISO/IEC 19796-1:2005. Information Technology - Learning, Education, and Training - Quality Management, Assurance and Metrics - Part 1: General Approach.* Geneva, Switzerland: ISO.

Keller, G., & Teufel, T. (1998). *SAP R/3 Process Oriented Implementation - Iterative Process Prototyping.* Reading, MA: Addison-Wesley.

Klett, F. (2007). Facing Learning System Design Complexity: Personalization, Adaptation and Reusability. In *Proceedings of the International Conference on "Computer as Tool" EUROCON 2007*.

Lewis, G. A., Morris, E., Simanta, S., & Wrage, L. (2008). Why Standards are not Enough to Guarantee End-To-End Interoperability. In *Proceedings of the seventh International Conference on Composition-Based Software Systems* (pp. 164-173). Washington, DC: IEEE Computer Society Press.

Madhour, H., & Wentland Forte, M. (2007). The Open Lausanne Model: A Reference Model for Open Adaptive Learning Object Systems. In *Proceedings of the 7th International Conference on Advanced Learning Technologies (ICALT 2007)* (pp. 747-749). Washington, DC: IEEE Computer Society Press.

Najjar, J., & Simon, B. (2009). Learning Outcome Based Higher Education: iCoper Use Cases. In *Proceedings of the Ninth IEEE International Conference on Advanced Learning Technologies* (pp. 718-719).

Scheer, A.-W. (1994). *Business Process Engineering – Reference Models for Industrial Enterprises* (2nd ed.). Berlin: Springer.

Tomberg, V., & Laanpere, M. (2007). Towards the Interoperability of Online Assessment Tools. In *Proceedings of the 29th International Conference on Information Technology Interfaces* (pp. 513-518). Washington, DC: IEEE Computer Society Press.

Tyrväinen, P., Warsta, J., & Seppänen, V. (2008). Evolution of Secondary Software Businesses: Understanding Industry Dynamics. In G. León, A. Bernardos, J. Casar, K. Kautz, & J. DeGross (Eds.), *IFIP International Federation for Information Processing Vol. 287, Open IT-based innovation: moving towards cooperative IT transfer and knowledge diffusion* (pp. 281-401). Boston: Springer.

UNESCO. (1998). *Forum on the impact of Open Courseware for higher education in developing countries. Final report*. Paris: UNESCO.

Vogten, H., Martens, H., Nadolski, R., Tattersall, C., van Rosmalen, P., & Koper, R. (2006). CopperCore Service Integration - Integrating IMS Learning Design and IMS Question and Test Interoperability. In *Proceedings of the Sixth International Conference on Advanced Learning Technologies* (pp. 378-382). Washington, DC: IEEE Computer Society Press.

Yin, R. K. (2008). *Case Study Research, Design and Methods* (4th ed.). Thousand Oaks, CA: Sage Publications.

This work was previously published in the International Journal of IT Standards and Standardization Research (IJITSR), Volume 8, Issue 2, edited by Kai Jakobs, pp. 1-20, copyright 2010 by IGI Publishing (an imprint of IGI Global)

Chapter 14

Key Challenges in the Design of Learning Technology Standards:
Observations and Proposals

Adam R. Cooper
University of Bolton, UK

ABSTRACT

This paper considers key challenges that learning technology standards must take into account: the inherent connectedness of the information and complexity as a cause of emergent behavior. Some of the limitations of historical approaches to information systems and standards development are briefly considered with generic strategies to tackle complexity and system adaptivity. A consideration of the facets of interoperability organizational, syntactic and semantic—leads to an outline of a strategy for dealing with environmental complexity in the learning technology standards domain.

INTRODUCTION

Many workers in the field of learning technology (LT) standards have a sense of dis-satisfaction at the amount of progress made to date, reflected in the call for papers of this special edition: "a growing awareness that standards experts and bodies have to improve both their processes and products" (Hoel, Hollins, & Pawlowski, 2009). It is, however, far from clear that other fields of IT standardization have made proportionately greater progress when considering the relatively small number of workers in the learning technology standards world. This paper considers some of the challenges arising from the character of the education system that future LT standardization must overcome or circumvent if desirable levels of future progress are to be made. In this paper, the word "standards" is used, not only for *de jure* standards, but for virtually any multi-laterally agreed set of technical conventions.

DOI: 10.4018/978-1-4666-2160-2.ch014

THE CHALLENGES OF LEARNING TECHNOLOGY STANDARDS

An Engineering Heritage

In the early stages of the development and use of the electronic computer, the biggest challenges were in the realm of engineering. Hardware, Operating Systems, compilers, data stores and programming languages/paradigms have all been developed to a phenomenal degree through engineering and use of objective measures of performance. In spite of early recognition that IT systems are not simply mechanical – they are socio-technical - in character, computing courses have generally continued to reflect the engineering heritage.

From the late 20th century, it has become progressively more clear that failure to account for complexity and socio-technical factors is severely limiting the effectiveness of ICT interventions and organizations (Bullock & Cliff, 2004) (Mumford, 2000). The recognition of this problem is not, however, a solution; the solution is hard and we live with the challenge of moving on from our engineering heritage in LT standardization as well as in IT systems design.

Connectedness of Concepts and Unknown Bounds

"Connectedness" is used to express the idea that almost anything that is the subject of a communication, i.e., is information, could also be the subject of a communication with different intent and effect. Any boundary around a collection of concepts is arbitrary. At best it is a commonly-adopted convenience, commonly it is an un-conscious artifact of a particular application or context, and at worst it is an insufferable impediment. When there is a high degree of uniformity in, and dominance of, a process, the "commonly adopted convenience" becomes a cause of greater efficiency and it may be possible to package the whole as a standard. In the absence of dominance and uniformity,

a conscious and reflective set of compromises becomes necessary.

The challenge for learning technology standardization is that the dominant and uniform processes are generally either not there or not easily seen. The typical case seems to be that any information about subject is used in many ways. For example, information about the content and structure of a university course appears in numerous processes/activities, each claiming some kind of authoritative status: design and validation, marketing, management information, e-learning platform, diploma/transcript, etc…. This appears as a general feature of information systems and is a problematical one if the large number of person-years spent on integration projects - where the consequences of un-conscious and un-reflective compartmentalization are partially compensated for - is taken as a measure.

There are some exceptions to this general challenge, counter-examples where there is a sufficiently isolated sub-domain and cost reductions that make for a proven business case. The most clear counter-example is content/delivery-platform interoperability in aviation maintenance and military training where the case for formalized approaches is clear (Jeffery & Bratton-Jeffery, 2004); a platform from which ADL SCORM could become widespread.

Complexity of the System

The education system is, of course, not an isolated system. Through the action of individuals, technology and social practices bleed-in to education from general civil life. Its inextricable binding into the social, political, technical and economic structures and collective intentions, combining elements of control, choice and autonomy, suggests that it should be considered a social enterprise.

Compared to a business enterprise, the workings of the education system as a whole are rather messier but it is worth considering the response of the business IT world to its far-from-simple environment. Historically, the problem of engineering IT in the business enterprise has been seen as a complicated task and approaches under the banner of Enterprise Architecture (EA) developed to increase the effectiveness of business IT developments. The inspiration for EA, according to John Zachman, the man credited with inventing it, arose from industries such as building and aerospace (Zachman, 2008), where the scale of operations had been previously overcome.

As time has gone on, the business world has become more complex and the problem of IT alignment to business need has presented business with more than a complicated engineering problem. One reaction to this change has been a move to see Enterprise Architecture as being more related to business strategy (Ross, Weill, & Robertson, 2006). This view emphasizes the identification of the core repeatable processes *vs.* those aspects of business operations that add value, i.e. competitive advantage.

More recent work is beginning to recognize, describe and model the complexity in the non-core rather than only identifying where the repeatable, stable and predictable processes occur (Paich & Parker, 2010). Increased interest in the "non-core" reflects an increasing motivation to understand and anticipate change rather than just to seek efficiency. The issue is that the market-place has become more complex and that change is less uniform, harder to predict. ICT and "the web" has radically reduced the transaction costs for business-to-business interactions and enabled greater customer-to-customer and commentator-to-customer communication. More recently, Cloud computing "infrastructure as a service" has significantly lowered the barrier to entry for innovators and enabled them to rapidly scale-up operations by incremental pricing models and instant availability. The ready availability of these services has the potential to dramatically increase dynamic behavior and overall system adaptivity.

The consequence of this is that network effects have become more important in ways that go beyond value creation by a multiplier effect;

networks behave in fundamentally different ways, they show emergent behavior (Bullock & Cliff, 2004).

Education is not isolated from these changes and has a supplementary problem: the scope of the enterprise is less well defined. This is illustrated by the example of efforts to expand work-based learning, where good intentions supported by cogent arguments for social and economic benefits have often failed to translate to success in practice. The map of stakeholders, their differing values and intentions, effective levers for change, their roles and relationships is messy: learner/employee, education institution, employer, professional/trade skills authority, government, funding agencies, etc.

Culture and Diversity

Educational practices and values are often quite deeply embedded in culture. In part this reflects about 1000 years of continuous existence for some universities but the sheer durability of practices dating back to the academies of ancient Greece, in the "Western World" at least, is remarkable. In the face of this, it seems surprising that there are significant differences between the organization of education among the countries of the European Union or between the United States of America and any EU state. "Significant differences" could also be expressed by saying that there is limited organizational interoperability.

Regional differences are a reality that must be accommodated. An ideal approach to learning technology standards should naturally and efficiently accomplish this objective. In contrast to complexity, this objective is widely apprehended and it will not be further elaborated upon.

Pedagogy

Pedagogy presents a particular problem for education. On the face of it, it seems that variation in the organization of education is more noticeable than differences in the pedagogic practices of lectures, essays, exams, presentations, seminars, discussion, problem-setting, reading etc... Beneath the surface description of these practices differences become more important: the pedagogic role of the activities differs between contexts and cultures. Furthermore, our understanding of the nature of learning and its relationship to the environment of teaching and technology is generally descriptive, lacks explanatory or predictive power and fails to account for its inherent complexity (Sharples, 2009).

Blandin makes the case that existing standardization practice and process, while intending to be neutral to context and culture, is actually incorporating "peculiar representations" of pedagogy and culture (Blandin, 2004). We need to find some way of dis-entangling these aspects and enable diversity while recognizing that differences of pedagogy are often latent in practice and poorly understood from a scientific perspective.

DEALING WITH COMPLEXITY AND ADAPTIVITY

Complexity and adaptivity – the idea that agents in the system interact and evolve according to their environment and consequently change the nature of the system – make it difficult to predict the behavior of a system. It is not sufficient to break it down into small parts, each of which can be independently addressed, as is possible for merely complicated systems.

Organization

Command-and-control approaches to managing, forming or exploiting complex adaptive systems either fail quickly, if the necessary information and system-understanding is lacking at the centre, or fail slowly under increasingly burdensome efforts at coordination and performance monitoring. Similarly, planned approaches fail due to plans that misunderstand the context or become bogged down in requirements gathering and study.

To deal with complexity and adaptivity, we need better ways of organizing our activities and institutions – principally decentralized models for planning and action - and to build-in the capacity for change. De-centralization is a general principle for dealing with complexity (Bullock & Cliff, 2004) and is not just about more people commenting and contributing; it is fundamentally about smaller and non-hierarchically-arranged self-organizing units with a greater capability to respond to signals from the environment.

Shearing Layers

Organization gives us the capability to apprehend change and to be concerted in our intentions and actions. "Shearing Layers", coined in relation to building design and architecture, is a metaphor to express the idea that changeability should be designed in to what we create. Enabling differential rates of change between the various components of a structure so that the whole does not have to be rebuilt is the goal of shearing layers. The idea has been applied to information systems design by IBM Research (Simmonds & Ing, 2000) on the grounds of similar observations –prevalence of discontinuous and unpredictable change and a view that enterprises are emergent organizations – to those made in this paper. Wilson and Velayutham interpreted and extended this argument in relation to educational technology systems (Wilson & Velayutham, 2009).

Understanding: Models

Complex Adaptive Systems may be difficult to predict and counter-intuitive but this does not mean that they cannot be understood. Models can be built and calibrated (Paich & Parker, 2010) but adaptivity is particularly challenging as time-dependent data is required for model-building and calibration. There has been little application of these kinds of modeling techniques in the education domain, although some work (Sklar & Davies, 2005) shows promise for this as a research topic.

Model-building operates at the level of most detail and is laborious; for the present time we should expect to use "Organization" and "Shearing Layers" to compensate for the deficiencies in our understanding.

PERILS AND PITFALLS

Learning Technology Architecture

Learning technology is a young concept at the intersection of the complex social enterprise of education and the rapid change of technology. The paradigmatic shift that is "the web" is still being played out and descriptions of its social and economic consequences continue to reveal new complexity and explanatory perspectives.

Attempts to define or describe an architecture for learning technology have been largely thwarted by change and difference of opinion arising from embedded cultural, technical or pedagogic perspective. These assumptions were either wrong or the cause of bogged down requirements gathering and study: out of date, inaccurate anticipation, recognized inadequacy, cause of dispute, etc…

The nature of the system, complex and adaptive, means that the architecture for learning technology is largely emergent. It may not be completely analyzed, anticipated or planned, although analysis, prediction and associated discourse are part of the process of emergence. Description and value-judgment as part of this discourse form a feedback loop that influences, but does not directly control, the emergence of the architecture. Description is part of the system.

The situation described above is a challenge to any would-be standards-maker; to decide where and how to make a standard, we need some view of architecture. This can be split into two: infra-

structural and application. The "architecture of the web" (Jacbos & Walsh, 2004) is clearly the infrastructural architecture for 21st century interoperability standards, quite a low-level description and a long way from an application architecture. This gives us a stable foundation and its adoption will improve the success that can be achieved from applying de-centralised organization and "shearing layers" to deal with the emergent application architecture.

Anticipatory Standardization

Anticipatory standardization has been identified as a necessary precursor in situations where products and services are only viable given a network effect but the causes of success and failure in anticipatory standardization are complex and poorly understood (Lyytinen, Keil, & Fomin, 2008). Telecommunications is the clearest domain where anticipatory standardization is necessary but it was also necessary for web standards to be developed in anticipation, although this was a process with many failures and false steps. Great care is taken to ensure that the low level protocols do not interfere with innovation and evolution but inevitably future innovation has to work around the limitations up to the point where a step-change occurs, as in mobile telephony "3G" networks. Whereas the products and services are strongly influenced by complexity and adaptivity, the low level standards are insulated (but not isolated) from these influences and are more suited to anticipatory standardization.

Anticipation at the level of products and services, where learning technology operates, must be undertaken with recognition that it will almost certainly be wrong without sense-making of potential futures and negotiated description of them. Whereas step-changes in infrastructural standards and technologies are seen to occur (3G, XML …), overlapping, phased, drift with incremental innovation and anticipation by degree is the rule within educational institutions as it is in the "perpetual beta" world of 21st century web applications. In learning technology standardization we should anticipate with care: the business case is difficult and the recipe for success unknown.

CONCERNING FACETS OF INTEROPERABILITY

Interoperability is generally viewed as being separable into syntactic and semantic interoperability. Organizational interoperability seems to have received early attention in relation to coalition warfare – e.g., Tolk (2003) - but now receives more general attention (Baird, 2009); this paper considers interoperability to be multi-facetted capability comprising organizational, semantic and syntactic interoperability. For education, a social enterprise, considerations of organizational interoperability – expectations of operational protocols, objectives, authority, etc - are not restricted to the educational establishments and must include ideas of social norms and values.

Each facet has different temporal properties, different sensitivity to network effects, etc ... and consequently a different implication for standardization, which relies on identifying points of stability. Table 1 suggests some key differences for the education domain.

Twitter (http://twitter.com) is an example, albeit outside the standards or education worlds, of a phenomenon that illustrates some of the above. Its organic growth in a sub-culture is predicated on a large degree of organizational interoperability within that sub-culture. Twitter's simple message syntax, for example "@username" to indicate a tweet is directed at a particular person, is now so well embedded that it is leaking out into other text-based communication such as email. On the face of it, Twitter introduces new concepts such as the "tweet" but this is a surface concept, too closely bound to a manifestation of a communication act. Beneath this thin veneer of novelty lies a broadly-applicable set of semantic units applicable to public communication acts that could be applied to email lists, web forums, blogs, etc... What is different between these are the constraints, structures and collections and, significantly, norms of behavior: organizational interoperability.

Table 1. Facets of interoperability

Facet	Stability	Implication
Organizational	The organizational structure of the education institutions is characterized by relatively stable differences, although some observers question the viability of existing models in the current social, technical and economic environment.	Diversity must be accommodated.
	If, however, we consider organizational interoperability to extend to the relationship between institutions and learner, significant and potentially disruptive changes are occurring.	Effort is needed to balance the supply-side (institutional), which often dominates standardization with the demand-side (learner) requirements.
Syntactic	Syntaxes become stable given sufficiently wide adoption and will be resistant to changing conditions, forcing the effect of the change elsewhere. In the early stages of adoption, competition is likely to add to the churn caused by environmental change.	The syntactic part of a standard, comprising the grouping of elements and their encoding must be changeable.
Semantic	Day-to-day activity tends to operate with implicit and surface semantic units and these lack stability. Working at this level will produce standards with poor semantic interoperability. Beneath the surface, there are core semantic units that are relatively stable.	Effort should be invested in identifying the stable, core, semantic units and standards should be built around these.

CONCLUSIONS FOR LEARNING TECHNOLOGY STANDARDS

In essence: LT standards should be developed to accommodate diversity and change and to be part-of the systemic processes from which learning technology emerges. This has two parts: the organizational aspects of standardization and the technical aspect of how standards are written. We can see this as a kind of formative evaluation; considering where we are now but looking into the future in recognition that no point in time has privileged status.

Learning Technology standardization, while learning ways to accommodate diversity and change is likely to succeed where change is least, in those areas that are least susceptible to change. These are where there is a higher probability that investment is justified; where there is a "business case". The challenge, in targeting activity, is not to cut ourselves off from the future by failing to build-in shearing layers and not to box ourselves in to single-application standards.

Organizational Aspects

De-centralized planning and action is partially a feature of the existing learning technology standards system but closer inspection reveals some limiting characteristics.

Learning technology R&D should be a good vehicle for de-centralized planning and action but neither public nor privately funded R&D is effectively integrated into an overall standards system. In addition, public funding program scoping and contracted obligations often impose a filter and constrain agility. We need to find better ways to harness R&D without assuming that its products are necessarily fit for purpose.

Research communities and industry consortia should fulfill a coordinating role, a higher order of structure in the de-centralized model. Well-established research communities exist but they are less successful at coordinating action than they are at supporting dissemination and networking within the community. On the other hand, industry consortia that behave as competitive enterprises reduce their value as coordinators in a de-centralized approach.

Public standardization (national standards bodies, CEN and ISO) impose a hierarchical structure and a highly regulated process. This structure works well to ensure fairness for mandated standards and particularly well for standardizing goods with well defined purpose – e.g., domestic waste pipes – but is ill-suited to the complex and inter-connected education domain. They have a role along-side more adaptive and de-centralized structures, from which the more stable and widely-relevant specifications can migrate.

Technical Aspects

The principal requirements, to accommodate diversity and change, should be met by similar or identical methods in the interest of efficiency and viability.

The "shearing layers" metaphor is well illustrated by building and architecture; foundations, superstructure, partitions, services, fittings and furniture form part of the whole in ways that reflect the speed of change people seek in their domestic or workplace environment. The same structural relationships also naturally support diversity and do so in an economical way if different elements can be composed in a modular fashion.

Bearing in mind the observations made on the facets of interoperability (above), and adopting the shearing layers metaphor, it is proposed that learning technology standards should be developed in a layered and modular style with core semantic units as the stable foundation and following the principles of web architecture (Jacbos & Walsh, 2004). The layers of the specification, as shown in Table 2 should build up from the general to the specific and each should have a well-defined and consistent shearing plane so that higher-up layers can change, or alternatives can be added, without disrupting the lower one.

Table 2. Proposed layering in the structure of standards

Layer	Character	Stability
Conceptual Model	Conceptual models relate to the way people conceive of things and their relationships independent of the way instances of those things may be described. They are abstractions over existing practice that draw out the essential similarities. They are shared within communities but may not be universal. They are application-neutral and usefully extend beyond the bounds of the specification that is to be written in order to situate it in the wider landscape.	Most stable if well executed; the concepts described are independent of the description.
Identified Semantic Units	The types of thing (classes) along with the properties and necessary value-spaces that will be used to describe them are enumerated and explained in relation to the conceptual model. These may be newly-defined or references to identified semantic units from other sources. All should be uniquely identified.	Slightly less stable as different groups will define different units for essentially the same concept.
Assemblies	The semantic units are assembled to specify how things are to be described, i.e. how the properties, classes and value-spaces fit together.	Different applications and changing requirements alter the description.
Encodings/ Syntax	These comprise the necessary binding to a method for exchanging the information in practice. Multiple bindings allow diversity of platform, for example JSON, RDF/XML, XML, LDAP, microformats …	Variable

Combining the Organizational and the Technical Aspects

There is a sensible correlation between the organizational components and layers outlined above. This suggests that we should target the public standardization bodies with specifications at the more stable layers, accommodating as much

diversity as possible through the range of bodies concerned. A role for research communities and industry consortia could usefully be developed in sense-making, teasing out the general from the specific, winnowing the viable from the un-viable and clarifying the shearing layers; initial R&D will inevitably not – and should not – take such a purist approach.

REFERENCES

Baird, S. (2009). *Organizational Interoperability is Key to a Successful eGovernment Strategy.* Retrieved April 5, 2010, from http://www.talk-standards.com/organizatlonal-Interoperability-is-key-to-a-successful-egovernment-strategy/

Blandin, B. (2004). *Are e-learning standards neutral?* In *Proceedings of CALIE 2004.* Retrieved April 1, 2010, from http://www-clips.imag.fr/calie04/actes/Blandin_final.pdf

Bullock, S., & Cliff, D. (2004). *Complexity and Emergent Behaviour in ICT Systems (HPL-2004-187).* Bristol, UK: Hewlett-Packard.

Hoel, T., Hollins, P., & Pawlowski, J. (2009). Special Issue on Learning Technoloy Standards. *The International Journal of IT Standards and Standardization Research.* Retrieve April 1, 2010 from http://sites.google.com/site/standardsgovernance/

Jacbos, I., & Walsh, N. (2004). *Architecture of the World Wide Web, Volume One.* Retrieved April 1, 2010, from W3C: http://www.w3.org/TR/webarch/

Jeffery, A. B., & Bratton-Jeffery, M. F. (2004). Integrated Training Requires Integrated Design and Business Models. In Armstrong, A.-M. (Ed.), *Instructional design in the real world: a view from the trenches* (pp. 218–249). Hershey, PA: IGI Global. doi:10.4018/978-1-59140-150-6.ch013

Lyytinen, K., Keil, T., & Fomin, V. (2008). A Framework to Build Process Theories of Anticipatory Information and Communication Technology (ICT) Standardizing. *Journal of IT Standards & Standardization Research*, *6*(1), 1–38. doi:10.4018/jitsr.2008010101

Mumford, E. (2000). A Socio-Technical Approach to Systems Design. *Requirements Engineering*, *5*(2), 125–133. doi:10.1007/PL00010345

Paich, M., & Parker, B. (2010). Using simulation tools for strategic decision making. *PricewaterhouseCoopers Technology Forecast*, *1*, 20–23.

Ross, J., Weill, P., & Robertson, D. (2006). *Enterprise Architecture as Strategy*. Boston: Harvard Business Press.

Sharples, M. (2009). Towards an Interdisciplinary Design Science of Learning. In Cress, U., Dimitrova, V., & Specht, M. (Eds.), *Learning in the Synergy of Multiple Disciplines* (pp. 3–4). New York: Springer. doi:10.1007/978-3-642-04636-0_2

Simmonds, I., & Ing, D. (2000). *A Shearing Layers Approach to Information Systems Development*. Retrieved March 30, 2010, from http://systemic-business.org/pubs/2000_IBM_RC21694_Simmonds_Ing_Shearing_Layers_Info_Sys_Dev.pdf

Sklar, E., & Davies, M. (2005). Multiagent Simulation of Learning Environments. In *Proceedings of the fourth international joint conference on Autonomous agents and multiagent systems* (pp. 953-959).

Tolk, A. (2003). *Beyond Technical Interoperability – Introducing a Reference Model for Measures of Merit for Coalition Interoperability*. Retrieved April 2, 2010, from http://citeseerx.ist.psu.edu/viewdoc/download?doi=10.1.1.79.6784&rep=rep1&type=pdf

Wilson, S., & Velayutham, K. (2009). Creating an innovation-oriented technology strategy. *Horizon*, 245–255. doi:10.1108/10748120910993277

Zachman, J. A. (2008). *The Zachman Framework: The Official Concise Definition*. Retrieved April 2, 2010, from http://www.zachmaninternational.com/index.php/the-zachmanframework

This work was previously published in the International Journal of IT Standards and Standardization Research (IJITSR), Volume 8, Issue 2, edited by Kai Jakobs, pp. 20-28, copyright 2010 by IGI Publishing (an imprint of IGI Global)

Chapter 15

Community–Driven Specifications:
XCRI, SWORD, and LEAP2A

Scott Wilson
University of Bolton, UK

ABSTRACT

This paper explores the issues and opportunities for specifications that develop outside of the traditional governance processes of industry consortia or formal standards organisations through a discussion and comparison of three specifications developed in the education sector: XCRI (eXchanging Course-Related Information), SWORD (Simple Web service Offering Repository Deposit), and LEAP2.0 (Learner Portfolios 2.0). In each case study, there are challenges, opportunities, and accomplishments, and the experiences of each project are compared to identify commonalities and differences. Based on these case studies, the paper applies the framework developed by Wilson and Velayutham (2009) to position the specifications against similar specifications from established consortia and formal standards. Finally, the topic of incubating specifications is discussed, with implications for funding agencies with an interest in supporting interoperability.

INTRODUCTION

The term "informal specifications" or "informal standards" is often used when discussing initiatives that take place outside the framework of de jure standards. However, this term is also applied to mature specification consortia such as the World Wide Web Consortium (W3C) and Internet Engineering Task Force (IETF); for example, Van Eecke and Truyens (2009) cite XML as an example of an informal specification.

DOI: 10.4018/978-1-4666-2160-2.ch015

Unlike specification consortia, the idea of "community specifications" or "community-driven specifications" is a fairly new characterization. While community-driven specifications are by definition also informal standards, they are also characterized separately from specification consortia.

For example, the Open Web Foundation describes its work as "an organization to facilitate community efforts to create technical specifications that conform to the ethos that anyone can use the specification and nobody "owns" the specification or its ideas" (Recordon, 2008).

While many of the characteristics set out by Recordon may be seen as aspirations rather than actual characteristics of such initiatives, there is a sense in which specifications such as OpenID, oAuth, OpenSocial and Microformats are developed differently from, for example, W3C or OASIS specifications.

It may be more accurate to describe the types of initiative the OWF supports as "single specification" communities; that is, communities formed to develop and promote a single specification to solve a single common problem, rather than an organisation that seeks to develop a range of specifications within some sort of agreed scope. However even this characterisation is not entirely satisfactory, as Microformats are commonly considered to be a community specification, and yet the Microformats community develops many different specifications in different areas.

Cooper (2010) characterises "Open Community Development" as: 1) very limited controls on participation by any interested party, either by minimal bureaucracy or peer pressure, 2) initiation by a group of people who have a common interest/need and form an ad-hoc group to meet the need, 3) development of prototypes/code interwoven with spec development, 3) an acceptance of rapid change, refactoring etc, 4) negligible formal process, 5) transparency/visibility of work in progress

(on public web), 6) online and often async (sic) rather than f2f or sync (sic) participation.

It could be argued that the main difference between a community specification and specification consortia is principally one of maturity; IETF, for example, could be considered to be a specification community in the sense that it has no official membership and anyone can contribute to specifications.

The picture is further blurred by the fact that community specifications may also be submitted to established specification consortia or to formal standardisation processes, or communities may choose to become consortia with official membership and processes.

Another approach is to simply consider community specification development as one end of a spectrum of informal standardisation, with consortia such as W3C and OASIS at one end, close to formal standards in terms of process and organisational stability, and community specification development at the other, but with no single defining characteristic. Using this approach, the characteristics Cooper describes are useful heuristics for placing specification development initiatives along the spectrum; any individual initiative may have one or more such characteristics to be considered a "community specification".

In the next section three initiatives are profiled that occupy the "community" end of the informal standards spectrum. The Joint Information Systems Committee of the UK Education Funding Councils[1] (JISC) supported each of these initiatives; JISC is an agency that supports the ICT infrastructure for UK universities and colleges. In the cases presented in this paper, JISC provided support through a combination of funding implementations, and supporting communities through two of its Innovation Support Centres (ISCs), CETIS and UKOLN; these support centres provide expertise in technology and standards in the technology-enhanced learning (TEL) and repository domains respectively.

XCRI

XCRI is the name of a community that formed to develop specifications related to course information (the acronym expands to "eXchanging Course-Related Information"), however it is mostly known for the XCRI Course Advertising Profile (XCRI CAP), which is a syndication format for courses. XCRI-CAP feeds provide the same type of information typically found in a course catalogue or prospectus in XML form, enabling third parties to aggregate them and provide services such as searching, recommendations and so on.

Origins

In 2005, XCRI spun out of a Special Interest Group organized by CETIS looking at integrating systems within higher and further education. It began life as a JISC project and subsequently joined the JISC e-Framework2 to address the lack of standard for representing course information. A community was formed to review current initiatives. Norway, Sweden and Finland were found to have mature representations but these were limited in their coverage of UK need.

The community developed an XML schema for representing courses based on site visits to UK universities, a review of 161 prospectus web sites and trials in colleges, universities and two regional LifeLong Learning Networks. Early deployments of the XML schema were reviewed and it was found that the majority of interest and usage lay in the area of Course Advertising. A lightweight schema optimised for this purpose (the XCRI Course Advertising Profile – XCRI-CAP) was released in August 2006.

Since then JISC has funded several waves of "mini projects" aimed at increasing implementation experience and participation in the XCRI community. Mini projects are 6 months long with funding of £10,000; since 2006 over 20 such projects have been funded 3.

The core specification has been supported through an XCRI support project; this began in 2007 to support implementation projects and the XCRI community, and has been extended several times. The most recent extension ended in March 2010. The support project is relatively small, essentially consisting of three persons each working one day per week.

Development Model

XCRI[4] was written as a flexible, light-weight XML specification that could be implemented by colleges with limited software development capacity, and was inspired by the success of RSS and Atom. The specification is developed largely through a public wiki and forum.

The initial specification was developed using a "bottom up" approach by mapping out the content found in electronic prospectuses in 161 institutions. Subsequent iterations have been influenced by implementation experience, particularly by sectors such as the UK 14-19 regional initiatives and lifelong learning and workforce development.

However the XCRI community did involve more experienced standards experts, which have directed the specification in a number of ways; first by maintaining an underlying modelling approach which is compatible with RDF, secondly by aligning the specification with the Dublin Core specifications where possible.

Sustainability Model

In 2008, the XCRI support project began liaising with other European initiatives in course information through the CEN Workshop on Learning Technologies; this was prompted by the submission to CEN of a competing standard developed in Germany through DIN (2006).

Prior to this, there was relatively little discussion of formal standardization in the XCRI community, although moving the specification towards an open governance model was a condition of JISC funding.

While the engagement may have initially been defensive in nature, the liaison proved highly successful, and resulted in a CEN workshop agreement for Metadata For Learning Opportunities in 2008 (see Wilson, 2008; CEN, 2008) that harmonized the common semantics of XCRI with initiatives from Norway, Sweden, France and Germany.

The workshop agreement was later submitted to CEN for ratification as a European Norm (EN) in 2009. It is anticipated that the standard will be ratified in late 2010. The formal standard defines the majority of the core concepts and information model used by XCRI.

The engagement of XCRI in CEN standards development has provided an opportunity and an impetus for the XCRI community to progress to formal standardization. The current roadmap of XCRI is to develop a British Standard for its course syndication format as a conforming binding and application profile of CEN Metadata for Learning Opportunities: Advertising (see Figure 1).

However in order to move to a formal standard, the XCRI community has to overcome a number of barriers:

The principle barrier to overcome in this model is that business model of BSI: traditionally BSI has operated by charging implementers for standards documents using a publishing industry business model. Either JISC would need to negotiate an alternative model with BSI to enable free access to implementers, or accept that the work that XCRI had conducted would no longer be freely available. (XCRI Support Project 2010 final report, unpublished).

If successful in a formal standardization strategy, the community would look for other areas of interest – there is some discussion of going back to work on the curriculum management issues that the community started with – and to continue work on supporting implementation and agreeing vocabularies and common practice. It remains to be seen how viable the XCRI community will be without significant central funding, and with an official standard in place.

SWORD

SWORD[5] stands for Simple Webservice Offering Repository Deposit, and is a profile of the Atom Publishing Protocol (APP, see IETF, 2007) aimed at enabling client applications to submit artifacts

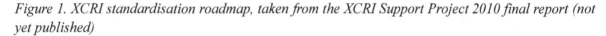

Figure 1. XCRI standardisation roadmap, taken from the XCRI Support Project 2010 final report (not yet published)

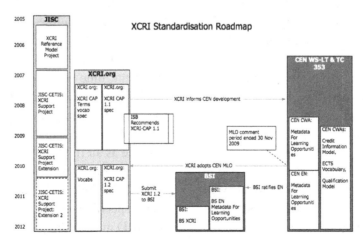

into scholarly publication repositories such as ePrints and Fedora, or into learning materials repositories such as IntraLibrary[6]. SWORD adds a number of custom extensions to APP to support a repository deposit workflow involving the selection of collections and feedback in the treatment of deposited materials, including scenarios involving direct deposit of scientific data from laboratory equipment (Allinson, Francois, & Lewis, 2008).

Origins

The idea for SWORD originated at a conference organised by JISC CETIS where participants identified the need for a common API for enabling content to be added to repository systems (Allinson & Heery, 2006).

The group identified a range of specifications that had some functionality that matched, but no exact fit, and several meeting and events were held to decide on a course of action to recommend to JISC. This group looked at a wide range of existing specifications before making the decision to recommend adapting APP. As a result of this JISC funded the SWORD project in several phases to develop the specification and support implementation.

The first phase of the project began in 2007; since then the project has since been extended twice, and is now in its third phase.

Today SWORD is managed as a project by UKOLN, a JISC innovation support centre, but with most of the technical contributions to the specification coming from a community of developers involved with various repository platforms. As with XCRI, this support project is quite modest, amounting to one part-time support officer.

Development Model

From the outset SWORD has been developed in close collaboration with implementations. As well as implementations in repository systems, this included developing code libraries and frameworks for both repositories and client applications. This lead to some early wins for the specification: the majority of open-source repositories (ePrints, DSpace, Fedora) implemented SWORD from an early stage (Lewis et al., 2009).

In general SWORD has tried to stick as close to the IETF APP specification as possible while supporting a wide range of repository-specific use cases, and has arguably focussed more heavily on practical interoperability within a fairly small number of influential implementations than on specification drafting. SWORD is developed primarily via a public mailing list.

Sustainability Model

In 2008, the CEN Workshop on Learning Technologies sponsored work developing a "Simple Publishing Interface" specification[7] that addressed the same problem space as SWORD, but initially defined completely independently of it.

As was the case with XCRI and CEN, this prompted an engagement with formal standards that was not previously under consideration in the SWORD community. A number of experts were put forward for the CEN SPI work that had experience of using SWORD as a means of ensuring that the resulting specification would not cause any difficulties for SWORD. This seems to have been fairly successful, with a CEN Workshop Agreement due to be published in 2010 that is compatible with SWORD; as with XCRI, the formal standard defines the core abstract model, leaving SWORD as a de facto specification for interoperability.

At the time of writing, the SWORD community is debating the way forwards for the specification. The main options being discussed are to progress as much of the specification as possible as an IETF Internet Draft, stressing the commonalities between SWORD and the core Atom Publishing Protocol and downplaying its sector-specific aspects. This option would place SWORD in a similar position to XCRI, in terms of pushing the majority of its technical work into an existing standards organisation.

The advantages for SWORD of this route are set out in a post by Ed Summers[8]:

- The SWORD effort would lose some of its JISC-centric-ness, and would be more about the Internet community.
- SWORD would be more clearly defined as an extension to AtomPub, and seen less as a re-branding of AtomPub.
- The specification would be hosted at a well known and trusted place that is likely to outlive JISC's interest in swordapp.org
- Going through the IETF process would probably tighten a few things up, and get more people involved doing implementations.
- It's quite possible that the bits that SWORD has added to AtomPub could be useful to people outside this little niche we call the Repository Community. Having them be an IETF RFC would allow people to discover and use them.

The principle barrier to SWORD becoming an IETF extension to APP is unfamiliarity with the IETF process among the SWORD community[9].

Another option under discussion is to continue SWORD as an independent specification community, and in this regard is discussing issues such as whether to adopt the Open Web Foundation agreement.

Leap2A

Leap2A[10] is "an open specification for transferring learner-owned information between different systems" (Smart, 2010). It is a specification based on the Atom Syndication Format, extending it for use to share feeds of portfolio information collected by learners. The specification is principally targeted as an open export format for ePortfolio

systems in use in institutions, in particular to enable learners to move information they have collected from one institution to another, or to keep personal archives.

Origins

Leap2A was to some extent a reaction to previous unsuccessful attempts at standardising ePortfolio information, which included the ePortfolio specification developed by the IMS consortium, and the Learner Information Package specification, which was temporarily ratified (as UKLEAP) as a British Standard by BSI but was not renewed. These previous approaches had not seen significant adoption, and interoperability was not evident when JISC trialled the specifications in pilot projects; as Grant (2009) notes:

Little experience had been gained of real users using such systems, and LIP was not developed in close collaboration with those who were developing the systems. When developers tried it out, they found that the specification was complex, and difficult to understand or implement consistently. Few people actually adopted it, and there was little sign of any practical and effective passing of information between systems using IMS LIP. Perhaps because both the IMS ePortfolio specification (2005), and the proposed British Standard UK LeaP ("Learner Profile", drafted 2004), were built on top of IMS LIP, they also suffered from a lack of adoption. In the UK, those involved with e-portfolio systems knew that they wanted a simpler, more straightforward specification, more in keeping with the nature of e-portfolio information.

The response was to develop a much simpler model by extending the IETF Atom Syndication Format, a widely-adopted specification for representing feeds of blog posts and other information.

As with XCRI, the starting point was a CETIS special interest group; the work of this group began in 2006, and in 2007 JISC started to provide funding for implementation pilots. As of writing, there have been three waves of pilot projects using Leap2A, the last of which run until July 2010[11].

Development Model

Leap2A took the Atom Sydication Format[12] as the basis of its technical work, while the conceptual model is to some extent inspired by the IMS ePortfolio specification[13], although the binding is completely different.

Leap2A is primarily developed using a public mailing list and Wiki site. Like XCRI, Leap2A has been supported by a series of phased interoperability pilots funded by JISC. The first wave of these took place in late 2007, with a second wave in late 2008, and a third wave in 2010 (Grant, 2010). Like SWORD, Leap2A has also benefited from implementation by key systems in use by the sector, including Mahara[14] and PebblePad[15].

There is a tension within the Leap2A community between the pragmatics of feed interoperability and a more theoretical semantic web approach, and the current specification is interesting as an example for how these worlds coexist within a single specification; as Simon Grant, the CETIS staff member who supports the Leap2A community puts it:

I had loads of conceptually neat ideas for Leap2A that were chucked out by the implementers on the grounds that they didn't do that. If the relevant practitioners can't relate to the spec, it is unlikely to fly. [16]

Recently, work has begun on a parallel RDF-based specification, Leap2R[17], using the same core model as Leap2A.

Sustainability Model

Unlike SWORD and XCRI, Leap2A is currently focussed primarily on establishing its viability as an independent specification community. While there is also the possibility of the specification entering formal standardisation or being adopted by one or more established consortia, these are not a central focus.

As the specification becomes more widely known and implemented, the Leap2A community has become more aware of potential IP and licensing issues. Also, up until recently no real governance mechanisms were in place, despite involvement in the specification by several commercial enterprises.

The Leap2A community is, at the time of writing, in the process of addressing these issues by establishing a more formal presence as a community, with a new web domain, a community membership process using Contributor License Agreements, and adapting the Open Web Foundation[18] agreement for licensing its work.

DISCUSSION

While each case study is of a specification developed to meet a different set of requirements, there are common elements.

Inspiration from Web Standards

Each of the specifications was inspired by – and in the case of both LEAP2A and SWORD, build upon – horizontal web specifications, particularly the IETF Atom standards[19]. This may be for pragmatic reasons – Atom is widely implemented, and so tools for working with the specification can be developed by simply adapting generic software, reducing the investment required to develop working implementations.

By positioning themselves with open web standards such as Atom, these communities may seek to align their work with other initiatives such as Microformats, OpenSocial and OpenID as an extension of the open web, rather than with TEL or repository vertical standardization.

XCRI has come "full circle" in the sense that it has now contributed to TEL formal standardization through CEN.

The Role of Funding Agencies in Incubating Community Specifications

XCRI, SWORD, and LEAP2A have all benefited from public funding; however, overall the amount invested in supporting the specifications has been quite modest. In each case funding has supported an individual or small team to devote part of their time to support the specification community. In the case of XCRI and LEAP2A, additional funding has also been specifically targeted at pilot implementations.

This might imply that, for a funding agency in the TEL domain, incubating a community specification may in some cases be a reasonable investment, and an alternative to either implementing or profiling existing TEL specifications.

However, in each of the cases above, support has been provided within the context of ongoing support for interoperability and open standards; the SWORD support role is provided by UKOLN, which advises the library and repository sector on interoperability and standardisation issues, while XCRI and LEAP2A support has been provided or assisted by CETIS, which performs a similar role in the TEL sector. This provided each community with links to both existing informal specification consortia and to formal standardisation processes, and also access to wider skills and experience in standardisation. While we cannot state categori-

cally that this is a critical success factor, agencies looking to incubate specifications in communities should consider absence of such experience and connections as a potential risk.

Staying Close to Implementation

In all the cases described here implementation experience has played a key role. SWORD has been very much driven by repository system implementations, and LEAP2A has been significantly driven by ePortfolio implementations; both specifications have incorporated significant feedback directly from developers implementing the specification. XCRI is slightly different in that there are a wider range of implementers but few "dominant systems" that drive the specification; XCRI has instead been shaped by a large number of small implementation pilot projects using a wide range of implementation techniques including bespoke software, extensions to existing databases, and ad-hoc integration.

Applying the Shearing Layers Model

To help understand the positioning of interoperability specifications in the education system, Wilson and Velayutham (2009) developed a "shearing layers" model of interoperability following the work of Brand (1994). This positions interoperability at different layers of the system – national, institutional, departmental, and personal. Interoperability technologies can operate both horizontally (between systems in the same layer, e.g., enterprise integration within institutions) and vertically between layers (e.g., using APIs and feeds to expose institutional systems to individuals).

While each of the specifications can be implemented in a purely "enterprise" fashion, as an internal interoperability specification between core systems, they have also all been designed for use in personal or "beyond the firewall" technologies. For example, XCRI feeds are designed to be exposed to the open web and harvested by third party aggregators. SWORD can be used to deposit resources from personal applications, such as FeedForward. Leap2A portfolios "degrade gracefully" and be read using standard Atom readers such as Google Reader. This contrasts strongly with sector specific standards (in both the TEL and Repository domains), which tend to focus on integration within established federations or within the enterprise, with perhaps an assumption that implementations are "native" to the sector and operated by experts, rather than being operated by individuals or small companies.

Applying the "shearing layers" model to the three specifications described in the case studies, we position them as shown in Figure 2.

These are the most likely positioning based on current implementation practice; if we take the closest related specifications within the TEL and repository domains and map these onto the

framework, there is a clear positional difference, as shown in Figure 3.

One question that immediately springs to mind looking at this is whether it is accidental that these community-driven specifications are more clearly concerned with bridging the internal space of their domain with personal technologies and the wider web?

Formal Standards as Exit Strategies

Cooper (2010), assert that the characteristics of open community specifications "make them suitable places to develop standards whereas FPS bodies have characteristics best suited to the codification of standards." The implication being that, as community specifications mature, the community is likely to look towards codification in established consortia or formal standards processes.

This assertion can to some extent be supported in the cases presented here; XCRI is in the process

Figure 2. XCRI, SWORD and LEAP2A positioned in the shearing layers model of Wilson and Velayutham (2009).

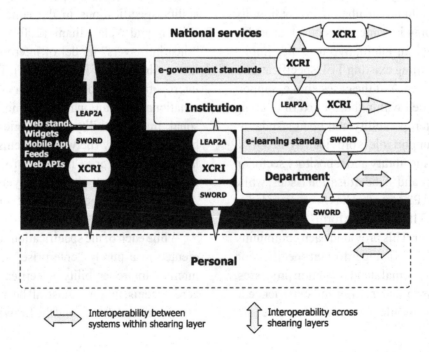

Figure 3. Prior specifications mapped to the same model. (Note that we have not included CEN MLO, which is a standard significantly based on XCRI, and which follows its usage pattern.)

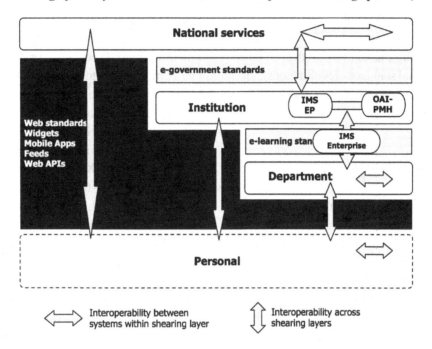

of transitioning its work to formal standardisation through CEN and BSI; SWORD is considering submission to the IETF process; LEAP2A, while pursuing an independent route, has not ruled out being incorporated into IMS or CEN processes. In each case we can see the potential interplay of standardisation at different levels of formality.

Such a conclusion points towards an approach to resolving the issue facing ICT standardisation in the EU as described by van Eecke and Truyens (2010):

The formal standardization bodies are reliable, open, neutral, and stable, but are also inherently slow and seem insufficiently equipped to meet the ICT sector's demands. The informal bodies, on the other hand, are often lightweight, do not need to take into account transparent processes, and do not need to reconcile different opinions from opposing stakeholders.

Supporting community specifications for incubating new work areas, and then easing their transition into codification through the formal standards process may be a viable strategy for policymakers, rather than attempting to make informal standardization initiatives meet WTO eligibility criteria (WTO, 1994). Blind and Gauch (2008) similarly conclude that informal and formal standardization are complementary rather than substitutive.

However, it should be noted that in the cases of XCRI and SWORD, the engagement began principally as a defensive move to protect the community specification from formal standardisation initiatives following a more typical anticipatory, research-oriented pattern that has been common in LET domain formal standardisation. It is also likely that, if the CETIS service had not been involved with both the XCRI and SWORD communities and with CEN that such an intervention may not have occurred, and that formal standards and informal, community-driven specifications would be at odds. This implies that for such a "best of both worlds" approach to work, there must firstly be a high level of awareness in both formal and informal standards development communities of the others' work, and secondly the ability and willingness to actively collaborate to avoid conflict.

An Honourable Tradition?

The initiatives discussed here are not an entirely new phenomenon, especially in the repositories field, where many specifications were developed by ad-hoc communities that later matured into stable organisations. For example, at a meeting in Santa Fe in1999 a group of researchers in the ePrints community started the Open Archives Initiative (OAI) to develop a common metadata harvesting specification for linking research paper collections, and secured funding from a range of education foundations (Van de Sompel & Lagoze, 2000; Kiernan, 1999; Luce, 2001).

5-Year Incubation Period

Each case study can be construed as the incubation of specifications that may eventually move into more formal processes, or move from an ad-hoc community into a more formal governance structure, or in some fashion execute an "exit strategy" from reliance on core funding form its initial sponsor. In which case, it may be useful to know how long such an incubation period may last.

In the case of XCRI, the incubation period has been around 5-6 years from initial community formation to the ratification of a European standard, and potentially also a national standard. For SWORD, an IETF RFP may be published in late 2010 or early 2011, an incubation period of around 5 years. For Leap2A, a more formalised consortium and governance model is currently emerging in 2010, around 4-5 years after initial community formation. This is illustrated in the timeline in Figure 4.

A period of 5 years (+/- one year) would seem to be the lifecycle of each of the specifications from initial requirements to transition from incubation into a more formal state. While not particularly rigorous, this may provide a useful

Figure 4. Timeline of the three specifications showing some of the key events.

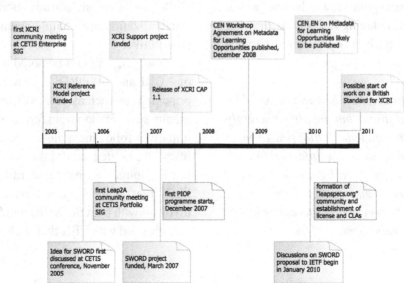

metric for funding agencies considering this approach to establishing interoperability, as it can be used to estimate the approximate lifetime funding requirement for such a specification.

Based on published budgets[20], we estimate the total funding of each project are as follows:

- **XCRI:** Support project and Reference Model project, 2005-2010: £255,000; Implementation mini-projects: £250,000.
- **Leap2A:** Support effort (via CETIS) 2006-2010: £150,000; Implementation projects (PIOP): £145,000
- **SWORD:** Support project (via UKOLN) 2007-2010: £120,000.

(It is more difficult to assess the implementation investment for SWORD, as there is no identifiable programme. However there have been projects funded that involve SWORD implementation)

CONCLUSION

While "community specifications" are problematic to define, the three cases presented in this paper represent initiatives at the more ad-hoc end of the informal standards spectrum. However, in each case we see connections with both formal standardisation processes and established specification consortia; in each case what is occurring can be construed as the incubation of specifications that may eventually move into more formal processes.

However, the cases we have described here are not entirely grassroots communities but have been deliberately incubated by a UK funding agency, and utilising the services of Innovation Support Centres with existing connections and expertise in more formal standards setting organisations and processes. With this in mind, tt would be incorrect to generalize from what may be a very unusual sample to the dynamics of specification communities in other sectors or that operate under a different support model. However we can draw some conclusions about the common characteristics of this small sample:

- Initial formation is ad-hoc, within an existing community, typically in a face-to-face setting such as a SIG meeting or conference
- Early engagement with sponsoring funding agency
- An incubation period of 5 years from initial idea to exit strategy
- Stable community support from 1-3 individuals (typically only funded one day per week) in receipt of funding from the primary sponsor
- Strong connections between the community and both formal standards and more established specification consortia through involvement of ISCs
- Building on or inspired by open web standards
- Developed principally via public mailing list and wiki
- Positioning of specifications in a wide range of interoperability scenarios, involving personal technologies and third-party services, not just enterprise integration
- Close engagement with implementers, and primacy of implementation and adoption as core concerns

Overall we feel that this model has been very successful for JISC, and may be of interest to similar agencies in other countries.

The approach has higher impact than a single project that develops a specification as part of typical research and technology development activity, yet also has a far lower cost than typical large-scale projects such as Framework 6/7 Integrated Projects (IPs). They operate over a far longer term than typical funded activities by formal standardisation projects and are consequently much more expensive; however the intent is different: such projects are aimed at drafting standards based on already-established requirements, rather than incubating specifications from an early stage.

When attempting to generalize or replicate this approach, the role of ISCs in connecting this work with wider standardisation processes and established consortia should also be taken into account; each community has been able to tap into a pool of wider expertise and intelligence on standards that have aided their progress and avoided potential conflicts with formal standards.

REFERENCES

Allinson, J., Francois, S., & Lewis, S. (2008). SWORD: Simple Web-service Offering Repository Deposit. *Ariadne, 54,* Retrieved from http://www.ariadne.ac.uk/issue54/allinson-et-al/

Allinson, J., & Heery, R. (2006). Deposit API. *UKOLN Wiki.* Retrieved March 30, 2010 from http://www.ukoln.ac.uk/repositories/digirep/index/Deposit_API

Blind, K., & Gauch, S. (2008). Trends in ICT standards: the relationship between European standardisation bodies and standards consortia. *Telecommunications Policy, 32*(7), 503–513. doi:10.1016/j.telpol.2008.05.004

Brand, S. (1994). *How Buildings Learn.* New York: Viking.

CEN. (2008). *CWA 15903: Metadata for Learning Opportunities (MLO) – Advertising.* Retrieved March 30, 2010 from ftp://ftp.cenorm.be/PUBLIC/CWAs/e-Europe/WS-LT/CWA15903-00-2008-Dec.pdf

Cooper, A. (2010). *The Best of Both Worlds: Formal Public Standardisation and Open Community Development.* Paper presented at JISC CETIS Future of Interoperability Standards workshop, Bolton, UK. Retrieved from http://wiki.cetis.ac.uk/images/e/e3/Best_of_Both_Worlds.doc

DIN. (2006). *DIN PAS 1068 (2006-12) Learning, Education and Training With Special Consideration Of E-learning - Guideline For The Description Of Educational Offers.* Retrieved April 1, 2010, from http://infostore.saiglobal.com/store/Details.aspx?ProductID=885033

Grant, S. (2009). *LEAP2A: A specification for e-portfolio portability and interoperability.* Retrieved March 30, 2010, from http://newsweaver.co.uk/alt/e_article001402921.cfm

Grant, S. (2010). Portfolio Interoperability Projects. *CETIS Wiki.* Retrieved March 30, 2010 from http://wiki.cetis.ac.uk/Portfolio_interoperability_projects/

IETF. (2007). *The Atom Publishing Protocol.* Retrieved from http://www.ietf.org/rfc/rfc5023.txt

Kiernan, V. (1999). 'Open Archives' Project Promises Alternative To Costly Journals. *Chronicle of Higher Education.* Retrieved March 30, 2010, from http://chronicle.com/article/Open-Archives-Project/32985/

Lewis, S., Hayes, L., Newton-Wade, V., Corfield, A., Davis, R., Donohue, T., & Wilson, S. (2009). If SWORD is the answer, what is the question?: Use of the Simple Web-service Offering Repository Deposit protocol. *Program: electronic library and information systems, 43*(4), 407-418.

Luce, R. (2001). The Open Archives Initiative: Interoperable, Interdisciplinary Author Self-Archiving Comes of Age. *The Serials Librarian, 40*(1/2), 173–182. doi:10.1300/J123v40n01_15

Recordon, D. (2008). The OWF Way. *OWF Wiki.* Retrieved March 30, 2010, from http://open-web.pbworks.com/The-OWF-Way

Smart, C. (2010). Leap2A: Enabling e-portfolio portability. *JISC website.* Retrieved March 30, 2010 from http://www.jisc.ac.uk/publications/briefingpapers/2010/bpleap2a.aspx

Van de Sompel, H., & Lagoze, C. (2000). The Santa Fe Convention of the Open Archives Initiative. *D-Lib Magazine, 6*(2). doi:10.1045/february2000-vandesompel-oai

Van Eecke, P., & Truyens, M. (2009). Standardization in the European Information and Technology Sector: Official Procedures on the Verge of Being Overhauled. *Shidler Journal. of Law, Commerce & Technology, 5*(11). Retrieved April 1, 2010, from http://www.lctjournal.washington.edu/vol5/a11VanEecke.html

Wilson, S. (2008). CEN endorses European Metadata for Learning Opportunities. *Scott's Workblog.* Retrieved April 2, 2010, from http://zope.cetis.ac.uk/members/scott/blogview?entry=20081021140752

Wilson, S., & Velayutham, K. (2009). Creating an innovation-oriented technology strategy. *Horizon, 17*(3), 245–255. doi:10.1108/10748120910993277

WTO. (1994, April 14). *Agreement on Technical Barriers to Trade, Marrakesh Agreement Establishing the World Trade Organization.* Geneva, Switzerland: WTO.

ENDNOTES

[1] http://www.jisc.ac.uk/

[2] http://www.jisc.ac.uk/whatwedo/programmes/eframework.aspx

[3] e.g., http://www.jisc.ac.uk/whatwedo/programmes/elearningcapital/courseinfo.aspx

[4] http://xcri.org

[5] http://www.swordapp.org/

[6] http://intrallect.com/

[7] http://www.cen-ltso.net/main.aspx?put=1048

[8] http://sourceforge.net/mailarchive/message.php?msg_name=f032cc0610032006220o385 3b646ya34a48e2f4e57e29%40mail.gmail.com

[9] Personal correspondence with Adrian Stevenson of the SWORD project, February 2010.

[10] http://www.leapspecs.org/

[11] http://wiki.cetis.ac.uk/Portfolio_interoperability_projects

[12] http://www.ietf.org/rfc/rfc4287.txt

[13] http://www.imsglobal.org/ep/

[14] http://mahara.org/

[15] http://www.pebblepad.co.uk/

[16] personal correspondence with Simon Grant, 2010

[17] http://wiki.leapspecs.org/2R

[18] http://openwebfoundation.org/

[19] The Atom Syndication Format (RFC 4287; see http://www.ietf.org/rfc/rfc4287.txt) and the Atom Publishing Protocol (RFC 5023; see http://www.ietf.org/rfc/rfc5023.txt)

[20] See http://jisc.ac.uk

This work was previously published in the International Journal of IT Standards and Standardization Research (IJITSR), Volume 8, Issue 2, edited by Kai Jakobs, pp. 74-86, copyright 2010 by IGI Publishing (an imprint of IGI Global)

Chapter 16
Concepts and Standardization in Areas Relating to Competence

Simon Grant
JISC CETIS, UK

Rowin Young
JISC CETIS, UK

ABSTRACT

This paper reviews terminology, motivation, history and current work in areas relating to skill or competence. Many useful services, clarifying pathways within and from education to employment, self-assessment, and selection would be facilitated by better standardization of the format in which related definitions are represented, and also by a standard approach to representing the structured sets often called frameworks. To be effective, information models underlying interoperability specifications must be based on common conceptual models; the authors propose one such model as a work in progress. The authors see the way forward as reaching greater consensus about the components of competence, including intended learning outcomes, agreement on a model for frameworks allowing reuse of and comparison between components in and between frameworks, and investigation of how requirements and claims for skill and competence can be coordinated in the light of common practice in recruitment.

INTRODUCTION

This paper is prompted by the sharp rise in interest in electronic representations of skills, competencies, learning outcomes, and related definitions. In response to this interest, the paper asks several fundamental questions about this whole area. The key question is, how can we progress through concepts and models towards the kind of useful specifications and standards that can enable the many real services that may well be demanded? The paper's approach is primarily to review and

DOI: 10.4018/978-1-4666-2160-2.ch016

synthesize existing work, but additionally the opportunity is taken to present a new proposal, for the representation of the many related kinds of "framework" structures of skills, competencies, etc., which are widespread across very many domains in education and employment. This is offered for further discussion and critique.

COMPETENCE: CONCEPTS AND TERMINOLOGY

This first main section addresses the different terms used, and offers first suggestions for drawing them together.

The term competence is subject to a range of subtly different interpretations across different standards and projects. In natural language, it refers to "the condition of being capable; ability" (HarperCollins, 1994), encompassing notions of possessing sufficient skill and knowledge in order to fulfil some role or perform some task. Interpretations used by standards in the competence domain (discussed below) share this general sense, but are complicated and diverge from each other in the detailed breakdown of its meaning. This can raise difficulties in sharing competence information as apparently synonymous terms may actually refer to somewhat different qualities. This poses a particular problem for competence information that is intended to be processed by machines rather than humans, whether because of mismatching terms or, potentially more seriously, different meanings assigned to the same term in different systems.

The HR-XML Consortium uses the term "competency" rather than "competence", specifying that competencies are "measurable characteristics" (HR-XML Consortium, 2007), and recognising that "some competencies can be objectively measured, whereas others may only be subjectively recognized." Although, as the name implies, the specification is particularly orientated towards business recruitment and recognition, it is eas-

ily adaptable towards educational and training contexts.

One issue that regularly arises is the question of whether competence is a binary quality or not. In natural language, and in other domains such as law and biology, competence is seen as a binary, someone is either competent or not. In the educational domain, however, some uses such as that of RDCEO (IMS, 2002) and IMS Learning Design (IMS, 2003) Level C suggest that competence or competency can be graded on a scale, and that it can have degrees or "dimensions" (RDCEO).

A competence may be made up of a number of sub-competences, for example, competence in a foreign language requires the separate skills of understanding written or spoken text and constructing written or spoken responses; these can be represented through the use of multiple linked elements. Whereas lower level competences may be seen as binary, these higher level ones might be seen as able to be partially fulfilled.

The TENCompetence project's definition of competence (TENCompetence, 2009) makes explicit the significance of context or community of practice, describing a competence as being a disposition or latent attribute of an individual, team or organisation that is situational and identified and defined in a community of practice. Similarly, the MedBiquitous definition of competence, "possession of sufficient and necessary knowledge, skill and attitude by an individual to allow her to safely and effectively perform a specific job" (MedBiquitous, 2009) is tightly focused on professional context.

HR-XML sees a statement of competency as very similar to a statement of Knowledge, Abilities, Skills and Other Characteristics ("KASOC") which formed the basis for their concept. The KASOC acronym is specifically excluded by HR-XML in part because the term competency is a far more familiar concept and was felt to be more meaningful (although this familiarity can be seen to lead to confusion and multiple meanings).

The Chartered Institute for Personnel and Development makes a distinction between *competency*, "the behaviours that employees must have, or must acquire, to input into a situation in order to achieve high levels of performance" and *competence*, "a system of minimum standards ... demonstrated by performance and outputs" (CIPD, 2009). This suggests that an individual can demonstrate competence without necessarily acquiring the expected competencies, or achieve competencies in a field without necessarily demonstrating competence.

The concepts of competence and competency are clearly closely related to, although not the same as, the concept of an intended learning outcome (ILO) from a course of study or vocational training. An ILO is a statement of the standard of knowledge, skill, etc. a learner is expected to acquire and to be able to demonstrate by the end of a course of study or training; it is equivalent to the objectives of a learning opportunity as defined by the Metadata for Learning Opportunities (CEN, 2008) specification and the European Learner Mobility work (EuroLM, 2009).

The relationship between the concepts is subtle. The European Qualifications Framework (Education and Culture DG, 2008) includes the acquisition of competence as a component of an ILO, along with knowledge and skills, defining competence in the context of the EQF in terms of responsibility and autonomy. This seems to be very similar to the more common definition of competence as encompassing knowledge and skill, but the distinction drawn within the EQF is that competence utilises skill and knowledge rather than being part of its construction. In this conception, competence transcends knowledge and skill because it utilises them selectively: competence is not "merely" the possession of knowledge or skill but the ability to take action according to the most appropriate information or perform the most appropriate action. Competence suggests the internalising of knowledge and skill to the point

at which they, and the instinctive selection of the most appropriate knowledge and skills, become an innate part of a person's responses.

In this paper, we see these views discussed above as being partially true, but needing to be drawn together. We understand both competence and competency as being related to the knowledge, skill and attitude or behaviour required for the effective performance of a task or role, as being measurable and certifiable, and composed of a number of individual components. From this perspective of drawing concepts together, it seems most straightforward to regard competence as a binary quality.

For technical implementation, a competence record may at minimum be represented as a single entry containing a unique identifier pointing to a description of the competence.

Later in this paper, we also discuss the relationships between competence or competency elements. The terms "competency framework" and "skills framework" have been used to describe a set of these elements related in a structure, where some are components of others, and we reuse the term framework. However, it should be noted that "framework" is also often used to denote an overarching structure, whereas here we may mean a relatively simple and small structure maintained by a single authority.

MOTIVATION FOR STANDARDIZATION IN THE AREA OF COMPETENCE

This section sets out the clear motivation for work in this area, which is ultimately to provide a firm foundation for many desired services, helping learners to manage information about the aspects of their competence, and to access relevant learning, employment, and potentially even leisure opportunities.

The Need for Common Languages

There are many reasons why people want to know about other people's, or their own, abilities. People hold positions, and perform roles, in industry, commerce, government, education, family life, wider social life – all walks of life in fact – and successful performance in these positions requires their holders to be able to do certain things to meet the needs, and conform to the expectations, of others playing related roles in related positions. In older societies much more static that our modern one, children may have learned to fulfil the roles of their parents by observation, imitation, and correction. Also frequent in the past were periods – possibly long periods – of training or apprenticeship, whereby less experienced people could learn about occupations or trades from more experienced people that were not necessarily their parents. This form of society may have worked adequately where just about anyone could in principle fill any role, and it was just a matter of accident of birth who actually got to fill the roles – as persists in the institution of monarchy today. However, it is not difficult to see that, particularly when societies compete with each other, it makes more sense to place into positions those most suited to fill them. Moreover, in a changing society, new positions arise. To operate most effectively, society as a whole needs some means of matching available people with available positions, and this needs knowledge about the abilities of all concerned.

It seems that the mechanisms in our society have not kept up with this need, if indeed they ever did work effectively. There are several different views about the nature of education, only one of which is that what is taught and learned as part of education should be what is required to fill roles in working life. And even where that is that view, what is required in working life keeps changing, so that it is difficult for an educational system to keep up. At the same time, increasing mobility of jobs, and increasing change in employment, means that employers are less and less likely to take on those leaving school or university, keep them for a good part of their working lives, and therefore have the motivation to train them adequately on the job. There is increasing pressure for educational institutions to provide work-ready graduates.

Looking at this more generally, there is an increasing need overall for a common language about abilities, to be used for communication between educators, trainers, employers, learners, assessors / evaluators, professional bodies, awarders of licences or certificates, customers / clients, careers advisors, and any other stakeholders, when referring to what individuals want to or should learn, or what they have learned, in terms of ability, capability, competence, or whatever the most relevant term is in a particular context. This common language is needed for the expression of requirements for jobs, requirements for prospective students on higher courses, the outcomes of learning processes (whether connected to formal education, or to informal learning in the workplace or in wider society), and the claims made by (or about) individuals to have attained the outcomes, to have the abilities, to be competent, etc.

Matching Claims and Requirements

It is not just the language which needs to be harmonised, to relate together claims for competency and requirements for it, because both requirements and claims have significant structure, and the corresponding elements of those structures need to be matched against each other. So it is vital to specify just what those elements are, even to start to enable automatic matching that is neither simply text-based, nor using arcane artificial intelligence.

The matching currently done in this area, as part of recruitment, tends to be either labour-intensive or of variable quality or both. One of the persistent problems is that requirements, particularly as specified by employers, tend to bear little relationship to what learning opportunities aim at giving, or what they actually give, learners who complete them. Learners who want to provide evidence for their abilities turn readily to what they see defined as the learning outcomes, and therefore risk missing connecting with employers' requirements.

The Need for Agreed Frameworks

Going along with the increasing diversity, change and potential fragmentation of occupations and their requirements, is the need to recognise quite small units of ability, and to be able to build these up in different ways to express the needs of different roles and positions. We see such frameworks being expressed, for example, as National Occupational Standards (NOSs) in the UK. Conventionally, these are all expressed in similar ways, with the requirements in a particular area being analysed in terms of what a person needs to be able to do, and what underlying knowledge is needed to support effective performance of what they are doing. But though these have similar form, they vary enough to greatly hinder putting them into a common format capable of distinguishing the parts that seem to be important to distinguish.

From Common Language to Common Specifications

The introduction of ICT tools into this area of life brings an extra set of requirements. If IT systems supporting the areas mentioned above are to work together, the common language necessary for human mutual understanding needs to be more tightly defined so that it is machine processable in some way. It needs to be clear when an ability referred to is the same, or different, or related, in a way that is not dependent on human background knowledge and ability to process language in an extremely sophisticated manner. If tools use frameworks, and if those frameworks are to be decoupled from the tools, they would ideally be expressed in a standard format which is readable or importable by any tool implementing that standard. E-portfolio tools are a good example of the

kind of tool that would benefit from a standard format for frameworks.

This paper is not concerned with the processes of agreeing occupational standards themselves, such as NOSs, which are the province of bodies representative of industry and education. Rather, we are looking for the possible standardization of

- Formats for definitions related to competence, and their exposure
- Formats for frameworks related to competence, and their exposure
- Relationships across frameworks
- Claims and requirements related to competence

Facilitated Services

We could expect various services to be greatly facilitated by widespread adoption of common definitions of competence or competency, if they were expressed, singly and in frameworks, according to common formats. These could easily include:

- Establishing whether something is claimed to fulfil a requirement;
- Searching for and matching people and opportunities;
- Searching for pathways to get from a low state of achievement to fulfilling a higher requirement;
- Assessment / assignment / recruitment for employment positions, external or internal;
- Skills gap analysis, and management of corporate competency profiles;
- Self-assessment of abilities / knowledge / skills / competences in conjunction with preparing CVs etc.;
- Selection of students to participate in educational opportunities;
- Selection of learning materials to help towards learning objectives.

There are probably several more.

HISTORY AND BACKGROUND OF STANDARDIZATION IN THE AREA

Any standardization effort should start by looking at related efforts that have been made in the past, and current initiatives that may have related objectives, to try to ensure that standards do not multiply and diverge. The following two sections address this.

IMS RDCEO and IEEE RCD

The IMS Reusable Definition of Competency or Educational Objective (RDCEO) (IMS, 2002) specification "defines an information model for describing, referencing, and exchanging definitions of competencies." It attempts to identify a set of core or key contextually neutral characteristics of competencies that can be shared across different learning systems. Released in 2002, this work was subsequently further developed as IEEE Reusable Competency Definitions with the most current version being released in 2008 (IEEE, 2008). Both IMS RDCEO and IEEE RCD avoid attempting to specify how a competency should be defined, but allow generic statements within a definition. It is not clear how this approach of including some detail in the definitions sits with trying to keep all definitions separate and able to be referred to separately, to avoid duplication and the errors liable to build up in potentially having several versions of the same wording.

IMS Learning Design

IMS Learning Design (IMS LD) (IMS, 2003) is a specification for modelling and designing learning processes, consisting of three levels of which the third, most extensive (and least implemented) is Competency Based Learning. IMS LD does not itself define competency but instead refers to the IMS RDCEO definition, but it is noteworthy as it interprets competencies as being potentially gradable and therefore not necessarily binary.

XCRI

The eXchanging Course-Related Information (XCRI) project (XCRI, 2010) has developed an XML schema to enable learning providers and information services to easily share information on learning opportunities, increasing access to and potential participation in education and training. Competence statements are clearly a significant aspect of this, both for establishing entry requirements and in relation to the course's intended learning outcomes. However, XCRI does not define any particular structure to a statement of what the objective, or intended outcome, of a learning opportunity might be.

Leap2A

The Leap2A (Grant, 2010) specification supports interoperability between e-portfolio tools and similar systems and the exchange of information between them. It is specifically intended for systems that allow users to manage their own portfolios, rather than for institutions to define institution-wide information. In line with its intentions, Leap2A allows the transport of portfolio information referring to skills or competencies, which are called "abilities" in Leap2A. In most cases, the definition of an ability is envisaged as given at a URL on the server of the body responsible for that definition. But in cases where the learner wishes to define their own skill, this is also allowed.

PROJECTS IN THE AREA, AND THEIR OUTCOMES OR OBJECTIVES

There are several projects active in this area. The brief notes here give a sense of what the ones we know about are doing.

TENCompetence

The TENCompetence project (TENCompetence, 2010) has worked on the development and implementation of infrastructure to support individuals, groups and organisations in lifelong competence development. The project takes a competence-based approach to lifelong learning which is tightly tied to a specific work, educational or other context. The ability to effectively exchange competence-related information is therefore a significant factor in this work as it is crucial for supporting transition between learning or training providers.

ICOPER

The ICOPER (ICOPER, 2010b) project is developing best practice in the use of educational standards for the exchange and reuse of competence models, learning designs and educational content. As part of the Needs Analysis stage, the Competency Development working group (ICOPER, 2010a) is building on existing competency specifications to develop a standard description of Educational Learning Offerings based on learning outcomes.

MedBiquitous

The MedBiquitous Competences working group (MedBiquitous, 2010) develops standards and good practice guidance for linking educational content to a competency framework within medical education. The working group wiki provides extensive information on the work of the group.

ECOTOOL

The eCOTOOL project aims to develop an information model of the Europass Certificate Supplement, within which skill or competence is a central feature. It will therefore be investigating how to structure definitions of competences effectively, taking the agriculture sector as a working example.

CONCEPTUAL MODELS OF COMPETENCE FOR INFORMATION MODELS

Conceptual models provide a vital underpinning for information models, helping ensure that the concepts represented in different information models are compatible, and that specifications built on those information models will actually help with interoperability and portability.

There are some existing conceptual models that deal with competence in some way, but none of them go into any detail, for instance, about what the difference is between the different kinds of competency – whether one follows the EQF in distinguishing learning outcomes in terms of knowledge, skills and competence, or the other approaches mentioned in earlier sections.

Schmidt and Braun (2008), for example, beyond allowing tree structures of competencies, distinguish only levels and scales, and we have found levels tricky in similar contexts. Other authors identify various kinds of "qualifier" for competencies, but are not so clear about the conceptual model surrounding this. Representing things simply as "qualifiers" fits well into an information model approach, where they would be sub-elements of the competency element, but more important at the conceptual modelling level is to understand what the qualifier concepts really mean, and how they relate to each other and to other related concepts.

One possibility for qualifiers, similar to what is being proposed within the ICOPER project, is to abstract common elements that are frequently referred to across different definitions of skill or competence. Whether these are then called "context", as in current ICOPER drafts, or use some other term, is less important than the idea itself.

Our own cognitive modelling work has detailed the relationships across a range of potentially formal processes surrounding the individual, including opportunities for learning or work, assessment, and recognition, which includes the award of credit and qualifications. The distinction between knowledge, skills and competence finally makes sense only in terms of an analysis of the processes within the individual – even if this analysis is relatively superficial by any standards of psychology.

Figure 1 is a selection from a more detailed conceptual model (see, for example, Grant, 2009). Here, a knowledge learning outcome is understood

as being about a desired pattern of belief of the individual. A skill learning outcome is about individual behaviour patterns, but also needs to be supported by knowledge. Competence, on the other hand, is always described in terms of a real world situation, and seems to be about behaviour patterns and knowledge that together produce outcomes conforming to agreed quality criteria, in agreed real-world contexts.

An area where this model does not attempt to delve is whether frameworks can be conceptually distinguished from individual definitions. Two considerations argue rather for the idea that they are interchangeable. First, practically any competence-related definition could in principle be broken down to a set of related components. This is true as much of practical skills, where sewing skill could be analysed in terms of threading a needle, handling fabric, accuracy in locating

Figure 1. A concept map of several concepts related to competence, drawn from a wider model.

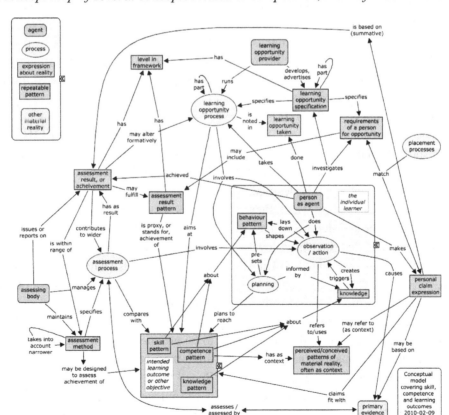

the holes in a button, and many more; or cognitive skills, where to do long division you have to multiply, subtract, etc. But while some people might be interested in the finer details, many people would not be. Looking the other way, a framework that is normally used as a structure may be relevant to someone else only as a single, high-level definition.

These considerations point away from a rigid distinction between frameworks and individual definitions. In consequence, if a definition can be seen ambivalently as a single entity or as a framework, when it is included in another framework, it has to be clear which is meant. One can include just the top-level title and definition, or import the detailed structure as well. Importing the detailed structure will entail not only the subsidiary competence concepts and definitions, but also the parts of their competency map that relate them together.

This duality between individual definitions and frameworks may also in part account for the very wide variation in the degree to which definitions are detailed. Some programmes of education or development use only very broad headings for the skills and competencies that are proposed for learning, perhaps because there are many acceptable ways to develop them. It is up to the individual learner to decide the detail. This is in contrast to specific qualifications, licences, or tests, which may set out in considerable detail not only the precise skills that are to be learned, but also the means of assessment by which they are to be verified. Given these differences of application, it is not surprising that some high-level skill and competence terms are vague and not well specified.

One reason why people may use high-level definitions that may seem vague is that competence in certain roles can be fulfilled in several different ways. People rarely discuss management competence without mentioning management style, and it is reasonable to suppose that different styles of managing require a different set of skills. Thus,

assessment of management competence in practice cannot simply consist of assessing one particular set of sub-skills, which would be relevant only to one management style. Competence in any artistic endeavour is also likely to have a large style component, as may other creative competences, even extending to computer programming. All these examples warn us that a competence does not necessarily have a single decomposition.

A final point follows from the observation that people like creating their own maps, their own frameworks, and their own definitions. To get useful inferences across frameworks, in the style of the Semantic Web, there will need to be many other relationships specified, as well as the relationships necessary for individual maps, and the mapping of inclusion of externally defined competence concepts. For instance, it would be very useful to know, of two competence-related definitions, whether either one covers more than the other.

One way of representing both framework structure, and relationships between parts of different frameworks, would be by using the W3C's Simple Knowledge Organization System, SKOS (W3C, 2009). This is discussed further below.

THE WAY FORWARD FOR STANDARDIZATION IN THE AREA OF COMPETENCE

In this section we will bring together the issues introduced above in a general discussion, arguing that there are certain areas that could now be taken forward towards standardization. It is useful to distinguish between separate definitions related to competence, and frameworks related to competence. Jobs and roles require abilities that tend to be grouped together rather than isolated, and this is the motivation for representing frameworks. Recall that when we use the term "framework", we do not mean a large, overarching structure, but just a set of definitions and documentation related to a particular application area, role, industry, educational programme, etc.

In anticipation of the emergence of definitions and frameworks of competency, it also makes sense to explore a common format for what could perhaps turn out to be the most practically useful standardization effort, namely, the common ground linking claims by individuals to possess aspects of competence, and employer or institutional requirements for aspects of competence in those applying for relevant positions – jobs or courses.

Individual Definitions in the Area of Competence

For laying down a detailed standard model for separate concept definitions in the area of competence, there is a great deal of practice already established, and as this practice does not follow a common model, a detailed standardization would require the restructuring or even rewriting of many, if not most, currently used definitions and frameworks related to competence.

Given the current diversity of practice, two approaches are plausible. First, it is possible to standardise on the common elements evident across current practice. This is a remarkably straightforward task, given the lack of common elements. In effect, the common ground is the same ground as is common to very many documents, and can be concisely expressed as a few elements from Dublin Core (DC): title, content or description, authorship, dates of publication, etc. What is generally missing, in order to turn these elements into a specification workable for learning (and other) technology is a universal identifier, and what is commonly accepted as the most useful form of identifier is the http URL or URI, as in the widespread semantic web related vision of "linked data". Given this basis, any atomic definition can be given a URI, and at the URL that is arrived at by dereferencing that URI, there can be the DC metadata, together with either the actual content

of the definition, perhaps in HTML or XHTML format, or a link to a document designed for printing, in any common format.

The second approach would be to look at the extra features that often appear within definitions related to competence, and to construct a permissive schema to allow representation of these in a way in which information which is common is recognised as such. To be standardized effectively, such features have to be clearly distinct.

Looking at the features of models that are currently proposed, alongside existing specifications such as HR-XML and IEEE RCD (as IMS RDCEO), some features appear that could perhaps be seen as distinct. But substantial further work would have to be done, and the consensus processes followed, to facilitate people moving towards agreement on them. Here is a list of potential features (or "facets") of competence:

- Professional, occupational or educational context
- Level of responsibility, or role
- Constraints above those inherent in the context
- Knowledge of subject matter required
- Tools or equipment provided
- Other support provided.

Some of these might, in some frameworks, be bound up in the concept of "level", but as there is no universal standard level scheme, the meaning inherent in levels would have to be broken down in terms of the level descriptors, so that it could be compared in terms of the features or facets above.

RDCEO does not specify particular facets. Instead, it provides a more general purpose structure. Not to be confused with the common identifier, title and description, RDCEO's definition element allows a model to contain statement names and texts. However, this effectively ducks the challenge of providing agreed facets. RDCEO adds nothing towards defining what facets are actually useful and potentially agreed. Rather, it could be taken as a warning that it may in practice be impossible to agree any universal facets at all.

However, there is one aspect of competence-related information that comes up over and over again: some division along the lines of knowledge, skill, and something else (competence, attitude, other attributes...). This is loosely related to the method of assessment. Knowledge and cognitive skills can be assessed through ordinary paper and computer-based tests, or direct question and answer. Practical, transferable skills can be assessed through practical tests, given appropriate equipment. The other aspects of competence are those that can only be fully assessed in the context of use, or something very like it. But competence as a whole involves the use of knowledge and skill, so other forms of assessment may still be relevant.

Relationships between Definitions

Relationships between terms in the same framework seem to raise few issues of difficulty. People envisage greater and lesser, broader or narrower, definitions, and when frameworks related to competence are documented, this is clear in the structure of the documentation. Typically, a framework may consist of several areas, and each area may consist of a set of descriptors, which may cover either or both of what people are expected to do to fulfil that definition, and what people are expected to know, perhaps to support their effective actions. When definitions are used electronically, however, it can easily happen that parts of definitions are reused outside their original context. If the definition components are to be understood correctly outwith their original context, the relationships between the parts and their whole needs to be made explicit, and included when the part is taken away from its natural context.

As this is an example of a general knowledge representation structure, it would seem reasonable to use the most widespread general definitions for these relationships. SKOS, mentioned above, has relationships that seem to be good contend-

ers for this role. The properties skos:broader and skos:narrower are generalised from general knowledge organisation systems, and applied to competence components, "A skos:broader B" would mean that B is a broader term than A, which could mean that A is a component of B. Conversely, "A skos:narrower B" could reasonably be taken to mean that B is a component of A. This would fit well with a view that definitions are just concepts, and concepts as such cannot contain other concepts.

However, while this may be an adequate start, simply having broader and narrower relationships does not capture the distinction between, on the one hand, a greater competency comprising a set of lesser competencies, and on the other hand, a competency having different "styles", each involving a potentially different set of lesser competencies. This remains as further work.

An Information Model for Frameworks Related to Competence

There appears to be an obvious and immediate need here – the case of e-portfolio tools was introduced above. The question is what is a general purpose structure for a framework format, which will cover existing frameworks adequately so that they need only to be fitted in to the format, not radically restructured, and which will allow e-portfolio and other tools to use the framework?

The first requirement to consider is to specify the relationships between different parts of the same framework. If the parts of the framework are thought of as concepts, rather than expressions, SKOS relationships are well suited. If, rather, they are thought of as parts of a larger document, some whole-part relations may be preferred. Probably some work will have to be done to reach consensus on this, but it seems likely that the SKOS broader-narrower relationships might be initially acceptable, with the possible later addition of a mechanism to distinguish components of a competence from styles of a competence.

Different people, organisations or bodies may want to create different frameworks using, and reusing, some of the same definitions, or even whole frameworks. The relationships in each framework may differ. To allow for this, three considerations may be helpful.

1. Care needs to be given to whether given relationships are really inherent in a definition, that is, valid in all situations, or whether they might differ in different frameworks. The safer choice is the latter.
2. As a consequence, the preference will be to define the relationships as part of the framework, but not as part of the individual definitions. Conceptually, therefore, we should distinguish a relationship map, attached to the framework, but separate from the individual definitions.
3. A definition within a framework must be able to refer to an external one within its definition, and preferably without the need to duplicate all the information associated with the external definition.

In many ways it seems an obvious choice to use the SKOS mapping properties. As a relationship, skos:exactMatch can express your intention that your definition means just the same thing as, and is interchangeable with, someone else's definition. You could use skos:closeMatch to indicate that evidence for one is likely to be evidence for the other, albeit less reliably. The object of a skos:broadMatch relationship is a concept which satisfies more than your original concept, and therefore other people could provide evidence for the broader concept that automatically is taken to satisfy the narrower one. Conversely, you could suggest, using a skos:narrowMatch relationship, that your concept covered more than the external one, and attributing it implied attributing the narrower one. If two authorities agreed on reciprocal broadMatch-narrowMatch relationships between

competence concepts in their respective areas, it would give added confidence to inferences across the two.

Thus, a likely specification for frameworks related to competence could include these features.

- A framework could conceptually include a set of concepts and a structure map, though these need not necessarily be represented in separate sections of XML.
- The map could use skos:broader and skos:narrower relationships between the concepts in the same framework, with the possibility of refining that later to distinguish components from styles.
- The map could use any of the SKOS mapping properties for documenting relationships between your competence concepts and those belonging to others.
- External concepts and frameworks could be reused and extended in a structure map created by you.
- Metadata could be given in each framework, referring particularly to the structure map: some metadata could also be carried in the competency concepts.
- When reusing external frameworks, there could be a way of specifying whether just to take the top concept and definition, or to import the whole framework as it is.

These points are illustrated in Figure 2.

This is perhaps not quite as simple as could be imagined, but anything simpler would risk losing some important feature. Another question is whether this is simple enough, or can be represented simply enough, to be processed by tools such as e-portfolio systems, where there is the desire to incorporate a framework into their tools and related practice. But in any case, this seems like a plausible suggestion for a conceptual model of how skill and competence concepts and structure could be related.

Figure 2. The structure of competency frameworks – a possible model

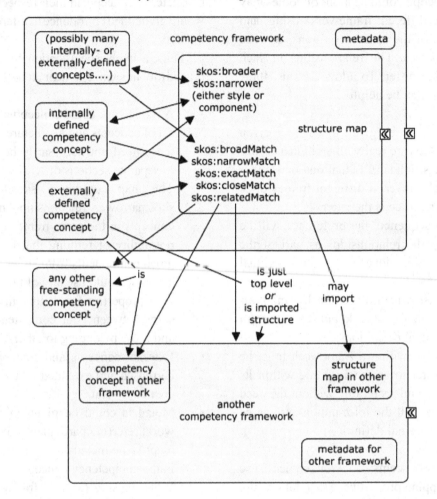

Claims and Requirements Related to Competence

We can now attempt to specify a common format at least for claims and requirements. The conceptual model in the previous section has been drawn to include "personal claim expressions" and the attributes of people wanted for opportunities. The model illustrates the view that there is significant correlation between these two.

Helpful ideas on claims come from PDP and e-portfolio practice. Often, an individual wants to claim an ability of some sort, usually related to some kind of competence, and the e-portfolio medium allows linking from that claim directly

to some kinds of evidence to support the claim. There are a small number of obvious sources for supplying relevant evidence which might be accepted by those relying on it, and which are often used in evidence.

- Qualifications (and other professional grades, certificates, or other public recognition of status) are perhaps the most classic form of evidence. Vocational qualifications may even be based around definitions related to competence, though what academic qualifications are evidence of is more uncertain.

- It is possible that an assessment is designed directly to assess a competency, or it may be more or less related to that competency.
- Trusted witnesses have always played a part in evidence. This varies from expert judgement on whether a performance is itself expert, which can often only be judged by a human expert, to witness statements merely confirming that something actually took place.
- One of the things that witnesses can attest is to experience relevant to an ability, and particularly to a competency. It may be that it is not feasible to hold down a particular role without a certain competency, in which case simply holding the post is evidence. Or it may be that competency generally grows as a result of certain experiences.
- E-portfolio practice increasingly allows more primary evidence to be presented to interested parties. Clear examples of this could be videos of performances; links to discussion fora; links to informational artefacts produced; news or other web sites documenting the public results of a person's actions or interventions.

But at the same time, it must be recognised that one particular person's ability – in anything but the most mundane tasks – is never quite the same as another's. Personal style differs, but often also the particular mix of abilities that people use, say in management, is personal. The contexts in which experience is gained vary widely. Thus, a true and full claim of competence will almost always need to bridge the gap between the competency definition itself and the actual competence or component of competence claimed, with an individual explanation and clarification of what the claim is for. This also takes into account the fact (discussed above) that competence concepts vary wildly in their specificity. One can have a "definition" that merely states "team work" as a topic heading, in which case a personal claim needs to bridge a long way to explaining exactly what team working ability is actually claimed. In contrast, another definition of team work may go into great detail about the exact interpersonal skills used or required, and the context in which they are needed. In those cases, much less personal explanation is likely to be needed. In any case, an information model for a competency claim should include a free text field for this kind of explanatory detail.

Turning now to requirements, there seems to be some significant common ground with recruitment and interviewing practice. Reviewing sample person specifications reveals a grid, there are usually two columns, for "essential" and "desirable" characteristics (or a column stating whether a particular characteristic was essential or desirable), and each row represents a characteristic heading, with essential attributes and/or desirable attributes. Frequently, there is a third column, something like "method of assessment". This might be chosen from "application form", "interview", "presentation" if there is one, "reference" or possibly "certificates". Obviously, something like "assessment centre" could feature for applicable practice. The exact grouping of the rows varies, but a full model could easily include categories such as

- Qualifications
- Experience
- Knowledge
- Skills
- Attitudes and other qualities
- Other characteristics, attributes or criteria.

What is very promising for standardization about current practice is that, despite differences in detail, there seems to be a fundamental agreement about the nature of a person specification, in that anyone who has been involved in recruiting, or been recruited, with the help of a person specification would probably recognise all of them as reasonable examples. The underlying agreement gives the basis on which standardization is feasible, while the differences present the challenge to achieving consensus.

Perhaps the key to useful as well as viable standardization here is to allow the external form of the structures to remain recognisably the same, while trying to ensure that what could be matched automatically is represented in a format that allows sufficient machine processing to do the matching. Though the details remain to be investigated more thoroughly, it does appear that there is substantial overlap, which could be maximised in a number of ways.

- Qualifications would probably need a standardised representation of subject area, together with an internationally recognised or cross-referenced level.
- Assessment other than through recognised qualifications might benefit from categorisation of the general assessment method, and of the type of evidence taken into account, as well as a clear specification of the results that can come out of the assessment process. This can be combined with cohort performance information to get useful information about where applicants stand in relation to the norms of their peer groups.
- Experience would need a common model of occupational categories, plus an agreed scheme for level of responsibility.
- Knowledge, skills, attitudes and other qualities need to refer to commonly acknowledged definitions of the kind that have been discussed above.
- References might benefit from some common scheme for recognising status of the referee.
- Other primary evidence needs to be clearly connected with what it is presented as evidence for, though in any case it is difficult to see it being used in any automatic matching process, but rather in the conversion of a list of "possibles" to a short list for interview.

For many of these, it would only become viable to put them into practice given effective tools to help with the categorisation, labelling, classification, etc., based on the agreement of a good number of categories, balancing ease of understanding with sufficient discriminating power.

CONCLUSION

We have reviewed a range of issues relevant to potential standardization in the area of competence-related information. The way seems open now to integrate the work of several projects and initiatives, to feed in to proposed international standardization work. We conclude by briefly summarising the key points we believe should be taken into consideration.

Competence Concept Definitions

There needs to be more exploration of what consensus is possible around the different features/ qualifiers/facets proposed for competence concept definitions, including the knowledge/ skill/ context dependent distinctions. If genuinely common features become clear, a consensus will need to be reached on an information model for their representation, which might be quite simple.

Competency Frameworks

First, a minimal set of relationships needs to be agreed to cover good practice in relating the components of competence concepts to each other. SKOS properties should be considered, and may initially be adequate. Second, a set of relationships needs to be agreed for relating competence concepts within a framework to those in a different framework. The SKOS mapping properties should be considered, and again may well be adequate. This may lead towards an agreed specification for competence frameworks, in the foreseeable future.

Competency Claims and Requirements

The line of enquiry outlined above needs to be taken further, to reach a broad consensus on appropriate approaches to enhancing the automatic processing of the various elements potentially shared between a competency claim and a person specification, or similar document used in a selection process.

It remains as further work to investigate the requirements for and uses of the distinction between framework relationships indicating components, and those indicating styles.

REFERENCES

W3C. (2009) *SKOS Simple Knowledge Organization System home page*. Retrieved February 9, 2010, from http://www.w3.org/2004/02/skos/

CEN. (2008). *Metadata for Learning Opportunities (MLO)*. Advertising.

CIPD. (2009). *Competency and competency frameworks*. Retrieved February 11, 2010, from http://www.cipd.co.uk/subjects/perfmangmt/competnces/comptfrmwk.htm

Education and Culture DG. (2008). *The European Qualifications Framework for Lifelong Learning*. Retrieved February 8, 2010, from http://www.qcda.gov.uk/libraryAssets/media/Leaflet_on_the_EQF_en.pdf

Euro, L. M. (2009). *European Learner Mobility*. Retrieved February 8, 2010 from http://wiki.teria.no/confluence/display/EuropeanLearnerMobility

Grant, S. (2009). *Development of a conceptual model 5*. Retrieved February 10, 2010 from http://blogs.cetis.ac.uk/asimong/2009/12/11/development-of-a-conceptual-model-5/

Grant, S. (2010). *Leap2A Specification*. Retrieved February 8, 2010 from http://wiki.cetis.ac.uk/LEAP2A_specification

HarperCollins. (1994). *Collins English Dictionary*. Glasgow, UK: HarperCollins.

HR-XML Consortium. (2007). *Competencies (Measurable Characteristics)*. Retrieved February 15, 2010 from http://ns.hr-xml.org/2_5/HR-XML-2_5/CPO/Competencies.html

ICOPER. (2010a) *Competency Development WG*. Retrieved February 8, 2010 from http://www.icoper.org/icoper-big-picture/needs-analysis/Competency%20Development%20WG

ICOPER. (2010b). *ICOPER Best Practice Network*. Retrieved February 8, 2010 from http://www.icoper.org/

IEEE. (2008). *Data Model for Reusable Competency Definitions*. Washington, DC: Retrieved February 8, 2010 http://www.cen-ltso.net/main.aspx?put=652

IMS. (2002). *IMS Reusable Definition of Competency or Educational Objective Specification*. Retrieved 8 February 2010 from http://www.imsglobal.org/competencies/

IMS. (2003). *IMS Learning Design Specification*. Retrieved February 11, 2010 from http://www.imsglobal.org/learningdesign/

MedBiquitous. (2009). *MedBiquitous Competency Framework Specifications and Description Document Version: 0.3*. Retrieved Febrauy 13, 2010, from http://www.medbiq.org/working_groups/competencies/CompetencyFrameworkSpecification.pdf

MedBiquitous. (2010). *Competencies Working Group*. Retrieved February 8, 2010 from http://www.medbiq.org/working_groups/competencies/index.html

Schmidt, A., & Braun, S. (2008). People Tagging & Ontology Maturing: Towards Collaborative Competence Management. In *Proceedings of COOP '08, the 8th International Conference on the Design of Cooperative Systems*, Carry-le-Rouet, France. Retrieved February 152010, from http://publications.andreas.schmidt.name/ Braun_Schmidt_CollaborativeCompetenceManagement_COOP08.pdf

TENCompetence. (2009). *TENCompetence Frequently Asked Questions*. Retrieved February 15, from http://tencompetence-project.bolton.ac.uk/ node/123/

TENCompetence. (2010). *TENCompetence Foundation*. Retrieved February 8, 2010, from http:// www.tencompetence.org/

XCRI. (2010). *eXchanging Course-Related Information*. Retrieved February 8, 2010 from http:// www.xcri.org/

This work was previously published in the International Journal of IT Standards and Standardization Research (IJITSR), Volume 8, Issue 2, edited by Kai Jakobs, pp. 29-44, copyright 2010 by IGI Publishing (an imprint of IGI Global)

Chapter 17
Application Profiles and Tailor–Made Conformance Test Systems

Ingo Dahn
University Koblenz-Landau, Germany

Sascha Zimmermann
University Koblenz-Landau, Germany

ABSTRACT

This article examines the potential of application profiles and domain profiles as means to adapt technical specifications of data structures to particular needs. The authors argue that application profiling is better suited to increase the use of formal specifications than the creation of new specifications. The authors also describe a method to generate specific conformance test systems for machine-readable application profiles. The authors describe the respective tool set of the SchemaProf Application Profiling Tool and the Generic Test System and report on the experience of their usage in developing and introducing the IMS Common Cartridge domain profile.

INTRODUCTION

Application profiles are adaptations of specifications to the needs of particular communities. While there are many communities that develop application profiles, few only have the resources to implement a dedicated test system for testing conformance with these profiles. This becomes

even more severe if the profile involves several XML schemas or uses restrictions that cannot be expressed by XML schemas. The paper describes the role played by application profiles in the specification process. The development of the IMS Common Cartridge specification (IMS, 2008) serves as an example. Then SchemaProf, a tool to capture machine readable application

DOI: 10.4018/978-1-4666-2160-2.ch017

profiles, is described. Based on these profiles a Generic Test System can be instantiated to create a profile-specific Test System. The final section describes the actual experience gained with this technology. All views expressed in this paper are solely those of the authors and do not express any position of the mentioned organizations.

APPLICATION PROFILES – THEORY AND PRACTICE

Application Profiles and Alternatives

Only seldom general specifications meet exactly the needs of particular communities. Most existing specifications have been designed to support all cases of data exchange that could be envisaged as being relevant. Consequently, these specifications tend to become complex. From the point of view of a community, that intends to adopt a specification for its internal data exchange, such specifications are overloaded with many features which are not used (yet) by this community. While this rarely makes using the specification impossible – as most of the unnecessary features are usually optional – it makes implementing the full specification often complex without delivering additional benefits.

However, even the most generic specification shall miss to specify some issues that are needed for a particular community. Also this does not hinder the use of modern specifications as they contain extension points where the community may extend them at will, assuming that their extensions shall be tolerated by conformant systems designed for other communities and based on the same base specification.

These two modifications – eliminating superfluous elements from the specification and extending it with specific additional definitions – are the fundamental operations of application profiling as discussed below. Building the specifics needed by a community into an application profile offers important benefits:

- The application profile can be easily extended, should additional demands occur which have been foreseen in the generic specification.
- Bringing the own specific demands into the development of the base specification helps making it more usable.
- Data exchange beyond the boundaries of the envisaged community is directly supported since other systems, using different application profiles based on the same specification, can immediately re-use those data which are relevant for them.
- Understanding the generic specification helps understanding the needs of neighboring communities and appreciating the real value of the available data.
- Working with application profiles opens up the possibility of getting an affordable conformance test system (as explained below).

The price to pay for these benefits is the effort to understand the existing specification, to select what is needed and to add what is not there yet.

The alternative to the development of an application profile is to develop a new specification from scratch. While this may save time in the development of the specification, since no needs of the wider world have to be considered, it guarantees non-interoperability with whatever systems exist, respectively it creates the need for the implementation of additional mediator systems which translates the data formats between the different "standards".

Unfortunately, this happens all too often. For example there are at the time of this writing (April 2010) four specifications how to encode learning-related personal data - IMS LIP/IMS ePortfolio (IMS, 2005; IMS, 2005a), CEDEFOP Europass (CEDEFOP, 2004), UK LEAP 2.0 (CETIS, 2009), HR-XML 3.0 (HR-XML, 2009). As there is an obvious need to re-use such data in the course of lifelong learning, having such a variety of specifications even in this restricted field can hardly be perceived as optimal.

By far the most frequent argument for starting a re-specification project is, that existing specifications are "too complex and are therefore not taken up". In recent discussion this is often seconded by a more fundamental criticism on the use of complex and deeply nested data structures, advocating the use of simple re-usable and interrelated "core components" as proposed by UN/CEFACT (UN/CEFACT, 2003), essentially consisting of name-value pairs. Of course, working with such simple structures cannot eliminate the need to encode the complexity that lies in the domain to be modeled – in fact the complexity is shifted from the complexity of data structures to the complexity of the network of relations between those structures.

There is still a need to provide tools with a power similar to the wide variety of available tools for structural analysis, exploiting technologies like XML Schemas, XPath, Schematron, XSLT and XQuery, in order to ease maintaining a large network of structure definition – often scattered over a large number of files for one specification.

Theoretical Concepts

The following discussion of theoretical concepts, relevant for understanding essentials of application profiles, is adapted from the IMS Application Profiling Guidelines (Riley, 2005). We shall make use of these concepts when we illustrate the development of application profiles in the following sections. As this paper is mainly concerned with issues of automated conformance testing, we concentrate in the following on the discussion of precisely defined and testable concepts. This does not mean that we underestimate the critical importance of more "soft" descriptions of application profiles, like use cases, best practice documents and examples of conformant data structures.

The relation with the alternative theoretical approach taken by M. Nilsson and the Dublin Core

Educational Metadata Application Profing Group shall be discussed at the end of this subsection.

According to (Riley, 2005) the semantics of a specification and of an application profile is defined by the *set of conformant documents*. Therefore specifications and application profiles can be compared by comparing the respective set of conformant documents which they define.

In particular we call an application profile a *restrictive* profile of a specification if each document that conforms to the profile is also conformant with the specification. For reasons to be explained below, restrictive application profiles are the ones most commonly in use. By analogy, an application profile is *extensive* with respect to a specification if each document that conforms to the specification is also conformant to the profile. Extensive profiles are, for example, obtained if a vocabulary of values permitted by the specification is extended in the profile to admit additional values.

Systems can read and write documents. The set of all documents which a system can write is specified by its *write profile*. Similarly the set of all documents which a system can read is defined by its *read profile*. Two systems – a sender and a receiver – are (syntactically) *interoperable* if all documents produced by the sender can be read by the receiver, i.e. if the write profile of the sender is restrictive with respect to the read profile of the receiver.

It is often required that different specifications are used together. In particular, for example in the case of the Common Cartridge specification discussed below, application profiles of several specifications are combined in what is called a *domain profile*. Such a domain profile does not only collect a number of application profiles. It has, moreover, to define the ways in which they are connected.

The Dublin Core Metadata Initiative (DCMI) uses so-called Description Set Profiles (DSP) as a constraint language to define application profiles for the Dublin Core Metadata Specification

(Nilsson, 2008). A DSP consists of Description Templates, selecting resource definitions, and of Statement Templates constraining the usage (optional, mandatory) and the values permitted for specific data fields. This includes the definition of constraints on the possible targets of relations between data objects.

The DCMI approach is an example of the core-components-related approach discussed above. It is designed to be supported mainly by semantic-web like tools based on RDF (W3C 2004). Conformance test systems based on this approach are under development. Complex data structures, domain profiles and the structure of packages containing a variety of files of different types – as used in the Common Cartridge specification discussed below – are out of scope for these core components approaches to application profiling.

Practical Issues

More than a decade of technical specifications in the eLearning domain has led to a wealth of mixed practical experiences. The metadata specification has made it into the IEEE LOM standard (IEEE, 2002). Others, like SCORM 1.2 (ADL, 2001) and IMS Content Packaging (IMS, 2009a), can be considered as de-facto standards. Some, like IMS QTI (IMS, 2006) or IMS Learning Design (IMS 2003), are generally accepted as dominating approaches to the description of relevant data, but are hardly implemented with their full power.

Since the first specifications emerged, they had to struggle with two conflicting requirements.

- Specifications should be general enough to cover all currently relevant or foreseeable use cases
- Specifications should be easy to use and implement.

The first of these requirements seemed even more complicated when it was realized that even with the best intention foreseeing all applications was simply impossible. The soon emerging need to extend given specifications was satisfied early by introducing extension points. Extension points are locations in specified data structures where it was foreseen that user communities can request that their own additional data structures should be used if any. All systems which claim to be conformant with the base specification are requested to at least tolerate any structure that may occur at a specified extension point. Still today using extension points is one of the most important ways to profile a specification.

Most specifications achieve the highest level of generality by introducing a large set of optional elements. In some cases, for example IEEE LOM, even all elements are optional. Therefore another major profiling activity is making a certain set of elements mandatory and declaring others to be prohibited. Such modifications, which redefine the permitted number of occurrences of an element, are called *cardinality modifications*.

Similar to XML elements also optional XML attributes can be declared to be required or prohibited. Also the permitted content of an attribute or element can be restricted. We call such modifications *attribute usage modifications*. A particularly important restriction of this kind is the requirement to use in a particular place only values from a particular restricted enumeration of values (often called a controlled vocabulary).

All modifications we have described so far add new requirements to the base specification, thus leading to restrictive application profiles. Note that this is even true when extension points are used since the base specification allows for arbitrary data structures at such points, while the actual use of the extension point puts more restrictive requirements.

The use of restrictive profiles has the perceived advantage that all data that conform to a restrictive profile can be processed by each system that conforms to the base specification, i.e., which can read all data that conform to the base specification. Note, however, that this perceived advantage evaporates if the reading system itself accepts only data that conform to its own restrictive read profile. In particular, when systems and tools are built specifically to process data from a special community which uses a restrictive profile there is little incentive for developers to implement the full power of the specification. This has turned out to be a major obstacle to the take-up of specifications and application profiles. As a consequence, application profiles are the principal method to ensure interoperability between tools of a community, the practice of which is covered by the profile while cross-community interoperability is at best restricted to the parts which are shared between the interacting communities. Even this restricted interoperability gets lost when different communities rely on different base specifications.

The restriction of interoperability resulting from the incomplete implementation of the specifications, i.e., having systems with a restrictive read profiles, as well as the observation that for many data structures well-thought specifications exist, has led to an important paradigm change for the work of IMS Global Learning since ca. 2005. Since then IMS has put less efforts on developing new specifications that cover all potentially relevant use cases of a specific kind.

Instead emphasis was directed to the development of application profiles of already existing specifications. These profiles are determined to describe those parts of specifications that are in current use at a given point in time. It was made a strict requirement that no development of a specification or application profile shall be started unless a defined number of members of the specification working group committed own resources to its full and independent implementation already during the specification or profiling phase. The IMS Common Cartridge Specification, discussed below, is the first developed following this policy.

This paradigmatic change had major consequences. It blocked a number of specification requests no-one was willing to implement. It also made sure that specifications are based on independent implementations. This in particular helps avoiding ambiguities by detecting possibilities of ambiguous interpretations already during the specification work. Further it restricts the number of features that make it into the specification, which in turn makes it easier for the eLearning community to take up the specification or profile and to fully implement it.

The balance to pay for this ease of uptake, obtained by priority support for current practice, is that the specification/profile must evolve as current practice proceeds. This implies that new versions are required in shorter cycles. An Application Profile Management Group is needed to capture user experience and to incorporate it into the development of the next version. As practice becomes richer there is a fair chance that new versions of specifications shall be backward compatible, handling more rich data structures. In these cases data providers shall be compatible with future versions of the specification while tool providers shall have to update their tools in order to remain conformant to the latest version.

In the following section we use the recent IMS Common Cartridge Specification as an example to illustrate the different types of modification that are in use. Further on it will be shown how these modifications are supported by the SchemaProf Application Profiling Tool to create testable domain profiles.

THE COMMON CARTRIDGE CASE

The Common Cartridge Specification (IMS, 2008) has been developed to support the exchange of the most important types of content data between content providers and content users – learners and courses. The primary objective of the Common Cartridge specification is the support for teachers and instructors who are setting up a learning environment for their students.

Content types supported in Version 1.0 of the specification are

- **Web Content:** This is all content that is located on the web or within a Common Cartridge and that can be launched with a standard application, for example images, documents or animations
- **Assessment and Question Banks:** These contain test items that can be used for assessments or self-tests
- **Discussion Topics:** These can be used to initiate discussion forums.

Moreover, Common Cartridge provides the conditions to connect to an authorization web service before importing a cartridge or before using some of its resources.

Using a Common Cartridge requires a Common Cartridge Player or a Common Cartridge aware Learning Management System. At the time of this writing end of 2009 the first editors and players for Common Cartridges have emerged. Providers of major Learning Management Systems have announced to implement Common Cartridge support.

A discussion of the purpose and benefits of Common Cartridges is beyond the scope of this paper. For the following paragraphs we shall discuss the relation of the Common Cartridge specification with other specifications and its character as a domain profile.

Common Cartridges are content packages. In fact, the main part of the Common Cartridge specification is a restrictive profile of the IMS Content Packaging specification. Moreover, the Common Cartridge Specification incorporates two application profiles of the IEEE LOM Metadata Specification – one to describe the cartridge as a whole and another one to be used for describing individual resources which are packaged in

the cartridge. These profiles are connected with the main Common Cartridge Content Packaging profile through extension points of the Content Packaging schema. Another schema for describing information to authorize access to the cartridge content is also connected to the Content Packaging profile through an extension point. There is more profiles part of the Common Cartridge specification which is not integrated through extension points but through another mechanism – additional constraints – which we shall discuss below.

Each content package can have several tables of content, named organizations where a cartridge can have only one. This is an example for a restrictive cardinality modification as described above.

Attribute usage modifications may either make the use of an optional attribute mandatory or prohibited or they may redefine the set of values which an attribute can take. The Common Cartridge specification uses the former, for example, to prohibit use of the deprecated attribute *isvisible* of item elements in an *organization* table of content. The latter type of attribute usage modification is applied to request that the *type* attribute of a *resource* element can hold only one of a small set of strings which each uniquely identifies one of the content types allowed in a Common Cartridge.

*Item*s in the *organization* table of content can be of two different types – those, called *folder items*, which contain other *items*, and those, called *learning resource items*, which do not. Only the latter are allowed to point to resources. Hence for folder items the attribute *identifierref* is prohibited while it is allowed for learning resource items. It is worth noting that such a profiling modification, depending on the context of whether an *item* element has further *item* sublements, cannot be expressed by modifying the Content Packaging base schema. *Assertions* are a new type of modifications that is capable of handling such definitions in a testable way: An assertion is an XPath expression that is bound to a type or element definition. For example the XPath expression can be bound to the *item* type to test that an *item* does not contain simultaneously a *subitem* and an *identifierref* attribute. Such an assertion can be encoded into a Schematron rule and a Schematron processor can be configured to flag an error if the XPath expression evaluates to *true*. Assertions turn out to be a very powerful profiling tool. Their usage requires special care, in particular since they must address positions in test instance documents which are only available at test time but not at the time when the assertion is defined as part of the profiling process.

Conditions are another way of using instance document XPath expressions in application profiles. They add a whole new level of flexibility to application profiling: Conditions are XPath expressions which are added to the types of modifications described above with the understanding that the modification must only be respected (i.e., tested) if the XPath expression evaluates to *true*. This makes it possible to define for the same type not just one but several modifications in order to test for the first whose condition is *true*; if no condition is *true*, the definition of the base schema applies and must be tested.

In some cases, for example for cardinality modifications or assertions, additional conditions can be integrated into specific Schematron rules. For other modifications, like attribute usage modifications requesting values of a specific simple type, adding conditions requires the use of specific tests beyond what XML Schema and Schematron can provide.

For the Common Cartridge specification conditions are essential to integrate further application profiles. A cartridge is a zip package which contains, aside of a manifest file, a number of other files. The specification restricts which types of files are allowed. For example a cartridge may contain assessments or question banks but those must conform to the Common Cartridge profile of the IMS Question and Test Interoperability (QTI) specification. Such requirements, which do not just concern a specific file but rather the structure of a package, are called *additional constraints*.

The simplest additional constraints require that particular files exist in a particular place in the package. For example the Content Packaging specification, and hence also the Common Cartridge specification, requests that a file named *imsmanifest.xml* exists at the root of the package. Such additional constraints, working with fixed parameters only, are called *static constraints*. In some cases, however, constraints may depend on parameters which are only found in instance documents at test time – these are called *dynamic constraints*. In Common Cartridge a dynamic constraint is that the *href* attribute of a *resource* may have to point to a file in the package which must conform to the Common Cartridge QTI profile. But that cannot be requested for all resources but only for those for which the *type* attribute indicates that the respective resource is an assessment or question bank. This can be achieved by making the additional constraint, dependent on an XPath condition testing the type of the resource.

Additional constraints cannot be expressed in XML schemas or Schematron rules. Their verification requires specific test systems. The same holds for another type of requirements which is part of the IMS Content Packaging specification. This specification requests that each file in a content package, with the exception of the file *imsmanifest.xml*, is referenced in this file by an *href* attribute of a *file* element. Also this requires specific tests.

The next section describes how the modifications just described can be captured in machine readable format with the *SchemaProf* tool.

CAPTURING APPLICATION PROFILES WITH SCHEMAPROF

In order to support interoperability and conformance testing, application profiles and domain profiles must be captured in a machine readable format. The SchemaProf tool allows just this. It has been developed in the European project Telcert and adapted to the needs of IMS GLC after the end of the project.

The tool has a graphical user interface that provides a visualization of schema files as well as methods to attach modifications to the displayed components of the schema. The user can choose between different views for viewing the structure of the schema or its components in form of element, attribute and other definitions.

Definitions of the base specification which have been modified in the application profile are highlighted. Highlighting of elements on the paths to these modifications make it easy to locate the modifications made, even from the top level of the specification and even for complex specifications which span over a number of files. The base schema of the application profile is visualized as a tree structure with expandable nodes.

One view provided is the *"Elements view"* displaying all global element definitions as root nodes. Elements of the XML Schema Language used by an element definition are displayed using its path inside the schema. Figure 1 shows the path to the modified element *location/metadata*.

For every selected schema element a panel containing a list and buttons is shown right of the tree view. This list shows all attached modifications. Buttons provide support for attaching new or removing / editing already present modifications.

Definition re-use is a common feature in XML schemas, i.e., the same definition is re-used in different contexts. However for application profiles it is often desirable to only modify a definition in a particular context while leaving it unchanged for others. Referenced definitions are shown in SchemaProf grayed out and inactive, i.e., they can be inspected but not modified until they are activated which can be done by a right click. Activating a definition, for example of an element type, in a particular place lets SchemaProf create a copy of the original type for local use and modification in the specific context.

The tool will check automatically if a modification to be made is valid with respect to a particular compatibility level – restrictive, extensive or undefined – as defined above. By default SchemaProf works with restrictive compatibility level but that can be overwritten in the tools' settings.

Figure 2 shows the panel used to attach a cardinality modification, thus changing the *minOccurs* and/or *maxOccurs* attribute.

Figure 1. Visualization of the path to a schema element

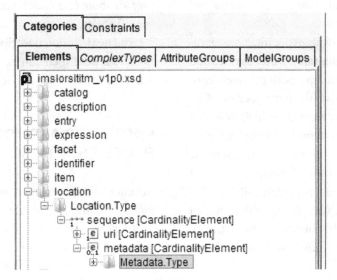

Figure 2. Dialog for adding or editing a cardinality modification

Changing the minimal occurence to a value greater than 0 would *restrict* the set of valid documents because the element is no longer optional. Increasing the maximal occurence *extends* the set of valid documents. Increasing both values would result in a profile of compatibility level *undefined*. The tool will validate the modification when confirming the dialog. As shown in the dialog a condition can be defined for a modification. Such conditions are evaluated when validating an instance document and affect whether the modification should be taken into account by the test system responsible for the validation. A Con-

dition Manager allows the definition of conditions as XPath expressions for re-use.

Besides editing a single profile file, SchemaProf also supports the handling of domain profiles. The XML Schema Language already allows specifying that at an extension point only elements of a particular namespace are allowed. SchemaProf takes this further – valid contents regarding the extension point can be restricted to contents conforming to another profile. With the help of IMS SchemaProf this can be done in a guided way. Also the profiles referenced through modifications of the base profile can be viewed and a referenced profile can be directly opened through SchemaProf's profile manager for editing.

Additional constraints, as introduced in the previous section, are saved as part of the profile. Besides the mere existence of a file given either by value or by reference in a text element, additional constraints in SchemaProf can specify a variety of features like Mime type or file size, but also that the file should validate against another profile.

The example in Figure 3 shows constraints that specify file existence and requirements that referenced files must conform to auxiliary application profiles. The latter are dependent from conditions. SchemaProf guides the user through the process of defining additional constraints.

Conformance tests are initialized by a set of rules that can be edited in SchemaProf. Such a rule contains file criteria for matching files and defines the type of test to create for files that fulfill the criteria. It has regular expressions defining for which file names and XML namespaces specific tests (like XML validation or reference testing) should be applied initially. It is foreseen to allow for additional types of tests in the future. The Figure 4 shows the step of configuring the rule for triggering schema tests for all XML files with a particular namespace.

SchemaProf creates these rules automatically from the analysis of the available namespaces and derived schemas. Nevertheless the application profiler is urged to inspect the generated rules to

resolve cases where there are several derived schemas defining the same namespace.

SchemaProf and the language for describing machine readable application profiles are extensible to incorporate new types of tests. Currently besides XML schema validation Schematron validation and reference testing are implemented. In the future, communities may design their own specific additional tests should the existing ones not suffice (Figure 4).

Application profiles are saved by SchemaProf as zip-compressed folders. They contain, besides the machine readable application profile in XML format, a subdirectory with derived schemas capturing modifications of a profile. But not all modifications that can be defined with the help of SchemaProf can also be expressed by a derived schema.

Therefore profiles may also contain Schematron files. The derived XML schemas and the derived Schematron files may be used separately with third-party XML and Schematron validators. It is worth noting that Schematron rules are generated such that comments in the profile on the respective modifications appear as error messages during Schematron validation.

In order to support testing for additional constraints and future test types, the generated Schematron rules may also contain "technical messages" which just issue the message that some additional test is required. For example for the Common Cartridge profile there is a Schematron

Figure 3. Additional constraints of common cartridge profile V1.1

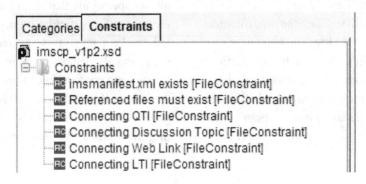

Figure 4. Creating or editing a rule for schema related tests

rule which is applied if a resource of type assessment or question bank is found. In such a case this rule will issue a technical message stating that an additional QTI profile compliance test is required for the referenced file of this resource.

Once SchemaProf has been used to describe a domain profile, techniques described in the next section can be applied to produce a profile-specific test system.

GENERATING CONFORMANCE TEST SYSTEMS

In order to provide even communities without software developers with conformance testing capabilities for their specific application profiles, a software has been developed that automatically creates test systems for application profiles that have been configured with SchemaProf. Such a *Testsystem Bundle* or simply a *bundle* in the following contains test systems for executing tests defined in the profile, a control system capable of launching test systems and an initial launcher with a graphical user interface for configuring and executing it.

The final test system (configured bundle) is created from an unconfigured bundle and a profile through a packager program (Figure 5). For domain profiles, the configured test system bundle shall contain test systems for each individual application profile in the domain profile.

A test system being part of a bundle has to be able to return a self description in a well defined way in order to be recognized by the control system. A so called *System Scanner* exists as part

Figure 5. Packager program

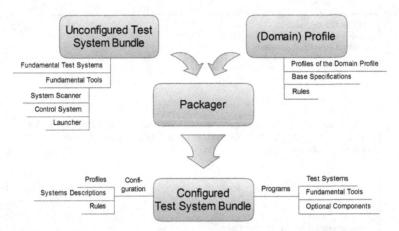

of every bundle that uses the descriptions returned by such systems in order to provide a self description of the whole bundle. These self descriptions may contain required parameters that need to be provided before the test can be called.

This mechanism allows for the integration of further specific tests. Integrating a new test system into an unconfigured bundle requires the development of the system itself and the integration of test rules that define the circumstances for triggering tests of files using the new system.

In the following the term *"test"* is used for a test to be carried out in form of an execution of a bundled test system while the term *"test run"* is used to refer to the set of tests that are necessary to run in order to test the conformance of a set of documents with respect to a domain profile. A test run is specified by:

- The set of files to test for conformance
- The rules which define what files in a package should be tested and what kind of tests should be created for them.

The control system starts the execution of the test run with the process of applying the rules of the main profile on all documents that are part of the packages to be tested. As a result of this process, appropriate tests are selected and executed. Figure 6 shows the architecture of a packaged test system bundle:

Figure 6. Packaged test system bundle

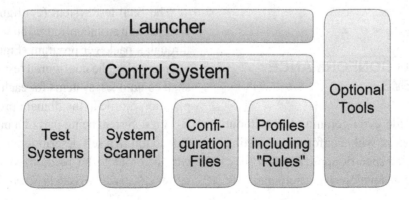

The launcher makes use of the control system in order to execute tests requested by the user. The control system uses the packaged test systems, the descriptions of those created by a run of the system scanner, the profiles to test against and the rules to fulfill its task.

The set of files to test for conformance as well as the report directory to write the html reports to can be configured with the launcher. The execution chain of the control system is the following:

1. Apply the *rules* in order to determine the files to consider and the tests to create for those files.
2. Create a task list containing the abstract representations of the tests. An abstract representation of a test can be used to build up an appropriate command line for calling a bundled system in order to execute the test in a separate process.
3. Execute the tests in the created task list by creating a command line for each test and executing it. Listen during the execution for requests for the creation of new tests:
   a. If a request for another test is created by the called system, create the abstract representations of the requested tests and add them to the task list.
   b. Continue with the next test.
4. Analyze the log files produced by the test runs and generate the html reports.

A request from a running system can also be one for validating a set of files against a profile registerd at the system executing the test run. Such a request would make statements about the profile to test against and the files to test. In this case step 3.1 involves the application of the rules of that profile on the specified files and adding the created abstract test representations to the task list under execution. During the whole process the control system informs the user about the progress of the task list execution and about errors that might occur.

After each test the specific test system generates a test report. These report files are converted into HTML pages using stylesheets for formatting the validation results. By changing the style sheets, test reports can be aligned to reflect the corporate identity of the profiling community.

While using SchemaProf requires some understanding of the potential of the XML schemas of the base specification, the generated test systems are designed for ease of use. As soon as the user has unzipped the test system he/she can in most environments just load the items to be tested, launch the test and view the test results without further configuration. Summary pages show for each item under test which test systems reported errors. Error messages are given with references to the file names and line numbers where the error occurred.

USER EXPERIENCE

Developing application profiles in a machine readable form using SchemaProf proved to be very useful. It led to increased precision and disambiguation during the Common Cartridge specification process. As test data became available, the packaged test system enabled early testing. It was particularly helpful that the test system could be rapidly adapted as the specification evolved. This is an important feature for specifications which are determined to change as they reflect current practice.

In order to support Common Cartridge developers, the specification group decided to provide a set of sample cartridges demonstrating all features of the specification. The generated test system was a valuable help to get these cartridges correct. On the other hand, in order to be sure that the SchemaProf profile captured the specification correctly, a number of incorrect cartridges was developed to make sure that the known errors in these cartridges get trapped by the test system.

The IMS Approved Schemaprof tool is available from the IMS web site (IMS, 2010). The Common Cartridge Test System is distributed to members of the IMS Common Cartridge Alliance (IMS, 2009). Though there is no statistics available, feedback suggests that the Common Cartridge Test System is used successfully by many content providers producing cartridges. Since cartridges are frequently produced in an automated packaging process, the major application of the test system was to eliminate systematic errors from these packaging processes.

Future work on the technology described in this paper is directed towards adding more test systems, for example to test usage of external vocabularies, and to producing a test service that can be used as a filter for documents before they are uploaded to a repository.

REFERENCES

W3C. (2004). *W3C Resource Description Framework Specification*. Retrieved from http://www.w3.org/RDF/

ADL. (2001). *ADL, Sharable Content Object Reference Model Specification, V 1.2*. Retrieved from http://www.adlnet.gov/Technologies/scorm/SCORMSDocuments/Forms/AllItems.aspx?Root Folder=%2fTechnologies%2fscorm%2fSCORMSDocuments%2fPrevious%20Versions%2fS CORM%201%2e2%2fDocumentation%20Suite%20%28SCORM%201%2e2%29&FolderCT ID=0x0120007F801FCD5325044C89D912405 19482D7&View=%7b4D6DFFDE%2d3CFC%2d4DD9%2dA21A%2d4B687728 824A%7d

CEDEFOP. (2004). Retrieved from http://europass.cedefop.europa.eu/img/dynamic/c1399/type.FileContent.file/EuropassDecision_en_US.PDF

CETIS. (2009). *UK LEAP 2.0*. Retrieved from http://wiki.cetis.ac.uk/LEAP_specification

HR-XML. (2009). *HR-XML 3.0 Specification*. Retrieved from http://www.hr-xml.org

IEEE. (2002). *IEEE 1484.12.1-2002, Draft Standard for Learning Object Metadata, Piscataway 2002*. Retrieved from http://ltsc.ieee.org/wg12/files/LOM_1484_12_1_v1_Final_Draft.pdf

IMS. (2003). *IMS Learning Design*. Retrieved from http://www.imsglobal.org/learningdesign/index.html

IMS. (2005). *IMS Learner Information Package Specification*. Retrieved from http://www.imsglobal.org/profiles/index.html

IMS. (2005a). *IMS ePortfolio Specification*. Retrieved from http://www.imsglobal.org/ep/index.html, 2005

IMS. (2006). *IMS Question and Test Interoperability 2.1*. Retrieved from http://www.imsglobal.org/question/index.html

IMS. (2008). *IMS GLC Common Cartridge*. Retrieved from http://www.imsglobal.org/cc/index.html, 2008

IMS. (2009). *IMS GLC Common Cartridge Alliance*. Retrieved from http://www.imsglobal.org/cc/alliance.html

IMS. (2009a). *IMS GLC Packaging Specification 1.2*. Retrieved from http://www.imsglobal.org/content/packaging/index.html

IMS. (2010). SchemaProf. *Version 2.0*. Retrieved from http://www.imsglobal.org/profile/IMSSchemaProf-2.0.zip

Nilsson, M. (2008). *Description Set Profiles: A constraint language for Dublin Core Application Profiles*. Retrieved from http://dublincore.org/documents/dc-dsp/

Riley, K. (2005). *Application Profiling Guidelines*. Retrieved from http://www.imsglobal.org/ap/

UN/CEFACT. (2003). *Core Components Specification*. Retrieved from http://www.unece.org/cefact/ebxml/CCTS_V2-01_Final.pdf

This work was previously published in the International Journal of IT Standards and Standardization Research (IJITSR), Volume 8, Issue 2, edited by Kai Jakobs, pp. 60-73, copyright 2010 by IGI Publishing (an imprint of IGI Global)

Chapter 18
A Data Model for Describing and Exchanging Personal Achieved Learning Outcomes (PALO)

Jad Najjar
WU Vienna, Austria

Bernd Simon
WU Vienna, Austria

Michael Dernt
University of Vienna, Austria

Michael Totschnig
WU Vienna, Austria

Tomaž Klobučar
WU Vienna, Austria

Simon Grant
JISC CETIS, UK

Jan Pawlowski
University of Jyväskylä, Finland

ABSTRACT

Employers seek people that match particular qualifications and graduates seek jobs that match their qualifications. This market is currently managed primarily using paper certificates and heterogeneous university management systems that capture achieved learning outcomes as well as corporate information systems that capture required qualifications. In light of trends toward increased student mobility, employability and lifelong learning, this situation is less than satisfactory. Therefore, in this paper, the authors propose a schema that facilitates interoperable storage and management of Personal Achieved Learning Outcomes (PALO) based on a common data model. This paper presents use case scenarios and implementations addressing these challenges and demonstrating the added value of using such a common model.

INTRODUCTION

Nowadays, the management and interoperability of data about learning outcomes (knowledge, skill and competence) in outcome based learning are of high importance for both education and employ-ment sectors. By managing and sharing data about their profiles, learners in higher education and lifelong learning can better plan their careers and enhance their employability potential. In order to achieve this goal, the information about learning outcomes associated to learning opportunities and

DOI: 10.4018/978-1-4666-2160-2.ch018

units of learning as well as the learning outcomes achieved by learners need to be captured, managed and exchanged in common formats (Paquette, 2007; Van Assche, 2007; Sampson, 2009; Lindgren et al., 2004).

Currently, in the context of online learning, higher education institutions have yet adopted neither a common format for describing learning outcome definitions nor formats for describing achieved learning outcomes of learners. Such data are gathered in personal profiles and give information about the context where the outcomes were achieved (Richter & Pawlowski, 2007) by taking a learning opportunity, the achieved outcome level, and assessment information (Crespo et al., 2010; Grant, 2002).

Using a common format for describing, referencing and sharing learning outcome definitions enables exchange and comparison of learning outcome definitions across systems, domains and sectors. For instance, data about learning outcomes achieved in one course or by one student and stored at a university database may be exchanged with a Human Resources (HR) system of an employment agency. In other words, the two systems can refer to a common definition of a learning outcome with a common meaning. By this way, a lifelong learner would be able to access his/her achieved learning outcomes from the school, the university, the training agencies and the employer in one profile. This work would enable the matching between what people learn in universities (and schools) and what they need to know and be able to do at work. The gap in learner skills and knowledge may be easily identified (Paquette, 2007).

Following the European initiatives like European Qualification Framework (EQF, 2000), Europass (2010) and European Learner Mobility (EuroLM, 2009), the aim of this paper is to introduce a specification that captures information on knowledge, skills and competences achieved by a person (a lifelong learner) in higher education and training institutions or in the workplace. The

specification represents data on relations between a learner's achieved learning outcomes. In addition to that, information on the context where the learning outcomes are obtained or applied is covered by schema. Evidence (assessment) records and levels (e.g. proficiency level) associated to the outcomes are also a core part of this schema. This specification is an important step towards the enhancement of the interoperability and transparency of such personal data of a lifelong learner between higher educational and workplace applications and services.

The Personal Achieved Learning Outcomes (PALO) specification presented in this paper went through at least three iterative expert evaluations by the ICOPER consortium and at relevant international workshops by standards experts, teachers and learners to make sure that it captures data needed for increased employability of learners and higher interoperability with different learning systems.

Prototypes of outcome based learning applications like widgets and modules of Learning Management Systems (LMS) are being developed, to produce and import data about achieved learning outcomes of learners in systems like Moodle (2010), Elgg (2010) and Clix (2010). The data of learner achieved learning outcomes profiles are stored in ICOPER's PALO repository. These data can be consumed by learning systems to provide learners with relevant material, recommendation of other teachers and learners based on similarity of learning outcome profiles, or to enable learners to share their achievement profiles with social or recruitment systems.

This paper is structured as follows: In the second section, related work regarding outcome-based learning, competence and learning outcome specifications is provided. Then, in the third section, the outcome based learning components and features are introduced. The fourth section provides a scenario of learner achievements in outcome-based learning. Afterwards, fifth section, the Personal Achieved Learning Outcomes

(PALO) data model is presented. This data model captures information, in a profile, on learning outcomes achieved by a learner after successfully following a learning opportunity (unit of learning). The data presented in a PALO profile can be imported to different learning, training and recruitment systems or social applications like LinkedIn (2010) and Facebook (2010) for presentation purposes, or for recommendation of relevant units of learning, people or jobs. The sixth section presents prototypical implementations being developed in ICOPER (2010) project for learning management systems like Moodle (2010) or Social applications like Facebook. Conclusions and future directions are drawn at the end. A detailed description of the PALO elements, data types and values can be found at http://www.icoper.org/schema/palov1.1.

RELATED WORK

The importance of capturing data about life-long learners' knowledge, skills and competencies has been stated by several national/international initiatives, standardisation bodies and researchers. The European Qualification Framework (EQF, 2000) was proposed as an instrument to make learning outcomes more transparent and comparable across Europe. This is an important step towards outcome-based learning and mobility. Following the recommendations of EQF, the European Learner Mobility (EuroLM, 2009) stated the importance of including data on intended learning outcomes to the Europass Diploma Supplement record. Personal achieved learning outcomes specifications can be seen as a complementary part to the Europass Diploma Supplement (DS). Specifications and services for management and exchange of personal achievement information should be developed to support the expression of the European lifelong learner achievement information across higher education, training and employment sectors, this should result in:

- Promoting transparency of lifelong learner achievements across higher education systems;
- Providing an evidence-based and up-to-date on an individual achievements (what he/she knows and is able to do);
- Exchanging of learner achievement information between educational systems and workplace systems;
- Refereeing to common skills, knowledge and competences across higher education institutions and workplace.

Metadata for Learning Opportunities (MLO, 2008) specification covered, to some extent, the linkage of learning outcomes to metadata of learning opportunities.

The important role of personal competence profiles in human resource management and education was emphasised by Paquette (2007), who demonstrates how a gap in learner skills can be identified in competence-based ontology-driven e-learning systems.

With a focus on linking metadata records of learning resources to intended competences of courses, Van Assche (2007) and Sampson (2009) extend the IEEE Learning Object Metadata (LOM; IEEE, 2002) records with some attributes that capture generic characteristics of an intended competence, like title, type, description, proficiency level and context.

Emphasising the importance of aligning organisation level core competences with individual level job competence, in competence management systems, (Lindgren et al., 2004) develop an integrative model of competence that incorporates a typology of competence-in-stock, competence-in-use, and competence-in-making). The authors found company systems substantiating the job-based approach with predefined job descriptions and taxonomies of formal competence create barriers to the use appropriate use of a competence management system, On the other hand, authors suggest that HR systems that adopt the skill-based approach must be accompanied by sufficient user control over the information that represents her competence.

Regarding competence standards and specifications, IEEE LTSC Reusable Competency Definitions (IEEE RCD, 2007) is a world-wide standard that defines a data model for describing, referencing and sharing competence definitions, primarily in the context of online and distributed learning. IEEE RCD specification has a rather narrow scope, focusing on representing the key characteristics of a learning outcomes, it offers technical and semantic interoperability and (to some extent) extensibility. IEEE RCD is based on the existing IMS Global Learning Consortium specification entitled IMS Reusable Definition of Competency or Educational Objective (IMS RDCEO, 2002).

HR-XML (2008) is a world-wide standard for the formalization and ranking of competences, supported by HR-XML Consortium. This standard is used to capture information about evidence used to substantiate a competence, their ratings and weights and reusable data typed for referencing competences. Competence data elements of this schema are designed in order to be used in process-oriented environments and can be used to rate, measure, match and asses competence against one that is demanded, required (e.g., as a prerequisite, skill requited to take training). HR-XML has a strong focus on management and business and makes use of very clear non-extendable semantics expressed by the XML structure, which is likely to make the standard less flexible, but easier to maintain compatibility on a basic level. This is obviously a result of the firmly demarcated scope and focus of HR-XML.

As far as e-portfolio data is concerned, (LEAP2A, 2008) sets up the framework for the e-portfolio data interoperability. The purpose of LEAP2A specification is to represent e-portfolio information collected by the individual (learner) and not the information stored by the others (in-stitutions/teachers) about this individual. This information can be digital artefacts and users reflection to some kind of information. This specification extends ATOM syndication format to allow representation of such rich data. More analysis of competences and learning outcomes related specifications is provided in (Najjar & Klobučar, 2009).

BACKGROUND

Learners and Learning Outcomes

A learner's knowledge is about what the learner knows, or is presumed to know. Knowledge or belief does not automatically turn into behaviour, but needs to be applied to be of practical use. Skills, in contrast, are about patterns of behaviour in the learner's actions. In practice, all skills are supported by knowledge. Competences are more complex; they involve the application of knowledge and skill, but they are also about the kinds of situations (context) in which the knowledge and skill are applied. These kinds of situation are patterns that are instantiated in the world just at those times and places where the competence is applicable (EQF, 2000).

To exemplify the distinction of knowledge, skills and competence, consider this medical nurse scenario:

- A nurse learns about different types of medicine and its use during her study; here, she gains knowledge;
- She learns also how to administer intra-muscular medication; here, she obtains a skill.
- When she can correctly recognize which treatment is to be given to a particular patient (taking the context into account), we talk about competence.

Learning Needs

Learning needs are the skills, knowledge and competences that need to be attained by an individual in order to function at the desired level when performing a particular task or job. Learning needs cover also the skills, knowledge and competences that need improvement (Grant, 2002). The successful involvement of a learner in the learning and assessment process enables the learner to attain those needs. Those needs are also defined in terms of the learning outcomes of a learning process according to the European Qualification Framework (EQF, 2000):

Learning outcomes are statements of what a learner knows, understands and is able to do on completion of a learning process.

Following the EQF, in the ICOPER (2010) project, the term learning outcomes is used to refer to knowledge, skills and competences intended or achieved by learners. This model enables management of those definitions to enable and facilitate their finding and reuse across different units of learning as intended learning outcomes. In the coming sections of this paper, we introduce a data model for describing a profile of learning outcomes achieved by an individual (learner). This data model enables learners to share their profile of achieved outcomes with third-party applications for applying to future learning opportunities or employment or for recommendation of relevant information or services.

Learning Outcome Definitions

The Learning Outcome Definitions (LOD) data model has been defined in ICOPER as a conceptual base schema for describing and sharing learning outcome definitions in the context of online and technology enhanced learning. The data model provides a way to capture the key characteristics of a learning outcome, independently of its use in any particular context or target group (persons). This model should enable the storage, retrieval and exchange of learning outcomes across systems that deal with learning outcomes data.

The LOD model has been based on the IEEE Reusable Competency Definitions standard (IEEE RCD, 2007). IEEE RCD is a widely accepted standard for describing generic learning outcomes. In a nutshell, the LOD schema includes four descriptive elements:

1. **Identifier:** A unique identifier for this learning outcome definition
2. **Title:** A single text label of the learning outcome definition, e.g., "principles of academic writing"
3. **Description:** A human readable description of the learning outcome, e.g. "Students are able to explain the basic principles of academic writing"
4. **Type:** A label that captures the type of the learning outcome. According to the EQF, learning outcomes either relate to knowledge, skill or competence.

Role of Assessment

In universities, it is common practice for every taught module to have an associated assessment activity. This may lead to the assumption that an assessment is somehow an integral part of a learning activity (Crespo et al., 2010). However, a variety of formal, informal or self-study activities may all be preparation for the same assessment. Indeed, some assessment processes (such as psychometric tests) may be expected to be taken without any associated learning process.

Where learning and assessment are related, the logic would seem to be that the learning process aims at producing the intended learning outcomes in the learner, while the assessment method is designed to assess the learner's attainment of those outcomes. Formal assessment produces some formal result, according to a formally defined process. That result may fall into a certain pattern (pass/fail, or being over or under a certain percentage mark, for instance) and this is taken as an evidence for whether the learner has attained the intended learning outcome. The evidence is recorded and issued by the institution that has offered the learning opportunity.

Claims about Achievements

One of the useful applications of technology based on these models is for matching people with opportunities, that is, trying to get people into situations to which they are suited.

What is called here a personal achievement is intended to represent the way in which people claim that they are good at some thing. Achievements may have different forms and characteristics, e.g.:

- Achievements are about attainment of intended learning outcomes.
- Achievements may be based on assessment results achieved by the individual.
- Achievements may be backed up by primary evidence drawn from the material world.
- Achievements often are scoped in terms of the contexts in which an ability or competence is claimed.

Most formally defined opportunities – opportunities of employment as well as learning – have some kind of selection process, and that process typically specifies the kinds of knowledge, skill or competence that people are expected to have. A process of comparison can be undertaken between achievement and requirement. Does the assessment result in the achievement fit into the required pattern? Does the knowledge, skill or competence claimed to be achieved match the ones which are required? Do the contexts referred to in the achievement match the contexts expected in the requirement? The greater clarity about this

matching process that is achieved through modelling can potentially serve as the basis for a greater degree of effective automation in the initial stages of recruitment or selection.

SCENARIO OF LEARNER ACHIEVEMENTS IN OUTCOME-BASED LEARNING

Let us motivate our work on developing a model that captures learner's achieved learning outcomes by a scenario. The scenario gives an insight into outcome-based learning from a learner's point of view. It also serves as the basis for describing concrete examples of data model elements in the next section.

Peter Smith is a motivated young computer professional from the United Kingdom, working as a programmer in a big software company. Already as a teenager he was dreaming about becoming an entrepreneur in the area of computer games development and founding his company before the age of 30. The computer science programme Peter attended at a local university lacked many learning outcomes Peter needs to obtain while pursuing his goal, especially non-computer science related ones, for example in management and finances. Peter also has to regularly update his computer science knowledge and skills to be able to follow the rapid scientific and technological development.

In an attempt to organize an individual learning path, Peter wants first to analyse his knowledge, skills and competence gaps and clearly define his learning needs in terms of learning outcomes. A free on-line service at a career development agency helps him analysing those gaps by automatic-semantic matching of his achievements stored in his personal achieved learning outcome profile to the data the agency has for different occupations and positions. His profile includes both obtained learning outcomes formally assessed by educational institutions and other achievements obtained at work or in informal learning; for example, developed open source games. Peter updates his profile by importing missing learning outcomes as intended learning outcomes.

Based on the identified learning needs, he decides that his first goal is to obtain competences in project management on EQF level 6. Since Peter's university studies he has been maintaining his personal learning environment (PLE) that supports self-directed learning and collaboration. The PLE's tools and services enable Peter to find learning opportunities that best suit his intended learning outcome at different educational institutions as well as other users. They also keep notifying Peter about the changes and upgrades of the computer science programme from his alma mater and suggest topics he should learn to stay in touch with the latest developments. His achievements are taken into account during selection of the best suited learning opportunities. As Peter does not speak other languages than English and German, the search engine, for example, shows only courses in those two languages when presenting search results.

From the list of found courses Peter selects a blended course on project management that also enables him to obtain competences in group leadership. As the course is given by Vienna University of Economics and Business (WUW) he takes an opportunity to use his three months stay in Vienna also for learning purposes. Peter uses a variety of social software tools from his PLE when interacting with a teacher, his assistant and other learners. For the final assessment in the course he has to prepare a small project and lead a group of peer students who will help him implementing the project. His project management and group leadership competences are assessed by the learner supporters and peer learners.

Data collected about personal achieved learning outcomes are generated by learning system after Peter has successfully completed the course, as shown in Figure 1. Based on the assessment results the university issues Peter a certificate in German that proves obtained learning outcomes and register's Peter's achievement in the form of an achievement record. The achievement states attainment of all learning outcomes Peter obtained in a certain context in the course, and can be verified on the basis of assessment record (e.g., certificate). The achievement is stored in Peter's personal achieved learning outcome profile in WUW's PALO repository. Peter can import the achievement also in his personal profile and enhance it with English descriptions.

DATA MODELS FOR PERSONAL ACHIEVED LEARNING OUTCOMES (PALO)

Purpose and Scope

The Personal Achieved Learning Outcomes (PALO) data model is a simple schema proposed to capture information on knowledge, skills and competences achieved by a person (a learner), and the relations between those outcomes. Furthermore, information on the context where the learning outcomes are obtained or applied, evidence records (assessment), and levels (e.g. proficiency level) associated to the outcomes are also part of this schema.

One of the main challenges of communities and systems that deal with learning outcome information is the interoperability issue. Different communities and systems may use different data models to represent information on skills, knowledge or competence obtained by a person or that is required for a job or a task. The PALO specification is a step towards a common model supporting the exchange of such data, to enhance interoperability of personal learning outcome information between, for example, learning management systems, e-portfolios, social applications and recruitment systems.

The PALO data model enables capturing the following information:

Figure 1. Generation and use of personal achieved learning outcomes data

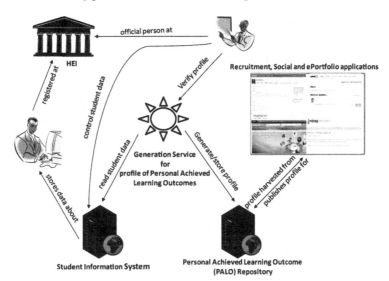

- *Relations* between achieved learning outcomes, regardless of the taxonomies or ontologies they belong to;
- *Contextual information* on where the achieved learning outcome is obtained or applied;
- Information about all types of *evidence and assessment* that prove the achievement of a learning outcome;
- Information about *levels and ranking* of an achieved learning outcome, like proficiency level.

The PALO data model covers (with some customization) data elements and concepts related to learning outcomes from other specifications like:

- IEEE RCD (2007) and ICOPER LOD (presented earlier), which describe the characteristics of learning outcomes;
- HR-XML (2008), which describes evidence records of learning outcomes.

The data collected in person's PALO profile can be used in different ways:

- They can be used in person specifications in the course of recruitment.
- Individuals can claim to have attained them.
- Evidence can be assembled by or about individuals to support a claim to their attainment.
- They can be used by employers or professional bodies as the basis for review processes that tie in with career progression.
- This data can also be used for recommendation of relevant learning opportunities for the learner based on his achievements.
- This data can be used as part of a learner diploma supplement; European Learning Mobility (ELM) Diploma Supplement (EuroLM, 2009).

PALO Data Elements and Types

In this section, we briefly describe the main PALO data elements and types. Figure 2 presents a graphical representation of the Personal Achieved Learning Outcomes (PALO) data model, the for a detailed description see http://www.icoper.org/schema/palov1.1. There are 6 main elements in the model:

Figure 2. The PALO data model

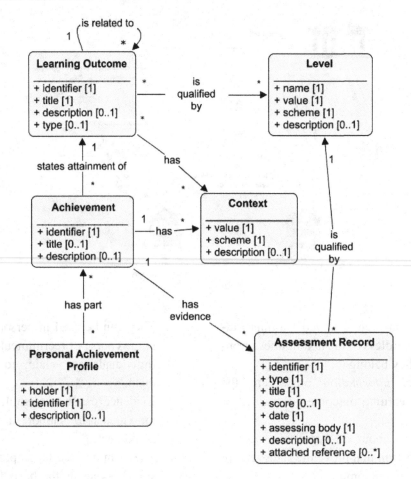

- **Personal Achievement Profile:** This element represents a collection of learner's *achievements*. Additional information about the profile is given by a title and optionally a human readable description of the profile. Both title and description can be repeated in multiple languages.

- **Achievement:** This element represents an achievement record, normally, of an attained learning outcome. Information about the achievement may be taken directly from a related *learning outcome*, rather than being given particularly. Personalised versions of a title and description may be used to supplement learning outcome. The element is also related to the *contexts*

where the achievement is claimed to be attained, and to *assessment records* that stand as evidence of the achievement.

- **Learning Outcome:** This element represents the learning outcome that is attained by the learner. Its type defines whether the learning outcome is knowledge, skill or competence. Further information about the element is provided by human-readable title and description of the learning outcome. The outcome can be related to other *learning outcomes*, e.g. with a relation narrower or broader, *contexts* and *levels*.

- **Level:** This element captures ranking information about the learning outcomes and/or assessment records of learners. This includes proficiency level, interest level, weight, ageing. The element also defines a schema used to describe the level values. Textual description about the level is useful to be provided when a level value provided is not part of a common ontology or taxonomy.

- **Context:** This element is a set of factors that are external to and give meaning to a learning outcome and/or achievement. For instance subject domain and location (e.g., lab, classroom) are textual information that gives meaning to the learning outcomes. The element also defines a schema used to describe the context values. A textual description about the context domain is useful to be provided when a context value/term provided is not part of a common ontology or taxonomy.

- **Assessment Record**: This element captures information of evidence that a learner has obtained a learning outcome. The record constitutes of evidence of the verification of the attainment of a certain achieved learning outcome by a certain learner. Thus, assessment records allow to associate learners and learning outcomes, in a formalised way, e.g., as a certificate, license or official record. Apart from the learner data and learning outcome data, an assessment record provides information about the type of test performed for verifying the achieved learning outcome, the responsible expert or institution who endorses it, and the date the record was created. The record is qualified by a level.

All six elements are uniquely identified; the context and the level by a combination of a scheme and its value, and the other four element by means of URIs. Figure 3, using a concrete example, demonstrates how the PALO specification

(shown in Figure 2) can represent the data about the learning outcome achievements of a lifelong learner like Peter, the character presented earlier in the scenario section.

PROTOTYPE APPLICATIONS USING PALO

Current work in ICOPER (2010) includes building software prototypes, services and modules that use the PALO model to capture, store and exchange learning outcome data between systems. The prototypes use the Open ICOPER Content Space – OICS (Totschnig et al., 2009) as an open repository containing different kinds of educational resources collected from distributed providers, ranging from small-scale assets like pictures and documents to complete units of learning, as well as PALO learning outcome profiles of learners and teachers. There are two types of prototype being developed:

1. Design-time applications that enable people to plan and design outcome-based units of learning, and
2. Run-time applications that enable implementing and running those units of learning.

The PALO model is primarily targeted towards run-time applications: the idea is that the applications use and update the PALO profile of a learner, e.g., when evidence or context for the achievement of an intended learning outcome is available. Therefore, applications that use PALO are dependent on units of learning that have their intended learning outcomes explicitly stated. This is where the design-time applications come into play. The design-time prototypes being developed enable learning designers to enrich units of learning with definitions of intended learning outcomes,

Figure 3. Concrete example of schematic representation of personal achievement profile and learning outcomes

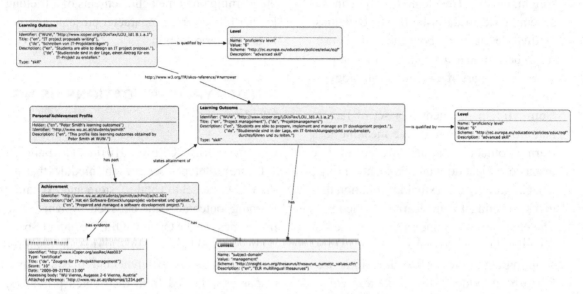

assessment resources, learning resources, and so forth.

To "pick up" as many existing users as possible, the plan was to enable the design and delivery of outcome based learning by extending functionality of *existing* systems that are already used by teachers and learners. To illustrate this approach of implementing PALO, this section presents a set of extensions to Moodle Learning Management System (Moodle, 2010), which were implemented as prototypes:

Search and Import Module

This is a Moodle module that enables searching and importing units of learning from the OICS. These units of learning come with intended learning outcomes in their metadata. A screenshot clipping of the search interface is displayed in Figure 4. The screen shows a list of units of learning that have "school geography" in their metadata. In addition it is possible to filter the query by selecting a specific portion of metadata to be queried for the given search string.

Figure 5 shows a screenshot of the details of a unit of learning after the user clicked on one of the items in the query results. The section most relevant to PALO is the list of intended learning outcomes connected to this unit of learning.

After importing the unit of learning, Moodle "knows" what outcomes are to be added to the PALO profiles of learners who pass the course assessment. In the optimal case this can achieved fully automatically, if the intended learning outcomes are linked to the learning assessment in the metadata of the unit of learning. For instance, the unit of learning may include an IMS QTI compliant assessment resource (e.g., a multiple choice test on geography basics) that can be used by Moodle to do the actual assessment and subsequently automatically create an assessment record with information like scores, assessing body and verification date (see Figure 2) that forms an evidence for the achievement of specific learning outcomes.

Figure 4. Unit of learning search interface in Moodle

Units of learning search for "school geography"
Search results: 20
school geography
Search
Filter by
learning outcomes
teaching methods
assessment
School geography: exploring a definition
education, geography, school, school_geography
Geography in education: exploring a definition
education, geography, school, school_geography
Rating:
Import to moodle
Loodusgeograafia, Physical geography
education, geography, school, school_geography
Rating:
Import to moodle
Eesti Bioloogia- ja Geograafiaopetajate Liit a definition
education, geography, school, school_geography
Rating:
Import to moodle
School geography: exploring a definition v2
education, geography, school, school_geography
Rating:
Import to moodle
1 2 3 4

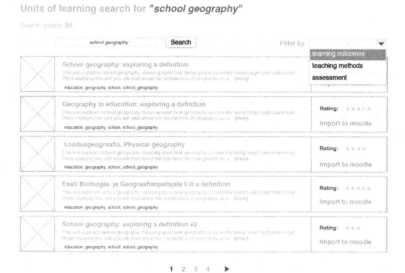

Figure 5. Unit of learning detail display based on available metadata

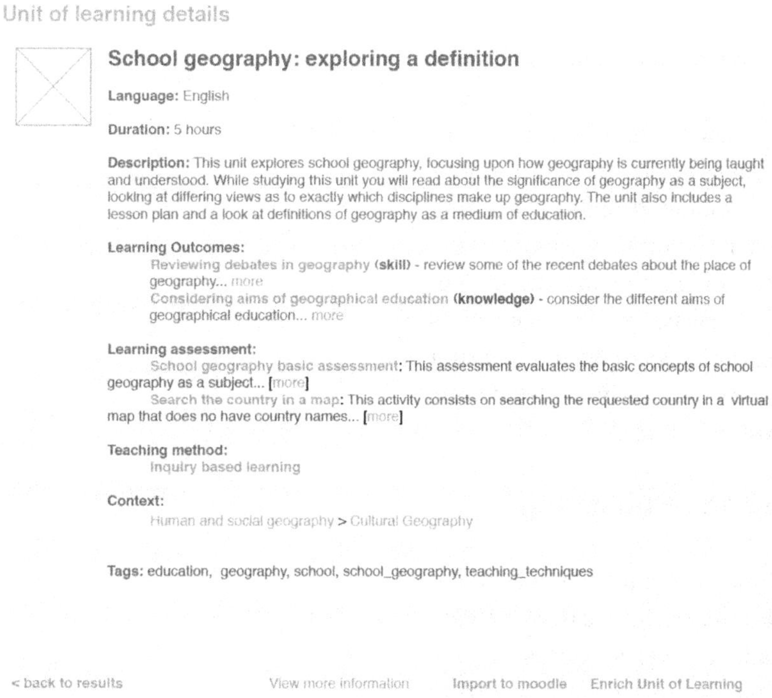

Unit of learning details
School geography: exploring a definition
Language: English
Duration: 5 hours
Description: This unit explores school geography, focusing upon how geography is currently being taught and understood. While studying this unit you will read about the significance of geography as a subject, looking at differing views as to exactly which disciplines make up geography. The unit also includes a lesson plan and a look at definitions of geography as a medium of education.
Learning Outcomes:
Reviewing debates in geography (skill) - review some of the recent debates about the place of geography... more
Considering aims of geographical education (knowledge) - consider the different aims of geographical education... more
Learning assessment:
School geography basic assessment: This assessment evaluates the basic concepts of school geography as a subject... [more]
Search the country in a map: This activity consists on searching the requested country in a virtual map that does no have country names... [more]
Teaching method:
Inquiry based learning
Context:
Human and social geography > Cultural Geography
Tags: education, geography, school, school_geography, teaching_techniques
< back to results
View more information
Import to moodle
Enrich Unit of Learning

Recommendation Widgets

After the unit of learning is successfully imported into Moodle, several additional benefits of PALO can be exploited: the system can keep a PALO profile of intended learning outcomes of units of learning that are – or have been – taught by the logged-in teacher user. If this is available for a large group of users (potentially also outside the current Moodle instance), Moodle can recommend other teachers who have similar profiles of taught learning outcomes. This enables teachers to create practitioner communities around the learning outcomes they teach simply based on the intended learning outcomes linked to courses where they have a teacher role in Moodle. A screenshot of a Moodle sidebar widget that recommends similar teachers is given in Figure 6.

Another, potentially, even more powerful recommendation approach, can be implemented for the learners: based on outcomes of courses currently being attended, and outcomes already in the PALO profile of a learner, Moodle can instantly recommend other learners, e.g., learners with similar background knowledge who are currently working on achieving the same or similar outcomes. Depending on the richness of user profile data, the recommendation approach can be simple or sophisticated, e.g., filtering the recommendation by physical proximity. Additionally, Moodle can recommend units of learning which address the same learning outcomes as the ones attached to units of learning that the student is currently using. This way, students can access additional resources during learning. A screenshot of a Moodle widget recommending related units of learning is shown in Figure 7.

PALO Updating and Publishing

After a unit of learning is completed in Moodle, the system can, depending on the local policy (e.g., after explicit clearance is given by the teacher, the institution, and/or the student), update the PALO

profile of the learner in the PALO repository. In addition, newly achieved learning outcomes can for instance be published to social networking sites like LinkedIn (2010) and Facebook (2010). To demonstrate this, an Atom XML binding (ATOM, 2010) of the PALO schema was defined. This binding is used to publish PALO profiles to Facebook using a custom Facebook application. The application retrieves the user's public PALO profile and displays it in a separate tab of the personal profile page in Facebook. The screenshot in

Figure 6. Moodle widgets displaying recommended units of learning and recommended teachers

Figure 7. Moodle widgets showing personal learning outcomes and related units of learning

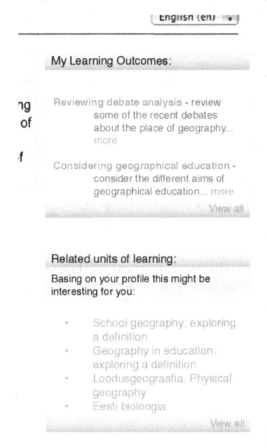

Figure 8 shows a screenshot mockup of the user's public PALO profile in Facebook.

The Moodle extensions presented in this serve as a hint to the potential world of powerful person-centred, outcome-based applications that can be developed building on PALO. On the other hand, the use of PALO data in social applications support the portability and transparency of personal achieved learning outcomes data.

CONCLUSION

The knowledge, skills and competences achieved by the learner play an increasingly important role as the professional life introduces new lifelong formative challenges. In this paper, we introduced a data model for capturing information that enables management and exchange of personal data on achieved learning outcomes. The Personal Achieved Learning Outcome (PALO) schema describes the relations between achieved learning outcomes, context where outcomes are achieved or applied, and evidence records of the obtained learning outcomes. Information on levels like

Figure 8. Profile extended with learning outcomes

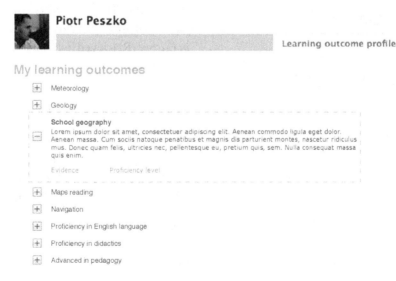

proficiency level of learner mastering for the learning outcomes are also captured.

The PALO schema went through at least three iterative expert evaluations by the ICOPER consortium and at relevant international workshops by standards experts, teachers and learners to make sure that it captures data needed for increased employability of learners and higher interoperability with different learning systems.

Currently, prototypes of outcome based learning applications like widgets and LMS modules are being developed. These prototypes produce data about achieved learning outcomes of learners in systems like Moodle (2010), Elgg (2010) and Clix (2010) and store it in ICOPER's PALO repository. These data can be consumed by learning systems to provide learners with relevant material, recommendation of other teachers and learners based on similarity of learning outcome profiles, or to enable learners to share their achievement profiles with social or recruitment systems.

Future work will include the dissemination and validation of the prototypes in real-world environments. The PALO model is being prepared to be discussed in the CEN Workshop on Learning Technologies for standardization, as an EU specification for capturing data of personal achieved learning outcomes.

ACKNOWLEDGEMENT

This work was supported by the ICOPER Best Practice Network. (http://icoper.org), which is co-funded by the European Commission under the eContentplus programme, ECP 2007 EDU 417007. We thank Piotr Peszko for creating and providing the mock-up screens.

REFERENCES

ATOM. (2010). *The Atom Syndication Format.* Retrieved February 3, 2010, from http://www.ietf.org/rfc/rfc4287.txt

CEN. (2010). *CEN Workshop Learning Technologies*. Retrieved February 5, 2010, from http://www.cen-isss-wslt.din.de.

Clix. (2010). *Clix IMC Learning Management System*. Retrieved February 3, 2010, from http://www.im-c.de/en/products/learning-management-system/product-overview/what-is-clix

Crespo, M. R., Najjar, J., Derntl, M., Leony, D., Neumann, S., Oberhuemer, P., et al. (2010, April 14-16). Aligning Assessment with Learning Outcomes in Outcome-based Education. In *Proceedings of the Engineering Education Conference (EDUCON)*, Madrid, Spain.

ELGG. (n.d.). *Social Networking Platform*. Retrieved February 3, 2010, from http://elgg.org/

EQF. (2000). *The EQF for lifelong learning, Office for the publication of the EC*. ISBN 978-92-79-0847-4

Euro, L. M. (2009). *European Learner Mobility*. Retrieved February 5, 2010, from http://wiki.teria.no/confluence/display/EuropeanLearnerMobility

Europass. (2010). *Europass - Initiative for Transparency of Qualification and Mobility of Citizens in Europe*. Retrieved February 3, 2010, from http://europass.cedefop.europa.eu/

Facebook. (2010). *Facebook Social Network*. Retrieved February 3, 2010, from http://www.facebook.com/

Grant, J. (2002). Learning needs assessment: assessing the need. *BMJ (Clinical Research Ed.)*, *324*, 156–159. doi:10.1136/bmj.324.7330.156

HR-XML. (2008). *HR-XML Competency data model*. Retrieved February 5, 2010, from http://ns.hr-xml.org/3.0/.

ICOPER. (2010). *ICOPER Best Practice Network*. Retrieved February 3, 2010, from http://www. icoper.org/.

IEEE. (2002). *1484.12.1 – IEEE Standard for Learning Object Metadata*. Washington, DC: IEEE.

IEEE RCD. (2007). *IEEE LTSC Reusable Competency Definitions (RCD)*. Retrieved February 3, 2010, from http://www.ieeeltsc.org/working-groups/wg20Comp/

LEAP2A. (2008). JISC LEAP 2A Portfolio Interoperability Projects (PIOP). *Educational Technology & Society, 9*(1), 23-37.

Lindgren, R., Henfridsson, O., & Schultze, U. (2004). Design Principles for Competence Management Systems: A Synthesis of an Action Research Study. *Management Information Systems Quarterly, 28*(3), 435–472.

LinkedIn. (2010). *LinkedIn Social Network*. Retrievd February 3, 2010, from http://www. linkedin.com/

Moodle. (2010). *Moodle Learning Management System*. Retrieved February 3, 2010, from http:// moodle.org/

Najjar, J., & Klobučar, T. (2009). *ISURE: Report of study of learning needs building blocks and the standards to be used*. ICOPER Project Deliverables.

Paquette, G. (2007). An Ontology and a Software Framework for Competency Modeling and. Management. *Journal of Educational Technology & Society, 10*(3), 1–21.

Richter, T., & Pawlowski, J. M. (2007, October). The Need for Standardization of Context Metadata for e-Learning Environments. In *Proceedings of the e-ASEM Conference*, Seoul, Korea.

Sampson, D. G. (2009). Competence-related Metadata for Educational Resources that Support Lifelong Competence Development Programmes. *Journal of Educational Technology & Society, 12*(4), 149–159.

Totschnig, M., Klerkx, K., Klobučar, T., Law, E., Simon, B., & Ternier, S. (2009). *Open ICOPER Content Space Implementation of 1st Generation of Open ICOPER Content Space including Integration Mini Case Studies*. ICOPER Project Deliverables.

Van Assche, F. (2007). Linking Learning Resources to Curricula by using Competencies. In *Proceedings of the First International Workshop on Learning object Discovery Exchange*, Crete, Greece.

This work was previously published in the International Journal of IT Standards and Standardization Research (IJITSR), Volume 8, Issue 2, edited by Kai Jakobs, pp. 87-104, copyright 2010 by IGI Publishing (an imprint of IGI Global)

Compilation of References

ABET. (2006). *Criteria for the evaluation of engineering programs*. Retrieved from http://www.abet.org

Abrahamson, E., & Fombrun, C. J. (1994). Macroculture: Determinants and Consequences. *Academy of Management Review, 19*(4), 728–755.

Abrahamson, E., & Rosenkopf, L. (1993). Institutional and Competitive Bandwagons: Using Mathematical Modeling as a Tool to Explore Innovation Diffusion. *Academy of Management Review, 18*(3), 487–517.

Abrahamson, E., & Rosenkopf, L. (1997). Social Network Effects on the Extent of Innovation Diffusion: A Computer Simulation. *Organization Science, 8*(3), 289–309. doi:10.1287/orsc.8.3.289

ADL. (2001). *ADL, Sharable Content Object Reference Model Specification, V 1.2*. Retrieved from http://www.adlnet.gov/Technologies/scorm/SCORMSDocuments/Forms/AllItems.aspx?Root Folder=%2fTechnologies%2fscorm%2fSCORMSDocuments%2fPrevious%20Versions%2fSCORM%201%2e2%2fDocumentation%20Suite%20%28SCORM%201%2e2%29&FolderCTID=0x0120007F801FCD5325044C89D912 40519482D7&View=%7b4D6DFFDE%2d3CFC%2d4DD9%2dA21A%2d4B687728 824A%7d

Adolphi, H. (1997). *Strategische konzepte zur organisation der betrieblichen standardisierung*. Berlin, Germany: Beuth Verlag: DIN Normungskunde Band 38.

Advanced Distributed Learning. (2009). *Shareable Content Object Reference Model SCORM 2004* (4th ed.). Alexandria, VA: Advanced Distributed Learning.

Alcácer, J., & Gittelman, M. (2006). Patent citations as a measure of knowledge flows: The influence of examiner citations. *The Review of Economics and Statistics, 88*(4), 774–779. doi:10.1162/rest.88.4.774

Allinson, J., & Heery, R. (2006). Deposit API. *UKOLN Wiki*. Retrieved March 30, 2010 from http://www.ukoln.ac.uk/repositories/digirep/index/Deposit_API

Allinson, J., Francois, S., & Lewis, S. (2008). SWORD: Simple Web-service Offering Repository Deposit. *Ariadne, 54*, Retrieved from http://www.ariadne.ac.uk/issue54/allinson-et-al/

Allison, J., & Lemley, M. (2002). The growing complexity of the United States patent system. *Boston University Law Review, 82*, 77.

Allison, J., & Tiller, E. (2003). The business method patent myth. *Berkeley Technology Law Journal, 18*(987), 1082.

Al-Qirim, N. (2005). An Empirical Investigation of an e-commerce Adoption-Capability Model in Small Businesses in New Zealand. *Electronic Markets, 15*(4), 418–437. doi:10.1080/10196780500303136

Angeles, R., Corritore, C. L., Basu, S. C., & Nath, R. (2001). Success factors for domestic and international electronic data interchange (EDI) implementation for US firms. *International Journal of Information Management, 21*(5), 329–347. doi:10.1016/S0268-4012(01)00028-7

ANSI. (1959). *ANSI Patent Policy*. Retrieved from http://publicaa.ansi.org/sites/apdl/Reference%20Documents%20Regarding%20ANSI%20Patent%20Policy/02-Apr1959%2011.6PatentsASA.pdf

ANSI. (2006, June). *Activities Related to IPR and Standards. Paper presented to the* Global Standards Collaboration -11, IPR Working Group Meeting, Chicago.

ANSI. (2010). *ANSI Essential Requirements.* Retrieved from http://publicaa.ansi.org/sites/apdl/Documents/Standards%20Activities/American%20National%20Standards/Procedures,%20Guides,%20 and%20Forms/2010%20ANSI%20Essential%20 Requirements%20and%20Related/2010%20ANSI%20 Essential%20Requirements.pdf

ANSI. (n.d.). *Domestic Programs (American National Standards Overview).* Retrieved from http://www.ansi. org/standards_activities/domestic_programs/overview. aspx?menuid=3

APEC. (2006). *The eighteenth APEC ministerial meeting joint statement.* Singapore: APEC.

Arborio, A.-M., & Fournier, P. (1999). *L'enquête et ses méthodes: l'observation directe.* Paris: Nathan Université.

Arthur, W. B. (1984). Competing Technologies and Economic Prediction. In MacKenzie, D., & Wajcman, J. (Eds.), *The Social Shaping of Technology* (2nd ed., pp. 106–112). Buckingham: Open University Press.

Arthur, W. B. (1989). Competing technologies, increasing returns, and lock-in by historical events. *The Economic Journal, 99*(394), 116–131. doi:10.2307/2234208

Arthur, W. B. (1990). Positive feedbacks in the economy. *Scientific American, 262*(2), 92–99. doi:10.1038/scientificamerican0290-92

Asami, H., & Sasaki, M. (2006). Outline of ISDB systems. *Proceedings of the IEEE, 94*(1), 248–250. doi:10.1109/JPROC.2005.859690

ATOM. (2010). *The Atom Syndication Format.* Retrieved February 3, 2010, from http://www.ietf.org/rfc/rfc4287.txt

ATSC. (2009). *Mobile DTV standard, part 1 – ATSC mobile digital television system.* Retrieved from http://www.atsc. org/cms/standards/a153/a_153-Part-1-2009.pdf

Attewell, P. (1992). Technology Diffusion and Organizational Learning: The Case of Business Computing. *Organization Science, 3*(1), 1–19. doi:10.1287/orsc.3.1.1

Augustine, N., & Vest, C. (1994). *Engineering Education for a Changing World.* Washington, DC: ASEE.

Baird, S. (2009). *Organizational Interoperability is Key to a Successful eGovernment Strategy.* Retrieved April 5, 2010, from http://www.talkstandards.com/ organizational-interoperability-is-key-to-a-successful-egovernment-strategy/

Bakhuizen, M., & Horn, U. (2005). Mobile broadcast/multicast in mobile networks. *Ericsson Review, 1.*

Bamberg, U. (2004). Le rôle des syndicats allemands dans le processus de normalisation national et européen. *Newsletter du BTS, 24-25,* 12-16. Retrieved December 10, 2008, from http://hesa.etui-rehs.org/fr/newsletter/ files/Pages12-16.pdf

Barn, B., Dexter, H., Oussena, S., Sparks, D., Petch, J., & Stiles, M. (2006). *COVARM – Course Validation Reference Model* (Final Report). *JISC Collections.* Retrieved March 31, 2010 from http://www.jisccollections.ac.uk/ media/documents/programmes/elearningframework/ covarm_final_report_v1.pdf

Baumol, W., & Swanson, D. (2005). Reasonable and nondiscriminatory (RAND) royalties, standards selection, and control of market power. *Antitrust Law Journal, 73*(1).

Beauvais-Schwartz, N., & Bousquet, F. (2010). *France – Fostering competitive intelligence.* Retrieved from http://www.iso.org/iso/iso-focus-plus_index/iso-fo-cusplus_online-bonus-articles/the-2009-iso-award/2009-award_france.htm

Beck, R., & Weitzel, T. (2005). Some Economics of Vertical Standards: Integrating SMEs in EDI Supply Chains. *Electronic Markets, 15*(4), 313–322. doi:10.1080/10196780500302781

Behrens, H. (2010, March 9). *Education about standardization – Competency of standards body staff.* Paper presented at the First Meeting of the CEN/CENELEC/ETSI Joint Working Group on Education about Standardization, Brussels, Belgium.

Behrman, J., & Taubman, P. (1976). Intergenerational transmission of income and wealth. *The American Economic Review, 66*(2), 436–440.

Bekkers, R. (2001). *Mobile Telecommunications Standards: GSM, UMTS, TETRA, and ERMES.* Boston: Artech House.

Bekkers, R., & West, J. (2009). Standards, patents and mobile phones: Lessons from ETSI's handling of UMTS. *International Journal of IT Standards and Standardization Research, 7*(1). doi:10.4018/jitsr.2009010102

Belleflamme, P. (2002). Coordination on formal vs. de facto standards: A dynamic approach. *European Journal of Political Economy, 18*(1). doi:10.1016/S0176-2680(01)00073-8

Ben Youssef, H., Grolleau, G., & Jebsi, K. (2005). L'utilisation stratégique des instances de normalisation environnementale. *Revue Internationales de Droit Economique, 4,* 367–388. doi:10.3917/ride.194.0367

Benjamin, R. I., de Long, D. W., & Morton, M. S. S. (1990). Electronic Data Interchange: How Much Competitive Advantage? *Long Range Planning, 23*(1), 29–40. doi:10.1016/0024-6301(90)90005-O

Bensaou, B., & Venkatraman, N. (1995). Configurations of Interorganizational Relationships: A Comparison Between U.S. and Japanese Automakers. *Management Science, 41*(9), 1471–1492. doi:10.1287/mnsc.41.9.1471

Berkowitz, L. (1980). *A survey of social psychology.* New York: Holt, Rinehart and Winston.

Besen, S. M. (1992). AM versus FM: The battle of the bands. *Industrial and Corporate Change, 1*(2), 375–396. doi:10.1093/icc/1.2.375

Besen, S. M. (1995). The Standards Processes in Telecommunication and Information Technology. In Hawkins, R., Mansell, R., & Skea, J. (Eds.), *Standards, Innovation, and Competitiveness: the Politics and Economics of Standards in Natural and Technical Environments.* Cheltenham, UK: Edward Elgar.

Besen, S. M., & Farrell, J. (1991). The role of the ITU in standardization: Pre-eminence, impotence or rubber stamp? *Telecommunications Policy, 15*(4), 311–321. doi:10.1016/0308-5961(91)90053-E

Besen, S. M., & Farrell, J. (1994). Choosing how to compete: Strategies and tactics in standardization. *The Journal of Economic Perspectives, 8*(2), 117–131. doi:10.1257/jep.8.2.117

Bijker, W. E. (1993). *Dutch, Dikes and Democracy: An Argument against Democratic, Authoritarian and Neutral Technologies.* Lyngby, Denmark: Unit of Technology Assessment, Technical University of Denmark.

Bijker, W. E. (1995). *Of Bicycles, Bakelites and Bulbs. Toward a Theory of Sociotechnical Change.* Cambridge, MA: MIT Press.

Biswell, K. (2004). Consumers and standards: increasing influence. *Consumer Policy Review, 4*(6), 177–185.

Blandin, B. (2004). *Are e-learning standards neutral?* In *Proceedings of CALIE 2004.* Retrieved April 1, 2010, from http://www-clips.imag.fr/calie04/actes/Blandin_final.pdf

Blind, K. (2008). A Welfare Analysis of standards Competition: The example of the ECMA OpenXML Standard and the ISO ODF Standard. In K. Jakobs & E. Soederstroem (Eds.), *Proceedings of the 13th EURAS Workshop on Standardisation* (pp. 1-17). Aachen, Germany: Wissenschafts Verlag Mainz.

Blind, K. (2004). *The economics of standards: theory, evidence, policy.* Cheltenham, UK: Edward Elgar Publishing.

Blind, K. (2004). *The Economics of Standards: Theory, Evidence, Policy.* Cheltenham, UK: Edward Elgar.

Blind, K., Cremers, K., & Mueller, E. (2008). The influence of strategic patenting on companies' patent portfolios. *Research Policy, 38,* 428–436. doi:10.1016/j.respol.2008.12.003

Blind, K., & Gauch, S. (2008). Trends in ICT standards: the relationship between European standardisation bodies and standards consortia. *Telecommunications Policy, 32*(7), 503–513. doi:10.1016/j.telpol.2008.05.004

Blind, K., & Thumm, N. (2004). Interrelation between patenting and standardisation strategies: Empirical evidence and policy implications. *Research Policy, 33*(10), 1583–1598. doi:10.1016/j.respol.2004.08.007

BmcoForum. (2008). *The bmcoforum articles of association.* Retrieved from http://www.bmcoforum. org/fileadmin/user_upload/Forms/bmcoforum_Articles_2008_06_17_English.pdf

BmcoForum. (2009). *Recommendation for implementation profile: OMA BCAST system adaptation: IPDC over DVB-H.* Retrieved from http://www.bmcoforum. org/fileadmin/user_upload/Downloads/Implementation_profiles/bmcoforum_profile_-_DVB_Adaptation_V1.2_20090107-A_-_OMA_BCAST_V1.0.pdf

BmcoForum. (2010). *Profile documents, version 2.0.* Retrieved from http://www.bmcoforum.org/index. php?id=191

Boström, M. (2006). Regulatory credibility and authority through inclusiveness: Standardization organizations in cases of eco-labelling. *Organization, 13*(3), 345–367. doi:10.1177/1350508406063483

Bouchard, L. (1993). *Decision Criteria in the Adoption of EDI.* Paper presented at the Fourteenth International Conference on Information Systems, Orlando, FL.

Boynton, A. C., Zmud, R. W., & Jacobs, G. C. (1994). The Influence of IT Management Practice on IT Use in Large Corporations. *Management Information Systems Quarterly, 18*(3), 299–318. doi:10.2307/249620

Bradford, M., & Florin, J. (2003). Examining the role of innovation diffusion factors on the implementation success of enterprise resource planning systems. *Accounting Information Systems, 4,* 205–225. doi:10.1016/S1467-0895(03)00026-5

Brand, S. (1994). *How Buildings Learn.* New York: Viking.

Brehm, J. W., & Cohen, A. R. (1962). *Explorations in cognitive dissonance.* New York: Wiley. doi:10.1037/11622-000

Brons, T. F. (2007). *Effective participation in formal standardization: A multinational perspective.* Rotterdam, The Netherlands: Rotterdam School of Management.

Brunsson, N., & Jacobsson, B. (Eds.). (2000). *A World of Standards.* New York: Oxford University Press.

Brynjolfsson, E., & Hitt, L. M. (1998). Beyond the productivity paradox. *Communications of the ACM, 41*(8), 49–55. doi:10.1145/280324.280332

Bullock, S., & Cliff, D. (2004). *Complexity and Emergent Behaviour in ICT Systems (HPL-2004-187).* Bristol, UK: Hewlett-Packard.

Burkart, M. (1995). Initial shareholdings and overbidding in take-over contests. *The Journal of Finance, 50*(5), 1491–1515. doi:10.1111/j.1540-6261.1995.tb05186.x

Cable & Satellite International. (2009). *3 Italia launches OMA BCAST service.* Retrieved from http://www.csi-magazine.com/news-19-02-2009-oma.php

Cabral, L., & Salant, D. (2008). *Evolving technologies and standards regulation.* Retrieved from http://ssrn.com/abstract=1120862

Caliste, J., & Farges, G. (2007). A French University: Encouraging hands-on experience. *ISO Focus, 4*(11), 13–14.

Callon, M., Lascoumes, P., & Barthe, Y. (2001). *Agir dans un monde incertain. Essai sur la démocratie technique.* Paris: Seuil.

Canadian Engineering Accreditation Board. (2007). *Canadian Accreditation Criteria.* Retrieved from http://www.ccpe.ca/e/files/report_ceab.pdf

Canadian Engineering Accreditation Board. (2007). *CEAB Questionnaire for Evaluation of Engineering Programs.* Retrieved from http://www.ccpe.ca/e/acc_supp_1.cfm

Case C-336/07 Kabel Deutschland [2008] ECR I-10889 para 46.

CEDEFOP. (2004). Retrieved from http://europass. cedefop.europa.eu/img/dynamic/c1399/type.FileContent. file/EuropassDecision_en_US.PDF

CEN. (2008). *CWA 15903: Metadata for Learning Opportunities (MLO) – Advertising.* Retrieved March 30, 2010 from ftp://ftp.cenorm.be/PUBLIC/CWAs/e-Europe/WS-LT/CWA15903-00-2008-Dec.pdf

CEN. (2008). *Metadata for Learning Opportunities (MLO).* Advertising.

CEN. (2010). *CEN Workshop Learning Technologies.* Retrieved February 5, 2010, from http://www.cen-isss-wslt.din.de.

CEN/ISS. S (2008). *CWA 15903:2008. Metadata for Learning Opportunities (MLO) – Advertising.* Brussels, Belgium: The European Committee for Standardization.

Center for Global Standards Analysis. (2004). *Report on a survey of schools of engineering in the United States concerning standards education.* Washington, DC: The Catholic University of America.

CETIS. (2009). *UK LEAP 2.0.* Retrieved from http://wiki.cetis.ac.uk/LEAP_specification

Chappatte, P. (2009). FRAND Commitments—The Case for Antitrust Intervention. *European Competition Journal, 5*, 319–340. doi:10.5235/ecj.v5n2.319

Chen, A. N. K., Sen, S., & Shao, B. (2003, August 4-6). *Identifying Factors to improve effective XML adoption in Electronic Businesses.* Paper presented at the Ninth Americas Conference on Information Systems, Tampa, FL.

Chiao, B., Lerner, J., & Tirole, J. (2005). *The rules of standard setting organizations: An empirical analysis.* Retrieved from http://ssrn.com/abstract=664643

Chin, W. W., Marcolin, B. L., & Newsted, P. R. (1996, December 16-18). *A Partial Least Squares Latent Variable Modeling Approach for Measuring Interaction Effects: Results from a Monte Carlo Simulation Study and Voice Mail Emotion/Adoption Study.* Paper presented at the Seventeenth International Conference on Information Systems, Cleveland, OH.

China Mobile Multimedia Broadcasting (CMMB). (2009). *List of promulgated industry standards.* Retrieved from http://www.cmmb.org.cn/knowledge/105/

Chircu, A. M., Kauffman, R. J., & Keskey, D. (2001). Maximizing the Value of Internet-Based Corporate Travel Reservation Systems. *Communications of the ACM, 44*(11), 57–63. doi:10.1145/384150.384162

Choi, D. (Ed.). (2008). *APEC SCSC education guideline 1: Case studies of how to plan and implement standards education programs.* Singapore: Asia Pacific Economic Cooperation.

Choi, D., & de Vries, H. J. (2011). Standardization as emerging content in technology education. *International Journal of Technology and Design Education, 21*(1), 111–135. doi:10.1007/s10798-009-9110-z

Choi, D., de Vries, H. J., & Kim, D. (2009). Standards education policy development: Observations based on APEC research. *International Journal of IT Standards and Standardization Research, 7*(2), 23–42. doi:10.4018/jitsr.2009070103

Chowdry, B., & Jegadeesh, N. (1994). Pre-tender offers share acquisition strategy in takeovers. *Journal of Financial and Quantitative Analysis, 29*, 117–129. doi:10.2307/2331194

Chwelos, P., Benbasat, I., & Dexter, A. S. (1997). *The Adoption and Impact of Electronic Data Interchange: A Test of Internal and External Factors.* Paper presented at the International Conference on Information Systems (ICIS), Atlanta, GA.

Chwelos, P., Benbasat, I., & Dexter, A. S. (2001). Research report: Empirical test of an EDI adoption model. *Information Systems Research, 12*(3), 304–321. doi:10.1287/isre.12.3.304.9708

Ciganek, A. P., Haines, M. N., & Haseman, W. D. (2005, January 3-6). *Challenges of Adopting Web Services: Experiences from the Financial Industry.* Paper presented at the Hawaii International Conference on System Sciences (HICSS 38), Waikoloa, HI.

Ciganek, A. P., Haines, M. N., & Haseman, W. D. (2006, January 4-7). *Horizontal and Vertical Factors Influencing the Adoption of Web Services.* Paper presented at the Hawaii International Conference on System Sciences (HICSS 39), Kauai, HI.

CIPD. (2009). *Competency and competency frameworks.* Retrieved February 11, 2010, from http://www.cipd.co.uk/subjects/perfmangmt/competnces/comptfrmwk.htm

Clix. (2010). *Clix IMC Learning Management System.* Retrieved February 3, 2010, from http://www.im-c.de/en/products/learning-management-system/product-overview/what-is-clix

Cochoy, F. (2000). De l'AFNOR à NF ou la progressive marchandisation de la normalisation industrielle. *Reseaux, 102*, 63–89.

Cochoy, F. (2002). Une petite histoire de client, ou la progressive normalisation du marché et de l'organisation. *Sociologie du Travail, 44*, 357–380. doi:10.1016/S0038-0296(02)01238-4

Cochoy, F. (2005). A brief history of 'customers,' or the gradual standardization of markets and organizations. *Sociologie du Travail, 47*, S36–S56. doi:10.1016/j.soctra.2005.08.001

Cochoy, F. (2006). The industrial Roots of Contemporary Political Consumerism: The Case of the French Standardization Movement. In Micheletti, M., Follesdal, A., & Stolle, D. (Eds.), *Politics, Products, and Markets: Exploring Political Consumerism Past and Present* (pp. 145–160). London: Transaction Publishers.

Cofrinex v Helary, Paris Court of Appeal 12 July 1977; Sec. 139 Para. 2 German Patent Act.

Cohen, W. M., & Levinthal, D. A. (1990). Absorptive capacity: A new perspective on learning and innovation. *Administrative Science Quarterly, 35*(1), 128. doi:10.2307/2393553

Cooklev, T. (2010). The role of standards in engineering education. *International Journal of IT Standards and Standardization Research, 8*(1), 1–9. doi:10.4018/jitsr.2010120701

Cooper, A. (2009). *Evaluating Standards – A Discussion of Perspectives, Issues and Evaluation Dimensions.* Bolton, UK: JISC CETIS. Retrieved April 21, 2010 from http://wiki.cetis.ac.uk/images/e/e7/Evaluating_Standards_Public_v1p0.doc

Cooper, A. (2010). *The Best of Both Worlds: Formal Public Standardisation and Open Community Development.* Paper presented at JISC CETIS Future of Interoperability Standards workshop, Bolton, UK. Retrieved from http://wiki.cetis.ac.uk/images/e/e3/Best_of_Both_Worlds.doc

Cooper, R., & Zmud, R. (1990). Information Technology Implementation Research: A Technological Diffusion Approach. *Management Science, 36*(2), 123–139. doi:10.1287/mnsc.36.2.123

Corbin, A. L. (1952). *Corbin on Contracts.* St. Paul, MN: West Publishing Company.

Council of the European Union. (2007). *Draft council conclusions on "strengthening the internal market for mobile television (Mobile TV)" (15201/07).* Retrieved from http://register.consilium.europa.eu/pdf/en/07/st14/st14398.en07.pdf

Council of the European Union. (2008, September 25). *Council conclusions on standardisation and innovation: 2891st competitiveness council meeting.* Brussels, Belgium: Council of the European Union.

Cour de Cassation. (1991). Sté Ets Delaplace et Sté Sicma c. Sté Van Der Lely. *Annales de la Propriété Industrielle, 4.*

Cowan, R. (1992). High Technology and the Economics of Standardization. In Dierkes, M., & Hoffmann, U. (Eds.), *New Technology at the Outset. Social Forces in the Shaping of Technological Innovations* (pp. 279–300). New York: Westview.

Crane, R. J. (1979). *The politics of international standards: France and the color TV war.* New York, NY: Ablex Publishing.

Crespo, M. R., Najjar, J., Derntl, M., Leony, D., Neumann, S., Oberhuemer, P., et al. (2010, April 14-16). Aligning Assessment with Learning Outcomes in Outcome-based Education. In *Proceedings of the Engineering Education Conference (EDUCON)*, Madrid, Spain.

Cronbach, L. J. (1951). Coefficient Alpha and the Internal Structure of Tests. *Psychometrika, 16*, 297–334. doi:10.1007/BF02310555

Czaya, A., Egyedi, T., & Hesser, W. (2010, June 8-9). The current state of standardization education in Europe. In *Proceedings of the 7th International Conference on Standardization Protypes and Quality: A Means of Balkan Countries Collaboration*, Zlatibor, Serbia (pp. 85-90).

Damsgaard, J., & Lyytinen, K. (2001). The Role of Intermediating Institutions in the Diffusion of Electronic Data Interchange (EDI): How Industry Associations Intervened in Denmark, Finland, and Hong Kong. *The Information Society, 17*(3), 195–210. doi:10.1080/01972240152493056

David, P. A. (1985). Clio and the economics of QWERTY. *The American Economic Review, 75*(2), 332–337.

David, P. A. (1995). Standardization policies for network technologies: The flux between freedom and order revisited. In Hawkins, R., Mansell, R., & Skea, J. (Eds.), *Standards, innovation and competitiveness - The politics and economics of standards in natural and technical environments*. Aldershot, UK: Edward Elgar.

David, P. A., & Greenstein, S. (1990). The economics of compatibility standards: An introduction to recent research. *Economics of Innovation and New Technology*, *1*(1), 3–41. doi:10.1080/10438599000000002

Dawar, K. (2006). Global governance and its implications for consumers. *Consumer policy review, 16*(1), 2-4.

De Vries, H. J. (2005). Standardization education. *Homo Oeconomicus (EURAS Yearbook of Standardization, Vol. 5), 22*(1), 71-91

De Vries, H.J., & Simons, J. (2006). Effectiveness of participation in Standardisation. *Synthesis Journal*, 15-20.

de Vries, H. J. (1999). *Standardization – A business approach to the role of national standardization organizations*. Boston, MA: Kluwer Academic.

de Vries, H. J. (2002). Standardization – Mapping a field of research. In Bollin, S. (Ed.), *The standards edge* (pp. 99–121). Ann Arbor, MI: Bollin Communications.

de Vries, H. J. (2003). *Kenbaarheid normalisatie en normen – Deelproject 9b HBO-onderwijs – Tussenrapportage*. Delft, The Netherlands: NEN.

De Vries, H. J. (2006). IT Standards Typology. In Jakobs, K. (Ed.), *Information Technology Standards and Standardization Research* (pp. 1–26). Hershey, PA: Idea Group Publishing. doi:10.4018/978-1-59140-938-0.ch001

de Vries, H. J., Blind, K., Mangelsdorf, A., Verheul, H., & van der Zwan, J. (2009). *SME access to European standardization - Enabling small and medium-sized enterprises to achieve greater benefit from standards and from involvement in standardization*. Brussels, Belgium: CEN and CENELEC.

de Vries, H. J., & Egyedi, T. M. (2007). Education about standardization – Recent findings. *International Journal of IT Standards and Standardization Research, 5*(2), 1–16. doi:10.4018/jitsr.2007070101

Dedrick, J., & West, J. (2003, December 12-14). *Why Firms Adopt Open Source Platforms: A Grounded Theory of Innovation and Standard Adoption*. Paper presented at the International Conference on IS Special Workshop on Standard Making sponsored by MISQ, Seattle, WA.

DeLacey, B., Herman, K., Kiron, K., & Lerner, J. (2006). *Strategic behavior in standard-setting organizations*. Retrieved from http://ssrn.com/abstract=903214

Denardis, L., & Levin, A. (2009). *Bridging the standardization gap – ITU-T research project: Measuring and reducing the standards gap*. Geneva, Switzerland: International Telecommunication Union.

DeNicolo, V. (2008). Revisiting Injunctive Relief: Interpreting *eBay* in High-Tech Industries with Non-Practicing Patent Holders. *Journal of Competition Law & Economics*, *4*, 571. doi:10.1093/joclec/nhn028

Deutsches Institut für Normung. (2010). *DIN-Preise*. Retrieved from http://www.din.de/cmd?level=tpl-rubrik&menuid=47388&cmsareaid=47388&menurubricid=47468&cmsrubid=47468&languageid=de

Devaraj, S., & Kohli, R. (2003). Performance Impacts of Information Technology: Is Actual Usage the Missing Link? *Management Science, 49*(3), 273–289. doi:10.1287/mnsc.49.3.273.12736

Dewatripont, M., & Legros, P. (2008). *'Essential' patents, FRAND royalties and technological standards*. Retrieved from http://ncomprod.nokia.com/NOKIA_COM_1/Press/Legal_News_(IPR_news)/IPR_News/pdf/Dewatripont_Legros-frand-march16-2008.pdf

Die Bundesregierung. (2009). *Normungspolitisches konzept der bundesregierung*. Berlin, Germany: Die Bundesregierung.

DIN. (2006). *DIN PAS 1068 (2006-12) Learning, Education and Training With Special Consideration Of E-learning - Guideline For The Description Of Educational Offers*. Retrieved April 1, 2010, from http://infostore.saiglobal.com/store/Details.aspx?ProductID=885033

Dolmans, M. (2008). Standards, IP, and Competition: How to Avoid False FRANDs. *Fordham IP Law Institute, Standard Setting — The Interplay With IP and Competition Laws,* 12-13.

Dutson, A. J., Todd, R. H., Magleby, S. P., & Sorensen, C. D. (1997). A review of literature on teaching design through project-oriented capstone courses. *Journal of Engineering Education, 76*(1), 17–28.

DVB-H.org. (2010). *DVB-H global mobile TV: Services, trials & pilots.* Retrieved from http://www.dvb-h.org/services.htm

Dym, C. L., & Little, L. (2003). *Engineering Design: A Project-Based Instruction.* New York: John Wiley & Sons.

Dym, C., Agogino, A. M., Eris, O., Frey, D. D., & Leifer, L. J. (2005). Engineering design thinking, teaching and learning. *Journal of Engineering Education, 94*(1), 103–120.

E & L Consulting, Ltd. v. Doman Indus. Ltd., 472 F.3d 23 29 [2d Cir. 2006].

Education and Culture DG. (2008). *The European Qualifications Framework for Lifelong Learning.* Retrieved February 8, 2010, from http://www.qcda.gov.uk/library-Assets/media/Leaflet_on_the_EQF_en.pdf

Edwards, P. N., Jackson, S. J., Bowker, G. C., & Knobel, C. P. (2007). *Understanding Infrastructure: Dynamics, Tensions and Design* (Report of the Workshop on History & Theory of Infrastructure: Lessons for New Scientific Infrastructures). Ann Arbor, MI: School of Information, University of Michigan.

Egan, M. (1998). Regulatory strategies, delegation and European market integration. *Journal of European Public Policy, 5*(3), 485–506. doi:10.1080/135017698343938

Egyedi, T. M. (1996). *Shaping Standardization: A study of standards processes and standards policies in the field of telematic services.* Delft, The Netherlands: Delft University Press.

Egyedi, T. M. (2001). Why JavaTM was -not- standardized twice. *Computer Standards & Interfaces, 23*(4), 253–265. doi:10.1016/S0920-5489(01)00078-2

Egyedi, T. M. (2007). Experts on causes of incompatibility between standard-compliant products. In Doumeingts, G., Müller, J., Morel, G., & Vallespir, B. (Eds.), *Enterprise interoperability* (pp. 553–563). Berlin, Germany: Springer-Verlag. doi:10.1007/978-1-84628-714-5_51

Egyedi, T. M. (2007). Standard-compliant, but incompatible?! *Computer Standards & Interfaces, 29*(6), 605–613. doi:10.1016/j.csi.2007.04.001

Egyedi, T. M. (2008). An implementation perspective on sources of incompatibility and standards' dynamics. In Egyedi, T. M., & Blind, K. (Eds.), *The dynamics of standards* (pp. 181–189). Cheltenham, UK: Edward Elgar.

Egyedi, T. M., & Blind, K. (2008). Introduction. In Egyedi, T. M., & Blind, K. (Eds.), *The dynamics of standards* (pp. 1–12). Cheltenham, UK: Edward Elgar.

Egyedi, T. M., & Hudson, J. (2005). A standard's integrity: Can it be safeguarded? *IEEE Communications Magazine, 43*(2), 151–155. doi:10.1109/MCOM.2005.1391516

Egyedi, T. M., & Koppenhol, A. (2009). Concurrerende standaarden een goede zaak? In Sleurink, H., & Stedehouder, J. (Eds.), *Open Source Jaarboek 2008-2009* (pp. 119–130). Gorredijk, The Netherlands: Media Update Vakpublicaties.

Egyedi, T. M., & Verwater-Lukszo, Z. (2005). Which standards' characteristics increase system flexibility? Comparing ICT and batch processing infrastructures. *Technology in Society, 27*, 347–362. doi:10.1016/j.techsoc.2005.04.007

Ehlers, U. D., & Pawlowski, J. M. (2006). Qualiy in European E-Learning – An Introduction. In Ehlers, U. D., & Pawlowski, J. M. (Eds.), *European Handbook of Quality and Standardisation in E-Learning.* Berlin: Springer. doi:10.1007/3-540-32788-6_1

ELGG. (n.d.). *Social Networking Platform.* Retrieved February 3, 2010, from http://elgg.org/

Elsen, I., Hartung, F., Horn, U., Kampmann, M., & Peters, L. (2001). Streaming technology in 3G mobile communication systems. *IEEE Computer, 34*(9), 46–52. doi:10.1109/2.947089

Emerson, R. M. (1962). Power Dependence Relations. *American Sociological Review, 27*(1), 31–41. doi:10.2307/2089716

Endress & Hauser, Inc. v Hawk Measurement Sys. Pty. Ltd. 892 F. Supp 1123, 1130 [S.D. Ind. 1995].

EQF. (2000). *The EQF for lifelong learning, Office for the publication of the EC.* ISBN 978-92-79-0847-4

Erard, L.-O. (2008). Sécurité: Fumer n'est pas jouer. *FRC Magazine, 12*, 4.

ETSI. (n.d.). *ETSI IPR Policy.* Retrieved March 7, 2010, from http://www.etsi.org/WebSite/document/Legal/ETSI_IPR-Policy.pdf

Ettlie, J. E. (1980). Adequacy of Stage Models for Decisions on Adoption of Innovation. *Psychological Reports, 46*(8), 991–995. doi:10.2466/pr0.1980.46.3.991

Euro, L. M. (2009). *European Learner Mobility.* Retrieved February 5, 2010, from http://wiki.teria.no/confluence/display/EuropeanLearnerMobility

Europass. (2010). *Europass - Initiative for Transparency of Qualification and Mobility of Citizens in Europe.* Retrieved February 3, 2010, from http://europass.cedefop.europa.eu/

European Commission. (1992). *Communication of the Commission: Intellectual Property Rights and Standardization.* Brussels, Belgium: Author.

European Commission. (2002a, March 7). Directive 2002/21/EC of the European Parliament and of the council on a common regulatory framework for electronic communications networks and services (Framework Directive). *Official Journal of the European Communities, L108*, 33–50.

European Commission. (2002). List of standards and/or specifications for electronic networks, services and associated facilities and services. *Official Journal of the European Communities, C331*, 36–49.

European Commission. (2007). *Memo/07/389.* Retrieved from http://europa.eu/rapid/pressReleasesAction.do?reference=MEMO/07/389

European Commission. (2008, March 17). 2008/286/EC: Commission decision amending decision 2007/176/EC as regards the list of standards and/or specifications for electronic communications networks, services and associated facilities and services. *Official Journal of the European Union. L&C, L93*, 4.

European Commission. (2009). *MEMO/09/516.* Brussels, Belgium: Author.

European Commission. (2009). *MEMO/09/549.* Retrieved from http://europa.eu/rapid/pressReleasesAction.do?reference=MEMO/09/549&format=HTML&aged=0&language=EN European Commission. (2010). *Guidelines on the applicability of Article 101 of the Treaty on the Functioning of the European Union to horizontal cooperation agreements (DRAFT).* Retrieved from http://ec.europa.eu/competition/consultations/2010_horizontals/guidelines_en.pdf

European Telecommunications Standards Institute (ETSI). (1997). *EN 300 421 V1.1.2: Digital video broadcasting (DVB): Framing structure, channel coding and modulation for 11/12 GHz satellite services.* Sophia-Antipolis, France: European Telecommunications Standards Institute.

European Telecommunications Standards Institute (ETSI). (2004). *ETSI EN 302 304: Digital video broadcasting (DVB): Transmission system for handheld terminals (DVB-H).* Sophia-Antipolis, France: European Telecommunications Standards Institute.

European Telecommunications Standards Institute (ETSI). (2005). *ETSI TS 102 427: Digital audio broadcasting (DAB); Data broadcasting - MPEG-2 TS streaming.* Sophia-Antipolis, France: European Telecommunications Standards Institute.

European Telecommunications Standards Institute (ETSI). (2005). *ETSI TS 102 428: Digital audio broadcasting (DAB); DMB video service; user application specification.* Sophia-Antipolis, France: European Telecommunications Standards Institute.

European Telecommunications Standards Institute (ETSI). (2006). *ETSI EN 300 401 V1.4.1: Radio broadcasting systems: Digital audio broadcasting (DAB) to mobile, portable and fixed receivers*. Sophia-Antipolis, France: European Telecommunications Standards Institute.

European Telecommunications Standards Institute (ETSI). (2007). *ETSI TS 102 005 V1.3.1: Digital video broadcasting (DVB); Specification for the use of video and audio coding in DVB services delivered directly over IP protocols*. Sophia-Antipolis, France: European Telecommunications Standards Institute.

European Telecommunications Standards Institute (ETSI). (2007). *ETSI TS 102 468 V1.1.1: Digital video broadcasting (DVB); IP datacast over DVB-H: Set of specifications for phase 1*. Sophia-Antipolis, France: European Telecommunications Standards Institute.

European Telecommunications Standards Institute (ETSI). (2007). *ETSI TS 102 474 V1.1.1: Digital video broadcasting (DVB); IP datacast over DVB-H: Service purchase and protection*. Sophia-Antipolis, France: European Telecommunications Standards Institute.

European Telecommunications Standards Institute (ETSI). (2007d). *ETSI TS 102 563 V1.1.1: Digital audio broadcasting (DAB); transport of advanced audio coding (AAC) audio*. Sophia-Antipolis, France: European Telecommunications Standards Institute.

European Telecommunications Standards Institute (ETSI). (2009). *ETSI TR 102 377 V1.3.1: Digital video broadcasting (DVB); DVB-H implementation guidelines*. Sophia-Antipolis, France: European Telecommunications Standards Institute.

European Telecommunications Standards Institute (ETSI). (2010). *ETSI TS 102 471 V1.4.1: Digital video broadcasting (DVB); IP datacast over DVB-H: Electronic service guide (ESG)*. Sophia-Antipolis, France: European Telecommunications Standards Institute.

European Telecommunications Standards Institute. (2006). *ETSI directives: Version 20*. Retrieved from http://portal.etsi.org/directives/

EZ. (2007). *Nederland Open in Verbinding: Een actieplan voor het gebruik van Open Standaarden en Open Source Software bij de (semi-)publieke sector*. 's-Gravenhage: Ministerie van Economische Zaken.

EZ. (2008). *Actielijn 6 ODF-invoering Toelichting op actieplan Nederland Open in Verbinding. 's-Gravenhage*. The Netherlands: Ministerie van Economische Zaken.

Fabisch, G. (2003, December 8-9). *Consumers and standards: Consumer representation in standards setting*. Paper presented at the Cotswolds Conference. Retrieved December 10, 2008, from http://www.stanhopecentre.org/cotswolds/Fabisch%20Paper%202003.pdf

Facebook. (2010). *Facebook Social Network*. Retrieved February 3, 2010, from http://www.facebook.com/

Faria, G., Henriksson, J. A., Stare, E., & Talmola, P. (2006). DVB-H: Digital broadcast services to handheld devices. *Proceedings of the IEEE, 94*(1), 194–209. doi:10.1109/JPROC.2005.861011

Farquhar, B. (2006). Consumer representation in international standards. *Consumer Policy Review, 16*(1), 26–30.

Farrell, J. (2007). Standard Setting, Patents, and Hold-Up. *Antitrust Law Journal, 74*, 603–638.

Farrell, J., Hayes, J., Shapiro, C., & Sullivan, T. (2007). Standard setting, patents, and hold-up. *Antitrust Law Journal, 603*(3).

Farrell, J., & Saloner, G. (1985). Standardization, compatibility, and innovation. *The Rand Journal of Economics, 16*(1), 70–83. doi:10.2307/2555589

Farrell, J., & Saloner, G. (1986). Installed base and compatibility: Innovation, product preannouncements, and predation. *The American Economic Review, 76*(5), 940–955.

Farrell, J., & Saloner, G. (1988). Coordination through committees and markets. *The Rand Journal of Economics, 19*(2), 235–252. doi:10.2307/2555702

Farrell, J., & Saloner, G. (1992). Converters, Compatibility, and the Control of Interfaces. *The Journal of Industrial Economics, 40*(1), 9–35. doi:10.2307/2950625

Federal Trade Commission. (2008). *Negotiated Data Solutions LLC, Order and Decision, No. C-4234*. Retrieved on March 7, 2010, from http://www.ftc.gov/os/caselist/0510094/080923ndsdo.pdf

Festinger, L. (1957). *A theory of cognitive dissonance*. Palo Alto, CA: Stanford University Press.

Fettke, P., & Loos, P. (2003). Multiperspective Evaluation of Reference Models – Towards a Framework. *Computer Science: Conceptual Modeling for Novel Application Domains* (LNCS, pp. 80-91). New York: Springer.

Fettke, P., & Loos, P. (2003). Classification of Reference Models - A Methodology and Its Application. *Journal of Information Systems and e-Business Management, 1*(1), 3-53.

Fettke, P., & Loos, P. (2006). *Using Reference Models for Business Engineering - State-of-the-Art and Future Developments. Innovations in Information Technology.* Washington, DC: IEEE Computer Society Press.

Fettke, P., & Loos, P. (2007). Perspectives on Reference Modeling. In Fettke, P., & Loos, P. (Eds.), *Reference Modeling for Business Systems Analysis* (pp. 1–22). Hershey, PA: Idea Group.

Fichman, R. G., & Kemerer, C. F. (1993). Adoption of Software Engineering Process Innovations: The Case of Object Orientation. *Sloan Management Review, 34*(2), 7–22.

Fichman, R. G., & Kemerer, C. F. (1997). The Assimilation of Software Process Innovations: An Organizational Learning Perspective. *Management Science, 43*(10), 1345–1363. doi:10.1287/mnsc.43.10.1345

Fichman, R. G., & Kemerer, C. F. (1999). The Illusory Diffusion of Innovation: An Examination of Assimilation Gaps. *Information Systems Research, 10*(3), 255–275. doi:10.1287/isre.10.3.255

Fleck, J. (1995). Configurations and standardization. In Esser, J., Fleischmann, G., & Heimer, T. (Eds.), *Soziale und ökonomische Konflikte in Standardisierungsprozessen.* Frankfurt, Germany: Campus Verlag.

Fleddermann, C. B. (2000). Engineering Ethics Cases for Electrical and Computer Engineering Students. *IEEE Transactions on Education, 43*(3), 284–287. doi:10.1109/13.865202

Flint v Lovell [1935] 1 K.B. 354 (CA) (Greer, L.J.)

Flyvbjerg, B., Bruzelius, N., & Rothengatter, W. (2003). *Megaprojects and Risk. An antomy of ambition.* Cambridge, UK: Cambridge University Press.

Forman, C., & Gron, A. (2005, January 3-6). *Vertical Integration and Information Technology Adoption: A Study of the Insurance Industry.* Paper presented at the Hawaii International Conference on System Sciences (HICSS 38), Waikoloa, HI.

Fr. Civil Code Art. 1121

Franklin, T., Beeston, M., Dexter, H., & van Harmelen, M. (2008). *Final Report of the Reference Model Projects Synthesis and Evaluation Projects.* London: JISC Collections. Retrieved March 21, 2010, from http://www.jisc.ac.uk/publications/publications/finalreportreferencemodelsynthesis, retrieved 2010-03-21

Fridenson, P. (1991). Selling the innovation: French and German color TV devices. *Business and Economic History. Second Series, 20*, 62–68.

Froyd, J. E., & Ohland, M. W. (2005). Integrated engineering curricula. *Journal of Engineering Education, 94*(1), 147–164.

Funk, J. L. (2002). *Global competition between and within standards: The case of mobile phones.* New York, NY: Palgrave MacMillan.

Funk, J. L., & Methe, D. T. (2001). Market- and Committee-based Mechanisms in the Creation and Diffusion of Global Industry Standards: The Case of Mobile Communication. *Research Policy, 30*, 589–610. doi:10.1016/S0048-7333(00)00095-0

Furman, J., & Stern, S. (2006). *Climbing atop the shoulders of giants: The impact of institutions on cumulative research.* Cambridge, MA: National Bureau of Economic Research. doi:10.1257/aer.101.5.1933

Furukawa, Y. (2007). A Japanese university: Educating standardization strategists in business. *ISO Focus, 4*(11), 15–16.

Ganeva, L., Sandalski, B., & Kotev, R. (2010, June 8-9). Contributions of the Bulgarian Union of Standardization for the European Integration of the Republic Bulgaria. In *Proceedings of the 7th International Conference on Standardization Protypes and Quality: A Means of Balkan Countries Collaboration*, Zlatibor, Serbia (pp. 29-38).

Garrard, G. A. (1998). *Cellular Communications: Worldwide Market Development.* Boston: Artech House.

Garud, R., & Karnøe, P. (Eds.). (2001). *Path Dependence and Creation*. Mahwah, NJ: Lawrence Erlbaum Associates.

Gefen, D., & Straub, D. (2005). A Practical Guide to Factorial Validity Using PLS-Graph: Tutorial and Annotated Example. *Communications of the AIS, 16*, 91–109.

General Tire & Rubber Co. v Firestone Tyre & Rubber Co. [1975] F.S.R. 273

Georgia-Pacific Corp v US Plywood Corp. 318 F Supp 1116 1120-21 [SDNY 1970]

Geradin, D. (2006). Standardization and Technological Innovation: Some Reflections on Ex-ante Licensing, FRAND, and the Proper Means to Reward Innovators. *World Competition, 29*, 511.

Geradin, D. (2008). Competing Away Market Power? An Economic Assessment of Ex Ante Auctions in Standard Setting. *European Competition Journal, 4*, 443. doi:10.5235/ecj.v4n2.443

Geradin, D. (2008). The Complements Problem Within Standard Setting: Assessing the Evidence on Royalty Stacking. *Boston University Journal of Science & Technology Law, 14*, 144.

Geradin, D. (2009). Pricing Abuses by Essential Patent Holders in a Standard-Setting Context: A View from Europe. *Antitrust Law Journal, 76*, 329.

Geradin, D., & Rato, M. (2007). Can Standard-Setting Lead to Exploitative Abuse? A Dissonant View on Patent Hold-up, Royalty-Stacking and the Meaning of FRAND. *European Competition Law Journal, 3*, 101.

Geradin, D., & Rato, M. (2009). *FRAND Commitment and EC Competition Law: A Reply to Philippe Chappatte.* European Competition Journal. doi:10.5235/ecj.v6n1.129

Gerst, M., & Bunduchi, R. (2005). Shaping IT Standardization in the Automotive Industry - The Role of Power in Driving Portal Standardization. *Electronic Markets, 15*(4), 335–343. doi:10.1080/10196780500302872

Gerundino, D. (2010). Standards in economic development and trade. *ISO Focus, 1*(1), 35.

Ghosh, R. (2005). *Free/Libre/OpenSource Software: Policy Support: An Economic Basis for Open Standards*. Maastricht, The Netherlands: MERIT, University of Maastricht, FLOSSPOLS Project. Retrieved from http://flosspols.org/deliverables.php

Giossi, S., & Papastamatis, A. (2010, June 8-9). The effective teaching of standards in a lifelong learning world. In *Proceedings of the 7th International Conference on Standardization Protypes and Quality: A Means of Balkan Countries Collaboration*, Zlatibor, Serbia (pp. 118-125).

Gogan, J. L. (2005). Punctuation and Path Dependence: Examining a Vertical IT Standard-Setting Process. *Electronic Markets, 15*(4), 344–354. doi:10.1080/10196780500302880

Goldstein, L., & Kersey, B. (2004). *Technology patent licensing: An international reference on 21st century patent licensing, patent pools and patent platforms*. Boston, MA: Aspatore Inc.

Gosain, S. (2003, December 12-14). *Realizing the Vision for Web Services: Strategies for Dealing with Imperfect Standards*. Paper presented at the International Conference on IS Special Workshop on Standard Making sponsored by MISQ, Seattle, WA.

Grant, S. (2009). *Development of a conceptual model 5*. Retrieved February 10, 2010 from http://blogs.cetis.ac.uk/asimong/2009/12/11/development-of-a-conceptual-model-5/

Grant, S. (2009). *LEAP2A: A specification for e-portfolio portability and interoperability*. Retrieved March 30, 2010, from http://newsweaver.co.uk/alt/e_article001402921.cfm

Grant, S. (2010). *Leap2A Specification*. Retrieved February 8, 2010 from http://wiki.cetis.ac.uk/LEAP2A_specification

Grant, S. (2010). Portfolio Interoperability Projects. *CETIS Wiki*. Retrieved March 30, 2010 from http://wiki.cetis.ac.uk/Portfolio_interoperability_projects/

Grant, J. (2002). Learning needs assessment: assessing the need. *BMJ (Clinical Research Ed.), 324*, 156–159. doi:10.1136/bmj.324.7330.156

Graz, J. C. (2004). Quand les normes font loi. Topologie intégrée et processus différenciés de la normalisation international. *Revue. Etudes Internationales*, *35*(2), 233–260. doi:10.7202/009036ar

Graz, J. C. (2006). International standardisation and corporate democracy. In Giesen, K. G., & van der Pijl, K. (Eds.), *Global Norms for the 21st Century* (pp. 118–133). Cambridge, UK: Cambridge Scholars Press.

Greenstein, S., & Rysman, M. (2007). Coordination costs and standard setting: Lessons from 56K modems. In Greenstein, S., & Stango, V. (Eds.), *Standards and public policy*. Cambridge, UK: Cambridge University Press. doi:10.1017/CBO9780511493249.005

Grindley, P. (1995). Framework for standards strategy: Establishing standards and maximizing profits. In Grindley, P. (Ed.), *Standards strategy and policy: Cases and stories* (pp. 20–54). Oxford, UK: Oxford University Press. doi:10.1093/acprof:oso/9780198288077.003.0002

Grinter, L. E. (1956). Report on the evaluation of engineering education. *English Education*, *46*(1), 25–63.

Grover, V. (1997). *A Tutorial on Survey Research: From Constructs to Theory*. Retrieved from http://dmsweb.badm.sc.edu/grover/survey/MIS-SUVY.html

Grube, M., Siepen, P., Mittendorf, C., Boltz, M., & Srinivasan, M. (2001). Applications of MPEG-4: Digital multimedia broadcasting. *IEEE Transactions on Consumer Electronics*, *47*(3), 474–484. doi:10.1109/30.964136

Grundmann, S., & Mazeaud, D. (Eds.). (2006). *General Clauses and Standards in European Contract Law – Comparative Law, EC Law and Contract Law Codification*. Frederick, MD: Aspen Publishers.

Hall, B., Jaffe, A., & Tratjenberg, M. (2001). *The NBER patent citation data file: Lessons, insights and methodological tools*. Retrieved from http://www.nber.org/patents/

Hall, B., Trajtenberg, M., & Jaffe, A. (2005). Market value and patent citations. *The Rand Journal of Economics*, *36*(1), 16–38.

Hallier, J., Lauterbach, T., & Unbehaun, M. (1994). Multimedia broadcasting to mobile, portable and fixed receivers using the Eureka 147 digital audio broadcasting system. In *Proceedings of the 5th IEEE International Symposium on Personal, Indoor and Mobile Radio Communications: Wireless Networks - Catching the Mobile Future*.

Hanseth, O. (2001). Gateways — Just as important as standards: How the Internet won the "religious war" over standards in Scandinavia. *Knowledge, Technology & Policy*, *14*(3), 71–89. doi:10.1007/s12130-001-1017-2

Harhoff, D., Narin, F., Scherer, F. M., & Vopel, K. (1999). Citation frequency and the value of patented inventions. *The Review of Economics and Statistics*, *81*(3), 511–515. doi:10.1162/003465399558265

HarperCollins. (1994). *Collins English Dictionary*. Glasgow, UK: HarperCollins.

Hauert, C. (2008). *Normalisation: quelle place pour les consommateurs? Etude de la participation des associations de consommateurs aux comités miroirs établis en Suisse en 1987, 1997 et 2007*. Lausanne, Switzerland: Mimeo.

Hausman, J., Hall, B. H., & Griliches, Z. (1984). Econometric models for count data with an application to the patents-R&D relationship. *Econometrica*, *52*, 909–938. doi:10.2307/1911191

Hay, D. C. (1996). *Data Model Patterns - Conventions of Thought. New Yorks*. Dorset House.

Heckman, J., Ichimura, H., Smith, J. A., & Todd, P. E. (1998). Characterizing selection bias using experimental data. *Econometrica*, *66*, 1017–1098. doi:10.2307/2999630

Heckman, J., Ichimura, H., & Todd, P. E. (1997). Matching as an econometric evaluation estimator: Evidence from evaluating a job training programme. *The Review of Economic Studies*, *64*, 605–654. doi:10.2307/2971733

Hesser, W. (1997). *The need for interdisciplinary research on standardization*. Paper presented at the SCANCOR/SCORE Seminar on Standardization, Lund, Sweden.

Hesser, W., & Czaya, A. (1999). Standardization as a subject of study in higher education. *ISO Bulletin, 30*(6), 6–11.

Hevner, A. R., March, S. T., Park, J., & Ram, S. (2004). Design Science in Information Systems Research. *Management Information Systems Quarterly, 28*(1), 75–105.

Hills, B. (2000). Common message standards for electronic commerce in wholesale financial markets. *Bank of England Quarterly Bulletin, 40*(3), 274–285.

Hilton, M. (2008). The Death of a Consumer Society. *Transactions of the Royal Historical Society, 18*, 211–236. doi:10.1017/S0080440108000716

Hoel, T., Hollins, P., & Pawlowski, J. (2009). Special Issue on Learning Technoloy Standards. *The International Journal of IT Standards and Standardization Research.* Retrieve April 1, 2010 from http://sites.google.com/site/standardsgovernance/

Hommels, A. (2005). *Unbuilding Cities. Obduracy in Urban Sociotechnical Change.* Cambridge, MA: MIT Press.

Hommels, A., Peters, P., & Bijker, W. E. (2007). Techno Therapy or Nurtured Niches? Technology Studies and the Evaluation of Radical Innovations. *Research Policy, 36*(7), 1088–1099. doi:10.1016/j.respol.2007.04.002

HR-XML Consortium. (2007). *Competencies (Measurable Characteristics).* Retrieved February 15, 2010 from http://ns.hr-xml.org/2_5/HR-XML-2_5/CPO/Competencies.html

HR-XML. (2008). *HR-XML Competency data model.* Retrieved February 5, 2010, from http://ns.hr-xml.org/3.0/.

HR-XML. (2009). *HR-XML 3.0 Specification.* Retrieved from http://www.hr-xml.org

Hughes, T. P. (1983). *Networks of power: Electrification in western society, 1880-1930.* Baltimore, MD: Johns Hopkins University Press.

Hughes, T. P. (1998). *Rescuing Prometheus.* New York: Pantheon Books.

Hunt, R., Simojoki, S., & Takalo, T. (2007). *Intellectual property rights and standard setting in financial services: The case of the single European payments area.* Retrieved from http://www.philadelphiafed.org/files/wps/2007/wp07-20.pdf

Iacovou, C. L., Benbasat, I., & Dexter, A. S. (1995). Electronic Data Interchange and Small Organizations: Adoption and Impact of Technology. *Management Information Systems Quarterly*, 465–484. doi:10.2307/249629

ICES. (2008). *Workshop Presentations.* Retrieved from http://www.standards-education.org/workshops/ices2008/presentations

ICOPER. (2010). *ICOPER Best Practice Network.* Retrieved February 3, 2010, from http://www.icoper.org/. ICOPER. (2010) *Competency Development WG.* Retrieved February 8, 2010 from http://www.icoper.org/icoper-big-picture/needs-analysis/Competency%20Development%20WG

IEC. (2005). *IEC lecture series – International standardization in business, industry, society and technology.* Geneva, Switzerland: International Electrotechnical Commission.

IEC. (2007). *IEC lecture series II – The importance of standards.* Geneva, Switzerland: International Electrotechnical Commission.

IEEE Educational Activities Board Standards in Education Committee. (2008). *Standards Education.* Retrieved from http://www.ieee.org/web/education/standards/index.html

IEEE RCD. (2007). *IEEE LTSC Reusable Competency Definitions (RCD).* Retrieved February 3, 2010, from http://www.ieeeltsc.org/working-groups/wg20Comp/

IEEE. (2002). *1484.12.1 – IEEE Standard for Learning Object Metadata.* Washington, DC: IEEE.

IEEE. (2002). *IEEE 1484.12.1-2002, Draft Standard for Learning Object Metadata, Piscataway 2002.* Retrieved from http://ltsc.ieee.org/wg12/files/LOM_1484_12_1_v1_Final_Draft.pdf

IEEE. (2008). *Data Model for Reusable Competency Definitions.* Washington, DC: Retrieved February 8, 2010 http://www.cen-ltso.net/main.aspx?put=652

IETF. (2007). *The Atom Publishing Protocol.* Retrieved from http://www.ietf.org/rfc/rfc5023.txt

IMS Global Learning Consortium. (2003). *IMS Learning Design, Version 1.0 Final Specification.* Lake Mary, FL: IMS Global Learning Consortium.

IMS Global Learning Consortium. (2004). *IMS Content Packaging Specification, Version 1.1.4 Final Specification*. Lake Mary, FL: IMS Global learning Consortium.

IMS Global Learning Consortium. (2006). *IMS Question and Test Interoperability Specification, Version 2.1 Public Draft Specification*. Lake Mary, FL: IMS Global Learning Consortium.

IMS Global Learning Consortium. (2008). *IMS Common Cartridge, Version 1.0 Final Specification*. Lake Mary, FL: IMS Global Learning Consortium.

IMS. (2002). *IMS Reusable Definition of Competency or Educational Objective Specification*. Retrieved 8 February 2010 from http://www.imsglobal.org/competencies/

IMS. (2003). *IMS Learning Design Specification* Retrieved February 11, 2010 from http://www.imsglobal.org/learningdesign/

IMS. (2003). *IMS Learning Design*. Retrieved from http://www.imsglobal.org/learningdesign/index.html

IMS. (2005). *IMS Learner Information Package Specification*. Retrieved from http://www.imsglobal.org/profiles/index.html

IMS. (2005). *IMS ePortfolio Specification*. Retrieved from http://www.imsglobal.org/ep/index.html, 2005

IMS. (2006). *IMS Question and Test Interoperability 2.1*. Retrieved from http://www.imsglobal.org/question/index.html

IMS. (2008). *IMS GLC Common Cartridge*. Retrieved from http://www.imsglobal.org/cc/index.html, 2008

IMS. (2009). *IMS GLC Common Cartridge Alliance*. Retrieved from http://www.imsglobal.org/cc/alliance.html

IMS. (2009). *IMS GLC Packaging Specification 1.2*. Retrieved from http://www.imsglobal.org/content/packaging/index.html

IMS. (2010). SchemaProf. *Version 2.0*. Retrieved from http://www.imsglobal.org/profile/IMSSchemaProf-2.0.zip

Institute of Electrical and Electronic Engineering (IEEE). (1990). *IEEE 610.12:1990 IEEE Standard Glossary of Software Engineering Terminology*. Washington, DC: IEEE.

Institute of Electrical and Electronics Engineers (IEEE). (2007). *IEEE 1484.20.1 Draft Standard for Learning Technology - Data Model for Reusable Competency Definitions*. Washington, DC: IEEE.

Institute of Electrical and Electronics Engineers. (2002). *IEEE 1484-12.1:2002 Standard for Learning Object Metadata (LOM)*. Washington, DC: IEEE.

Intellor. (2001). *XML Adoption: Benefits and Challenges*. Retrieved from http://www.dad.be/library/pdf/intellor2.pdf

International Organization for Standardization. (2003). [*Information and documentation - The Dublin Core metadata element set*. Geneva, Switzerland: IOS.]. *ISO*, *15836*, 2003.

International Organization for Standardization. (2011). Society for standards and standardization launched. *ISO Focus*, *2*(1), 36.

International Organization for Standardization. (2011). *The ISO 2011 award for higher education in standardization*. Geneva, Switzerland: International Organization for Standardization.

International Organization for Standardization/International Electrotechnical Commission (ISO/IEC). (2005). *ISO/IEC 19796-1:2005. Information Technology - Learning, Education, and Training - Quality Management, Assurance and Metrics - Part 1: General Approach*. Geneva, Switzerland: ISO.

ISO. (n.d.). *What COPOLCO does*. Retrieved May 22, 2009, from http://www.iso.org/iso/resources/resources_consumers/what_copolco_does.htm

ISO/IEC. (1991). *Guide 2*. Geneva, Switzerland: Author.

ISO/IEC. (2004). *ISO/IEC Directives, Part 1, Procedures for the technical work* (5th ed.). Geneva, Switzerland: Author.

ISO/IEC. (2008). *ISO/IEC Directives, Part 1, Procedures for the technical work* (6th ed.). Geneva, Switzerland: Author.

Iversen, E. J. (1999). *Standardization and Intellectual Property Rights: ETSI's controversial search for new IPR-procedures*.

Jacbos, I., & Walsh, N. (2004). *Architecture of the World Wide Web, Volume One.* Retrieved April 1, 2010, from W3C: http://www.w3.org/TR/webarch/

Jaffe, A., & Lerner, J. (2001). Reinventing public R&D: Patent policy and the commercialization of national laboratory technologies. *The Rand Journal of Economics, 32*(1), 167–198. doi:10.2307/2696403

Jaffe, A., & Trajtenberg, M. (1999). International knowledge flows: Evidence from patent citations. *Economics of Innovation and New Technology, 8*, 105–136. doi:10.1080/10438599900000006

Jakobs, K., Procter, R., & Williams, R. (1997, July). Users in IT-Standardisation: A Myth Revised. In *Proceedings of the 1st International Conference on Managing Enterprise Stakeholders, Mech. Eng. Publications*, Loughborough, UK (pp. 599-604).

Jakobs, K., Procter, R., & Williams, R. (1998). User participation in standards setting – the panacea? *ACM Standard View, 6*(2), 85–89. doi:10.1145/301688.301693

Jastrzebski, R. (1993). Europese harmonisatie van communicatiestandaarden op komst. *Alert, 5*, 26–27.

Jeffery, A. B., & Bratton-Jeffery, M. F. (2004). Integrated Training Requires Integrated Design and Business Models. In Armstrong, A.-M. (Ed.), *Instructional design in the real world: a view from the trenches* (pp. 218–249). Hershey, PA: IGI Global. doi:10.4018/978-1-59140-150-6.ch013

Jennings, R., & Mazzeo, M. (1993). Competing bids, target management resistance and the structure of takeover bids. *Review of Financial Studies, 6*, 883–909. doi:10.1093/rfs/6.4.883

Johnson, D., & Popp, D. (2003). Forced out of the closet: The impact of the American inventors protection act on the timing of patent disclosure. *The Rand Journal of Economics, 34*(1), 96–112. doi:10.2307/3087445

Jones, M. C., & Beatty, R. C. (1998). Towards the development of measures of perceived benefits and compatibility of EDI: a comparative assessment of competing first order factor models. *European Journal of Information Systems, 7*(3), 210–220. doi:10.1057/palgrave.ejis.3000299

Jones, P., & Hudson, J. (1996). Standardization and the Cost of Assessing Quality. *European Journal of Political Economy, 12*, 355–361. doi:10.1016/0176-2680(95)00021-6

Joris, E. (2008). Institut suisse de recherche ménagère. In *Dictionnaire historique de la suisse.* Retrieved December 10, 2008, from http://www.hls-dhs-dss.ch/textes/f/F16503.php

JTC1. (2007). *ISO/IEC JTC 1 Directives, Version 3.0* (5th ed.). Geneva, Switzerland: ISO/IEC JTC1.

Kallet, A. (1956). Standards for rating consumer goods. In Reck, D. (Ed.), *National Standards in a Modern Economy* (pp. 275–291). New York: Harper & Brother.

Karahanna, E., Straub, D. W., & Chervany, N. L. (1999). Information Technology Adoption Across Time: A Cross-Sectional Comparison of Pre-Adoption and Post-Adoption Beliefs. *Management Information Systems Quarterly, 23*(2), 183–213. doi:10.2307/249751

Katz, M. L., & Shapiro, C. (1985). Network Externalities, Competition, and Compatibility. *The American Economic Review, 75*(3), 424–442.

Katz, M. L., & Shapiro, C. (1994). Systems competition and network effects. *The Journal of Economic Perspectives, 8*(2), 93–115. doi:10.1257/jep.8.2.93

Kaufmann, A., et al. (2004). De la gestion à la négociation des risques. Apports des procédures participatives d'évaluation des choix technologiques. *Revue européenne des sciences sociales, 130*, 109-120.

Keil, T. (2002). De-facto Standardization Through Alliances - Lessons From Bluetooth. *Telecommunications Policy, 26*(3-4), 205–213. doi:10.1016/S0308-5961(02)00010-1

Keller, G., & Teufel, T. (1998). *SAP R/3 Process Oriented Implementation - Iterative Process Prototyping.* Reading, MA: Addison-Wesley.

Kelly, W. E., Bickart, T. A., & Forselius, R. (2006). *Standards Education: An Industry, Government, University Partnership.* Paper presented at the American Society for Engineering Education Mid-Atlantic Conference.

Kerwer, D. (2005). Rules that many use: Standards and global regulation. *Governance: An International Journal of Policy, Administration and Institutions, 18*(4), 611–632. doi:10.1111/j.1468-0491.2005.00294.x

Ketchell, J. (2010, July 5-9) *Education about standardization – developing future generations of standardisers.* Paper presented at the WSC Academic Week, Geneva, Switzerland.

Kiernan, V. (1999). 'Open Archives' Project Promises Alternative To Costly Journals. *Chronicle of Higher Education.* Retrieved March 30, 2010, from http://chronicle.com/article/Open-Archives-Project/32985/

Kindleberger, C. P. (1983). Standards as Public, Collective and Private Goods. *Kyklos, 36*, 377–396. doi:10.1111/j.1467-6435.1983.tb02705.x

Klett, F. (2007). Facing Learning System Design Complexity: Personalization, Adaptation and Reusability. In *Proceedings of the International Conference on "Computer as Tool" EUROCON 2007.*

Klopfenstein, B. C. (1989). The diffusion of the VCR in the United States. In Levy, M. R. (Ed.), *The VCR age: Home video and mass communication.* London, UK: Sage.

Komiya, M. (1993). Personal Communications in Japan and its Implications for Asia. *Pan-European Mobile Communications, Spring,* 52-55.

Koppenhol, A., & Egyedi, T. M. (2008, April 9). Een standaardenoorlog met alleen verliezers. *Automatisering Gids.*

Krechmer, K. (2007). Teaching standards to engineers. *International Journal of IT Standards and Standardization Research, 5*(2), 1–12. doi:10.4018/jitsr.2007070102

KSA. (2003). *International workshop to develop a standardization education model.* Seoul, Korea: KSA.

Kuhn, T. (1962). *The structure of scientific revolutions.* Chicago, IL: University of Chicago Press.

Kurokawa, T. (2005). Developing human resources for international standards. *The Quarterly Review,* 17.

La3tv. (2007). *Samsung P910: Accendi il TVfonino.* Retrieved from http://www.la3tv.it/la3Live/HM/Offerta/TVfonini/Samsung_SGH-P910

Langer, W. (2008, February 28). Open Standards, Open Source, Open Documents: Experiences in Format Conversion. In *Proceedings of odfworkshop.nl.* Retrieved from http://www.odfworkshop.nl/files/20080228-ODFworkshop-WernerLanger.pdf

Lanjouw, J., & Schankerman, M. (1999). *The quality of ideas: Measuring innovation with multiple indicators.* Retrieved from http://www.nber.org/

Lanjouw, J., & Schankerman, M. (2001). Characteristics of patent litigation: A window on competition. *The Rand Journal of Economics, 32*, 129. doi:10.2307/2696401

Layne-Farrar, A., & Lerner, J. (2010). To join or not to join: Examining patent pool participation and rent sharing rules. *International Journal of Industrial Organization, 29*(2), 294–303. doi:10.1016/j.ijindorg.2010.08.006

Layne-Farrar, A., Padilla, A. J., & Schmalensee, R. (2007). Pricing patents for licensing in standard setting organizations: Making sense of FRAND commitments. *Antitrust Law Journal, 74*(3).

LEAP2A. (2008). JISC LEAP2A Portfolio Interoperability Projects (PIOP). *Educational Technology & Society, 9*(1), 23-37.

Lee, K. (1996). Cooperative standard-setting: The road to compatibility or deadlock? The NAFTA's transformation of the telecommunications industry. *Federal Commission Law Journal, 487.*

Lee, G. (2007). Universities in the Republic of Korea: Training the next generation of professionals. *ISO Focus, 4*(11), 17–18.

Lee, W. C. Y. (2001). *Lee's Essentials of Wireless Communications.* New York: McGraw-Hill.

Leibowitz, S., & Margolis, S. E. (2002). *Winners, losers, and Microsoft.* Oakland, CA: The Independent Institute.

Lelong, B., & Mallard, A. (2000). Présentation. *Reseaux, 102*, 9–34.

Lemley, M. (2006). *Ten things to do about patent holdup of standards (and one not to).* Retrieved from http://ssrn.com/abstract=923470

Lemley, M., & Shapiro, C. (2006). *Patent holdup and royalty stacking.* Retrieved from http://ssrn.com/abstract=923468

Lemley, M. (2002). Intellectual property rights and standard-setting organizations. *California Law Review, 90*, 1889. doi:10.2307/3481437

Lemley, M. (2002). Intellectual Property Rights and Standard-Setting Organizations. *California Law Review, 90*, 1889–1909. doi:10.2307/3481437

Lemley, M. A., & Shapiro, C. (2005). Probabilistic Patents. *The Journal of Economic Perspectives.* doi:10.1257/0895330054048650

Lemley, M. A., & Shapiro, C. (2007). Patent Holdup and Royalty Stacking. *Texas Law Review, 85*, 1991–1996.

Lemley, M., & Shapiro, C. (2006). Patent holdup and royalty stacking. *Texas Law Review, 85*, 2007.

Lepper, M. R., Zanna, M. P., & Abelson, R. P. (1970). Cognitive Irreversibility in a dissonance-reduction situation. *Journal of Personality and Social Psychology, 16*, 191–198. doi:10.1037/h0029819

Lerner, J., Tirole, J., & Strojwas, M. (2003). *Cooperative marketing agreements between competitors: evidence from patent pools.* Retrieved from http://www.nber.org/papers/w9680.pdf

Levy, D. A. L. (1997). The regulation of digital conditional access systems: A case study in European policy making. *Telecommunications Policy, 21*(7), 661–676. doi:10.1016/S0308-5961(97)00035-9

Lewis, G. A., Morris, E., Simanta, S., & Wrage, L. (2008). Why Standards are not Enough to Guarantee End-To-End Interoperability. In *Proceedings of the seventh International Conference on Composition-Based Software Systems* (pp. 164-173). Washington, DC: IEEE Computer Society Press.

Lewis, S., Hayes, L., Newton-Wade, V., Corfield, A., Davis, R., Donohue, T., & Wilson, S. (2009). If SWORD is the answer, what is the question?: Use of the Simple Web-service Offering Repository Deposit protocol. *Program: electronic library and information systems, 43*(4), 407-418.

Liebowitz, S. J., & Margolis, S. E. (1990). The fable of the keys. *The Journal of Law & Economics, 33*, 1. doi:10.1086/467198

Liebowitz, S. J., & Margolis, S. E. (1995). Path dependence, lock-in, and history. *Journal of Law Economics and Organization, 11*(1), 205–226.

Lindgren, R., Henfridsson, O., & Schultze, U. (2004). Design Principles for Competence Management Systems: A Synthesis of an Action Research Study. *Management Information Systems Quarterly, 28*(3), 435–472.

LinkedIn. (2010). *LinkedIn Social Network.* Retrievd February 3, 2010, from http://www.linkedin.com/

Lord, R. A. (2009). *Williston on Contracts.* St. Paul, MN: West Publishing Company.

Luce, R. (2001). The Open Archives Initiative: Interoperable, Interdisciplinary Author Self-Archiving Comes of Age. *The Serials Librarian, 40*(1/2), 173–182. doi:10.1300/J123v40n01_15

Lyytinen, K., & Damsgaard, J. (2001, April 7-10). *What's Wrong With the Diffusion of Innovation Theory: The Case of a Complex and Networked Technology.* Paper presented at the International Federation for Information Processing (IFIP), Banff, AB, Canada.

Lyytinen, K., & Fomin, V. V. (2002). Achieving high momentum in the evolution of wireless infrastructures: The battle over the 1G solutions. *Telecommunications Policy, 26*(3), 149–170. doi:10.1016/S0308-5961(02)00006-X

Lyytinen, K., Keil, T., & Fomin, V. (2008). A Framework to Build Process Theories of Anticipatory Information and Communication Technology (ICT) Standardizing. *Journal of IT Standards & Standardization Research, 6*(1), 1–38. doi:10.4018/jitsr.2008010101

MacKenzie, D., & Wajcman, J. (1999). Introductory Essay: the Social Shaping of Technology. In MacKenzie, D., & Wajcman, J. (Eds.), *The Social Shaping of Technology* (pp. 3–27). Buckingham, UK: Open University Press.

Madhour, H., & Wentland Forte, M. (2007). The Open Lausanne Model: A Reference Model for Open Adaptive Learning Object Systems. In *Proceedings of the 7th International Conference on Advanced Learning Technologies (ICALT 2007)* (pp. 747-749). Washington, DC: IEEE Computer Society Press.

Mallard, A. (2000). L'écriture des normes. *Reseaux*, *102*, 37–61.

Mallard, A. (2000). La presse de consommation et le marché. Enquête sur le tiers consumériste. *Sociologie du Travail*, *42*, 391–409. doi:10.1016/S0038-0296(00)01087-6

Marcus-Steiff, J. (1977). L'information comme mode d'action des organisations de consommateurs. *Revue Francaise de Sociologie*, *18*(1), 85–107. doi:10.2307/3320870

Market Based Rates, para. 6, 72 Fed. Reg. 33906-33907.

Markus, M. L., Steinfield, C. W., & Wigand, R. T. (2003, December 12-14). *The Evolution of Vertical IS Standards: Electronic Interchange Standards in the US Home Mortgage Industry.* Paper presented at the International Conference on IS Special Workshop on Standard Making sponsored by MISQ, Seattle, WA

Markus, M. L., Steinfield, C. W., Wigand, R. T., & Minton, G. (2006). Industry-Wide Information Systems Standardization as Collective Action: The Case of the U.S. Residential Mortgage Industry. *Management Information Systems Quarterly*, *30*, 439–465.

Mata, F. J., Fuerst, W. L., & Barney, J. B. (1995). Information Technology and Sustained Competitive Advantage: A Resource-Based Analysis. *Management Information Systems Quarterly*, *19*(4), 487–505. doi:10.2307/249630

Maxwell v J. Baker, Inc. 86 F 3d 1098, 1109-10 [Fed. Cir. 1996]

MedBiquitous. (2009). *MedBiquitous Competency Framework Specifications and Description Document Version: 0.3.* Retrieved Febrauy 13, 2010, from http://www.medbiq.org/working_groups/competencies/CompetencyFrameworkSpecification.pdf

MedBiquitous. (2010). *Competencies Working Group.* Retrieved February 8, 2010 from http://www.medbiq.org/working_groups/competencies/index.html

Mendoza, R. A., & Jahng, J. J. (2003, August). *Adoption of XML Specifications: An Exploratory Study of Industry Practices.* Paper presented at the Americas Conference on Information Systems (AMCIS), Tampa, FL.

Meyer, J., & Rowan, B. (1977). Institutionalized organizations: Formal structure as myth and ceremony. *American Journal of Sociology*, *83*, 340–363. doi:10.1086/226550

Micro Chem., Inc. v Lextron, Inc. 317 F 3d 1387, 1394 [Fed Cir 2003].

Miller, J. (2006). Standard setting, patents, and access lock-in: RAND licensing and the theory of the firm. *Indiana Law Review*, 40.

Mobile, L. G. (2005). *Mobile meets TV: LG Mobile V9000* [Product Brochure]. San Diego, CA: LG Mobile.

Mock, D. (2005). *The Qualcomm Equation: How a Fledgling Telecom Company Forged a New Path to Big Profits and Market Dominance.* New York: AMACOM.

Monsanto Co. v Ralph 382 F 3d 1374, 1383 [Fed Cir 2004].

Moodle. (2010). *Moodle Learning Management System.* Retrieved February 3, 2010, from http://moodle.org/

Moore, G. C., & Benbasat, I. (1991). Development of an Instrument to Measure the Perceptions of Adopting an Information Technology Innovation. *Information Systems Research*, *2*(3), 192–222. doi:10.1287/isre.2.3.192

Moore, K. (2005). Worthless patents. *Berkeley Technology Law Journal*, *20*, 1521.

Morgan Stanley Capital Group, Inc. v Public Utility District 1 of Snohomush County 128 S Ct 2733, 2746 [2008].

Morikawa, M., & Morrison, J. (2004). *Who develops ISO standards? A survey of participation in ISO's international standards development processes.* Retrieved December 10, 2008, from http://www.pacinst.org/reports/iso_participation/iso_participation_study.pdf

MPEGLA. (2010). *Summary of AVC/H.264 license terms.* Retrieved from http://www.mpegla.com/main/programs/avc/Documents/AVC_TermsSummary.pdf

Mueller, J. (2001). No 'dilettante affair': Rethinking the experimental use exception to patent infringement for biomedical research tools. *Washington Law Review (Seattle, Wash.)*, 76.

Müller-Römer, F. (1997). *DAB progress report*. Retrieved from http://www.ebu.ch/en/technical/trev/trev_274-m_romer.pdf

Mumford, E. (2000). A Socio-Technical Approach to Systems Design. *Requirements Engineering*, 5(2), 125–133. doi:10.1007/PL00010345

Najjar, J., & Simon, B. (2009). Learning Outcome Based Higher Education: iCoper Use Cases. In *Proceedings of the Ninth IEEE International Conference on Advanced Learning Technologies* (pp. 718-719).

Najjar, J., & Klobučar, T. (2009). *ISURE: Report of study of learning needs building blocks and the standards to be used*. ICOPER Project Deliverables.

Nambisan, S., & Wang, Y.-M. (1999). Roadblocks to Web technology adoption? *Communications of the ACM*, 42(1), 98–101. doi:10.1145/291469.291482

National Science Foundation. (1995). *Restructuring Engineering Education: A Focus on Change*. Arlington, VA: Author.

National Standardization Strategic Framework. (2008). *British National Standardization Strategic Framework*. Retrieved from http://www.nssf.info/resources/documents/Guide_to_NSSF.pdf

NBF. (1993). *Programme of requirements third generation communication networks for the fire brigade*. Author.

Nelson, M. L., Shaw, M. J., & Qualls, W. (2005). Interorganizational System Standards Development in Vertical Industries. *Electronic Markets*, 15(4), 378–392. doi:10.1080/10196780500303045

NEN. (2010). *Annual report 2009 – Crisis & control*. Delft, The Netherlands: NEN.

Nickerson, J. V., & Muehlen, M. Z. (2003, December 12-14). *Defending the Spirit of the Web: Conflict in the Internet Standards Process*. Paper presented at the International Conference on IS Special Workshop on Standard Making sponsored by MISQ, Seattle, WA.

Nickerson, J. V., & Muehlen, M. Z. (2006). The Ecology of Standards Processes: Insights from Internet Standard Making. *Management Information Systems Quarterly*, 30, 467–488.

Nigel Christopher Blayney (t/a Aardvark Jewellery) v (1) Clogeau St Davids Gold Mines [2003] F.S.R. 19.

Nilsson, M. (2008). *Description Set Profiles: A constraint language for Dublin Core Application Profiles*. Retrieved from http://dublincore.org/documents/dc-dsp/

Noam, E. M. (1992). *Telecommunications in Europe*. New York: Oxford University Press.

Nokia. (2010). *Nokia N96 tech specs*. Retrieved from http://europe.nokia.com/find-products/devices/nokia-n96/technicalspecifications-nseries#tv-lt

Nolan, D. (1997). Bottlenecks in pay television: Impact on market development in Europe. *Telecommunications Policy*, 21(7), 597–610. doi:10.1016/S0308-5961(97)00037-2

Nonaka, R. (2010, March 19-20). New approach on the pedagogy for standards education: A case of Applied Standards Education at TUAT. In *Proceedings of the International Symposium on Standardization Education and Research*, Hangzhou, China (pp. 156-167).

NO-REST. (2005). *Networked organisations – research into standards and standardisation*. Retrieved May 10, 2008, from http://www.no-rest.org/Documents/D05&6_Final.pdf

NRG Power Marketing v Main Public Utilities S Ct 693, 696 [2010].

O'Brien, V. E. (2000). Economics & Key Patent Damages Cases. *University of Baltimore Intellectual Property*, 9.

O'Callaghan, R., Kaufmann, P. J., & Konsynski, B. R. (1992). Adoption correlates and share effects of electronic data interchange systems in marketing channels. *Journal of Marketing*, 56, 45–56. doi:10.2307/1252041

Odjar Ratna Komala, D. (2011, February 28). *Mechanics of developing a university level standards education program in Indonesia*. Paper presented at the PEC SCSC PAGE – ANSI CoE Workshop, Washington, DC.

Open Mobile Alliance (OMA). (2009). *Releases - Mobile broadcast services V1.0.* Retrieved from http://www.openmobilealliance.org/Technical/release_program/bcast_v1_0.aspx

Open Mobile Alliance (OMA). (2009). *Service guide for mobile broadcast services (1.0).* Retrieved from http://www.openmobilealliance.org

Orgalime. (2010). *Draft Orgalime comments on EP IMCO report on the future of European standardization.* Brussels, Belgium: Orgalime.

Orgalime. (2010). *Review of the European standardization system.* Brussels, Belgium: Orgalime.

Paich, M., & Parker, B. (2010). Using simulation tools for strategic decision making. *PricewaterhouseCoopers Technology Forecast, 1,* 20–23.

Panduit Corp v Stahlin Bros. Fibre Works 575 F 2d 1152, 1158 [6th Cir 1978].

Paquette, G. (2007). An Ontology and a Software Framework for Competency Modeling and. Management. *Journal of Educational Technology & Society, 10*(3), 1–21.

Patterson, M. (2003). Antitrust and the costs of standard-setting: A commentary on Teece and Sherry. *Minnesota Law Review, 87,* 1995.

Peretz, H. (1998). *Les méthodes en sociologie: l'observation.* Paris: La découverte & Syros.

Pinch, T. (2001). Why Do you go to a Piano Store to Buy a Synthesizer: Path Dependence and the Social Construction of Technology. In Garud, R., & Karnøe, P. (Eds.), *Path Dependence and Creation* (pp. 381–399). Mahwah, NJ: Lawrence Erlbaum Associates.

Pinch, T. J., & Bijker, W. E. (1984). The Social Construction of Facts and Artifacts: Or How the Sociology of Science and the Sociology of Technology might Benefit Each Other. *Social Studies of Science, 14*(3), 399–441. doi:10.1177/030631284014003004

Pinch, T. J., & Bijker, W. E. (1987). The Social Construction of Facts and Artifacts: Or How the Sociology of Science and the Sociology of Technology Might Benefit Each Other. In Bijker, W. E., Hughes, T. P., & Pinch, T. (Eds.), *The Social Construction of Technological Systems. New Directions in the Sociology and History of Technology* (pp. 17–50). Cambridge, MA: MIT Press. doi:10.1177/030631284014003004

Porter, M. E. (1990). *The Competitive Advantage of Nations.* New York: The Free Press.

Premkumar, G., & Ramamurthy, K. (1995). The Role of Interorganizational and Organizational Factors on the Decision Mode for Adoption of Interorganizational Systems. *Decision Sciences, 26*(3), 303–336. doi:10.1111/j.1540-5915.1995.tb01431.x

Premkumar, G., Ramamurthy, K., & Crum, M. R. (1997). Determinants of EDI adoption in the transportation industry. *European Journal of Information Systems, 6*(2), 107–121. doi:10.1057/palgrave.ejis.3000260

Project, D. V. B. (2002). *DVB-Mobile commercial requirements CM391v5: DVB-CM ad-hoc group DVB-Mobile.* Retrieved from http://www.dvb.org/groups_modules/commercial_module/cmavc/index.xml?groupID=51

Project, D. V. B. (2010). *Rules and procedures of the DVB project (SB 1699 rev. 4).* Retrieved from http://www.dvb.org/membership/mou/Rules-and-Procedures-of-the-DVB-Project.pdf

Qui est l'association pour le lable de qualité ? (n.d.). Retrieved December 10, 2008, from http://www.guete-siegel.ch/

Rahnasto, I. (2003). *Intellectual Property Rights, External Effects and Anti-trust Law.* Oxford: Oxford University Press.

Raines, S. (2003). Perception of legitimacy and efficacy in international environmental management standards: The impact of the participation gap. *Global Environmental Politics, 3*(3), 47–73. doi:10.1162/152638003322469277

Ravichandran, T. (2005). Organizational Assimilation of Complex Technologies: An Empirical Study of Component-Based Software Development. *IEEE Transactions on Engineering Management*, *52*(2), 249–268. doi:10.1109/TEM.2005.844925

Recordon, D. (2008). The OWF Way. *OWF Wiki*. Retrieved March 30, 2010, from http://open-web.pbworks.com/The-OWF-Way

Reddy, N. M. (1990). Product of Self-Regulation. A Paradox of Technology Policy. *Technological Forecasting and Social Change*, *38*, 43–63. doi:10.1016/0040-1625(90)90017-P

Reding, V. (2007). *Commission strategy for mobile TV in Europe endorsed by member states.* Retrieved from http://www.europa.eu/rapid/pressReleasesAction.do?reference=IP/07/1815&format=HTML&aged=0&language=EN&guiLanguage=en

Reding, V. (2007). *Mobile TV: The time to act is now.* Retrieved from http://www.europa.eu/rapid/pressReleasesAction.do?reference=SPEECH/07/154&format=HTML&aged=0&language=EN&guiLanguage=fr

Reimers, K., & Li, M. (2005). Antecedents of a Transaction Cost Theory of Vertical IS Standardization Processes. *Electronic Markets*, *15*(4), 301–312. doi:10.1080/10196780500302740

Restatement (Second) of Contracts (1981) § 213.

Richter, T., & Pawlowski, J. M. (2007, October). The Need for Standardization of Context Metadata for e-Learning Environments. In *Proceedings of the e-ASEM Conference*, Seoul, Korea.

Riley, K. (2005). *Application Profiling Guidelines*. Retrieved from http://www.imsglobal.org/ap/

Rite-Hite Corp v Kelley Co., Inc. 56 F 3d 1538, 1554-55 [Fed Cir 1995].

Roe, M. (1996). Chaos and evolution in law and economics. *Harvard Law Review*, *109*, 641. doi:10.2307/1342067

Rogers, E. M. (1983). *Diffusion of Innovations* (3rd ed.). New York: The Free Press.

Ross, J., Weill, P., & Robertson, D. (2006). *Enterprise Architecture as Strategy*. Boston: Harvard Business Press.

Ruffat, M. (1987). *Le contre-pouvoir consommateur aux états-unis*. Paris: PUF.

Ruwet, C. (2009). *Des filetages à la RSE. Normalisation et démocratie. Sociologie du processus d'élaboration d'ISO 26000*. Unpublished doctoral dissertation, Université Catholique de Louvain.

Rysman, M., & Simcoe, T. (2005). Patents and the performance of voluntary standard setting organizations. *Management Science*, *54*(11), 1920–1934. doi:10.1287/mnsc.1080.0919

Rysman, M., & Simcoe, T. (2008). Patents and the performance of voluntary standard setting organizations. *Management Science*, *54*(11), 1920–1934. doi:10.1287/mnsc.1080.0919

Sampson, D. G. (2009). Competence-related Metadata for Educational Resources that Support Lifelong Competence Development Programmes. *Journal of Educational Technology & Society*, *12*(4), 149–159.

Sampson, T. (2007). The "Adjusted Future Free Income Ratio": A New Methodology for Determining IPR Royalty Rates? *European Intellectual Property Review*, *1*(371), 377.

Samsung. (2008). *Samsung introduces P960, the first mobile TV slider phone for Europe.* Retrieved from http://www.samsung.com/uk/news/presskitRead.do?news_seq=8460

Scheer, A.-W. (1994). *Business Process Engineering – Reference Models for Industrial Enterprises* (2nd ed.). Berlin: Springer.

Schepel, H. (2005). *The constitution of private governance – Product standards in the regulation of integrating markets*. Portland, OR: Hart Publishing.

Scherer, F. M. (1992). Schumpeter and Plausible Capitalism. *Journal of Economic Literature, 30*(3), 1416–1433.

Schilling, M. A. (2002). Technology success and failure in winner-take-all markets: Testing a model of technological lock out. *Academy of Management Journal, 45*(2), 387–398. doi:10.2307/3069353

Schmidt, A., & Braun, S. (2008). People Tagging & Ontology Maturing: Towards Collaborative Competence Management. In *Proceedings of COOP '08, the 8th International Conference on the Design of Cooperative Systems*, Carry-le-Rouet, France. Retrieved February 152010, from http://publications.andreas.schmidt.name/ Braun_Schmidt_CollaborativeCompetenceManagement_COOP08.pdf

Schmidt, S. K., & Werle, R. (1998). *Coordinating technology: Studies in the international standardization of telecommunications*. Cambridge, MA: MIT Press.

Seo, D., & Lee, J. (2007). Gaining Competitive Advantage through Value-Shifts: A Case of the South Korean Wireless Communications Industry. *International Journal of Information Management, 27*(1), 49–56. doi:10.1016/j.ijinfomgt.2006.12.002

Seo, D., & Mak, K. T. (in press). Using the Thread-Fabric Perspective to Analyze Industry Dynamics: An Exploratory Investigation of the Wireless Telecommunications Industry. *Communications of the ACM.*

Serenkov, P. (2010). *Belarus – Training tomorrow's experts today.* Retrieved from http://www.iso.org/iso/iso-focus-plus_index/iso-focusplus_online-bonus-articles/ the-2009-iso-award/2009-award_belarus.htm

Shapiro, C. (2001). Setting compatability standards: Cooperation or collusion? In Dreyfuss, R., Zimmerman, D., & First, H. (Eds.), *Expanding the boundaries of intellectual property*. New York, NY: Oxford University Press.

Shapiro, C., & Varian, H. (1999). *Information rules: A strategic guide to the network economy*. Boston, MA: Harvard Business School Press.

Shapiro, C., & Varian, H. R. (1999). The Art of Standard Wars. *California Management Review, 41*(2), 8–32.

Sharples, M. (2009). Towards an Interdisciplinary Design Science of Learning. In Cress, U., Dimitrova, V., & Specht, M. (Eds.), *Learning in the Synergy of Multiple Disciplines* (pp. 3–4). New York: Springer. doi:10.1007/978-3-642-04636-0_2

Shiraishi, Y., & Hirota, A. (1978). Magnetic recording at video cassette recorder for home use. *IEEE Transactions on Magnetics, 14*(5), 318–320. doi:10.1109/ TMAG.1978.1059827

Shuman, L., Besterfield-Sacre, M., & McGourty, J. (2005). The ABET "professional skills" – can they be taught? Can they be assessed? *Journal of Engineering Education, 94*(1), 41–55.

Silberston, A. (1972). Economies of scale in theory and practice. *The Economic Journal, 82*(325), 369–391. doi:10.2307/2229943

Simmonds, I., & Ing, D. (2000). *A Shearing Layers Approach to Information Systems Development.* Retrieved March 30, 2010, from http://systemicbusiness.org/ pubs/2000_IBM_RC21694_Simmonds_Ing_Shearing_Layers_Info_Sys_Dev.pdf

Sklar, E., & Davies, M. (2005). Multiagent Simulation of Learning Environments. In *Proceedings of the fourth international joint conference on Autonomous agents and multiagent systems* (pp. 953-959).

Smart, C. (2010). Leap2A: Enabling e-portfolio portability. *JISC website.* Retrieved March 30, 2010 from http://www.jisc.ac.uk/publications/briefingpapers/2010/ bpleap2a.aspx

Smerdon, P. (2000). *An action agenda for engineering curriculum innovation.* Paper presented at the 11th IEEE-USA Biennial Careers Conference, San Jose, CA.

SNV. (2007). *Jahresbericht 2006.* Retrieved December 10, 2008, from http://www.mysnv.ch/document_show. cfm/Jahresbericht%202006?wm=c%28614%29cl%282 %29cv%28200706181518%29&ext=.*

Song, M. (2007). Guest view. *ISO Focus, 4*(11), 4–7.

Spivak, S. M., & Kelly, W. E. (2003). Introduce strategic standardization concepts during higher education studies … and reap the benefits! *ISO Bulletin, 34*(7), 22–24.

SS Tech., Inc. v PC–Tel, Inc., No. C-99-20292, 2001 WL 1891713, 3–6 [N.D. Cal. November 28, 2001].

Stango, V. (2004). The economics of standards wars. *Review of Network Economics, 3*(1), 1–19. doi:10.2202/1446-9022.1040

Steen, H. U. (2009). Technology convergence, market divergence: Fragmentation of standards in mobile digital broadcasting carriers. *Information Systems and E-Business Management, 7*(3), 319–345. doi:10.1007/s10257-008-0099-8

Steinbock, D. (2003). Globalization of Wireless Value System: From Geographic to Strategic Advantages. *Telecommunications Policy, 27*, 207–235. doi:10.1016/S0308-5961(02)00106-4

Steinfield, C. W., Wigand, R. T., Markus, M. L., & Minton, G. (2004, May 13-14). *Promoting e-Business Through Vertical IS Standards: Lessons from the US Home Mortgage Industry.* Paper presented at the Workshop on Standards and Public Policy, Chicago.

Stickle v Heublein, Inc. 716 F 2d 1550, 1563 [Fed Cir 1983].

Stone, R. (2007). Notes from Region 2. *Journal of Contemporary European Studies, 15*(1), 5–14. doi:10.1080/14782800701273292

Stulz, R., Walking, R., & Song, M. (1990). The distribution of target ownership and division of gains in successful takeovers. *The Journal of Finance, 45*, 817–833. doi:10.1111/j.1540-6261.1990.tb05107.x

Sumner, M. (2000). Risk factors in enterprise-wide/ERP projects. *Journal of Information Technology, 15*(4), 317–327. doi:10.1080/02683960010009079

Swann, G. M. P. (2010). *The economics of standardization – An update report for the UK Department of Business, Innovation and Skills (BIS).* London, UK: Innovation Economics Limited.

Swanson, D. G., & Baumol, W. J. (2005). Reasonable and Nondiscriminatory (RAND) Royalties, Standards Selection, and Control of Market Power. *Antitrust Law Journal, 73*(1), 10.

Swanson, E. B., & Ramiller, N. C. (1997). The Organizing Vision in Information Systems Innovations. *Organization Science, 8*(5), 458–474. doi:10.1287/orsc.8.5.458

Swatman, P. M. C., Swatman, P. A., & Fowler, D. C. (1994). A model of EDI integration and strategic business reengineering. *The Journal of Strategic Information Systems, 3*(1), 41–60. doi:10.1016/0963-8687(94)90005-1

Tamm-Hallström, K. (2004). *Organizing international standardization: ISO and the IASC in quest of authority.* Cheltenham, UK: Edward Elgar.

Tan, M., & Teo, T. S. H. (2000). Factors influencing the adoption of Internet banking. *Journal of the AIS, 1*(1).

Tanriverdi, H. (2006). Performance Effects of Information Technology Synergies in Multibusiness Firms. *Management Information Systems Quarterly, 30*(1), 57–77.

Taubman, P. (1976). Earnings, education, genetics, and environment. *The Journal of Human Resources, 11*(4), 447–461. doi:10.2307/145426

Taubman, P. (1976). The determinants of earnings: Genetic, family, and other environments: A study of white male twins. *The American Economic Review, 66*(5), 858–870.

Telecommunications Industry Association (TIA). (2006). *TIA-1099: Forward link only air interface specification for terrestrial mobile multimedia multicast.* Arlington, VA: Telecommunications Industry Association.

Telecoms Korea. (2006). *Korea has 29% of terrestrial DMB patents.* Retrieved from http://www.telecomskorea.com/service-4855.html

Temple Lang, J. (2007, April 13-14). Licensing, Antitrust and Innovation under European Competition Law. In *Proceedings of the Fordham IP Property Conference* (pp. 2-6).

TENCompetence. (2009). *TENCompetence Frequently Asked Questions*. Retrieved February 15, from http://tencompetence-project.bolton.ac.uk/node/123/

TENCompetence. (2010). *TENCompetence Foundation*. Retrieved February 8, 2010, from http://www.tencompetence.org/

Thomson, P., & Fox-Kean, M. (2005). Patent citations and the geography of knowledge spillovers: A reassessment. *The American Economic Review, 95*(1), 450–459. doi:10.1257/0002828053828509

Tolk, A. (2003). *Beyond Technical Interoperability – Introducing a Reference Model for Measures of Merit for Coalition Interoperability*. Retrieved April 2, 2010, from http://citeseerx.ist.psu.edu/viewdoc/download?doi=10.1.1.79.6784&rep=rep1&type=pdf

Tomberg, V., & Laanpere, M. (2007). Towards the Interoperability of Online Assessment Tools. In *Proceedings of the 29th International Conference on Information Technology Interfaces* (pp. 513-518). Washington, DC: IEEE Computer Society Press.

Tornatzky, L. G., & Klein, K. J. (1982). Innovation Characteristics and innovation Adoption-Implementation: A Meta Analysis of Findings. *IEEE Transactions on Engineering Management, 29*(1), 28–45.

Totschnig, M., Klerkx, K., Klobučar, T., Law, E., Simon, B., & Ternier, S. (2009). *Open ICOPER Content Space Implementation of 1st Generation of Open ICOPER Content Space including Integration Mini Case Studies*. ICOPER Project Deliverables.

Trajtenberg, M., Henderson, R., & Jaffe, A. (1996). University versus corporate patents: A window on the basicness of invention. *Economic Innovation New Technology, 5*.

Trajtenberg, M. (1990). A penny for your quotes: Patent citations and the value of innovations. *The Rand Journal of Economics, 21*(1), 172–187. doi:10.2307/2555502

Trajtenberg, M., Henderson, R., & Jaffe, A. (1997). University versus corporate patents: A window on the basicness of invention. *Economics of Innovation and New Technology, 5*, 19–50. doi:10.1080/10438599700000006

Troxel Mfg. Co. v Schwinn Bicycle Co. 465 F 2d 1253, 1257 [6th Cir 1972].

Tunze, W. (2005). *The DMB story. Deutschland Online: Forum für Politik, Kultur und Wirtschaft*. Retrieved from http://old.magazine-deutschland.de/magazin/OZ-IFA_5-05_ENG_E4.php?&lang=eng&lang=eng&lang=eng

Tyrväinen, P., Warsta, J., & Seppänen, V. (2008). Evolution of Secondary Software Businesses: Understanding Industry Dynamics. In G. León, A. Bernardos, J. Casar, K. Kautz, & J. DeGross (Eds.), *IFIP International Federation for Information Processing Vol. 287, Open IT-based innovation: moving towards cooperative IT transfer and knowledge diffusion* (pp. 281-401). Boston: Springer.

U.S. Department of Justice and FTC. (2000). *Antitrust guidelines for collaborations among competitors*. Retrieved from http://www.ftc.gov/os/2000/ 04/ftcdoj-guidelines.pdf.

U.S. House of Representatives. (2005). *Europe, and the use of standards as trade barriers: How should the US respond?* China: Congressional Hearing.

UN/CEFACT. (2003). *Core Components Specification*. Retrieved from http://www.unece.org/cefact/ebxml/CCTS_V2-01_Final.pdf

UNESCO. (1998). *Forum on the impact of Open Courseware for higher education in developing countries. Final report*. Paris: UNESCO.

Valletti, T. M., & Cave, M. (1998). Competition in UK mobile communications. *Telecommunications Policy, 22*(2), 109–131. doi:10.1016/S0308-5961(97)00063-3

Van Assche, F. (2007). Linking Learning Resources to Curricula by using Competencies. In *Proceedings of the First International Workshop on Learning object Discovery Exchange*, Crete, Greece.

Van de Sompel, H., & Lagoze, C. (2000). The Santa Fe Convention of the Open Archives Initiative. *D-Lib Magazine, 6*(2). doi:10.1045/february2000-vandesompel-oai

Van Eecke, P., & Truyens, M. (2009). Standardization in the European Information and Technology Sector: Official Procedures on the Verge of Being Overhauled. *Shidler Journal. of Law, Commerce & Technology, 5*(11). Retrieved April 1, 2010, from http://www.lctjournal.washington.edu/vol5/a11VanEecke.html

Verman, L. C. (1973). *Standardization – A new discipline.* Hamden, CT: Shoe String Press/Archon Books.

Vizio Inc. v Funai Elec. Co. No. CV-09-0174, 2010 U.S. Dist. LEXIS 30850 [C.D. Cal. February 3, 2010].

Vogten, H., Martens, H., Nadolski, R., Tattersall, C., van Rosmalen, P., & Koper, R. (2006). CopperCore Service Integration - Integrating IMS Learning Design and IMS Question and Test Interoperability. In *Proceedings of the Sixth International Conference on Advanced Learning Technologies* (pp. 378-382). Washington, DC: IEEE Computer Society Press.

Volvo Trucks N. Am., Inc. v. Reeder-Simco GMC, Inc., 546 U.S. 164 176 [2006].

Vrancken, J., Kaart, M., & Soares, M. (2008). Internet addressing standards: A case study in standards dynamics driven by bottom-up adoption. In Egyedi, T. M., & Blind, K. (Eds.), *The dynamics of standards* (pp. 68–81). Cheltenham, UK: Edward Elgar.

W3C. (2004). *W3C Resource Description Framework Specification.* Retrieved from http://www.w3.org/RDF/

W3C. (2006). *Extensible Markup Language (XML) 1.0* (4th ed.). Author.

W3C. (2009) *SKOS Simple Knowledge Organization System home page.* Retrieved February 9, 2010, from http://www.w3.org/2004/02/skos/

Walking, R. (1985). Predicting tender offer success: A logistic analysis. *Journal of Financial and Quantitative Analysis, 20,* 461–478. doi:10.2307/2330762

Wareham, J., Rai, A., & Pickering, G. (2005). Standardization in Vertical Industries: An Institutional Analysis of XML-Based Standards Infusion in Electricity Markets. *Electronic Markets, 15*(4), 323–334. doi:10.1080/10196780500302849

Warner, B. (2008, January 9). HD-DVD v Blu-ray: Is the battle over? *Times Online.* Retrieved from http://technology.timesonline.co.uk/tol/news/tech_and_web/the_web/article3159432.ece

Webster, J. (1995). *The Development of EDI.* Paper presented at the PICT/COST A4 International Research Workshop, Brussels, Belgium.

Weitzel, T. (2003, December 12-14). *A Network ROI.* Paper presented at the International Conference on IS Special Workshop on Standard Making sponsored by MISQ, Seattle, WA.

Weitzel, T., Beimborn, D., & Konig, W. (2006). A Unified Economic Model of Standard Diffusion: The Impact of Standardization Cost, Network Effects, and Network Topology. *Management Information Systems Quarterly, 30,* 489–514.

Werle, R., & Iversen, E. J. (2006). Promoting legitimacy in technical standardization. *Science. Technology & Innovation Studies, 2,* 19–39.

Wicklund, R. A., & Brehm, J. W. (1976). *Perspectives on cognitive dissonance.* Hillsdale, NJ: Erlbaum.

Wigand, R. T., Steinfield, C. W., & Markus, M. L. (2005, January 3-6). *Impacts of Vertical IS Standards: The Case of the US Home Mortgage Industry.* Paper presented at the Hawaii International Conference on System Sciences (HICSS 38), Waikoloa, HI.

Wilcock, A., & Colina, A. (2007). Consumer representation on consensus standards committees: a value-added practice. *International Journal of Services and Standards, 3*(1), 1–17. doi:10.1504/IJSS.2007.011825

Wilson, S. (2008). CEN endorses European Metadata for Learning Opportunities. *Scott's Workblog.* Retrieved April 2, 2010, from http://zope.cetis.ac.uk/members/scott/blogview?entry=20081021140752

Wilson, S., & Velayutham, K. (2009). Creating an innovation-oriented technology strategy. *Horizon, 17*(3), 245–255. doi:10.1108/10748120910993277

World, D. M. B. (2010). *Country information for DAB, DAB+ and DMB - Germany.* Retrieved from http://www.worlddab.org/country_information/germany

WTO. (1994). *Agreement on Technical Barriers to Trade of the WTO Agreement: Annex 3: Code of Good Practice for the Preparation, Adoption and Application of Standards.* Geneva, Switzerland: Author. Retrieved from http://www.wto.org/english/docs_e/legal_e/17-tbt.pdf

WTO. (1994, April 14). *Agreement on Technical Barriers to Trade, Marrakesh Agreement Establishing the World Trade Organization.* Geneva, Switzerland: WTO.

XCRI. (2010). *eXchanging Course-Related Information.* Retrieved February 8, 2010 from http://www.xcri.org/

Yamada, H. (2011, February 28) *Development of education on standardization in Japan.* Paper presented at the PEC SCSC PAGE – ANSI CoE Workshop, Washington, DC.

Yang, Y. (2010) China institute of metrology's educational model for standardization. *China Standardization, 37*(1), 15–21.

Yin, R. K. (2008). *Case Study Research, Design and Methods* (4th ed.). Thousand Oaks, CA: Sage Publications.

Zachariadou, K., Zachariadis, A., & Latinopoulou, M. (2010, June 8-9). Contributions of the Bulgarian Union of Standardization for the European Integration of the Republic Bulgaria. In *Proceedings of the 7th International Conference on Standardization Prototypes and Quality: A Means of Balkan Countries Collaboration,* Zlatibor, Serbia (pp. 78-82).

Zachman, J. A. (2008). *The Zachman Framework: The Official Concise Definition.* Retrieved April 2, 2010, from http://www.zachmaninternational.com/index.php/the-zachmanframework

Zhao, K., Xia, M., & Shaw, M. J. (2005). Vertical E-Business Standards and Standards Developing Organizations: A Conceptual Framework. *Electronic Markets, 15*(4), 289–300. doi:10.1080/10196780500302690

About the Contributors

Kai Jakobs joined RWTH Aachen University's Computer Science Department in 1985. His current research interests focus on various aspects of ICT standards and the underlying standardisation process. Over time, he (co)- authored/edited a text book on communication networks and, more recently, seventeen books on ICT standardisation. More than 200 of his papers have been published in conference proceedings, books, and journals. He has been on the programme committee and editorial board of numerous international conferences and journals, respectively, and has served as an external expert on evaluation panels of various European R&D programmes, on both technical and socio-economic issues. He is also Vice President of the European Academy for Standardisation (EURAS). Kai holds a PhD in Computer Science from the University of Edinburgh and is a Certified Standards Professional.

* * *

Tineke Egyedi is senior researcher Standardization. She has participated in several EU projects (the last one was on EU ICT standardization policy, finalised in 2007), industry projects (e.g. Dynamics of standards; Sun Microsystems), and Dutch government projects (e.g. Trends in Standardization). Her current research interests projects include standards and infrastructure flexibility (Next Generation Infrastructures project, TU Delft), and the interaction between international standardization and national innovation projects (Dutch National Science Foundation). She is president of the European Academy for Standardization (EURAS) and chair of the International Committee for Education about Standardization (ICES). She has chaired standardization seminars, workshops and conferences. Currently she is associate editor of the International Journal of IT Standards and Standardization Research (Idea Group) and member of the editorial board of Computer Standards and Interfaces (Elsevier).

Aad Koppenhol is Senior Principal IT Architect and Open Source & Standards driver for Sun in the Netherlands. He has 35 years of experience in ICT sector. During his ICT career he has played different roles. He strongly believes that, in view of the current changing role of the Web towards a Social and Cultural utility, more than ever Human Values need to be protected. In his PhD on Value Sensitive Design and Information Architectures at the Delft University of Technology he argues that technology's first role is to facilitate mankind. His motive is based on co-creation or 'Collaboration & Knowledge Sharing', which are key in many developments. The combination of his interest in Technology and Philosophy feed him with fresh insights. As an IT- Architect he is very conscious of dealing in human values. His broad experience and technical skills are to his advantage and match his relation-building capacities.

Henk de Vries is Associate Professor of Standardization at the Rotterdam School of Management, Erasmus University, Rotterdam, The Netherlands. He is Vice-President of the European Academy for Standardization EURAS, Vice-Chair of the International Cooperation for Education about Standardization ICES, and Special Advisor of the International Federation of Standards Users IFAN.

Todor Cooklev is the Founding Director of the Wireless Technology Center at Indiana University-Purdue University Fort Wayne, Fort Wayne, Indiana, USA. He received his Ph.D. degree in electrical engineering from Tokyo Institute of Technology, Tokyo, Japan in 1995. In addition to his academic experience, he has worked for several years in industry. He has received research grants and as a consultant has performed technology and business development for several major corporations and government organizations, including Hitachi America, France Telecom, Agilent Technologies, the US Air Force Research Laboratory, the Government of Canada, ITT Corporation, and other smaller technology and investment companies. He has served on the board of start-up companies. In 1999 he received the 3Com Inventor Award for his contributions to 3Com's intellectual property. He has been involved with the development of the Bluetooth and the IEEE 802 standards for wireless communication and has served on the IEEE Standards in Education Committee since 2006. T. Cooklev has published over 70 journal and conference papers, as well as the book "Wireless Communication Standards," published by IEEE Press, New York, NY, 2004. Among his honors, he received the Best Paper Award at the 1994 Asia-Pacific Conference on Circuits and Systems, and a NATO Science Fellowship Award in 1995. He is the recipient of the 2006 Wireless Educator of the Year Award from the Global Wireless Education Consortium.

Christophe Hauert (1978) is Ph.D student of political science at the University of Lausanne. He joined the research team "Standards and international relation" in 2008 following his MA degree in Political Science from the University of Lausanne and a Dissertation on consumer's participation in the Swiss standardization process between 1987 and 2007. His research interests focus on standardization, stakeholders involvement, and political consumerism.

Anique Hommels (1972) is assistant professor at the Department of Technology & Society Studies, University of Maastricht (since 2003). She was trained in the interdisciplinary Arts and Science programme of the University of Maastricht (1991-1995). In her PhD thesis she concentrated on the resistance to change ('obduracy') in urban sociotechnical transformation processes. A book (Unbuilding Cities - Obduracy in Urban Sociotechnical Change (2005). Cambridge, MA: The MIT Press), based on her thesis, has been published by MIT Press in 2005. After her PhD, she worked as a researcher at MERIT/Infonomics (Maastricht Economic Research Institute on Innovation and Technology) (2001-2004). Her research focuses on processes of sociotechnical change and resistance to change. Her work is interdisciplinary in combining perspectives from history, sociology and philosophy. At MERIT/Infonomics, her empirical focus shifted to the network society, but her theoretical focus on sociotechnical change remained. In 2003, she was awarded the Brooke Hindle Fellowship from the American Society for the History of Technology (SHOT). In 2005, Hommels was commissioned by the Dutch Ministry of the Interior (BZK) to monitor the final evaluation of the C2000 project. Together with Dr. T.M. Egyedi and Prof.dr.ir W.E. Bijker she received an NWO-grant for the project "Complex interactions between international standardization and national innovation projects" (2007-2010). Hommels is also involved in the ESF/Eurocores project "Europe goes Critical: The emergence and governance of critical transnational European infrastructures" (2007-2009).

DongBack Seo is currently an assistant professor in the department of Business and ICT at the University of Groningen, the Netherlands and fellow of the SOM research school. Her research interests include modeling and analyzing competitive dynamics in rapidly changing industries, organizational standards strategy, converge in information and communications technology (ICT) areas, analysis of organizations' and users' behaviors toward ICT, and data-mining. She published two books in Korean, as well as a class manual and several chapters. Her papers were published many journals and conference proceedings including *Communications of the ACM, European Journal of Information Systems (EJIS), and Telecommunications Policy*. She has worked as a software engineer at a wireless telecommunications company in Silicon Valley and as an entrepreneur in Seoul, Korea. She holds a Ph.D in Management of Information Systems from University of Illinois at Chicago.

Jan Pawlowski works as Professor in Digital Media - Global Information Systems at the University of Jyväskylä, Finland. Born in 1971, originally from Essen, Germany. Masters' Degree and Doctorate in Business Information Systems (University of Duisburg-Essen). Since 10.2007 working as Adjunct Professor within the Faculty of Information Technology. Since 12.2009 Professor of Digital Media with the specialization "Global Information Systems". This includes the research coordination of several national and European projects. Main research interests and activities are in the field of Global Information Systems, E-Learning, Modeling Learning-related Processes, Procedural Models, Learning Technology Standardization, Quality Management and Quality Assurance for Education, and Mobile / Ambient Learning. Actively involved in research organizations (AACE, GI, IEEE) and in standardization organizations (DIN, CEN, ISO/ IEC JTC1 SC36). Acting chair of the CEN/ISSS Workshop Learning Technologies.

Denis Kozlov is a PhD candidate at the University of Jyväskylä, Finland. He received his Master degree (2001) in Information Systems Science from the Polytechnic University of Tomsk, Russia. He has authored a number of journal, international conference and workshop papers. His research interests include global information systems, reference modeling in the TEL domain, open educational resources, open source software quality and maintenance and quality management

Adam Cooper's professional history has included a range of roles within further and higher education and educational technology. Following several years teaching chemistry in further education and developing computer-based simulations, interactive tutorials and self-tests he focussed on educational technology and joined Farnborough College of Technology (a HE and FE institution) in 1998 as the first head of their new Teaching and Learning Technology Centre. In this role he worked closely with the heads of the library and computing services to develop the use of technology in teaching and learning within the college and thorough local partnerships. While at Farnborough, he became interested in the opportunities offered by the newly emergent field of activity in XML based interoperability in education and in 2000 he moved into the commercial sector to work on European collaborative R&D projects under the 5th Framework Programme with interoperability as a cornerstone principle. Through this work he became involved in IMS, contributing to and co-leading a number of project teams, and first met some of the CETIS colleagues he now works with. Following these R&D projects, he spent time working on education sector bids and projects, both in formulating the solution and in its technical implementation. He has broad interests in pragmatic educational technology and interoperability and a strong belief that educational technology developed in tandem with progressive educational methods has a great deal of unrealised potential. He is a member of the Education Schools and Childrens Services Information Standards Board and chair of the British Standards Institute Committee IST/43

Simon Grant is a Learning Technology Advisor with CETIS, the JISC's Centre for Educational Technology and Interoperability Standards. Over the last 10 years, he has developed a particular expertise in electronic portfolio systems and their interoperability. Since 2006, he has led work that has resulted in the CETIS-managed Leap2A specification, now widely adopted, for the portability of learner-owned information across e-portfolio and other systems. It has become increasingly apparent that competencies need to be handled well to deliver more of the potential of e-portfolio systems for personal and professional development, and after writing several relevant papers and presentations, Simon is now involved in several relevant European and international initiatives to explore the standardization of information and structures related to competence as well as e-portfolios. His book, "Electronic Portfolios: personal information, personal development and personal values" was published in 2009.

Rowin Young is a learning technology advisor with the JISC Centre for Educational Technology and Interoperability Standards innovation support centre (JISC CETIS), with a particular interest in issues relating to assessment and the use of virtual worlds and games for learning. She has participated actively in the development of interoperability specifications for assessment, including metadata for describing assessment resources, and has contributed to the development of models for the infrastructure and workflow for item banks. She has also managed a number of small projects in the area of assessment tools. Before joining CETIS she taught English and Scottish Language and Literature at several universities, supporting both face-to-face and distance learning students.

Dr. Ingo Dahn received PhD and habilitation in Mathematics from Humboldt University in Berlin, Germany. He has been working in Mathematical Logic, Automated Theorem Proving and personalization of teaching materials. He is the CEO of the Knowledge Media Institute of the University Koblenz-Landau in Koblenz/Germany. As a member of the Technical Advisory Board of IMS Global Learning he concentrates on issues of Application Profiling and Conformance Testing.

Sascha Zimmermann is studying Computer Science at the University Koblenz-Landau. He has been among the key implementers of the Generic Conformance Test System and has been actively involved in its design.

Jad Najjar obtained his PhD from Katholieke Universiteit Leuven (K.U.Leuven), Computer Science Department, Belgium. He was also a post doctoral fellow at Hypermedia and Database research unit of K.U.Leuven and afterwards has been working as a senior researcher at Institute for Information Systems and New Media, WU Vienna, Austria. Jad has been working as a work package leader of Learning Needs and Opportunities of the European ICOPER eContentPlus Project. He was also involved in other European projects like ARIADNE, MACE and MELT. His recent work focuses on modelling, design and evaluation of learning outcome based educational systems and specifications. He is a co-author of the Contextualized Attention Metadata (CAM) specifications; a schema and framework for tracking and managing data about user attention and interest across systems and contexts. He is involved in standards workgroups like the European CEN/ISSS Workshop on Learning Technologies and IEEE LTSC. Jad is a reviewer of several international journals and conferences, and served as a chair of international (IEEE/ACM) workshops around attentions metadata, learning needs and learning outcomes.

Michael Derntl holds a PhD in Computer Science from the University of Vienna. He is a Lecturer and a Researcher at the Faculty of Computer Science, University of Vienna. He has worked and published extensively on topics related to learning technologies in international journals, books and conference proceedings. His current research interests include educational design, particularly the role of people, design languages, tools and standards for technology enhanced learning, as well as Web 2.0 and social software for teaching and learning.

Tomaž Klobučar is a researcher at Laboratory for Open Systems and Networks at Jožef Stefan Institute, an assistant professor at University of Maribor and Jožef Stefan International Postgraduate School, and head of SETCCE research group. His main interests are technology enhanced learning and information security and privacy. Lately, he has been actively involved in several EU Framework Programme projects, such as iCamp (social software in technology enhanced learning), ELENA (creation of a smart space for learning), PROLEARN (professional learning) and UNIVERSAL (building of a platform for exchange of learning resources), as well as in eContentPlus ICOPER (learning outcome-driven educational framework) and OpenScout (open content for management education and training) projects. His publication list includes 65 conference contributions, journal papers, books and book chapters.

Bernd Simon holds a PhD in Information Systems from Wirtschaftsuniversität Wien. He is also a graduate of the International Management Program of New York University's Stern School of Business. Dr. Simon is senior researcher at Wirtschaftsuniversität Wien and managing director of Knowledge Markets Consulting GesmbH. In his professional activities he is involved in research in the area of technology-enhanced learning and knowledge management. He has been specifically contributing to areas such as (1) assessment of corporate learning environments and learning processes, (2) success factors for implementing technology-enhanced learning, and (3) interoperability of knowledge repositories. As expert in the field of technology-enhanced learning, he provided consultancy to clients including Daimler AG, Erste Group, Volksbank Group, and the Austrian Ministry of Education.

Michael Totschnig, PhD, currently works for Wirtschaftsuniversität Wien (WU) as a senior researcher in the ICOPER project, where he is managing the development of the Open ICOPER content space, a repository architecture providing access to a critical mass of high-quality, re-usable content. He has been working as a system architect for Learn@WU, the e-learning platform of WU, where he was responsible for designing the content authoring environment and for standards implementation (SCORM and IMS QTI). At Knowledge Markets Consulting GesmbH he has managed the development of learning object repository technologies, based on established open source components that have been deployed for Bildungspool, the Austrian national repository for learning ressources for schools, and for Educanext, an exchange platform for higher education learning material. He earned his PhD in communication at the Université du Québec à Montréal. He is participating in the work on the SPI standard of the CEN/ISSS workshop on learning technologies.

Index